The UNIX Industry and Open Systems in Transition

A Guidebook for Managing Change

The UNIX Industry and Open Systems in Transition

A Guidebook for Managing Change

Ed Dunphy

A Wiley–QED Publication

John Wiley & Sons, Inc.

New York • Chichester • Brisbane • Toronto • Singapore

Copyright © 1994 by Edward P. Dunphy
Published by John Wiley & Sons, Inc.

ISBN 0 471-60608-1

Printed in the United States of America

10 9 8 7 6 5 4 3 2 1

To all the hackers in the world who have been too busy hacking to write a book that someone like me could understand

and

to all the Information Systems professionals who have to deliver on the promise of Open Systems.

Trademarks

Trademark Acknowledgments

Acer Incorporated—ACER

Adobe Systems Incorporated—Display PostScript, PostScript and TranScript

Altos Computer Systems—Altos, Series 1000, Series 2000

Amdahl Corporation—UTS

Apollo Computer Inc.—APOLLO, DOMAIN/IX, Aegis, Domain/IX, Domain/PC, PA-RISC

Apple Computer—A/UX, Mac, MacOS, Macintosh, LaserWriter

Arix Corporation—Arix

AT&T—Open Look, System V Interface Definition (SVID), 3B2, Programmer's Workbench, Tuxedo, ABI UNIX, System V and AT&T

Charles River Data Systems—UNOS

Convex Computer Corp.—Convex, ConvexUNIX

Commodore—Amiga, AmigaDOS

Compaq—Compaq 386, SYSTEMPRO

Cray Research, Inc.—Cray

Data General Corporation—Data General, DG/UX

Dell Computer Corporation—Dell

Digital Equipment Corporation—DECwindows, DECnet, ULTRIX, VAX, VT100, DEC, PDP, MicroVAX, Digital, VMS, VT100, VT200

Digital Research, Inc.—CP/M

Evans and Sutherland—ESIX

Excelan, Inc.—EXOS

Frame Technology Corp.—Framemaker

Gould, Inc.—UTX/32

Hewlett-Packard Corporation—HP-UX, NewWave, HP 9000 Series, HP Windows, Precision Architecture

Independence Technology, Inc.—Turbo

Informix Software, Inc.—Informix, C-ISAM, Informix-4GL, SQL

International Business Machines Corporation—IBM, IBM RT System, PS/2, OS/2, AIX, AS400, S36, S38, BSC3270, SAA, Andrew, Token-Ring, PC/XT, DB2, VP/SP, RS/6000, MVS, PS/2, RT, SNA, SNA RJE, CADAM, CATIA, CAEDS, CIEDS

Interleaf, Inc.—Interleaf

Institute of Electrical and Electronic Engineers, Inc. (IEEE)—POSIX

Intel Corporation—Intel, 80386, 80486, 386

INTERACTIVE Systems Corporation—386/ix, IN/ix and VP/ix

IXI Limited—X.desktop

Language Processors, Inc.—LPI

Locus Computing Corporation—X Sight

Massachusetts Institute of Technology—X Window

MicroFocus Ltd.—MicroFocus

Microport Corp.—DOSMerge, Microport, System V/AT, System V/386

Microsoft Corporation—MS-DOS, XENIX, MS, Windows-386, Windows-3.0, LAN Manager

MIPS Computer Systems, Inc.—RISC

Motorola Computer Systems—MC68010, MC68020, MC68030, Motorola

NCR Corp.—NCR, TOWER, TPSX, System 3000, ITX

NeXT—NeXT

Novell—NetWare, UnixWare

Open Software Foundation—Motif

Open Systems Inc.—Open Systems

Oracle Inc.—Oracle

Radioshack—TRS80

The Regents of University of California—Berkeley 4.2BSD, Berkeley 4.3BSD

Relational Technology, Inc.—INGRES

The Santa Cruz Operation, Inc.—SCO, SCO VP/ix, Open Desktop, SCO UNIX, and SCO XENIX

SPARC International Inc.—SPARC

Sun Microsystems, Inc.—SunOS, ONC, X11/NeWS, Open Windows, NeWSprint, Network File System (NFS), Sun 3, Sun 4, SunLink and PC-NFS and NeWS, SPARC, SPARCstation, Sun Microsystems

Sybase, Inc.—Sybase, Data ToolSet, DataServer, Data WorkBench

Tolerant Systems, Inc.—TX, Pathway

Transaction Processing Performance Council—TPC Benchmark

UniForum—UniForum, /usr/group

Unicorn—UniKix

Unify—Unify

Unisys Corporation—Unisys 6000

Visionware Inc.—X Vision

VISystems Inc.—VIS/TP

The Wollongang Group, Eunice, WIN

Xerox Corporation—Ethernet

X/Open Company Ltd.—XPG3, X/Open, UNIX

Zilog—Z80

All other products and services mentioned herein are identified by the trademarks as designated by the companies that market those products. Inquiries concerning such trademarks should be made directly to those companies.

Contents

List of Figures

Preface

The first edition of this work, *The UNIX Industry*, was written between 1987 and 1990. In this second edition, the basic structure of the book is the same, but its emphasis has been shifted. All sections have been updated, and many new topics are covered including microkernel technology and multiprocessing on the technical side, and there is extensive new material on business reengineering and the impact of Open Systems on information architecture. An overview of COSE, the common Open System software environment is also provided.

The computer industry, perhaps one of the most dynamic and fast paced, continues to undergo significant change. Developing strategies to manage this change is what this book is all about. It is intended for a wide variety of professionals. In rewriting the book, I have increased its relevance to MIS professionals who are faced with the daunting task of delivering on the promise of UNIX and Open Systems-based technologies. To do so requires a major rethinking of the approach to systems planning, design, and implementation. This book is not about systems management methodology; it is about developing strategies for managing different types of change:

> The technology is changing—so how do you keep abreast of what is happening, and how do you separate truly significant trends from marketing hype and press coverage?

> The computer industry is changing. A paradigm shift is accelerating that promises to restructure the nature of cooperation and competition.

Fortunes are changing on the supply side of the industry. The dynamics between systems and software are changing. There is a growing recognition that software—and more specifically a solutions orientation—is required to meet customer needs. COSE, described at the end of Chapter 1 promises to accelerate this trend.

Customers themselves (the demand side of the industry) are changing as they are impacted by the availability of enabling technology that accelerates change. Companies are accepting the necessity to re-examine their business and re-engineer business processes as they adopt this new information technology in order to achieve the maximum benefits.

The way computers are used is changing. New styles of computing are emerging; old methods such as online transaction processing are being reinvented but within a more advanced, open, networked enterprise computing environment. Such changes demand a reorientation and rethinking of how information systems are architected to meet business objectives.

Open Systems standards are changing and evolving as are the processes through which they are developed. The adoption of a standards-based information architecture is one of the keys to avoiding lock-in and technological obsolescence. But standards are not always what they appear to be.

The UNIX and Open Systems industries are quite complex. Understanding these topics within the normal context of information overload, retraining, and gaining new skills will be a requisite for most computer professionals as the paradigm shift to Open Systems and interoperability takes place.

How to read this book

To better understand the structure of this book, a brief synopsis of each chapter is included here. The UNIX industry is organized into the following seven chapters, an extensive glossary, and a bibliography.

CHAPTER 1—UNIX COMES OF AGE

The history of UNIX and events leading to the present are used to provide an understanding of UNIX in relation to general advances in computer science. Our treatment of UNIX history deals with the evolution of the UNIX operating system and with critical sociological and commercial factors that have helped shape today's UNIX industry.

The concept of a layered systems architecture is introduced, which is then used repeatedly in later chapters to explain the UNIX operating system, portability, and important emerging standards and standards bodies relevant to UNIX and Open Systems. This explanation is directly relevant to developing an understanding of COSE.

CHAPTER 2—BASIC UNIX CONCEPTS AND PHILOSOPHY

This chapter provides the reader with a high-level, user-oriented view of UNIX. It explores all of the major components of the operating system and how they interrelate and operate. It does not provide specific instructions on command usage, nor does it attempt to describe technically how the UNIX system works. Rather, it concentrates on describing the key elements in UNIX from the point of view of layered systems and Open Systems architecture. Numerous references are provided for the reader interested in more technical details.

CHAPTER 3—THE SUPPLY SIDE OF THE UNIX MARKET

This chapter begins by describing system elements that should be considered when comparing various UNIX system alternatives. A system evaluation methodology is recommended that details considerations that should be made during the process of system evaluation and selection. There is a brief summary of the major commercial UNIX systems suppliers. The supply side of the UNIX industry is explored by analysis of the strategies of seven major computer systems vendors. Other leading systems and software suppliers are also provided.

CHAPTER 4—THE DEMAND SIDE OF THE UNIX MARKET

This chapter is an in-depth discussion of major trends and characteristics of the UNIX market. The UNIX market is segmented and sized in terms of geography, industry, application, and establishment size. Key market participants' strategies are highlighted.

CHAPTER 5—NEW STYLES OF COMPUTING

This chapter provides an introduction to rapidly advancing areas of computing, including networked computing, the client-server architecture, windowing graphical user interfaces, and transaction processing.

Simplified explanations and examples of these relatively new concepts in computer usage are provided. This section also analyzes how these new styles of computing are contributing to a shift in the way computer systems are being deployed.

New styles of computing will allow more cost-effective utilization of computer power, ease of use, and flexibility for the next generation of application solutions based on UNIX. Further, new styles of computing—together with an Open Systems strategy—based on a set of vendor-independent, internationally established data communication and operating system standards will yield many benefits. Most important among them will be more leverage and buying power with computer vendors, lower costs, and a much stronger network-capable basic system platform for integrating information resources.

CHAPTER 6—OPEN SYSTEMS, STANDARDS, AND THE UNIX INDUSTRY

This chapter discusses the evolution and importance of standards as they relate specifically to UNIX. It gives an overview of several major standards bodies and describes the work they are performing. Among the topics discussed are UNIX System V, IEEE's POSIX, FIPS, and X/OPEN, as well as OSF and UNIX International, two consortia of prominent computer systems and software vendors. The chapter concludes with a comprehensive discussion of software portability in UNIX environments.

CHAPTER 7—OPEN SYSTEMS AND INFORMATION ARCHITECTURES IN TRANSITION

A great challenge lies ahead for business executives and MIS professionals in determining how they can best design and implement information technology. This chapter deals with one of the most important elements in this regard—business process re-engineering. This section provides insights into the impact Open Systems will have on information architecture.

CHAPTER 8—GETTING CONNECTED

There are many resources available to learn more about UNIX. This chapter provides a road map of where to go and how to get additional information. Sources of UNIX market research, professional societies and user groups, trade shows, application software, and educational services are all described. This information will steer the interested reader to valuable resources that will help him or her remain current with the rapidly changing UNIX industry.

GLOSSARY AND BIBLIOGRAPHY

The glossary (Appendix A) sets forth easily understood, high-level definitions to help the reader with terms and concepts. The bibliography (Appendix B) lists 33 works the reader may want to refer to.

How different readers can approach this book

This book provides a considerable amount of information and is unlikely to be read cover to cover in one sitting. Depending on your area of interest, you might want to read chapters in a different order. Here are some suggestions.

- If you are a manager or sales professional, you will find the chapters are pretty much already organized in a logical progression.
- If you are technically familiar with UNIX, you might want to start with later chapters, which discuss the supply and demand side of the market, and return to the early chapters afterwards.
- If you are an end user and new to UNIX, you might want to start by reading the glossary to become familiar with terminology and then read Chapter 7 first.
- If you are an MIS professional or business executive, you should start by reading Chapter 7.

In any case, the Introduction that follows will set the stage for the remainder of the book. It is divided into two parts. Part I examines the paradigm shift that is occurring in business with the movement toward open, networked enterprise organizations. Part II examines in greater detail the important role that UNIX and Open Systems will play in facilitating this transition to a new way of integrating information technology and business systems.

ACKNOWLEDGMENTS

The UNIX Industry and Open Systems in Transition was written in two phases over the past six years, during which time I worked at Sun Microsystems Computer Corporation. Because Sun focuses solely on the UNIX market, when I first joined Sun it was necessary for me to become as knowledgeable as possible about both the technology and business aspects of UNIX. As I learned, I realized that most of the sources of UNIX information were highly technical, oriented specifically toward technical end users and software developers. I became aware of the need for a higher-level, more business-oriented analysis.

Over the past few years, I have sensed there was a considerable amount of confusion among commercial users and MIS professionals in understanding the impact of Open Systems and UNIX and Open Systems, standards, and how all of these relate to information systems strategies. This situation is only made more difficult because of the rapid pace of change and confusion created to some extent by the popular press. The UNIX industry is experiencing change on the supply side of the market due to rapid technological advancement. At the same time UNIX is being *pulled* into the commercial market at a time when computing is becoming an integral part of most businesses. MIS professionals are trying to figure out how UNIX fits at a time when conventional Information Architecture and strategies are being radically impacted by client-server computing and Open Systems.

At no time has change been so prevalent, and never has it been more challenging to manage the change while moving forward.

My career in computing began in the early 1970s, a period when mainframes were the norm and time-sharing was still somewhat new. Over the next two decades, as my career evolved from systems design and programming to technical marketing and business, I became more interested in how technology could be applied to business problems. I realized that tremendous opportunities lay ahead for UNIX as a result of the industry shift toward Open Systems—opportunities that would benefit not just programmers and technicians but also systems managers, purchasing managers, and executive decision makers, as well as marketing, sales, and support specialists.

I frequented the bookstores and libraries, seeking more information about UNIX, but I could not find the sort of industry and technology overview I was looking for. I decided to write the original book, *The UNIX Industry*, not only for myself but for others like me who wanted a broader understanding of UNIX technology and industry from management and business perspective. As the first version of the book went to press, I felt it was particularly challenging to include up-to-date information that would have longer-term value for the reader. The week I froze the text of the first version, major industry announcements were still being made (the ACE consortium in particular). As it turned out, these particular announcements never came to fruition ... but it started me thinking about the rapid nature of change in the industry.

That is when I decided to work on a sequel, a book about Open Systems and UNIX industry transitions and how people can better understand and predict these transitions and factor them into their planning.

Thanks are due to the many people who helped me along the way. I would especially like to thank James Callan of the Albert Consulting Group for his continuous support as a collaborator on the original project as well as the sequel. There are many people who read the first book and offered advice and insight. Acknowledgments and thanks go to Todd Bernhard, Collette Moquette Ricks, Colleen Sullivan, and Gina Davis for their support early in the project. I'd also like to thank Gordon Short (Hitachi) and Mike Dierker (Independence Technology, Inc.) for their feedback on reviewing early drafts of the manuscript. Thanks also to Eric Herr, Pat Harding, Norm Eaglestone, Andy Hall, Xavier Candia, Marleen McDaniel, Herb Hinstorff, Michelle Aden, and many others at Sun. I would also like to thank Roger Gourd, vice president of engineering for the Open Systems Foundation, Inc., who read the manuscript and provided insight and perspective that balance my Sun-nurtured views.

I would like to thank the following people who provided valuable input on the second version of this work: David Smith and members of The Context Group were extremely supportive on the new sections on client-server database systems and applications re-engineering. Michelle Aden, Larry Baker, and Andrew Maisel provided valuable insight in the area of Open Systems standards. Thanks go to Brad Jacobs of Breakaway Software, a firm in San Francisco specializing in UNIX system administration. Craig Stouffer, president of Mobius Computer, provided excellent feedback on PC UNIX and the need for information on networking. Thanks also to Mark Gorenberg of Hummer Winblad Venture Group for his insights into the UNIX and PC software industries.

Many thanks also to Richard Fichera, an independent consultant, and to James M. Spitze, CIO of Tri Valley Growers and president of The Systems Consulting Consortium, Inc. Jim has been a source of deep practical knowledge on the complex subject of Information Architecture. I would also like to thank all the vendors who provided input and feedback. A special thanks to my brother Charles H. Dunphy, Jr., for working with me from the first draft manuscript and throughout the project, and to my wife Janet and my family for their ongoing support and encouragement.

It is my hope that readers of *The UNIX Industry and Open System in Transition* will gain a fundamental understanding of UNIX concepts and deeper appreciation of the relevance of UNIX, Open Systems, and leading-edge technology on information systems strategies, on end users, and on the computer industry in general.

Thanks to InfoCorp and in particular to Lewis Brentano, Group vice president for his support and permission to use certain data especially on market sizing, and to Richard Fichera for his contributions to the industry's demand-side analysis.

The author also acknowledges the support of Sun Microsystems, Inc. for permission to access Sun's computers in the development of this work and for permission to use graphics icons in some of its illustrations.

Ed Dunphy

Introduction

PART I—FOCUSING ON BUSINESS

Perhaps the most challenging requirement in gaining competitive advantage from computers and in using information technology effectively is focusing more on business and less on technology.

As we move into the 1990s, major changes will occur as a consequence of the intensified competitive business environment. Just as a major technological shift is predicted in terms of new technology supporting open, networked computing, there will also be a modification in the nature of organizations.

The 1990s will be the decade of major transition in terms of the way business is conducted. Major industry shifts will occur as companies restructure their cost base and look for ways to use information technology for competitive advantage. Major business transformations will occur in which management and production processes will be streamlined and redefined.

Paper-based systems, bureaucratic approval processes, clerical activity, multilayered decision-making processes, and the like will be replaced by source data capture, integrated transaction processing, electronic data interchange, real-time systems, online decision support, document management, and expert systems.

Computers will become ubiquitous. Information technology will be used in many new ways to improve the productivity of knowledge and service workers. It will become increasingly easy to use and therefore will accommodate a much wider range of end uses.

Companies understand the need to react to rapidly changing market conditions. Attention to quality in manufacturing and production environments, for example, is recognized in terms of the integrated nature of the production process where quality problems can back up, causing a chain reaction of problems along the supplier network. Information technology must address the need to support distributed business operations and serve as a means of connecting to other companies and their information systems.

The global nature of most major businesses necessitate 24-hour-a-day, worldwide networks to link business divisions, customers, and suppliers and to support the needs of the business infrastructure. Applications must become network intrinsic to fulfill the requirements of these environments.

Considerable attention is being paid to the ability to integrate the product or services of suppliers—allowing offloading of previously internal processes to outside suppliers. Companies realize that no single vendor can do it all. The era of proprietary systems is coming to an abrupt end.

What is behind the move to enterprise computing?

In the past, vertical integration within an enterprise was attempted to gain self-sufficiency and competitive advantage. The enterprise of the 1990s, however, is shifting the focus to horizontal integration across organizations, including alliance partnerships, sales and distribution relationships, key supplier relations, support organization, and generally tighter integration of divisions within the enterprise.

The enterprise is becoming "extended" based on new kinds of relationships with suppliers, customers, affinity groups, and even competitors. Today's enterprise is opening up. This implies many dimensions of change, and organizations will tend to move at different paces along these dimensions. The structure of the new enterprise is moving from a multilayered hierarchy to a set of integrated yet relatively autonomous business units. The new organization paradigm is one of a global, open, networked business environment.

An era of profound change that will test leadership lies ahead

The business application of computers, the nature of the technology and the leadership required to successfully plan, control, and use it, will be going through profound change. In the 1950s through the 1970s, information technology for data processing was primarily viewed as offering cost reductions by reducing clerical costs. In the 1980s and early 1990s, information technology has become both ubiquitous and strategic. It is now a necessary component for the execution of the business outside of traditional areas of data processing. Computing has expanded well beyond back office data processing to the front line delivery of services and products to customers.

A change has occurred in terms of who uses computers. The new users are business users—not just technicians or professionals. Business users want to shape the technology implemented in their personal computing environment, their work group environment, and their organizations, and they are not content to depend completely on traditional MIS departments to achieve the benefits technology can bring. As computing in the workplace—and related computing outside the workplace—change, the traditional approach to MIS is being outmoded.

The industry has seen a succession of shifts from centralized to decentralized computing, from batch to interactive, from timesharing to personal computing, and now from personal computing to work group computing. Work group systems streamline the work process or work flow and thereby change the nature of the jobs in a business unit. One of the key goals in work group automation is to reduce the turnaround time or cycle time. In essence, get the job done faster. Electronic mail, integrated office automation and Lotus Notes are all examples of this today.

With the move to work group computing, a major task lies ahead in integrating islands of automation. Often, these islands are found in the form of departmental computer solutions. For example, manufacturing systems, financial systems, sales and marketing systems, personnel and payroll systems, and engineering systems are developed separately, and they each provide specific information system functions and often require separate administrative support. The major systems are usually organized around the lines of functional management and control systems.

An enterprise architecture, which provides the backbone for the new open, networked enterprise, enables moving beyond the traditional organizational hierarchy. As a transitional step, many companies are implementing executive and management decision support systems—building links between various existing systems.

The new technology that supports work group computing will be extended to allow the recasting of relationships with external organizations. Computer systems between enterprises are beginning to talk to each other. Corporate computing is becoming interenterprise computing, with an electronic value-added network that links affinity groups such as business partners and customers. Interenterprise databases, voice response systems, electronic messaging, and automated point-of-sale devices are all examples of emerging technologies that support the interenterprise.

Computer-to-computer interchange of business documents through electronic data interchange is transforming the way companies work together. Using EDI a company can communicate purchase orders, shipping notices, invoices, remittance and inventory advice, text messaging, and changes to purchase order inquiries and status reports. Companies can link to not only their suppliers but to networks of other companies as well through value-added networking services.

Information technology hierarchy is rapidly evolving in numerous dimensions including the following:

- Personal computing—especially mobile computing
- Work group computing
- Corporate computing
- Interenterprise computing (private)
- Interenterprise computing (public)

It used to be that only large companies with private networks could implement interenterprise computing strategies. But these capabilities are becoming available to any size company and even individuals. Public interenterprise computing is facilitated by providers of public internetworking (Compuserve, PSI, the Internet, etc.), providing a new means for cost-effective interenterprise computer communications.

Important changes are occurring in microprocessor technology, in multiprocessing, in the transformation of host-based to networked-based computing, in software development, and in many other technology areas. There will be accelerated change in the way people work with computers and in the dynamics of both the supply side and demand side of the industry.

Information technology sourcing strategies will change from reliance on a single, proprietary vendor to multivendor. There will be a higher reliance on industry standards for vendor-neutral solutions. Shrinkwrap software—or at least the serious consideration to buy versus make in all but the most sophisticated applications will be more widely utilized. In the 1990s, a revolutionary change will occur in terms of computer-aided software development and application interoperability, with the emergence of commercial quality, object-oriented technology.

The greatest challenge lies in managing this change

Research has shown that the real problems are less technological and more organizational for managing computing, along with the knowledge skills, resource base, and new approaches required for systems and network planning and applications re-engineering. Users also will have to play a more involved and proactive role in information systems from the definition phase through assuming responsibility for their own system administration—or at least adhering to new computing policies.

How will this change occur?

A survey by DMR showed that 75 percent of the Information Systems managers surveyed admitted that their organizations did not have the necessary information to understand and evaluate the relative merits of moving to Open Systems. Surveying their investments in legacy systems, most IS managers are struck by the enormity of the challenge. Managing, planning, and controlling this change are responsibilities that will be shared at many levels within the organization. The challenge is not just to learn a new model of computing but rather to set out a new way of doing business in which the ability and flexibility to change is built into the planning process.

There are two dynamics at work here. First, there will be a technology push from the supply side. Second, there will be demand pull from the new business-team-oriented organizations. It is interesting to consider these changes in the way people and work groups will function in terms that bear metaphorical relationships to the technology itself. An open-networked organization will be based on cooperative multidisciplinary teams and businesses. Business teams are both clients (to upstream teams) and servers to other teams, both inside and outside the organization.

The team approach has been used for years. In the automotive industry, teams of engineers are assigned to new car development projects that are treated as business programs where the team leader has real power and responsibility. Teams are a way of empowering people instead of relying on hierarchical executive management.

Changes in information technology will enable companies to redesign their business processes and remove the barriers normally associated with hierarchical organizational structure. But technology will only facilitate and provide a support infrastructure. Companies must re-evaluate both their business and their business processes. Establishing effective work groups supported by work group computing will result in high-performance teams that will be of real strategic value to meeting corporate objectives. The greatest gains will not come from technology but from the changes in the way people work and work together.

Re-engineering the Workplace and the Work Group

Call it re-engineering or re-architecting or business process redesign, it all implies the same sort of planning, design, and implementation of changes in business process. Business processes are a set of work activities that are logically related and executed to create a business outcome such as creating a product or providing a service. Work systems result from combining business processes to achieve broader business objectives.

As we will see later when we discuss change management, the beginning of change occurs when a careful assessment of the current situation is carried out. It may seem stereotypical, but in some medium- to large-scale organizations, it is not uncommon to find out no one is really sure "why we do it that way." The typical response could be "but we've been doing it that way for as long as anyone around here can remember." It is often the case that the relationship between information systems and business process and architecture is never explicitly documented. As a result, anything that would help the business planner or system developer understand why something is done a certain way is lost.

The objectives of work group re-engineering include the following:

*   Streamlining communications
*   Improving inter-work group communications and synergy
*   Improving decision making
*   Increasing the efficiency of the division of labor
*   Eliminating unnecessary activities
*   Reducing the time it takes to get the job done
*   Increasing the speed of the response systems (e.g., customer support)

The technology push

Work group computing is a major supply side technology push driven by the rapidly increasing power of desktop workstations and servers plus the maturing of networking technology. The work group will not be restricted to an office or campus location. Wide area networking allows work groups to function with team members in geographically remote locations. The graphical user interface technology that improves ease of use and reduces training costs is yet another factor. All of these base technologies are being exploited by a new type of software known as groupware. This software takes a variety of forms including the following:

- Teleconferencing
- Electronic mail and document distribution
- Calendar planning tools
- Electronic data interchange utilities, services, and linkages
- Powerful new scheduling tools

For those familiar with personal computers, this may not seem so new. But the shift from personal to work group computing is a notable departure from the ways PCs are traditionally used, even in PC-LAN environments.

PCs facilitate standalone word processing; work group computing will help coauthoring and shared document creation. Desktop computing with PCs today is largely restricted to the capabilities of the PC. PC-LANs offer only basic file and print sharing capabilities compared to work group computing. Applications sharing of multimedia (data, text, voice, and image) information access and networked applications software access will be the norm for groupware applications. Spreadsheets in a databased work group environment will facilitate multiuser decision support.

The emphasis on work group computing will require better access to information. Real-time alarms or threshold indicators that advise a user when an important event occurs will be used with expert systems to aid in decision making in a wide range of applications. In these types of applications, software and hardware subsystems will monitor events as they occur in real time. When a preprogrammed event occurs, such as an indicator that is out of range, an intelligent alarm will be set off that could take any of a number of different forms. It might take the form of a pop-up window on a display and/or an audible alarm to notify the operator something is wrong.

Implications of work group computing

Work group computing will have profound effects on organizational structure. Organizations will need to be re-architected to concentrate more on business teams and less on functional and hierarchical lines. A shift from personal computing to group-oriented computing will take place given the availability of groupware, desktop computing, and networking technology. The emphasis will shift from the individual to the team. A change in application will occur from technocentricity to re-engineering the way work is performed. A wider group of users will develop, and this will further accelerate the pace of change. New applications, such as geographical information systems, will spring up providing completely new ways of looking at data.

Perhaps the most significant shift will occur in the way information system technology is planned, designed, and implemented. The installation of technology will be accompanied by changes in the very nature of the business process. All of these events will require forward-thinking management to lead the way and plan the migration from existing systems to new styles of computing as well as plan the migration of the human skill base that uses these systems.

The challenge for integrated information systems

The demands of future business environments will force continual reinvention of the business structure. Companies will need to function as a single enterprise rather than being a collection of business units for effective information sharing and communication. Yet, at the same time, the new enterprise will be based on a client-server model, which is built around empowered business teams with a higher degree of autonomy. This is an apparent paradox that will only be resolved if there is an overall strategy and information architecture for the business, the work organization, information, and technology.

Since it will be information technology more than any other factor that enables this new integrated system, an enterprise-wide information architecture is required. This architecture must incorporate a migration path forward from legacy systems and past investments as well as ensure the integration of new systems. Effective coordination through ongoing user-driven process is proving to be the best way organizations can develop and evolve their technology infrastructure to support their business objections.

There are numerous dimensions to the challenges faced by IS professionals who seek to develop future information architectures. The impact of Open Systems on information architecture, the subject to which most of Chapter 7 is dedicated, implies significant changes must be made in a number of areas:

- Change must be driven from the top of the organization.
- A new recognition of the role of open systems standards must be developed.

In order to deal with the real-world complexity of business processes, basic systems theory tells us to begin by dismantling (functionally decomposing) the overall business process and systems into a number of standard functions with well-defined behavior and interfaces between people and work groups. The methodology we suggest is similar to that of a layered systems architecture with the development of clean, documented set of business policies and procedures between empowered work groups. The focus should be on integration between these business processes and information systems. One of the key goals of the Information Architecture must be to foster cooperative business processing.

PART II—INTRODUCTION TO UNIX AND OPEN SYSTEMS

This book was originally written during a critical time in the evolution of not only the UNIX operating system but of the UNIX industry as a whole. It provides a comprehensive overview of one of the most exciting stages in the evolution of the computer industry. It is hoped that the reader will benefit by obtaining a wide business perspective of these changes and their practical significance. The work has been expanded to increase its relevance to MIS professionals and general management as well.

This book has been developed specifically for managers, executives, users, and sales and support professionals in the computer industry who have a basic level of computer literacy. It will also serve as a thorough overview of the UNIX industry and technology for college students who desire a broader understanding.

Today's computer market is experiencing major change caused by a movement toward Open Systems and what some have called free-market computing. Only in the last decade has this phenomenon and philosophy begun to move out of the research labs and into the real world—out of the realm of marketing and sales hype and into commercial reality. A new, consistent language—or paradigm—of computing is emerging. It is difficult to keep abreast, let alone stay in the forefront, of the technology, the trends, or even the terminology. This book has been written to help its readers better understand not only UNIX technology and terminology but the structure of the UNIX industry and Open Systems.

Pinning UNIX down

UNIX is a trademark of X/Open Company Ltd., now owned by Novell. It is the name of an operating system. There are numerous operating systems based on UNIX, but they can only be called UNIX if they are licensed from USL and comply with their licensing terms. In this book,

UNIX is often used to refer to suppliers of software or systems products based either formally or informally on the Novell UNIX product or its specifications.

AT&T historically (and now Novell) didn't allow the name UNIX to be used as a noun, only as an adjective. The reason is a legal one having to do with trademark protection. There are many different meanings to the term "UNIX," and restricting the use of the label requires one to be more precise. But in conversation and sometimes in print people didn't heed AT&T's warning. Defining UNIX is a most confusing task. Experienced programmers describe their feelings and judgments about it. Users talk about its user interface or their UNIX applications. Vendors tell you about their particular variant and its distinct features rather than about UNIX in general.

The attention UNIX is getting now is due as much to advances in hardware and systems as it is to UNIX software. With the 80x86 and 680x0 and RISC processor chips, we finally have realistic, low-cost, multiuser, microcomputer-based systems. A resurgence of interest in UNIX can also be attributed to growth in the workstation and high-performance computer market and, more recently, to the trend toward Open Systems.

An Open Systems architecture is one built from a set of vendor-independent, internationally recognized and established standards as well as a standard application platform. Vendor-independent standards have become known in the industry as "Open System standards." There should be no doubt as to the increasing rate of change occurring in the computer marketplace. This growth is fueled by both technological advancements and commercial factors. Recent years have also seen the growing influence of standards bodies. Nowhere are these changes creating more opportunity than in the UNIX marketplace.

The widening array of commercial products is making it harder for the average professional user and manager to become and remain informed. A dozen new books appear monthly about UNIX and Open Systems, and there are now several established professional monthly periodicals dedicated specifically to it. Articles abound in industry publications, tracking the progress of products and the standards movements, providing details from the soap opera being acted out by vendor consortia battling for public mind share, and extolling the virtues of the industry high fliers' very latest developments. The sheer amount of data itself is staggering. Nearly all of the computer industry's major market research companies are now actively developing and promoting UNIX-oriented services to meet the needs of system and software vendors. Such services are too expensive for all but the largest end-user organizations.

In the last five years, companies have moved significantly beyond the evaluation stage. UNIX is no longer restricted in its application to academic, scientific, or technical communities. It has achieved commercial momentum and is now having a major impact in the computer marketplace. While UNIX gained early acceptance in areas of technical computing and applications, it is poised for explosive growth in commercial markets where proprietary operating systems have been dominant. UNIX is now verging on penetration into the PC and PC LAN markets.

UNIX System V Interface Definition, or SVID, specifications that define UNIX are rapidly becoming nonnegotiable elements in users' requests for proposals for their future computer systems. Many companies are making strong commitments in terms of capital outlay for systems, applications, and personnel, all of which are based on new, emerging standards. As a result of unprecedented cooperation between vendors, these standards are set not only by formal standards bodies such as IEEE and ISO but also by vendor consortia such as the Open Software Foundation (OSF) and UNIX International (UI). Finally, large or progressive companies are first establishing their own internal standards. They have in recent years banded together in industry groups and are becoming much more involved in the standards process.

So what is behind this change? Haven't we been hearing for years now that widespread use of UNIX is just around the corner? UNIX is far from being the new kid on the block. It is in its mid-20s. As a result of the way it developed, both technically and commercially, there have been numerous versions of UNIX—probably more than 100 of them, all the same or similar in terms of being based on the UNIX System V Interface Definition. All have differed, however—sometimes significantly—in terms of implementation. Only in the last year has there been a convergence of the most popular versions of UNIX and general industry agreement on UNIX standards.

SVID and POSIX are now the accepted standard specification for UNIX. POSIX represents the lowest common denominator in operating systems' call interface. It will become the standard not only for UNIX but for most other proprietary operating systems such as VMS and MVS as well. Agreement on standards by multiple UNIX vendors has expanded well beyond communications and the UNIX operating system interface and into wider specifications of computer systems environments such as those from X/Open. This is simply a recognition on the part of the industry that a standard application programming interface for the operating system is necessary but not sufficient to ensure portability of user applications across a range of systems and their layered software environments.

But why has there been so much in the trade press about UNIX? Is there really something to it, or is this simply more hype from the marketing departments of systems vendors? While there *is* an enormous amount of marketing hype, UNIX is now recognized as a commercially viable alternative to proprietary operating systems. The reason computer companies started believing UNIX was important was that the two largest segments of the market buying computers, namely the U.S. government and the regional Bell operating companies, as well as many other large corporations, were demanding UNIX.

Why UNIX? Cost—Application solutions—Consistency

Cost reduction is one of the principal driving factors in the UNIX market—especially from the user's point of view. UNIX holds the promise of reducing user dependence on a particular supplier who has been locked into an operating system. "Locked into" means that applications the user runs are only available on that particular brand of hardware, and changing hardware is a costly and difficult undertaking since it ultimately means scrapping one's investment in systems, software, and user training. Why is it that most new hardware products come to market first supporting UNIX? With UNIX, migrating to new technologies—for example, to more powerful multiprocessing computer system architectures—becomes considerably easier for any user both technologically and in terms of cost. This benefits customers and the systems vendors alike. Another major reason for this migration lies in the large number of applications that are available and that run on UNIX-based systems, as well as the relative ease with which they can be ported between different system environments.

UNIX can help build consistency

Consistency can get results. What are people really going to get out of IBM's SAA or DEC's NAS or any of the umbrella architectures? Can they point to something and say, "That's what I was able to do with SAA?" The benefit most people derive from an architecture is consistency. It forces manpower and skill to be focused in a common direction. UNIX is going to play a very important role in bringing consistency to an otherwise complex world of multiple technologies and multiple platforms.

Portability and cost benefits are driving the trend toward UNIX

The single most important element in the movement toward UNIX as a standard lies in its achieving a degree of portability. This makes it easier than in the past to move work and applications software freely to less expensive and/or higher-function hardware platforms available from a far wider range of suppliers. This makes UNIX an attractive alternative for users. Application portability reduces the costs for system suppliers as well as for users.

Software costs are skyrocketing. For the hardware vendor, a standard operating system reduces the expense in redeveloping operating systems for new and different system architectures. The amortized cost to a system vendor to design, develop, and support a proprietary operating system can run to 50 percent of total product cost. It can equal the cost of hardware development. While this savings to the systems vendor is an enormous benefit, an even greater plus comes from tapping into the UNIX applications market.

Users and systems vendors alike benefit from the ability to reuse software from other UNIX systems environments. Unlike proprietary system environments, UNIX gives the application user the potential to use the same software or procedures on multiple UNIX systems often with little or no change. Proprietary operating systems such as VMS, OS/2, MVS, MS-DOS, Windows, and Windows/NT are called proprietary because their future evolution and licensing is controlled by a single company. One test of openness is "clonability." A sure sign of an open standard is when you can point to more than one reference model or implementation of the standard.

Current systems are fragmented by different proprietary technologies, which make it very difficult to merge and synthesize information. The current situation is like a modern-day Tower of Babel. Such barriers must be removed for information technology to fulfill its critical role in producing and supporting real productivity improvements for individuals and work groups. UNIX is increasingly being viewed as a viable solution and a key part of information system strategies to address this problem. UNIX itself has also been fragmented with many variants and environments.

While UNIX does offer an attractive alternative from a cost standpoint compared to minicomputers and other systems historically, its popularity hasn't been commercially driven. If it had been, surely UNIX would have a much larger market than it has today. UNIX market acceptance has been gradually built up over the last 24 years by users who preferred the freedom and openness of using UNIX as an alternative to any of the proprietary operating systems that were available. This base of users has expanded to include a very wide range of users over time.

AT&T originally licensed UNIX to hundreds of universities for a nominal fee. An estimated 500,000+ students worldwide are graduating from universities annually, and of these, tens of thousands have become proficient in UNIX. These people are entering the work force in significant numbers, and their influence will be increasingly felt as they become more influential in the purchasing decisions of large industrial concerns. A review of any technical UNIX conference proceedings will illustrate that the research and scientific community, in addition to major industrial corporations, are still exerting a strong influence on the technological advancement of UNIX.

While AT&T's licensing of UNIX to universities and institutions increased its availability and popularity, the computer industry had never before experienced the adoption of any operating system software architecture like UNIX. Even MS-DOS was never adopted by such a diverse number of vendors offering such a wide spectrum of hardware. Growth in UNIX systems is coupled with growth in networked computing, and the fastest-growing computer companies in the industry have UNIX as their primary (or only) operating system.

Hundreds of computer systems vendors have announced a commitment to UNIX and Open Systems on their hardware products. Virtually every major computer company today offers some variant of UNIX. The industry's largest vendors have recently moved from a position of treating UNIX as a stepchild to their proprietary operating systems to that of treating it as a nearly equal "strategic" product. For example, IBM has announced that AIX (their variant UNIX implementation) is available on several (but not all) lines of their computers. IBM has publicly stated that they support UNIX as an architecture just as they support SAA! DEC's UNIX variant, called ULTRIX, has received considerable attention as DEC has announced new higher-performance system, workstation, and fault-tolerant system products that only run one of the variants of UNIX they support (e.g., ULTRIX, SVR4), not their mainstay proprietary operating system known as VMS. More recently, DEC has announced the support of System V Release 4 on their new high-availability (fault-tolerant) systems. While the traditional computer systems vendors support some variant of UNIX in addition to their proprietary operating systems, newer companies like Sun Microsystems support *only* UNIX. Even the traditional companies are now launching product lines that run only versions of UNIX.

Today's computers, from personal computers to mainframes, are being networked together. There are natural advantages to having networked systems share as many characteristics as possible. The more commonality, the more potential for interoperability. During the 1990s, networked computing will advance rapidly from today's technology, which permits data and file sharing, to fully distributed applications processing. UNIX will play a major role in facilitating this trend toward interoperability not only for individual computer system product lines but across diverse heterogeneous networks of computer systems. UNIX promises to do for the work group computing environment what MS-DOS did for personal computing.

Interoperability means that the components from different vendors will work together to form systems that support the overall applications solution. It refers to the notion of connecting disparate hardware platforms and providing compatible data types and consistent protocol levels. Interoperability implies that users can easily access data anywhere in the network without having to worry about where in the network the data actually resides. Demand for interoperability is being driven by users and will benefit them by increasing the ease with which data can be shared and manipulated.

The UNIX and Open Systems information explosion

There is a considerable amount of data available to anyone interested in UNIX. Most of it has historically been technically oriented and narrowly targeted to the computer user or technician. Technical reference manuals and command reference manuals for both novice and power users (programmers) crowd the shelves of technical bookstores and libraries. Even the introductory material currently available is targeted primarily at the reader who has to learn to *use* UNIX.

The UNIX Industry and Open Systems in Transition is motivated in large part by the recognized need of many people for a synthesized, tightly focused body of information about UNIX. Many people neither need nor seek to be UNIX experts in a technical sense. Rather, they need to understand UNIX basics in order to better perform in other professional, managerial, or supervisory functions. *The UNIX Industry and Open Systems in Transition* provides a management summary of UNIX to fill the need for a wider, management-minded view of UNIX.

Managers should become more aware of what is meant by Open Systems and how this may affect their computing environment. Users should purchase UNIX-compatible products and understand the benefits of this in terms of software compatibility. Large and most smaller organizations alike should pay more attention and participate as best they can in the standards process. They should adopt standards internally as the basis for their longer-term information technology strategies. This is an important way to protect the assets associated with information technology systems, including hardware, systems software, applications solutions, and user training.

Open Systems management information technology strategy

In an ideal implementation of Open Systems, components would plug in and play with each other like the components of modern sound systems (for example, stereos). This would allow one to mix and match components in creative ways, leveraging the relative strengths of several suppliers to get the desired result (optimizing price, performance, reliability, and so forth). The strength of Open Systems is vendor independence. Independence is achieved through standardization in the way components from different vendors plug and play. There is growing and broad-based support for standards in the computing and communications industries. This is particularly true in the UNIX segment of these industries.

It is always difficult to predict the future, and this is particularly true of the computing industry. The research that led to the original work, *The UNIX Industry*, indicated that major change would continue to occur over the next decade in the information technology arena, and it has in the form of mergers and acquisitions, technological advancements, and so forth. The goal of *The UNIX Industry and Open Systems in Transition* is to help managers understand and respond to new industry directions and position their businesses to achieve maximum advantage from this continuing evolution in computing.

Research indicates that as a whole the computer industry is still in an application development crisis, an application programming backlog crisis that isn't new but has been around for more than a decade and is only getting worse. Neither traditional tools nor today's generation of high-productivity proprietary tools provide an adequate solution to the needs of the next wave of integrated and GUI-oriented, network-intrinsic applications. Today's tools are much better than they used to be, and the application development crisis has been the driving force behind the tools, which are just now coming to market. A new model for networked application development is needed. This will be one of the major driving forces behind the continued push toward UNIX and Open Systems standards. These powerful catalysts will focus the energies of the software industry to produce tools to handle the complexity of future applications developments.

Just as the personal computer stimulated tremendous development of personal productivity applications, Open Systems will stimulate the development of "organizational" systems, focusing first on logical work groups and eventually on entire enterprises. Today's focus on work group computing is in contrast to the traditional "departmental" structures. Applications will be run on many vendors' platforms, increasing market share potential for software vendors and stimulating new software developments. MIS and in-house developers will also take advantage of this same technology as they replace their aging systems and internally developed applications. According to Bill Joy of Sun Microsystems, "Open Systems are the way to go. They are the best way of adapting to the incredible changes and innovation that lie ahead."

UNIX represents a new model of computing—a formalized, industry-defined, and verifiable standard operating system that can run on many types of hardware. However, much of the talk about UNIX and Open Systems fails to address how computers and information technology actually create and add value.

This has to do with innovation and technology change. All the innovation and change isn't going to occur at once, or in one company. No one can predict when or where it is going to occur. Companies and people need to take advantage of innovation, or they will rapidly fall behind. Technology in most industries means more reliable, cheaper, faster, and so forth. To succeed, the business model and structure has to take advantage of innovation that occurs elsewhere. No company can hire all the best people. In this context UNIX is an industry and a community that transcends a specific commercial implementation. Windows/NT by comparison is a new technology, but its technological evolution is controlled by Microsoft.

Open Systems and standards are simply techniques that remove the roadblocks that prevent technological innovation from getting to the end user. A platform is valuable when it is based on widely accepted standards, which increases the likelihood that someone who knows how to solve a problem will solve it using the latest innovation in information technology.

Open Systems is the birth of free enterprise of ideas in the computer industry. It is critical that computer system platforms be compatible so that valuable people developing innovative technology can spend more time innovating instead of fighting to get their software solutions to run. Successful UNIX and Open Systems vendors will be those who are not just committed to UNIX and Open Systems with rhetoric but who are committed to a philosophy of working together internally and externally with people in other organizations.

Standards allow innovation to be moved around. This is possible even with competing sets of standards. It may even be better to have more than one standard to generate competition and thus encourage faster and more sophisticated developments. The objective is to ensure that technological innovation moves forward at the lowest cost. The important issue is not that of *open* versus *closed* systems. Rather, it is the task of making it possible for users to take full advantage of all the advances technology is able to offer.

Open Systems isn't as "pie in the sky" as one might think. The basic concept of Open Systems is closely linked to software interchangeability and portability across hardware platforms. Interchangeability will become real when the functions of each module and the interfaces between various modules are defined by industry consensus and when software vendors provide products that comply with such standards.

Developing an Open Systems strategy

Most large companies have an MIS group responsible for the selection, assimilation, and utilization of information technology. Open Systems is a fundamentally different approach from the "preferred vendor" strategy followed by many companies. An Open Systems strategy will allow computer companies to provide their customers with computing capabilities that will meet and exceed their requirements at the lowest possible "life cycle cost." Open Systems strategies do not rule out the use of proprietary de facto standards, but it rejects the idea that an entire architecture would be based on them.

The economic advantages of Open Systems include the following:

- Improved flexibility for addressing different business needs while enhancing the economies of scale from departmental and corporate-wide support functions.
- Greater control of business operations such as pricing, production, and inventories, as well as potential for exploitation of new markets through external customer-supplier integration.
- A flatter, more responsive organization through improved networking.
- Reduction of systems' life-cycle cost.

Cost savings from adopting an Open Systems environment will include the following:

- Increased leverage of technical resources by eliminating multiple proprietary environments, all of which require full-range support.
- Reduced effort and hardware dollars expended on "gateways"

or other integrating components that are "built on" instead of "built in."
- Reduced training costs as a consequence of common "look and feel" components and company standard software.
- Volume discounts on common hardware and software.

Open architecture

The highest-level principle of an open architecture is to optimize the whole rather than the parts. Given the high level of specialization within the information system function, the natural tendency is to concentrate on parts—the best local area network, the best PC, the best operating system, the best database management system, the best application generator, and so forth.

Working in isolation, the best components will not make the best whole. The ability of these individual parts to operate as segments of a unit is the key purpose of an Open Systems architecture. Applications built on standard interfaces and services will achieve the highest levels of portability and interoperability. Portability is the ability to port or move an application to multiple vendor platforms.

Why users want and what they expect from Open Systems

- They believe UNIX provides an architectural framework that provides an extensible collection of interfaces.
- They want nonproprietary interfaces defined, supported, and available to any vendor or user in the development of products.
- They expect Open Systems to provide a consensus-based evolution and process regarding the definition and specification of these interfaces.
- They want a user-friendly interface to the operating system and in their applications that provides a common human interface, integrating the execution environments and application-enabling tools.
- They expect common applications programming interfaces and tools for building graphical windowing interfaces.
- They expect a wide range of interoperable components available from different vendors.
- They want vendor-neutral solutions—interoperability with, and application transportability to, hardware and operating systems that are likewise Open Systems.
- They expect that in order to be called "open", systems standards and specifications are recognized by independent standards bodies, such as X/Open, IEEE, and NIST.

UNIX creates momentum for an "Open Systems industry"

Computer communication is perhaps one of the most highly developed and recognized areas of standardization in computer systems technology. True Open Systems will go far beyond communications and the operating system. By the end of the century, Open Systems standards will include virtually all areas in which technology can be seen as a commodity. Unfortunately, the term Open Systems is overloaded today. There are as many definitions of Open Systems as there are people ask to define the term.

Computer buses such as the PCs ISA, EISA, and MCA buses have been called Open Systems. Sun calls its SPARC processor an Open System. Open Systems aren't limited to hardware or software standards. The idea of Open Systems in computing came long after UNIX was invented.

The original ideas that led to the development of UNIX—specifically, that the operating system was portable and could be licensed to anyone who paid a reasonable price for it, and that its source code was available—have since spilled over into many other areas. This is what an "open" UNIX means commercially.

From an applications perspective, the original idea of UNIX was to promote portability of application software. Your application could run on any computer that supported a compatible version of UNIX or at least was much easier to port between different UNIX systems than between proprietary systems. The result was an environment far more open to applications. From a systems perspective, UNIX offered a smooth path for scalability because the same operating system could be run virtually on any computer from laptop to supercomputer. Other operating systems environments supported a much more restricted, or less open, range of computer technology.

Finally, as UNIX and standards for networking such as TCP/IP and Sun Microsystem's NFS combined to allow networked computers to share files and applications, interoperability, even with non-UNIX systems, opened up the computer environment to a new set of network computing possibilities.

As the International Standards Organization came up with the seven-layer Open Systems Interconnection (OSI) stack, the idea of offering interoperability among heterogeneous systems in a standards-based way was born. These systems, however, are not required to have anything else in common except for the OSI communications capability. When UNIX came along, it significantly extended the promise of portability across different and incompatible hardware platforms. The basic operating system was recognized as the next fundamental means of accomplishing applications portability. But true applications portability, even at the source level, requires more than a standard operating system. Such a standard environment is the objective of X/Open's CAE (Common Application Environment). Now the stage is set for the next logical step—assuring not just applications portability but also interchangeability among the components that make up the standards-based environment.

UNIX isn't Open Systems

To many, UNIX has become synonymous with Open Systems, but it is only one part of it. Indeed, a freely available, portable, scalable UNIX operating system has helped create tremendous momentum towards a new world of highly interoperable systems. The UNIX industry has helped to create, and now exists as one part of, the Open Systems market.

UNIX is a subset of Open Systems. The question is not just "Will vendor X put UNIX on all its hardware platforms?" but rather "Will end users be able to buy machines from multiple vendors and plug and play them together, thereby minimizing their training and applications investments?" Open Systems does not necessarily require UNIX on all platforms. The interoperability of systems discussed above is precisely the key to Open Systems. As a matter of fact, it is naive to assume that the advanced commercial needs of end users (e.g., in the banking environment) could have been met with most UNIX systems solutions until fairly recently. UNIX just wasn't up to it in terms of supporting large centralized transaction processing applications. Those vendors in the forefront of computing in the 1960s and 1970s met their customers' needs in other ways, inevitably proprietary in nature.

IBM, DEC, HP, Microsoft, and Novell have all historically succeeded by selling "closed systems" based on proprietary operating systems and/or hardware designs. The reality of the current situation—that end users are now demanding Open Systems—has not been lost on these companies. But a migration process rather than a revolutionary switch in operating systems is required by these vendors to protect their installed customer base. (As the joke goes: *Q*: How could God have created the earth in only seven days? *A*: Easy. He had no installed base.)

UNIX's Open Systems Moniker: Is It Myth or Reality?

The very expression Open Systems is like a high-tech riddle. Nobody knows exactly what the phrase means. Most vendors used to use the term liberally in their marketing as a means of distinguishing themselves from proprietary systems. But today, with what used to be considered proprietary systems supporting standards (another complex term), Open Systems seems to be evolving to characterize whatever the vendor using the phrase wants it to mean. A few years ago, the OPEN VMS would have seemed an oxymoron, but not today; DEC has actually given this name to the new version of VMS.

Defining Open Systems

How it is defined depends on who is defining it. Vendors tend to use 'open' and 'open systems' to describe whatever they are selling. There will never be a coherent definition from the supply side of the industry for this very reason. However it is defined, there are other terms and concepts that are closely aligned to openness and Open Systems.

Openness is normally related to industry standards, especially official or government standards (e.g., IEEE, OSI, FIPS) or de facto standards (e.g., SVR4, NFS). Calling a specification or a product implementation 'standard' has become commonplace. The only real measures for how standard something is based on two factors. The first is compliance with a documented and published interface specification (and increasingly with technology like software verification suites, benchmarks, or other tests that actually test compliance). The second measure has to do with the extent to which something that is claimed to be a standard actually exists. "Exists" can be a measure of both the number of companies that license a technology as well as the number of actual installations where the standards-based product is in use.

Openness may also be measured in terms of licensing and commercial practices. If a company or consortium freely documents and makes readily available its interface definitions, and even its source code or hardware design, then it is more open than a company that has expensive or restrictive licensing practices. An open standard is one whose price is based on cost rather than value. UNIX was open because it could be licensed to anyone who paid a reasonable price for it. UNIX source code was also available and was not prohibitively priced.

How standards come into being also has to do with commercial practices and impacts their legitimacy. An open standards development process is questionably open when it is in fact a cartel of vendors picking and choosing largely from the best of breed of their own technologies. This isn't Open Systems, it's closer to antitrust. Calling something standard because the institution promulgating it is nonprofit is nonsense. There is no such thing as a purely philanthropic computer industry group, especially when it is composed of and bankrolled by the largest and most powerful industry incumbents.

For many years, AT&T's UNIX has been the Open Systems policy direction within the U.S. federal government and closely associated with the original concept of an open operating system. UNIX from Novell is also a commercial product. It must be licensed and royalties paid by its OEMs. It is documented, and its specification and source code are readily available. Hundreds of companies use it as a code base or at least use some version of the UNIX System V interface definition. POSIX is a very generic, UNIX-like system interface definition standard. POSIX compliance is also normally associated with the concept of openness.

The debates around openness will go on for a long time. However, it is widely agreed that UNIX does support a larger number of de jure standards than any other operating system. It is also a fact that UNIX System V is the de facto standard for UNIX.

So why should anybody care? Given a choice of a $100 proprietary operating system and a $1000 open, standards-based operating system for the same hardware, which would you choose? Does being proprietary imply that a product is less valuable than a standards-based product? These are excellent questions. As in art, beauty lies in the eyes of the beholder. The answer is really different if you are a casual user of personal computers in your home or if you are responsible for running a business that spends enormous amounts of capital on information technology. It all comes down to what your requirements are.

Open Systems is a way of thinking about how you evolve information technology solutions. It is not achieved simply by buying a product. It is best to think of it as a process where you are thinking ahead toward your future requirements.

Is Proprietary UNIX an Oxymoron?

In this book, proprietary UNIX is used to describe UNIX variants that are not based on AT&Ts System V.

Information technology-related productivity challenges of the 1990s

The learning curve for systems, system software, and application software is still steep. With graphical user interface technology, UNIX variants are getting closer to Macintosh ease of use as far as the end user is concerned, but it is still much more complex—given its sophistication, for example, in multiuser and networking functionality—from the systems administration point of view.

The cost of ownership and administration remains high. This is true of all computer products, not just UNIX. Perhaps the ultimate solution will come from a new approach to the problem where the total cost of support of nodes on the network is amortized over utilities that work on all platforms. So long as the human resources and skill set for system administration and the tools are proprietary to specific platforms, the cost of ownership cannot be reduced below a relatively high threshold.

The cost of developing and integrating software is still high. No matter how you look at it, software is expensive whether you acquire it shrinkwrapped, buy and tailor it, or build it from scratch. Software is quickly being viewed as a key asset and a key cost driver. The cost of migrating to new software and retraining users often creates a barrier to the adoption of new and much better technology. Developing and supporting software on multiple platforms has become a technical as well as business expectation that is still difficult to achieve.

Finally, the industry has produced more sophisticated technology than the users have figured out how to exploit. The ability of people to absorb and utilize technology can be easily overestimated. The challenge for the supply side of the industry is to produce solutions users can grow with. This implies an ability to scale across prevalent base platforms be they hardware or software and the ability to interoperate with existing systems.

How do you evaluate the comprehensiveness of distributed computing alternatives?

With all the product claims and marketing messages around distributed computing, it has become difficult to appreciate and evaluate the comprehensiveness of alternative environments. A comprehensive environment is one that addresses the above productivity issues from the point of view of the end user, the developer, and/or system integrator and the system and network administrator.

It should be clear by now that no single vendor, no matter how big they are, can do it all. It will also become clearer that the pace of technological innovation is not going to let up. These are times when the benefits of new technologies are capable of being achieved (e.g., electronic mail and global networking is here and now) and where even more radical and innovative technology is migrating toward the mass market (e.g., object-oriented technology holds the promise of radically changing the nature of software development and distribution).

Summary

Why should you care about the operating system? Because the operating system does the following:

- Protects hardware and software investments
- Enables rapid adoption of new technologies
- Provides integration for multivendor environments
- Allows scalability across a wide variety of system platforms
- Addresses the requirements of diverse work groups
- Reduces software development and deployment costs

Why care about standards? Because they do the following:

- Promote lower-cost, higher-quality products and services
- Open interfaces increase the potential for interoperability
- Make it possible to have multiple sources—a form of insurance
- Provide a common set of benchmarks for evaluating alternatives
- Offer greater selection—common solution elements from multiple vendors
- Increase the potential to exploit interoperability at various levels within the system architecture

UNIX Comes of Age

The origins of UNIX explain why it initially came into being and how it has progressed technically and commercially to the present. This chapter explores the basis of the controversial positions held by several of the major industry players, which will surely be validated by future events. At a minimum, the reader will be alerted to critical areas of development on which to focus in the industry press and in wider news coverage.

UNIX was first developed at AT&T's Bell Laboratory and was originally designed using a process of informal and piecemeal development. There was no committee that decided to write the operating system for the coming decades. UNIX was sheltered within Bell Labs Research for five years before its design was described and subjected to the outside world.

The evolution of UNIX was also interlinked with the evolution of microcomputer developments such as the Intel 386, the Motorola 68000 (a.k.a. "68K"), and RISC chip-based processors. It benefited from the growth of both the minicomputer and the workstation market. Systems based on the 68K chip with its flat address space could run code that a large DEC VAX computer could run. A 68K-based workstation was as powerful a CPU as a DEC VAX 750. UNIX proved to be the most easily portable operating system, which could take advantage of the 68K's power as well as its address space. The evolution of UNIX continues with UNIX usually being the first operating system ported to new hardware platforms and architectures including today's multiprocessor systems. UNIX continues to serve as a model for other new operating systems, most interestingly including Window/NT whose design was based in part on Mach, and hence a UNIX-clone in many respects. But the history of UNIX and the UNIX industry has been shaped by factors other than technology.

UNIX has struggled for years to gain credibility, market share, and the widespread acceptance and respectability many had predicted it would achieve during the late 1970s and early 1980s. The explosive growth of UNIX seemed always just around the corner. In the late 1980s UNIX has also been at the center of the battle waged over industry standards. With the acquisition of USL by Novell, a new era opens for UNIX. Novell has the market position and marketing capability to do for UNIX what AT&T never could.

UNIX has a rich history of use and development spanning nearly 24 years. Until the mid-80's there has never been massive marketing efforts behind UNIX equivalent to those of IBM's MVS, DEC's VMS, the Macintosh, MS-DOS, or Windows. While UNIX has historically enjoyed widespread popularity in certain circles of computer users, it is still not well understood by a broad group of computer users, data processing professionals, and other interested people.

For years, the development and licensing of UNIX were dictated by AT&T. As more companies licensed the technology and used it in their products, AT&T's power to control its development and licensing became an increasingly serious issue. For UNIX to gain greater acceptance, its future development needed to become an open development process addressing the specific interests of both UNIX end users and those companies that were basing all or part of their strategies on UNIX. This represented a change for AT&T, which had a history of changing UNIX and its licensing terms with little regard for UNIX users or licensees, who included many of the largest corporations and computer companies in the world.

There are many companies and users who will be impacted by the future evolution of UNIX. This is causing a significant move away from the way the UNIX system has historically been developed and enhanced. UNIX has evolved a great deal over the last 24 years, and, as explained later, it can be expected to continue to evolve rapidly in the future.

The roots of UNIX history spring from laboratory and practical utilization of computing in the user environment. Early users were mostly programmers and technical computer users in engineering and research environments. Some have jokingly referred to UNIX as "a 24-year-old scientific experiment (since it was invented some 24 years ago), a 13-year-old sociology experiment (since 1980 is about when it became generally popular), and a 10-year-old business experiment."

The current commercial momentum behind UNIX indicates an acceleration in multiple trends—technical, social, and commercial—that is unquestionably having a major impact on the whole of the computer hardware and software industry as we know it.

1.1. THE ANCIENT HISTORY OF UNIX

Figure 1.1 summarizes four major stages in the evolution of UNIX. This section provides an analysis of the development of both UNIX the operating system and UNIX the industry.

When UNIX was being conceived, the counterculture had already peaked at Berkeley. In 1969, America had reached a technological zenith by putting men on the moon. It was only beginning to come to terms with its earthly powers by starting a retreat from Vietnam. Joe Namath and the underdog New York Jets came home from Miami after winning Super Bowl III. Against what seemed like all odds, baseball's lovable losers, the New York Mets, won the World Series. Bill Gates wasn't even in high school yet.

Before the era of the video game, programmers were hacking away and writing software when they didn't like the software that was available. These early hackers continually pushed the bounds of what could be done with computers.

1.1.1. UNIX Was Adventure—Programmers Were Paid to Play

Adventure is the name of a sophisticated computer game that one can spend hundreds of hours playing. At first, UNIX was like a game. It found popularity among the technologically advanced users and programmers. Technically, it offered a fairly straightforward development environment for programmers, especially those programming in the C language.

UNIX enjoyed an almost cult-like status, attracting many programmers who had "dared to be different" by working with something technically challenging and deep, yet elegant, because of its simplicity in comparison to other operating systems. This simplicity was owed in large part to the fact that UNIX was written by only two people.

UNIX was first described in a 1974 *Communications of the ACM* article by Ken Thompson and Dennis Ritchie. But work had started much earlier. In 1965, at Bell Telephone Labs, General Electric, Bell Telephone, and Project MAC at MIT had joined together in the develop-

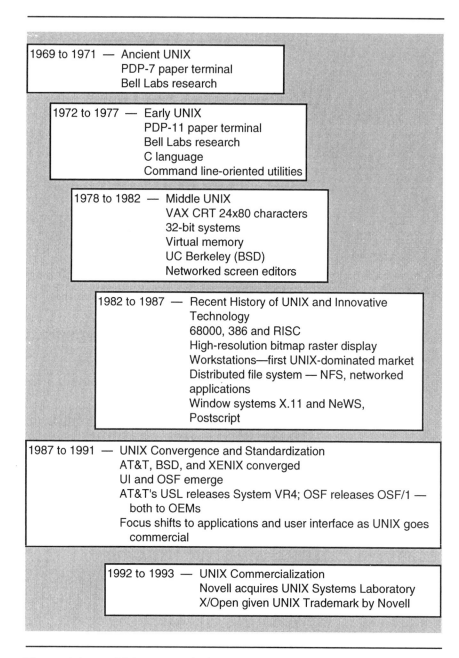

1969 to 1971 — Ancient UNIX
PDP-7 paper terminal
Bell Labs research

1972 to 1977 — Early UNIX
PDP-11 paper terminal
Bell Labs research
C language
Command line-oriented utilities

1978 to 1982 — Middle UNIX
VAX CRT 24x80 characters
32-bit systems
Virtual memory
UC Berkeley (BSD)
Networked screen editors

1982 to 1987 — Recent History of UNIX and Innovative
Technology
68000, 386 and RISC
High-resolution bitmap raster display
Workstations—first UNIX-dominated market
Distributed file system — NFS, networked
applications
Window systems X.11 and NeWS,
Postscript

1987 to 1991 — UNIX Convergence and Standardization
AT&T, BSD, and XENIX converged
UI and OSF emerge
AT&T's USL releases System VR4; OSF releases OSF/1 —
both to OEMs
Focus shifts to applications and user interface as UNIX goes
commercial

1992 to 1993 — UNIX Commercialization
Novell acquires UNIX Systems Laboratory
X/Open given UNIX Trademark by Novell

Figure 1.1. Major stages in the evolution of UNIX. UNIX has gradually progressed from its early applications at Bell Labs and internal use within AT&T to the primary operating system in engineering and scientific environments, and it is now one of the key growth areas in the computer industry.

ment of the MULTICS operating system. MULTICS stood for Multi-plexed Information and Computing Service.

The goal of MULTICS was to provide multiuser interactive comput-ing, something that today we all take for granted on most computer systems, but which at that time was a significant advance over batch computing. A multiuser operating system allows simultaneous com-puter access to a large community of users who want to work online and interactively with their computer instead of just running batch jobs. By 1969, MULTICS ran on the GE645 computer, but it was far from a general-purpose computing solution. It didn't meet all of its goals, so AT&T (Bell), MIT, and General Electric, the companies collaborating on the project, eventually dropped it. Thompson was quoted as saying, "For us it ended up being a million dollar PC." No one was devastated when AT&T dropped out of the project in 1969, but Thompson re-mained very interested in the computing utility. Much of the work done for MULTICS laid the groundwork for UNIX. Thompson had worked on operating systems before. In a matter of a few months, Thompson, in collaboration with Ritchie and colleague Rudd Canaday, proceeded to design a new kind of file system that begged for hardware to give it life. That problem was solved when he got hold of a discarded DEC PDP-7 computer, which he and Ritchie ambitiously programmed.

1.1.2.   UNIX Was a Classic Backroom Development

Ken Thompson and Dennis Ritchie had also wanted to improve their programming environment and continued their work on a GE645 com-puter. Thompson was writing a game called *Space Travel* in FORTRAN for the GECOS operating system that ran on the GE645. In *Space Travel*, a player toured the solar system right down to the numerous moons of the various planets. The game ran in a rather jerky fashion on the GE645. Thompson was having trouble controlling his spaceship, and the game was incredibly expensive to run. He wanted a better medium. He found it in the PDP-7 and decided to port *Space Travel*. But this was not as simple a task as originally thought. So Thompson and Ritchie picked up where MULTICS had left off and implemented a very simple operating system for the PDP-7. They started by implementing their new file system design, which was an early version of the UNIX file system and a small set of utility programs. This effort was enough to satisfy the basic requirements of *Space Travel* as well as provide a bare bones development environment for it.

With only a PDP-7 to work on, the researchers wanted another machine. To get funds for a PDP 11/20, they had to come up with some justification. Bell Lab's legal department, which was located close to Thompson's and Ritchie's Murray Hill office, was looking for a text processing system. The researchers interested the legal department in a UNIX-based system. The UNIX project got the machine it needed, and the legal department got the text processing system it wanted along with high-powered support from the system's original developers.

Thompson set out to implement a FORTRAN compiler for the system but instead came up with a new language he called B. Ritchie saw ways to improve on B and came up with a derivative compiler and a language he called C. UNIX and C developed together.

In 1972, the UNIX operating system itself was rewritten in C. An operating system written in a higher-level language was practically unheard of at the time. Most operating systems were developed in the assembly language of the target machine. This was done for both efficiency and performance. This rewriting of the UNIX system in C proved very significant, since it made the UNIX operating system relatively easy to port to computers that supported a C compiler.

In 1972, mainframe computers offered performance measured in a few million instructions per second, processing power we have now come to expect from today's desktop computers. Operating systems had to be painstakingly developed in low-level assembly language in order to get reasonable performance. As the hardware itself got faster, and with the introduction of higher-level languages, developing operating systems in higher-level languages became possible for the first time. UNIX was one of the first operating systems to benefit.

What's in a name? There are two popular stories as to how UNIX came to be named. Some claim UNIX came to life as a pun on the name MULTICS and was coined by Brian Kernighan, a member of Bell Telephone Labs' Computing Sciences Research Center. The name "UNIX" was a play on the idea that UNIX was a castrated version of MULTICS. Others have suggested that UNIX was an acronym similar to MULTICS. Brian Kernighan purportedly referred to UNIX jokingly as "UNICS," meaning Uniplexed Information and Computing System, since UNIX was much smaller and less complex than MULTICS.

The term UNIX connotes different things depending on the context in which it is used. It is commonly used as a collective noun to refer to the systems that support a standardized specification. UNIX also has a very specific meaning, which is why you invariably see an accompanying trademark symbol when you see the word UNIX in print. From the moment AT&T recognized its potential value and made UNIX one of its registered trademarks, only vendors who formally complied with AT&T

licensing terms for a particular version of UNIX could call their derivative product "UNIX." As we will discuss later, there are actually many versions or variants of UNIX.

Who needs support? Today, when you make a major hardware or software purchase, you automatically expect the supplier to provide support for it in terms of documentation, training, problem determination, and so forth. In the early days, however, there was no vendor support for UNIX. Since Bell Labs' operations people were building their own system, they had to support it themselves.

Independently of the research potential, Bell was aware of the need for minicomputer support for its telephone operations. With the number of systems being considered, being tied to multiple-system vendors (e.g., Univac, DEC, and IBM) induced a kind of paranoia. Berkeley Tague, a manager at Bell Labs, suggested that they consider writing their applications on the UNIX operating system instead of writing them for multiple proprietary operating systems. The idea gained support in the operations group during 1971 and 1972, and in September 1973, a UNIX Development Support Group was formed to support the first "standard UNIX." The first UNIX applications were installed in 1973. This system updated directory information and intercepted calls to numbers that had been changed.

Very quickly, the number of UNIX installations grew within Bell to the point where the dedicated internal support team grew and continued to develop UNIX while providing maintenance and support to approximately 25 installations. A key reason for the rapid spread of UNIX within Bell Labs was the low price of minicomputers relative to mainframes. History would repeat itself when workstation vendors later provided UNIX-based systems as an alternative to minicomputers and mainframes for certain applications.

Because of the 1956 consent decree* that prohibited AT&T from

---

*In 1949, the Justice Department sued AT&T because it wanted the company to divest itself of Western Electric's manufacturing operation. In order to keep from doing that, AT&T entered into a consent decree in 1956. This consent decree allowed AT&T to keep Western Electric and the Bell system intact so long as AT&T agreed to be restricted to U.S. regulated businesses and to cross-license all of its patents. In the 1970s AT&T realized the need to address other business areas and saw the computer market as an obvious choice. In 1974, the Justice Department again sued AT&T and again wanted the company to divest itself of Western Electric. In a 1982 consent decree, AT&T agreed to divest itself of the Bell Operating Companies in order to keep Western Electric which AT&T felt was critical to its entry into the computer and office systems business.

marketing computer products, UNIX was made available only to universities who requested it for educational purposes. Nevertheless, UNIX was gaining popularity and visibility through papers such as the one by Thompson and Ritchie in the Communications of the Association for Computing Machinery in 1974.[1]

Bell was dragged kicking and screaming into providing UNIX to the world. In the early 1970s, Bell Labs, through Western Electric, made UNIX available to research institutions and universities for a nominal fee. As minicomputers grew in popularity, so did UNIX. By 1974, copies of Version 4 found their way into a few universities and nonprofit organizations. The people who picked up UNIX were the type who could deal with the lack of support offered. Back then, it was basically "Here's a tape—take it." In 1975, AT&T began officially licensing UNIX for use in universities and nonprofit educational institutions for a nominal fee and under a strict license.

With the introduction of UNIX Version 4 in 1974 at Western Electric, porting activity began to increase. In 1974, the University of California at Berkeley took Version 4 of UNIX, which Bell Labs had ported to DEC's PDP system and began enhancing it.

At Berkeley, Keith Standiford first converted Version 4 to the PDP-11/45 for the computer science, math, and statistics department in 1974. The system had to be scheduled to run UNIX part of the time for the computer scientists and DEC's RSTS the rest of the time for the mathematicians and statisticians. The INGRES database project was among the first to move from the batch machines to the interactive environment provided by UNIX. As all these activities were competing for time, they quickly ran into machine shortage problems, and this led to the purchase of a PDP 11/40 to run Version 5. The INGRES project was the first group to distribute its software. Several hundred tapes were shipped over the six years following 1974, helping to establish Berkeley's reputation in designing and building real systems.

UNIX—the wonder years. By 1977, there were over 500 sites running UNIX, with approximately 20 percent of these located in universities. UNIX was being used on these systems mainly for software development, network transaction operating services (especially within Bell), and for support of near real-time services. In the university environments, UNIX was proving to be the best means through which research groups could gain access to state-of-the-art software engineering and electrical engineering design software that was either public domain or very inexpensive. The use of UNIX on projects for DARPA provided a strong incentive: if one wanted to be compatible with research institutions also engaged with DARPA, UNIX had to be used.

In 1977, AT&T began to license UNIX to commercial institutions. That year, INTERACTIVE Systems Corporation became the first value-added reseller of the UNIX system, although it originally intended to use UNIX to penetrate the office automation market. In 1977, commercial NIX was first ported to a non-PDP machine, the INTERDATA 8/32. AT&T marketed its first commercial UNIX system targeted at software developers in 1978.

UNIX market share increases with adoption of microprocessors.
In the early 1970s, microprocessors didn't use UNIX. CP/M from Digital Research, Inc., was the first popular operating system for the 8-bit microprocessor world. In 1978, Onyx Systems licensed UNIX for a 16-bit multiuser microprocessor they had developed.

With the increasing popularity of microprocessors, other companies took advantage of the simplicity of UNIX and began to enhance it in their own way. This resulted in several derivative products. Some of them were modified versions of UNIX licensed from AT&T, while others were UNIX clones.

UNIX is a multilayered set of procedures, utilities, and applications that are isolated from the particular hardware upon which they are implemented—with the exception of the kernel. UNIX clones are usually compatible at the system call level with the kernel completely rewritten. (Chapter 2 explains what the "kernel" is.)

XENIX, one of the most successful clones, was announced in 1979 by Microsoft, best known at the time for its Basic language. Based on UNIX Version 7, XENIX was originally ported to Intel's 8086 microprocessor and was later adapted to Motorola's 68000, Intel's 80286, and Zilog's Z8000. XENIX was based on Microsoft's proprietary architecture. In August 1981, IBM launched the PC, which supported MS-DOS, also written by Microsoft. XENIX was momentarily forgotten.

In 1982, Bell Labs combined several AT&T UNIX variants into a single system dubbed System III. Many new features were later added, resulting in UNIX System V, and AT&T announced official support for System V in January 1983. "System V" is commonly understood to mean one of two things: the operating system offered by AT&T or the System V Interface Definition (SVID). The first is a software product, the second a formally documented specification.

In 1983, AT&T introduced System V Release 1 and announced its intention to maintain upward compatibility from release to release. As a result of the AT&T divestiture in 1984, which permitted AT&T Information Systems to participate in the computer and semiconductor markets, AT&T began to market UNIX and UNIX-based systems more aggressively. AT&T's actions helped to make UNIX a competitive commercial operating system and also established AT&T UNIX as the standard.

Microsoft eventually announced support of both AT&T System III and System V.2. XENIX continued to be adapted to run on microprocessors powerful enough to support a small number of timesharing users. These versions contained the editor vi, the C shell, and other enhancements. XENIX grew in popularity and installed base as it was remarketed by several companies including Tandy, Altos, Compac, and IBM. XENIX and other PC-derivative UNIX products made it possible to give multiple users access to shared programs and data. Many early XENIX and SCO users used microprocessor-based low-end multiuser systems with cheap character-based terminals and serial cables.

The Santa Cruz Operation (SCO) combined SCO XENIX UNIX, and UNIX System V from AT&T. SCO UNIX System V/386 Release 3.2 was the first operating system licensed by AT&T to carry the UNIX trademark. In January of 1987, Microsoft and AT&T announced their agreement to develop UNIX System V for 386-based computers, which was intended to be upwardly binary compatible with UNIX System V/ 386 Release-3 and XENIX System V from Microsoft and SCO.

1.1.3.   The Best Thing That Ever Happened to UNIX

The best thing that ever happened to UNIX was handing it over to a bunch of kids. Not long after the first versions of UNIX were created, UNIX was taken up by an unaffiliated group: students. These students, primarily at the University of California at Berkeley spawned a number of new technologies and tools like full-screen editing, networking, graphics, and relational database management. UNIX was fun; it was something the students got to work on. UNIX source code found its way to universities all over the world under the banner of research. UNIX was and still is one of the largest and most fruitful collective technical projects of all time.

BSD UNIX. Under contracts from the U.S. government, the University of California at Berkeley was developing a variant of UNIX, which became known as BSD (Berkeley Software Distribution). BSD was first developed for VAX machines. Computer science students at Berkeley began shipping BSD releases to various universities and government research groups. What started as a sort of grass roots effort began to catch on. The BSD release offered performance enhancements over the AT&T version of UNIX, and BSD extensions made it more suitable for software development. BSD UNIX was being accepted as an efficient means of sharing software and new developments at an accelerated pace. Although Berkeley UNIX was not commercially supported as a product, several computer companies used or modified it for their own purposes and supported it themselves. Berkeley UNIX included support of virtual memory, a full-screen text editor, and other enhancements such as networking functions not found in AT&T's version of UNIX.

The tools that came with BSD versions of UNIX, which included compilers and editors unique to BSD, along with "free market" software developed and freely exchanged among technical users, helped BSD gain rapid acceptance in technical research and development computing environments within universities and the government. BSD was also increasing in popularity as DEC's VAX computer line achieved market acceptance.

The Stanford University Network and Sun Microsystems, Inc.
By 1982, a California start-up company called Sun Microsystems, Inc., combined new hardware designs from Stanford with the BSD system from Berkeley. These hardware designs, which have become known as networked workstations, offered outstanding price performance, especially when combined with the powerful BSD UNIX operating system. Sun Microsystems based its entire product line on UNIX. Sun's success and rapid growth, as well as the growth of the workstation market where UNIX had become the standard, helped stimulate considerable interest in UNIX. As explained more fully later, Sun's aggressive support of UNIX and its relationship with AT&T triggered an unprecedented formation of a consortium of major computer vendors known as OSF (Open Software Foundation.)

UNIX—generally less expensive than proprietary alternatives.
UNIX has historically been used on midrange computers and microprocessor-based, low-end multiuser systems, as well as workstations ranging in price up to $100,000. By comparison to the application software available on proprietary systems above $25,000, UNIX application software is also generally less expensive than similar software on minicomputers and larger machines. These cost savings have contributed to the rapid spread of UNIX.

By 1984, UNIX systems installations numbered around 100,000 worldwide. There were three significant variants of UNIX. The first was the version available from AT&T. It was being licensed to a number of computer systems vendors. The second was XENIX, developed by Microsoft and marketed by various low-end systems vendors, including IBM. The third was BSD, which was achieving something akin to cult status within the universities and defense research establishments.

AT&T announced UNIX System V Release 2 in February 1984 and continued to enhance and refine its definition of System V. By June of 1986, AT&T announced System V Release 3. In the fall of 1989, AT&T announced System V Release 4 (SVR4).

Each AT&T and BSD release has led to numerous variants or clones of UNIX, which are listed in Table 1.1.

UNIX systems and vendors, past and present. UNIX industry history is actually much more complex. The partial list of companies in Table 1.1 that have licensed or used UNIX in their products includes extinct products and companies and is intended to illustrate the number of UNIX implementations that have at one time or another been on the market. No wonder there was concern over the sporadic proliferation of UNIX.

Even with the explosion of UNIX variants and clones, UNIX itself was proving to be readily portable. However, there was a danger that application software running on one version of UNIX might not easily port to another version. This drew UNIX users together in the common desire for the development of standards specifications for UNIX to ensure the highest level of portability and consistency from one version to another. Equally important, it was a move to prevent AT&T from enhancing UNIX without taking the users' interests into account.

While the software and system vendors were interested in avoiding AT&T's licensing fees or practices, UNIX users, on the other hand, have been very clear and proactive in making sure the advantages that drew them toward UNIX in the first place wouldn't disappear. As AT&T raised license fees and imposed increasingly restrictive terms, it pressured commercial implementers to look for alternatives.

1.2. THE MIDDLE AGES OF THE UNIX INDUSTRY

As already mentioned, UNIX was initially developed by a very small group. Early UNIX was developed to be a bare bones yet efficient time-sharing operating system. It was first developed to support the porting of a program, *Space Travel*, from one computer to another. UNIX itself was later made portable by being written in the C language. It was and still is supplied with a C compiler. As C compilers were implemented on different computer systems, virtually anybody could license UNIX from

Table 1.1. Variants of UNIX. There have been a large number of UNIX-deriative operating systems.

AIX — IBM	Serix—CMI Corp.
Auros—Auragen	Sphinx—Data General
A/UX—Apple Computer, Inc.	SunOS—Sun Microsystems, Inc.
Regulus—Alcyon	Sysb—Plexus
4.1 BSD and 4.2 BSD—Berkeley	System V/AT—Microport Systems, Inc.
Coherent—Mark Williams	TI System V—Texas Instruments, Inc.
CPIX—IBM	TI System V for System 1500—Texas Instruments, Inc.
Cromix—Cromemco	
Domain/OS—Apollo	TNIX—Tektronix
Enix System V—Everex Systems Inc.	ULTRIX—Digital Equipment Corporation
Eunice—Wollongong	
FOR:PRO—Fortune	Unidos—Unidos
Genix—National Semiconductor	Uni-Dol—DMC
HP/UX—HP	Unisis—Codata
Idris—Whitesmiths, Ltd.	Unity—HCR
IS/1, IS/3—INTERACTIVE Systems	UNIX System III—AT&T
IN/ix—INTERACTIVE Systems	UNIX System V—AT&T
Mach—MT XINDU, Inc.	UnixWare—Novell/USG
Merge 386—Locus Computing Corp.	Unos—Charles River Data Systems
Micronix—Marrow Designs	UTS—Amdahl
Microport 286—Microport Systems, Inc.	Venix 386—Venturcom
Microport 386—Microport Systems, Inc.	UNIX Version VII—AT&T
Minix—Prentice-Hall, Inc.	VM/IX—IBM/INTERACTIVE Systems
Personal Mainframe—Opus Systems	Writers Workbench—AT&T
Oasis—Phase 1	XENIX—Microsoft
Onix—Onyx	XENIX 286—Intel Corp.
Opus5—Opus Systems	SCO XENIX 386—The Santa Cruz Operation, Inc.
OS-9—Gimix	
OSX—Pyramid	SCO XENIX System V/386—The Santa Cruz Operation, Inc.
PC/IX—IBM/INTERACTIVE Systems	
Perpos—CCI	SCO UNIX Venix System V— VenturCom, Inc.
PNX—Perq Systems	
QNX—Quantum Software Systems, Ltd.	Zeus—Zilog
RTU—Concurrent Computer Corp.	386/ix—INTERACTIVE Systems Corp.

AT&T and get it running on their hardware. Portability and effective software development were key factors in the evolution of UNIX and remain today the most widely regarded of its strengths.

MS-DOS is about 11 years old; OS/2 is a little over 5 years old; UNIX is nearly 24 years old and very mature in contrast to these other "youngsters." It has gone through quite an evolution and is therefore somewhat complex. There is software in UNIX to support paper terminals, dumb ASCII terminals, and smart terminals like the new X Terminals, PCs, and workstations as well. UNIX is supporting five generations of interactive devices, only one example of the baggage it is carrying in the interests of the upward compatibility its users have demanded. Recent history has seen the convergence of the most popular versions of UNIX into a single System V Interface Definition and release called SVR4. The next section takes a brief look at how this evolved.

1.2.1.   How Many UNIX Variants Would There Be?

The genealogy of UNIX is summarized in Figure 1.2, which shows the evolution of various versions of the UNIX system. It can be easily seen that from about 1973 to the present there have been several versions of UNIX on the market.

Almost from the beginning, the UNIX market has suffered from a plethora of versions. Lack of consistency was a continual problem as the popularity of UNIX spread. The first bout of expansions and contractions occurred within the Bell System, where versions 1 through 7 were developed. From these research versions sprang UNIX versions controlled by the Programmers Workbench (PWB) group, the USG UNIX support group, and by the CBUNIX group at Bell Labs in Columbus Ohio. The three nonresearch UNIX versions converged into USDL System II just as Berkeley splintered research version 7 into BSD. AT&T then launched System V, advertising it as "System V, Consider it Standard." But System V was not powerful enough to deal with then-current hardware innovations and user needs. There were also many users in the scientific and research community who favored BSD.

Three major categories of UNIX-based systems emerged. The first category was AT&T System V-based systems. Vendors in this camp include AT&T, DEC (which has supported early versions of AT&T System V Release 3 for regional Bell operating companies), IBM, and HP. Several other vendors are also in this category, providing several of the extensions to AT&T's System V.

The second category was BSD based. This group used the Berkeley version of UNIX that resulted from the DARPA development project sponsored by the Department of Defense. This group most notably includes Sun Microsystems' SunOS and variants such as DEC's ULTRIX and HP's HP/UX.

The third category, XENIX-based, was developed by Microsoft initially for Intel's family of microprocessors. The Santa Cruz Operation (SCO) has also marketed XENIX, which falls in this category.

There have been numerous other variants of UNIX, most of which have received only limited market acceptance to date. With the exception of INTERACTIVE Systems (shown as INTERACTIVE IS/1 UNIX in Figure 1.2), most of these are relatively new variants, including AIX, originally developed by INTERACTIVE Systems and later licensed to IBM. Also in this category is Mach, a variant of UNIX being developed at Carnegie-Mellon. Mach was chosen by NeXT as the operating system for its workstation product and more recently was selected by OSF as the kernel for the first release of the OSF product in place of the AIX kernel.

The importance of compatibility. While UNIX gurus liked seeing UNIX change with the times, UNIX users wanted it to sit still and keep working today like it did yesterday. Changes in UNIX often caused users to lose time getting their applications to run under new versions. To AT&T's credit, it took care of users and applications vendors by making most of their changes to System III and System V upwardly compatible, more compatible than Berkeley releases of BSD. While it might be argued that some of Berkeley's lack of accommodation came from a desire to track current technology, some of their frequent rewrites were quite annoying to BSD's user base. Most of the major system vendors undertook to integrate the AT&T UNIX and BSD systems.

AT&T was controlling the evolution of System V. Berkeley controlled the BSD project officially, but many people thought of the UNIX systems offered by Sun and DEC as synonymous with BSD. There have been hundreds of other vendors who have AT&T UNIX and Berkeley BSD source licenses, and many mutated the UNIX operating system to their own liking.

Concern over proliferation of UNIX variants. UNIX users grew concerned about the proliferation of UNIX variants during the 1980s. /usr/grp, a UNIX user group that recently changed its name to UniForum, formulated a standards committee to try to influence AT&T and other companies working with UNIX to adhere to standards. Their objective was for software to be portable across the systems offered by these companies. They developed the specification for a UNIX standard to prevent the chaos that was spreading throughout the UNIX industry.

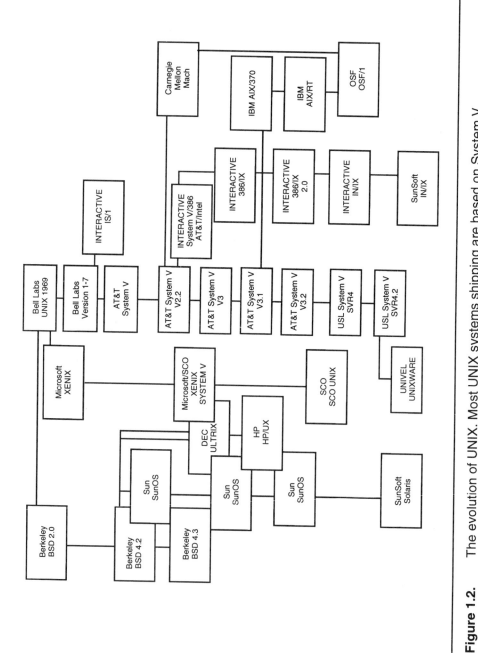

Figure 1.2. The evolution of UNIX. Most UNIX systems shipping are based on System V.

AT&T responded by progressing further with its definition of UNIX System V. But the UNIX landscape was proving to be quite different from MS-DOS landscape, for instance, where software comes in shrinkwrap packaging and where the same software supplied on a floppy disk can run on systems from multiple vendors. For example, spreadsheet software can be run on any PC clone that runs MS-DOS. While UNIX has a similar goal, the current reality is one of conditional portability at best, although there is progress being made as system vendors define and the industry adopts so-called application programming interface, or "APIs."

There are some major reasons for lack of interoperability in UNIX compared to MS-DOS. The first is the higher level of commodity products in the PC world and standardization of distribution media. The second reason is that there is one MS-DOS operating system rather than myriad variants. In addition, MS-DOS systems are based on Intel processors, whereas UNIX systems run on multiple merchant chip technologies, such as Intel, Motorola, SPARC, and so on. On the other hand, in the PC world, there are a myriad of combinations of hardware options, floating point accelerators, networking interface hardware and software, graphics cards, and so forth. The PC operating system can support a wide variety of these devices, but the traditional PC environment is typically far less integrated than the workstation. It is therefore misleading to compare PC operating systems to workstation operating systems or PC hardware to UNIX hardware. The operating systems and hardware levels of integration are discussed in Section 3.7.

UNIX variants differ from one another in subtle ways. While some applications can be ported from one UNIX variant to the next, portability as a goal has been pushed largely by software developers and systems vendors.

Developers and users of AT&T System V and BSD might be said to resemble evangelists. They adhere to UNIX and one particular variant or base as one would a religion. Indeed, it is very typical in a meeting of technical personnel to see hours spent arguing over particular features of one system versus another, such as streams versus sockets, the subtleties of which would be lost on all but the most technical programmers.

By 1985, UNIX splinter groups were converging rather rapidly, the result of a combination of factors—sometimes via natural selection or survival of the fittest but more often as the result of commercial market forces and users' buying power. Many of the small system vendors who offered UNIX or UNIX clones went out of business or never really went anywhere. There were only a few major players with UNIX strategies.

Sun Microsystems helped popularize UNIX and, through its approach to technology licensing, popularized other developments such as its Network File System (NFS) in the workstation market. Microsoft, INTERACTIVE, and SCO helped promote UNIX in the multiuser microprocessor systems market as a very attractive alternative to minicomputers. Many of the traditional computer systems companies (prominently including IBM and DEC) offered UNIX to customers who demanded it but derived most of their business from their proprietary operating systems.

UNIX by the mid-1980s. In the mid-80s the dominant UNIX platforms were AT&T System V, BSD, SunOS, Ultrix, and Xenix. The main system platforms these were supported on were Dec Vax, Sun Sparc workstations, and Intel-based small systems like Altos. The major applications included CASE, electronic mail, word processing, database management, communications, and CAD/CAM/CAE. At the time, over half of all UNIX systems were networked and over 85 percent of the commercial software sold on UNIX systems involved software maintenance agreements.

UNIX gained popularity in the 80s because of the following advantages:

- Cheaper computing power, throughput, and multitasking functionality
- Filled a gap between PCs and traditional minis and mainframes
- Support for networking and computer communications in general
- UNIX was the leader in the movement toward open computing standards.
- Innovative applications and tools were available:
  — CAD/CAM/CAE (computer aided design, manufacture and engineering)
  — Scientific applications
  — Database Management especially Relational Database management
  — CASE (computer aided software engineering)

These innovative applications needed UNIX because of all the earlier reasons cited. Indeed, these were the "killer" applications that really kicked off the UNIX workstation industry and set the stage for future UNIX industry growth and expansion. This market growth did not go unnoticed by major vendors like IBM, DEC, and HP.

Carnegie-Mellons' Mach. Starting in the mid-80s, Carnegie-Mellon was involved in extensive research into distributed computing. A network operating system was developed called ACCENT. The culmination of the research resulted in a UNIX-like operating system called Mach in 1988. Mach looked the same to users as UNIX. What was really different about Mach was its kernel design which Carengie-Mellon developed from scratch. Mach featured object-oriented programming, threads, and messages (see glossary for explanations of these terms). A program is considered to be a collection of concurrent computing routines. Each routine is known as a thread. Programs are composed of a set of threads running concurrently. The message-passing mechanism enables the facility to indicate what commands can be used while executing and allows computers with multiple processors to use different processors for different threads of execution.

One of the first implementations of Mach was seen in the fall of 1988 when NeXT introduced its computer that used Mach technology. Mach would come to be examined closely by Microsoft's development team as they began work on Windows/NT.

Convergence represented a major threat to traditional system vendors. In 1987, AT&T, Sun, and Microsoft agreed to combine the predominant variants of UNIX back into a single system to be manufactured by AT&T. This new release was called AT&T System V Release 4, more commonly referred to as AT&T SVR4. Sun coupled this strategy with an announcement that it would optimize UNIX for its recently announced SPARC (Scalable Processor Architecture) CPU design. This caused an outcry from other system vendors who supported UNIX and were concerned about the market potential in an alliance between AT&T and Sun, which could give Sun a time-to-market advantage over other companies.

Responding to the announcement of the AT&T and Sun alliance, a group of major system vendors banded together defensively in a consortium called the Hamilton Group. They were concerned about AT&T licensing policies, about the manner in which AT&T was advancing UNIX without any clear open process, and about the possibility that Sun might enjoy an advantage by having earlier access to UNIX as well as the ability to optimize UNIX for its SPARC RISC architecture. When talks with AT&T failed to achieve the desired result, the Hamilton Group formalized the incorporation of OSF (Open Software Foundation), which was aimed to compete directly with AT&T and its development partners in providing a standard version of UNIX for its own members. OSF is dominated by the "big three": IBM, DEC, and HP. (OSF is described in more detail in Section 6.5.)

There were other system vendors who hadn't joined OSF who were equally concerned about the direction being taken by AT&T and who shared OSF's concerns about how AT&T would continue to develop and license UNIX. A group of companies, many of which had been licensing AT&T's System V, were similarly concerned about AT&T's licensing practices and development process as well as the formation of OSF. The Archer Group, as it was called, was reportedly named after the hotel suite in which initial group meetings were held.

By the end of 1988, AT&T and the Archer Group reached several points of agreement. The Archer Group formalized itself as a nonprofit corporation called UNIX International Inc. (UI). UI (see Section 6.4) was set up to provide AT&T with licensing policy guidelines and marketing direction for UNIX and to ensure that no vendor, including AT&T's Computer Systems division and Sun, would have any built-in advantage. Before these vendors endorsed the continued support of AT&T's System V version of UNIX as their base system, they were able to influence AT&T to break out its UNIX systems development to a development group independent of the AT&T Computer Systems division. This UNIX software group has been through a succession of names, but is now called the UNIX Software Laboratory, Inc., or USL. AT&T also agreed to let the UI consortium take a lead role in driving System V's direction and marketing promotion efforts. AT&T, in conjunction with USL, then took steps to address many of the concerns that led to the original formation of OSF.

1.2.2. How Many Versions of UNIX Were Actually Making It?

Clearly, with SVR4, USL's System V Interface Specification (SVID) is now regarded as the de facto UNIX standard today. AT&T, Sun, and Microsoft have successfully driven the unification of the most popular versions of UNIX (i.e., System V, BSD, and XENIX). Even the UNIX variants offered by OSF's principals IBM, DEC, and HP comply with SVID. While much has been made of the splintering effect caused by two versions of UNIX, one from USL and one from OSF, variants of UNIX based on OSF have been very slow to find widespread support and adoption in the industry. USL's System V interface definition as well as its code base is clearly dominant in today's UNIX industry.

However, no specification can be all-encompassing. SVID addresses the issue of interfacing to UNIX from higher-level software but leaves to the developer other important operating system issues such as security, system administration, multiprocessor support, and so on. POSIX (see Section 6.2) addresses issues of this kind in it standards-setting process, but it is conservative in its approach. It awaits consensus before issuing standards definitions and, to more advanced developers, represents a lowest common denominator of operating system functionality—to which even proprietary operating systems may comply.

Meanwhile, users demand more advanced functions, and in the absence of a standards roadmap, each UNIX vendor in the past took its own road in implementing them. These proprietary extensions threatened the most essential foundations of UNIX's popularity: interoperability and application program portability. They also cost each vendor time and development expense. More functionality constantly awaits development.

Some of these extensions will remain proprietary for some time to come because they are of concern to fairly few vendors (e.g., fault tolerance). It was in an effort to consolidate the more mainstream of them in an orderly and predictable fashion, however, and hopefully to drive the development of new standards, that both UI and OSF were formed. Internally, each group's members cooperate though they might compete fiercely for customers' business. UI has a significant head start with a major proportion of the installed base and with System V already in existence as an indisputable standard, while each of the OSF members has its own variant of UNIX and far fewer customer installations. OSF lost more time by changing its mind from IBM's AIX to Carnegie-Mellon's Mach as the kernel for OSF/1. Meanwhile, the divergence of OSF members' UNIX variants continued.

In the fall of 1990, OSF released OSF/1, and its members were quick to pledge support. The "big three" then announced their intentions to release OSF/1-compatible versions of their respective UNIX variants, but after three years only DEC and HP have launched OSF/1-based products, later than expected and without much apparent interest from paying customers.

Finally, convergence has replaced divergence, and there will be only two versions of UNIX for all practical purposes. UI, USL, and OSF are moving away from single-vendor specifications and towards industry standards and specifications, most notably X/Open's XPG. Most major commercial UNIX products will be based on either AT&T's System V. Traditional vendors have not converged their products and will likely offer multiple variants of UNIX in addition to their proprietary operating systems.

System V, BSD, XENIX, and SunOS constitute the installed base of UNIX systems. Interestingly, IBM and DEC do not have large percentages of the installed base of UNIX (looking at the operating system itself and not just the system hardware). To be sure, they now view UNIX as strategic, however. A merger of the System V, BSD, XENIX, and SunOS commands—all commands except for machine-specific ones—is found in AT&T's USL's SVR4. A merge of System V, BSD, and Mach is found in OSF/1.

It is unrealistic to expect companies such as IBM, DEC, and HP to make an overnight switch in operating systems. These vendors must protect their installed base; therefore, a migration plan must be carefully considered prior to making public statements. DEC appears to be further ahead than most vendors in announcing its intention to base its next major release of ULTRIX (i.e., 5.0) on OSF/1.

When AT&T announced the availability of SVR4, The New York Times reported that the battle was all but over and that AT&T and its partners appeared to be the winners in the race to establish the preeminent UNIX software standard. Despite the market confusion created by OSF, there was no real doubt that UNIX is now in the mainstream and that AT&T's System V Release 4 was well in the lead.

Figure 1.3 summarizes important milestones in the evolution of UNIX. The current UNIX customer base is concentrated in XENIX, UNIX System V, BSD which includes derivatives HP-UX and ULTRIX, and SunOS. The UNIX solution that offers the most attractive upgrade path to these users, and to UNIX software developers, will have the largest installed base and therefore attract the most independent software developers (ISVs) and eventually win the most market share.

- 1965 MIT, AT&T, and GE developed MULTICS—Interactive OS for GE 645
- 1969 Thompson & Ritchie developed Multitasking OS, UNICS, in assembler language with Bell Labs financial support
- 1970 Name changed to UNIX, written in Assembly Language
- 1972 Initial UNIX product–Single-user UNIX
- 1973 Kernel rewritten in C languages, AT&T makes operating system available at low cost. Pipes implemented.
- 1974 Fourth Edition used at Bell Labs, UNIX V is released and licensed to educational institutions by AT&T—unsupported
UNIX proliferates inside Bell System and AT&T
UC Berkeley involvement begins with DARPA funding
"Communications of the ACM" UNIX paper appears
- 1975 Development of BSD Distribution
- 1976 Different UNIX start to proliferate versions
- 1977 Fifth and sixth editions of UNIX released
500 sites running UNIX, 20 percent at universities
- 1978 600 nodes now running UNIX, based on the seventh edition
Virtual memory, ported to VAX 11/780

Figure 1.3.   Milestones in the evolution of UNIX.

		AT&T licenses UNIC to INTERACTIVE systems and other commercial institutions.
		Onyx Systems licenses UNIX for 16-bit multiuser microprocessor
•	1979	UNIX Version 7 is released by Bell Labs, UNIX 32V for DEC Vax, and Berkeley incorporates 32V into BSD
		Microsoft licenses UNIX Version 7 and develops XENIX
•	1980	Microsoft introduces XENIX for the IBM PC (8-bit micro version)
		SCO becomes a XENIX distributor
•	1981	AT&T releases UNIX System III, combination of PWB and Version 7
		Amdahl develops UTS—first mainframe UNIX
		First 16-bit PC version
•	1982	AT&T commits to UNIX—announces official support
		AT&T's first commercial release, UNIX System III
		Sun Microsystems releases SunOS based on BSD 4.2 and 4.3
		DEC releases ULTRIX based on BSD UNIX.
		INTERACTIVE Systems works with IBM on AIX, based on System V.2 and BSD 4.3
		IBM releases CPIX
•	1983	AT&T releases System V Release 1
		4.1/4.2 BSD released
		AT&T publishes System V Interface Definition (SVID)
		HP releases first version of HP-UX
		Berkeley 4.2 BSD released
		AT&T divestiture allows AT&T to enter computer market
		X/Open is formed
•	1984	AT&T releases System V Release 3 and SVID
		INTERACTIVE develops PC/IX for IBM, IBM also launches VM/IX
		More than 400 applications running on UNIX
		Over 100,000 UNIX installations worldwide
		DEC releases ULTRIX based on BSD4.2
		XENIX first released by IBM for the PC
		IBM releases IX/370
•	1985	XENIX moves to System V Base
		POSIX standard is introduced
		INTERACTIVE Systems ports System V to 386
		More than 700 applications on UNIX
		Sun and AT&T start work on System V release 4
•	1986	AT&T releases System V Release 3
		AIX released by IBM on the RT
		More than 1100 applications

Figure 1.3.   *Continued*

- 1987   AT&T, Microsoft, and INTERACTIVE collaborate on UNIX System V/386
          AT&T and Sun collaborate on joint development of UNIX System V release 4 to merge XENIX, System V, BSD, and SunOS
          4.3BSD released
          SCO ports XENIX to 80386 platform
          Microsoft & AT&T effort
          System V Release 3.2
          Hamilton Group forms
          IBM launches AIX on PS/2
- 1988   UNIX International (UI) forms
          Open Software Foundation (OSF) from Hamilton Group
          A/UX is introduced
          Carnegie Mellon University Mach introduced
          NeXT computer uses Mach
          HP releases HP/UX based on BSD4.2
          IBM releases AIX/370 and AIX family definition
- 1989   AT&T ships System V Release 4
          OSF/1 changes its mind on AIX kernel—decides to use Mach instead
          UNIX International forms to promote System V
          AT&T breaks out UNIX development from its computer business
          Intel introduces first shrinkwrap UNIX System V/386R3.2
          More than 3000 applications on UNIX
- 1990   OSF introduces OSF/1 to its OEMs based on Mach Kernel and AIX
          AT&T forms USL
          SVR4 developer releases from AT&T and Sun
          Motif shipped from OSF to OEMs
          OpenLook developed by Sun and AT&T
          IBM releases AIX 3.1 and RISC System/6000
- 1991   ACE consortium announced
          Sun creates SunSoft as subsidiary, SunSoft announces Solaris
          Sun acquires INTERACTIVE Systems
          Novell and USL form Univel joint distribution company/venture
          DEC only major system vendor to ship OSF/1 variant
          OSF/USL peace talks on and off
- 1992   USL releases SVR4.2 and Univel distributes UnixWare
          Novell acquires USL
- 1993   All major UNIX vendors move to support X/Open and COSE

Figure 1.3.   *Continued*

1.2.3.   SVR4 Becomes the de facto Standard

By early 1992, it became clear that OSF/1 was not going to take off. It was plagued by delays and the normal life cycle problems associated with major new pieces of software. Many OEMs underestimated the complexity of merging their own technology and porting application software to the new platform. Many choose a conversative path of releasing "developer versions"—which basically indicates performance or stability problems that render the release not ready for prime time in customers' production environment.

OSF would seem to have served the purpose of getting AT&T to look differently on their product.

AT&T's USL division established SVR4 and SVID as the standard for UNIX. SVR4 (1) is: the industry standard (de facto) UNIX operating system base specification and technology, (2) has established itself as a major market force, (3) is now and will be available from multiple vendors and on multiple platforms, and (4) is destined to continue to change with the industry.

USL's SVR4 provided so much functionality that SVR4 vendors had only a few ways to differentiate their operating system, competing on the basis of the following:

* Feature completeness
* Hardware differentiation
* Ease of installation
* Documentation
* Support
* Performance
* Quality (few bugs)
* Price

It is not trivial to keep track of the players in the Intel/UNIX SVR4 field let alone all the other platforms and software vendors.

In 1990, Intel declared it would use vanilla UNIX. INTERACTIVE later took over this project. USL named INTERACTIVE as the "Principal Publisher" (or the publisher of the Intel Reference part of UNIX for Intel-based UNIX.) INTERACTIVE produced a developers release by summer of 1991. Shortly thereafter, SunSoft purchased the relevant development group within INTERACTIVE. SunSoft also announced that it planned to release Solaris 2.0, an Intel-based version of SunOS and SVR4. SunSoft also announced a marketing agreement with Novell where Sun would offer a version of Netware on Solaris and Novell would help Sun with marketing Solaris to its distribution channel.

Meanwhile, USL and Novell formed a joint venture called Univel. The idea was that Univel would develop a more highly integrated version of SVR4 including Novell Netware as an integrated feature. USL would OEM this product while Univel (now the Novell UNIX Systems Group (USG)) would sell binaries to distributors or other channels.

It would appear that smaller Intel/SVR4 vendors like ESIX, Microport, and UHC will have problems competing with Sun and Novell-Univel. The era of the vanilla SVR4 release-based products may be short lived as vendors feel a need to differentiate themselves. UNIX International and USL have to stay alert lest the SVR4 community diverges into similar but incompatible offerings. SVR4 blends AT&T, Berkeley, Sun, and XENIX features.

The marketing strategies of the major system vendors are the primary cause of the current widespread confusion. The confusion will continue to be fostered by the rival marketing activities of the OSF and UI organizations.

Figure 1.4 illustrates estimates of the size of the installed base and the relative maturity of each major UNIX-based commercial product. Note that the few production-ready versions of OSF/1 have actually been released and none have yet had any signifcant commercial success.

XENIX is definitely in the aging category and will be replaced in part by SCO UNIX. System V could also be viewed in the aging category, from a basic technology point of view, except that it now includes a significant amount of new code.

Neither System V nor OSF/1 will be able to stand still technologically. Both operating systems have yet to include an accepted standardization of symmetrical multiprocessing support, however. Mach provides full symmetrical multiprocessing capability, as do various versions of SVR4 from vendors such as International Computers Ltd. and Encore, to name only two, but full support of process synchronization has yet to be fully developed in either System V or OSF/1. Similarly, issues of high levels of computer security and the modularity of the UNIX kernel are creating intense current technical (and marketing) debate within the industry.

The relevance of such leading edge technology for most end users is another matter. For example, not everyone needs the ultimate in secure operating system functionality. Many of today's computer systems, especially desktop machines and distributed computing system environments, are not multiprocessor architectures. Where multiprocessing systems can be found in some installations, there are still many uniprocessors for every one such multiprocessor machine. Today's networks consist mainly of uniprocessor machines, and uniprocessors also

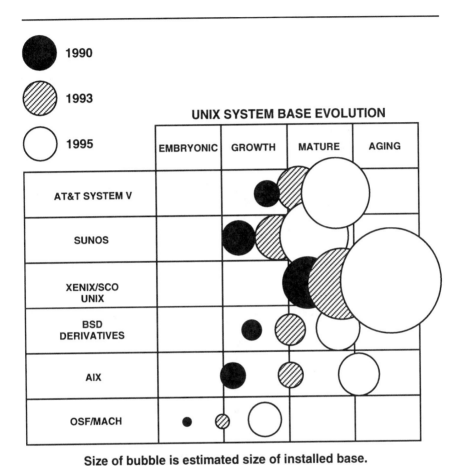

Size of bubble is estimated size of installed base.

Figure 1.4.   Adoption of different versions of UNIX. In terms of installed base growth, over the next few years, it is clear that System V-based systems will represent major growth and consitute the largest installed base of UNIX users in the UNIX industry.

represent the predominant desktop platform architecture and will continue to do so for the next several years. The important point here is that the technological leading edge, while of current development interest to system hardware and software vendors, is years ahead of the mass market. It is easy for an end user to get confused. For example, purists can argue that the System V kernel is bloated with unnecessary and difficult-to-support functionality, especially compared to Mach. But this argument is of questionable relevance to today's end user who is not in the business of porting UNIX.

1.2.4.   UNIX, Acquisition by Novell—What are the Implications?

By 1990 USL revenues were around $100 million and were estimated to be as high as $160 million in 1992. USL had around 600 employees based mainly in the United States with about 50 employees in its European and Pacific operations. Pacific rim companies represented the bulk of the outside investment in UNIX System Laboratories. The Asian holdings were equivalent to the combined United States and European holdings.

On December 22, 1992, Novell, Inc. and AT&T jointly announced they had signed a letter of intent for Novell to acquire UNIX Systems Laboratories (USL). Under the terms of the letter of intent, existing shares of USL common stock would be exchanged for up to 12.3 million newly issued shares of Novell common stock in a tax-free merger accounted for as a purchase. Novell would issue approximately 11.1 million shares of common stock to the current non-Novell USL shareholders. In addition, the outstanding USL stock options and other equity incentives would be exchanged for Novell stock all in accordance with the terms of USL employee plans and the definitive agreement.

Prior to the acquisition of USL by Novell, AT&T owned approximately 77 percent of the outstanding shares of USL. Novell held approximately 5 percent of USL's outstanding stock, and 11 other investors held approximately 18 percent.

1.2.5.   UNIX, Open Systems, and Standards

An open system is a compliant implementation of an evolving set of vendor-neutral specifications for interfaces, services and protocols, and formats which is designed to enable the configuration, operation, and substitution of the whole system, or parts of the system, in a layered systems architecture with applications and / or its components with equally compliant implementations, preferably available from many vendors.

Gartner Group

Standards are formed to help eliminate confusion and achieve consensus among the various interests of the members of the standards-forming bodies. There is considerable activity in the area of computing standards. Several standards have come about as the direct result of computer users' desire to see UNIX standardized and to see it evolve in a direction compatible with present use as well as future needs. Standards are at the basis of the concept of Open Systems.

In both government and private industry, standards in the computer industry are of critical importance to anyone interested in effectively planning information systems for the future. There are several standards bodies and organizations working to define specifications and test suites that can be used to demonstrate whether products are in conformance with specifications. Test suites such as SVVS (System V Verification Suite) are programs that, when successfully run on a version of UNIX, demonstrate conformance, in this case to the System V specification.

Government computer procurements demand the most rigid adherence to specifications and that conformance be validated. The government's FIPS (Federal Information Processing Standards) committee has recently adopted specifications regarding UNIX. Some companies are setting their own internal standards. For example, large corporations such as General Motors have adopted UNIX as one of their internal standards. This is because of their desire to preserve their investments in applications software developments and to preserve their pool of educated users, especially when they change computer platforms or vendors.

Some standards are acknowledged when the product technologies they specify are so widely accepted and used commercially that they become de facto. In order for standards to come into being, there has to be a desire on the part of those creating the standards to accept the same specification and for those receiving the standard to accept and comply with it. When specifications are openly available for anyone, they are "open." When they are protected and private, and commercially restricted, they are "proprietary." UNIX is open; OS/2, VMS, and MVS are proprietary.

The challenge of verification. The proof of compliance with SVID lies in the successful certification of any particular implementation via the SVVS, or System V Verification Suite, which is supplied, at additional cost, to licensees of System V X/Open. The U.S. government demands such compliance formally in its Federal Information Processing Standards applied to its procurements. Standards specifications that do not provide such a means of verification make it difficult to measure the extent of any given vendor's implementation and, consequently, its compatibility with other vendors' implementations. Without some means of formal verification, supported by running a set of software test programs, most users have no way of really understanding whether implementations are really compliant with various standards. Most standards-setting bodies have addressed this issue, but there are still many specifications that people will call standards even without any formal means of measurement. The original purposes of SVID and SVVS were to provide compatibility and a method to measure compatibility with and between existing System V implementations.

Upward compatibility is a serious issue, not only for the installed base of System V, XENIX, BSD, and SunOS users, but also for new users. True system compatibility from an end user perspective rests not only with the provision of standard application programming interfaces but also with the compatibility of UNIX shell scripts. If a vendor changes the way UNIX commands format their output, then there is a chance that shell scripts will be incompatible between systems, even though software programs are compatible. The issue of compatibility and portability is extremely important and is covered at length in Chapter 6. Chapter 6 also provides an in-depth discussion of important standards-making bodies and standards that will impact the UNIX industry of the 1990s.

Who will call the shots in the future? Historically, the field of computing has been dominated by proprietary technology. But today, with UNIX, we are seeing examples of unprecedented openness and multivendor cooperation. While the term "Open Systems" has perhaps been overused, what it represents is very important: (1) companies will adhere to standards, and (2) vendors will license new technology and describe interfaces openly. This holds the promise of continued cooperation between vendors. The Open Systems approach is inherently multivendor, competitive, and multisourced, all of which should result in much better and longer-lasting value for the customer.

UNIX has been accepted as a standard operating system, with Novell's USL System V, the de facto standard. There will continue to be debates as well as marketing warfare waged over the "standard UNIX." However, the existing base of users will call the shots and, most likely, will choose to migrate to System V-conforming versions of UNIX. They will do so for reasons of applications compatibility.

Will there ever be convergence on a single version of UNIX? During the late 1980s there were hundreds of articles and analyses that made predictions about the convergence of UNIX. It seemed at that time that the industry would settle on one or two versions of UNIX, one based on the original AT&T (now USL) and one on OSF. Yet here we are today still with SVR4, evolved from the original version, and with dozens of variants. Virtually all of them are based on the same set of standards including POSIX, XPG, and SVID, run TCP/IP over Ethernet, and so on.

In retrospect, OSF suffered continual slips, and only one major vendor, DEC had a version ready for production use by the end of 1992. Most other versions were development only. Major vendors are finding it difficult to make the migration. These migrations are taking the vendors much longer than they originally predicted.

UNIX International and OSF appear to be much more interested in aligning with each other than some of their respective backers. OSF has been participating in UNIX International technical meetings in a variety of areas, but on an ad hoc basis. As the end of 1992 neither group had actually joined the other in any official capacity. To do so would require the consensus of their respective memberships. Both groups realize that while the feud between them may serve some of their corporate sponsors, it does not please the end users who are by now completely alienated from UNIX feuds. They realize the only way to compete with Microsoft and to expand the UNIX market to new levels is to demonstrate mutual respect and look for ways to increase their synergism.

1.2.6.   How Widespread Is UNIX?

There are hundreds of computer companies that support UNIX variants today. Industry forecasters predict that the market for UNIX-based systems, software, and services will be the fastest-growing segment of the industry, experiencing growth rates in the range of 30 percent per year. Some computer industry analysts feel the UNIX market already commands more than 30 percent of the entire computer market.

Until UNIX, no operating system was adaptable enough to accommodate a wide range of hardware. UNIX is available on a broader range of computer systems than any other operating system (see Figure 1.5). It runs on personal computers such as IBM's PS/2, Apple's MAC SE, numerous PC clones, Radio Shack's TRS-80, and several laptops, to name only a few.

UNIX runs on Intel-based and smaller systems, on the biggest iron around, including those as dissimilar as IBM and Cray. It runs on new networked I/O architectures, multiprocessed CPU architectures, and fault-tolerant architectures. Versions of UNIX are available for most of

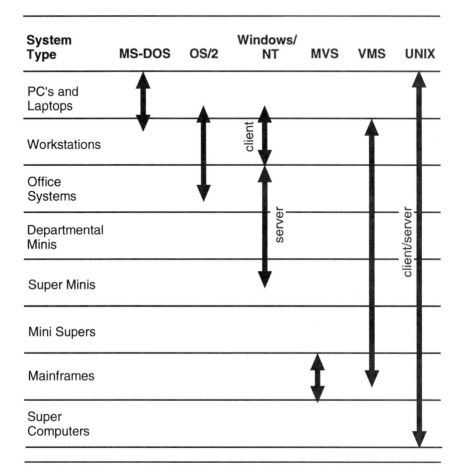

Figure 1.5. UNIX system technology range. UNIX runs on a wider set of computing platforms than any other operating system.

the standard mainframes—AIX on IBM 3090s and UTS on Amdahl. Virtually all of the minisupercomputer and supercomputer vendors, such as Convex and Alliant, support UNIX.

UNIX is an automatic first-choice operating system when any new CPU is designed. You will probably never see VMS run on any machine but a VAX, and the same is true of most of the other proprietary operating systems, although it is theoretically possible. If VMS were ported, would DEC freely license and port it to multiple architectures?

UNIX is currently regarded as the standard operating system for the workstation market. It has gained the greatest market share in engineering-oriented environments like software development and CAD/CAM/CAE.

UNIX is fast becoming the industry standard for a new generation of multiuser systems. Sophisticated applications are available and continue to be ported and developed for these systems. As new applications are written in conjunction with relational database systems, they are often being made available on UNIX in addition to the proprietary operating systems such database software often runs on.

UNIX is having a tremendous impact in the minicomputer market. Virtually all the major midrange minicomputer vendors offer UNIX as either a primary or secondary operating system. UNIX is fast becoming the preferred computer operating system.

1.2.7.   UNIX Applications—How Many and How Mainstream?

Many companies first choose the application software that will satisfy their needs and then make a selection of the hardware and operating system on which to run the application. Computer vendors recognize that there are limits to the number and types of applications they can profitably sell and support under their own brand name. This motivates their making "third-party software" available on their systems. Having the software the customer needs greatly increases the likelihood that the vendor's hardware and system software products will be purchased. In fact, this has rapidly become "do or die" for any new computer.

UNIX applications, taken as a whole, now rival both MS-DOS and MacOS in terms of applications availability. Given the software recruitment efforts of prominent UNIX vendors (especially AT&T, Sun, DEC, NCR, and Unisys), there are more applications now available on UNIX than on any other multiuser operating system in existence. Estimates range up to 15,000. If one includes MS-DOS applications, since MS-DOS runs as a guest under many UNIX systems, the number of applications approaches 30,000. Individual system vendors' software catalogs usually list from a few hundred to a few thousand. By comparison, there are perhaps 5,000 applications running on DEC's VMS operating system.

There are several sources of UNIX-based applications, and systems vendors are working diligently to convince independent software vendors that porting solutions to UNIX is in their strategic interest. Application software development itself has been and will continue to be a key driver and critical success factor for UNIX. Not all applications are bought from independent software vendors. There are many cases where application software is internally developed by users either as standalone applications or to augment other purchased application software. Such UNIX users are interested in exploiting the rich development environment of UNIX in building their own internal application solutions. Chapter 8 contains suggestions on locating UNIX software.

Still, however, it remains true that UNIX has not attracted the volume of off-the-shelf "shrinkwrap" software available on MS-DOS. This situation is now changing, and the battle between UNIX and MS-DOS/Windows, and to a lesser extent OS/2, is bound to intensify. Software capabilities will make it easier to port applications from MS-DOS to UNIX.

1.3.   THE FUTURE OF THE UNIX INDUSTRY

UNIX and key standards, formal and de facto, will form the basic glue for interfacing computing platforms and application solutions in the future. UNIX will promote levels of portability, interoperability, and interchangeability (openness) seen today only in the area of personal computers and MS-DOS.

By the mid-1990s, a far wider range of applications software will be readily available on UNIX. Consequently, PC software vendors in particular will find UNIX an attractive growth market opportunity. UNIX now runs on virtually every type of hardware, from the personal computer to the mainframe and the supercomputer. UNIX will first be made available on new hardware designs such as very powerful desktop computers, multiuser microprocessor-based systems, and specialty systems. Whether UNIX will be applicable to the most advanced computer architectures of the future, however, such as massively parallel CPUs (transputers), is not as clear.

On some system environments, UNIX will be the "second choice" operating system. As its library of applications software grows to truly rival that of the now leading operating systems, these systems will increasingly be challenged and replaced. UNIX systems will continue to offer price/performance advantages over other proprietary alternatives. By the mid-1990s it will have substantially increased its market share and it will compete quite successfully with OS/2.

1.3.1.   Strong Points

The impact of UNIX and Open Systems on the users of computer systems will be significant. The "good news":

1. Virtually every (over 250 at present) computer system and software vendor will support a UNIX offering. For some companies, UNIX will be the primary (or only) operating system offered. Other com-

panies will provide UNIX as a secondary operating system, as an alternative to their primary proprietary operating system.

2. Porting software from one machine to the next will be measured in hours or days instead of months and years. The greater the compliance with accepted standards, the less time and complexity when porting.

3. Advances in hardware and core technologies will be wholly applicable both quickly and consistently, with UNIX the primary operating system.

4. Price/performance competition among system vendors will increase, driven by advances in processor design and manufacturing process engineering and also because UNIX will tend to level the playing field in favor of new high-performance processor architectures such as RISC (Reduced Instruction Set Computers).

5. Programmer availability will not be the issue it once was. Once committed to a UNIX strategy, it will be far easier for a company to leverage its investments in hardware, software, training, and personnel when switching to new computer systems and solutions. By some estimates, there are currently over 300,000 programmers who know UNIX.

6. The collective rate of UNIX development and enhancement as well as vendors' added value will allow UNIX to rival and surpass investments in operating systems made by the largest computer companies today. By "collective" we mean that, unlike a proprietary operating system, which is developed and maintained by only one relatively small group of software engineers, UNIX is being worked on and developed by many groups of software engineers and academic and research professionals.

7. More than ever before, users will have a clear path for cost-effective management of their assets in the face of technological obsolescence. Their databases and applications software will be more easily protected and preserved and (when necessary) migrated to new systems.

8. The installed base of UNIX users will continue to increase from over 7.2 million systems now, at more than 1.2 million sites.

But even under the best-case scenario, it won't all be good news. There remain significant challenges and drawbacks to UNIX in certain computing environments and applications.

1.3.2. UNIX Limitations

Dennis Ritchie was once quoted as saying, "UNIX is a simple, coherent system that pushes a few good ideas and models to the limit." While UNIX is a comparatively simple operating system, it will continue along a path of rapid technological advancement. Several factors will combine to increase the usefulness of UNIX but at the price of increasing its complexity. This stands to affect users in several ways:

1. Despite the value of several layers of standards-based systems, vendors will be compelled to differentiate their products with proprietary extensions to their UNIX operating system implementation. It will be up to the customers to avoid or take care in using proprietary extensions in order to keep their software portable. Independent software vendors will have the same challenge in supporting software in multiple UNIX environments. The challenge is to develop not just a generally accepted operating system standard (e.g., POSIX), but also a standard environment (e.g., X/OPEN XPG) above the level of the UNIX operating system, as well as a user interface standard. (See Sections 6.2 and 6.3 and the Glossary for explanations of POSIX and X/OPEN.)

2. UNIX system administration will continue to be a significant area of responsibility requiring skilled technical professionals to ensure the successful implementation of UNIX installations. Better documentation will also be important in this area. This will be a special challenge where UNIX is to be used to support corporate-level data processing or "mission-critical" applications.

3. UNIX market penetration in mainstream commercial data processing, the heartland of IBM and DEC proprietary operating system products, will occur as more traditional software applications become available on UNIX. In certain areas, such as centralized transaction processing, the use of UNIX may be limited unless facilities such as transaction monitors analogous to IBM's CISC become available. However, as the computer systems market matures and network computing spreads, new decentralized applications will be architected to fully exploit Open Systems standards and modern styles of computing (windowing and client server).

4. UNIX functionality can be expected to increase, and in a much more orderly fashion than in the past. Major enhancements can be expected in UNIX ease of use, international language support, security, and many other areas.

1.3.3. Arguments For and Against UNIX

The popularity and success of UNIX are due to several factors:

- It is written in the high-level C language, which is itself highly portable.

- It has a simple (albeit cryptic) command structure.
- It features a hierarchical file system that is relatively easy to implement and maintain.
- Its files follow a consistent format, making it very easy for applications and programmers to interact with them.
- It provides a large number of primitive commands and utilities from which one can construct complex programs from simpler ones.
- It possesses a simple, consistent interface to peripheral devices. Similar consistency is also found in other areas, such as software development tools.
- It has multiuser and multitasking functionality, enabling several interactive users to be supported simultaneously.
- It provides an interface to application software to hide specific hardware characteristics.
- It runs on more computers than any other operating system.
- It has a large, growing portfolio of application software.
- It is portable and enables a high level of application software portability.
- It offers advanced features for use in a network computing environment.
- It is highly scalable; that is it runs on computers from laptops and PCs to supercomputers (e.g., Cray).
- It is available on systems that usually cost less and offer better performance for departmental and corporate applications.
- It offers its commercial users a large and growing pool of trained professionals and university graduates who know UNIX.

Balancing these positive attributes are many problems that UNIX doesn't solve, or doesn't solve very effectively at present. For example, UNIX isn't nearly as easy to use as MacOS, but it is much more powerful. Most users don't use MacOS—they use the Mac's Desktop Interface. It is commonly believed that UNIX will be much easier to use as graphical user interfaces are used in conjunction with UNIX shells. UNIX functionality pales when measured against mainframe transaction processing capabilities found on MVS, but then it costs a small fraction of what MVS costs. UNIX was never intended to replace MVS or support the exact same types of mainframe applications or the large centralized system style of computing typical to traditional mainframe environments.

The following are common complaints about UNIX.

"UNIX is comparatively user unfriendly; it is cryptic and employs somewhat unnatural mnemonics (commands)."

This is mostly true for casual users or others who are already versed in some other operating system. While UNIX commands are terse, they are not notably more obscure than those of other systems. Graphic user interfaces will help improve ease of use. UNIX shells will also be available to make UNIX closely resemble the user interface on other operating systems (e.g., the DEC VMS Command Language (DCL) shell). Finally, in many applications, UNIX will be hidden altogether from the user.

"UNIX will let you hang yourself. . . . It doesn't adequately protect a user from himself / herself."

This is true to some extent, but the same can be said of other operating systems as well. For example, you can type in a command that will delete all user files without the system ever asking you for verification that you really mean it. There are things you can do to minimize problems that result from putting power tools in the hands of the unskilled. The command interface can be controlled by modifying the UNIX shell (explained in the next chapter). The cryptic command line UNIX user interface will increasingly be hidden by window systems that are being used to front-end UNIX. As this occurs, one can expect many of the "rough edges" to be smoothed over.

"UNIX doesn't handle database applications very well. For example, large files can become excessively fragmented, and there are limits on the maximum allowable size of files."

This is true of database software that uses the UNIX file system instead of what is called raw I/O. Most commercially available database software packages use raw I/O not only to solve these problems but also to gain performance.

"UNIX doesn't handle error conditions well. For example, it doesn't handle recovery of bad disk blocks."

Until recently, most versions of UNIX have not had so-called "high availability" features. Early variants of UNIX were nowhere near as sophisticated as the operating systems running on mainframes and minicomputers in this regard. In recent years, however, most vendors have made meaningful advances, and this is no longer as significant a difficulty as it once was. In fact, many variants of UNIX provide many high availability features.

"UNIX documentation and the software itself are of low or uneven quality, buggy, and incomprehensible to new users."

This has been true in the past, but UNIX documentation and quality are now receiving considerable attention.

"UNIX is not a very secure environment. It assumes all users are friendly and cooperate with each other. UNIX offers only a modicum of security features."

In UNIX, security is implemented for the most part from a personal point of view by granting others the right to access one's own files. Security has not been a major requirement in environments that have historically used UNIX. Unlike other commercial operating systems, which tend to come out of the box "tightened up," UNIX comes out of the box wide open and has to be tightened up by the system administrator. This has contributed to UNIX's poor reputation with regard to security. Section 2.9 describes security features of UNIX and new secure versions of UNIX that are commercially available. A discussion of the recent computer virus or worm that hit UNIX installations in 1989 is described in Section 2.9.1.

"Generic UNIX does not support real-time."

UNIX has been advocated and used as a real-time operating system since early in its use at AT&T for switching systems. UNIX has traditionally been considered a poor choice for real-time applications. Unless specially modified, generic UNIX is probably not appropriate for such applications. Several vendors have enhanced UNIX to function in real-time environments, however. Much more will be happening as standards efforts are focused on UNIX real-time support. Many companies already offer real-time support in UNIX.

"UNIX lacks the bells and whistles that are available on other operating systems."

This is certainly true with respect to the "big" operating systems that run on sophisticated mainframes. Conversely, it is certainly not true when examined from the viewpoint of the much more numerous general-purpose, multiuser computer systems. In this latter case, UNIX now has most of the key required features.

"UNIX puts constraints on interprocess communications."

Again, only when compared to operating systems that run on the large mainframes, which are far more sophisticated and costly.

"There is a lack of mainstream applications software available on UNIX."

Not true. There are many thousands of application programs on UNIX. Indeed, many key applications are only available on UNIX.

"The cost of conversion to UNIX isn't justified."

This could be true in special cases. One must be willing to examine the long-term implications, however. Once converted to UNIX, customers will find they have more flexibility than is possible with proprietary operating system alternatives.

Flying in the face of the facts are these arguments against UNIX:

"Our programmers don't know UNIX and C."

"UNIX is too complex."

The only way to overcome such arguments is through education.

1.4.   WHY UNIX?

In 1989, UNIX became the largest installed multiuser operating system worldwide with over one million installations, according to DMR. In a survey of over 100 sites, DMR researchers found that UNIX is being implemented more for competitive than for cost-cutting reasons. The survey found that many companies are instituting Open Systems strategies, including UNIX, for competitive reasons associated with applications availability.

In the 1990s, UNIX and microprocessors are givens. The 1990s will likely see the demise of proprietary minicomputer-oriented computing in favor of distributed network computing. The 1990s will also see a shift from personal to workgroup-oriented computing. UNIX will play a key role in this evolution as well. Ritchie reflected on the origins of UNIX, ". . . what we wanted to preserve was not just a good environment in which to do programming, but a system around which a fellowship could form. We knew from experience that the essence of communal computing, as supplied by remote-access, time-shared machines, is not just to type programs into a terminal instead of a keypunch, but to encourage close communication. . . . A common environment makes it much easier for people to take advantage of each other's work."

About 10 years ago, UNIX growth underwent a qualitative change. It became a commercial product, and that was the end of the age of innocence for the system. The User Group and USENIX (described in Chapter 8) became real communities instead of ad hoc groups. The availability of a portable operating system made possible the start-up of a lot of new companies.

UNIX-based systems have now become a credible alternative in the computer systems marketplace. While UNIX offers numerous advantages in the short term, including cost savings, its real benefits come over the long term. Management's responsibility is to set out long-term direction. Management's understanding of UNIX will be increasingly important in planning information technology strategies and controlling the acquisition of future technology.

UNIX has become a leading contender not just in technical computing applications but also as a platform for supporting typical office support tasks, because of its portability and its flexible set of commands and utilities (which are discussed in the next chapter). There are obvious benefits to be gained from using the same operating system to support both office automation and software development functions. UNIX systems are also going to be used extensively to handle electronic mail and document processing.

There are several benefits to be derived from the addition of UNIX to today's data processing environments. It allows users to gain greater access to computing capabilities and to gain more control over their own information needs. Even nontechnical users can become knowledgeable enough to develop their own tools to automate routine tasks—tools they might never have been able to develop otherwise. Most development staffs find the transition to UNIX quite easy. Developers will find it easy to develop online applications under UNIX.

UNIX provides great flexibility in configuring system components, including the support of terminals. The combination of UNIX and smaller processors allows computer capacity to be increased in smaller, more cost-effective increments.

1.5. ASSET PROTECTION IN INFORMATION TECHNOLOGY REQUIRES STANDARDS

Just as the government and standards bodies set standards and expect the vendor community to comply with them, so too should the MIS or system planning function set standards for computer systems and software. Attention to such internal norms will increase the return on investment through the following results:

- Cost reduction (short term and long term)
- Greater leverage from a common skill base

- Improved integration and communications between systems and applications
- Protection against technological obsolescence
- Greater focus on strategic applications of Open Systems computing

X/Open UNIX is the de facto open UNIX standard. Many users consider UNIX a strategically correct decision. These customers include the General Services Administration of the U.S. government (more than 70 percent of federal RFQs (requests for quotation) specify UNIX and USL System V) as well as major private firms such as General Motors/EDS. UNIX will continue to sell well where presently used, and it will increasingly make inroads into other markets as it is enhanced.

1.6.   DESKTOP UNIX: A NEW FRONTIER

UNIX has not historically made serious inroads on the desktop. Unlike DOS, which runs on any PC, and Windows, which runs on most PCs (e.g., 386 and more powerful systems), UNIX requires high-end PCs for use as personal workstations and requires high-end PC-based configuration for use as file servers. Software developers also need to create versions of their software for each major variant of UNIX. Binary compatibility is only possible when application vendors or users adhere to the specifications of the APIs and ABIs for a given processor architectures. For example, well-behaved applications will be binary compatible (possibly shrinkwrap) for SPARC-based systems.

Intel PC versions of UNIX are now available from a number of companies including Berkeley Software Design Inc., Falls Church, VA; Dr. Dobb's Journal, San Mateo, CA; ESIX Computer Inc., Santa Ana, CA; SunSoft, Mountain View, CA; Mt. Xinu Inc., Berkeley, CA; NeXT Computers, Redwood City, CA; The Santa Cruz Operation, Inc., Santa Cruz, CA; UH Corp., Houston, TX; and Univel, San Jose, CA.

The operating system is *not* the frontier for the 1990s. UNIX will be taken for granted as one component of the new model of computing, an operating system that anyone can run on standard microprocessors that anyone can buy. But don't expect UNIX to take over the world of computing. Although predicted to represent over 20 percent of the systems market worldwide by 1992, UNIX is not expected to completely displace other major operating systems such as DOS, VMS, or MVS. However, even where these other systems are used, UNIX is expected to help in better integrating these environments in a more cohesive, overall network-aware information system.

Management rethinks UNIX. In 1989, Computerworld surveyed 211 top MIS executives who already had UNIX, SunOS, ULTRIX, or XENIX in their shops. Almost two-thirds felt that UNIX would continue to play an important role in their information strategies. They see UNIX as a cost-effective alternative for multiuser computing and as an alternative to PCs strung all over and networked together.

1.6.1.   Microsoft Windows NT—Will It Kill UNIX?

In October of 1992, Microsoft chairman Bill Gates finally admitted what had become obvious, that the much-hyped Windows/NT software promised by the end of 1992 had slipped.

This event naturally raised speculation as to whether Microsoft was simply overoptimistic in its original schedule or if was in fact calculated as a means of maintaining its market dominance. It was reported that in mid-1991, Bill and his staff huddled and weighed the risks of losing the high end of the market against a risk of a little embarrassment and the latter strategy won.

Microsoft is competing with IBM OS/2, with Novell, and with UNIX for the high end of the market. The hype associated with Windows/NT should be a case study in the annals of computer marketing. Windows finally becoming multitasking and supporting 32-bit architecture is not exactly earth-shaking. Should companies like Microsoft act more responsibly toward their customers and the industry? Should the press act more responsibly in more accurate reporting (read conservative) reporting on futures? Does the press have a responsibility to large organizations and to the software development community on which the computer industry depends, especially on major announcements, which matter a great deal to the industry?

When you get an industry powerhouse—such as a Microsoft—announcing its future roadmap, and other companies follow suit and aggressively engage in futures marketing, the press has almost no choice but to go along with it. Truth in reporting would seem more to do with faithfully representing the story than its reality. All of this tends to snowball to the point where customers can't make meaningful decisions based on what they read. Industry analysts are often no less objective than the press in this regard.

The lesson for managing change should be clear. As in politics, people tend to want to believe and follow their candidates. Traditional hardware and software platform vendor relationships have similarities. The movement toward open systems has been changing this dynamic. Customers are becoming less wedded to particular vendors. They are becoming more sophisticated and knowledgeable.

1.6.2. UNIX in LAN Environments

Over the last several years, UNIX was predicted to be embraced by the LAN community. UNIX offered numerous advantages not found on DOS-based network operating systems, such as true multiuser and multitasking capabilities, built-in communications, and so on. But UNIX failed to excite LAN managers for a number of reasons. Early PCs lacked RAM memory sufficient to run UNIX. Many versions of UNIX made it difficult for software developers to commit their limited development and support resources. UNIX has a reputation for being complex and requiring well-trained network management. The complexity of NetWare and LAN Manager have closed this "complexity gap" over the last few years, however. The introduction of graphical front-end interfaces on UNIX systems has also helped UNIX to overcome some of these complexity issues.

Many corporations today are creating enterprise-wide networks. These networks require capabilities long associated with true 32-bit multitasking, directory services, efficient network management, and security. As Microsoft enters this market with its new technology, Windows/NT, Novell is embarking on a strategy based on UNIX. Novell will continue its strategy with NetWare, providing its network operating system for use with DOS and Windows clients and believes UNIX variants in general and its USG subsidiary's UnixWare specifically, will find a place in LAN environments running NetWare today. UnixWare is intended to run on high-end Intel systems as application specific servers that will provide information and services requested by "client" networked PCs. Applications currently running in NetWare environments that will likely incorporate UNIX application servers include information management, office automation, general business data processing, accounting, and CAD/CAM/CAE.

1.7. STRATEGIC QUESTIONS CONCERNING CHANGE IN THE INDUSTRY.

What operating system environment will most effectively support a client-server environment?

Which networking architectures will most effectively support a client-server environment?

How will application development technologies facilitate development of client-server application development and deployment?

Will traditional mainframes and midrange systems evolve to support client-server or will they be replaced by networked computing environments?

What are the most common mistakes that will be made in implementing client-server?

How will vendors' positioning be impacted by the markets move to client-server?

What opportunities and challenges do vendors face in adapting to client-server market evolution and demand?

Which are the application areas that offer the most promise in exploiting client-server?

Is "middleware" a fad, or will it evolve into a position of greater importance than operating systems?

These and other strategic questions will be explored throughout the rest of this work.

1.8. MANAGING CHANGE

Many companies have undergone some sort of evaluation of UNIX and UNIX system platforms. They may have even conducted pilots or have applied UNIX in some initial application area or in some limited applications area like CAD/CAM. Pilot UNIX projects can enable a company's personnel to gain insight into the problems associated with migrating from their existing platform supporting legacy applications.

To make a change to a new architecture without taking full advantage of that architecture will probably result in user frustrations. If users never encounter new services and the business is still being carried out the same way it was performed with older systems, the cost of migration in disruption and the elimination of a familiar environment may not be offset by the benefits. Changing the look rather than the function itself can be a mistake. Users will ask, what did we change the environment for? MIS or systems implementors should be concerned that they have successfully led a change that has resulted in an effective solution to known business problems and processes.

The business strategy needs to be redrawn identifying those strategic business functions and areas for improved services. This may involve the following:

1. Determine today's requirements for automated functions and responsiveness.

2. Capture requirements and put them into perspective. Explore different alternatives and technological plans for these requirements.
3. Look at the organizational infrastructure and the current information flow so that the impact of information systems automation can be analyzed as new services are injected into the flow.
4. Establish productivity and maintainability objectives to assess system effectiveness. There is no substitute for well-defined requirements and architectural mapping.
5. Define goals based on a time line and series of events looking for opportunities to maximize software reusability and allow scalability.

The bottom line is to integrate as close as possible to users and provide user-service-oriented solutions.

The way to meet today's needs for information systems and distribution is computer and information systems technology. New business processes require technology transformation. The key factors that must exist for a technology transformation to occur include the following:

- Information/applications backlogs
- Organizational change
- New technology alignments
- The empowerment of people by management to change

Many of today's computers are aged systems straining under the present load. The applications backlog industrywide has increased from around six months in 1988 to one year in 1993. Today's legacy systems, their networking capabilities, their software environments are going to be able to accommodate just so much change. These systems were never designed for certain modern applications.

Organizational transformation will take place with the introduction of technological innovations. Organizational change takes many forms. Flatter and more matrixed organizations are a symptom of simply having to do more with less. No company is recession-proof. Businesses are rapidly decentralizing. Technology has become a key enabler for such organizational transformation.

The alignment of processor, database, and network technology has created incredible potential for technological transformation. Workstation, databases (especially relational and object oriented), and networking technology have all reached a sort of technological zenith simultaneously. In 1984, 44 MIPS cost about $14 million dollars. By 1992, you could buy a 25 MIPS workstation for around $10,000. This processing power has created the opportunity to accomplish database and networking functions that were only recently available to a privileged few.

In the 60s and 70s, new business developments such as credit card clearing, reservation systems, telemarketing, and many other functions were made possible by the first wave of these three technologies. These new business developments demonstrated the characteristics of technology transformation and involved leading edge technology, high dollar investment (creating a new computing environment), and changes to the way business is done. Today these same three technologies promise to support a new wave of technology transformation involving client-server applications based on distributed computing environments.

This type of computing promises higher productivity and flexibility. It consists of "clients" that are connected to a network and have access to a wide range of services, and "servers" that store, process, and distribute information. These environments employ high-performance systems and networks that allow users to distribute the computing workload across the network. Processing is divided into separate functions that communicate with each other across high-speed networks. The advantages for users lie in direct access to information quicker and more easily through the use of desktop tools. As applications change and grow, additional resources can be added or deployed with minimal incremental investment.

1.9.   OPEN SYSTEM ARCHITECTURE

Openness is confusing. The term "open" is widely confused among the following contexts:

- Interoperability
- Portability
- Standards-based
- Availability on multiple platforms
- Availability from multiple companies
- Well defined, published, and available
- Available from more than one source
- No tax—free from huge or unreasonable royalties
- Publicly documented interfaces
- Reference implementation available
- Future evolution controlled by independent organization
- The presence of compatibility testing framework

Rightsizing. Some combination of upsizing and/or downsizing.

Upsizing. Relates to upgrading low-end systems to more powerful systems with added services and increasing productivity.

Downsizing. Relates to relocating data and applications from a mainframe or large centralized system to local servers.

A distributed architecture is the key to a rightsizing project. It delivers flexibility and performance needed where clients and servers are tuned to the specific business tasks. Rightsizing is not an autonomous project. It is a consistent re-engineering supporting numerous projects. Some projects will create new user applications and others will enhance existing applications.

No matter how you look at it, rightsizing will involve expanding information technology along two dimensions: new platforms and new business processes and services. The goals of such expansion should be carefully established:

1. Information services should support the demands of the business.
2. Innovative use of information services should be used to make the business more productive.
3. An information strategy should ensure that users are able to interact with their information systems.

New challenges and increased responsibilities are encountered in managing the change to a new environment.

1.10.   MANAGING MIGRATION

Distributed processing model should allow the use of different types of heterogeneous system components. Information systems need to be re-engineered to run in a new environment in a clear, time-triggered strategy. What is migrating is the way people do their jobs. Attention to user requirements and assisting them in carrying out their business function during the transition and after the transition are fundamental to migration planning.

What actually needs to be done, and in what order, is not always straightforward. Before systems can be decommissioned or centralized systems downsized, an information system re-engineering program needs to be carried out to redefine the information architecture in strategic and tactical detail.

This cannot be done without a reasonable understanding of the company infrastructure and the specific targets of the re-engineering process. The goal of the re-engineering process is to produce an architecture that supports information services and does so in a reliable, secure, and cost-effective manner.

A vision of the future computing environment should be documented and formalized together with goals, objectives, and with assumptions concerning justification. It is important that executive management and the users understand the vision of the future computing environment as well as the reasons for the upcoming change. This process should convince all of the key people that the change is for the better.

Each aspect of the process needs to be covered. All key people should be aware of critical decisions and be sure that expectations are managed consistently and all aspects of the process are properly planned. Each project element should be documented with clear phrases, milestones, and responsibilities with people's names next to them.

1.10.1. Resistance to Change

In computing environments, as everywhere in life, people naturally resist change. Part of the problem with UNIX and Open Systems architecture as we describe it is that it forces the information system to be triggered by end user needs. Users are presented with vast amounts of tools, and many possible interactions exist. When architecting a new system or application, the bottom line is the re-engineering process should be user driven. This is in marked contrast to a tradition of users being told what they need and how to accomplish their tasks. Users are not used to thinking this way and may assume there are only a few ways available to do things.

The one investment that is commonly overlooked, but in reality is one of the largest expense items, is end user education. Not only is it costly to train users sufficiently to the point that they make independent conclusions about their own needs but the time they must devote to being trained is time away from some other revenue-generating activity.

Computers can take in and grind out enormous amounts of data, but people have to look at it, analyze it, and decide if the data is relevant to their decision process. As we enter the decade of the 90s, we have seen an explosion in the amount of raw information. We can also see an explosion in the distribution of this data. As this information wave comes down in the 90s, a new way to analyze the flood of information is needed.

The new technology encompasses not just computing architecture and software products but also an administrative infrastructure, processes, and human skills. Identification and access to information, extraction and integration of disparate information, analysis and synthesis of this information must all be accommodated. Client-server is splitting applications into tasks that are performed on separate computers. Open Systems are an important trend in information technology and should be considered in planning any client-server architecture.

1.11. THE POWER OF INFORMATION

The words "power of information" are used so frequently one might think of them only as an advertising claim or cliché. But advances in information processing are acting as a catalyst for economic and social change. The sudden evolution of traditional computing promises to play a major role in transforming the traditional corporation, its employees, and its customers. Information processing is now advancing every decade equivalent to the 4,000-year path in transportation from horse cart to the bullet train. The power to control information is now moving so fast we are able to use different kinds of data we have never been able to use before.

1.11.1.   Emerging Forms of Information

Consider the forms of information that have been used in a manufacturing environment. First, because of limitations on processing data, historical information had to be used. So called "content information" was stored in cabinets or on punched cards. "Form information" represented the next step up in sophistication of information. This form information might describe the shape of every component in the vehicle as well as the precise shape of components, information used to design the tools to manufacture these components. Whereas content information to describe the car might take hundreds of bytes, form information might take millions. Minicomputers and personal computers were able to handle this new type of form information.

With the massive amount of processing power and storage now possible, manipulation of multiple forms of information becomes feasible. "Behavioral information," used to predict the behavior of physical objects is used as a means of testing new designs. Increasingly complex simulations, such as predicting the weather or the analysis of atomic interactions can take trillions of computations with terabytes of information being generated, stored, visualized, and so forth.

Another form of information might be called "action information." This is information that is instantly converted to an action. Automatic teller machines provide a present day concrete example of an action system. But this is only the beginning. With new technologies as diverse as machine vision, speech recognition, improved sensors, and neural networks, computers will increasingly be able to learn from experience, interact with the environment and produce adaptive products and services.

The explosive advance of technology, new forms of technology, information technology, thinking machines—all are propelling traditional businesses toward a transformation. That process can be expected to radically redefine what it means to be an employee and to be a customer. Technology and business infrastructure are co-evolving to a world of electronic markets. Experts believe that object-oriented technology will be inexorably linked to these electronic markets. This technology will foster the transition from software development as fabrication, to a broader community that accomplishes system/application development through a new assembly process. Information services will evolve from passive information that readers interpret and manipulate to active objects or components that developers or users will assemble that will cooperate by themselves.

1.12. STAYING ON TOP OF INDUSTRY CHANGE

The battleground for the "open networked" operating systems war of the 1990s has formed. The competition for the desktop market will begin to heat up in the next few years. The linkage between the desktop and the midrange systems market will become more apparent. There are several major forces in the desktop market, some relatively new that promise to reshape the very way we think about using computers.

Microsoft will continue to be a dominant force. Microsoft *is* the dominant desktop operating system vendor. It is pushing MS-DOS, Windows 3.x. Now Windows/NT is poised to expand Microsoft's reach from the personal computer world into the enterprise. NT is new technology for Microsoft, but it's not really that new when viewed from the perspective of UNIX. The Mach microkernel has been around awhile, and there are probably more robust microkernel technologies in the labs and even on the market (e.g., Chorus). Windows/NT is very similar in many ways to OSF/2. Our analysis indicates that Microsoft should be especially concerned that NT become the platform for the major portion of their installed base. Why else all the support for 16- and 32-bit windows and OS/2, or that Windows 3.x is even better under NT than without it and that OS/2 is as good or better than OS/2 on NT? So in a sense, Microsoft Windows/NT has to compete with Windows for Workgroups and with DOS version 6 (which will be out about the same time as NT). In essence, it has to compete first with other Microsoft products.

Novell (and its friends) will emerge as Microsoft's biggest competitor. Novell is the dominant PC-LAN network operating system with almost two-thirds of the networked PC market. Novell which recently acquired UNIX System Laboratories now sells UNIX System V release 4 to OEMs and USG, a division of Novell packages and distributes UnixWare, versions of UNIX with integrated NetWare for Intel-based PC's.

SunSoft is also entering the Intel market in a big way. First SunSoft bought INTERACTIVE Systems and continued selling its products that have been highly competitive with SCO UNIX. SunSoft also plans to ship Solaris 2.x for Intel platforms during 1993.

SCO, meanwhile, having decided to move away from UNIX System V, would seem to be in danger of having its strategy change so quickly it will loose market share to Novell, to OEMs, and to SunSoft. We aren't convinced it will stick to its stated strategy of moving to OSF/2. With Microsoft's stake in SCO, SCO has a big enough reason to once again modify its strategy, this time to be more synergistic withWindows/NT. Is it possible that SCO might implement SCO UNIX for NT and still claim to be OSF compliant without using any OSF/2 base software? We see SCO as being vulnerable to product transition issues, and it will face competitors that it has never encountered before in its installed base.

IBM and Apple are working on their own new technology. In the meantime, IBM is pushing OS/2 on its desktops and AIX on its RS/6000 workstations and working long term with Apple on PowerOpen. Apple is pushing System 7 and A/UX and working with IBM on PowerOpen. Taligent has an enormous task of coming to market late and to be successful has to demonstrate innovation beyond that available from Microsoft and Novell and UNIX implementers like SunSoft.

1.12.1. Three Operating System "Camps" to Watch

Each camp will be pushing its own operating system platform and frameworks for future object-oriented environments.

1. Microsoft will be there with Windows/NT, which will be packaged as both client and server versions. The client side will slip in under Windows 3.x and help overcome some MS-DOS limitations. The server side will be ported to a number of servers. There will be versions of Windows/NT servers on Sequent, DEC, HP, and likely as third-party-supported products on other platforms including Sun. Windows/NT is a major threat to the Open Software Foundations OSF/2 since technologically there won't be much difference,

and NT will run more traditional PC software than OSF/2 will. Microsoft will continue to be a company that sets its own standards. It will support POSIX and some government standards like FIPS, but it is not going to be X/Open branded, and will not conform to UNIX SVID or many of the UNIX industries accepted standards.

2. IBM and Apple will slowly converge on PowerOpen. How smoothly they will migrate the Mac-installed base and the AIX base to PowerOpen remains to be seen, but the microkernel technology will probably be similar to OSF/2 and NT. Time-to-market will be a critical issue for IBM and Apple.

3. The third camp will be the SVR4 gang lead by Novell/USL and SunSoft; System V release 4-based UNIX with Novell, Sun/SunSoft, and other vendors supporting SVR4. If these vendors figure out how to work with each other, the basic success factors are in place to give Microsoft some competition it hasn't seen in the past. Novell has the distribution channel to help users integrate UNIX into their PC-based Novell environments. SunSoft is likely to continue to gain market share at SCO's expense, and depending on its marketing relationship with Novell, able to reach the larger corporations with its direct sales force providing the level of integration and leading edge technology that seems to always be expected of Sun. SunSoft can be expected to continue a long-standing Sun legacy of innovation.

Will UNIX and Open Systems experience healthy market growth in the coming years? The answer is an unqualified yes. UNIX has had the greatest market share penetration in the workstation, midrange systems, and small business markets. The greatest opportunity for success and the greatest risk for failure for UNIX vendors over the next few years will be in the office desktop market. Most market analysts predict that UNIX is well positioned not only because of the acceptance of RISC-based workstations but also because of the increasingly strong movement toward client server in which UNIX has the decided lead.

During the difficult economic times of the past few years, UNIX has continued to experience positive growth because of the trend toward client-server and open-network computing. So the battle lines will be drawn between Microsoft and Windows/NT on the one side and a cadre of UNIX SVR4 vendors in Novell, Sun/SunSoft, and other OEMs of Novell.

It is probably Microsoft's market share to lose with Windows/NT on the desktop. Windows users who understand its benefits will be able to utilize Windows/NT for application software that is "well behaved" without much difficulty. Window/NT does not create a binary-compatible migration path by a long shot. This means it is not likely to take off like a rocket—by Microsoft standards—until the applications are there. Windows/NT on Mips RISC architecture, if it succeeds wildly, won't compare to the number of Intel desktops Windows/NT will capture.

On the other hand, the UNIX community is not going to flip over to Windows/NT any time soon. It will continue to consolidate and innovate around SVR4. Exactly whether and how the UNIX Intel market expands has less to do with technology than with marketing. If users perceive that UNIX offers price/performance advantages and believe that UNIX "openness" is clearly differentiated from Microsoft "openness," then UNIX desktop acceptance could accelerate, and the UNIX camp could do well given their relative time-to-market advantage over both of the other camps in terms of delivery product.

1.12.2.   Measuring "Openness" and "Proprietariness"

We believe that the answer in corporate computing environments will have to do with overall network integration and the software development capabilities for distributed application software development. As will be discussed in Chapter 5, networking is all the rage, but it is by no means trivial. Anyone who works with this technology will tell you that the marketing claims of vendors and the realities of systems and network integration, implementation, and administration are very different. With the move to work group, client-server applications, internetworking of desktop and server platforms has to go through a period of major change. Openness will be judged in terms of the ability to plug and play standards-based networked desktop and server technologies. "Proprietariness" will be measured in terms of the licensing practices, the free availability of standards that evolve through a process of industry consensus so that multiple companies can innovate within the standard and drive competition in the marketplace.

We believe that UNIX technology and vendors like Sun/SunSoft and Novell have the ability to fuel significant market share penetration for UNIX in networked desktop environments. They have the technology, but more importantly, the distribution channels and the requisite experience. What is more, even though they will offer products that compete, the companies recognize there is more to be gained through a competitive collaboration than by going it alone. Sun is selling its SPARC RISC against Intel-based platforms. SunSoft has quickly established itself as a major force in innovation in UNIX and surrounding technologies that are critical in the evolution of object-oriented computing.

The way we see it is that if MS-DOS and Windows users want to network today, most of them (maybe two-thirds by some estimates) are already implementing their networks using Novell NetWare. They aren't going to just throw this away for Windows/NT. It is natural for them to continue to use NetWare and adopt an Open-Systems-based migration strategy to UNIX with UnixWare and other SVR4 compatible plug and play compatibles offering the benefits of UNIX without as many integration problems. Sun/SunSoft on the other hand will be expected to remain "UNIX agents of change," especially in terms of enhancing the de facto standards for "open network computing" based on ONC+/NFS and TCP/IP—which at 3.1 million nodes is what OSF hopes DCE will be in three to five years. SunSoft, in a competitive collaboration with HP, can also be expected to push the state of the art in object-oriented technology within the UNIX and Open Systems industry.

To TCP or the SPX—that will be one question. TCP/IP is a world totally different from Novells' SPX/IPX. The transport layer becomes critical when you want to extend networking beyond the work group. TCP/IP or SPX/IPX can handle the work group transport layer connectivity equally well. But TCP/IP is an open industry standard that is only increasing in terms of market share and is supported on a very wide spectrum of system platforms. TCP/IP is going to continue to be perceived as the "open" way to network. Novells' success with UnixWare may depend on its ability to deliver a migration path for its NetWare users to "open systems" and to better leverage the fact that TCP/IP has the potential to replace SNA as the de facto enterprise networking standard.

Levels of openness in Open Systems. A hierarchy of Open Systems has been described by 88open and the following definitions have been adapted from these.

Network interoperability. The lowest level of openness and perhaps one of the most developed involves sharing data between system environments or architectures.

Network interoperability provides the ability to transfer data from one environment into another. SNA, SQL, and TCP/IP are examples of standards that support this form of interoperability. ONC(NFS) and DCE are similarly middleware that promotes data and file sharing. But network interoperability says nothing of the underlying operating system or hardware. This level of openness is important but constitutes only one dimension of openness related to computer communications.

Source level compatibility. Another level of openness deals with applications programming interfaces (APIs) or so-called source-level standard interface definitions. Examples of this level of openness can be found in POSIX, in FIPS, in X/OPEN, and other standards. Source-level compatibility assures that the source code of software that adheres to a standards specification will be able to be moved from one environment to another necessitating recompilation and testing. Porting activities are minimized but not totally eliminated. Applications that can be ported in this way are usually written in a higher-level language, and the application must be written to a standard set of source-level interfaces. It is assumed that these interfaces will be available on the target environments. In this sense, both the application and the target environments must adhere to the standard(s).

Compatibility through emulation. This level of openness is afforded by special software that will emulate software in one environment in another. DOS emulation under UNIX is a good example of this. Application software binaries from the DOS environment are run in binary form in the UNIX environment by an emulation program. Emulation normally carries with it numerous special considerations and/or limitations. These may be in terms of performance and/or functionality. Undocumented interfaces or functionality can present problems with the stability and quality of emulation.

Application binary interfaces. Binary compatibility is like binary compatibility through emulation, but the concept with an ABI is that both the application and the system it runs in conform to an established standard. ABIs rigidly enforce compatibility at the lowest possible level.

1.12.3. A New World with NT?

The press and industry analysts will have their honeymoon with Windows/NT—but what are the real issues? No one is underestimating the great opportunity that Windows/NT will represent for Microsoft. But if we are correct in the way users will measure openness, then Microsoft has a lot of promises to deliver on before it can compete head-on in the traditional UNIX market and emerging Open Systems market. First, Microsoft Windows/NT for servers will have to provide superior functionality and robustness to SVR4 UNIX.

- Will there be one Windows/NT server product, or will there be a variant from DEC, one from Sequent, one from HP, and so on?
- Where will the innovation on the server side of NT be coming from? Will it be from Microsoft, or will it come from Microsoft's partners at DEC and HP?

Is Microsoft going to put a bullet into OSF's heart with NT? In terms of OSF/2, we believe the answer is already a 95 percent certainty.

OSF can be expected to keep OSF/2 alive only in the minds of its OEMs as the standards alternative to SVR4. Windows/NT, being OSF "compliant" from a specifications point of view—which it is not—will be all OSF should care about. OSF can't seriously expect Microsoft to license OSF/2 from it anymore than Microsoft is paying Carnegie Mellon a licensing fee for Mach even though Microsoft has stated that it took a "hard look" at Mach before they implemented their own microkernel in NT. OSF can be expected to redirect its emphasis with a strong push behind DCE/DME as it deemphasizes OSF/1 and OSF/2.

There are a lot of issues that Microsoft has to work through—NT is not an NB (no brainer). While the prevailing wisdom says that no one company can do it all, Microsoft—"the IBM of the software industry"—seems intent on being more than an operating systems company. Microsoft is also an application software company.

- Can Microsoft attract software vendors to innovate on their platforms and face an all but certain future of competition from Microsoft itself?
- What chance does Microsoft really have of making Windows/NT viable technology for enterprise-oriented server and midrange systems?
- Is NT going to be principally wedded to the Intel architecture, and if so, what are the implications?
- Will there be any champion for NT on RISC? If not, what implications will that have on its potential to capture market share in servers and midrange systems environments?
- Will desktop users really need NT for the next few years given the benefits they get out of the Win32s API's?
- Will NT be able to be sold and supported by Microsoft's traditional dealer channel? We doubt it.
- Will users perceive or even care about Microsoft's proprietary lock on its technologies like NT?
- Will Microsoft really be able to migrate MS-DOS users and OS/2 users to NT? When will the applications that make NT attractive be there?
- Could the U.S. government break up Microsoft into an operating system company and an applications software company? Does Microsoft carry unfair competitive advantage in its applications software business because it is in the operating systems business?

Microsoft Windows Versus X Windows in the Long Term. Any direct comparison of these two technologies is difficult since MS Windows is an operating system while X Windows is a protocol. This discussion focuses on the positioning of these technologies as they relate to application architectures within future distributed computing environments.

Windows and Windows/NT are operating systems and complete environments. Programmers targeting Intel-based PC platforms write applications to the Windows API (and there are several—Win16, Win32S, etc.). Alternatively, programmers who are targeting workstations, servers, and host systems platforms write applications for X Windows because X Windows is used in virtually all of the UNIX graphical user interface and window management system environments. Now with COSE, there will be some consolidation around Motif and application development tool kits for Motif. Perhaps the most fundamental and interesting thing to consider has less to do with the window environment and application development tool kit and more with the flexibility and cost of bringing applications to the desktop.

X Windows on PC desktops. With X Windows-based applications, an application can be written to run on a host computer with only the user interface running on a terminal, PC (running X windows server software), or a workstation. By contrast, the Microsoft Windows-based application has to run on the desktop. So what are the consequences?

X offers flexibility since applications can run on a desktop, a server, or split between the two. Applications that needs more "horsepower" can be run on a higher-performance host like a server, a supercomputer, or even on a legacy system such as a minicomputer or mainframe (although these architectures are not usually as optimized as UNIX servers to support X windows in an open networked environment).

What this means for X Windows-based applications users is that the cost per user of an application could be quite a bit less expensive and carry additional benefits due to the inherent flexibility of X Windows. By the time you add the cost of Windows + Excel + Word + etc. the cost per seat begins to add up. Customers have begun to understand the cost dynamics in utilizing software servers with applications licensed for a specific number of concurrent users, for example. This way, even software like spreadsheets can be placed on the server and run either on the desktop or from the server. As a result, customers can cut costs through application sharing.

Microsoft Windows in the UNIX environment. Windows/NT provides no remote windowing or networked window services. But this doesn't preclude the potential for using DOS and MS Windows applications in a UNIX environment through the use of emulation technology or application conversion tools.

Why Windows/NT has limited appeal to customers with Open Systems IT strategies. Customers with Open Systems strategies have to ask themselves a number of questions when they consider using Windows/NT.

Do we want to use a brand new operating system or one that is time tested (SVR4 implementations, for example)?

As standards are important to us, does our operating system suppliers' commitment to standards make any difference to us? Don't we care about POSIX 1003.2, 1002.4, POSIX.2, POSIX.4, X/Open's XPG3 and XPG4, the UNIX System V Interface Definition, Federal processing standards, X Windows, and so forth?

Do we care how portable the operating system is and the number of architectures it runs on?

Do we want a wide choice of microprocessor and system architectures to choose from?

Do we want to have multiuser capability on our client and/or your server systems?

Are we planning to implement a transaction processing application that needs a transaction monitor?

Do we need terminal emulation capabilities beyond the most basic and do we require true multiuser capabilities on our desktop systems and servers?

Do we expect our operating system to fully support TCP/IP?

Do we want our desktop and server operating system to support a high level of security in a consistent fashion?

Are we planning to use international language variants of your application and operating system in the near term?

Do we expect native support for any of the following: SNA, OSI, X.25, DECNet?

Are high availability and redundancy features important to us?

Will we require a batch subsystem facility?

Do we expect to have a large file space?

The answers for many companies that already have or plan to embark on an Open Systems Information Architecture will be "yes" to many of the above questions. Windows/NT is deficient in many of these respects and will therefore have to be considered quite carefully to ensure that it offers the functionality you require. While NT has some nice features, and the press and many ISVs believe it represents a significant opportunity, Windows/NT offers little groundbreaking or new technology, and while software vendors may hope that it will provide volume sales for their software, its functionality may fall well short of what many commercial computer users expect in their information systems. At the time of this writing, NT was being supported by NCR, HP, COMPAQ, Sequent, the Intergraph Clipper, and DEC Alpha.

In 1996, despite the pundits tolling the bell in anticipation of UNIX's demise, UNIX desktops will be close to 2.4m units, versus around 900,000 for NT according to IDC. Acceptance could be even slower on servers with annual UNIX shipments reaching around 100,000 compared to UNIX's over 800,000 by 1996.

Other than the IBM AS/400, and to some extent DEC VAX, the midrange and high-end systems market is basically all UNIX today. Some analysts are equally pessimistic about Microsoft's abilities to penetrate this area as the UNIX vendors ability to penetrate the desktop.

IBM and Apple are going to be late for the party, but they will both continue to be forces in the marketplace in their own right.

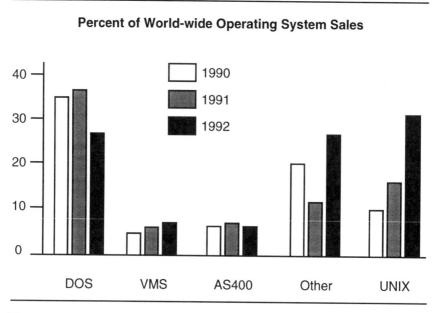

Percent of World-wide Operating System Sales

Figure 1.6. The evolution of the UNIX market in system revenue terms. *Source:* InfoCorp and Networked Publications

Figure 1.6 shows the evolution of the UNIX operating system compared as a percent of sales with other leading operating systems. While other midrange operating systems remain flat, UNIX is growing. UNIX will play an important role in evolving the base of DOS and Windows systems and will help DOS and Windows clients tie into networks in which UNIX will play an important integrating role.

Our bottom lines:

- OS/2 will lose market share.
- OSF/1 is not worth talking about, but OSF is here to stay especially with Motif.
- NeXT and NeXTStep, despite being interesting software technology, are not viable.
- Novell can be counted on to accelerate UNIX SVR4 momentum.
- Sun/SunSoft are going to continue to innovate and grow.
- Microsoft is going to ramp Windows/NT up, but it won't compete with UNIX in most traditional UNIX environments.

1.12.4. Where Will the Significant Changes Be in the UNIX Industry and Open Systems?

Some of the most significant technology changes in the UNIX industry and Open Systems will continue to be fueled by the following advances:

1. Advances in microprocessor and multiprocessing technology (RISC and MP)
2. Rapid shift toward distributed network computing (internetworking)
3. Radical shift to distributed object-oriented applications (interoperability)

At the same time, there will be an unprecedented set of changes in the industry dynamics. The acquisition of USL by Novell was being predicted for some time by several analysts. The pace of industry change in the UNIX industry, because of Open Systems, is increasing due to the following factors:

1. A shift toward commodity in hardware systems driving margin pressure for systems vendors to look for more leveraged business models. The types of company restructuring like those at Sun and IBM will continue, and the traditional system vendor will gradually evolve toward a business model that is focused on fewer core competencies.

2. Profound shifts are occurring in distribution. Many customers will be buying UNIX and applications and sourcing support and integrated (embedded) applications from resellers. The changes in the commercial distribution models will only hasten the requirement for the systems vendors to accelerate the rate of change in their own shift toward a different set of business models.

3. The UNIX software industry, while representing a challenge to software vendors, will emerge as a lucrative market opportunity for ISVs that understand how to design a business model for profitability. We believe the UNIX software market's distribution structure will begin to gel during the next few years.

4. The impact of all these changes on the users of UNIX systems and of computer users in general will be equally profound. Margin pressure in the systems and software businesses will have a direct impact on the customer's relationship with suppliers. Gone will be the days of traditional models of customer support and "one-stop shopping."

DESKTOP UNIX on the move. While there have been numerous versions of UNIX for the Intel architecture, the memory and hard disk requirements were too large for most PC users. UNIX was criticized for its cryptic command syntax, the high cost of UNIX and UNIX applications, and its complex system administration and installation procedures. For these reasons and because there has never been a major marketing push behind UNIX on PCs, UNIX market penetration in the PC market has been low. Unless users required specific networking capabilities, multiuser functionality, or were interested in purchasing an application only available on UNIX, PC users, PC ISVs, and PC hardware vendors and distributors have not historically seen UNIX as a volume market opportunity.

Many vendors understand this and have moved aggressively to address these deficiencies. Versions of UNIX designed specifically for the PC market are rapidly emerging. These new versions of UNIX offer most of the functionality of full-featured UNIX but are highly optimized to run in less memory, require less disk, address ease of use, installation, and administration, and continue to offer new state-of-the-art functionality for networking, distributed object management computing functionality, and support for DOS and Windows through emulation.

Novell, SunSoft, and SCO will all be aggressively addressing the PC market with versions of UNIX optimized for use on the Intel architecture.

UNIX has witnessed some of its greatest market share penetration in the workstation, midrange, and small business markets. The greatest opportunity for success and the greatest risk for failure for UNIX suppliers over the next years are in the office workstation market. Growth in the UNIX workstation segment will continue to be strong due to increasing movement toward client/server computing and continued acceptance of workstations in all markets.

UNIX in low-end commercial desktop applications has a window of opportunity of two to three years. If UNIX doesn't make it in that time, it will be relegated to a niche product status in terms of volume applications and market share. Even if this happens, it will not diminish the importance of UNIX as an operating system for servers and for networked environments.

UNIX is now entering the mainstream and an era of commercialization. It will not be eclipsed by any new operating system. Those that don't understand this probably don't understand the unique personality and characteristics of the installed base of UNIX. UNIX is going to continue to change. The pace of change is going to increase as will the commercial acceptability of UNIX. Novell is going to help UNIX in ways AT&T never could.

To those that point to UNIX as a low-volume, fragmented market compared to MS-DOS and Windows, they need to understand that UNIX isn't MS-DOS or Windows and probably never will be. UNIX is less about a single implementation of a product for a commodity hardware industry and more about a standards-based enabling technology infrastructure that will drive interoperability in networked computing environments. UNIX will emerge in the next few years as the premier scalable, heterogeneous network operating system of choice.

UNIX is going to continue to dominate niche markets. But to become commercially successful in the market at large, UNIX can be expected to take on new focus because of the way it is being deployed. One of the major changes that we predict will be the evolution of separate but related client-side and server-side UNIX implementations.

UNIX will be strategically important to companies because it will continue to stimulate innovation in information technology. People will continue to develop application solutions on UNIX for deployment in cross-platform environments. Innovation will not be restricted to technical or niche markets.

1.12.5.   The Only Thing That Is Constant Is Change

The following questions illustrate the changes we can expect to see over the next year or two and beyond.

Will Intel's Pentium catch up with RISC only to lag again?

Will Novell heal the divisions within the UNIX world? Is Ray Noorda, the unpretentious billionaire, going to be the Moses of the UNIX industry?

Will Novell invest in developing and evolving UNIX for the good of everyone in the industry, or will it have a strictly pragmatic business orientation and use UNIX only as a way to create greater profitability for itself?

Will Novell support TCP/IP in its UnixWare and NetWare products, or will it continue to push IPX/SPX protocols first and TCP/IP only for compatibility?

Will Novell invest in growing USG, or will it collapse back into Novell or spin parts of it off?

Is Windows/NT going to be used in production-oriented server environments? How will it it impact the UNIX market?

Will Microsoft start supporting industry standards fully like X/Open XPG, TPC/IP, Posix (other than 1003.1), SVID, FIPS, NFS, OSI, X.25, and X Windows?

Will OSF survive in its present form? Can it become self sustaining with Motif and DCE?

When will DEC and IBM be able to stop their losses and regain their momentum?

Will Sun "engineer its way out of Novell's SVR4" in the next few years as it moves to an object-oriented operating system?

1.13.   MIGRATING TOWARD A COMMON OPEN SYSTEMS ENVIRONMENT

1.13.1.   The Move Toward a Common Open Systems Environment

The adoption of UNIX hasn't been as rapid as it should have been because of inconsistencies in different implementations. Nowhere has this been more visible than in the area of the UNIX desktop computing environment and particularly in the area of graphical user interface. The COSE promises to remove several of the most significant inconsistencies. This helps to explain why the COSE announcement has such a strong desktop computing focus.

For the past five years the UNIX industry has been the scene of pitched battles. With all the rhetoric paid to Open Systems and standards, pride of authorship and NIH (Not Invented Here) syndrome have made it difficult for vendors to accept and standardize on other vendors' technology. Until now, UNIX has been plagued by incompatible user interfaces and application programming interfaces that slowed its acceptance and added to the cost of training software developers and users.

The Common Open Software Initiative and Environment (COSE). COSI is an acronym for the Common Open Software Initiative. It was first announced at UniForum on March 17, 1993 in a joint announcement by HP, IBM, SCO, SUN, and Novell. These vendors all steadfastly insisted that there was no COSI consortium, that they were coming together and agreeing on a set of specifications for the industry that will be known as COSE. COSE has been endorsed by a large number of other systems and software vendors including DEC.

At the time of its announcement, the following companies announced their support and endorsement of the Common Open Software Environment:

Adobe Systems, Inc.

Autodesk, Inc.

Computer Associates International, Inc.

ComputerVision Corp.

Convex Computer Corp.

Cray Research, Inc.

EDS

Fujitsu, Ltd.

Hitachi, Ltd.

ICL, Plc.

Integrated Computer Solutions

Interactive Multimedia Association

Ingres

Mead Data Central

Object Management Group

OKI Electric Industry Co., Ltd.

Oracle Corp.

Samsung

Siemens-Nixdorf

Stratus Computer, Inc.

Sybase, Inc.

Toshiba

Unisys Corp.

UNIX INTERNATIONAL, Inc.

XSoft, a division of Xerox Corp.

Open Systems are based on freely available, vendor-neutral interface standards and therefore offer users a wide range of product choices from multiple vendors. COSE represents a pivotal statement on the part of the largest and most significant UNIX vendors that they will be standardizing on an open interface and will compete on the basis of implementation.

COSE represents a major change in terms of greater convergence between the major suppliers of UNIX systems and represents one of the most significant milestones in the evolution of Open Systems that has occurred in years. While it will take time for details to be announced, and with commercial products planned for release in the future, the announcement represents a strong endorsement for the premise of Open Systems—that is, unencumbered specifications that are freely available, independent branding and certification, multiple implementations for a single product can be created enhancing competition.

75 percent of the UNIX industry—United? The six companies that initiated COSE, and other computer companies and software vendors who have publicly endorsed it, have agreed to a common open software environment and on software technologies as defined by a set of standard software interfaces for a common UNIX desktop environment. These vendors account for almost 75 percent of the UNIX industry. But just how cozy are these vendors in this initiative? Does this really mean that the UNIX industry is becoming unified? And why is this happening now?

Why COSE now? If there was ever a group of vendors that needed to get cozy, it was the vendors in the UNIX industry. While the companies indicated that the motivation for this was in responding to their customers—software developers, end users, and systems administrators—there was considerable speculation that the real motivation was the common enemy that these companies perceive in Microsoft. DEC, which has been working with Microsoft on NT for Alpha, was noticeably missing from the initial announcement but did issue a press release the day following the initial announcement endorsing COSE. Some press reports indicated that DEC was appraised of the COSE announcement only a day or so before it took place. COSE, at least on the surface, would appear to expand the opportunities for Open Systems products and would appear to be a catalyst in enabling cost-effective technology evolution.

However, COSI and COSE can be somewhat difficult to understand. COSI is not a foundation like OSF. It is not another consortium like UNIX International. It is not a development company. According to its constituents, it is not even an "initiative," despite the word appearing in the phrase. There are some analysts in the press and industry who discount COSI as another ACE Consortium, as so much marketing hype.

The companies involved with COSI position it as a means of accelerating the Open Systems process. This is achieved by accelerating the supply side of the industry's response to customers' and software developers' demands.

By agreeing to adopt common networking products to increase interoperability across heterogeneous computer environments, they have endorsed specifications, standards, and technologies in the areas of graphics, multimedia, and object technology.

What is interesting about COSI is how quickly it appears to have developed. What is significant about COSI is the concurrence of the industry's major forces in the principles upon which Open Systems are based and commitments demonstrated, including the following:

- Unencumbered freely available specifications
- Independent branding and certification process
- Multiple competitive implementations
- Competitive market terms and conditions

Following the announcement of COSE, the following were popularly perceived as the most significant immediate implications of the agreement:

X/Open would be accepted as the holder and architect of Open Systems standards. OSF would submit the Motif specification to X/Open's "Fast Track" process as well as make certain changes to its licensing terms and conditions. Sun announced that it would support Motif. Novell announced that it would submit Netware UNIX client specifications to X/Open. These new specifications will be covered in X/Open's Portability Guide (XPG). All vendors agreed to sell and support NetWare for UNIX, DCE, and ONC compliant networking solutions.

The X/Open Fast Track process allows high-quality specifications with broad industry support to be integrated quickly into the XPG architecture. From the time submissions are made to X/Open, it takes as little as three months for X/Open to incorporate these new specifications into

X/Open's XPG architecture, which is supported by every Open Systems vendor and integrates the most comprehensive set of international and de facto standards to provide seamless interoperability to users as they implement open information systems.

The principal goals of COSE are unified UNIX and Open Systems application software interfaces (APIs). The main goal of COSI is to send a message to ISVs and end users that they can preserve their investments in terms of offering compatibility with existing applications written to HP-UX, IBM's AIX/6000, SCO Open Desktop, SunSoft Solaris, Novell's UnixWare, and Novell's UNIX SVR4.2 as these products evolve toward the Common Desktop environment. All of the interfaces and technologies adopted under this effort will be turned over to X/Open. X/Open will architect and publish the full specifications of these new standards.

1.13.2. A General Technical Overview of the COSE

COSE will be constituted by a combination of established technologies such as networking, graphics, and desktop environment and new emerging technologies such as multimedia, objects, and systems administration.

COSE can be viewed as a sort of common framework for distributed computing. COSE is a set of APIs in the following areas:

- Common desktop environment
- Networking
- Graphics
- Multimedia
- Object technology
- Systems management

1.13.3. Common Desktop Environment—A Common UNIX Dashboard

The desktop environment will scale across a range of client-server platforms providing a common look-and-feel "UNIX dashboard" of capabilities such as electronic mail, text editing, productivity tools, window management, and provide a unified framework for graphical object and file management.

The common desktop environment or CDE will incorporate technologies from OSF's Motif, Sun's DeskSet productivity tools, and ToolTalk interapplication communication facility, IBM's Common User

Access model and Workplace Shell, USL's Desktop Manager and HP's Visual User Environment (VUE), and its Encapsulation capability.

In the past, there have been several UNIX desktop managers to choose from. ISVs have had to write their applications to take advantage of the specific features of each UNIX windowing environment. A common desktop manager should help ISVs overcome objectives of having to port to numerous UNIX desktop management environments.

The common desktop specification incorporates existing technology from participating suppliers. It is intended to support distributed computing across an enterprise that runs applications on numerous platforms. As such, it will scale across client and server platforms.

The following technologies will be incorporated:

- OSF's Motif tool kit and Window Manager with modifications to support users familiar with OPEN LOOK applications. This is very significant toward expediting the formalization of a GUI standard based on X-Windows. With Motif part of X/Open's XPG, X/Open assumes responsibility for the Motif specification as a standard. X/Open would license certification test suites that verify Motif compliance. These suites would be used in X/Open's Branding Program to certify implementations as compliant with the X/Open Motif-based standard specification and allow the use of the Motif trademark.
- MIT's X11 Window system, Version 11, and more generally, support for the X Consortium's imaging and graphics facilities.
- SunSoft's OPEN LOOK and DeskSet productivity tools, and ToolTalk Message Service and interapplication communication facility to support encapsulation capabilities.
- Novell's UNIX SVR4.2 Desktop Manager.
- Elements of HP's Visual User Environment (VUE), and HP encapsulation, which will be used with SunSoft's tool kit.
- IBM's Common User Access model and Workplace Shell.

Alternate approaches to encapsulation. HP's approach to encapsulation externalizes message logic. This requires extra program logic to monitor an applications input-output stream. Sunsoft's Tooltalk approach is embedding messages into application source code. Most of the message integration development effort is the same whether messages are embedded in source or the application is encapsulated. HP-style encapsulation is most appropriate when working with command-line-oriented applications. GUI-based or forms-based applications may be more appropriate for using Tooltalk.

These different approaches to message encapsulation represent fundamentally different models. Programmers need to be careful to understand the limitations and implications of messaging. Message encapsulation does not magically support sophisticated levels of application integration. There are many considerations that should be factored into the use of this type of technology. The level of effort required and complexity of implementing messaging, the cost of the base technology, performance implications, and the appropriateness of different approaches in specific applications environments all need to be carefully considered. None of this technology is magic. There is no panacea.

The developer using encapsulation to integrate applications has to understand the functionality of the application, how users interact with it, and decide what messaging functionality is required. Encapsulating programs at the command line level is relatively straightforward. For graphical and forms-based applications, however, monitoring complex screen interactions can be difficult, and adding message to the source code of applications may prove a better approach. One element of the complexity of approaches lies in the tools that are used. Some schemes require the use of proprietary languages that are not necessarily compatible with existing debuggers, profilers, source code managers, and so forth. Encapsulation is also prone to duplication of effort by development groups that tend not to communicate. Maintenance issues also need to be considered since depending on the approach used, encapsulation may be impacted by changes to the application's input-output stream.

Taken together, the above technologies will combine to form the specification for a common desktop environment that will support the following capabilities:

- Electronic mail, group calendaring, text editing, audio, and other productivity tools
- Task and window management and online help
- Procedural and object-oriented application integration with drag and drop, linking, embedding, and data interchange capabilities
- Dialog and forms building with icon editing
- Graphical object and file management
- Security features including start-up, login, locking, and authentication
- End user installation automation and runtime configuration

This environment is already demonstrable and a preliminary specification for this environment is being developed and submitted to X/Open for incorporation of X/Open's portability guide.

In summary, the Open Systems desktop environment promises to accelerate the specification, joint development, and introduction of an environment for UNIX on desktop computers in particular.

By basing the CDE on Motif and the Motif tool kit, there will now be one graphical user interface API for UNIX developers. This is going to turn out to be one of the most important industry developments this year and should be expected to have a significant impact on the ISVs and in-house software developers. The CDE will eventually feature one set of APIs for the CDE and all the other COSE areas with the exception of networking.

1.13.4. Networking

Distributed networking technology provides the fundamental infrastructure that allows information and computing resources to be shared. It includes services necessary to ensure that information is transmitted in a secure and efficient manner and that resources, such as storage subsystems, specialized servers, and printers, can be transparently accessed over the network. It also provides the necessary tools to enable developers to build distributed applications.

In the area of networking, COSE offers three choices in the form of leading technologies. Three sets of APIs are provided that users can chose from: Sun's ONC+, OSF's DCE, and Novell's NetWare for UNIX. All three of these technologies offer services and tools that support the creation, use, and maintenance of distributed applications in heterogeneous, distributed computing environments. Each of these three technologies will be sold and supported by all of the vendors participating in COSI.

In the area of networking, COSE will support existing products and provide a higher level of compatibility in networking for de facto standards such as NFS and Netware as well as emerging standards such as DCE. It is up to each individual company to announce pricing and availability of products in each of these areas. X/Open will develop the means through which vendor implementations will be certified as compliant with these standards.

There is still considerable work to be done in the area of networking. A common naming scheme, common network services for time and security, and interoperability between the various schemes still need to be addressed. As sophisticated new applications that incorporate advanced graphics, multimedia, and object-oriented programming advance, these underlying networking technologies must certainly have to change and evolve. We predict that to accommodate future applications, even the Remote Procedure Call (RPC) technology that is *new* today will likely be made obsolete by far more efficient interprocess communication mechanisms.

1.13.5.   Graphics

In the area of graphics technologies, fundamental programming utilities are needed by developers who need to produce graphic-intensive applications while shielding them from specific hardware dependencies.

A common and consistent graphics application environment is envisioned that will run across multiple platforms through a common API and interoperability protocols. Support for the X Consortium's imaging and graphics facilities as a part of the overall graphical capabilities, which will also include X consortium graphics facilities, include the following:

- Xlib / X for basic 2D pixel graphics
- PEXlib / PEX for 2D and 3D geometry graphics
- XIElib / XIE for advanced imaging

Consistency is expected to extend to areas of programming, documentation, validation testing, and test suites over time. Companies participating in COSI are expected to share validation and test suites. The COSE initiative in graphics is attempting to enable a consistent implementation of high-performance graphics software and promote wider availability of applications. Notably absent from the graphics area is SGI's OpenGL. SGI, which uses the SCO operating system, did not participate in the initial announcement of COSI.

1.13.6.   Multimedia

Multimedia encompasses the creation, editing, playback, and synchronization of distributed audio, video, graphics, image, speech, and telephony. An infrastructure is being defined and specified that will include the Desktop Integrated Media Services (DMS) and the Desktop Integrated Media Environment (DIME) for multimedia access and collaborative tools for the user. DMS is network independent and supports an integrated API and data stream protocol. Supported on DMS, DIME will provide basic tools for each data type such as audio, video, and so on supported in the DMS infrastructure.

The multimedia specifications will be delivered to the IMA's request for technology. Implementations will then be built by suppliers ensuring compliance with the International Multimedia Association's (IMA) "best practices" as they are established. It is expected that multimedia desktop tools will be integrated into the common desktop environment such as multimedia email, for example. The multimedia initiatives are intended to enable developers to create next-generation applications that use multimedia as data.

1.13.7. Object Technology

Distributed object technology presents a new paradigm for software development and deployment. By working together, the companies involved are hoping to accelerate the development and delivery of object-based technology. This will be accomplished in part by each of the companies supporting the efforts of the Object Management Group (OMG), an industry standards organization that has helped define the Common Object Request Broker Architecture (CORBA). CORBA is a specification that provides a stable foundation for independently developed objects to plug and play in a heterogeneous, distributed environment. CORBA will foster application interoperability, define a common mechanism for managing objects across multiple platforms, enable multiple software implementations based on standard, open interfaces and promote wide availability of distributed object technology.

The companies are also expected to establish common style guidelines to simplify developer transition, specify common core capabilities for object construction and development, and further the adoption of common testing and certification through industry standards organizations. All vendors that support COSE in terms of object management will implement OMG-compliant Object Request Brokers. In summary, all companies are committed to accelerate development and delivery of object-based technology. All endorse the OMG process and will ship CORBA-compliant products.

1.13.8. Systems Management

As the trend toward distributed computing moves out of the work group and into the enterprise-scale environments, companies view distributed systems management as a critical requirement to the successful deployment of distributed, heterogeneous computing networks. Systems management involves such tasks as performance monitoring, data backup and restore, configuration management, security, fault determination, and recovery. The proliferation of distributed networks has led to an increased demand for more consistent management tools across heterogeneous platforms. As corporations' computing resources have become more distributed, the problem of effectively managing these installations has increased exponentially.

Systems management technologies have not kept pace with the rapid evolution of distributed computing. System administration today is often expensive, labor intensive, and messy. As the number of distributed computer systems increases, traditional means of system administration becomes increasingly impractical and potentially a barrier to effective system performance.

Through a working group, the companies involved in COSI have agreed to focus on defining a systems management framework and associated tools to support improved interoperability and management of distributed systems. The following are some of the key areas to be address:

- User and group management including security
- Software installation and distributed management
- Software license management
- Storage management (backup and restore)
- Print spooling and management
- Distributed file system management

Today there are existing products and emerging specifications that address some aspects of systems management. The goal is to have these applications interoperate among all supported platforms. The goal should be one system manager for 30 to 300 or more nodes in a network.

While network management tools are becoming more sophisticated, they tend to focus on managing the physical connections between systems and monitor network traffic. Above the level of basic systems management, rudimentary software applications are available from independent software vendors that typically target a specific area such as backup/restore or print spool management. Systems' managers must often develop their own scripts or simple applications that also address pieces of the systems management problem. Many applications are supplied with tools for basic systems services (utilities for backing up databases, for example). This patchwork quilt can actually contribute to the complexity of the systems management problem since "point" applications are often incompatible, complex, and poorly integrated.

While there are several companies planning to provide products that address the requirements of systems management, Tivoli Systems Inc. of Austin, Texas, has one of the most widely endorsed technologies.

The Tivoli object-oriented Management Framework and graphical desktop services form the core of the Open Software Foundation's DME. Tivoli is working with SunSoft in developing an object-oriented systems management framework for Solaris. The Tivoli framework was endorsed by UNIX International as the key systems management technology for UI-Atlas.

A distributed network is represented as a collection of objects or groups of programs and data describing attributes and actions within the Tivoli Management Framework. Users, groups of users, servers, devices, and other physical and logical resources in the network are modeled as self-describing objects. All the information necessary to manage the network resources is encapsulated as objects rather than as programs and files. These objects interrelate to share information and capture associations between the entities they represent. Object services manage how objects interrelate to share information. Dialog services determine how applications communicate with the objects and the user interface. Authorization services parcel out different levels of access to system resources. Authorization services, based on MIT's Kerberos distributed authentication protocol, verify users as they bid to access system resources. Notification services allow system managers to subscribe to feedback about various events that happen in a distributed system. These core services form the basis of Tivoli's systems management applications. Applications can be creating using these services, which will work with other applications built on the same framework.

The object-oriented framework approach demonstrated by Tivoli has been establishing itself as a core technology in several open operating systems environments and is already compliant with the OMG's Object Request Broker standard. The frameworks' interoperability with common network management protocols, including the Internet SNMP and ISO/OSI CMIP, as well as POSIX 1003.7 and X/Open Systems Management standards, gives it advantages in being considered as a basis for rapidly developing standards for systems management. As has been seen in the case of OSF Motif and DCE, Tivoli may have to become quite flexible in terms of licensing its technology as well as submitting it to the X/Open standards process before its framework will be adopted into COSE.

Tivoli has proposed a common applications programming interface based on its object-oriented framework and to submit it gratis to X/Open as part of the COSE standard. Tivili is not alone, however, in trying to establish a new standard in the area of systems management. Computer Associates and OpenVision are also angling into this market.

COSE's systems management technology will be determined by X/Open's systems management group, a committee that will include all the current COSE companies.

1.13.9. Analysis of COSE

COSE represents perhaps the most significant change in the UNIX industry in years. It promises to accelerate the industry's convergence toward the adoption of "best of breed" technology and shift the focus from vendors talking about technology to delivering solutions. The COSE announcement provides developers and end users with a clear direction for the nineties and brings closure to the "UNIX wars" of the last five years.

Prior to the COSE announcement, Sun had adamantly refused to support Motif. Sun was concerned that Motif was not an open specification, had multiple potentially incompatible implementations, and involved royalties it considered excessive. Scott McNealy had often explained that Sun would support Motif only if it became a standard. With the submission by OSF of Motif to X/Open, customers will now benefit from Motif being an open specification.

The common desktop environment will bring together "best of breed" desktop tools from participating vendors. COSE is likely to have profound impacts over time on the alignment and relationship of technology suppliers. Competitive collaborations and cross-licensing will become even more commonplace. While vendors will continue to evolve their marketing "umbrella" strategies, new investments in component technologies will involve much more in the way of make/buy analysis.

COSE will first have ramifications on the strategies of suppliers. The market for GUI application builders and environment managers that helped bridge Motif and OPEN LOOK, for example, may experience short-term benefit as OPEN LOOK customers migrate to Motif but they are going to go away in the long term as the UNIX industry consolidates around Motif and X Windows and, we believe, even Microsoft Windows in the future.

Another group that will be significantly impacted by COSE will be software developers, both independent software vendors and in-house software developers. The UNIX industry will now have new COSE specifications, COSE developers conferences, and numerous other events and programs aimed to increase software developers' understanding of and migration to COSE. Software professionals will become increasingly interested in COSE. They will have a better defined set of

APIs and tools with the potential to lower certain development costs for system vendors, ISVs, and in-house developers.

Some users will start to see the impact of COSE on commercial software during 1993, and major commercial application software will begin to take full advantage of COSE by early 1994. Examples are easily found—for example, Sun customers will be able to more easily source Motif applications, and NetWare users will find it easier to integrate UNIX solutions into Novell NetWare environments.

Business decision makers are going to want to believe that there is real commitment from industry leaders to deliver common standards-based and innovative Open Systems products. As they gain confidence in the industries' commitment, it will make it easier to base decisions on business needs rather than arbitrary technical differences between products. It will preserve and leverage existing investments and lower business risks.

1.13.10. Exploring Questions about COSE

Isn't COSE a reaction to Microsoft's NT?

There has been considerable speculation that COSI is really a reaction to Microsoft's impending announcement of NT. The agreements are about Open Systems. NT is not open; it is a proprietary environment that does not really adhere to industry standards. Vendors involved with COSI for the most part are evolving the UNIX operating system. The UNIX industry was founded on Open Systems, and this is a natural evolution for the industry. Developers and end users will have in COSE a clear direction for the 1990s, and the announcement brings to a close the "UNIX wars" that were providing a disservice to customers.

No doubt that Microsoft and, at the time, its impending announcement of Windows/NT played some role in motivating a more rapid consensus on COSE. The UniForum 1993 trade show may also have served as a major industry event to launch the announcement.

Is COSI/COSE just another ACE Consortium?

One of the first things people may question is whether COSI is another ACE. COSI is very different from ACE in several respects. ACE was focused on the ABI. It was comparable to SPARC International or the more recent PowerOpen, which are tied to the SPARC chip and IBM RS/6000 chip architecture, respectively. COSE is at the API, not the

ABI level. COSE solves problems ACE wasn't able to solve in the UNIX environment. All of the major players in the UNIX industry are involved in COSI, which wasn't true of ACE. One of the things that killed ACE was that is was tied to hardware in the form of the Mips RISC chip, which clearly disenfranchised many major UNIX vendors who had competitive chip architectures. ACE grew to the point that it collapsed under its own weight. COSI by contrast is a comparatively small group of the truly major players in the UNIX industry. Finally, COSE is using many established technologies—most of which are here today.

Is COSI another Open Systems consortium?

Not really. It is simply a set of relationships that are being established in connection with existing Open Systems consortia. A new set of business relationships are likely to occur between participants in COSI.

How does a company join this initiative?

There is nothing to join, per se. Vendors participate in existing consortia and standards bodies and support this commitment by implementing products based on the X/Open specifications that result. Most ISVs and user organizations participate through X/Open and associated bodies.

How do you get additional information on COSE and on the status of new product offerings based on COSE?

Specifications will be made available by X/Open. In the case of implementations of the COSE standards, you should contact the public relations or product marketing representative from the appropriate hardware or software supplier.

Who will emerge as key players in COSE?

Sun/SunSoft, Novell, IBM, HP, USL, and OSF would appear to be the most influential of the participants in COSE in terms of providing its base technology. Whether and how SCO and other vendors will become more involved remains to be seen. X/Open, OMG, IMA, and the X Consortium have all achieved a higher status and wider industry recognition (at least from the supply side of the industry initially).

How will various major players in the industry be impacted by COSE?

DEC certainly hasn't done much to gain credibility in the UNIX industry. It would seem that DEC's relationship to Microsoft may have played some part in its low-profile role in COSI.

HP would not appear to be impacted much by COSE. The use of parts of HP VUE and encapsulation in the Common Desktop Environment (CDE), from the end users' point of view, will resemble what HP ships today, but there will be enough new functionality in CDE that users will need to make some migration.

IBM will have some parts of its OS/2 environment incorporated in CDE. IBM's UNIX products may not be the only ones impacted by COSE. There is speculation that IBM may use parts of COSE in both OS/2 and even in its new PowerOpen environment.

Novell is positively impacted by COSE. By submitting the UNIX NetWare stacks through Novell to COSE, Novell is proliferating greater support in the UNIX community for Netware. The end result will be that Novell will get even more UNIX systems to use its networking protocols and offer compatibility with NetWare, which is the de facto standard in today's PC LAN environments.

OSF benefits by the acceptance of Motif and DCE. The emphasis on higher-level standards does little for OSF/1 and could create a situation where OSF will place more of its emphasis at higher levels.

The Santa Cruz Operations plans to buy in many ready-made COSE components and use the interfaces that will be made available through the COSE specification.

SGI was conspicuously absent. SGI's GL graphics library would seem to have lost support in the UNIX community.

Sun will now support Motif. People at Sun were saying Scott McNealy was looking pretty good for a dead man. Over the last several years, McNealy maintained a very hard line "Motif over my dead body." Sun will need to migrate many of its own applications over to Motif. COSE represented a face-saving way for Sun to support Motif. Sun's ONC networking will gain a new level of support from other vendors. Its low cost and significant market momentum and existing installed base (estimated at over 4 million ONC nodes) may slow acceptance of DCE unless OSF does something to reduce DCE's ultimate cost to customers and finds some way to accelerate market acceptance.

SunSoft has several products in COSE including ToolTalk, DeskSet, and Solaris and can be expected to add more along with subsidiaries of Sun's SunTech Inc., which can be expected to offer technology to COSI in the future.

Novell stands to benefit from the inclusion of Netware for UNIX client support in the networking portion of COSE. Novell's aggressive marketing push of UnixWare may be impacted by customers waiting to see how the Novell product may change as a result of COSE and in particular in terms of its support of a native implementation of Motif.

UNIX International's role as the marketing and requirements definition front end to Novell would seem to have been impacted not only by X/Open's clear role as the holder of the COSE specifications but also as a result of the transfer of the UNIX trademark to Novell. UNIX International still has a role to play in supporting proliferation and customer acceptance of SVR4 and may be in a unique position to help increase customers' understanding of X/Open in the future as well.

Novell could be impacted by COSE only in the sense that since COSE focuses on APIs—a higher level and therefore with less dependence on the SVR4 kernel—COSE does nothing special to increase other vendors' movement to SVR4. However, it does nothing to slow it down either. It is possible that vendors will determine that their own investment in UNIX system software should go into areas other than the kernel. If this happens, Novell and other kernel providers may have new opportunities open up.

X/Open benefits from COSE in several ways. X/Open is crucial in the process of COSE's evolution. X/Open will continue to be the standards integrator for the industry. Its job just became easier especially in the area of graphical user interface in its upcoming desktop standard specification. X/Open becomes the keeper of the COSE specifications and gains much more influence in the UNIX and computer industry as a whole. X/Open also has a major revenue opportunity opened to it in the areas of testing and certification for COSE. X/Open has provided an industry-wide set of specifications and test suites in the XPG3 and XPG4. X/Open's XPG is the leadership brand for Open Systems products. COSI endorsees have agreed to build on top of specifications and test suites provided by X/Open to implement products. This will create opportunities associated with economy of scale, fast time to market, and vastly improve the prospects for interoperability of systems and applications software in Open Systems environments.

1.13.11. Conclusions about COSE—Its Success Is Far from Guaranteed

This agreement is a major step forward for the UNIX community in reducing the fragmentation in the UNIX industry, which has been growing as a key concern to software developers and end users alike over the past years. The Common Open Software Environment will allow application developers, be they ISVs or in-house developers, to increase investments in developing and delivering UNIX-based applications without maintaining multiple costly versions of software.

While the focus of this announcement is on UNIX system platforms, we believe they will have a major impact on other desktop and networking environments. COSE, a major step toward Open Systems, will accelerate the acceptance of Open Systems and UNIX as a viable platform for mission-critical applications.

COSE is far from a panacea, and its success is by no means secured because of the announcement. It is not clear whether companies that endorse COSE must be for or against everything it ratifies or whether a company can pick and choose from components within COSE. Perhaps the single most significant question about COSE concerns how it is going to go about selecting technologies. HP, for example, lost out to IXI when the ACE Consortium selected the IXI X.desktop manager over HP VUE. Until the workings of the COSE "inner circle" are clearer and the COSE requirements setting process becomes better understood, additional support for COSE may be slow in coming.

The unification of the UNIX market may finally be taking place. Previous unification efforts tended to dwell on differences between UNIX kernel designs. COSE is clearly focused on the API or source level of standards.

We expect COSE to roll out in a number of phases. Initial focus will be on the desktop environment. Networking will come next followed by systems management. The other areas will follow.

One of the most interesting questions involving COSE will be the cost structure that emerges from this "unified UNIX." It remains to be seen if through technology exchange and cross-licensing focused on a rich set of application programming interfaces, the vendors participating in COSE will have a comprehensive, relatively unified UNIX environment priced competitively, especially against Microsoft's Windows/NT. UNIX will have to be priced competitively against Windows/NT.

Unlike the ACE initiative, there's a tangible threat in the form of Windows/NT to keep the COSE vendors compliant. Although inspired by the threat of NT, the participating companies claim that COSE grew out of pressure from large end users and ISVs demanding UNIX standardization. The Novell acquisition of USL made the COSE desktop effort easier. With the possible exception of DEC, agreement among the UNIX suppliers was relatively painless and occurred in a matter of weeks prior to UniForum. Within weeks of the announcement, technology and licensing agreements between the vendors were already being announced.

But not everyone is so optimistic about COSE. The pessimists are quick to point out that this is just the latest in a number of efforts in the past to unify UNIX. These folks will likely choose to adopt a "wait and see" approach. An interesting perspective was pointed out by one UNIX engineer who commented:

> *"I'm not too sure that a unification of UNIX is a good thing. UNIX has done this spiral dance of separation and unification for quite some time. The separations allow greater innovation and development, and the unifications filter out all the good stuff to be used across many platforms. I see unification as a possible means of stagnation."*

Another most curious comment from a researcher following the announcement of COSE:

> *"What's this COSE coalition, in what sense is UNIX not unified, and what do UNIX and Windows/NT have to do with one another? Personally, I'd be just as glad if NT kills off UNIX as a commercial system; it will let the people UNIX was designed for, researchers and hackers, have their system back without having to fight off the tidal wave of four-color-glossy UNIX-alikes that are utterly hopeless for research and hacking."*

Well, at least this shows the UNIX cult is still alive and well in some research establishments.

Whether COSE has real clout depends on how much effort the UNIX vendors are really willing to put out in terms of:

1. Marketing the benefits of UNIX, rather than their own particular brand of UNIX.
2. Actually ensuring their products are truly interoperable.
3. Whether commodity-style pricing for UNIX and UNIX applications will be possible.
4. How quickly COSE evolves and real products begin to roll out.

REFERENCES

1. Ritchie, D. M., and K. Thompson. *The UNIX Time-Sharing System*, Communications of the ACM, Vol. 17, No. 7, July 1974, pp. 365–375.

Basic UNIX Concepts and Philosophy

Before diving into UNIX concepts, philosophy, and technology, we start this chapter with a look at a typical organization and at different levels of computer literacy within it. As we then introduce the concept of a layered organization and relate these concepts with layered systems, this approach should help even the most novice user understand the basic components of the UNIX operating system, how they fit together, and how different people relate to the technology and philosophy of UNIX in different ways. As was described in Chapter 1, UNIX is going to play an important role in PC LANs and increasing the interoperability of individual users and work groups within an enterprise. This is another reason why it's important to understand UNIX within the context of its application in an organization.

A manager's first concern should be people. A computer manager's concern centers on how computers support these people. To take advantage of what technology has to offer, the managers and the people in an organization need a fundamental understanding of the technology and understand its potential impact and implications on the way they work. Acquiring such knowledge in the UNIX industry has not, heretofore, been easy.

The issue faced by the typical professional or manager is not *whether* to learn about UNIX but, rather, *how much* to learn about it. Before presenting an overview of the UNIX operating system, we introduce two concepts that should be especially useful to the less technically oriented reader.

The first concerns the levels of computer literacy of people in any company, organization, or group that uses computers. The second concept is layered systems architecture. These factors underlie a better understanding of how individuals at various levels of computer literacy see and use UNIX in different ways and tend to be most concerned with specific layers in the overall architecture of the system. The concept of layered systems architecture is also useful in understanding the function of standards in defining clean interfaces between the layers.

Developing a view of the users in the organization

Consider the various types of computer literacy of individuals in an organization (see Table 2.1). Let's assume a decreasing level of computer literacy, from "type A" people—for example, programmers—to "type E" people who have at best a very limited knowledge of how to use applications on a computer system. "Type F" is the person who has no interaction with computers in any way. Many workers have no need to master the programming of computers or even use computers at all. This classification highlights how different users require different levels of knowledge with computer systems. Managers of computer systems should keep each individual's computer needs and requirements in mind. Such needs are likely to be different for people, based not only on their job function but also on their level of computer literacy. They should also bear in mind that computer literacy can be easily increased through education.

Type A and B users can be thought of as power users. Their on-the-job productivity is directly affected by information systems and technology. These power users are most productive using power tools, and their productivity is greatest when their computer maximizes their efficiency.

Table 2.1.   Types of computer literacy. Most organizations have a relatively diverse community of users, from a computer literacy point of view and from a "knowledge worker" perspective.

A	— Formal computer science degree
B	— College education and experience with computers
C	— Minimal work experience with computers
D	— Training in general use of software and OS
E	— Training in use of a particular application program
F	— Training only in limited data input functions or no training at all

They are most likely to use dedicated computer systems such as PCs or workstations. Classical examples are programmers and systems engineers. More recently, managers and analysts have adopted this same style of computing to support database analysis and decision support.

User types C, D, and E either don't know how to, or don't want to have to, program computers. They expect programmers to do this for them. They need to be trained both in the use of the computer system and in the use of one or more applications. It can be difficult or costly to use much of their time for even this type of training because of the other skills they employ on the job. Examples include doctors, dentists, architects, professional managers, and so forth.

Type E users may use a system, but the extent of their knowledge of the system may be learning to push the right buttons or enter data, without any need for a deeper understanding of the underlying application or system. This type of user's view of the system is sometimes referred to as a "terminal view," since the only required knowledge of the system relates to interacting with menus on a terminal or graphics screen.

Figure 2.1 illustrates the varying levels of computer literacy required in different functions in a company as an example. By taking into consideration the different types of computer users in the organization, the manager will be better able to match system capabilities to user needs and to understand the potential impacts that UNIX will have on the different types of users.

Just as people in a group or department interact with each other, computers that support people have gradually become more and more connected via computer networks. Networking provides the means to let users send and receive mail messages or various types of data between computers and other types of devices connected to the network.

One of the great advantages of UNIX is not that it provides every feature known. Rather, it is that it creates an environment in which the user can build the right applications with maximum flexibility. In addition, it offers the advantage that these applications, when written with portability in mind, can be deployed on a wide range of existing or new technologies. The next section further develops this concept by explaining the overall environment in increasingly greater detail.

Layered organizations in flux

Most organizations consist of a set of functions that ultimately are described in terms of functional hierarchies. If you look at the way computers are deployed in these functions, there is often a similar hierarchy in

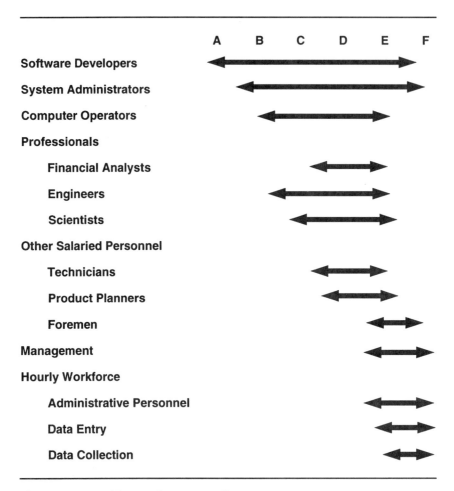

Figure 2.1.   Types of computer literacy.

terms of a layering of expertise levels. For example, the casual user may gain assistance from another user in their department if they need to learn how to use a particular software application or access data files. Application users tend to know just enough to get by in terms of operating system commands, and they rely on the operations support personnel (operators in the traditional mainframe world) to make sure the software and hardware they need is up and working properly and to perform basic functions like backup or restoring of files. The system (and/or) network administrator is the next layer. These people implement business policies as regards the use of the computers, the level of access to data, and/or other computing resources in the network. They might not have much knowledge of the programs that end users work with in terms of actually using the application software, but the system administrator does know where that software is, who has access to it, what typical computer resources it requires to be run, and so on. Programmers might represent another layer in this model.

In technical environments, engineers could represent all of these functions in one. In commercial data processing environments, there is often a support infrastructure as described above within the company and extending out into the supplier's customer support organizations for systems hardware and software, peripherals, and all the different forms of software.

As will be developed in Chapter 7, perhaps one of the most important issues in managing computer systems is having the right people involved and to have their roles and responsibilities clearly spelled out. But organizations are transforming and becoming more matrixed and more interenterprise oriented. Computers are everywhere, and the traditional model of MIS support is quickly becoming outmoded. Users often want to take full advantage of the information technology that is available to them and the demand is already outstripping MIS's ability to manage it.

At the same time, Open Systems are coming along, and suppliers are paying more attention to standards. As anyone who has played with personal computer systems integration can tell you, it takes a lot of expertise to determine the right combination of components when building a system. Someone has get the computer and software setup for the average computer user. Now we add to that the additional requirement to network everything. We have PCs and a few Macintoshes—now let's add in a UNIX database server. The current level of system complexity demands real expertise to design and administer the whole network computing environment correctly. The traditional responsibility matrix no longer fits since almost anybody can just buy another PC or UNIX workstation. But what about adding that device into the network, allowing it access to other devices, and tying it into enterprise-level computing like electronic mail.

Companies do not usually want to spend a great deal of time trying to make computers work for them. They want computers that work with a minimum of expertise on their part. Change in the human infrastructure of computer support organizations is normally required.

Many companies choose to simply outsource the integration headaches to other service companies, but no matter how you look at it, your organization's traditional support infrastructure will be impacted, and it will need to have layered responsibilities that must leave the end user community with more freedom and autonomy than has traditionally existed. The philosophy of support and putting computing into the hands of the end users has changed and will continue to do so.

UNIX Philosophy

UNIX has a large following, and its supporters claim it is the operating system platform for the 90s. UNIX also has detractors that claim it is archaic and not the panacea UNIX fanatics would have you believe. UNIX has advantages and disadvantages. There are certain philosophies that are somewhat unique to UNIX. Understanding some of them is important in determining the advantages of UNIX for you.

UNIX provides a lot of tools for users. While the core of UNIX is a small number of programs called the kernel, UNIX consists of a large number of short programs known as utilities which perform basic functions by calling the kernel using a standard set of interfaces. There are a large number of commands and utilities in UNIX. These tools can be used together to form powerful utilities without programming. More sophisticated utilities may be built up by using a set of lower-level utilities. Reusable, easy to construct tools built out of utilities that can communicate with each other are what UNIX is all about. The philosophy of system use historically was to string these utilities together to do whatever you wanted to do rather than having to write software.

Another basic idea in UNIX concerns the way the user interacts with the operating system. Traditionally the user types in commands and the operating system performs functions. These commands can often be put into scripts so command sequences can be built up to perform functions. UNIX takes the concept to the next level. You don't actually interact with the UNIX operating system, you interact with the UNIX shell. The shell, which is explained later, is really an environment that can be as simple as a traditional operating system interface or as complicated as a full-blown programming language.

Shell scripts and the shell environment allow a very high level of customization. Graphical user interfaces are a newer addition to UNIX. A graphical user interface can be used to execute commands or sequences of commands by pointing and clicking on ICONs within windows. This is an alternative method, especially suitable to new users or casual users, and it frees the user from remembering UNIX command syntax and/or shell script syntax. Modern UNIX systems are no more difficult to use for the average user than a Macintosh or a PC running Microsoft Windows. Most typical users alternate between using the graphical user interface and windows and interacting with one or more UNIX shells.

UNIX support philosophy—users and superusers

UNIX has a definite philosophy around system administration. As we will see in later sections on UNIX system administration, certain users have the power to do just about anything. These are people known to the system as superusers. Superusers have access to specials user accounts that require passwords to get into, and once in superuser mode, the user can perform many special functions. Unless steps are taken to customize the UNIX environment, users have powerful capabilities, some of which can get them into trouble. UNIX is not really any different from most operating systems in this regard. UNIX users should avoid trying to do system administration on their own—it is too easy to get into trouble. The graphical user interface technology that has been integrated with UNIX over the past several years is reaching the point where most users can do almost anything with point and click and a window-based user interface. The client-server model, for which UNIX is ideally suited, has also become a sort of philosophy of UNIX. For example, clients are provided access to their data stored on file servers. These file servers may be backed up by the systems administration or operations support group. This frees individual users up from having to implement their own backups and so forth. Client-server and how it is evolving within network computing environments is discussed in Chapter 5.

2.1. LAYERED VIEWS OF COMPUTER SYSTEM ENVIRONMENTS

A layered systems architecture consists of various hardware and software technologies that are layered on each other in order to form a complete system. A model of such an architecture can be useful in drawing attention to the major elements of an information system. Two layered system architectural models that vary in level of detail are described here. The first is a macro view of a generic system architecture. The macro view illustrates major components in the overall system ranging from the hardware and operating system up through the general-purpose, or horizontal, application software (such as office automation) and the industry-specific (often called vertical software, such as a CAD/CAM package or an engineering analysis program).

Modularity of subsystems and interface definitions. Application and system software solutions are made out of many pieces of functionality. These pieces are herein called subsystems in a layered systems architecture. Each subsystem is made up of pieces of functionality. These pieces can be called modules, which come in many types and sizes. Modules are connected via interfaces. Changing interfaces can be a costly business, and software systems tend to have lots of interfaces.

Higher-level programming tools help. Source management systems help teams of programmers change a system at the same time. Some changes force other changes. Evolving a system is a complex activity that can be helped by using software tools. Applications all need certain common services. Machine resources need to be shared by multiple applications: memory, processors, disk, floppy disk, network connection, display, keyboard, mouse, tablet, and so on.

Machine resources need to be shared by multiple users to control access to information and to enforce policies for sharing the machines resources. An operating system manages shared resources and application software providing access control and security and giving applications as much of the functionality and speed of the underlying hardware as possible. Shared resources are managed though special functionality. For example, memory is shared through support of virtual memory, access control, and shared libraries. CPUs are shared using separate processes that are given slices of time, multithreading that allows each process to do more than one thing at the same time, and multiprocessing where more than one thread can be run at the same time. Disk space is shared and managed by file systems, access control mechanisms, and so forth. Network access is facilitated by the operating system that acts as a mail carrier for short messages. A network's transport capacity is shared among programs by the operating system. The operating system enforces security that is extremely important in network computing environments.

The second layered system model illustrates the interrelationship of the major components of the UNIX operating system at a more detailed level and is called the micro view. By looking at the way systems are layered, the reader can see how each category of user has a different "system view." It will also become clearer that standards tend to address the interfaces between specific layers in the architecture through specifications that describe the application programming interfaces between layers. This makes the layers less dependent on each other and, to the extent the interface standards are adhered to, allows for more freedom in substituting certain components in the architecture with little or no impact on the others.

2.1.1. The Macro View of Layered Systems Architecture

The macro, or highest-level, view of the system is shown in Figure 2.2. The lowest layer is the network and the system hardware. Above it is the operating system, and above that are various tools and capabilities such as data management, window management, software development tools such as compilers and libraries, and capabilities for supporting networking.

The next layer, called the application layer, consists of different types of applications depending on the purpose a given system is being used for. Vertical application software includes general-purpose software that provides solutions that may be industry or function specific. For example, in a manufacturing environment, software for manufac-

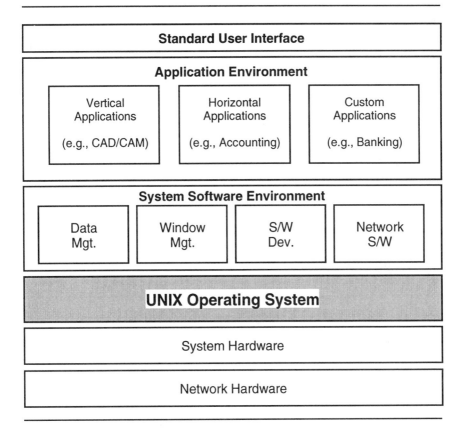

Figure 2.2. Macro view of layered system.

turing resource planning or cost accounting would be examples of vertical software. This type of software is generally available from independent software vendors, although it has historically had to be developed and/or highly customized in-house. Horizontal application software consists of general-purpose capabilities like spreadsheet programs, calculator programs, technical publishing software, word processing, and other capabilities. Custom applications are those not necessarily generally available and written by the user or some other agent specifically for the user.

The user interface is the highest layer within the architecture. Well-integrated applications share a consistent user interface in the sense that they all have a similar look and feel to them. As explained later, window systems provide a powerful means of standardizing the user's interface to the system. The orthogonality of the various layers makes the UNIX environment highly modular so that different parts of the environment can be swapped in or out without other parts being affected.

The orthogonality of UNIX is enforced by software interfaces. For example, there are only a few very simple interfaces to the file system: open, close, read, write, and so forth. This forces modularity in the software that is layered above the file system. There are no "sneak paths" in the file system. This permits powerful flexibility in swapping layers, like a new file system into the overall environment, without significant programming effort. This capability is particularly important when one considers the high level of innovation that is taking place in UNIX software.

From a technical perspective, UNIX achieves a separation of ideas and concepts through clean interfaces. This accommodates both simplicity and change and is the result of the basic system having been designed by only two people who shared common goals. UNIX has a long and rich history, as already explained in Chapter 1. This rich legacy of innovation required internal changes to UNIX functionality, which were always made easier as the result of its clean interfaces.

2.1.2.   The Micro View of Layered Systems Architecture

In the micro view of the system architecture (see Figure 2.3), we look more closely at the components of each layer and how they interface with each other. The more heavily shaded areas surround the major elements of UNIX.

Layer I. At the lowest level, there are one or more physical networks, assuming the system is tied into a network. Attached to the network are usually devices such as printers, terminals, and gateways. Gate-

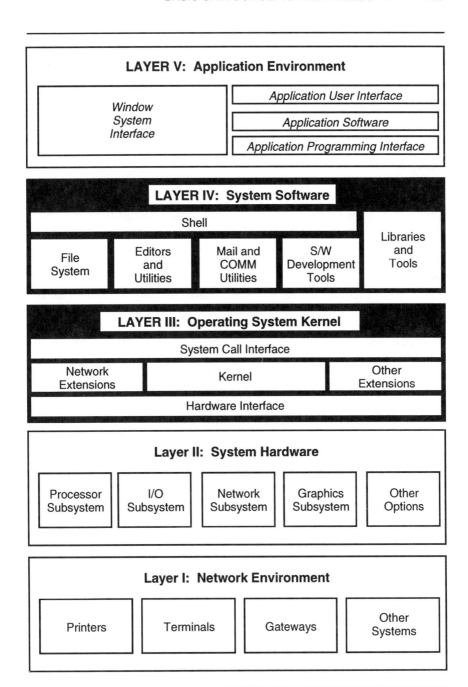

Figure 2.3. Micro view of layered system.

ways are special-purpose, dedicated computers that support inter-computer communications.

Layer II. The computer system hardware, at the next level, consists of a combination of subsystems and options.

Layer III. The lowest-level software interface consists of machine-dependent hardware interfaces contained in the operating system. These interfaces are designed to make it possible to easily interchange the "parts" or, more precisely, to reimplement the operating system on different hardware configurations or architectures. These machine-dependent interfaces connect the machine-independent software above them to the specific architectural details of the present machine and support the use of these machine-independent elements of UNIX on many computers of widely varying configurations and architecture.

The heart of the operating system—what you might think of as the engine—is called the kernel. The kernel is a program that has to run for anything to work. It usually has extensions to support networking, graphics, any special devices, or other hardware options. Above the kernel is the system call interface level. Like the hardware interface, this interface serves the purpose of cleanly separating the higher levels of software from the core of the operating system.

Layer IV. In the next layer, there are usually a number of tools and capabilities. In UNIX, these are accessed through the shell. This system software, which includes hundreds of commands and utilities, is most easily thought of as the environment supplied with the operating system. Different systems are supplied with different system software options and capabilities.

Layer V. In the application layer, each piece of software usually has some user interface, although this is not necessarily the case. The actual application software, if written to the API (Application Software Interface) specification, should be portable (in source form) between different system environments.

When the applications software uses a common user interface (for example, the same window system) then users will more readily understand how to operate the software. The range of technical sophistication of users is extremely broad—ranging from kernel programmers to people only interested in their specialized application such as word processing.

These various types of users typically have very different views of the layered architecture.

Layer V: Application Environment. Most versions of UNIX support multiple-user interfaces. The most modern are windowing systems that utilize high-resolution bit map displays. Most modern application software is written to support multiple-user interfaces. The application software also makes calls to subroutine libraries that in many cases have been standardized across different UNIX variants. This layer of the application software makes use of one or more APIs, or application programming interfaces. For example, an application may use a combination of SQL for data management and also make calls to the UNIX operating system kernel through the system call interface.

Layer IV: System Software. System software as used here denotes standard utilities and commands normally supplied with the UNIX operating system. This includes basic file system functionality, editors, and utilities for text preparation, programs for electronic mail, basic software development tools and utilities, as well as a large number of other specialized utilities and tools. As new enhancements have been added to UNIX and as different variants have converged, support of additional functions is usually added to promote portability of application software. This has a drawback in terms of complexity. UNIX carries several generations of utilities around with it for the sake of compatibility.

Layer III: Operating System. Much of the UNIX system software is written to the system call interface layer. This allows the utilities and any layers of software above it to be shielded from changes in the lower layers. Depending on the particular variant of UNIX, the kernel may contain certain functionality such as support for lower-level networking services or graphics. These can alternatively be implemented at a next higher layer of system software.

Layer II: System Hardware. System hardware includes the base platform as well as options and add-ons such as floating point accelerators, mass-storage subsystems, graphics accelerators, and other options. These are typically different depending on whether the system configuration is intended to support desktop/end-user computing, to function as a node in a network, or to function as a multiuser system.

Layer I: Network Environment. Most UNIX systems today are connected in local area and/or wide area networks. The nodes in these networks may provide services remotely to the system hardware on which UNIX is running. Such nodes may themselves run versions of UNIX or other operating systems.

2.1.3. Relating Layered Systems Architecture to Organization

Where you are in the organization will have a major influence on your view of the system. Figure 2.4 illustrates the relationships between the various classes of users and the macro view of the systems architecture presented in the last section.

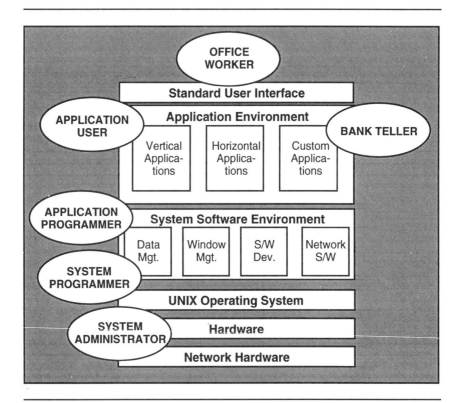

Figure 2.4. The macro view of users with different computer literacy. Different classes of users tend to have very different views of the overall system environment. Applications shield the typical user from direct interaction with underlying layers.

There is an interesting and important message in Figure 2.4. Most people interact with application software of one form or another, and their proficiency in the operating system itself does not have to be high. With the aid of window systems, both the application and the operating system have become much easier to use. The user no longer has to remember long command lines and sequences. It is increasingly the case that a majority of UNIX computer users don't have to know much about UNIX (the operating system) at all!

2.1.4.   An Overview of Computer Systems and Networks

As described earlier, UNIX is supported on a wide variety of computer systems ranging from laptops to supercomputers. These computer systems break down into three broad categories:

1. Desktops (single user)
2. Servers (single or multiuser)
3. Hosts (multiuser)

This section will first focus on a typical host multiuser configuration. Other hardware configurations typical in networked computing environments will be discussed. A typical multiuser UNIX-based computer system is quite similar to a traditional minicomputer or midrange system. The main differences are that the traditional minicomputer system (1) typically runs a proprietary operating system and has multiple terminal users, and (2) is often not connected to a network, especially a local area network.

Figure 2.5 shows a modern configuration for a typical UNIX-based departmental computer system. Such a system typically supports several users, operates standalone in that no other computer system is required to support its operation, and is connected to a local area network in which it functions as a server for the personal computers or workstations that may also be attached to the local area network.

UNIX Server. A node in the network that provides other nodes with file, compute, database, or some combination of these services in the local area network. The server may support options such as floating point accelerators and except for small work group servers will increasingly be multiprocessor architectures.

Multiport Connections. Circuit boards that support multiple serial ports. Intelligent adapters use local processors and require extra software but relieve the main processor of many tasks required in handling asynchronous devices such as terminals, modems, and so forth.

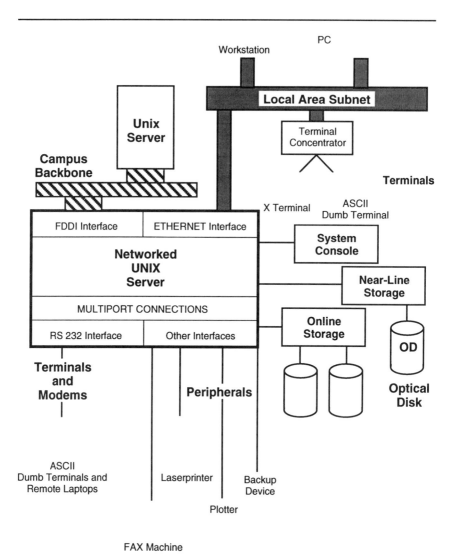

Figure 2.5.   Typical UNIX networked system environment. UNIX
helps to bridge the desktop and server computing
environments.

System Console. Typically, a terminal used by the computer operator or system administrator to control the system start-up, shut-down, diagnostics, and other privileged user functions.

Output Devices. High-speed printers, laser printers, impact printers, plotters.

Disk. Device on which the file system resides. Magnetic disk is currently the most common form of mass storage; high-density media such as optical disk are being used increasingly in certain applications.

Terminals. Either character or window-based display with keyboard.

Local Area Network. Hardware and software for connecting systems and supporting high-speed data transfer between network nodes. See Chapter 5.

Site Backbone. A high-speed network, now often employing fiber optic technology, usually supporting server-to-server communications.

Wide Area Network. Similar to local area network, except data transfer is across telephone or other medium for connecting systems that may be great distances apart.

PC. Personal computer, for example, an IBM PC or PC clone, or a laptop.

Workstation. A desktop computer system offering high performance and support of multitasking—for example, products from Sun, IBM, DEC, HP/Apollo, SGI, MIPS, and so on.

Online/Near-Line Storage. Disks or other mass-storage devices (OD stands for optical disk).

Modem. Device used to modulate signals from a computer for transmission across telephone lines. These signals are demodulated by a modem on the computer at the other end.

Network. Subsystem that carries signals between nodes, handling routing, transport, and physical connectivity.

Peripherals. Printers, plotters, or other input or output devices. CD-ROM players are one of the most interesting new peripherals to come along. CD-ROM is increasing in use because of the cost savings and efficiency it offers software developers. CD-ROMs can store an incredible amount of information and provide benefits to customers as well.

UNIX System Configurations. The following summarizes typical personal computer, workstation, server, and multiuser system configurations used with UNIX.

Personal Computers Running UNIX. An Intel PC, featuring a 486 processor, comes close to offering the same performance as midrange workstations. Add-on graphics and networking are not as well integrated in most cases.

PC's graphics performance and features are limited compared with those options available on workstations.

PC's disk I/O needs improvement relative to workstations. Ethernet through a PC is 80 percent of what it is on a Sun workstation, for example. Workstations use the same drives and interfaces as on the PC but feature better integration and better benchmarks.

PCs are not well suited for computationally demanding 3D solids modeling or I/O and CPU-intensive image processing.

PCs have a performance ceiling compared to workstations.

A personal computer is distinguished from workstations by its adherence to hardware and software compatibility. This compatibility drives high-unit volumes of commodity like products. High-performance features such as networking, graphics, floating-point coprocessors, virtual memory, multiuser, and multitasking functionality in the operating systems are normally optional and not integral system features.

Uniprocessor Hardware

  1—Processor (16 or more typically 32-bit processor)

  1—Up to 640K bytes memory (max) without expansion

  1—6 Mb add-in memory (a typical configuration is more like 12 to 16 Mbs)

  1—Ega/Vga display adapter and monitor

  1—80 Mb hard disk minimum (usually 500Mb and a fast SCSI controller are typical)

  1 or 2—8-port multiport boards (for multiuser support)

  1—Tape backup unit with controller

  2 to 12—Dumb ASCII terminals (as terminal server)

  1—Parallel print

Software

Typical UNIX

S/W—SCO XENIX, SunSoft IN/IX or Solaris 2.x, Univel UnixWare

Spreadsheet S/W—Lotus, 20/20

Database—Foxbase, Oracle, Sybase

Windowing S/W

Workstation Configuration Running UNIX.

Uniprocessor Hardware

1—Processor (32-bit or 64-bit processor)

Math coprocessor option

8 to 12 Mbs of memory (128+ Mbs for RDBMS applications)

1—Gigabyte of hard disk

Multiple multiport cards (for multiuser support)

2 to 40—Dumb ASCII Terminals (as terminal server)

Note: Multiprocessor workstations are now becoming widely available.)

Software

Typical UNIX S/W—Solaris 2.x, ULTRIX, AIX

Database S/W—Oracle, Sybase, INGRES

Windowing S/W

UNIX multiuser server configuration running UNIX.

1—Uniprocessor or multiprocessor (32-bit)

Math coprocessor option

16 Mb of memory base plus 2 to 4 Mb per user

1 to 10 Gigabytes of hard disk

Multiple multiport cards

Tape backup

UNIX multiuser server configurations usually accommodate multiple serial ports and intelligent multiport adaptors that use local processors and software on the circuit board, which relieve the main processor of many of the tasks required in handling asynchronous terminals.

Server configurations provide much greater expandability in terms of memory, I/O subsystems, and backplane slots than do desktop or deskside configurations of personal computers or workstations. Servers are often optimized for their primary role as file, compute or database servers.

UNIX and Computer Processor Architectures. UNIX is being implemented on most emerging computer processor architectures, including multiprocessors and RISC microcomputers. This is happening because UNIX is fairly inexpensive to port, it has lots of readily available application software, and users want it and not a proprietary operating system.

The design of the UNIX system is based on a central (uniprocessor) processor architecture. A multiprocessor has two or more CPUs that share common memory and peripherals. The UNIX system cannot run unchanged in a multiprocessor system and still take full advantage of the hardware's capabilities. Multiprocessor system (MP) vendors must rewrite portions of the UNIX operating system to ensure effective use of their hardware.

2.1.5. Multiprocessing

What Is Multiprocessing? Multiprocessing is not just a matter of hardware. As we will see, there are operating system implementation issues, parallel programming and tools, parallel utilities, and parallel applications. There are many forms of multiprocessing architecture. A complete explanation is well beyond the scope of this book. The following summarizes the major categories of multiprocessing architectures at a high level.

- Tightly coupled microprocessing
  - Coarse grain (2 to 4 processors)
  - Medium grain (6 to 20 processors)
  - Fine grain (1000s)
- Loosely coupled microprocessing
  - Cluster computing

To fully support MP, architectures require a preemptible kernel or some other mechanism and the design of data structures and algorithms that handle locking protocols to avoid deadlock and starvation between processes. MP support in UNIX is one of the most active areas of new research and development and is still awaiting standardization. There are two different ways to implement MP in UNIX: asymmetric MP (ASMP) and symmetric MP (SMP).

In an ASMP implementation, the kernel is run on only one processor, which means that processes running on other processors must wait on this "master processor," for example, to process I/O. In an SMP implementation, the kernel itself is multithreaded and can therefore be executed on multiple CPUs. See Figure 2.6. To take full advantage of the hardware, the operating system itself must be implemented as a symmetric multiprocessor (SMP). Symmetric multiprocessing enables multiple tasks to take full advantage of multiple CPUs. This translates to high-application throughput and allows performance to scale efficiently as CPUs are added.

The benefits of multiprocessing include the following:

- More performance
  — Decreased time-to-completion

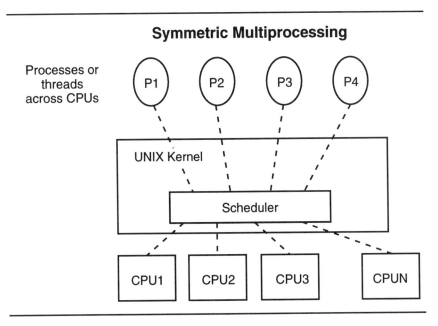

Figure 2.6.   Symmetric multiprocessing.

- — Higher throughput
- — Higher transaction throughput
- — More simultaneous users
- Smooth upgrades
- Lower overall cost of computing
  - — Sharing of system resources
  - — Fewer copies of software may be required

2.1.6. Multitasking

Some operating systems that claim to support multitasking actually support what is sometimes referred to as cooperative multitasking. This means they rely on the application programs you run to cooperate, working out how they are going to share the systems processor(s) on their own. For well-behaved programs, this sort of electronic democracy approach works satisfactorily. Badly behaved programs stick an hour glass or some other icon up on your desktop GUI and lock you out of the system while they are running. Under preemptive multitasking offered by 32-bit operating systems, the operating system is in control—not the application programs. If one program is busy for a long time, you can hot-key to the operating systems and do other things.

2.1.7. UNIX and RISC

RISC microprocessor technology has become synonymous with high-performance computing. RISC (Reduced Instruction Set Computer) is a type of processor architecture that comprises a relatively small number of instructions by comparison to CISC (Complex Instruction Set Computer) processors found in traditional microcomputers, minicomputers, and mainframes. In recent years, RISC architectures have achieved new levels of price/performance in the computing world. A few examples of RISC processors are Sun Microsystems' SPARC, Hewlett Packard's Spectrum, and IBM's RS/6000. UNIX is ported to RISC architectures without any particular problems.

What are the changes ahead for RISC? The SPARC technology is nearly dominant in today's RISC market. SPARC accounts for almost two-thirds of this market, followed by MIPS, IBM, Intergraphs Clipper, the Motorola MC88x00, and the HP-PA Prism. All of these combined were equal to slightly half of the SPARC market share in 1990. Other vendors seem to be following Sun's strategy to license their RISC technology. From Sun's experience it would seem clear that licensees are concerned about the openness of the architecture. Sun spun out its architecture and helped form SPARC International. This move together with the spin-out of its operating systems business into SunSoft were both designed to provide neutrality and more responsiveness to SPARC licencees.

RISC is here to stay. Every major vendor now offers systems based on RISC. Digital has completed this by moving to RISC with Alpha. One of the changes coming over the next few years will be 64-bit RISC implementations. We expect a relatively slow migration to 64-bit architectures depending on the number of applications that are available that really exploit 64-bit architecture.

The next section provides an overview of UNIX. It begins with a high-level description of the UNIX operating system. Each of the major components is defined, including the typical hardware configurations, the UNIX system kernel, UNIX commands and utilities, and UNIX shells. Subsequent sections provide more detailed discussions of these components and explain when and to whom various components of the system are important.

2.2.   BASIC CONCEPTS OF UNIX

This section provides an introduction to the major components of the UNIX operating system. These include the kernel, shells and shell scripts, and commands and utilities.

Windowing systems, commonly referred to as GUI's or graphical user interfaces, have not been an original, fully integrated part of UNIX. Instead it is usually a distinct layer over the command line interface.

The environment the typical user normally sees is really a shell that surrounds the operating system, as illustrated in Figure 2.7. Window systems were not historically part of UNIX. They are invariably supplied with UNIX software today, however, either bundled with the operating system or offered separately. More than one window system can be supported simultaneously. The shell interprets all commands, letting the user navigate through the file system, manipulate files through the use of editor programs, and run programs like electronic mail (email), technical publications software, calendar programs, spreadsheets, and the like.

The UNIX programmer typically finds the UNIX environment to be a rich one, especially when programming in the C language. Since C was originally designed specifically to write UNIX, and since UNIX is now written in C, the programmer will find the C development environment under UNIX a rich and robust computer-aided software develop-

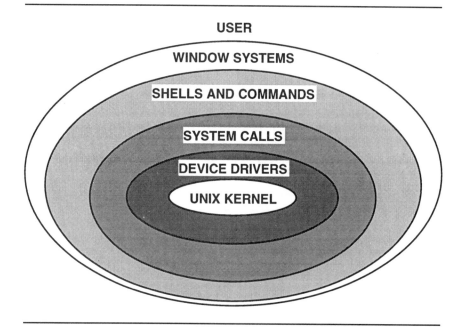

Figure 2.7.   UNIX system environment. UNIX users interact with the shell command interpreter or a window system. Various shells can usually be run in different windows as well.

ment toolset. This toolset is part of the standard UNIX release and provides sophisticated functionality such as test coverage analysis, profiling, debugging and complex text substitution, and search methods.

The UNIX programmer will often write software that uses the extensive software libraries available with UNIX. The programmer will also find powerful capabilities like the "pipe," which makes it possible to string commands together to accomplish tasks that would require traditional programming on most operating systems.

The system administrator's UNIX environment is relatively straightforward, although historically much of the documentation on system administration of UNIX has been less than user friendly. Several books have recently been published to address this. Vendors understand this issue and are working on making UNIX-based systems administration easier. The system administrator has to set up and manage both the hardware and the software environments for all other users. Managing disks, tapes, terminal and serial lines, user accounts, and security is a function typically accomplished using special shell scripts that have either been supplied with the system or, more likely, written by the administrator to fit the needs of the specific installation.

2.3.   THE KERNEL IS AT THE CENTER OF IT ALL

The UNIX kernel is the heart of the UNIX system. Strictly speaking, the kernel is the UNIX operating system. Utilities and the shell are really just ordinary programs, although they are critical to the completeness of the UNIX environment from the user's point of view. The kernel hides the underlying hardware. It provides a collection of services independent of the particular hardware it is implemented on. The kernel is loaded from a storage device and runs in memory all the time. The size of the memory required to support a given version of UNIX is therefore very important. Typical UNIX kernels consume one or more megabytes of random access memory (RAM). Without enough memory, the system will spend much of its time paging instead of doing useful work.

The kernel performs low-end functions that support the UNIX environment by directly interacting with the system hardware. The kernel implements the UNIX file system, managing the system's mass storage, and schedules and executes all the jobs that run in the system. It manages the multiuser operation of the system, schedules the central processor, and processes the work of each user. The UNIX job scheduler controls the execution environment, deciding how to allocate CPU and system resources to processes.

Processes are in different states of execution—running or waiting to run. If the process requires CPU only, it will be put on a run queue; if the process is waiting for some other resource, it will be put on the system sleep queues. Each process is given a finite amount of CPU time. At the end of the time slice, the process has to relinquish control of the CPU to the next-highest-priority process that is ready to run (next in line on the run queue).

Processes can either voluntarily or involuntarily context switch. An example of a voluntary context switch is when a process blocks for a system resource such as disk. If a process exhausts its CPU quantum, then it is forced to do an involuntary context switch. The next-highest-priority process in the run queue is executed in a round robin fashion. Priorities are shifted all the time depending on the amount of CPU time a process uses. This priority is one of the factors that determines where a process gets placed on the run queue. UNIX commands are available for the user to run jobs in the background, defined as the lowest-process priority, or to set priorities for different processes.

Scheduling algorithms may differ between UNIX implementations. Other differences in kernel implementation are most commonly found in memory management software, I/O device drivers such as disks, and system timer clock access. These interfaces are schematically shown in Figure 2.8 as the binary interface layer below the UNIX kernel. Since this layer of software has to be written for specific hardware, it is quite hardware dependent. The Binary Call interface allows this layer to be easily changed without the layers above it being affected.

UNIX is the only widely accepted demand-paged, virtual memory operating system in the computer industry. A demand-paged virtual memory is a technique where the length of the page swapped in and out of memory depends on how much code is required for any given opera-

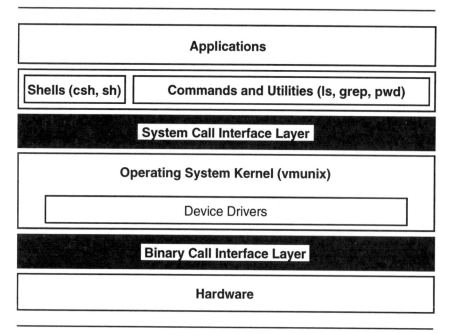

Figure 2.8.   System and binary call interfaces. The system interface layer shields the function above it from changes in the operating system kernel itself. Examples are shown in parentheses of the commands and utilities and device drivers that can be added in transparently to other layers of functionality.

tion. Most UNIX implementations use virtual memory to enable programs and data sets to be processed in physical memory. Programs and data that do not fit are swapped on and off disk in a process called paging. A disk partition called swap is set aside for this paging process. A memory management unit (mmu) is used to map virtual memory addresses to physical memory pages that are active.

PCs and I/O buses are slow because time is wasted while code is moved back and forth between the disk and the I/O bus. If only one line of code is needed in the next page, the PC memory management requires the entire 64K-byte page to be swapped in. UNIX is normally implemented with much larger page sizes and is far more efficient and therefore achieves much higher levels of performance, particularly in handling large applications. It is important that the UNIX kernel is configurable, allowing it to be tuned to the particular requirements of the system engineer.

This section has discussed the traditional UNIX kernel. The SVR4 kernel (depending on configuration) may be substantially larger than one megabyte. Fundamental changes in kernel structure are found in Mach and OSF/1 and in commercially available versions of SVR4 today. These are not discussed in any detail here. Interested readers should consult their system vendors for more information if the UNIX system kernel is of particular importance to them for some reason. The kernel is one area where the state of the art of technology is being advanced. The OSF/1 kernel still uses code that required a System V Release 2 or 3 source license. The command set, taken from AIX3.1, also incorporates code taken from System V Release 2. The OSF/1 kernel will be about the same size as the ULTRIX kernel on a DECstation 3100. Even though the heart of the OSF/1 kernel has been replaced by Mach 2.5, the remainder and largest portion of the kernel involves the UNIX system and related services, which have not shrunk but grown by comparison to Mach itself.

The UNIX kernel services requests by processing system calls. UNIX system calls are the interface between the kernel and all of the application programs, utilities, and shells that run above it in the layered structures described earlier. The kernel supports approximately 80 system calls depending on the implementation. Usually, these system calls are identical among UNIX systems. A basic set of system calls make up a key interface standard that permits interoperability between UNIX applications. Such calls are intended to be as vendor independent as possible. This allows a vendor to modify any part of the kernel internals as necessary, while it prevents any disturbance of the layers of software above the system call interface.

2.3.1.   The Future of the UNIX Kernel

To cope with the increasing demands placed on it, the UNIX kernel has become more modular over time. Future enhancements will be incorporated providing enhanced capabilities without disrupting the software above the system call interface. This provides a framework through which Novell, SunSoft, or other organizations can provide the base UNIX operating system to hardware or software companies that in turn will integrate their own enhancements within the standards framework of either one or both of (1) the system call interface and (2) the binary call interface.

The AT&T kernel was written before modern software engineering practices were well defined, but it is well structured. For the past several years, each new UNIX release from AT&T has introduced new enhancements and improved modularity. The well-defined interfaces now serve to effectively isolate various software components such as the file system, device drivers, communications and networking, and memory management. The orthogonality of the various layers or functions make UNIX highly modular. For example, the virtual memory system can work with different file systems unaffected by the choice of networking protocol used.

2.3.2.   Microkernels

Now that UNIX has become the de facto operating system for addressing new computing challenges, it is being incorporated into increasingly elaborate, large-scale transaction processing and speed-of-light computers. As the computing environment shifts from large general-purpose systems to collections of sophisticated and specialized nodes, the original monolithic UNIX model becomes less adaptable. Researchers have been working for years to develop a software model to realize the potential of modern distributed computing environments.

The spectrum of applications for traditional UNIX applications is expanding. Microkernels are being developed to address the requirements of applications at these extremes. Examples include real-time, embedded systems on one end of the spectrum and high availability and support for massively parallel architectures at the other extreme.

Traditional Kernels—UNIX SVR3, SCO UNIX, AIX, HP/UX, SunOS. Traditional UNIX kernels use a lot of memory. Performance is fast, but the monolithic kernels give system programmers a difficult time getting around the memory limitations. Various services such as graphics, networking, and so on have to be kernel based to achieve high performance.

Microkernel Technology—OSF/1, MACH, Windows/NT. In microkernel technology, virtual memory support means that less real memory is required, but performance can easily suffer. Microkernels would seem to offer a much simpler—albeit restrictive—environment for programmers. An implementation that provides a hardware abstraction layer means that the programmer no longer has to code around memory limitations and/or accesses devices directly. For example, UNIX databases often use raw I/O rather than the UNIX file system for performance reasons. With microkernel technology, this will be more difficult if not ill-advised. This places significant demands on microkernel architectures to offer excellent performance and tuning.

Dynamically configurable kernels—Solaris 2.x. Finally, there are architectures that feature smaller modular kernels through the use of dynamic loading. Device drivers, for example, are loaded when required and are otherwise not in the kernel. This approach yields excellent performance but does not necessarily involve the ease of programming possible with a microkernel. This approach, however, offers many of the benefits of microkernel technology in terms of supporting smaller hardware configurations and featuring clean programming interfaces.

What Are Microkernels? Microkernels are the software equivalent of the reduced instruction set in hardware. A microkernel is a small central core of essential services that allow the creation of highly modular operating systems. A key element in the original design of the UNIX operating system was that the operating system could provide a majority of the services that are required by user-level processes. As more services such as graphics, networking, and so forth were added into the kernel for new applications, the kernel became larger requiring more memory to run efficiently. It also became more complex for system programmers.

The key industry trends toward the rapid technology advancement of microkernels have been to achieve higher levels of computer power and functionality. The main drivers consist of the following:

1. Tightly coupled, fine-grain multiprocessor system architectures
2. Loosely coupled multiprocessing
3. High-level integration of network resources—services to manage replicated systems for high-availability cluster processing
4. Real-time and embedded applications

Most UNIX system vendors have future plans for smaller, more modular operating systems. This is not unique to UNIX. Most future operating systems will feature microkernels.

This technology is advancing rapidly. USL has invested in Chorus Systems S.A., a French software company, in a joint technology agreement for their future microkernel architecture. OSF selected the MACH microkernel. Small sophisticated companies like Tenon Intersystems have implemented a version of the MACH kernel for the Macintosh.

A microkernel, as the name implies, has a small kernel because services provided by the conventional kernel are delegated to other operating system services. This smaller kernel is ideal for executing the operating system and its basic kernel on processors with limited memory. It also means that specific user-level server processes can be run on specific server (read any computer node's) processor in essence making these nodes customized server processors. Microkernels will permit the contouring of operating system functionality uniquely for different nodes in a multiprocessing system or computer complex.

How does the Microkernel work? Figure 2.9 shows the layered architecture of generalized microkernel architecture. The applications and utilities at the top of this diagram make the same UNIX system calls they always do. This call interface then invokes the services of operating system servers. These are independent servers that can be run in user space or system space (depending on the sophistication of the microkernel).

Such operating system servers might run locally or remotely on other processors. They provide services such as process management, file (and object) management, streams management, interprocess communications, and so forth. These servers communicate with each other through message passing. They also make calls to the microkernel call interface. The microkernel itself manages all process communications and usually supports a real-time executive, a machine-dependent supervisor, a memory-management subsystem and machine-dependent, memory-management support.

Figure 2.10 illustrates how the microkernels work together in a multiprocessing environment. The basic microkernel and applications code can be configured for different nodes which require fewer operating system resources other than communications. The microkernel for a node providing I/O services would be augmented with servers that provide I/O servers and device drivers that provide file system functions.

Are Microkernels THE Answer? Even with the benefits offered by microkernels, they are not expected to replace the more conventional monolithic kernels. This is because the conventional kernels offer higher performance. This is especially true today in shared memory,

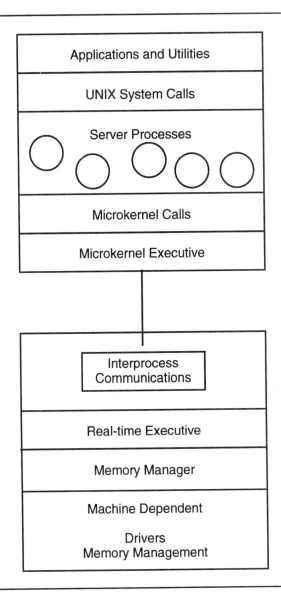

Figure 2.9.   UNIX microkernel architecture.

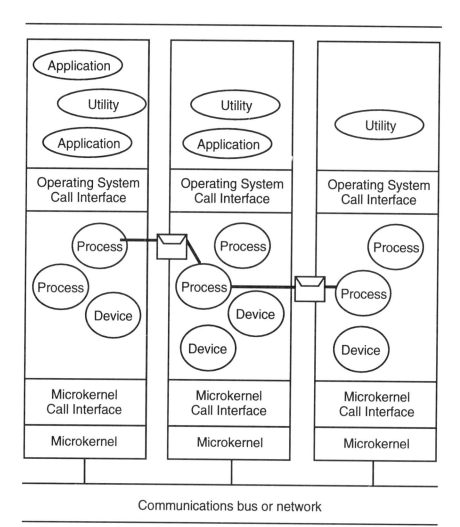

Figure 2.10. Microkernel in distributed or multiprocessor environment. Communication between different kernels could take place across either the MP system bus or a very high-speed network connection on such as that found in loosely coupled clustered computing environments.

coarse and medium grain, shared memory multiprocessors and in uniprocessor architectures.

One of the key technologies in microkernels is the message-passing mechanism needed to support node-to-node communications and distributed memory. Special communications support is required for microkernels to find use in loosely coupled systems. There is still considerable technological hurdles to overcome in this area.

Microkernels are relatively new technology. While their initial use will be in systems that require economical memory and software modularity such as real-time and embedded systems and fine-grain, tightly coupled multiprocessors, it is unclear whether they will displace conventional UNIX kernels.

The keys that will determine whether microkernel technology will be successful has to do with compatibility with existing and evolving standards and the extent to which performance can be enhanced. The basic technology of microkernels offers real promise for the future of distributed multiprocessing in tightly and loosely coupled multiprocessing systems. Since microkernels are theoretically simpler, the kernel itself should be highly portable to multiple architectures.

A Note on Parallel Processing. Today's fastest computers work at dizzying speeds performing hundreds of millions of arithmetic operations each second. But that's just not fast enough for some applications. There are scientific problems that would take 20 years to run on existing supercomputers.

Computer designers have come close to squeezing almost all of the speed they can out of single computer processors. Significant increases in computing speed will likely require computers that have more than one processing unit. Instead of solving problems step by step, computers will need to divide problems into parts that can be solved simultaneously by different processors. This concept is called parallel processing.

Dramatic speedups are possible by allowing the problem size to increase with the number of processors. In this way, all of the processors can work at maximum efficiency.

Researchers at Sandia Laboratory in Albuquerque, New Mexico have shown that they can solve problems on a 1,024 processor NCUBE/ ten machine at about the same speed as a CRAY supercomputer. The CRAY features only a few processors, but they operate at a much faster speed and require more rapid and expensive memory.

The NCUBE machine's processors, therefore, can make use of slower memory. Because slow memory costs less than fast memory, large memories become more affordable. This work showed the promise that fine-grain multiprocessing holds. But the massively parallel fine-grain configurations may be held back in terms of overall speed by the overhead required for processors to talk to each other.

How UNIX Variants Differ. The kernel is usually ported from a licensed version of UNIX available from one of several sources, including Novell and its licensees, notably software vendors like Sun, Microsoft, SCO, and The Wollongong Group, among others.

Between 10 and 50 percent of the traditional UNIX kernel has to be implemented specifically for a given hardware platform. In the future, with more modular versions of the UNIX kernel, system vendors will have to implement fewer kernel modes than they did with the traditional UNIX kernel, as more functionality migrates to outside the kernel.

Different versions of UNIX contain certain algorithms and data structures supported by the kernel and are likely to differ from version to version. While every UNIX kernel is theoretically supposed to support the same set of system calls, there are usually a few that reflect these kernel differences—for example, calls to system timers. Different versions of UNIX may vary in the areas summarized in Table 2.2.

The following people are most likely to be interested in the UNIX kernel:

- System vendors—because kernel differences impact the portability of UNIX to a specific computer architecture.
- Software developers—because software relies on specific kernel structures, algorithms; developers are often required to write specific I/O drivers.
- System administrators—who must periodically rebuild the kernel via an operation called MAKE.
- Programmers—who may be required to make system calls from programs they develop.

Threads. Multithreading allows a single process to be broken into modular tasks (see Figure 2.11). Tasks can run on one or multiple CPUs. In uniprocessor architectures, tasks complete when the longest thread finishes, so the computation is complete as soon as the longest task completes.

Using multithreading, you get higher performance. A single application can take advantage of preemptive multithreading. It can divide itself up into several subprograms. The application is more efficient since it can execute subprograms concurrently.

Table 2.2.   Kernel features that may differ between UNIX variants.

PROCESS CONTROL	May be required by application software
JOB CONTROL	
SEMIPHORES	
SHAPED LIBRARIES	May be important for software development purposes
INTERPROCESS COMMUNICATIONS	
FILE SYSTEM	
LOW LEVEL FILE SYSTEM	Performance implications
MAXIMUM FILE SIZE	Limits size of files or databases
SERIAL I/O	Ability to support dumb terminals
SYSTEM CALLS AND STRUCTURE	
SYSTEM V CALLS	Application software or software development implications
XENIX CALLS	
BSD CALLS	
SHARED MEMORY IMPLEMENTATION	Better performance
DEVICE DRIVERS	Off-the-shelf support of peripheral devices
MULTIPROCESSOR SUPPORT	Supports multiprocessor system hardware

In multiprocessor architectures, both processes and tasks can run on multiple CPUs.

2.4.   SHELLS AND SHELL SCRIPTS

In UNIX, "shell" is the name given to a command interpreter. One or more shells are usually made available with the operating system. The UNIX shell is similar to the DCL interpreter in the DEC VAX environment or to CICS executives in the IBM environment.

A shell accepts commands from the user and translates them into appropriate system calls to the kernel. Shell scripts are simply files that contain combinations of commands together with any special programming constructs the shell supports (for example branching and conditional expressions).

MULTITHREADING

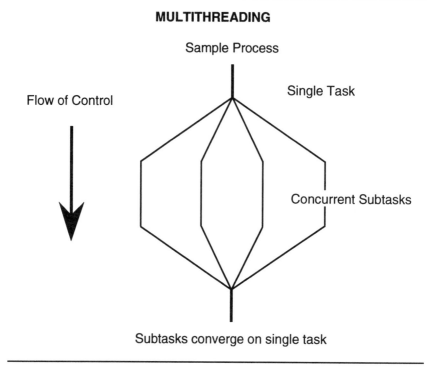

Figure 2.11. Typical UNIX networked system environment. UNIX helps to bridge the desktop and server computing environments.

There are a few popular shells that are commonly supplied with the UNIX operating system. Some of the most common shells are the Bourne shell, developed originally for use with System V, and the C shell, originally developed to support programming environments at Berkeley. There are other shells, such as the Korn shell, which features a programming environment, and the Tshell. In addition to UNIX shells, some vendors have begun to market shells that emulate the environment of other systems. A good example is a VAX DCL shell marketed on UNIX by the Boston Consulting Group.

A shell is usually a C program. Different shells provide different functionality. The C shell is one of the most popular. In the C shell, a start-up file is included that provides aliases for various commands, environment variables, setup program calls, and pathnames defining the location of various files within the UNIX file system. These start-up files can be easily modified to customize the shell. This allows the user to design the environment so that abbreviated or special commands can be entered by the user that will then be interpreted by the shell to match preprogrammed meanings.

UNIX shells differ in their specific syntax and in certain constructs they will interpret. They all, however, perform the same function of interpreting commands given by the user and translating them into calls to UNIX commands and utilities.

Shells are excellent habit-preserving mechanisms for users. They ensure that the ls command does the same thing (lists the files in the user's directory) on every UNIX system. They are the prime vehicles permitting users to move easily from system to system without having to relearn a new command syntax.

Shell scripts, as mentioned earlier, allow UNIX commands to be combined in a programming fashion. System administration utilities or much-repeated command sequences are often put into shell scripts to increase ease of use. Shells must be portable in order for shell scripts to be portable.

Even with the advent and widespread adoption of window systems and applications and system software that feature GUI-based interfaces, UNIX shells continue to be used and supported by system vendors. This is not just to provide backward compatibility. Shell environments offer very powerful tools for customizing the UNIX users environment. Shell programming isn't something UNIX novices have to master, but the more sophisticated users will continue to rely on it for years to come.

The Most Popular Shells.

Bourne Shell (sh). Originally developed at Bell Labs, the Bourne shell is one of the most popular shells and almost always available on UNIX systems. It provides simple Algol-68-like programming capabilities. Many people write scripts for the Bourne shell but choose to use other shells as well. The Bourne Shell is named after Steve Bourne.

C shell (csh). Originally developed to support C language development environments at Berkeley and NASA, csh is distributed with most Berkeley and AT&T-based UNIX systems. csh has C-like programming constructs as well as features for maintaining command histories, job control for multiple processes running in the foreground and background, and supporting command aliases. Aliases are names given to command lines that when issued to the shell are replaced by the command lines. This cuts down on the amount of typing the user needs to do to make things happen. Bill Joy of Sun Microsystems and previously of Berkeley is credited with the development of the C shell.

Korn Shell (ksh). Developed after the Bourne and C shells, ksh provides many of the C shell's best features. It is usually available as an unbundled product.

New Shells. A DCL shell became available from Boston Consulting Group in late 1989. There is a good possibility there will be a REXX SAA shell released in 1991. These shells will help ease the transition from other operating systems to UNIX by mimicking the non-UNIX system environments command interpreter.

Examples of shell scripts may be found on every UNIX system. They are used to run batch jobs; to perform repetitive tasks like compile, link, and execute in a software development application; to carry out system administrative functions like archiving old disk files to tape and performing system backups; and to simplify system installation. In UNIX, shell scripts provide a faster way to implement new software applications or utilities instead of writing them in a higher-level language.

Shells are of particular interest to system programmers who make heavy use of shell scripts in conjunction with their software development activities. Most other users' interests will be confined to using one or two shells and writing shell scripts, not developing software.

Shell scripts are of interest to a wide group of users, not just programmers or system administrators. Casual users should understand what shells are and how to execute them, but they will usually not have a need to write shell scripts. The casual user, with the aid of the UNIX systems administrator, may find it useful to customize his or her start-up file. This capability permits a tailoring of the commands the system will accept and process without any software modification. In UNIX, shell scripts are intended to do things that can't otherwise be done with standard UNIX commands.

Shells and Window Systems. Today, users can interact with UNIX via window systems as an alternative to using shells. They can also be used in conjunction with each other, as different shells can be run in different windows. Windowing systems, which will be covered in Chapter 5, are important tools that, when used correctly, can greatly improve the user friendliness of the UNIX user interface. In fact, window systems can allow UNIX commands to be completely hidden from view!

Bourne and C Shell Features. As previously described, the shell is a command interpreter. The Bourne shell has a default prompt of a "$," while the C shell's default is "%."

Foreground and Background. As has been discussed, commands typed on the command line are interpreted by the shell and run as separate processes. Command line options and arguments are passed to the command being processed. Commands are usually run in the foreground; that is, the user waits for the current command to be completed before typing another command. The user can specify to the shell that the command should be run as a job in the background. Running commands in the background releases the shell from waiting for the command to complete. The shell prompt returns immediately, ready for another command.

Redirection. The default input and output devices for commands are the keyboard and the screen (or window), respectively. The user can redirect the standard input and output of any shell command. Redirection is accomplished using the following special symbols in a command line:

< change source to specified file or device

> change destination to specified file or device

>> change source and append to specified file

<< change destination and append to specified file

Pipelines. Pipelines allow the user to build new commands by chaining the output and input of many commands together:

| *"pipe" standard output of one command to standard input of another*

Consider the following example of how pipes are used. The command is "ls", "-c" is the option. However, to list the files of a particular directory named "edward" in the order they were last edited, the command is

ls -c edward

In listing the contents of a very large directory so that the system pages through the listing a screenful at a time (which is what the more command does), the following command is typed:

ls -c edward | more

A number of commands can be strung together using a succession of pipes.

Filename Expansion. To save typing and to speed access, shells offer special characters to match single or multiple ranges of characters when command arguments are entered. These are sometimes referred to as "wild card" characters. For example, the example:

fgrep -i intro /usr/edd/book/chapter2

could also have been entered with the "*" wild card character as:

*fgrep -i intro /usr/edd/book/*2*

such that any file name ending in the letter 2 would be examined.

Search Paths and Environment Variables. The shell must know where to look in the hierarchical directory structure to find a specified command. A user-defined search path designates the place in the shell's start-up file. Without a search path, the user has to type in the absolute pathname for every command entered.

Most shells have environment variables. C shell environment variables are set using the set command. Bourne shell variables are set using the *setenv* command or *set* directly by typing a command such as my_var = value.

2.5. COMMANDS AND UTILITIES

There are over 200 programs typically supplied with the UNIX system, and some UNIX systems come with as many as 400. These are UNIX commands and utilities that are invoked through a shell. UNIX utilities may be executed like commands and implemented as shell scripts and as ordinary programs.

In theory, UNIX commands and utilities are quite similar between different variants and can be a key factor ensuring portability between UNIX variants. In practice, there are fundamental differences in the implementation of UNIX variants, which are usually reflected in the characteristics of the UNIX kernel. So while variants may look the same from the command level, they can actually be very different.

UNIX commands and utilities can be used in conjunction with each other to form powerful sequences or scripts in lieu of time-consuming, error-prone, high-maintenance programming in a high-level language. The ability to combine UNIX commands and utilities is a feature strikingly different from what is found in other computer operating systems today. All UNIX commands are written to use standard input, standard output, and standard error handling. This greatly facilitates the ability to string commands together into constructs where the standard output of one command is "piped" as standard input into the next command.

There are several excellent command reference guides available, some from computer vendors and some from book publishers. Many vendors also support online help in the form of man pages. The man command takes as an input the name of a UNIX command and displays the pages of the manual explaining how that command can be used.

The advanced user may need to know 80 to 90 percent of UNIX commands and utilities. The more typical user needs to know from 50 to 100 commands. The casual user or the user who spends most of his or her time working with an application program only needs to know a handful of commands. As window systems are used in the future, the requirement to know UNIX commands will be diminished, especially for the less advanced user. UNIX will essentially be hidden from this type of user.

DOS versus UNIX—Command Syntax

The following provides a brief commentary on UNIX versus MS-DOS command syntax. This is provided as an illustration that MS-DOS has borrowed many ideas from UNIX. If we were to compare the UNIX window system environments to Windows, there would also be a very similar set of functionality. Almost any user of Windows could easily learn to use any UNIX window system and vice versa.

Navigating Around the File System

— Change directory—cd

MS-DOS uses \ to indicate directory path name

cd \DIR\SUBDIR

— File names are limited to 8 characters including extensions.

In UNIX the / is used instead of the \

cd /DIR/SUBDIRECTORY

File names are usually 32 characters max and even more.

Table 2.3. Major categories of commands.

Category	Typical Commands	Function Performed	DOS Equivalent
File System	mkdir	Create Directory	MKDIR
	rm	Delete file	DEL
	cp	Copy file	COPY
System Security (none)	chmod	Set file permission	
(none)	passwd	Set login password	
File Navigation	cat	Concatenate/Print	TYPE
	sort	Sort/merge	SORT
Shells DOSSHELL	csh, sh	Starts shell	
Text Editors	vi	Full screen editor	EDIT
Text Processing	nroff, troff	Formaters for printer or laser printer	(none)
Process Control (none)	kill	Stop a process	
	nice	Run job in background	(none)
	bg	Run job in background	(none)
	fg	Run job in foreground	
(none)			
Networking	ftp	Network file transfer	(none)
	rcp	Remote copy	(none)
	uucp	Intersystem copy	(none)
Programming	make	Maintain/rebuild programs	(none)
	prof	Display performance data	(none)
	lex, yacc	Program parsers and code generator	(none)
Other Functions	spell	Spell checker	(none)
	bc and dc	Calculators	(none)
	bas	Basic Interpreter	QBasic
	ac, sa	Accounting tools	(none)

Print the Working Directory—pwd

— In MS-DOS, the cd command does this.

In UNIX, cd prints the pathname of the working or current directory.

— List directory contents— ls

This UNIX command lists the contents of the directory.

The MS-DOS equivalent is the DIR command.

Type the Contents of a File—cat

— This command is called TYPE in MS-DOS.

— cat in UNIX displays the contents of the specified files in a given sequence.

Controlling the Viewing of a File

— The UNIX command is more. MS-DOS has an equivalent command that displays the contents of a text file one screenfull at a time. The more command displaces another line or another screen in UNIX if the user enters a carriage return or a space bar respectively.

— Head in UNIX displays a specified number of lines at the start of a file. There is no equivalent MS-DOS command.

— Tail is a UNIX command that displays a specified number of lines at the end of a file. There is no equivalent MS-DOS command.

Moving and Renaming Files

— In UNIX the mv command is used to move (rename a file).

— REN is the equivalent command in MS-DOS.

Copying Files

— In UNIX the cp command creates a duplicate of the source file or directory and puts the duplicate into the destination directory.

— The equivalent MS-DOS command is copy.

Remove (Deleting Files)

— In UNIX, rm removes one of more files.

— In MS-DOS, the equivalent command is DEL.

Making a New Directory

— In UNIX, mkdir creates an empty directory in the current directory unless a full pathname is specified.

— In MS-DOS, MKDIR provides similar functionality.

Deleting a Directory

— In UNIX, rmdir removes an empty directory in the current directory, unless a full pathname is specified.

— In MS-DOS, RMDIR provides similar functionality.

Determining Information about Current User, login name, and so on

— In UNIX, the following commands are available:

    who—displays information on current users
    whoami—displays login name
    users—displays the current users

— There are no equivalent MS-DOS commands.

Display the Time and Date.

— In UNIX, the date command displays or sets the system date and time. DATE in MS-DOS provides similar functionality.

Calender Command

— UNIX has the cal command which displays a calendar for the specified year, or if a month is specified, a calendar for that month.

— There is no MS-DOS equivalent.

Finding a File

— In UNIX, whereis (filename) searches a list of standard system directories for the filename. If found the full pathname to the file(s) is displayed.

— There is no equivalent MS-DOS command.

Print a File

— In UNIX, lpr is the command. In MS-DOS, it is PRINT.

Print Print Queue Status

— In UNIX, lpq. In MS-DOS, no equivalent.

The next section provides an overview of the major categories of UNIX commands. It also points out where there can be differences or extensions to UNIX provided by different vendors.

2.5.1.   Basic Utilities and Commands

Basic UNIX commands tend to be the same no matter whose version of UNIX you use. Several examples of basic commands were given in the last section. UNIX syntax is actually quite rich and powerful. Many of the features you would expect in an operating system are available. The remainder of this section describes some of the most basic utilities and commands.

2.5.2.   Traditional and New UNIX Editors

Certain editors are universally available with UNIX systems. They form what might be thought of as a lowest common denominator in terms of compatibility. UNIX editors "ed," "ex," and "vi" have a common foundation. The basic line editor in the UNIX system is "ed." Although it has been superseded by "ex" and "vi" for most purposes, "ed" is still used by system utilities such as "sccs" (source code control system).

The "ex" editor is a common line-oriented text editor that is the root of a family of editors including "vi" (the display or visual editor). The no-frills editor "ex" is notable for its very terse user interface. It is commonly used with slow dial-up lines and character-oriented terminals.

Another common editor is "vi." Originally created for Berkeley UNIX, "vi" is a screen-oriented editor. It is suitable for use with higher-speed terminal connections, for example, above 1200 baud.

While these editors might not be considered the most user friendly or comprehensive in existence, they provide a common and somewhat rudimentary capability that, once mastered, applies to all UNIX environments. They are often embedded in shell scripts and like other basic UNIX utilities are key to the upward compatibility of existing software. More sophisticated text editors, word processing, and electronic publication software are available on UNIX. Several provide what is called WYSIWYG (What You See Is What You Get) capability, where what you see on your screen (usually a bit-mapped display graphics device) is identical to what will print on an output device.

New UNIX Editors

UNIX veterans usually opt for either the traditional UNIX editors like vi or emacs, or the editors supplied with desktop tool kits. But there are newer-to-UNIX editors that might be useful to programmers, system administrators, and users dealing with ASCII files.

Editors available from third parties are often supported on numerous platforms and tend to sell that as a benefit for users. Many are available on both MS-DOS and UNIX versions. While the traditional UNIX editors come free with UNIX, these editors can cost anywhere from the low $100s up to $500 list price per copy.

Some of these editors have their origins in other environments. The compatibility they offer with traditional editors from non-UNIX environments may be a real plus for some users who don't want to deal with training issues or the redevelopment of libraries of macros they have developed and working on another non-UNIX system.

Some of the more popular editors include:

Slick Edit from Microedit of Raleigh, NC

Epsilon from Lugaru Software, Pittsburgh, PA

Professional Edit from Buzzwords International, Cape Girardeau, MO

Vedit Plus from Greenview Data Inc. of Ann Arbor, MI

Edix from Emerging Technology Consultants Inc., Boulder, CO

EDT+ from Boston Business Computing Ltd, Andover, MA

nu/TPU from A/Soft Development, Salem, NH

There are no hard and fast rules, but here are some of the things to think about when evaluating editors.

- What systems do they run on? What OS release levels?
- Licensing and pricing terms and conditions
- Quality of implementation of emulation
- Integration with C programming tools
- X-support and speed of X-based interface
- Built-in support for programming languages
- Quality of documentation
- Undo functionality
- Macro language
- Dynamic window resizing and window environment integration in general
- Support, 800#, support hours, BBS available

2.5.3. Programming Tools

Certain compilers, an assembler, a linker, and debuggers are standardized within UNIX. Figure 2.12 shows the flow of a source file through various programming utilities and tools in the UNIX programming environment.

Preprocessors. General-purpose macro preprocessors handle arguments, conditional expressions, arithmetic, file manipulation, and string processing. They are usually invoked by a shell script invoking a compiler and expand certain commands into entire sequences of commands.

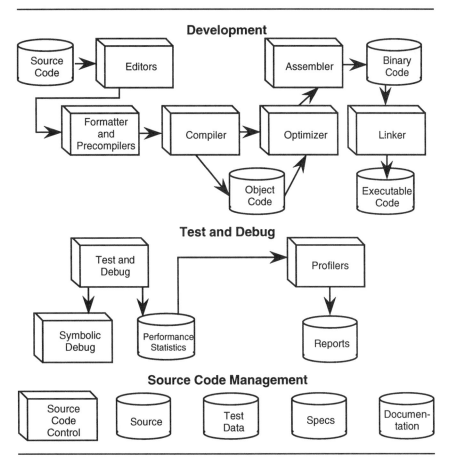

Figure 2.12.   Software development process.

Compilers. Depending on the supplier, various compilers may be bundled with UNIX. The C compiler may be bundled in with the UNIX operating system or offered as an option, as are FORTRAN compilers. Other compilers such as COBOL, Ada, Lisp, or PL/I are not usually provided with the operating system but can be obtained separately for a charge. A compiler accepts a high-level source code file as input and generates the lower-level assembly language for a target processor.

Assemblers. Assembly language is most commonly found in the UNIX kernel where particular machine instructions must be used. An assembler accepts an assembly language source input file and generates a machine language program for a target processor.

Optimizers. Optimizers are usually postprocessing phases of compilers or assemblers that eliminate unnecessary instructions and rearrange a sequence of instructions without changing their intent. This is done to eliminate unnecessary branches or statements and has the effect of decreasing a program's size and potentially increasing its speed.

Linkers. The linker combines compiled files, resolves references to system calls or libraries, and builds the final application program's binary file, which can then be executed.

Debuggers. A debugger is a tool that can be used to monitor and control the execution of a compiled program. This allows the programmer to step through the execution of the program and see each line of source code as it is executed. Such tools aid in finding bugs.

Profilers. When a program is compiled, a profile option can be invoked to trace the operation of the program so that a profile of its execution can be generated. Various utilities can then be used to reduce and analyze the output of special files that are generated when the profiled program is executed. This is commonly done to identify performance bottlenecks that occur when a program is running.

Source Code Management. The UNIX system includes special utilities for managing software. Large programs may consist of hundreds of independent modules, which are combined to create one large program. SCCS is a source code control system historically supplied with BSD-based versions of UNIX, while AT&T System V-based systems historically have RCS. These utilities help track successive versions of a program. Another utility called MAKE is used to automatically recompile modules of a program affected by source code changes.

How software is represented in a computer. There are three ways that software is represented in a computer:

- Source code
- Object code
- Binary code

Source code (of higher-level languages like C and FORTRAN, for example) is written to cross multiple instruction set and operating system combinations through recompilation. The code is the most flexible means of moving applications between systems or system environments, but it does have some drawbacks. Source code written to a specific machine is often more optimized and therefore faster, but such modifications may decrease the compatibility of the source across different architectures. This in turn increases the complexity of software maintenance as well as future development. Source code also suffers from the risk of piracy, which is unacceptable to most companies that consider their source to be proprietary and confidential.

Object code is an intermediary form between binary and source. It requires some additional processing by the user to run, but does not need to be completely recompiled. Performance, compatibility, and copy protection are, again, drawbacks.

Binary code is loaded directly into computer memory and runs without any additional processing or recompiling. Binary code offers the highest level of performance, compatibility, and copy protection. The trade-off is that the code is usually targeted at a specific instruction set, which means the software supplier has to maintain different versions for every machine and operating system combination it wants to support.

Commercial software is usually supplied in binary or object code formats. Programmers work with source code when it is available. The UNIX operating system source code is not usually required, but system administrators may have a need to reconfigure the operating system to add functionality, like special device drivers, or to delete unneeded capabilities.

There is considerable work underway on ABIs (Application Binary Interfaces) and architecture-neutral distribution formats. Application binary interfaces enable software developed for one chip architecture to run on all computer models using that architecture. This leads to the possibility of ISV's packaging their software for UNIX in a manner that is comparable to IBM PC software that runs on clones. An architecture-neutral distribution format defines a common format in which software is physically manufactured independent of any particular vendor or architecture.

2.5.4. Filters

The UNIX command set is a well-integrated tool for working on byte stream files. Filters and pipes provide excellent flexibility for working with files that contain ASCII text.

Many UNIX utilities can be classified as filters. Filters read standard input, transform the input data in some way, and then write the transformed data out as standard output. Filters perform relatively simple types of operations and can be used individually or in combination to create complex functions or utilities.

The most common UNIX filters are grep, sed, awk, and sort. While these names (except for the last) sound obscure, the functions they perform usually have equivalents in other operating systems.

The grep filter is used for pattern matching. It is commonly used to match a pattern supplied by the user with the lines of one or more files. This function can be used to find a file containing the specified pattern (like a name or phrase). It is commonly used to locate a file whose name or location has been forgotten but whose contents are still partially known.

Sed, which stands for "stream editor," is a filter that applies a set of editor commands to the lines in one or more files. This is a shortcut for using the functionality of UNIX editors instead of having to build some specific application program to perform a specific function. The sed filter is a time saver in situations where editing operations need to be done repeatedly over a set of files.

Awk was designed for the fast production of code for simple tasks. The awk language derives its name from the last names of its creators, Al Aho, Peter Weinberger, and Brian Kernighan. Awk is a filter, like grep, which can be used for pattern matching and substitution and as a report generator. Having selected a line of a source input file, awk programs specify actions to be taken to operate on fields or variables declared by the user. Awk is usually used instead of writing and compiling programs to make text transformations in data files. Few UNIX users use the full power of tools like awk and sed. This is partly the result of poor documentation. These tools are rarely used in any but the most simple ways by casual users.

Sort is a UNIX filter, and as the name implies, it is used to sort the lines of a file. Various options are provided that allow for the definition of multiple fields or specific bytes within fields on which sorting should be based. Sort is also able to merge sorted files, optionally eliminating duplicate records.

2.5.5.   Formatters

Formatters are utilities that translate a file containing ordinary text with special embedded commands into formatted documents. Two standard UNIX formatters are nroff and troff. Nroff is for use with line printers, terminals, and daisy wheel impact printers. Troff is for use with typesetters or devices like laser printers that can emulate typesetters.

While native UNIX formatters are widely used, there are several excellent software products commercially available on UNIX such as Interleaf and FRAME. These software products are gaining increased popularity because they offer WYSIWYG (What You See Is What You Get) capability. This means that the user can design documents with sophisticated text and graphics and view the document online exactly the way it will appear on paper once printed.

2.5.6.   Communications and Electronic Mail

UNIX has always implied connectivity, and programs for UNIX-to-UNIX communication are part of the base system. UNIX normally comes with email as a utility. Although it is common to have your UNIX machine as part of a small network of machines, few people want to pass up the opportunity to connect to "the net," or USENET. Electronic mail and NetNews are commonly used by the casual and the professional user alike. NetNews is the largest electronic news organization in the world, the UNIX market's equivalent to the Bulletin Board System (BBS).

UNIX includes utilities for sending and receiving electronic messages to users in a UNIX network. There are several types of UNIX networks. They can be private, for example, restricted to UNIX systems in a given company, or public, meaning available to anyone.

The UNIX network is called USENET and other networks such as CSNET and ARPANET are examples of these public networks. USENET is an informal organization that comprises the largest worldwide network of computers. Thousands of machines of all types connect over a million users. USENET is a distributed network, as opposed to other networks such as BIX or CompuServe. The USENET network consists of backbone sites for collecting and forwarding messages to other regions. Branch sites cascade information to other branch and leaf sites. NetNews and USENET have been adopted by Bell Labs, HP, DEC, IBM, NCR, Motorola, Unisys, Sun, and many other companies and institutions of industry and education around the world.

In 1987, the USENIX organization funded the first public UUNET site. New UNIX systems can now subscribe to the network service from this single site for a fixed monthly fee. (See Section 8.9 for details on how to get "plugged into" USENET and UUNET.)

The UNIX MAIL utility provides a simple mechanism for users to send and receive mail in a UNIX network. Each user has a mailbox where messages are stored.

USENET is a voluntary cooperative network implemented with dial-up telephone lines. A transfer program called UUCP (UNIX to UNIX Copy) is used to transfer data across telephone connections. Each node in the USENET network maintains a list of nearby sites to which it periodically agrees to transfer data.

UUCP-Net and its subnet USENET are composed of a large, loosely knit group of machines that voluntarily call each other and transfer data on an ad hoc basis. UUCP-Net is used mostly to pass electronic mail (email) messages back and forth. USENET consists of "newsgroups" that essentially make up an electronic bulletin board that is passed around from machine to machine. This type of information, known as NEWS, is transferred via USENET. NEWS is similar to an electronic bulletin board and carries, for example, articles organized into one of over 200 different groups. NEWS moves through the network the same way mail does.

UUNET was started by the USENIX user group. The basic idea behind it is that it is a nonprofit communications service designed to provide access to USENET news, UUCP mail, ARPANET mail, and various source archives at low cost through volume discounts.

Machine-to-machine file transfer is made possible by the UNIX "ftp" facility, a program that facilitates the transfer of files between systems by making the computer on which it is executed emulate (or look like) a terminal to another computer. UNIX also contains a program called "tip," which provides a terminal emulation capability.

2.5.7.   Other UNIX Utilities

Depending on the version or variant of UNIX, the operating system environment will be supplied with different bundled utilities. Systems vendors and independent software suppliers provide many other utilities for a price.

We expect to see several major software companies begin to address the UNIX market as the number of UNIX variants diminishes. These companies will offer software applications that embed typical system utilities. For example, many data management software packages include functionality for database backup.

2.5.8.   The UNIX Software Development Environment

From history, we know that UNIX was originally designed by and for software developers. It flourished in universities and research establishments because it supported a rich, simple environment for software development. One of the key benefits associated with UNIX is the portability of software largely made possible by the software development environment. Early versions of UNIX were shipped with free compilers for what, at the time, were new languages like C and PASCAL. Suffice it to say that the UNIX software environment has been one of the reasons for its success in the past, and this will likely continue into the future. Difficult problems are difficult on any platform. UNIX offers more tools with which to tackle them.

The software engineering environment—one of the key strengths of UNIX. In the last decade, much attention has been focused on the process of software engineering. There is a large and growing market for software development tools and productivity aids. Today, there are power tools for programmers. There are discrete tools, like third-generation languages (FORTRAN, COBOL, C), fourth-generation languages (FOCUS, NOMAD, etc.), software design, analysis and specification tools, source code management tools, project management tools, and so forth. There are integrated tool kits called software developer workbenches. These provide a set of tools with a common underlying mechanism that enables the tools to work together, sharing information and passing control from one to the other. Often, these integrated tool kits adhere to a methodology for modeling software at a higher level of abstraction, for example, entity relationship diagrams or process flow diagrams. Tools for software development, whether discrete or integrated, tend to address specific problems inherent to parts of the software or system life cycle. Figure 2.13 shows various phases in the software development life cycle. Also shown are tools typically provided as a standard part of the UNIX system. There are also several tools provided by third-party software companies, as shown under the phase of the life cycle to which they apply.

Many experts feel that there will be a shift in emphasis away from traditional languages. New technologies will be developed to address the unique needs of the design and prototyping activities at the beginning of the cycle and the maintenance and re-engineering of code at the end of the cycle. Powerful design and analysis tools will be used for structured design of both databases and process flow. Design information, coupled with standard sequences of code, will be used to generate

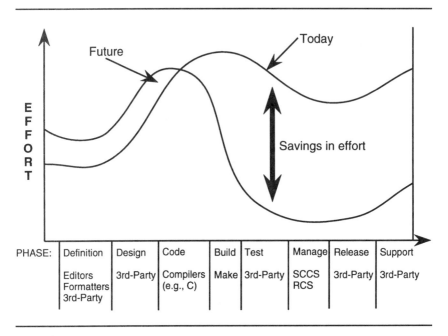

PHASE:	Definition	Design	Code	Build	Test	Manage	Release	Support
	Editors Formatters 3rd-Party	3rd-Party	Compilers (e.g., C)	Make	3rd-Party	SCCS RCS	3rd-Party	3rd-Party

Figure 2.13. Software development life cycle and UNIX tools. Modern development tools will require additional effort in definition and design phases but will offer great savings downstream in terms of higher-quality reusable code.

large portions of code automatically. Concurrently, new tools are now emerging that can be used to re-engineer old code. Primarily targeted at programmers who spend most of their time maintaining code, these tools aid in analyzing source code and abstracting from it higher-level process information. This high-level information can then be changed and new code automatically regenerated from it.

Shell scripts and other basic commands and utilities in UNIX provide tools and an environment for rapid prototyping. This is especially the case for both technical and system software development today and will likely be the case for other commercially oriented software development in the near future.

Part of the base definition of the UNIX standard is formed by the UNIX libraries. These are essential in facilitating software portability between UNIX variants. UNIX system libraries are included in the operating system. The UNIX shell, as earlier described, actually translates commands entered by the user, or read from a shell script file, and makes the appropriate calls to the UNIX system libraries. The user interacts with the UNIX shell, which in turn interacts with the operating system.

A programmer can also call routines in the UNIX system library. UNIX system libraries are composed of several libraries that handle a number of diverse functions such as math calculations, file and device I/O, terminal control, and so forth.

2.5.9. UNIX and Software Languages—from C to C++

The C programming language is the undisputed champion of both UNIX and PC-application development today. C++ is the object-oriented programming language extension of C and is one of the hottest new markets in the software industry.

Object-oriented technology has come out of years of work in academia that predates UNIX. C++ was developed to address the oldest problems in programming—code reuse and management of change.

The concept is that a programmer can create a program that can then be reused by other programmers in the same way software libraries used to be designed and used. Similarly, software that called these subroutine libraries could be recompiled and relinked to take advantage of enhancements, bugfixes, or other changes, C++ programs can be developed so that changes can be localized and controlled and extensions do not make the system too complex to maintain.

In traditional languages like C, Fortran, and Pascal, procedures and functions are written to manipulate data and calculate some result for example. In object-oriented programming such as C++, classes are first defined to represent the underlying abstract types. Each class is comprised of an associated set of operations (like procedures) and functions that characterize the behavior of the subject type.

Objects are what C++ makes more usable than non-object-oriented programming approaches. Once the developer has created a particular component or class, it is easy to use it in other applications by understanding the interface (not necessarily the internals).

The push to object-oriented programming is coming from the need to be able to program for multiple hardware platforms, multiple graphical user interface environments, and multiple network interfaces. This creates a need for very disciplined software development practices so that code is portable, maintainable, and more generic in terms of functionality that can be used across all the combinations of platforms and lower-level software technology.

C++ is now being used extensively in the commercial software industry. It can be most useful in creating programs that take advantage of graphical user interfaces. Large companies are also using C++ extensively. C++ compiler technology and programming environments are popular on MS-DOS and Windows-based PC's as well as UNIX. Borland, Symantec, Microsoft, Lucid, and others offer C++ compilers. Many system vendors also offer C++ compilers.

UNIX history is repeating itself. C++ represents a new paradigm of programming and yet a logical way to transition from C (and other languages today) to C++ or other object programming environments in the future. Many UNIX operating systems are being reimplented in whole or in part with C++. We will see the object-oriented approach catch on and accelerate as new tools become available. UNIX is helping to drive rapid innovation in this area.

2.5.10.   UNIX and Cross-Development

Cross-development includes the porting of code and the development of embedded systems applications. UNIX is being used extensively for software engineering both in cases where UNIX is the target operating system for the application being developed and also where the application will ultimately be deployed on some other type of operating system of almost any kind.

Sophisticated software engineering environments on UNIX can be used to significantly aid in the software development process independent of the target platform.

In cross-development, in addition to the normal code construction and debugging tools, it is helpful to also have code compression that analyzes and provides information about the architecture of the code being converted, and prototyping that aids design and allows unit testing.

With code comprehension, developers don't have to rely only on design documents that are often outdated or nonexistent, or from reading the source code itself.

Rapid prototyping gives programmers a mechanism for implementing and testing proposed changes to code structure and logic. Edit and test cycles can be improved, allowing for testing at the component level before incorporating these changes on application basis.

The movement to C++ and advanced programming tools. According to primary market research conducted by Lucid, 60 percent of all users of C are estimated to now be using C++. Twenty percent are still using C only, and 20 percent are estimated to be using C++ only. So what is behind the rapid movement to C++?

The complexity of C++ increases the need for advanced programming tools. However, programmers tend to adopt new tools relatively slowly. Advanced tools need to fit in with the programmers' environment rather than imposing a new methodology.

As applications themselves become larger and complex, there is a need for advanced programming systems that allow the developer to work more productively with their existing standalone tools. The past few years have seen the advent of software technology to address the requirements of advanced programming environments.

Computer-aided programming (CAP) tools automate the routine programming tasks and allow developers to focus more on complex aspects of software development and less on managing the tools being used. These CAP tools differ from CASE in that the latter focuses on the analysis and design portion of the software life cyle, while CAP focuses specifically on programming tasks.

CAP focuses on the back end of the life cyle. They speed up the critical coding activities, the iterative edit-compile-debug-get information loop in the third-generation language environment. The focus on CAP systems is on tasks that include editing source code, building executable programs, debugging the program, and enhancing the software. CAP systems usually include best-in-class implementation tools (e.g., incremental compilers and linkers, editors, debuggers) to accomplish the core tasks while providing robust program information through browsing and graphing utilities. The use of tightly integrated tools that access a common base of fine-grained program information gives the user a task-driven toolset that focuses on the problem being solved rather than on the tools being used. CAP systems are available today from workstation and UNIX software vendors including Lucid, HP, and Sun's subsidiary SunPro.

2.5.11. UNIX Desktop Environments

The Desktop environment is a collection of utilities that are supported within a common graphical user interface environment. When comparing UNIX variants, don't forget to examine the types of desktop utilities that come built in. These include but are not limited to the following:

- Electronic mail
- Text editors

- Calculator tools
- Clock(s)
- Work group-oriented calendar and scheduling tools
- Print tools
- Multilevel, context-sensitive help facilities
- Performance meter(s) and profiling tools
- File manager
- Audio tools
- ICON editing utilities
- Tape archival and restore tools
- Screen saver(s)
- Screen image capture tools
- Games and demonstrations that show features

What to look for in desktop utilities

Electronic Mail. Look for how the environment can be customized. Facilities to store mail in folders for easy categorization and subsequent retrieval should be provided. How the email system is integrated with other desktop utilities—for example, supporting a drag and drop metaphor is an important ease-of-use consideration. A notification system should be provided that tells you when new mail has been received. Email systems differ in terms of the types of media that can mailed or included in mail. Binary files, audio, image, and documents in native binary file formats should all be capable of being transmitted and received. Finally, the adherance of the mail system to standards should be carefully investigated.

File Manager. File manager functionality should allow complete file system navigation and browsing. It should be able to launch applications. It should feature a graphical user interface and be capable of displaying file types and file system hierarchy graphically. A find facility should be included.

2.6. THE UNIX FILE SYSTEM

The UNIX file system is a simple hierarchical file system. It is different from other file systems in that it treats all files as consisting of a string of bytes. Managing the growth of files dynamically, it supports basic protection mechanisms to control users' access to the system or their ability to manipulate files. Peripheral devices look like any other type of file to the UNIX operating system. In other operating systems, there are usually many different file types, which add to their complexity.

UNIX commands and utilities may be used in conjunction with peripheral devices in a powerful and elegantly simple way without requiring additional, specially written software.

Many of the features of the UNIX file system were unique when UNIX was first developed. Over time, certain of these features were adopted by other operating systems. If much of this discussion seems familiar, it may not be coincidental.

The UNIX file system provides the means of organizing a hierarchical file structure. UNIX files are allocated dynamically. This frees the user from having to plan ahead how large files must grow and, therefore, how much disk space to allocate for them. UNIX files have no specific fixed internal structure. They are simply a string of bytes. UNIX does not structure files, except for directories, with any special formats. This allows all file-related utilities to be used on all files.

UNIX allows all devices to be read from or written to in the same way as ordinary disk files. This allows the redirection of input or output to and from any device as though it were a disk file.

UNIX files are organized into directories. Directory files contain a list of files (and directory names) that are contained in the directory, pathnames, and file information used to manage the operations on the directory. This information consists of owner data, security information such as who has access rights, creation date, date last modified, and date last accessed.

The following is a list of certain characteristics or limitations that exist in different versions of UNIX file system implementations:

Max size of a file

Max size of a file system or directory

Ability for files to span physical disks

File system's ability to span disks

Max number of characters in a file name

Max number of files in a file system

Max depth of nesting directories

2.7.   SINGLE AND MULTIUSER SYSTEM OPERATION

UNIX has been designed, since its inception, as an operating system to support programming groups. Thus, it is inherently a multiuser operating system. UNIX can support from one to several hundred simultaneous users depending on the underlying hardware that is being used. Several multiuser features have been built into UNIX.

A UNIX user can execute multiple programs concurrently. Multiple users are supported through concurrent execution of multiple programs. When a group of users intends to share a system, UNIX system security provides a password protection scheme to control file access. User passwords can be used to control access to the system when users log in.

UNIX system utilities manage access to shared devices such as printers, tape drives, or plotters. System administration utilities for system maintenance and administration, such as backup and recovery, are also provided, as are basic system accounting utilities. Commands are available to status a system and see exactly who is running what on the system.

2.8. SYSTEM ADMINISTRATION

System administration is a topic that should be of special interest to management. This section explains why you may need a UNIX system administrator and describes the system administrator's role and functions, particularly in a UNIX-based system.

A UNIX superuser is a user with special privileges granted if he or she supplies the correct password when logging into the system. The superuser is the overlord and master of the system and is able to perform functions ordinary users—no matter how smart they are—can't. A superuser is the only user allowed by UNIX to perform the following types of functions:

Backing up and restoring system files

Editing sensitive files, like the kernel configuration file or password files

Changing permissions for directories or files

Adding, modifying, or deleting users of the system

A system administrator is a superuser from time to time, but there could be other individuals with superuser access in an installation—for example, the system programming staff. The system administrator's responsibility is simply to keep the system (and all the attached equipment) running smoothly. But the UNIX system administrator also tends to be the "guru" who understands all the UNIX commands and utilities and how they interact with each other. When something goes wrong, the system administrator is usually the one to figure things out—to pinpoint where the problem is—and to wear several hats: operator, guru, liaison to vendor, and Mr. Fixit.

The system administrator (or group charged with this responsibility) has a direct impact on the quality of the system for all the system's users. It is an important function, and forward-thinking management will take care to ensure that those responsible for system administration have the proper qualifications.

A representative sampling of the primary UNIX system administration tasks is shown in Table 2.4 as well as how often these tasks are called for. The tasks and frequency will vary depending on the nature of the work performed. The responsibilities of a UNIX system administrator are summarized in the following generic job description:

1. Order and install new hardware and software releases, including acceptance testing for functionality and reliability.
2. Provide training and support to the general user community regarding generic system and application software.
3. Plan and coordinate ongoing system maintenance functions, including posting of DUMP and preventative maintenance.
4. Set up new user accounts and update system files for users' electronic mail and networking.
5. Plan resource and capital equipment requirements to accommodate growth of the organization.
6. Respond to requests for assistance on critical system software projects.
7. Provide direction and assistance to junior members of the staff who perform day-to-day operator support functions.
8. Normally, receive no instructions on routine work and only general instruction on new assignments. Must be capable of coordinating own work within the group with only minor assistance required from management.
9. Establish procedures for users to request services and define key contacts for services. Such services to include: new account setup, planning new machine installation, software installation, file restoration, expediting repairs of broken hardware, answering UNIX questions, software licensing, making available equipment for home use, and ensuring availability of commercial software.

The required qualifications of a senior UNIX system administrator typically include the following:

Computer science or equivalent degree, or equivalent experience as a UNIX system administrator.

Minimum of two years of UNIX system administration experience.

Table 2.4. UNIX system administration tasks.

TASK	FREQUENCY
Install operating system or major software releases	1 or 2 time/yr.
Install bug fixes, new releases and other software patches	As required
Install new hardware	
Major new systems and servers	Infrequently (aided by vendor)
Add-on boards, printers, etc.	As required
New terminals, users	Weekly, monthly
Diagnose and fix problems	As they occur
Maintenance and file system checks	Weekly
Creating new accounts	As required
Allocating disk storage space to users	As required
Maintenance of printers, modems, etc.	Monthly or as required
System Backups	Daily (incremental) Full (weekly)
Programming (and shell script development or maintenance)	Daily/Weekly
Setting up new user accounts or maintenance	Daily/Weekly
Restore files from backups	As required
Network Administration	
Creating UUCP/Dialup accounts	As required
Creating and moving clients partitions around between servers	As required
Arrange other services for users	
Installation of ethernet or TTY drops	As required
Repairs of simple broken hardware	May be required
Installation of application software, license management	As required

Knowledge of software, documentation, and utilities of the UNIX operating system.

C language capability, plus demonstrated ability in writing shell scripts and in performing tasks manually that are normally done using a script.

Excellent written and oral communications skills in interacting with users and vendors, especially under pressure situations.

The UNIX system administrator might be seen as having the knowledge and creativity of the so-called hacker but with one important difference. The system administrator must ensure that the system is maintained at a high level of reliability and with excellent data integrity; the typical hacker is normally not very interested in these mundane "business" issues. A system administrator's creativity is channeled into ensuring that the system continuously meets the needs of its users.

A clear lesson can be learned from the past history of UNIX. UNIX encourages technical innovation. It can be a hacker's or programmer's dream since it makes rapid prototyping of an application easy. However, the system administrator must be perceived by the other technically oriented system users as a value-added function that has a legitimate interest in knowing about everything that is going on in the environment.

Several good books are now available on UNIX system administration. Your system administrator should acquire such reference material as well as specific training from your suppliers as your installation grows.

Finally, a word on incentives for your system administrator. A competent systems administrator is a valuable corporate asset, and you will compete with others inside and outside your company to keep him or her. Worse, you will likely lose people you have brought in and trained at just about the time they become proficient (in a year or two). While there is a an adequate pool of qualified system administrators, you should hire the most senior person you can, who in turn will train new recruits. Other than the "lead" person, systems administrators can be trained on the job, but should not be allowed to put your system at risk while receiving their training. You should plan in advance a career progression for the system administrator because, sooner or later, this vital employee is apt to move on to become a system programmer, application programmer, or manager.

The following list shows typical yearly salary ranges for computer operators, system administrators, and programmers. Significant fluctuations exist depending on job location and local demand. Average salaries are shown in Table 2.5. Salaries tend to be higher in certain locations.

Hiring experienced UNIX programmers and systems administrators is beyond the capability of many companies. A cottage industry of UNIX resellers usually called VARs (Value Added Resellers) exists to

Table 2.5. 1993 U.S. dollar salary ranges. Salary ranges for personnel associated with development and operations.

Operator	$18K to 40K
Entry-level system administrator	$24K to 45K
Senior system administer	$35K to 65K+
Entry-level C programmer	$28K to 60K+
Senior C programmer	$40K to 90K+
Network administrator	$35K to 90K
Combined system/network administrator	$50K to 90K+

help small customers get their networks set up and their applications installed just as they do with PCs. Even large corporations often turn to outsourcing contracts with integrators to assist them in program managment and project developments involving UNIX.

2.8.1. UNIX System Administration Framework—A Summary

This section provides a list that will be useful in planning analyzing your UNIX system administration framework.

Systems administration considerations shown in Table 2.6 can become sophisticated especially in multiuser environments.

2.9. COMPUTER SYSTEM AND NETWORK SECURITY

Simply defined, computer security is the process, procedures, or tools that ensure that data entered into a computer today will be retrievable at a later time by, and only by, those authorized to do so. The procedures for ensuring security should additionally include systems by which computer system managers will be notified of attempts to penetrating security. Security is violated when some person or persons succeeds in retrieving data without authorization. Security is breached when the subverter manages to destroy or alter data belonging to others, making retrieval of the original data impossible.

Although a substantial effort has been spent in academic and computer research communities exploring issues of computer security, little of what is understood has been put into practice on a wide scale. Computers are not inherently insecure, but there is a great temptation

Table 2.6.   UNIX system administration considerations.

1.0   Application Support
    1.1   Hardware Requirements
        1.1.1 Systems Configuration(s)
            — Processor Architecture
            — System model/type
            — System function
            — Operating System (release levels)
            — Power requirements (type)
            — Memory
            — Swap space
        1.1.2 Disk Storage
            — Controller(s) and type(s)
            — Capacity
            — Partitioning
            — Mirroring
        1.1.3 Network
            — 10 Base T
            — Leased lines
            — Bisync connections
            — Ethernet
            — Fiber Optic (backbone)
    1.2   Peripherals
        1.2.1 Printers
            — Number and type
        1.2.2 Modems
            — Number and type
        1.2.3 Other
            — Backup devices
            — Plotters
            — Computer output microfilm
            — CD-ROM for software
    1.3   Clients supported
        1.3.1 Diskless
        1.3.2 Dataless
        1.3.3 Datafull
        1.3.4 Terminal concentrators or terminal servers
2.0   Software Requirements
    2.1   System Software
        2.1.1 Operating system release level(s)
        2.1.2 Other required system software

Continues

Table 2.6.   *Continued*

2.2   Application Software
    2.2.1 Title/description/release level(s)
    2.2.2 File size requirements
    2.2.3 Directory location
    2.2.4 Compatibility issues
       — Operating system releases
       — other
2.3   Database Software
    2.3.1 Title/description/release level(s)
    2.3.2 Database size
    2.3.3 Partition requirements
    2.3.4 Backup
2.4   Acquired Software
    2.4.1 Support agreement from vendor
    2.4.2 Response time from vendor
    2.4.3 Bug list availability
    2.4.4 Escalation process for bugs
    2.4.5 Source
    2.4.6 Documentation
    2.4.7 Maintenance release schedule
    2.4.8 Vendor upgrade/testing processor
3.0   Operations
  3.1   Job Control
    3.1.1 Job Scheduling
       — Description of scheduled jobs
       — Frequency/Dependencies
       — Run time requirements for jobs
       — Other requirements
    3.1.2 Job Accounting
    3.1.3 Activity reporting and logging
  3.2   Backup Requirements
    3.2.1 Backups
    3.2.2 File restores
  3.3   Resource Usage
    3.3.1 Frequency of backups
    3.3.2 Tape volume management
    3.3.3 Print queue management
  3.4   Daily operations
  3.5   Database Tools
  3.6   Disaster and Recovery

Table 2.6.   *Continued*

to build and run computers with lax security procedures, since this often results in simpler, faster, and friendlier operation.

When a computer system is intended for use by many people, the operating system must distinguish between users to prevent them from interfering with each other. For example, multiuser operating systems should not allow one user to delete the files belonging to another user unless the files' owner gives explicit permission to do so. Most operating systems require that a user enter both the account name and a "password" in order to use the account. Account names are generally public knowledge, while the passwords are secret.

Most medium to large computers support a multiuser operation and provide access to private or public data networks. Data stored in computers and on computer networks is accessible to anyone who has access to these networks.

UNIX was originally designed with system security in mind, and the UNIX system administrator can establish how secure, on the one hand, or how open, on the other, the system will be. In UNIX, a balance has to be struck between a totally secure computer environment and one that permits, and even encourages, users to share data. With the introduction of networked computing, UNIX system security is best illustrated in a hierarchical arrangement:

Network management

System management/administration

System operations

System programmers

Application programmers

Users

The federal government is one of the key driving forces behind computer security and through its procurement process is helping to drive the state of the art regarding secure UNIX implementations. Another driving force is concern about the loss of data, data integrity, and computer time caused by breaches in system security.

UNIX's historical weakness in the area of system security is a serious issue. The next section discusses the infamous invasion of the Internet Network by a young programmer. UNIX is not the only operating system that is susceptible to attack. All computer systems are susceptible to some extent. What is interesting in the story of the computer worm is that the problem was simultaneously investigated by a very large number of specialists all competing to be the first to make the discovery. Once isolated, the problem was quickly fixed, and changes were incorporated in the basic software to prevent a recurrence. UNIX system administrators implemented the fixes published over the same networks that the virus had itself spread over.

"UNIX security" was considered an oxymoron until recently. Because security was not a concern for early UNIX developers, adding security features beyond the basic file protection schemes has required extensive modifications to the operating system. It is well known that skilled, persistent UNIX practitioners can transgress the protection of most carefully designed systems. Earlier versions of UNIX had more security gaps than designers cared to admit, but over the years, many, although not all, of these have been closed. Since vendors have built security into their systems in different ways, an uneven situation exists regarding the protection levels and security features of different UNIX versions.

The famous Internet worm that caused a stir in late 1989 exploited bugs in the mail system and a C library routing. These problems had existed for many years, and only after the Internet experience were protection levels upgraded from previously lax security and administrative practices for systems on the Internet.

In the last few years, there has been a dramatic expansion of UNIX installations and a corresponding heightened awareness of system vulnerabilities. Significant changes to security provisions have been made to most UNIX products. In addition to bug fixes and security-related enhancements, versions of UNIX are now provided by system vendors that address the requirements of the NCSC (National Computer Security Council). The sophisticated security features offered include:

Discretionary Access Control—allows users to determine who has access to data files and the type of access granted for each type of user.

Identification and Authentication—gives all users unique login names and passwords, and users' actions are tracked and, recorded by the system.

Administrative Controls—requires system administrators to progress through a set of levels, permitting increasing privileged access, which can also be restricted to designated system consoles.

Audit Trails—records each command initiated, by a user for future review.

Restricted environment—imposes only a subset of commands and other limitations for special situations where users do not need access to total system facilities.

There are many other services available that reflect the increasing commitment to security.

2.9.1. The Story of the Computer Worm

On Wednesday night, November 2, 1988, the Internet Network was attacked by a software program that exploited weaknesses in the UNIX BSD (and derivative) systems. The Internet Network is a collection of unclassified research and defense networks, including ARPANET, MILNET, and NSFnet. It is a government-sponsored network that allows various military, government, educational, and research organizations to communicate with each other and share information.

Security loopholes in the UNIX operating system environment allowed the worm program to enter and replicate itself, effectively taking over the control of the system by "glutting up" the file system and running so many copies of itself that the processor couldn't do anything else.

This story was widely reported in the press. A computer virus had attacked these networks, causing systems to stop working. Technically, it wasn't a virus but a worm. The difference is this: a "virus" is a program that replicates itself by exploiting weaknesses in the operating system by adding itself to other programs, including the operating system itself. It requires a "host" to live on. When the host is activated, so too is the virus, analogous to the biological virus. The virus invades host cells (programs) and takes over, making these programs generate more viruses.

On the other hand, a "worm" doesn't destroy any data or program. Instead, it only impairs (or kills) the performance of the machine it attacks by running an excessive number of jobs or by using all of the available resources of one sort or another. A worm can run by itself and propagate a fully working version of itself onto other machines. A worm typically triggers a system to run so many processes that it will eat up all available disk space or processor cycles of memory or whatever other resource it attacks.

In the November 1988 episode, hundreds of machines at major universities and laboratories were attacked by the Internet worm, including Lawrence Livermore National Labs, Digital Equipment Corporation, and numerous universities.

Once the worm was isolated, a "swat" team from Berkeley, MIT, and Purdue investigated the problem to learn more about the worm code. They quickly disassembled it and were able to determine how it worked and how a patch could be devised to kill it and prevent reinfestation.

The Internet worm was designed by a 23-year-old doctoral candidate at Cornell, Robert Tappan Morris. His father, ironically, is head of the National Computer Security Center, the NSA's public effort in computer security. His father has lectured widely on security aspects of UNIX, and, surely, this will give him subject matter closer to home to talk about in the future. Associates of the student claimed that the worm was a "mistake"—that he had intended to unleash it, but that it was not supposed to move so quickly or spread so widely. The worm, however, proved incredibly virulent, attempting to introduce itself to every system it could find. It was only able to infect VAXes and Suns running Berkeley UNIX simply because that was all it was programmed to attack.

You knew it had hit you when you could see hundreds of jobs running in your system and the system was no longer responding properly.

The worm spread rapidly over the MILNET and reached over 10 sites across the country in a matter of three to four hours.

The worm was a program that used a hole in the UNIX "sendmail" utility. From a distant host, a message was sent to start up an editor. A 99-line C program was sent through the mail. The distant host then sent a command to compile this C program. The program started looking to replicate itself by searching for other system addresses, and once it found another host, it replicated itself and the process started all over again. The worm "forked" copies of itself as it spread, and the load on the infected machines skyrocketed.

The worm was successful in finding its way into other systems by taking educated guesses about passwords. Unfortunately, most people don't choose passwords very well. Once the worm got into someone's account, the process started over again. Within a matter of days, the worm was fully understood and eradicated, and the fix was transmitted across electronic mail. Knowing the security loopholes that allowed the worm into their systems, most installations and vendors took precautions to prevent any reinfestation, and the vendors who supply operating systems took steps to ensure that the loopholes were closed in their next operating system release.

Not all UNIX machines were hit by this worm. Berkeley UNIX 4.2 and 4.3 systems seemed to be the only ones that were infected. Almost all operating systems have flaws and can be attacked. Secure versions of the UNIX operating systems were not infected, but most nonmilitary systems don't require the level of security provided by B1 as defined by the NSA.

During the summer of 1990, Robert Tappan Morris was indicted and convicted of felony trespass—unauthorized computer access. In May, he was put on three years' probation, ordered to perform 400 hours of community service, and fined an inconsequential amount of money. In his defense, Morris contested that once he had released the worm, he had no contact with it and couldn't control it. As reported in MIS World, July 8, 1990, the Morris' trial became the trial of an entire generation and philosophy of computers and information. Some security experts, friends and associates of Robert's father, said that his son's experiment was a harmless and overdue warning of gross gaps in computer security, and they argued that the son should be cheered, not convicted. "If Morris had wanted to do damage, there would have been nothing left ... all the computers would have gone up in smoke," some suggested.

Historically, UNIX has come out of R&D organizations with administratively lax security. Unfortunately, this practice has continued as UNIX has gained in popularity. UNIX is fundamentally no less secure than most operating systems if administered properly. Most operating systems arrive from the vendor highly secured, and the system administrator or user must relax the security as deemed necessary. UNIX, on the other hand, generally arrives "wide open" and must be tightened up administratively.

The Internet (and networks in general) has also opened new holes in system and network security. Any network is only as secure as its weakest link. One node on a network with a security problem leaves the entire network open to problems.

Software written for UNIX is sometimes not secure in its own right. In the future, we will see much more offered in the way of software tools and applications to further improve the security and system administration of UNIX systems and networks.

2.10. APPLICATIONS

"The myth of the frontier in the United States is very strong. In some sense we've had a succession of operating systems and the new operating systems represented opening up new territories. However, the frontier for another operating system is closed. If we're the cowboys, it's time for the farmers and the ranchers to move in—the people growing the applications."

—Bill Joy, Sun Microsystems

An application refers here to a computer program that provides some special function above and beyond the capabilities of the operating system. Applications come from one of several sources. They can be supplied by the system vendor, they may be acquired from independent software suppliers, or they may be developed by users. Applications generally refer to programs that will be invoked by the UNIX shell but may operate independently of it. Examples of applications software include spreadsheet programs, electronic publications software, accounting software, and so forth. UNIX applications are quite independent of UNIX itself. Different system vendors may offer different applications with their systems.

UNIX systems are often selected first on the basis of availability of applications that run on the specific version. For this reason, evaluating the applications available on a UNIX system platform is often one of the more important considerations faced by the user or manager of the system. This will depend on whether the user is writing the application or buying it, or both.

Section 4.3.5 describes the evolution of applications running on UNIX.

Subsequent sections in Chapter 4 describe applications in technical, commercial, and other markets. Chapter 5 describes some state-of-the-art applications, including distributed data management and imaging applications. Chapter 6 provides an overview of application's portability considerations. Finally, Section 7.4 provides pointers to some of the best sources of information on finding the applications you're looking for.

2.11. FURTHER EVOLUTION OF UNIX OPERATING SYSTEMS

UNIX is an operating system that has been developed with a special philosophy that makes it fundamentally different from other operating systems. It was designed for portability of the operating system itself and of the applications software that runs on top of it. This is in contrast to proprietary operating systems that run only on certain computers, such as OS/2 running on the Intel-based IBM PS/2.

The hierarchical file system and the lack of file structure and sizing mean that no special tools for reading special files with special structures exist—just simple sequential files. This is fundamental to the unification of file, device, and interprocess I/O supported by UNIX. The dominant file type is text. Once you have an editor, you can edit everything!

There is considerable power in the flexibility offered by the UNIX user interface via shells, which can be tailored by the user or replaced altogether. The shell provides rudimentary control structures and parameter passing and can be used instead of a higher-level programming language.

Commands and utilities in UNIX are simple and consistent, since they were programmed originally with the assumption that the output of one program might be used as input to another. UNIX was originally designed to be simple and small, so that even the kernel could be read and understood in its entirety by a single programmer. While other operating systems offer similar levels of functionality, UNIX is unique in terms of its simplicity, the philosophy on which it was built and with which it functions, and its openness and availability on a wide spectrum of computers and computer architectures.

UNIX will continue to evolve. In three to five years, the kernels of most UNIX systems will be restructured. All the facilities available in kernel mode will be available in user mode. Concurrency and multiprocessing extensions will be added, and the operating system itself will be implemented in a C++ object-oriented form. Finally, UNIX developments will address more of the issues of interoperability within network environments and will provide better support of distributed programs.

Beyond UNIX. During the 1990 UK UNIX User Group's summer conference in London, Dennis Ritchie, Ken Thompson, Rob Pike, and Brian Kernighan revealed the development of a new system named "Plan 9 from Bell Labs" after the 1950s cult science fiction film *Plan 9 from Outer Space.* Plan 9, which they claim is "culturally compatible" with UNIX but makes no attempt to follow standards, is a distributed system that focuses on file servers and intelligent terminals instead of workstations in local area networks. Although the system is highly portable, there appear to be no plans from AT&T to ship the system at the present time.

These UNIX pioneers condemned a number of trends that are currently transforming the UNIX industry in the commercial world. The natural desire of systems programmers to have free access to the source code for "hacking" purposes aside, in his keynote speech, Pike pointed to the X Windows standard that had been forced to develop too quickly due to commercial pressure, negating the possibility of a more technically elegant solution.

With its healthy disregard for standards, the Plan 9 system is unlikely to be offered as a commercial venture for the present at least, and, like UNIX itself, it might have to gather support in the academic community before it is taken seriously elsewhere. Papers on Plan 9 have been published in the UK UNIX User Group Conference Proceedings, available from the UKUUG Secretariat, Owles Hall, Buntingford, Herts, SG9 9LP, UK.

2.12.   Managing Change in Technology

The unrelenting nature of competition in a free market guarantees we will continue to see major changes in technology. These changes are driven by and will also drive changes in the way computers and information are used in business and in our personal lives.

Maintaining an awareness of significant technological change is extremely difficult. We believe service companies will spring up to provide the industry with informational "new bites" to help stay on top of all the change. It requires dedicated staff in market research and competitive analysis, and it requires tremendous expertise to spot significant technology as it germinates. This summary section outlines what we believe are the key UNIX and Open System technology areas. In each of these areas, it is possible to anticipate change by examining the nature of "technology creep" and the natural processes of product introduction on the supply side of the market.

Migration of Core Technologies. The most important new technologies are in the following areas:

Multiprocessing (hardware innovation in cluster computing)

Object-oriented programming (innovation in application development)

Microkernel architectures to support object-oriented applications (innovation in operating systems to support applications)

If the technology is object oriented, you can expect to see it appear first in compilers technology. Next it will appear in the operating system platform, then in other programming tools and environments—debuggers and system libraries, then in the utilities and tools surrounding the operating system, and finally in application software.

The Supply Side and Migration. History has demonstrated that new technology matures over time. Nobody wants to move to a new unproven technology if they are going to put their business at risk. Suppliers recognize the need to carefully manage the introduction of new technologies not only to preserve their relationship with existing customers but also for self-serving economic reasons. After all, suppliers are usually in business to turn a profit.

Our best advice in managing change in technology is to recognize that the press' job is to find and make the news. They have to speculate on future trends. Suppliers also tend to preannounce everything today. What you get is a lot of frenzy in the press and from market analysts that is often ahead of itself.

In the world of operating systems, the wheels of progress turn more slowly that you might think. Having taken years to develop, new operating systems remain lifeless until applications exist. People must learn to use the applications and the operating systems through documentation and training and experience—all of which take time and resources. This coupled with the delays common in developing applications for operating systems means that ordinary users often own and use operating system technology that is 10 to 20 years old.

Demand Side and Migration. As should be clear by now, the pace of innovation that is supply-side driven will not abate any time soon. Users will have become more adept at managing change associated with product migration. Even the staging of simple operating system upgrades will become a costly process if not approached professionally. UNIX and Open

Systems will give users a lot of flexibility at the time things are purchased, but they will require customers to stay on top of how they integrate new technology especially into their networked system environments. Customers and/or their systems/network administrators will have to learn to live with migration issues such as the following:

- Retraining users and systems/network administrators
- Application modification and recompilation
- Conversion of device drivers (if they have implemented any themselves)
- Conversion of kernel interfaces (if they deviate from using standard APIs)
- Conversion of windowing system and overall operating system environment files that are normally localized by corporations or individuals
- Addition of new libraries
- Testing and converting where necessary shell scripts
- Change of file system pathnames for new file system layouts (if required)
- Convert files to new filesystems (on time—if required)
- Check compatibility and/or licensing issues for application or any add-on software
- Identify and work on selected areas for performance optimizations

The list above is by no means unique to UNIX or Open Systems. However, UNIX differentiates itself by providing more tools for software management and systems administration than most operating systems. This is because customers have more choices for system/network administration tools than just the ones supplied by their operating system vendor.

Pioneers can end up with arrows in their backs. So as you try to stay abreast of the latest technology trends, remember from the time you hear about a future technology or standard, it may be years before the design is complete and implemented, a year before the bugs get shaken out of beta versions of the products, a year before the distribution channel can handle it, and a year before you are ready to go from pilot to production. It's not uncommon that a vendor is out of business, been acquired, or has killed the product you are about to take into production right about the time your pilot phase is over. All of this is not to imply that customers should be overly cautious. Indeed, time-to-production in information technology can translate in time-to-market and other commercial advantages in your business. The main suggestion in looking at areas of technological innovation is to assess the realistic time frames in which this innovation will roll out and to devise strategies for constantly managing changes associated with new releases, product migration as well as the training of the people involved in the change.

Processor Innovation.   *Merchant market microprocessors*. Economics has been a driving force in the evolution of computer processors. Before 1980, the marketing for merchant microprocessors was minimal. The explosive growth of PCs changed that. In the early 1980s, expertise was still concentrated in the proprietary vendor's engineering organizations. By 1985 the merchant market began to catch up. Today, only a few vendors have the resources to compete in microprocessor design. The rate of increase of merchant market processors architectures is higher than that of proprietary solutions because the large semiconductor vendors can bring vastly superior resources to bear in the areas of chip design and process technology, in addition to not being tied to compatibility with older architectures.

New architectures. Competition between CISC and RISC architectures will continue. Major innovation has occurred in RISC architectures, but this does not ensure the demise of CISC designs. There is a huge installed base of CICS processors. RISC will continue to outpace the growth in CISC and in particular in technical (computer-power hungry) markets. In commercial markets, RISC may grow at a lower rate, but given the immense size of the market, RISC will gather market share in commercial comparatively slowly. By no means does this mean that RISC in commercial will not become a more prevelant force in the general commercial market. While RISC processors hold a current performance advantage over CISC, there is a considerable amount of software written for CISC proccessors. CISC is not standing still in terms of development. Intel and other companies are still making serious investments in improving their CISC architectures.

The dominant RISC architecture is Sun's SPARC architecture. It is followed by SGI/MIPS (R4000), Motorola (MC88000 and 88110), Intel (I860 and I960), HP-PA-RISC and IBM's RS/6000.

Operating Systems Innovation. Microkernels will become the norm over the next three to five years. Early microkernels will have to evolve to scale up to the demands that will be placed on them. This is particularly true in terms of interprocess communication and distributed networking technology. It works now for small work groups, but what happens when you expect to distribute objects everywhere over 10,000 nodes in a large corporation?

We will see a classical and fairly predictable "technology creep" as object-oriented technology moves into the operating system itself (it will be programmed in C++), into the utilities of the operating system (indeed the file system will be an object-oriented database), through to the application development frameworks and finally into the application software.

Development Tools Innovation. Software tools that are cheap and easy to use will have become available for UNIX to succeed in the desktop world. Innovation like Pure from Purity Software represents this highly innovative new software that is used to find memory leaks in programs representing a new level of sophistication in the world of UNIX software debugging.

A new set of integrated object-oriented development tools and applications promise to radically change the world of programming. Innovation in object-oriented technology has been principally tied to UNIX. Tools like C++ compilers and development environments, object-oriented database management, and the like have all come out of UNIX. The promise will be realized as the Open development environments deliver on the promise of leaving the options open when it comes to deploying applications. NeXT has proven that a really nice tool for application software development won't sell if it only can be deployed on a limited set of platforms.

Applications Innovation. People don't just want the latest software tool or groupware solution for teleconferencing or whatever. They also need some pretty boring stuff that is available in the PC world. Word processors, spreadsheet packages, and other productivity software is going to be necessary. UNIX solutions don't have to be better than their MS-DOS/Windows counterparts, but they are going to have to coexist with them.

If more PC applications software developers use X Windows, then this could form part of the answer in bridging today's PC world to the new world of open network computing.

The Supply Side of the
UNIX Market

By the time of publication, any book providing a summary of available UNIX products is mostly out of date. It is practically impossible, even for the experts, to keep up with all the technical advancement on the supply side of the UNIX market. As a result, there are several trade magazines, journals, and specialized newletters that help track this dynamic industry (see Chapter 8 for details).

Nonetheless, this chapter provides information about the Open Systems and UNIX strategies of the dominant hardware and software vendors offering products. Emphasis has been given to vendors offering integrated computer hardware and UNIX operating system software. Within this group, the focus is on major computer systems vendors such as IBM, DEC, HP, and Sun, as well as the major operating system providers including Microsoft, SunSoft, Novell, and SCO.

To provide this overview of the supply side of the UNIX industry, we describe key industry players' products and strategies. These companies have the most to gain or lose as the UNIX market realizes its full potential, and they are also the ones that are likely to have the most profound impact on the UNIX market. The data presented here is based on publicly available information.

What is unique about this coverage is that we look at these vendors' UNIX strategies from a historical perspective. We attempt to track vendor commitments and will report situations where vendors announce things and then don't deliver or deliver late. The popular press tends to create an impression that events occur faster than they really do. For example, it could take two years from the time an announcement is made until a vendor finally brings a product to market that is capable of being shipped in volume. The memory of the popular press can also be rather short. In this chapter we also propose a detailed basis for UNIX product comparison as well as a methodology for system evaluation and selection.

3.1. THE NATURE OF CHANGE IN THE UNIX INDUSTRY

As UNIX matures into adulthood, in its mid-twenties, many experts seem to agree it has played a pivotal role in the restructuring that is now taking place in the entire computer industry. Change is occurring in parallel on many levels within the industry.

- UNIX-related mergers and acquisitions are on the increase. UNIX platform vendors are entering the software business with specialized divisions and taking equity stakes in strategic software ventures.
- Hardware vendors continue to increase their emphasis on software and services and integration as competition drives hardware margins lower.
- Vendors build differentiable solutions to meet special problems like security and transaction processing, areas where standards haven't advanced sufficiently, leaving their solutions quasi-proprietary.
- To meet customer needs, consultants and system integration companies provide multivendor bidding and systems integration support.
- The third-party distribution channel becomes a force in the marketplace as retailers and distributors move up-market with UNIX.

3.1.1. Evaluating and Comparing UNIX Solutions

There is a mind-boggling array of products in the UNIX market. It is not an easy job to evaluate and select a system solution consisting of application software, operating system environment, basic and add-on hardware, and so on. Nor is it easy to provide information to assist the various types of consumers. There is quite a difference between the needs of the home computer buyer and those of the institutional purchaser of a complex system costing hundreds of thousands to millions of dollars and supporting dozens to thousands of users. Therefore, we have made the following few assumptions about the reader of this section:

- Thinking of switching from a non-UNIX-based system.
- Interested in the name-brand vendors with commanding market share and offering pre- and post-sales support expertise.
- Would like a simple methodology to cut though all the combinations of vendors and product offerings.

- Probably would like to use UNIX in environments that currently use MS-DOS or traditional minicomputers today, or at a minimum expects UNIX solutions to interoperate with existing PC systems and legacy applications on proprietary computers.

Even if you think we've left you out, you might want to skip to Section 3.6 to see the sort of detailed comparison matrix we recommend for a survey of competitive Open System offerings.

UNIX vendors and customers seem to agree that support is a key factor in system selection. UNIX systems have relatively similar features, but the complexity of UNIX and the huge number of hardware configurations supported, coupled with the trend to configure aggressive systems with large numbers of peripherals, makes quick, effective vendor support a critical buying consideration. It is bad enough when a computer or software company supports only UNIX. It is even more challenging when UNIX is just one of the choices available to the customer.

3.1.2. System Evaluation and Selection

Entire books have been devoted to this subject. Consequently, it is not our goal to delve too deeply into the subject. Rather, we briefly address the issues users often face when they find themselves in organizations that are locked into computer systems and/or purchasing agreements with specific vendors.

There is too much going on in the market for even informed buyers to continue to conduct business as usual. UNIX is opening some significant new possibilities for companies that incorporate it correctly in their information technology strategies. Not all of the points of comparison suggested in Section 3.6 are necessarily relevant to every user's particular interests. Besides the operating system, there are many considerations in system selection, including for example:

- Processing power and speed
- Availability of application and system software
- Performance (e.g., overall throughput)
- System and data integrity and security
- Price
- Ease-of-use features
- Networking capabilities
- Support
- Serviceability
- Vendor reputation and market share
- Capacity and room for expansion

- Operating efficiency and memory usage
- Physical size, noise level, and other environmental issues
- Potential for integration of new systems and software with existing hardware and software

The first part of this chapter examines the most common impediments to change and then suggests a methodology for analyzing your requirements. The remainder of the section describes the strategies of the major UNIX system and software vendors.

Are You Under "House Arrest"? There are several reasons why people avoid evaluating alternatives and continue with the installed legacy systems and their traditional vendors even when there may be a better alternative. For many, the problem is just not being aware of what is actually happening in the marketplace. For others, it is the path of least resistance. They don't have any motivation to change.

After years of account management, and the building of personal relationships between their personnel and their vendors, many companies' information technology strategies are effectively determined for them by their suppliers. These companies may as well be under "house arrest." Other companies have negotiated master purchase agreements with their major vendors, which have the effect of putting more power into the hands of purchasing agents and less into the hands of those people who stand to gain or lose the most from actual purchasing decisions.

Not to be excluded are the outright "happy convicts" who almost irrationally depend on one vendor for all their needs. These people are typically very risk-averse and need to be educated. These are people who are happy with what they know best or learned first. If this is the case, only quality education will help to open their eyes to the benefits of UNIX and an Open Systems strategy. It is worth examining some of the rationales UNIX critics often use in defending their position against migrating toward UNIX and Open Systems.

Host-Dominated Thinking. Some companies feel that because they are so heavily invested in IBM's MVS, for example, they have no reason to look at UNIX. In such cases, hundreds of programs may be running on an IBM mainframe, making any change prohibitively expensive. It is a lot of work to move to UNIX. Recent painful moves to DEC's VMS may be fresh on their minds.

Precedent is clearly an obstacle in these downsizing situations. It will take vision and the involvement of the most senior management to push through changes to information technology strategies dominated by IBM or DEC proprietary operating systems. Yet even in these situations, UNIX advantages in portability and hardware independence can be persuasive arguments. An approach of augmentation as opposed to replacement may be an alternate course of action.

It is a mistake to always think of UNIX as replacing existing systems. It can often be employed in a compatible and coexistent manner, extending the useful life of existing equipment.

Waiting for the True Standard. A frequent rationale for putting off evaluation is the multiplicity of UNIX versions. Conservatives believe it is best to wait until standardization is resolved. While it is true that there are many versions of UNIX on the market, this is a pretty weak reason to put off considering any of them. This is like sticking to a horse and buggy because there are so many types of cars on the market.

The good thing about the UNIX International/OSF competition (see Chapter 6) is that the System V Interface specification has quickly emerged as the de facto standard. Even OSF users will be getting a Novell SVR4 UNIX license! In a perfect world, there would be one pure, well-defined standard, but this is highly unlikely to happen in the competitive commercial world of computing. What is "under the hood" of a particular implementation of UNIX should be of secondary interest to the application user. As long as system vendors follow X/Open standards such as COSE and XPG in implementing variants of UNIX, the benefits of portability still exist. The fact that UNIX is available on many systems platforms, and that systems and software vendors often enhance UNIX with special extensions, implies that careful system evaluation is required in selecting the UNIX product with a feature set to meet your specific requirements.

3.2. UNIX SYSTEM EVALUATION METHODOLOGY

A 10-step program for system evaluation and selection is outlined below. The objective of the process is a selection based on your requirements and other considerations that are important in setting out your future information technology strategy.

1. Define your overall information technology strategy based on a corporate Information Architecture.
   - Importance to the overall success of the company
   - Critical areas of current and future planned investment
   - Importance of industry, de facto, and internal company standards
   - Survey of equipment, networks, and facilities in place and determination of the importance of compatibility

2. Define for each major subsystem or application area and the requirements that must be satisfied: Application solution requirements (e.g., software functionality needed to support business functions).
   - Number and types of users to be supported
   - Desired life cycle of the system
   - System features and conformance criteria, with ranking of importance of each feature
   - Compatibility with installed systems
3. Investigate alternative solutions.
   - Who might be considered?
   - What are the strengths/weaknesses seen in each competitive offering?
4. Develop a short list of alternative solutions.
   - Establish a list of vendors and products (no more than top five) to be evaluated.
   - Prepare request for proposal or quotation and issue it to alternative suppliers.
5. Evaluate these alternatives by considering:
   - Rough "total cost of ownership," not just entry price
   - Fit with requirements and score based on weighting or ranking established in step 2
6. Generate a short list.
   - Narrow the set of choices based on vendor responses to no more than the top three alternatives.
7. Conduct initial negotiations with short-listed suppliers.
   - Analyze the total cost of ownership over three to five years (see next Section 3.2.3.)
   - Examine vendors' standards compliance and commitment.
8. Product demonstration and benchmarking:
   - Ask for reference customers—check references.
   - Visit the supplier's engineering and manufacturing facilities.
9. Negotiate from vendor's proposal and terms and conditions:
   - Type of discount
   - Type of upgrade options and cost
   - Specifics of acceptance and policy for warranty and returns
10. Select a vendor and conduct the previously agreed-on acceptance test upon installation.

3.2.1. Analyzing Total Cost of Ownership

Looking at the big picture means estimating total cost of ownership. Industry suppliers consistently tout their newest products as having price/performance leadership or the lowest cost-per-seat. Such claims are sometimes based on the supplier's view of the typical minimum configuration. Suppliers often fail to highlight hidden costs in these "typical" configurations such as hardware and software maintenance costs, cost of necessary system software, and other areas that affect the real cost over time of system ownership.

First Establish a Standards-Based Architecture. Chapter 7 provides a detailed discussion of the impact of Open Systems on information architecture. While this overall architecture does not specify specific projects or development programs, it should establish a profile of standards that should be developed which incorporate the "most likely" system requirements for each environment. Like space standards in a company's facilities plan, these are IT standards that in part establishes sets of requirements for information systems that might include the following considerations:

Desktop requirements

The number and type of desktop devices required

Response time desired/required

Memory requirements per user/application

Disk storage for every user

The number of printers for every *n* PCs or workstations

Application software—text editors, word processing, technical publishing software, electronic mail, spreadsheet, and computer-aided design and drafting

Graphics software or acceleration options required by the application software

Fit with existing network

Server / system requirements

System (model number)

Ability to support predetermined number of terminals, PCs, and/or workstations

Memory requirements

Disk storage requirements

Centralized printers, plotters, or other peripherals

System backup

Application software and fit with existing network. Various configurations should be evaluated by individual user, department, and/or business function. Given information on applications and numbers of users to be supported, vendors should supply memory and other configuration parameters, including disk, that may not be so obvious to the user. This analysis should help as follows:

How does the per-user cost vary as additional users are added (e.g., for 8, 16, 32, 64, and 128 users, etc.)? Memory capacity and recommendations from vendors may vary enormously. This will have a substantial effect on both the performance and cost of the system. Users should not assume similarity of memory requirements between vendors.

Competitive evaluations based on cost of hardware can be misleading. System evaluation should look at the three-to-five-year cost of ownership and consider system expansion up front. Other factors that should be considered include the following:

- Installation ease and vendor assistance and cost
- Education services, quality, and cost
- Hardware and system software maintenance costs
- Other costs of support
- Software costs
- Cost of networking hardware, software, and maintenance
- Upgrade costs
- Systems integration, porting, or consulting fees
- Quality and completeness of documentation
- Does the vendor have a user group?

Support considerations could prove to be extremely important. The following is a checklist to evaluate the short-listed vendors in terms of availability and cost:

- Hardware and software (800) number
- Software (special services)
- Installation assistance beyond the basics
- Disaster recovery (e.g., your file system gets corrupted)
- On-site service options
- Return policy (e.g., warranty)
- Update policy and cost
- Additional service options (e.g., network design, consulting, and programming)
- Information provided (e.g., published bug lists)
- Documentation (e.g., cost of extra copies)

No vendor can compete on an equally attractive price basis in all categories. Selecting a supplier based on hardware price leadership alone is likely to result in paying a premium in another area. Balancing price/performance against functionality is critical. It is also important to look at the total cost of ownership of a system over its financial life cycle of three to five years.

However, even cost of ownership cannot address one of the most important questions—how functionally rich the applications software is in satisfying the needs of the user. Under the prices and costs of the basic system lie a myriad of applications packages that may be functionally very different between competitors. Differing peripherals and styles of computing can also create significant functionality issues. For example, do dumb terminals really provide an appropriate solution? Such decisions can only be made by careful consideration of user requirements.

To insure that purchasing decisions are made based on value to the organization, weightings for factors that influence the system need to be developed. Only by applying a value to each component of the solution and ranking the sum against price will users really be able to determine what the actual cost of ownership will be.

Tough questions to ask UNIX suppliers about their UNIX operating systems:

- How much compatibility will there be between previous/current versions and the next one? Between their version and other current standards such as SVR4?
- Do they guarantee binary upward compatibility?
- What about standards compatibility and conformance:
  — X/Open XPG3 and XPG4?
  — SVID? Which edition?
  — Is your UNIX product licensed and available from other companies?
  — What other vendors' platforms does it run on?
  — Why is it open? Do you support COSE?
- Do you publish a bug list?
  — Can I get it?
- How many applications are supported?

If the vendor also supports a proprietary operating system or multiple versions of UNIX:

- How committed are you to UNIX?
- Can you compare the resource levels going into development, main-

tenance, and field support, and so on with your competitors for each operating system you offer?

- What is your operating system strategy?
- Do you have multiple UNIX offerings?
  — If yes, is there a plan to converge them?
  — If not, why not?
- What is the evolution path from today through the next two years?
- What sort of state-of-the-art features do you have?
  — Shared libraries?
  — Reconfigurable kernel?
  — Security features?
  — Does the remote file system support automounting?
  — Is there international language(s) support?
  — I/O performance enhancements?

3.3.   DOMINANT UNIX SYSTEM VENDOR STRATEGIES

This section provides an analysis of the major UNIX vendors and their strategies. This information is derived from public sources of information and represents our analysis of each vendor's strategies.

There are many other system vendors, as shown in Figure 3.1. Figure 3.2 shows suppliers by price class and category. Note how the relative rankings by vendor differ. Figure 3.3 shows the stage of evolution of the key variants of UNIX in conceptual terms. Clearly workstations are the dominant UNIX market by far, followed by a mature microprocessor-based multiuser market. PC and PC LAN markets are smaller but will have high growth potential over the next few years.

UNIX platform vendors can be divided into five major segments:

1. Operating system platforms. Software-only vendors include companies that market and support variants of the UNIX operating system on multiple platforms.

Examples: SCO, ESIX, SunSoft/INTERACTIVE Systems, Novell

Expectations: Low price, ease of use, available through all channels—distributors/value added resellers, 1000s of applications available.

Purchasing: By credit card or purchase order, evaluation and purchase same day or overnight shipment.

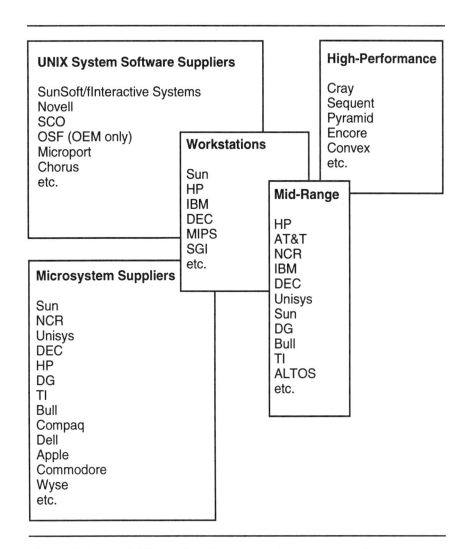

Figure 3.1.   UNIX suppliers by system class category. System vendors may be segmented in terms of system class.

Application Software Distribution: Retail, mail-order, distributors, VARs, and direct only to major accounts.

2. Microsystems suppliers. Microsystems include small multiuser systems (typically 5 to 10 users), small UNIX servers, and personal desktop systems. They typically run one or more of the commodity

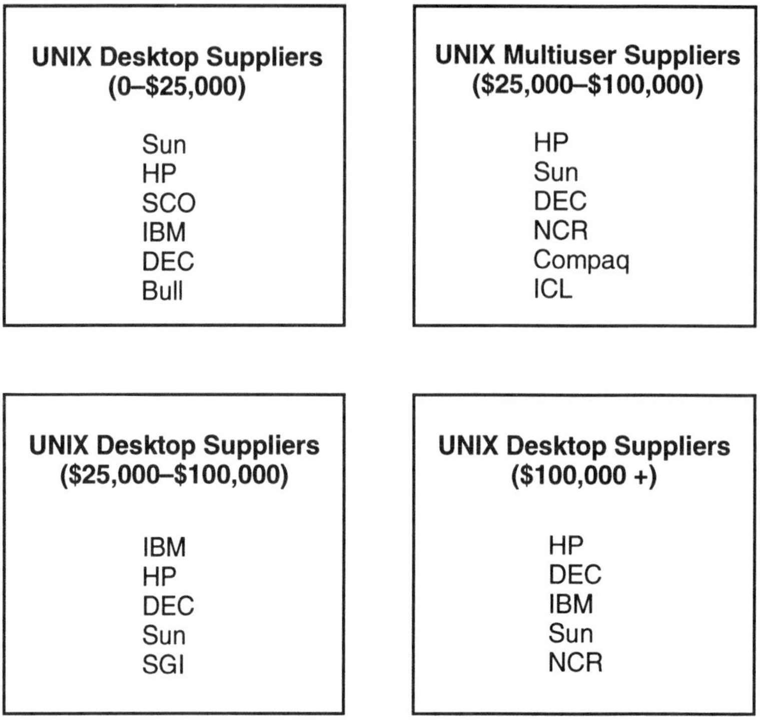

UNIX Desktop Suppliers (0–$25,000)	UNIX Multiuser Suppliers ($25,000–$100,000)
Sun HP SCO IBM DEC Bull	HP Sun DEC NCR Compaq ICL

UNIX Desktop Suppliers ($25,000–$100,000)	UNIX Desktop Suppliers ($100,000 +)
IBM HP DEC Sun SGI	HP DEC IBM Sun NCR

Figure 3.2. UNIX suppliers by price class and category. System vendors may be segmented in terms of system class.

microprocessor versions of UNIX available from SCO, INTERACTIVE Systems, or any of a number of other vendors.

Examples: Dell, Apple, Commodore, NCR, DEC, HP, DG

Expectations: Commodity price, ease of use, available through most channels, primarily indirect sales and value-added resellers, and many thousands of applications available.

Purchasing: By purchase order, evaluation, and purchase in days to months.

Application Software Distribution: Distributor for high-volume fulfillment to volume end users, VARs, and direct to major customers where special sales support of licensing is required.

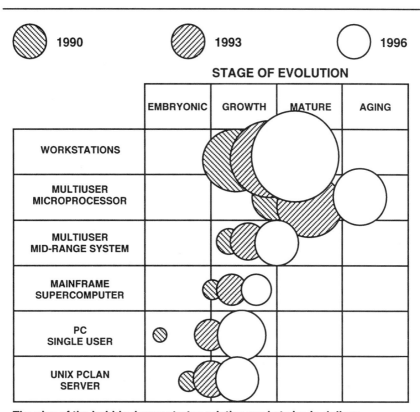

The size of the bubble demonstrates relative market size in dollars.

Figure 3.3. Evolution and market share by UNIX platform. Workstations and networked and communications-oriented platforms will continue to dominate the market.

3. Workstation and server suppliers. Workstations and servers dominate the UNIX market. This is largely because UNIX has become the de facto standard operating system for workstation platforms, and workstation platforms have been one of the hottest growth segments in the market. UNIX has also turned out to be an ideal fit with RISC architecture.

Examples: Sun, HP, IBM, DEC, MIPS, SGI

Expectations: Price range, ease of use, available through most channels, primarily sold direct and through value-added resellers, thousands of applications available.

Purchasing: By purchase order, evaluation, and purchase in weeks to months.

Application Software Distribution: Distributors for high volume fulfillment to volume end users or VARs, but primarily direct and through VARs.

4. Midrange system suppliers. Midrange system vendors sell larger (32 users and up) multiuser systems. With the notable exception of the IBM AS/400 and the 7370, virtually every system vendor in the mid-range systems market has supported some version of UNIX on its platforms since 1988 (see Figure 3.2).

Examples: HP, NCR/AT&T, IBM, DEC, UNISYS, Sun, Sequent, Pyramid

Expectations: Price range $25,000 to $250,000, available through direct sales, some value-added resellers, several hundred applications available.

Purchasing: By purchase order, predominantly corporate buyers, evaluation and purchase 3 to 18 months.

Application Software Distribution: VARs and direct.

5. High-End Platforms. High-performance UNIX systems are sold like mainframes for database or transaction processing applications. Some are also used for engineering and scientific applications such as supercomputing in numerically intensive calculations.

Examples: Amdahl, Cray, Encore, Convex, IBM, with costs from $250,000 upward into the millions

Expectations: High price, available through direct sales only with hundreds of applications available.

Purchasing: By purchase order, corporate buyers, evaluation months to years.

Application Software Distribution: Primarily direct.

Obviously, the lines of distinction blur between these categories. For example, Sun Microsystems offers products ranging from diskless workstations, like the SPARCstation SLC for a few thousand dollars, all the way up to multiuser servers that can cost hundreds of thousands of dollars when fully configured. The boundary between multiuser systems and personal computers blurs as well. There is no technical reason why a UNIX desktop can't function simultaneously as a server within its local area network or support one or more dumb terminals.

Even the term "microsystem suppliers" can be misleading, since almost all of these platforms use microprocessor technology. This category contains both platforms used as personal computers and derived servers or multiuser platforms that may be repackaged but are otherwise the same basic processor design as the desktop sans monitor.

The next sections summarize strategies of the major system suppliers. These include AT&T, Digital Equipment Corporation, Hewlett-Packard, IBM, NCR, Sun Microsystems, Inc., and Unisys, Pyramid, and Sequent. The reader is encouraged to contact specific vendors or sources referenced in Chapter 8 for more information.

3.3.1. AT&T

AT&T Computer Systems operations have been absorbed into NCR. This section provides background on AT&T strategy leading up to the acquisition by NCR. AT&T originally licensed source code for UNIX software before it was a software vendor and developed and supported UNIX for its own use before the 1984 divestiture allowed it to compete in the computer business.

Although AT&T, as a company, is considered a force as powerful as IBM, it has done a poor job of marketing UNIX. Walking away from the PC market and dropping support of UNIX on DEC equipment in an attempt to sell more of its own hardware helped to contribute to its past troubles (a $1 billion loss in its computer-related businesses in 1986).

AT&T secured patents, copyrights, and trademarks on UNIX, the software, the concepts, and the name. The largest developer of UNIX historically is AT&T's USL, although there are several other major developers, including IBM, Sun Microsystems, Inc., Microsoft, and numerous research institutions such as the University of California at Berkeley and Carnegie Mellon University. According to our research SunSoft and Sun Microsystems Computer Corporation has more UNIX engineers and support personnel than any other UNIX vendor or consortium.

AT&T was one of the leading midrange system suppliers of UNIX systems in commercial applications until its acquisition of NCR. Its strategy was linked to departmental and office computing where it also competed as a provider of telecommunications services. AT&T never captured a significant share of the computer market, although it has become a force in large government procurements.

AT&T was both a computer systems supplier and the principal stockholder in USL, which became the trademark holder and principle developer of UNIX System V. During 1989, AT&T formed a new division called the UNIX Software Organization (USO). About a year and a bit later it decided to incorporate a new subsidiary, UNIX Software Laboratory, Inc. (USL).

AT&T offered the MIPS-based Series FT for mission critical applications, and the i486-based multiprocessor Series E and i486 uniprocessor StarServer S systems. The StarServer FT Series E and S systems run UNIX System V Release 4.0. AT&T also offered the Series 7000 systems, which were repackaged MISservers from Pyramid Technology. The Series 7000 also ran UNIX System V and was targeted a commercial multiuser environments.

Here, we are mainly interested in the AT&T strategy as it relates to USL and to the development of UNIX, although AT&T was clearly taking more aggressive steps to increase its share of the computer systems market most notably through the acquisition of NCR and subsequent merger of its computer systems division into NCR.

A Succession of UNIX Product Releases. System V Release 3 was first introduced in 1986. There were two subreleases, 3.0 and 3.1. System V Release 3 in its time was the most widely used version and supported streams, RFS, and shared libraries.

System V Release 3.2, introduced in 1988, merged System V and XENIX SV/386 for PC 386-based machines. Source code was only made available for those 386 machines. This was developed in conjunction with INTERACTIVE Systems and provided a binary interface for the 386.

System V Release 4 merged System V with SunOS, which was based on Berkeley 4.2BSD. It was first released in the latter half of 1989.

By the early 1990s, AT&T's USL began working with several other computer vendors on enhancements to its standardized version of UNIX to support symmetric multiprocessing. Several system vendors, for example, ICL and Encore, already support versions of System V featuring their own implementations of symmetric multiprocessing. USL worked with Sun, with NCR and with many other companies continuing to enhance SVR4.

USL and UNIX International have a combined strategy to implement a binary standard for commodity microprocessors through an application binary interface, or ABI. This will ultimately allow software sharing, common media, and data exchange devices to read and execute the same software without any change, which provides the same sort of "shrinkwrap" software compatibility found today in MS-DOS and PCs, for example. This is extremely attractive to software developers and will no doubt cause many new applications to become available on UNIX System V, the most important applications being those that helped create phenomenal growth in the PC market.

AT&T Gets Aggressive. To increase its presence as a UNIX hardware supplier, AT&T acquired NCR. The merger made sense in terms of both companies' commitment to UNIX and interest in "transaction-intensive" applications like banking and retailing. On May 6, 1991, AT&T and NCR jointly announced that they have signed a definitive merger agreement for the acquisition of NCR by AT&T in an all-stock transaction valued at approximately $7.4 billion. Industry analysts estimated that the two companies had combined revenues, based on 1990 results, of $43.6 billion by 1992. This included AT&T revenues as a whole and not just that of its computer division, USL and NCR combined.

In April 1991, AT&T and USL announced that 11 industry vendors, including Sun, Amdahl, Motorola, Novell, ICL, Olivetti, Fujitsu, NEC, OKI Electric, Institute of Information Industry (Taiwan), and Toshiba had purchased shares of UNIX Systems Laboratories. AT&T remained the largest shareholder.

Industry analysts believed that AT&T's decision to make available shares of USL reinforced the concept of an open exchange of ideas between companies that support industry standard SVR4 UNIX. AT&T and USL also continued to focus on their international business strategy. AT&T UNIX Software Operation Pacific reported that a UNIX International, Inc. working group had begun consideration of the changes required to the Open Look user interface to meet Japanese and international requirements. The Open Look specification underwent review by 50 Japanese organizations in September 1990, and the draft internationalization and localization specification was prepared by AT&T, Fujitsu Ltd., Fuji Xerox Corp., Nippon Sun Microsystems, and Toshiba. The draft specification was shared by a working group that consists of 20 companies, including NEC Corp. and Oki Electric Industrial Co. The requirements include additional specifications for Japanese fonts and icons, vertical writing, Japanese input methods, systems messages in Japanese, and application installation commands.

As will be explained in a later section, in late 1992 Novell moved to acquire USL. AT&T will now be a major stockholder in Novell. Novell, previous to the acquisition had been working and investing aggressively in UNIX by forming a joint venture called Univel with USL.

3.3.2. Digital Equipment Corporation

DEC's UNIX revenues increased only 9 percent in 1992 to a little over $1.8 billion. UNIX-based business accounted for only 15 percent of DEC's revenues in 1992. A string of losses and the retirement of CEO Kenneth Olsen made 1992 a horrendous year for DEC which saw massive layoffs and resignations of key executives. Most analysts believe it would be 1994 before DEC comes back with its new Alpha-based 64-bit RISC product line which it introduced in 1992.

Historical Perspective. During the 1980s, DEC's strategy shifted from departmental systems to enterprise networking. DEC became the second-largest computer maker largely on the strength of its VAX architecture and VMS proprietary operating system software that was compatible from the top to the bottom of its product line. DEC began competing directly with IBM in the sale of large integrated systems. DEC now offers a wide range of UNIX-based systems, from workstations to large multiuser platforms.

DEC machines were originally used for the development of UNIX. DEC has historically been in an excellent position to capture UNIX market share but has failed to capitalize on it. Ken Olsen, DEC's president until his retirement in 1992, stated at one point that UNIX "was about as exciting as a Russian truck." That attitude changed—but not all that much—over the next several years.

DEC has offered its own UNIX implementation since 1982. In 1989, DEC offered its first UNIX-only workstation. However, DEC's resources were mainly focused on the VAX/VMS product lines. By the late 1980s, company officials claimed that they had made dramatic shifts toward UNIX, but that wasn't obvious from looking at growth in its revenue base for ULTRIX.

DEC's primary UNIX implementation is ULTRIX, which it sells mainly on its workstation products. DEC supports other versions of UNIX as well. System V is available on some VAX models for the telecommunications industry, and SCO UNIX is available for Intel 80x86-based desktop machines sold by DEC. DEC planned to make OSF/1 available and has claimed it will also support NT on Alpha which prompts many analysts and customers to wonder just what DEC's operating system and UNIX strategy really is.

DEC has assumed an "operating system neutral" attitude with customers, letting each determine on a case-by-case basis whether ULTRIX or the traditional VMS operating system is best. VMS is deeply ingrained in DEC's personnel, however, especially its sales force, so true achievement of a neutral attitude represents a major challenge for DEC for some time to come.

By the late 80s, DEC claimed that UNIX-based systems represented almost 10 percent of its overall sales. ULTRIX was a major part of this, while other UNIX software vendors like The Wollongong Group, which sells to the users of DEC systems. Third-party UNIX like Wollongong accounted for a substantial portion of DEC's UNIX business.

VMS/VAX remained a closely held technology. DEC killed its first internal RISC project and opted instead to OEM a variant of the MIPs computer chip. DEC publicly stated that half of its development resources were going into its UNIX offerings. In 1990, DEC released its first workstation which ran only UNIX, the RISC CPU DECstation 5000 series. ULTRIX has always been available only on DEC platforms. It is one of the more mature versions of UNIX.

Historically, DEC has benefited from UNIX and enjoys one of the largest installed bases of multiuser UNIX systems. Recall that UNIX was first developed on a PDP-7 in 1969. The first popular version of UNIX was its sixth edition, which was shipped on the PDP-11 in 1975. In 1976, Bill Joy, then working at the University of California at Berkeley, was shipping tapes from Berkeley to programmers in industry, universities, and research establishments running on PDPs.

DEC's first UNIX product, a BSD 4.2 derivative, was first released in 1984. ULTRIX, a merged System V and BSD version, was first released in 1985. DEC sees much of the UNIX market as being driven by the purchasing policies of major customers, like the U.S. government and large companies like GM. It also sees significant demand from technologically driven companies, especially those with engineering and technical environments. DEC has always had a "side business" catering to the telephone industry, which, because of this market's close alliance with AT&T, has required support of vanilla SVR4.

DEC's latest UNIX strategy is to integrate base technology from OSF and aggressively add functionality, while continuing to track and drive standards. This does not imply an end to DEC's commitment to and strategy for VMS. DEC's single VAX/VMS architecture is now a thing of the past. Windows/NT on Alpha is also a new strategy for DEC.

DEC, as expected, was one of the first vendors to offer a version of ULTRIX based on OSF/1. DEC has stated that by the end of 1991 it would merge ULTRIX and OSF/1 to create a new version of ULTRIX. But it didn't happen. In fact DEC tried to cancel its stated commitment to port OSF/1 to the Mips platform and backed down only after users became very vocal about DEC's reversal. DEC's strategy also expanded with its announcement of support for AT&T System V Release 4 on their hardware.

DEC is rather clearly positioning UNIX in markets where it has already gained momentum and where UNIX is being demanded. This will likely be in discrete manufacturing, medical, educational environments, and government, EDP services, transportation, and utilities. VMS is the flagship elsewhere, with ULTRIX used for defensive positioning.

In the 1980s, ULTRIX was estimated to account for 1 percent of the

11/7XX and MicroVAX sales, while other versions of UNIX running on DEC (e.g., Wollongong and AT&T System V) accounted for 9 percent. ULTRIX accounts for nearly the same percent of 8000 Series system sales as does UNIX, around 2.5 percent.

Over the past five years, the preponderance of DEC UNIX system sales have been in the DECstation product line, which ships exclusively with ULTRIX. DECsystems and DECstations support the OSF/Motif GUI and DECwindows, both of which are based on X Window System Version 11 from MIT. ULTRIX Version 4 also supports embedded database support with ULTRIX/SQL, a variant of INGRES Corporations' INGRES database.

By late 1992 Digital had been in the middle of a major reorganization and a major product transition. Digital's main priority has been to preserve and grow its installed base of VMS-based systems. For the foreseeable future, UNIX would appear to remain a diffused and secondary focus for Digital as it has been in the past.

DEC's Strategy for UNIX—How Real Is Its Commitment?

Digital's UNIX market share has steadily declined since 1987. Digital's strategy have changed frequently and have been confusing. Digital has traditionally viewed UNIX as a niche solution for technical markets, low integrity, low value-add, commodity-operating system.

During the past few years, Digital has faced intense competition in the technical market. The VAX/VMS product lines have not been able to keep up with the price performance advances of Digital's RISC workstation and server competition. Digital has had to drop prices, has seen profitability problems, and has actually been losing UNIX market share over the past few years, according to most industry analysts. Digital is a latecomer to next-generation RISC. Actually, Digital's early RISC-Alpha project was canceled and later restarted.

Digital has flip-flopped on whether it would support OSF/1 on its Mips-based product line, affirming to support it only after demands from its customers who feel they will be dead-ended otherwise. Digital is not expected to aggressively enhance this version of its operating system. Features like SMP and cluster support are not expected for years to come. Digital's 64-bit version of OSF/1 may never run on its Mips-based product lines.

Digital has preannounced Alpha, a new 64-bit RISC architecture. Digital must match and exceed other system vendors such as IBM, HP, and Sun in order to catch up. Digital's fundamental strategy for the 90s appears to be a multivendor systems integration company for large enterprises. This strategy would seem to reflect their anticipation of a decline in hardware profit margins necessitating a move to software and integration services. Digital's strategic initiatives for enterprise solutions, network applications support (NAS) middleware, and its porting of software to non-Digital platforms all seem to support this strategy. Like most major systems vendors, Digital's product strategy is fragmented and complex consisting of a number of hardware and operating system platforms.

Digital has recently renamed VMS as Open VMS. Open VMS has POSIX 1003.1-compatible system calls, POSIX 1003.2 shells and tools, POSIX 1003.4 real-time support, plus plans for VMS to be XPG3 branded. In addition, Digital is pushing OSF DCE and DME within its NAS strategy which spans VMS, UNIX, and other platforms.

Digital will position Alpha, Intel, and for the time being Mips, as three key architectures. With the apparent dissolving of the original ACE initiative, the strategy for Digital's operating systems is less clear. Digital will continue to support VMS (now being renamed and positioned as Open VMS), and has publicly stated it will support Microsoft's Windows/NT. Digital, who among major system suppliers has been most aggressive with OSF, can also be expected to provide an OSF/1-based product to which it can be expected to migrate ULTRIX users in the future. Digital will sell Open VMS first, OSF/1 to UNIX lovers, and NT for low-end desktops. Other operating systems may be sold and supported by Digital or made available as third-party software on a less strategic basis. Digital appears to be supporting making USL's Destiny SVR4 product available due to demand within their telecommunications-installed base. It's either that or lose the business. Digital announced it would develop a common set of APIs for USL's SVR4.2 recognizing key industries demand SVR4. This will become part of Digital's NAS product line.

UNIX on Alpha. ULTRIX users will be expected to migrate to OSF/1-based UNIX. Digital expects its UNIX business to regain momentum as it introduces a 64-bit version of OSF/1 UNIX on Alpha. Digital's first Alpha systems will be high-performance UNIX systems extending into mainframe class machines. Eventually, low-end systems based on Alpha will be introduced as Digital ramps down its Mips business. ULTRIX currently features SMP support, NFS and NCS, is XPG3 compatible, supports POSIX 1003.1 compliant.

While Digital is clearly one of the most aggressive proponents of OSF, it is also recognizing the fact that customers demand smooth product transitions and that with multiple architectures and operating systems, interoperability is a major issue. Digital announced it did not intend to support OSF/1 on Mips-based machines and then reversed itself when some customers made it clear that they wanted a better migration path. Digital's position on OSF/2 is very unclear especially since it has announced support for Windows/NT which is technologically quite similar to OSF/2.

In terms of interoperability, it seems as if Digital would have its customers believe that the operating system is almost irrelevant. VMS can be just as "open" as OSF UNIX since it is POSIX compliant, supports XPG3, and other standards. Maybe this line of reasoning even works with a few customers. Nonetheless, Digital has been a major proponent of OSF, as both a contributor of technology and as an OEM. More than any other major system vendor, Digital has used OSF to proliferate its technology as standards and has leveraged OSF as an R&D partner.

Digital was the first major vendor to provide OSF/1 development systems. Introduction of OSF/1 has been slower than expected with advanced development kits for early adopters and ISVs, followed by versions for end users that were to be deployed as products later in 1992. There has not exactly been a rush to OSF/1-based products. During 1990, DEC tried to circle the industries' wagons around the ACE consortium. This should go down as a case study in the love affair the press and industry analysts have with vendor consortia. As was described earlier, the ACE initiative, despite the visible support of industry powerhouses like Microsoft and DEC to form a binary standard around the MIPS architecture fell apart. A number of questions exist concerning compatibility of application programming interfaces for DEC's platforms versus existing platforms. DEC is claiming to support all sorts of operating systems and has now developed a new strategy under the marketing umbrella known as NAS.

What is NAS? Network Applications Strategy (or NAS) is a packaging of numerous tools including diverse software such as RPC mechanisms, database products, window systems, decision support, transaction processing software, and so forth.

Digital would like NAS to be seen as an architecture for development and deployment of client server applications. NAS packaging differs depending on the operating system it is based on. While most NAS modules run on multiple DEC platforms and may even run on competitive platforms, the NAS 400 collection of tools only runs on VMS and OPEN VMS. In effect DEC will support NAS clients on multiple operating systems while the server gives users a reason to continue to buy VMS.

Digital's strategy is to provide a mix of proprietary and standards-based layered software and tools. These will provide runtime services that user applications will depend on to execute. These runtime services will be supported best or exclusively on Digital server platforms. With so many operating systems, Digital is clearly shifting the focus from the operating system to a common set of what it calls middleware tools. These tools can run across different operating systems enabling applications to be more easily ported and to facilitate application interoperability. NAS is a key vehicle for Digital to use to create an image of a "single architecture" umbrella marketing strategy.

To be successful, NAS still has to be acquired and established as the network software architecture by customers. They will need to acquire NAS software on multiple platforms—with DEC likely the only source of supply.

Development tools are one of the most strategic investments companies make. Selling NAS packages will be time-consuming. While packaging makes the product set a little more understandable and easier to understand than, say, IBM's SAA, Digital may find it difficult to convince organizations to commit to NAS that aren't already Digital dominated. There may be redundancy between NAS product components and those available from third parties, especially in the areas of database, tools, and transaction monitors.

Much of the high availability and clustering technology and transaction processing of NAS 400 are completely proprietary to Digital and tend to blur Digital's Open Systems message for NAS when viewed as a whole. While some NAS product bundles are strategically intended for OSF/1, Windows/NT, HP-UX, AIX and SVR4, certain products will only be on VMS (e.g., NAS 400). Customers who commit to Digital's NAS middleware should be prepared to be a predominantly Digital shop. Digital may find it difficult to proliferate NAS until it supports a spectrum of server platforms and is able to ship and support software on other major platforms in volume. Given DEC's relatively poor financial position and its make or break challenge to migrate its product sales over to the Alpha architecture, it is not clear that DEC has the resources to carry out its NAS strategy as originally conceived.

Digital has to face a number of critical business changes in transitioning its installed base to Alpha over the next few years. The Alpha architecture will not offer binary compatibility with either its current Mips or VAX applications. While Alpha purportedly provides advanced translation technology, inevitably such technology has certain drawbacks most commonly associated with performance and compatibility. Digital also faces uncertainties in positioning Open VMS vs. OSF/2 versus Windows/NT. DEC has suggested that the choice of operating system depends on performance and features which are implemented in one operating system platform versus another. VAX cluster support is a good example of this. Which operating systems will support VAX clusters?

DEC and Microsoft. In a move that some believe is as close to a "kill UNIX" strategy as you can get, DEC and Microsoft would appear to be bordering on what might be best summarized as a Window/NT-on-Alpha strategy. Windows/NT will run on Intel, Mips, and Alpha (at a minimum) during 1993. Microsoft is to provide a full set of Alpha development tools. DEC has said it will port the DECtp Desktop for the ACMS transaction processing client environment to all Windows/NT platforms so programs can interact. Microsoft will put DEC's NAS-based eXcursion X-server on Windows/NT to enable interaction with X applications on UNIX, VMS, and other environments. So Windows/NT-on-Alpha has implications far beyond Microsoft's porting of the Windows/NT operating system to DEC. It represents a strategy for DEC to capitalize on supporting Windows and Windows/NT-based clients with DEC servers. DEC and Microsoft are jointly developing an SQL server gateway for Rdb/VMS so Windows users can access information residing in Rdb databases. Rdb will then be able to connect with the 125 or so applications designed for Microsoft's SQL server originally developed and based on Sybase.

As will be explained later, several of the core developers of Window/NT at Microsoft today were also the core team that developed VMS at DEC. This might also explain why DEC jumped into Windows/NT even at the risk of confusing its already confused strategy around ACE and OSF.

Summary

DEC ULTRIX:

Based on:	BSD 4.2
User Interface:	DECwindows, Motif, X Windows
Networking:	NFS, TCP/IP, RPC, NAS, TELNET, sockets, DECnet, OSI
Price:	~$60K
Notes:	Extensive ISV program

DEC OSF/1

Based on:	OSF/1

User Interface:	X Windows, Motif
Networking:	NFS, TCP/IP, sockets, NAS, RPC, ONC, streams
Price:	Not known
Notes:	Shared libraries, real-time, logical volume manager, threads

3.3.3.   Hewlett-Packard Corporation

Hewlett-Packard (HP) is well positioned as a large U.S. computer systems vendor to capitalize on UNIX. It attempted to jumpstart its workstation and UNIX business by acquiring Apollo and working on migrating a large portion of its installed base into HP-UX. Following the acquisition of Apollo, in 1989, HP had become the industry's second largest supplier of UNIX-based workstations, behind only Sun. Dataquest estimated the 1990 UNIX systems market to be nearly $18 billion. They also estimated that HP nosed out Sun in the number one spot with DEC, AT&T, and IBM in the other top five slots. Dataquest also estimated that these top five players accounted for 40 percent of the total market. By IDC estimates, however, Sun was still number one. According to IDC, Sun, HP, and IBM made up nearly 60 percent of the UNIX systems market growth in 1990. The bottom line is that HP has become a major force in the UNIX market through a combination of acquisition, technology investments, and ability to deliver a full featured version of UNIX with enhancements for its target markets.

HP was back in the number two spot in 1991 and depending on whose estimates you use was number one or two versus Sun in 1992. HP 1992 UNIX business was estimated at a little over $4 billion. HP brought in a new CEO, Lewis Platt replacing John Young in 1992. HP has continued to enhance and expand its workstation and server product lines based on the PA-RISC architecture. UNIX accounts for about 25 percent of HP's revenues overall.

Historical Perspective. HP has been historically more committed to standards than other larger U.S. vendors like IBM and DEC and has been selling UNIX for over 15 years. HP was one of the first major computer vendors to adopt RISC technology in 1983. This has helped HP achieve performance gains over the past few years. HP-UX has over 15 years of UNIX experience and over 3,700 UNIX applications ported mostly to its older Motorola-based architectures on DomainOS and HP-UX. But up until the early 90s, HP's proprietary operating system MPE was its cash cow, and HP has only recently moved from selling MPE first and then HP-UX to selling HP-UX first—in sales situations where MPE is not demanded. HP would appear to have done well in migrating a large part of its MPE installed base and ongoing sales to UNIX. This could be explained in part by the comparatively high pricing of MPE versus HP-UX on identical hardware.

HP has traditionally positioned HP-UX as preferred in engineering and technical market segments while it continues to invest in the enhancement of the proprietary MPE operating system. HP has become the first proprietary-based vendor to make a major commercial commitment to UNIX.

In 1990, HP introduced a series of minicomputers and servers known as the 3000 and 9000 range. These machines used HP's Precision Architecture (PA) RISC chip. The same hardware will support both HP's proprietary operating system MPE as well as UNIX.

The PA-based HP 3000-900 run MPE/XL and are targeted at multiuser OLTP applications. The PA-based HP 9000-800 runs HP-UX and is positioned as a midrange multiuser or UNIX server and as a workstation. HP continues to offer the PRISM-based Apollo DN10000 running the Domain operating system and positioned as servers and workstation. The PA-based HP 9000-700 then became HP's product line of workstations and servers which ran HP-UX. Finally, there are the Motorola 68K-based HP 9000-400 and Apollo DN4500, which are largely being phased out.

Many of the HP customers that came to HP from the Apollo acquisition are still running the DomainOS. HP must manage their transition since the new workstations from HP will run only HP-UX. Existing customers and ISVs have to decide whether to port to HP-UX now or wait for HP's version of OSF/1 to be available on its newer strategic platforms. But this isn't the only transition they will face. While HP migrates from HP/UX to OSF/1, they are also migrating from NCS to OSF/1 and DCE. This means migrating from NFS to AFS, NLB to DNS, and resolving other network service issues.

With the acquisition of Apollo, HP has had to resolve the differences not only in their competing hardware product lines but also in their operating systems, which include Aegis, Domain, MPE, HP-UX, SVR4, and, in the future, OSF/1. The migration of DomainOS to HP-UX has proved more difficult than the company originally expected.

HP's UNIX strategy has to accommodate four hardware architectures at the low end (Intel, Motorola, and two types of RISC) and three operating systems (Domain, HP-UX, and OSF/1 and Windows/NT in the future). Development of Domain is believed to be frozen, and HP-

UX is only available on HP platforms. HP's UNIX strategy is difficult to understand with so many variants. When HP-UX was released on the HP 9000 Series 700, their sales began to improve in 1991 and most of their UNIX revenues are coming out of their new systems sales and upgrades.

HP-UX is based on AT&T System V Release 2. HP has added several enhancements to the AT&T V.2 product. Not all extensions are supported on each HP processor configuration. Hardware configurations required to support the same number of users under MPE and HP-UX may also differ significantly.

HP positions HP-UX as a superset of System V Release 2 incorporating capabilities of Berkeley 4.2 and HP extensions in real-time and native mode support. HP strategically markets HP-UX where UNIX is demanded and generally for use in technical markets especially CAD/CAM and software development environments. HP continues to offer MPE as its primary operating system for commercial applications. They instruct their sales force to sell HP-UX to customers who are taking a long-term strategic view of their system purchases and have the sophistication to create end-user solutions out of basic tools provided with HP-UX, or who are best served with special functions supported by HP-UX such as real time.

HP-UX has several features that allow for real-time processing, such as improved kernel preemptibility, improved process scheduling, and memory locking. HP-UX supports 22 national languages, and its National Language Support was adopted by X/Open as an industry standard. HP has been slow to adapt the richer and far more flexible BSD commands and utilities, many of which have become "de facto" standards. They have offered GUI components such as X-Windows and Motif, the HP-VUE visual desktop is proprietary (only available from HP) and NewWave.

HP continues to support a number of operating systems including DomainOS (Apollo RISC version and Apollo Motorola version), HP-UX (a Motorola version and an HP-PA version), and a version of OSF/1 has been announced for the Motorola-based HP 400 and PA-based 700 current workstation product line as well as DOS and MPE/XL. HP will now be supporting four architectures: Prism, Precision (PA), Motorola, and Intel with five different ABIs: Domain, Domain/Prism, HP-UX, OSF, and SVR4 for the telecommunications industry.

HP is keeping its nose above the waves of change. HP has maintained revenues and profits during very difficult times in the industry, times that have seen its two major competitors, IBM and DEC, report repeated losses. The company appears to recognize that the commercial arena presents the best prospects for growth, and it has dedicated serious resources to UNIX. HP has become the darling of some industry consultants and is generally regarded now in the number two slot behind Sun in terms of overall market share. HP is investing aggressively in UNIX and in driving availability of software on its platforms.

One of HP's strengths derives from its world-class, in-house expertise in a wide range of technologies including printers, storage technology, processor architecture, and semiconductor production. HP is generally regarded as having the leading UNIX midrange multiuser systems market share, although Sun has narrowed the gap appreciably during 1992. HP's NewWave environment is an example of HP's leading edge, object-oriented technology, although NewWave has not achieved significant market penetration.

Is HP Opening Up? Imitating Sun's strategy of licensing its core technology, HP has licensed PA-RISC technology to a few companies including Hitachi. But HP has been able to garner only modest success for its PA-RISC architecture. PA-RISC continues to be third or fourth on the list of UNIX operating system environments that most ISV's are developing product for. HP has built a complete product line on PA-RISC, ranging from desktops to high-end servers.

HP has not been known for its marketing strength. For example, HP has been slow in countering the marketing strategies of its competitors IBM (SAA), DEC (NAS), SUN (ONC Plus), and NCR (OCCA) with its OSE (Open Software Environment). HP's product line consists of several incompatible operating system platforms including MPE, HP-UX, HP OSF/1, and probably support of Windows/NT on PA-RISC. HP-UX and HP OSF/1 are XPG3 branded. HP-UX is POSIX 1003.1 complaint and supports Motif and X11R5 as well as the DCE developers tool kit.

HP and Competitive Collaboration. Apollo originally developed the Network Computing System (NCS), which provided a remote procedure call technology. NCS has been licensed to competing vendors and has also been used in OSF's DCE. HP has devised a suite of products called Team Computing (the UNIX part of its NewWave computing strategy) which is in the early stages of release. It will be a while before it is available on non-HP platforms.

Hewlett-Packard and Sun signed a long-term joint software development agreement with the goal of allowing easy application interoperability on high-volume computers in the 1990s. Users will be able to seamlessly integrate data, for example, a spreadsheet, a graphic, and a block of copy, from systems made by different vendors located on one or more networks. This alliance moves the computer industry closer to the era of true open systems, overcoming the incompatibilities among software technologies that have frustrated users.

Perhaps the most significant result of the HP/Sun alliance is the spur to create distributed applications. These applications are designed so that pieces can be run by different systems on a network. An HP spokesman was quoted as saying, "Everyone agrees that distributed applications will realize the full potential of UNIX, but software firms have been holding back major development, pending some resolution of the multiple standards problem. By allowing developers to write to one interface rather than several, we expect the era of distributed applications to finally commence." This seems to indicate that the often reported debate about OSF/1 versus SVR4 isn't going to stand in the way of companies doing business. It also shows that the increased commitment to UNIX within the industry, no matter whose version it is, will only improve the potential for collaborative work that will ultimately benefit the end user.

Sun and HP reported that they are licensing their open software technology to vendors of other UNIX software and hardware platforms, thus extending the benefits of this technology to more computers and applications. This type of competitive collaboration is what has made COSE possible.

HP's Strategy for HP-UX and UNIX. HP now sells UNIX first and MPE if it is demanded. In the past few years, HP has focused on selling UNIX-based solutions for general-purpose commercial multiuser systems as well as workstations. They are generally regarded as the market leader in multiuser UNIX systems. HP's business expansion strategy is clearly based on high-end workstations and commercial OLTP. 1991 marked the first year that HP generated more revenues from UNIX-based midrange systems than from its proprietary system shipments. HP's UNIX-installed base is estimated to be between 300,000 and 400,000 users.

HP markets a wide range of general-purpose multiuser servers and UNIX workstations. HP is close to tying Sun for leadership in the UNIX systems market overall. HP has done very well in its UNIX business, leveraging an excellent business reputation, their ability to provide full solution sales and support, and their hot boxes based on PA-RISC technology.

In 1991, HP introduced new corporate business systems for the data center positioning these systems as mainframe alternatives. The HP 3000-990 and 992 systems run MPE/ix and the HP 9000-890 runs

HP-UX. HP has also announced that is has ramped up its support services. HP also announced a few dozen mainframe-class applications and tools that will run on these new high-end systems.

HP is following DEC's strategy of attacking the lucrative mainframe downsizing market. Whether HP can provide the level of product and services required to satisfy the demanding requirements associated with this market remains to be seen. HP has not been known as a mainframe supplier, and its capabilities in providing the high levels of data and system integrity, high availability, data conversion, and application re-engineering are unknown. How ready HP's sales force is for long sales cycles, sales to senior management, and MIS are also unknowns.

HP's strategic challenge is to break into the "glass house"—major enterprise OLTP applications that have traditionally been controlled and purchased by central IS groups in large corporations. In late 1992, HP introduced the Model 890 systems together with mainframe-oriented software applications and tools as well as special service offerings targeted at the conservative IBM-oriented IS community.

So what's HP's strategy for operating systems? HP has achieved success in RISC/UNIX because it has a full suite of products. HP is trying to be the first of the major system vendors to enter the mainframe replacement market with RISC/UNIX. Other vendors appear to be right behind HP including SUN, NCR, DEC, and IBM—NCR and IBM with the HACMP, or products like it, based on the RS/6000.

HP's product line consists of several systems and operating systems that are incompatible with each other. HP supports the Apollo Prism, Apollo Motorola (68K), Precision (PA), Intel in the HP Vectra, and Sequoia Motorola based system. Sequoia was OEM'd by HP in 1991. It is a fault-tolerant system. HP gained rights to Sequoia's multiprocessing and fault-tolerant technology as part of their agreement. Sequoia has other major agreements with Ultimate in the United States and Samsung in Asia. The Sequoia architecture is based on Motorola 680X0 microprocessors. The Topix multiprocessing kernel is layered beneath UNIX System V Release 3.2. It also conforms to 4.1 BSD and X/Open system interfaces. HP can be expected to implement the Sequoia technology on its HP PA-RISC chips in the future.

HP currently supports over five incompatible operating systems including MPE XL, Domain and Domain/Prism, Topix, RTE, HP-UX, OSF and even SVR4 for telecommunications. The migration path for these operating systems is not clear. For example, many users face a set of transitions first from Domain to HP-UX and then to OSF within a matter of a few quarters. HP also has three GUI strategies, NewWave, Motif and Open Dialogue, and a fourth on its way with Windows/NT. As previously mentioned, HP has different versions of HP-UX for 800 and 700 series systems products. Binary compatibility is only available for a special subset of "well-behaved" applications that use a common subset of features between the two versions. Interoperability and product releases suffer as a result of the complexity of supporting such a diverse range of technologies.

Despite early show of support, HP does not appear to be fully committed to OSF, particularly in multiuser environments. HP/UX is their focus currently. HP-UX has features for real-time processing and supports several national languages. HP-UX offers GUI components based on X windows and OSF Motif. The HP-VUE visual desktop is only available from HP.

HP on OSF. Almost two years after it began its involvement in OSF, HP concluded that OSF/1 would not be viable on the DN5500 product line. Reasons stated included that the product would be late, have insufficient system capability, and that it would not attract sufficient application support. (These points really articulate the underlying business case that drives product availability. It is easy for vendors to stand up and claim to support a standard or product, but all too often the real proof of commitment comes in the form of delivering real products—not on the marketing promises.)

HP continues to integrate OSF technologies into the HP-UX environment (e.g., Motif and DCE). When HP will move to the OSF kernel is unclear. HP has delayed plans to implement the MACH microkernel option and instead has stuck with SVR3 and BSD-based HP-UX. HP-UX lacks application services such as flexible memory management and dynamic code libraries and integrated support for PostScript. HP-UX provides a comparatively sparse user environment. System V commands and utilities dominate. Only a subset of the BSD facilities are implemented. The latest versions of HP-UX support SMP and multithreading.

HP announced in the first quarter of 1992 that it was delaying porting of OSF/1 to its machines. It stated that the OSF product was too immature and had no following among software houses. HP was likely trying to deal with the business of migrating the installed base of DomainOS users it inherited with its acquisition of Apollo. These DomainOS users are being told by HP to migrate to HP-UX even though there is not a clean migration process. DomainOS and HP-UX have incompatible file systems for example.

HP-UX 9.0 will comply with OSF's Application Environment Specification and will essentially be OSF/1 without Mach. The full OSF/1 kernel is projected for HP-UX 10.0, which will reportedly be backward compatible with other HP-UX releases. Even HP representatives admit that HP is not in any hurry to get to OSF/1 since users want UNIX and OSF isn't UNIX. HP will take other OSF technologies such as DCE but has to figure how to fit all of it together and how to develop interfaces that allow these products to interoperate within their environment(s).

Summary

HP/UX:

Based on:	System V.3
User Interface:	HP VUE, Motif, X Windows
Networking:	NFS, TCP/IP
Price:	~$60K
Notes:	Real-time support, disk mirroring

3.3.4.   IBM

IBM's UNIX revenues in 1992 were estimated at just under $2.9 billion, a 50 percent increase over 1991. UNIX still represents only a fraction (estimated at about 5 percent) of IBM's overall business. IBM has been having a succession of losses that culminated in early 1993 with the replacement of IBM CEO John Akers. IBM is plagued with reorganization, massive layoffs, and friction between competing business units. IBM is generally regarded as number three in the UNIX industry behind Sun and HP.

IBM spells UNIX A-I-X, for Advanced Interactive eXecutive. AIX was first introduced in 1986 and was associated with IBM specific platforms. AIX was largely associated only with specific IBM platforms and until 1990, AIX had no real impact on the UNIX market. AIX was largely discounted by the traditional UNIX community. Real questions existed in users' minds about IBM's overall commitment to UNIX and AIX in particular based on its slow delivery of products with only limited functionality compared to other UNIX offerings. By 1990, the concerns began to erode as the RS/6000 platform began to attain momentum. AIX and UNIX in general, however, did not occupy the same position as SAA in the IBM world. IBM originally had no intention of merging SAA and UNIX, but it has committed to support both and, as a consequence, has two "strategic architectures" to support.

1988 was the year that IBM actually first clarified its marketing position and entered the UNIX market. Anyone who has studied it knows that IBM has a history of following growth markets. It is clear that IBM is now getting in big because it sees that the market has achieved a given size and momentum.

If IBM was "getting religion" prior to the RS/6000, it was looking like a real "convert" as early as 1990. IBM had become a founding member of OSF and also seemed to be getting better at anticipating industry standards propelling its participation in standards consortia like X/Open and OMG to mention only a few.

IBM announced an across-the-board UNIX strategy from desktops to mainframes, but IBM does not support AIX on all platforms. Notably missing, for example, is the AS/400. AIX is central, however, to the RISC System 6000 workstation line, which went a long way toward putting IBM on the UNIX industry map.

AIX was chosen as the core component of OSF/1, which wasn't very surprising in that IBM was the largest of the founding members of OSF. OSF/1 plans weren't too far along before OSF announced its intention to use the MACH kernel and not the AIX kernel, although it would continue to use other technology from AIX.

IBM had stated plans to release a version of AIX that was compatible with OSF/1. This will be done first for the PS/2, followed by the RS/6000 and the 3090. The RS/6000 is the only platform on which IBM can claim real marketing success. AIX is only available on IBM platforms, although some of the technology, specifically commands and libraries, has been licensed to OSF.

In the past, IBM has offered a variety of versions of UNIX with no indication of which was more strategic. None of these versions was included in SAA. SAA is IBM's master plan to unify the application environment across all of its own product lines and stands for "Systems Application Architecture." IBM stated that AIX will not be part of SAA. SAA represents IBM's attempt to standardize the environment across its own product lines and as such is proprietary to IBM. Interestingly, the RS/6000 does not support SAA. IBM's strategy is to provide as much connectivity as possible between SAA and AIX by utilizing UNIX networking standards including TCP/IP or OSI protocols as well as IBM's SNA LU6.2.

There are several things in AIX that are not in SAA, like 3270 data streams, a database communications protocol, a protocol equivalent to RPC, XDR, or NFS, and other features that are part of UNIX, such as OSI, TCP/IP, and so forth. IBM has very recently begun to integrate some of this functionality into SAA. In some analysts' views, SAA has now become a general marketing umbrella or "markitecture" for anything IBM wants to throw into it. What is new and interesting is that IBM is publicly stating that AIX will have the same strategic status as SAA!

Prior to 1986, IBM had relatively little experience in UNIX. It selected INTERACTIVE Systems to assist in developing UNIX for the RT PC. INTERACTIVE Systems had provided a version of UNIX, IX, to run on the IBM PC XT in the early 1980s. AIX, originally created for the RT personal computer, was based on BSD4.3 and System V.2. It is a licensed System V product. At the time, System V had no virtual memory support, which IBM thought was important. However, IBM didn't have the internal expertise to undertake a rewrite of the kernel. It decided to keep a standard UNIX kernel but graft onto it code that supported virtual memory module (VRM) functionality. INTERACTIVE and IBM were codevelopers of AIX, IBM writing the VRM, and INTERACTIVE building UNIX on top of it. AIX is now IBM's only UNIX product. PC/IX was IBM's tactical response to the market. The same is true for its 370 version of PC/IX, introduced in 1988. PC/IX is now history.

AIX was originally based on AT&T System V Release 3. An important issue is that AIX does not offer a clear or simple migration path from BSD, XENIX, or System V Release 3 or SunOS. Users and ISVs will have to do substantial rewriting and porting to move to AIX, which might discourage some ISVs from porting to AIX-based systems. While the same challenge exists for most all vendors, IBM distinguished itself by reportedly investing over $40 million in porting fees as well as taking minority equity positions in a number of software companies in order to ensure applications are ported to AIX. IBM now claims that over 2,000 vendors support their products on AIX.

Another challenge for AIX (and some of the other UNIX implementations) is that there are relatively few people outside IBM who have any expertise with specific implementations of AIX. This is unlike System V/BSD, where a large body of expertise exists outside AT&T.

IBM has implemented AIX on several platforms, including mainframe 3090s, the mid-range 9370, the RT PC, and the PS/2 model 80. Most recently, AIX has been introduced on the RISC System 6000. On the 9370 and the 3090, AIX/370 runs on top of VM/SP as a guest. AIX/370 does not run in native mode—that is, as the primary operating system. Rather, it runs under the "umbrella" of IBM's VP/SP operating system and incurs as much as 25 percent additional overhead by doing so. AIX/370 follows the AT&T System V Interface Definition, and IBM licenses this release from AT&T. It also contains numerous features of BSD 4.2. AIX/370 was originally developed from System V.

IBM's UNIX business centers on the RS/6000. IBM's strategy will be to grow its RISC System 6000 (the successor to the RT PC line) into a general-purpose midrange system comparable to the 9370 or System 36 or 38. IBM is moving to expand the RS/6000 with what it calls loosely coupled multiprocessing—a form of cluster computing.

IBM mainframe sales with AIX account for a little less than half of their new mainframe sales when replacements and upgrades are factored out. These AIX mainframes function as huge servers to large networks of workstations and PCs. However, IBM does not publicly discourage the downsizing of mainframes and even those few AIX-based mainframes to RS/6000 servers. IBM has ported several applications to AIX, such as CADAM, CIEDS, CAEDS, and CATIA as part of this strategy. IBM is opening centers for UNIX training and AIX-based management consulting targeted at large-scale users.

IBM added tremendous credibility to UNIX by entering the market in the late 1980s. Until the RS/6000, it had historically had a small and fragmented installed base on the 370, PS/2, and RT PC platforms. The RISC System 6000 now accounts for most AIX installations. IBM's RS/6000 business represented almost a billion dollars in 1990.

In the last two years, IBM announced AIX/ESA for System/390 mainframes. It is marketed strictly as a technical and engineering operating system. AIX for the RS/6000, on the other hand, is the only operating system for the RS/6000 and is touted for its commercial features. AIX/ESA has an OSF/1 kernel derivative, while AIX/RS is based on AT&T System V.3. Their APIs are substantially the same, however.

IBM in the Place of Hamlet—"To AS/400 or to RS/6000, That Is the Question." Within IBM there is a fundamental schism between the AS/400 and RISC-based RS/6000. Internal issues aside, enhancements to the RS/6000 line including database performance, availability of CICS transaction processing software, high-availability, loosely coupled multiprocessing (HACMP) all seem to demonstrate the RS/6000 is positioned as more than a platform for technical applications and IBM's apparent willingness to tolerate competition between the AS/400 and the RS/6000.

A major deficit for IBM lies in its lack of any tightly coupled multiprocessing capability. IBM is not expected to introduce tightly coupled symmetric multiprocessing-based UNIX systems until 1994. IBM is trying to compensate with a strategy that emphasizes cluster processing based on a combination of IBM and third-party software. While experience is still being gained with clustering technology, this approach seems to work best when tuned for particular applications. It is not clear how flexible they are in supporting environments when application mix changes.

In 1991, IBM demonstrated a version of OSF/1 on an ES/9000. The native port was described as a "technological direction" rather than a product announcement. The OSF/1 port will run only on Enterprise architecture mainframes and not older models and is purportedly POSIX and XPG3 compliant. It included support for TPC/IP, NFS, X Windows, and Motif.

IBM Buys into Bull. In 1992 IBM took a $100 million investment for a little less than 6 percent of Compangie des Machines Bull. This deal included a wide range of 5- and 10-year agreements and contracts involving technology cooperation, licensing, and manufacturing. Bull would market and was licensed to manufacture systems based on the IBM RISC System/6000 architecture and AIX in the short term and would also be involved in IBM's future Power and PowerPC RISC architectures in the future. Bull was reportedly to lead cooperative development projects for symmetrical multiprocessing systems. IBM was also expected to leverage Bull's experience in Open Systems Interconnection (OSI) and related networking and interoperability technology. Also part of the agreement has Zenith providing IBM with customized portable personal computers.

IBM's Strategy for UNIX. IBM's RS/6000 constituted the company's major UNIX system platform. The success of the RS/6000 is largely due to the Power RISC microprocessor technology and less so to AIX. IBM in just two years had become the third-largest UNIX vendor behind Sun and HP. IBM's strategy seems to be SAA in the host world, AIX in the UNIX world, OS/2 in the PC world, with interoperability between them. But the interoperability hasn't quite been there. It is interesting to note that OS/2 is still positioned by IBM as the primary software development platform for SAA.

The RS/6000 has been popular as a multiuser system, but it continues to play a backseat role to IBM's AS/400. IBM has entered the OEM market with the RS/6000. It has been remarketed by Bull, for a short time by Wang, and by MAI. IBM now appears to be moving away from OSF and focusing instead on the new Taligent PINK operating system, on AIX, and OS/2. OSF-based operating system plans appear in a third tier of strategic importance.

AIX has a close adherence to UNIX System V SVID. It supports TCP/IP and Ethernet, Netware support, NFS and AFS, IEEE POSIX

1003.1, System V Korn and Bourne shells, 4.3 BSD C shell, X/Open XPG3 compatible compilers, Display Postscript, and MIT's X Windows system. Release 3.2 provided diskless and dataless support, asynchronous I/O, some OSF compliance in the form of AEC and OSF/1 file tree structures, diskquota, and FDDI support.

By mid-1992, IBM quietly introduced the HACMP/6000, a loosely coupled cluster multiprocessing high-availability system. This capability was not offered as a standard product, rather as a PRFQ (Program Request for Price Quotation). Targeted initially at only a few dozen commercial customers with high-availability requirements, IBM has preannounced support for increasingly sophisticated cluster configurations.

RS/6000s can be configured as warm backups to one another. The HACMP software provides a high-level set of services, tools, and application programming interfaces. The basic features have been in the RS/6000 and AIX/6000 generic products for some time, but this new software accesses these features. Generic failover scripts are provided that, depending on a customer's requirements, are modified to control basic failover.

IBM appears increasingly willing to leverage third-party developers, integrating their technology for time-to-market reasons. The HACMP/6000 products were developed by a company called CLAM of Boston, Massachusetts, for example. The AIX Windows user interface was adopted from VisualEdge. IBM is even using HP's Softbench and OpenView products.

Summary

IBM AIX

Based on:	System V
User Interface:	AIXwindows base on Motif, X Windows
Networking:	NFS, TCP/IP, RPC, NCS
Price:	~$10K
Notes:	DOS functionality supported

3.3.5.   NCR

NCR had UNIX revenues of just over $2 billion in 1992. We estimated that UNIX accounted for approximately 50 percent of total revenues, although this number is difficult to estimate. NCR is regarded as the fourth-largest UNIX systems vendor, edging DEC out of the fourth position it held in 1991. NCR has encountered some problems in rolling out its System 3000 product line, particularly with its multiprocessing systems and in assimilating AT&T's computer systems division, since NCR itself was acquired by AT&T. NCR acquired Teradata Corporation in 1992.

On May 6, 1991, AT&T and NCR jointly announced that they had signed a definitive merger agreement for the acquisition of NCR by AT&T. NCR's headquarters remained in Dayton, and AT&T intends that NCR's corporate structure, executive leadership, and name will remain intact.

NCR had 55,000 employees at the time of the acquisition and has become the fifth-largest U.S. computer company—most noted for its minicomputer products. The combined company by 1993 had shrunk to 54,000 employees.

Historical Perspective. NCR has been selling UNIX and multiprocessing for over 10 years. NCR was one of the first to offer UNIX for general business computing environments. NCR has also sold proprietary minicomputer and mainframe systems supporting UNIX, PICK, RM-COS, and TMX operating systems and must now help its customers make the transition to UNIX and the System 3000.

NCR products are generally targeted at banking and retail automation markets (automated teller and point of sale). NCR revenue growth in the mid-1980s was based on the company's strong market presence in these markets and on the Tower product line.

All of NCR's initial UNIX business was driven through alternate value-added reseller channels and the direct sales force was not allowed to sell UNIX. Significant investment in software and third parties was required before they began to see the payoff. By this time, UNIX was also becoming more interesting to the direct sales channel, and channel conflict problems ensued. These conflicts were largely settled through commissioning schemes.

In March 1990, NCR announced the Open Cooperative Computing Architecture or OCCA, which represents NCR's blueprint for open systems as it shifts from offering departmental minicomputers to enterprise-oriented systems.

NCR is now a $9 billion multinational computer systems vendor known for its strength in commercial markets, having assimilated the AT&T computer business. NCR is executing its plans to migrate their customers who have been running Motorola-based Tower systems to its newest systems based on Intel chips.

In its drive for market share in Open Systems computing, NCR announced the NCR System 3000 Series of Intel-based computer systems. UNIX System V Release 4, SCO UNIX, OS/2, and MS-DOS were all supported on the series 3000, which is intended to eventually replace the older Tower product line as more powerful machines are introduced over the next few years. The ambitious System 3000 product line spanning all computer categories from laptops through PC's, workstations, midrange and mainframe systems up to large-scale, enterprise-oriented, transaction-processing systems was modified following the assimilation of the AT&T computer business.

NCR expected the System 3000 would eventually replace not only the Tower lines but also earlier proprietary products such as NCR 9800 and 9500 machines. The NCR System 3000 Series supports NCR UNIX V.4, which features a multiprocessing version of AT&T's System V Release 4. According to NCR, NCR UNIX V.4 is the most powerful and feature-rich version of UNIX ever offered in NCR's history—supporting such capabilities as an enhanced NCR file system, a general-purpose transaction facility, mirrored disk facilities, power failure recovery, and other features that help satisfy the demanding commercial applications it is intended to address.

NCR's operating system strategy is also incorporating UNIX. NCR's Intel-based platforms will run combinations of DOS, OS/2, SCO UNIX, and UNIX SVR4 from USL. NCR also offers TOP END for OLTP solutions for small businesses up through high-end systems at the top of the 3000 series product line based on massively parallel technology called the Y-Net bus, which NCR has acquired and is jointly developing with Teradata. The joint development agreement between NCR and Teradata provided that both parties would share access to developed technology that would appear in the NCR 3000 model 3700 systems.

NCR's strategy is to offer a full spectrum of UNIX-based OLTP performance. Some industry analysts believe that NCR will offer TOP END on multiple UNIX system environments in order to create broader acceptance of OLTP based on the ANSI C and UNIX SVR4 standards. NCR is perhaps one of the first vendors to take a proprietary, feature-rich transaction processing system and move it to UNIX and Opens Systems standards including the X/Open API.

Industry analysts predict that NCR will be among the first vendors to offer UNIX systems capable of running the most demanding high-volume OLTP applications by 1994. The combination of TOP END and SVR4 in the future NCR fine-grain parallel engine could prove to be the most powerful OLTP system ever announced, not only on UNIX but even among non-UNIX systems.

NCR's Strategy for UNIX. Since May 1991, with the merger of AT&T Computer Systems Division and NCR, significant time has been spent with NCR absorbing the AT&T Computer Systems Division into its own operations. NCR now markets a converged product line called the System 3000 family. NCR's Open, Cooperative Computing strategy is based on the System 3000 server family, Cooperation, a suite of middleware software, and the Open Network Environment, a family of networking products. The System 3000 is based on Intel microprocessors and supports MS-DOS, MS-Windows, PenOS, OS/2, SCO, UNIX, and SVR4.

The System 3000 family actually consists of three different computing architectures. The Uniprocessor members of the family run the PenOS, MS-DOS, MS-Windows, OS/2, and UNIX SVR4. A product line of tightly coupled multiprocessors supports UNIX SVR4 with extensions. NCR claims its loosely coupled parallel processing can be configured with a thousand processors and supports SVR4.

NCR seeks to provide an integrated standards-based environment that consists of a combination of basic system software, administration utilities, application development tools, and even relational and object-oriented database management and decision support software. This is in contrast to other system vendors such as Sun that tends to rely on third-party software suppliers rather than price listing, selling, and supporting such variety of solutions.

NCR's UNIX SVR4 MP-RAS provides extensions to SVR4 for high availability and data integrity features required in commercial applications. NCR is focused on commercial markets; their systems are neither marketed nor sold into scientific or technical applications areas. NCR has still not offered any RISC-based systems at the time of publication.

NCR's high-end systems are positioned as enterprise-oriented database engines. These systems incorporate technology NCR has acquired from Teradata (acquired by NCR) and Sybase. These high-end systems are not conventional mainframes, but are designed for database application processors (APs). The parallel performance of these machines works best with the Teradata SQL engine based on up to 288 486 processors—the parallel architecture only applies to applications that are specifically architected for it.

Symmetrical Multiprocessing UNIX SVR4 is used for front-end processing across the System 3000 product line. NCR developed its SMP technology in conjunction with USL and licensed it to USL.

The NCR and USL merger was not without divergence in direction. NCR decided to go with TOP END as its UNIX-based transaction processing (TP) monitor relegating AT&T USL's Tuxedo /T product to support mode. The rationale was that TOP END was "product ready" and provided the best interfacing capabilities at a higher level than Tuxedo.

Another reason is that Tuxedo wouldn't support message-passing architecture between APs in the NCRs high-end parallel server.

NCR lacks a strong development environment. It may face a squeeze between mainframes and UNIX Superservers in the future. While NCR seems to have modest expectations for their high-end servers, history has shown that most customers prefer more general-purpose high-end systems. It is difficult to name many special-purpose computer systems that have even become that successful.

NCR must convince MIS to develop new types of applications for its proprietary open-database engine massively parallel architecture. NCR's shortage of tools and experience in selling this class of machine to MIS implies that NCR will have to refine their sales strategies, selecting account and vertical niche market applications with direct sales that can talk industry applications.

Summary

NCR UNIX System V release 4

Based on:	System V release 4
User Interface:	OpenLook, X Windows
Networking:	NFS, TCP/IP, RPC, UUCP, RFS, TLI, VPM
Price:	Not available
Notes:	SMP support for Intel-based MP

NCR SCO UNIX

Based on:	System V and XENIX
User Interface:	Open Desktop
Networking:	NFS, TCP/IP, UUCP, SCO XENIX-Net
Price:	Not available
Notes:	DOS file sharing, XENIX compatibility

3.3.6.   Sun Microsystems Computer Corporation (SMCC)

Depending on whose estimates you believe, Sun is either the leader or just behind the leader in the UNIX industry for many years now. Sun 1992 revenues were right around $4 billion. One hundred percent of Sun's revenues are based on UNIX systems, workstations, software, and related services.

1992 was a transition year for Sun as it reorganized some of its operations, completed its acquisition of the UNIX product portion of INTERACTIVE Systems, and launched its new Solaris 2.0 operating system for SPARC and Intel based on SVR4. Sun also rolled out a new line of multiprocessor desktops and servers.

Sun is the industry leader in RISC-based UNIX products, with approximately 38 percent market share in the UNIX workstation market. SPARC represents over 66 percent of the RISC market according to InfoCorp. Sun is a recognized leader in UNIX and Ethernet-based LANs, and its NFS product has become a de facto standard that is now widely supported on almost all platforms. Sun is also widely regarded as the "momentum" market leader in the UNIX and workstation marketplaces.

Historical Perspective. Sun initially grew at the rate of 80 percent a year from 1987 through 1990. At this run rate, Sun topped $3 billion in revenues during 1991. Sun was the first UNIX-only company to hit one billion dollars in annual revenues.

In the late 80s, Sun had licensed SunOS to be remarketed and supported by other companies, including INTERACTIVE Systems and numerous SPARC clones. By 1989, Sun had the second-largest installed base of UNIX systems behind Microsoft/SCO. It had a mature product in SunOS and a large number of third-party application software packages available. Sun was the first and is still the only major workstation vendor—indeed, the only full-line computer systems vendor—to offer only UNIX as its operating system.

Sun's longtime goal has been for UNIX to empower work groups in the 90s the way the personal computer empowered the individual in the 80s. As business users come to understand the cost savings and increased productivity of this approach to computing, Sun believes its workstations and servers will replace networked PCs and proprietary time-sharing minicomputers at an even greater pace.

Because it's a "pure play" in workstations, Sun, unlike most other companies in the business, doesn't have to worry about a workstation order that cannibalizes the sales of some other minicomputer or mainframe it sells. Since its incorporation in 1982, Sun Microsystems has become the recognized leader in the workstation market. Sun is also one of the most aggressive and outspoken forces causing change in the UNIX market.

SunOS was originally a derivative of Berkeley UNIX BSD 4.2 and 4.3. Sun worked with AT&T on SVR4 to converge AT&T System V and XENIX. Sun's focus is broadening as it grows to become a general-purpose distributed computer system company. Sun currently provides workstations, servers, and networks to professional work groups who demand more than a personal computer can offer and are also not satisfied with a style of computing typified by lots of slow-speed alphanumeric terminals time sharing off a central processor.

Sun first coined a phrase that stressed the importance of computer networks: "The Network is the Computer." Sun's strategy is best described as a pure play in client server. Sun has been very active in participating in formal standards bodies and in establishing "ad hoc" industry standards such as NFS (see Section 5.5 for a description of NFS). What has set Sun apart from other computer companies is its aggressive licensing practices. This plays well with the company's focus on heterogeneous distributed computing. Standards supported by Sun almost all have a common orientation toward supporting interoperability of products, both from Sun and from other vendors.

Sun has extended this philosophy even to its SPARC RISC system's architecture design. Sun has licensed several semiconductor companies to manufacture and sell SPARC chips. This is part of a larger strategy on Sun's part to provide, through UNIX, a single multivendor binary compatibility. This would promote a level of interoperability of applications for common microprocessor products such as Intel's 386 and Motorola's 68K as well as SPARC. This enables software developers to build one binary version of software for each unique processor architecture that can be executed on any system product running a unified version of UNIX and utilizing these commodity microprocessors.

In early years, UNIX was the single architecture that united Sun's three systems architectures on which its products have been based. Sun has used Motorola's 68K in the Sun-3 line of workstations and servers, Intel's 386 chip in its 386i workstations, and SPARC chips from different semiconductor manufacturers for its Sun-4 line of workstations and servers. However, Sun has, for all practical purposes, completed the transition from its Motorola and Intel microprocessor-based product lines to products based on the SPARC microprocessor.

During 1990, SPARC International, an independent consortium of companies licensing SPARC, released the SPARC Compliance Definition (SCD) specification. This defines the requirements for SPARC hardware and software compatibility which is at the center of Sun's and now SPARC International's compatibility strategy.

Sun's Open Systems strategy has continuously evolved. In the early 1980s, Sun was using standard commodity components like UNIX, Multibus/VME, Ethernet, and Motorola 68K microprocessors.

Sun then developed NFS, RPC, and XDR, which were intended to open up heterogeneous networks. Sun licensed NFS to over 200 companies and 3.1 million nodes (many competing systems vendors), and it has become a de facto standard through widespread availability and use in the industry.

In 1985, Sun first announced its intention to work with AT&T and Microsoft to merge AT&T System V, Berkeley BSD 4.2, and XENIX into a single UNIX. The result was a clean System V Interface Definition that supports System V's interprocess communications, BSD's networking and programming tools extensions, and Sun extensions for windowing, open network communications, and NFS, as well as other architectural extensions.

At the same time its AT&T relationship was strengthening, Sun was also beginning to aggressively market and license its SPARC RISC systems architecture. Several of Sun's competitors, and some industry analysts, saw this as giving Sun a significant advantage in that Sun and AT&T were now in a position to optimize UNIX for SPARC. There was also a growing frustration on the part of systems vendors about AT&T's increasingly stringent licensing policies for successive versions of UNIX. Whether these fears were justified is open to debate, but one thing is certain: Sun's work with AT&T had the effect of leveling the playing field and radically changing the traditional business model.

Sun Changes the Business Model Again. In February 1991, Sun Microsystems, Inc. announced that it had formed two new companies, SunSoft, Inc. and Sun Technology Enterprises, Inc., to develop, market, and manage its investments in UNIX-based software platforms and value-added, layered hardware and software products. The move seems to demonstrate Sun's commitment to other manufacturers of SPARC Compliance Definition (SCD) products, who need ready access to operating system and general-purpose, system-level products.

SunSoft offers an SCD-compliant application development and delivery environment for client/server computing. SunSoft also makes this software environment readily available, through sales, marketing, and licensing, to the SCD-compliant community, and, at some point in the future, to vendors of other volume platforms. The SunSoft platform consists of the industry's highest-volume RISC/UNIX platform, SunOS 4.1; the ONC networking standard; the X11/NeWS Window System; and the OpenWindows environment, including the OPEN LOOK graphical user interface.

SunSoft works with independent standards-setting bodies, including X/Open, IEEE, and NIST, to insure the compliance of its products with such standards as XPG3, POSIX, GOSIP, and SVID 3. The company also works with industry bodies, including SPARC International,

UNIX System Laboratories, and UNIX International to evolve the SCD definition.

SunTech Enterprises builds and markets general-purpose tools and products for SCD-compatible system users, including robust language and developer's tools, printing technology, PC and enterprise communications software, complementary accessories, and add-on products for the system administrator, software developer, and end user. Sun has also formed a subsidiary called Sun Laboratories. Its charter is to investigate and develop new technology and provide long-range vision for Sun's client/server solutions.

Sun continues to be the most successful UNIX vendor in terms of overall revenues and market share. Sun's strategic plan is to make the SPARC architecture a UNIX industry RISC standard much like Intel has accomplished with the 80x86. Sun has one strategic architecture in SPARC, one operating system strategy in terms of Solaris, and one approach to open network and distributed computing in terms of ONC Plus. This makes for an easily understandable and convincing strategy. Sun's technology and business focus combined with serious ongoing investments in R&D are without parallel in the computer industry. Sun is one of the only companies that has the engineering prowess to engineer itself out of any operating system royalty in a year or two, according to Scott McNealy. In early 1992, McNealy was quoted as saying that Sun would wait and see what Novell would do with USL and UNIX and six to nine months after the acquisition was completed would make a determination if they were getting what they were paying for in their royalties to Novell. Then they would make a make/buy decision.

Additional coverage of SunSoft and its Solaris product is provided under the next section on software vendors.

SunSoft Solaris	
Based on:	System V release 4
User Interface:	OpenLook, OpenWindows, X Windows
Networking:	NFS, TCP/IP, RFS, UUCP, RFS, TLI
Price:	Bundled
Notes:	Multithreaded Kernel, SMP, loadable modules, shared libraries

3.3.7. Unisys

Unisys was formed in 1986 from the merger of Burroughs Corporation and Sperry Corporation and has depended on selling proprietary mainframes and the proprietary CTOS and OS/1100 operating systems in its computer systems lineup.

Increased recognition of the importance of UNIX has been concurrent with efforts to improve low-end and midrange system products. UNIX workstations and departmental systems accounted for over a fifth ($2 billion) of total Unisys revenues for 1990 estimated at over $10 billion. Another $2 billion in revenue is attributed to software and services. Unisys positions itself as a supplier of value-added systems that address unique industry needs. Value-added products include software, development tools, and database products. Unisys products like LINC and MAPPER are provided on both UNIX as well as proprietary operating systems offered by Unisys.

Unisys has a good opportunity to capitalize on new products and UNIX within its own installed base. Three-quarters of Unisys product revenues were classified by the company as commercial information systems and one-fourth as Defense systems.

The growth of Unisys' UNIX sales has outpaced that of the computer industry overall and that of UNIX itself, making UNIX its fastest-growing business. Unisys system platforms now include mainframes, departmental systems and workstations, and personal computers.

The U5000 Series includes systems based on Motorola 68020. The business-oriented U6000 Series of systems offer Open/OLTP, which implements the X/Open DTP client server model of transaction processing. The U6000 system is based on Intel 80386 and 80486 processors. The U7000 is based on Computer Console Inc.'s Power 6/32. All of these platforms support versions of AT&T System V. At the time of this writing Unisys supported AT&T System V Release 3.2 with plans announced to migrate to System V Release 4.

As part of its multiuser UNIX strategy, Unisys is working on its Open/OLTP online transaction processing software, which is built upon an enhanced version of AT&T's Tuxedo System/T transaction monitor. Unisys System V is based on AT&T's System V Interface Definition and X/OPEN's interface standards for full portability across the Unisys product line and among other SVID certified hardware systems.

Unisys has joined UNIX International but reportedly continues to maintain a dialogue with OSF. Unisys is aggressively trying to influence AT&T into resolving what it sees as conflicts in source code availability and the extent to which UNIX is opened fully to the vendors that support it. Unisys participates in a number of trade groups including UniForum, the Transaction Processing Council, X/Open, X/Consortium and are founding members of UNIX International and Corporation for Open Systems (COS).

Unisys' strategy calls for the aggressive marketing and support of

UNIX on a complete range of hardware and leveraging its experience in commercial, real-time, transaction processing, and fourth-generation language environments as it builds its differentiation from a common UNIX operating system basis.

Unisys has found that even as the company has increased its sales, the dollar amount of each sale has been lower because of the rapid evolution toward smaller yet more powerful computers based on industry standards and UNIX in particular.

Unisys has targeted sales of UNIX-based systems for such commercial applications as document processing, banking, office automation, and distribution. Their approach is to provide customers with as close to one-stop shopping as possible, offering UNIX-based system hardware, software, and application software and service.

Unisys is still working to improve interoperability between the Convergent CTOS operating system and UNIX and MS-DOS-based systems. CTOS is slated to support Sun Microsystems' Network File System, enabling it to share applications with systems running under MS-DOS and UNIX, as well as applications developed for Microsoft's Windows graphical environment. Unisys is also said to be planning a distributed systems management product that will enable the management of networked CTOS workstations from a central hub.

Unisys is the largest UNIX supplier in Spain. Unisys Espana SA announced a plan to extend its plant in Catalonia and start manufacturing UNIX-based multiuser systems, thus becoming the first company to install a production plant in Spain for systems based exclusively on UNIX. The new factory is expected to supply the European market and will use the same production equipment as its counterpart in the United States—all of which means it can be ramped up to handle high volumes of production.

As part of its multiuser UNIX strategy, Unisys is working on its Open/OLTP online transaction processing software, which is built on an enhanced version of the Tuxedo System/T transaction monitor.

Unisys UNIX Strategy

Confounding the skeptics, Unisys returned to profitability in the fourth quarter of 1991 and through 1992. Unisys intends to increase market share on a global basis in financial institutions, airlines, communications carriers, and government agencies. These account for Unisys' current commercial business. Unisys hopes to build off its systems integration and services expertise in the government market. UNIX sales are increasing and approached $1 billion in 1991.

Unisys Corp. introduced upgrades to its Intel-based U6000 line, including a new entry-level system. Unisys OEM'd systems from Sequent for its top-end systems and reportedly has plans to offer high-end systems capable of replacing mainframes based on USL's ES/MP.

Currently, the U6000/65 runs the multiprocessing version of UNIX V release 4 while the 75 and 85 machines run DYNIX, Sequent's own multiprocessing UNIX implementation based on System V release 3.2. Unisys in the United Kingdom has predicted that UNIX will represent over 50 percent of its business by 1996.

Unisys introduced an enhanced version of Open/OLTP online transaction processing software that uses USL's Tuxedo TP monitor. Open/OLTP TM2 includes transactional desktop, terminal concentrator, and conversational transaction support features that Unisys believes will increase the options for integrating personal computers and UNIX systems into distributed client server networks.

Unisys is targeting transaction processing applications with a specific set of products with its Open/OLTP strategy. Informix's XA OnLine Relational Database, Tuxedo, its Ally applications, graphical performance monitors, and system administration tools are being bundled and integrated together with communications and database gateway products for IBM and Unisys mainframes.

Unisys has also launched new products that are designed to integrate UNIX and IBM systems network architecture. This allows mainframe users to add UNIX systems to their SNA networks with the risk and high costs of redundancy or re-engineering networks—existing SNA networks and terminals can be used to access UNIX. The processor also provides complete SNA-UNIX integration from the desktop devices in each environment.

In 1991 Unisys shipped a Chorus-based microkernel UNIX operating system.

Unisys UNIX System V release 4

Based on:	System V release 4 and Chorus
User Interface:	OpenLook, X Windows
Networking:	NFS, TCP/IP, RPC, UUCP, RFS
Price:	Not available
Notes:	

3.3.8. Pyramid Technology

Pyramid Technology, founded in 1981, is a small niche market supplier of UNIX multiuser systems. Pyramid was one of the earliest OLTP

UNIX system vendors. Pyramid implemented the first commercially available symmetric multiprocessing version of SVR4. Pyramid offers a family of RISC-based symmetric multiprocessing platforms running a UNIX variant called OSx. OSx was introduced in 1985 and was based on BSD 4.3 and SVR4. Pyramid was the first to offer symmetric multiprocessing based on SVR4. Pyramid sells most of its systems into telecommunications companies, financial services industry, and to the federal government.

Pyramids MIServer hardware consists of two product lines, the MIServer T series based on its proprietary Pyramid RISC architecture (which is being phased out) and a newer MIServer S series based on the Mips R3000 RISC architecture.

Since the late 1980s, Pyramid has been marketing high-availability SMP systems called the Reliant Series. These systems compete with fault-tolerant systems from vendors such as Tandem and Stratus. The Reliant series is mostly software added to configurations of T series systems. This software includes cluster monitoring software, disk mirroring, and disk and system management monitoring and management software. It features an intent logging file system, special power/fail/recovery software, and an intelligent console providing a single point of administration for the cluster.

Pyramids DataCenter OSx (DC/OSx) is based on UNIX System V Release 4 with numerous extensions including SMP support, virtual and mirrored disks, online backup, workload management, asynchronous I/O, and transaction management to satisfy high availability and other commercial OLTP applications requirements.

OSx is fully compliant with the AT&T Issue 2 SVID and passes the SVVS for SVR4. It is IEEE POSIX 1003.1 and NIST Fips 151-1 compliant. It supports X.25, AT&T DataKit I and II, NFS and Pyramids support of SNA BSC.

OSx since its creation has stayed on the leading edge of UNIX operating system technology. It was unique in having a SVR3/BSD mode switch early on. Pyramid has enhanced and rewritten much of the UNIX algorithms to enable support of thousands of concurrent users, support huge databases and disk farms and to support RDBMS software in achieving high transaction rates.

Pyramid added a virtual disk facility to the UNIX kernel enabling access to huge disk files spread over multiple disks and asynchronous I/O to reduce database bottlenecks and virtual disk management mirroring to reduce inherent storage limitations of most UNIX implementations. OpenNet NFS offers complete file server support for NFS workstations and PCs.

Pyramid supports more than 20 different databases including Oracle, Informix, Ingres, Sybase, Progress, and Unify. Pyramid was the first platform to run Oracles Parallel Server. Through the use of parallel cache management on Pyramid systems, Oracle's product allows multiple loosely coupled Pyramid servers access to a single database spread across multiple disks.

Pyramid, like other hardware vendors, has recently formed a database division to develop new software products for commercial database endusers. These consist of a set of tools to monitor and manage I/O performance bottlenecks where many databases are run under UNIX and other products including a TP monitor, fault tolerant distributed lock manager, and database backup and administration facilities.

3.3.9. Sequent

Sequent markets three models of Symmetrical Multiprocessor Systems, all based on the 50Mhz version of the Intel 486 microprocessor. Sequent's principal market focus is as a supplier of Open OLTP and UNIX RDBMS platforms. Most systems are sold and supported in commercial OLTP applications and decision support. File servers for decentralized Lan environments is a secondary market.

Sequent OEMs its products to other companies, in particular UNISYS. A large part of Sequent's revenues are reinvested into R&D related to software enhancements and specifically into developing parallelized versions of the DYNIX/ptx UNIX operation system. Sequent has relationships with both OSF/1 and with USL. Sequent and USL's technology agreement involves multiprocessor technology USL plans to adapt in its SVR4 ES/MP release.

DYNIX/ptx with its multithreaded kernel and parallel implementation of streams is optimized for load balancing and multiprocessing. It is well suited for tightly coupled symmetrical multiprocessing.

OLTP is Sequent's principle business, and most of Sequent's machines are purchased along with a UNIX relational database. Sequent either OEMs or has joint marketing relationships with leading RDBMS vendors such as Oracle, Ingres, Informix, Sybase, Unify, Progress, and Focus. Sequent TP monitors include Tuxedo /T from USL, VIS/TP from VISsystems, and UniKix from Integrix subsidiary of Bull HN.

Sequent also has a special focus on object-oriented technology working with ParcPlace Systems, Reusable Solutions, Tigre Object System, and Versant Object Technology. Sequent implements RAID and volume management software, provides disk mirroring and online replacement of disks without stopping the system but otherwise has not offered fault-tolerant systems, nor do they claim to have any leading high-availability solutions at this writing.

Despite its technological prowess and its clear market focus, Sequent has had some difficult financial problems during recent years, especially due to competitive challenges to the low end of its product line. Its OEM business has also been tailing off.

3.3.10.   Other UNIX Desktop and System Vendors

A brief summary of other UNIX vendors not covered in the preceding sections is outlined here in three broad categories:

1. Other workstation vendors
2. Personal computer- and microcomputer-based multiuser system vendors
3. Midrange and high-end multiuser system vendors

Other workstation vendors

Virtually all of the other workstation vendors, such as Silicon Graphics Incorporated (SGI) of which Mips is a wholly owned subsidiary, Stardent, Evans & Sutherland, MIPS, and others offer variants of UNIX. Evans and Sutherland are transforming their business focusing on graphics acceleration technology which is compatible with workstation technology, most prominently Sun Microsystems workstations.

The next companies we discuss include personal computer and multiuser microcomputer-based systems.

Altos. Altos has traditionally sold low-end microprocessor-based systems through value-added reseller networks. They have in the last few years brought UNIX systems to their traditional small multiuser commercial markets.

Apple. Apple's personal systems today are based on two product families: System 7 and A/UX. Apple first got into UNIX in 1988 when it introduced A/UX for Macintosh. A/UX will never have as significant a business commitment as System 7 does at Apple, as such, A/UX has not achieved significant market penetration within the UNIX industry. Early versions of A/UX, like IBM's AIX, were not really well received by the UNIX community. UNIX users did not see any real advantages to A/UX other than it ran on Apple's product line. By 1990 A/UX was more fully integrated with Macintosh, giving users the ability to run UNIX and the Macintosh user interface simultaneously. Apple also started a third-party software program for A/UX. A/UX provides the same user interface and runs the same application software as System 7 both with a UNIX foundation.

A/UX is based on AT&T System V R2.2. It is not clear how strategic UNIX really is for Apple, since the bulk of its sales continues to be based on its proprietary operating system, MacOS. A/UX is a stepchild to MacOS. To Apple, the window system is what matters most, and perhaps its idea of the ideal UNIX is that the user would never see it or even know it was there.

A/UX is positioned as a platform for Lan-based network services such as database management, image management, and X Window-based applications. A/UX 3.0 offers System 7 desktop as the user environment, and runs Macintosh System 7 binaries. Releases include libraries from IBM's AIX for future compatibility with A/UX 4.0. A/UX on the PowerPC architecture will provide high performance. The PowerOpen ABI is being implemented so AIX applications can run unmodified on Apple's future releases of A/UX.

A/UX is one of a very few implementations of UNIX available on the Macintosh and other Apple computers. Whether and how Apple capitalizes on A/UX remains to be seen. A/UX is usually at least a version or two behind where the rest of the UNIX industry is. For example, Apple does not yet have any version of the standard SVR4.

A/UX aside, Apple and IBM seem to have grand designs for the future. Apple has stated publicly that A/UX will be its server operating system of the future and has entered into a joint technology agreement with IBM.

Pink applesauce is coming. Apple and IBM's joint venture has created a new company called Taligent. Taligent is developing a new operating system (code-named Pink originally and later called PowerOpen) which is expected to hit the market in 1994 or even later. It will be based on object-oriented technology. The new program model reportedly incorporates networking and collaborative architecture. It will be made available as an open-industry standard which we believe means that Taligent will eventually make the software available on a wide variety of hardware platforms.

PowerOpen, will be a merged version of A/UX and AIX environments. Apple will release this new product as A/UX 4.0. This new product in the short term is expected to allow Apple, IBM, and other RS/6000 users to migrate to as yet unannounced PowerPC-based products that run UNIX.

Apple brings object-oriented development experience to the Pink project. IBM brings expertise in enterprise computing. Apple and IBM will develop a common look and feel across their PINK products. Pink is targeted for the Motorola 680X0, Intel 80X86, and the PowerPC RISC microprocessor based systems. A/UX is UNIX for Macintosh customers. It presents the familiar and intuitive Macintosh computer desktop and runs the familiar Macintosh shrinkwrapped applications.

Apple has taken the industry's lead in making operating systems essentially invisible to users. In the future, we expect Apple to pay particular attention to the upward compatibility of its applications. Apple can be expected to add to the midrange of the Mac line with a system built around the PowerPC based on IBM's RISC chip currently used in the RS/6000.

Apple customers will choose between two operating systems, one a new PowerPC version of System 7 and the other a new version of A/UX. Apple is likely to extend System 7 with a microkernel that will run on both PowerPC-based or 680x0-based systems. We expect that System 7's top layer will be a complete implementation of the Macintosh. We also expect Apple to continue to live in a proprietary world. Most of the functionality of System 7—like AppleScript, Quickdraw, Hypercard, and Interapplication Communications (IAC)—will continue to be available only from Apple.

Compaq. One of the largest master distributors of Intel-based systems, Compaq sells both PCs and low-end microprocessor-based multiuser systems with SCO XENIX and SCO UNIX. Compaq also markets an MP machine called SYSTEMPRO which runs SCO Open Desktop and SCO MPX (SCO UNIX with MP extensions).

Commodore. UNIX System Release 4 Amiga debuted at UniForum 1991. Commodore Business Machines, Inc., West Chester, Pennsylvania, demonstrated the 68030 machine, which comes preloaded with X Windows and Sun Microsystems' implementation of Open Look as well as AmigaDOS. Commodore has picked Open Look because of its programming consistency and superior number of applications. The company is hopeful of upgrading a portion of its installed base, numbering around 2 million Amigas, to UNIX.

Data General. Data General's Motorola 88000-based AViiON UNIX product line now accounts for as much as 75 percent of its UNIX business which was approximately 10 percent of Data General's overall revenues in 1991.

Intel. Intel began shipping its first shrinkwrapped UNIX System V/ 386 Release 3.2 for the OEM market in 1989. By the end of 1989, it announced a version of UNIX System V Release 4 that was made available in the spring of 1990. This version of UNIX System V for the Intel 80386 and 80486 processors signaled Intel's intention to actively market the software against products from SCO and INTERACTIVE Systems. Intel has limited software development experience and provides no significant features or value-added functions to SVR4. Its value-added is limited to a commercialization of its ABI UNIX for the 386 and 486. While Intel has long been known as a hardware component supplier, it is relatively inexperienced in the UNIX operating system. Intel relies heavily on third parties to support and service its products, sold primarily through OEMs.

SGI/MIPS. SGI is best known for its high-performance graphics workstations built on the MIPS chip. SGI acquired MIPS when MIPS future was in question since it depended completely on MIPS for the 64-bit processor for its workstation. SGI is highly focused in the engineering marketplace and uses a variant SCO UNIX adapted to its systems architecture.

Wyse. Wyse, perhaps best known for its terminal product line, also offers PCs and low-end microprocessor-based multiuser systems with SCO XENIX.

Midrange and High-End Multiuser System Vendors. There is a large and growing list of midrange minicomputer and minisupercomputer systems vendors who offer UNIX. These include multiprocessor UNIX compute server suppliers such as Arix, Encore, Convex, FPS, ICL, Pyramid, and Sequent, to name only a few, as well as supercomputing vendors such as Cray.

Mainframe and High-Performance UNIX System Vendors. UNIX has actually been accounting for as much as half of the new mainframe sales if replacement and upgrade sales are not considered. Mainframes are used in select scientific and engineering applications—in effect, as very high-end servers managing centralized databases. Over the next few years, with the introduction of new technology that addresses the requirements of demanding large-scale transaction processing applications, additional mainframes featuring UNIX can expect to find a market offering significant price performance over proprietary mainframes.

Amdahl. Amdahl's long history of IBM-compatible mainframe and data storage systems and its mainframe-based UNIX implementation (UTS) makes it one of the most significant players in bringing the advantages of open systems to enterprise-scale computing. With revenues over $2.5 billion, Amdahl is second in the mainframe market following IBM. Fujitsu is Amdahl's biggest stockholder with an estimated ownership of 49.5 percent of the company.

Amdahl's UTS and UTS Multilevel Security UNIX systems are designed to meet the requirements of large data center operations with respect to reliability, capacity, performance, and security.

UTS is a large-scale symmetric multiprocessing operating system initially based on AT&T's UNIX System V release 3.1 with enhancements from 3.2 and 4.0. It includes most of the features found in PC and UNIX versions of UNIX such as NFS support and BSD networking in addition to numerous enhancements for datacenter applications and environments. Amdahl now resells Sun products.

Other high-performance system vendors specializing in UNIX include companies like Encore, Sequent, and Pyramid. These companies offer some of the latest in multiprocessor server technology along with a focus on database management and transaction processing application solutions. Amdahl markets its UNIX operating system UTS into commercial and technical markets.

3.4.   UNIX SOFTWARE VENDORS

Software vendors are broken down into the following categories:

*   Operating system platform vendors
*   Enabling technology—especially Relational Database Management
*   Application solutions

The first two categories are discussed in this section. Application solutions on UNIX are discussed in Chapter 4.

The two main players in PC UNIX are SCO UNIX System V/386 and SunSoft INTERACTIVE UNIX for Intel also based on AT&T System V. These are the most truly portable (to hardware) versions of UNIX for PC's. Both run on a wide variety of hardware developed around Intel's 80x86 architecture and will support a broad array of standard industry peripherals and other devices although SunSoft INTERACTIVE has a slight edge in this respect. Both are limited to Intel-based platforms. SunSoft's new release of Solaris 2.x and Univel's

UnixWare are new UNIX System V release products that will expand the PC UNIX market significantly, both technologically and in terms of marketing. There are a number of smaller companies that cannot be discounted just because they are small who are also working hard on expanding the base of PC UNIX vendors.

UNIX and the Top 50 Software Companies Overall. Interestingly, in terms of who is making money off UNIX, it would seem that the application solution vendors are actually ahead of the operating system vendors.

We analyzed the top 50 software companies based on information published by Software Magazine. Table 3.1 shows how the top five UNIX software suppliers stacked up as of the end of 1990. While the data is slightly old, we believe it is relevant toward understanding the nature of UNIX software that we estimate is still largely similar today.

SunSoft revenues, which were not available at the time of publication, would probably place it ahead of SCO in the above analysis. Taken as a whole, Sun's total software revenues in terms of operating systems, compilers, networking, and other software is estimated as just under $200 million in 1990, which would make it a strong contender behind Oracle as the largest UNIX software vendor overall. It should be pointed out however that SunSoft and Oracle are not even competitors. Oracle, the leading relational database management and related tools and applications vendor happens to sell more software than any other company in the UNIX Industry.

Some interesting summary analysis included the following observations:

* 50 percent of the top 50 software vendors in the industry supported UNIX platforms
* 50 percent of these supported multiple UNIX platforms
* Most ISVs who didn't support UNIX were developing software expressly for IBM and in most cases for mainframes
* By far the largest UNIX software vendors were selling general commercial software tools and applications.

By 1990, the UNIX systems market had grown to over $15 billion. UNIX dominated the workstation and multiuser midrange server markets. Several hardware OEMs began to migrate toward ISVs and UNIX on the desktop and accounted for nearly half of all units and over half the revenues.

Table 3.1.   The largest UNIX software suppliers.

Rank	Vendor Name	UNIX Platforms Supported	Rank Overall	Percent Revenues were UNIX
1.	Oracle	Almost all UNIX platforms	4th	51%
2.	Informix	Sun, HP, AT&T	23rd	95%
3.	SCO	Intel platforms	26th	100%
4.	ASK	Most UNIX platforms	11th	50%
5.	Sybase	Sun, IBM, DEC	38th	60%

3.4.1.   Microsoft

Microsoft is primarily committed to NT, Windows, MS-DOS, OS/2, and XENIX in the past. In 1989, Microsoft took an equity stake in Santa Cruz Operation (SCO). Microsoft has done an excellent job of propagating UNIX (XENIX) in the small systems market. Microsoft licensed UNIX seventh edition from AT&T, and XENIX was launched in 1980. XENIX was enhanced by Microsoft for use on 80286-and 80386-based machines. XENIX is Microsoft's multiuser, multitasking operating system. It was positioned for use by small business systems where the main requirement intended for multiterminal access in accounting, low-end database, or other types of software solutions used with UNIX PCs. Since 1982, SCO has been a licensed second source for XENIX.

UNIX and Windows/NT. In a move clearly positioning Microsoft as a supplier of more enterprise-oriented solutions, Microsoft has bombarded the industry with its road map for the evolution of DOS and Windows over the next few years. Most prominent in this strategy is the Windows/NT family of products.

Microsoft's presentations and strategy seem very similar to Sun except the focus seems to be Intel, and if one looks closely, Mips RISC and Alpha. Microsoft has laid out its plans to develop a low-end version of DOS (based on microkernel technology) for use in embedded applications. It has developed Windows for Workgroups as an interim step toward Windows/NT and has adopted short-term positioning for Windows/NT as a product with two versions, one packaged for use on clients and one for servers.

The Background Behind NT. Windows/NT started in 1987 when Microsoft realized that OS 1.1 and Windows 2.0 has fundamental limitations tied to the 286 and Intel architecture. These products were not portable, they were not secure, they did not support MP, and they could barely be networked. Microsoft decided to develop an extensible OS technology to support OS/2, Windows, and POSIX API's.

In 1988, Microsoft took Mach from Carnegie Mellon and took it apart. They ported it to the 386 and rewrote pieces of it in C++. Then in 1988 a small group of developers who had worked on DEC's core VMS team joined Microsoft rather than forming a start-up they were planning after they left DEC.

The NT project was started with this core team, and OS/2 was chosen as the lead API. By 1990 Microsoft set the end of 1992 as its target date to ship Windows/NT. They were almost a year off their original schedule.

Windows/NT consists of around 3.8 million lines of code. NT claims to be threaded SMP, with support for networking, graphics, and a microkernel that supports multiple instruction sets. API's supported include Win32s, Win16, MS-DOS, OS/2, and POSIX. Each of these APIs is serviced by a "personality" subsystem that runs in nonprotected mode. The NT kernel executive and basic services run in protected mode and provide common services to the API subsystems. Applications call the subsystems which in turn call the executive. DOS, OS/2, and other applications cannot access the hardware directly, nor can they employ private device drivers in application space. This could be problematic for all the software that has for years employed undocumented features to get around DOS memory and other limitations.

NT features a layered device driver architecture that uses a hardware abstraction layer in order to support VME, ISA, EISA, and other bus architectures. This layer is all that needs to be changed to port the basic functionality of the microkernel to various platforms. NT claims to have generic drivers that make it relatively easy for device driver writers to implement drivers. Traditional UNIX drivers are often monolithic and more difficult to maintain by comparison. But it doesn't make sense to compare NT to UNIX of the past. The more modern UNIX kernels, such as SunSoft's SVR4-based Solaris, for example, feature dynamically loadable device drivers that represent as much a technology jump from previous kernel technology as NT is to MS-DOS. In terms of application interoperability, NT supports OLE, Object linking and embedding.

Windows/NT analyzed. In the short term, NT offers few functional innovations that would attract a major segment of the DOS installed base. NT does not deliver many of the improvements that would normally be expected of a major new operating system. In many ways, it is merely bringing DOS and Windows up to where they should have been a few years ago. Nonetheless, NT's success is almost inevitable given Microsoft's dominance of the PC desktop marketplace. NT as a client-side operating system is intended to slip in under Windows and help overcome some of the limitations of DOS. OS/2 personality mode will allow OS/2 applications to run—but not quite as well as under OS/2. NT on the server-side represents Microsoft's latest attempt to move into low-end networking, a market dominated by Novell. Microsoft faces a variety of challenges in addressing server environments that are distinctly different from what it understands in the PC community.

NT lacks support for Open Systems standards like X/Opens XPG and supports POSIX 1003.1 and not POSIX utilities or POSIX threads and other related standards like X Windows, OMG, and so on. Microsoft pays some attention to standards but believes it is big enough to set its own de facto standards. NT will not support native 32-bit applications initially. NT has immature networking technology at best. For example, NT supports no UNIX networking technology like that developed under BSD UNIX. No naming service is available. NT has no X.25 WAN or OSI support. It cannot run on one machine and display results on another. There is no heterogeneous network management scheme for Windows/NT, and it uses a desktop administration model, not a network administration model.

A Comparison of NT and SVR4

Graphical user interface. UNIX features scalable-font subsystem, NT will support Windows. UNIX GUIs are based on the X Window system and rely on bit-mapped fonts. SVR4.2 offers Adobe Type Manager. Some versions of UNIX also support Display PostScript.

Multiuser capabilities. To counter the criticism that NT does not support multiuser, Microsoft planned to include services such as incoming TFP server, telnet server, and remote login server functionality.

Distributable GUI applications. UNIX variant supporting X allows graphical applications to be intrinsically client server.

Network services. UNIX has well standardized basic network services. TCP/IP, sockets, RPCs work reliably across widely different platforms and operating systems. NT offers many options (named pipes, NetBIOS, sockets, RPC), but there is no path provided by NT for developers.

Email. UNIX offers a standardized version of Email. With NT this will likely be an add-on or third-party product.

Availability. UNIX is almost ubiquitous. It is everywhere and on almost every platform. NT will be on lots of platforms, but these will only come over time.

Will there be any vendor including Microsoft who is betting the ranch on Windows/NT? Few vendors will offer NT as their primary or only operating system. History has shown that from the time a company receives an early development release of an operating system to the time they release their own beta release (even with trivial enhancements of extensions) it is never shorter than six-months and may take over a year. A six month release assumes a very high-quality initial release and reliable intermediate releases of the production version of the OEM'd product. Beta test is usually at least three months before first shipments to customers. Volume shipment is usually three to six months following first production releases. So while early release and developer releases help to compress these time frames, it usually takes at least a year between the time the originator of the operating system ships and the licensee's are able to ship their products in any volume. Following this logic, it will be 1994 or 1995 before NT is available in volume from OEMs as a quality release ready for production use. The exceptions may be vendors like Sequent who have been using NT for some time and have enhanced it to the point it could be considered NT in name only.

Another consideration and cost for those who OEM and license operating systems is the "time-to-application." We can see from history that an OS without applications is slow to move to volume (OS/2 is offered as proof).

Microsoft has a talent for whipping up hype around its future products. Windows/NT is no exception. Microsoft market clout is considerable. As this book is being printed, Windows/NT is predicted to just be shipping after several slipped FCS dates. However we do not believe NT will not be ready to run mission-critical applications any time soon.

NT will be competing with Novell, Univel, and SVR4.2 from USL. It will not achieve significant market share as a server networked operating system for some period of time. It may be years before NT competes with UNIX as a fully functioned multiuser server operating system. Microsoft's entry into network operating systems for high-end (Intel 586 required) systems represents a whole new set of challenges and a new market for the company.

Experiences in Porting UNIX Software to Windows/NT. Today's version of UNIX support many technical features including support of a large address space, multiple protected processes, preemptive multitasking kernel, and networking NETBEUI and TCP/IP, threads, security, and SMP, and the experience of early ISVs converting to NT have surfaced interesting issues. The first problems they encountered were the typical ones you expect from an early beta release of software. The next problem came in the area of structured exceptions handling, and in the end, while the port only took a few weeks to go from 16-bit Windows to the 32-bit Windows API, the tools to make the conversion weren't there and were by no means comparable to those found on UNIX and available as third-party solutions on UNIX.

The personality subsystems are not quite the real thing. OS/2 emulation may not be quite as good as OS/2 and the POSIX subsystem will initially be very barebones and calculated to squeak by the letter of federal procurements.

In general, there is not a very good story for converting UNIX code to NT. But it's clear that Microsoft isn't all that concerned about that. What NT is about is moving up the food chain to a higher value server operating system. Clearly Lan Manager will be eclipsed over time by NT.

It's clear that Microsoft is aiming at 486 and Pentium-based servers in corporate enterprise architectures. Microsoft will develop a 32-bit version of DOS which will have overlapping features with NT. NT will be positioned as the network server for Banyon and Novell clients. Microsoft has licensed Novell's file system to ensure compatibility in this regard.

Even with the experiences of early users in one of the most extensive beta test programs ever undertaken, there are lots of questions around NT. Just how scalable will it be in supporting thousands of nodes in a network with its single name address space? Will NT's interprocess communications be up to meeting the demands of object-oriented applications?

From a marketing point of view, Windows/NT seems to be directly competitive with Novell and OS/2. It is also intended to be the "way forward" for Windows users. Get ready for a real marketing shoot out as Novell gets serious about UNIX and begins to leverage its very strong distribution channel into gaining time-to-market advantages over Microsoft.

3.4.2. SunSofts' Solaris Strategy

This section expands on the earlier section on Sun Microsystems Computer Corporation but focuses on SunSoft and its Solaris strategy. Sun had been selling SunOS for over 10 years. SunOS was based on AT&T System V and BSD 4.3 UNIX. Sun spun off the SunSoft subsidiary and changed the name of the operating system to Solaris during 1991 and

1992, respectively. SunSoft purchased the Intel Systems Division of IN-TERACTIVE Systems Corp., in the process acquiring the company's IN-TERACTIVE UNIX System V Release 3.2 for the Intel 386 architecture.

SunSoft is one of a group of independent wholly owned subsidiaries of Sun Microsystems. It was born in January 1991 but did not come into official status until July 1991. SunSoft sees its mission as client-server computing, providing the ability to have interoperable applications run in heterogeneous networks. Its first release, Solaris 1.0, was basically a repackaging of SunOS. Solaris 2.0 however represents a fundamentally new product which is based on SVR4. A variant of SunOS at one time ran on a Intel-based Sun workstation called the 386i. Solaris 2.0 is completely new and is being released on SPARC and Intel with other ports probably in the works.

SunSoft claims to have the largest number of UNIX installations at over 500,000+ and more software engineers (~1300) than any other UNIX operating system company or computer system company. SunSoft announced Solaris 2.0 in June 1992. SunSoft claims that development of Solaris 2.0 required over 1,000 man-years of software engineering and testing. Solaris 2.0 combines multitasking, multiprocessing, multi-threading, and network security with new ease of use, ease of installation, and new system administration features.

Solaris 2.0 ships in CD-ROM format. Solaris 2.0 was first shipped to SunSoft OEMs including Toshiba, CompuAdd, Solbourne, Tatung, and Sun Microsystems Computer Corporation. SunSoft also announced an OEM Multiprocessing Kit which allows OEMs to take advantage of (develop, tune, and verify) threaded symmetric multiprocessing features offered in the Solaris kernel for their hardware implementations.

Amdahl, Toshiba, NCR, Zenith Data Systems, Olivetti, Dell, AST Research, Everex, NetFRAME, and ICL have announced plans to support SunSoft's Solaris 2.0 on their 80x86 product lines. SunSoft claims that Solaris operating system is the volume leader in the 32-bit computing market in terms of volume and applications. Solaris has a run rate of over 300,000 units per year. Solaris 2.0 inherits over 4000 SPARC applications. By the end of 1992, over 1,000 applications were already well through the Solaris 2.0 migration program.

Solaris 2.x is SunSoft and Sun Microsystems Computer Corporation's System V release 4.0-compliant operating system environment. This product provides standards compliance, a dynamically configurable kernel and faster Network Information Service (NIS). Sun's challenge is to manage the migration of its customer base over to this new advance operating system and no one believes this is going to be simple. But Sun and SunSoft are taking creative steps to support their customers migration and in the process may be setting the stage for things to come.

Solaris 2.0 consists of three components, the foundation technology, the user environment, and developer environment. The foundation technology is based on SVR4. Solaris extends the base SVR4 kernel to feature numerous new technologies, designed to increase work group productivity. These include networking based on ONC Plus, a naming service called NIS+, industry standard file sharing with NFS, federated services that allow third-party network services (including DCE, Novell NetWare, and OSI) to plug into Solaris. Other features include network-independent protocols, multithreading, symmetrical multiprocessing, real-time support, Kerberos and other security features, international language support, ToolTalk, and OpenWindows. The foundation product complies with all the major industry standards including IEEE POSIX 1003.1, X/OPEN XPG3, ISO 9660, AT&T SVID 3, SPARC Compliance Definition (SCD) 2.0.

The Solaris User Environment features the Deskset capability. It features Multimedia Mail, an audio tool, a work group calendar manager, a help package, and numerous other utilities. SunSoft's Solaris is the industry's first shrinkwrapped distributed computing solution. Based on SunOS, Solaris gives users a powerful, simple graphical environment for high-performance computing with a path to the next generation of distributed objects technology.

Solaris 2.0 is offered on Sparc RISC and will be released slightly behind schedule in mid-1992 for Intel x86 platforms. Solaris 2.0 has three layers. The foundation consists of the SunOS operating system release 5.0. It contains an enhanced SVR4 kernel and ONC networking technology. The application framework includes the OpenWindows version 3 windowing product, the ToolTalk object-based application interoperability software, and other developer tools. The user environment incorporates the intuitive OPEN LOOK graphical user interface and DeskSet version 3 productivity tools including multimedia email, network-based calendar manager, and magnified help facilities. Neither Sun nor SunSoft had supported Motif directly, but it was available from third parties. Motif purportedly sells more licenses on Sun ironically than any other platform. As will be discussed later, neither Motif nor OPEN LOOK have become dominant in the UNIX GUI wars.

The Solaris development environment is based around what Solaris calls project DOE or distributed objects everywhere. DOE is SunSoft's strategy for next generation modular applications based on distributed objects that can be interpreted across multiple platforms. ToolTalk is the first component of Project DOE.

SunSoft seems to be squarely positioned against SCO. Perhaps this was a factor behind SCO's decisions during 1992 to move to support the OSF kernel and to suspend all work on the ACE initiative. SunSoft will

promote UNIX on the desktop. Sun has long been a distributed computing pioneer. Innovative software like NFS let the company lead the
client server parade. SunSoft will compete with IBM, Microsoft, and
Apple. Users who want to use Solaris or want applications that run on
Solaris will be able to evaluate Intel versus SPARC RISC.

Solaris offers a jumping-off point for symmetric multiprocessing and
multithreading. In moving from Solaris 1.x to 2.x, Sun has taken a novel
approach to assisting its customers in making a nontrivial transition.
There are applications to port, device drivers, driver kernel interfaces,
and windowing systems to convert, new libraries to add, and users and
systems administrations to re-educate. In its Solaris 2.x migration kit,
SunSoft has provided a mutlimedia demo and planning forms together
with tools that can be used by programmers to scan through C code and
suggest what needs to be done to make the code System V and ANSI C
compliant. The tools and plans generally breakdown into those for the
programmer and those for the systems administrator.

Solaris 2.x offers a number of major enhancements.

- NIS+
- New printing subsystem
- Default Korn Shell
- Simplified installation
- Symmetric multiprocessing
- Multithreading
- Message based application interoperability vis. Tooltalk
- Improved internationalization
- New features in Deskset like multimedia Mailtool

SunSoft and DCE. If you believe the press, then you might think that
the OSF DCE initiative is already the de facto standard for creating
and implementing distributed client server applications even before it
has shipped in any appreciable volume. As Sun has been quick to point
out however, hardly anyone is really using DCE—except for early developers as of the end of 1992. Sun on the other hand claims to have
over 4 million ONC licensees. Nevertheless, Sun has been criticized for
what appears to be a "not invented here" approach to technology. In the
past, although stopped short of adopting DCE, Sun—via its SunSoft
subsidiary operation—defined a new networking strategy that included the ability to "plug in" DCE components via what it calls federated services. With the introduction of its ONC Plus in early 1992,
among various enhancements SunSoft has provided a set of utilities
that allow users to develop ONC Plus or to plug-in alternative technolo-

gies such as DCE or Novell's NetWare. Since the formation of COSE, Sun has agreed to sell and support both DCE and Motif.

Solaris Overview. SunSoft now offers its 32-bit UNIX operating system on SPARC and Intel 80x86 platforms. The ONC Plus product suite together with federated services (see below) are central to its distributed computing strategy. SunSoft and Sun Microsystems Computer Corporation are both aggressively pursuing collaborative third-party relationships. Sun continues to maintain the lead in terms of the applications supported on its platforms. SunSoft has a development path defined for object-oriented technology and is working aggressively with HP and the OMG toward the goal of creating new standards for the future.

Tooltalk enables work group applications to work cooperatively in heterogeneous distributed computing environments. It represents SunSoft's first steps toward implementing an object-oriented computing environment. Tooltalk is a programmer's tool for facilitating interapplication communication. Its benefits for the end user is where the payoff comes. Tooltalk provides a means of interapplication messaging. It is already used in the Solaris Desktop environment and SunSoft is driving several alliances of software vendors who are leveraging Tooltalk and already providing integrated work group solutions in areas such as CASE, EDA, and CAD/CAM.

Between the Sun-installed base, its licensees, and third-party software companies supporting ONC and in particular NFS and PC NFS, the installed base of ONC has been estimated at 3.1 million nodes (by Dataquest in 1992).

Solaris, which employs by far the largest number of UNIX programmers of any company in the industry, can be expected to continue to innovate within official and de jure standards. For example, SunSoft claims that the Solaris file system is 50 percent faster than SVR4 and also supports RAM disk for extra speed. Solaris is POSIX 1003.1 compliant, XPG3 branded, IEEE 754+, conformant with SVID issue 3, and supports ANSI C among other standards.

Solaris has one of the industry's leading track records in terms of internationalization and localization. It supports numerous international languages and provides conformance to localization requirements and conventions. Solaris is designed with language-neutral packaging in mind and local binaries, source code, and documentation are all available.

Sun Microsystems Computer Corporation only sells SunSoft's version of Solaris UNIX. Solaris 1.x releases are based on SunOS 4.1.2, while Solaris 2.x and releases beyond it are based on UNIX System V release 4. Solaris 2.x is not completely binary compatible with Solaris 1.0 unless applications are "well behaved." Automated utilities have been produced by SunSoft to help software vendors and customers make the migration.

Sun has an extensive product line that seems to be completely replaced about every 18 months or so. Sun offers one of the easiest and least costly upgrade paths in the industry with cost-effective system upgrades or (MBus) processor module upgrades. Sun high-end desktops and servers employ new modular technology that helps to minimize costs and facilitate upgrades.

Solaris 1.x's leading features included dynamic linked modules and data structures, disk volume management, and state-of-the-art virtual memory support. They and other enhancements specifically designed for new commercial market opportunities have combined to help Solaris maintain its lead as the leading 32-bit UNIX implementation.

SunSofts' Solaris Federated Services Strategy for distributed computing. SunSoft is evolving its Open Network Computing strategy to accommodate the integration of other technologies for interoperability. In its approach to layered systems architecture, the Solaris APIs isolate applications from the various de facto and evolving network services. SunSoft has introduced a version of Netware based on collaborative efforts between Novell and SunConnect, a Sun subsidiary focused on PC NFS, connectivity tools, and other solutions. Sun markets and supports SunNET OSI solutions. Finally, Sun plans to accommodate DCE (e.g., via Transarc's AFS, Encina, and other tools) as well as solutions available from other third-party software vendors. All of these are dynamically pluggable into ONC Plus. This strategy is consistent with SunSoft's overall strategy to integrate with UNIX International Atlas, OSF's DME, and Tivoli, as well as to continue a pattern of collaboration with ISV partners who will build, sell, and support system and network administration applications based on the Solaris platform.

Sun closes the gap on commercial features. Solaris now incorporates features such as online backup, disk mirroring and logical volume support, and disk striping—all tools that enhance I/O performance, availability, and flexibility required in commercial applications.

SunSoft and NT. SunSoft's Interactive product and its Solaris-on-Intel port are both being promoted and sold aggressively through channel partners in anticipation of Microsoft's release of NT in 1993. SunSoft has developed third-party relations to provide Windows/NT on Solaris in addition to other Macintosh and Windows compatibility solutions.

Solaris on Intel and PowerPC. SunSoft's arguments for Solaris lie in the advanced Solaris architecture that features multithreading, multiprocessing, multitasking and multiuser, its compliance with the SVR4 ABI and API, the large number of applications it supports, its object-oriented technology, and its compatibility with multiprocessing. SunSoft is porting Solaris to what it believes will be the major volume architectures of the future, in addition to SPARC—that is, Intel and PowerPC.

Sun Microsystems brought out its Intel version of Solaris in mid-1993, a year after it was announced and several months late. Solaris on Intel requires at least a 33Mhz 386 with a math coprocessor, 12 MB of ram, 200 MB of hard disk, and an 800×600 pixel graphics display or better.

Sun Microsystems has reportedly laid out plans to port Solaris to the PowerPC over the next year or so. This in completing its strategy of supporting all the major volume chips that it expects to survive: Sparc, Intel, and PowerPC.

INTERACTIVE Systems Corporation (now part of SunSoft). INTERACTIVE Systems was the first commercial licensee of AT&T UNIX. Its first implementation was on DEC hardware in 1977. In 1978, INTERACTIVE introduced a hosted version of UNIX on VAX/VMS and by 1981 did one of the first native ports of UNIX to the IBM S/370. INTERACTIVE implemented the first symmetric multiprocessor port on S/370 in 1982 and developed PC/IX for IBM in 1984. In 1985, it developed AT&T's official port for UNIX System V for the Intel 386. By 1986, INTERACTIVE jointly announced AIX for the RT PC with IBM. Soon after, in 1988, it was acquired by Kodak. In July 1989, INTERACTIVE acquired Lachman Associates, a leading supplier of networking and telecommunications products and services. INTERACTIVE is one of the leading developers and suppliers of UNIX software products, technology, and services. It focuses on OEMs, VARs, and system integrators, including companies such as IBM, UNISYS, Fujitsu, and Teradyne. INTERACTIVE Systems also had agreements with Microsoft, making the company an OEM second source for XENIX System V/386.

INTERACTIVE, having been acquired by Sun, continues to sell their products but seems to be gradually merged into the overall SunSoft business. SunSoft/INTERACTIVE Systems is a powerful combination. The merger is resulting in a combination of the INTERACTIVE UNIX System and process independent version and the SunOS version which for several years has only been available on SPARC and in particular Sun SPARC RISC processors. SunSoft is in an enviable

position of managing the migration of an already aggressive INTERAC-
TIVE systems in penetrating the UNIX PC market.

Solaris, SunSoft's 32-bit UNIX, based on SunOS, is a fast, robust
UNIX implementation. The new version of Solaris 2.x will be truly portable UNIX for Intel as well as SPARC. SunSoft's willingness and ability
to migrate the code to other platforms remains a significant question that
could have implications on its ability to compete with other version of
UNIX from Novell, OSF and other core UNIX development groups.

SunSoft with Solaris 2.x represents one of the most significant
changes in the UNIX industry in years. It may have a dramatic effect on
the UNIX desktop market. Sun is a formidable force in workstations
and servers emerging as a full line computer systems vendor. Sun is
SunSoft's largest OEM. With its relationship to Sun, its acquisition of
INTERACTIVE and its aggressive technology and marketing orientation, SunSoft and Solaris are products to watch.

SunSoft's INTERACTIVE product and SCO UNIX with Open Desktop are compared in a later section of this chapter.

SunSoft Solaris

Based on:	System V release 4
User Interface:	OpenLook, OpenWindows, X Windows
Networking:	NFS, TCP/IP, RFS, UUCP, RFS, TLI
Price:	Bundled
Notes:	Multithreaded Kernel, SMP, loadable modules, shared libraries

SunSoft INTERACTIVE

Based on:	System V release 4
User Interface:	OpenLook, X Windows
Networking:	NFS, TCP/IP
Price:	

3.4.3.   OSF

The Open Software Foundation is now known for OSF/1, for the Motif
graphical user interface, and most recently for DCE, the Distributed
Computing Environment. Over the last few years, OSF has licensed
and integrated several software products through its so-called "open
process." Most of this software, with the exception of Motif, has not

become widely available commercially. In the meantime, OSF is bringing even newer technology based on the Mach microkernel out. OSF/1-MK is being based on the Mach 3.0 microkernel. OSF is described fully in Chapter 6.

OSF sells only to OEMs who add extensions, integrate, package, sell, and support the product. DEC is the first company to get to market with an OSF/1-based product. Other vendors released early versions and development versions of OSF/1—more on OSF in section 6.5.

3.4.4.   USL (USL, Univel, and Novell)

Rumors had circulated during 1992 about the acquisition of USL by Novell. Novell was already USL's largest single share holder. At the end of 1992, Novell, Inc. and AT&T jointly announced they had signed a letter of intent for Novell to acquire UNIX Systems Laboratories (USL). Perhaps now, under Novell, UNIX will get the marketing push AT&T never did provide. The purchase puts the weight of a major software company behind the marketing and development of the UNIX operating system.

The signing of the letter of intent was approved by the boards of directors of Novell and AT&T. The merger remained subject to the approval of USL stockholders, regulatory approvals, and the signing of a definitive merger agreement and other normal conditions to closing which were all but a formality. The acquisition was completed during 1993.

> *"Our support of UNIX systems, as evidenced by our earlier investment in USL and the joint creation of Univel, has been driven by the widespread use of UNIX at our customer sites and by our desire to work closely with our industry partners," said Raymond J. Noorda, president and chief executive officer of Novell. "This acquisition is being done at the urging of customers who have asked us to support the UNIX system directly and integrate it more fully within the NetWare environment. This reflects the growing importance of UNIX systems which are increasingly being used for rightsizing business applications on computer networks."*

Novell recognized and values the importance of UNIX as an open accessible technology to OEM partners and customers around the world. As part of Novell, USL's commitment to fair and neutral access to UNIX technology would not change according to press releases at the time.

Robert M. Kavner, AT&T group executive for communications

products, reiterated what the company had said since 1991 that AT&T intended to reduce its ownership in USL, but that AT&T remained firmly committed to the UNIX system. "Associating USL with Novell, another strong company, will allow USL to be an even more effective and flourishing force in the software industry."

Roel Pieper, president and chief executive officer of USL at the time, said: "The two best technologies for Open Systems and interoperability are coming together within one company. The UNIX system provides reliable, secure, sophisticated capabilities for network computing applications. The NetWare environment provides integrated cross-platform system services. The combination of the two enables distributed computing solutions to be deployed simply and cost effectively—from desktops to mainframes."

The Financial Times of London said the price to be paid is 270 million U.K. pounds. The value of the deal was estimated at $369 million. Novell exchanged 12.3 million shares of Novell common stock for USL common stock. AT&T will hold 3 percent of Novell's common stock after this transaction.

USL Produced Destiny—a "UNIX-lite" for the Desktop. USL's flagship product was UNIX System V Release 4 (SVR4). SVR4 supported system calls from AT&T UNIX, SunOS, and XENIX. Programs written for any of the systems based on SVR4 can be recompiled and run on SVR4 provided they use API's that are also available and assuming the appropriate runtime libraries are also available.

Univel slimmed down SVR4's size and price by unbundling. Univel integrated and distributed SVR4.2 under the name UnixWare. Novell USG now has the charter of recruiting independent software vendors for the new UnixWare release. At announcement, Univel had almost 70 companies lined up. With the exception of the rhetoric of major vendors, looking at the numbers of shipping systems, it would appear that SVR4 comes as close as it may ever to being the UNIX standard.

USL releases of SVR4 included SVR4MP, a version supporting symmetric multiprocessing, multithreaded kernel supporting up to 16 processors, SVR4.1ES, containing features of the MLS multilevel security normally provided in previous versions of SVR4. SVR4.1ES provided multiple methods of access control, trusted paths, and customized audit trails. It also incorporated features in a newly scrutinized and analyzed kernel and not merely as an add-on. This brought SRV4 much better performance and up to B2-level security. USL expected to merge these versions into a single product in 1993. The Destiny product, released in 1992 by USL, is a stripped-down version of UNIX SVR4.1ES that is targeted at Intel-based PC's.

SVR4.2. Novell USG now distributes UnixWare, a shrinkwrap version of SVR4.2 with enhancements that allow NetWare applications to be supported by UnixWare servers instead of MS-DOS servers, for example.

UnixWare features both Motif and Open Look graphical user interfaces and applications. A tool kit called MOOLIT allows developers to build applications that can dynamically switch between Open Look or Motif GUIs. MOOLIT allows the same binary application to run in either environment.

SVR4.2 provides graphics capabilities, utilities, and windowing based on the X11 Releases 4 and 5. A small number of desktop applications are bundled with the operating system including a mail package, calculator, clock, and so forth. An online hypertext help system supports online documentation. SVR4.2 provides a GUI-based system administration capability. SVR4.2 meets B1 security standards, and like OS/2 2.0, built-in protection prevents DOS or Windows applications from crashing the operating system. Backup and recover setup and scheduling functions are provided for use on a single system or on a network of machines.

A variety of networking protocols and environments are supported along with all the traditional UNIX networking services and functionality. SVR4.2 provides both client and server functionality. The server capabilities include multiuser services, disk management, high availability, and other features normally required in server environments.

SVR4.2 makes no assumptions about the PC hardware configuration it is installed on. This means someone needs to set up the system to work with a particular combination of hardware. There is no online documentation other than help menus. Networking is not completely plug and play and requires some level of integration to set up and manage.

USL did not sell to end users, so the support to end users was only as good as the support offered by USL's OEMs.

3.4.5.   Novell

Novell is a strong company with total assets of over $1 billion and $260 million in cash at the end of their fiscal year ending 1992 on October 31. Novell has very little debt and a low debt to equity ratio of 17 percent.

Novell is best known for NetWare, a proprietary PC-LAN networked operating system. In NetWare, Novell has a product that works and dominant market share in the PC-LAN market. UNIX and Open Systems seem to be the next step in their growth.

Novell has been making serious moves in the UNIX industry. Novell became the largest outside investor in USL holding 5 percent of USL's shares prior to acquiring USL. It has also recently joined UNIX International, OSF, the Object Management Group.

Prior to the acquisition of USL, Novell had formed a joint venture with USL called Univel. Univel moved quickly to release UnixWare, a shrinkwrap version of SVR4.2, featuring integrated NetWare support.

Univel and Novell. Novell originally formed Univel to focus its distribution to reach the mass market. USL and Novell had formed a distribution agreement for UNIX System V Release 4 (SVR4.2) through Univel. This allowed Novell to continue to focus on NetWare and continue with strategic marketing relationships with other UNIX vendors, most notably Sun Microsystems.

Originally called "Destiny," UnixWare is an operating system for Intel-based systems running the 386 or 486. Novell USG is charged with the development and marketing of UnixWare which incorporates a version of NetWare and increases the interoperability of UNIX System V Release 4 and NetWare. The Novell ventures seem focused on the client-server Intel market. Novell, with over 5,000 authorized resellers, will no doubt play a role in marketing and supporting UnixWare in the PC and PC LAN markets. Novell has the power to bring UNIX to the Intel desktop.

UNIX will be the application server environment and NetWare the best distributed services provider. Better integration of NetWare, the dominant PC-LAN network operating system in the world and UNIX SVR4, the dominant UNIX operating system can be expected. NetWare and UnixWare can be expected to become more tightly integrated in the future with common management, application frameworks, and infrastructure. NetWare will no doubt become more adapted for use with TCP/IP. Univel is unbundling TCP/IP and substituting NetWare hooks in UnixWare.

As Nina Lytton, Open Systems advisor, said at the time, "Novell is the shutout pitcher in the PC team's enterprise computing game. Novell has the potential to stall Microsoft's NT climb into enterprise computing." The buyout of USL by Novell was seen by most as one of the really bright spots.

3.4.6.   SCO (The Santa Cruz Operation, Inc.)

SCO revenues in 1992 were around $175 million, making it the fourth- or fifth-largest UNIX software supplier. SCO dominates the PC UNIX market although its competition appears to be gaining on it rapidly.

SCO was founded in 1978. Doug and Larry Michels founded the company without a business plan and without a clear vision. SCO's progressive early work on PC UNIX became the darling of the UNIX community. Over the first 10 years, Michels created a $70 million business. They sold PC UNIX to doctors, auto dealers, small businesses of all sorts. They put UNIX into small PC AT-based systems with inexpensive ASCII terminals attached. This was like a minicomputer at a much lower price. The business boomed in many directions. Eventually SCO realized that they were trapped. To expand, SCO realized they had to sell applications, but they didn't have enough applications. When SCO sold a system, it would promise specific applications. It would then hire the engineers to develop them or farm them out to third parties. As the resources were consumed in niche application development, they were gradually sapped from their core products. SCO could not convince big PC software developers like Lotus or Ashton-Tate to build or port their applications fast enough. This eventually would hamper SCO's growth.

As the PC UNIX market grew, SCO's market share and profits declined. Losses in the 1980s forced SCO to look for investors. Since the early 1980s, Microsoft had used SCO to distributed XENIX. In 1989, some venture capitalists and Microsoft made a deal. As part of this deal, SCO could rewrite Microsoft's applications for UNIX and Open Desktop. Microsoft put $25 million into the company and obtained 16 percent of the stock.

SCO has gradually shifted its focus to extend to large corporate accounts. It now claims around 30 percent of its revenues from major accounts with the balance coming from small businesses and distributors. SCO has been licensing XENIX from Microsoft since 1982. In retail software sales, SCO provides a final packaged product. For OEMs, the company provides either a packaged product or a license allowing them to adapt the product to their own hardware. SCO also provides support for OEMs, distributors, VARs, end users, and dealers.

In 1990, the Santa Cruz Operation was a $100 million-plus independent software vendor. By 1991, their revenues were estimated to be around $140 million, making it one of the largest UNIX software companies in the industry. The company has an installed base of over 500,000 SCO UNIX and SCO XENIX systems worldwide. According to some market research sources, this accounts for nearly two-thirds of the base of Intel-based PCs. As much as 80 percent or more of SCO's installed base is comprised of older XENIX systems running multiuser, small business systems on PC ATs. SCO UNIX, as it is often called, is really SCO UNIX System V/386 Release 3.2. It conforms to the AT&T SVID, POSIX 1003.1, X/Open XPG3, and the federal government's C2 security standard.

SCO has more than 2,500 value-added resellers and also distributes its products through MicroD and Merisel. DEC, HP, NCR, Unisys, and other computer companies have OEM agreements with SCO as well. SCO has been building up an infrastructure for UNIX/Intel, which is similar to what Microsoft has done with DOS/Intel. SCO is currently the leader in the PC UNIX market, with over 85 percent of the PC UNIX marketplace, but it is facing increasing competition from other vendors.

The Santa Cruz Operation is still one of the largest suppliers of Intel-based UNIX to end users and has been at the forefront of PC UNIX, that is, microprocessor-based UNIX operating systems since 1983, when it released the first version of XENIX for the PC/XT based on AT&T UNIX System III.

SCO UNIX System V/386 Release 3.2 was based on AT&T UNIX System V/386 and ported to Intel 80386 technology by Microsoft, AT&T, and INTERACTIVE Systems in 1987. SCO has been the exclusive distributor of this software. SCO has been successful by concentrating on one architecture and developing an off-the-shelf product.

Today, SCO still sells XENIX but mainly sells its own SCO UNIX based on System V Release 3.2. SCO is shifting its emphasis to the integrated environment above the operating system with Open Desktop. Open Desktop (ODT) attempts to package UNIX for users by bundling together the X Window system, networking support, OSF/Motif graphical user interface, a desktop manager, and the ability to run DOS programs.

SCO was a founding member of ACE, an initiative to create a binary standard version of UNIX for the Mips architecture. ACE was big news for about a year. Then it fell apart. Not long after Compaq withdrew its support for ACE, SCO followed suit. The ACE initiative fell into disarray because it was outpaced by industry events. SGI bought Mips, which had to have some impact on the way some OEM's viewed Mips. DEC, which has been a major proponent, and was to be the last "ACE mohicans." DEC seemed to be willing to give ULTRIX to ACE and buy it back from SCO. But DEC shifted its strategy if not its level of commitment by announcing Windows/NT would be ported to Alpha.

Indeed, with its Mips-based product line clearly going to be replaced by Alpha, and with its own customer base forcing it to port and support OSF/1 on its Mips product line, does ACE based on Mips really make any sense? But back to SCO.

In early 1992, SCO announced the suspension of all of its MIPS Computer Systems-based development work. This effectively ended SCO's participation in the ACE initiative. SCO's decision was primarily based on a decision to refocus on Intel and its next-generation chip, whose performance SCO believed would be comparable to the MIPS' R4000 RISC chip. SCO, possibly fearing competitive pressures from USL, SunSoft, and Novell, announced it would incorporate the OSF/1 operating system into its future products.

SCO UNIX System V/386 was the first commercially available version on UNIX for the Intel platform and has a significant share of the uniprocessor Intel-installed base. SCO had apparently decided not to implement all of the SVR4 and in the wake of the ACE initiative, its strategy is not clear. SCO is at a critical decision point. It must either commit to Microsoft Window/NT, OSF/1 or go back to SVR4. SCO participation in COSE may cause it to adopt a strategy of COSE on NT.

As the high-end PC market and the low-end workstation market overlap, SCO is likely to encounter severe competitive pressure from other companies offering 32-bit UNIX operating systems, most notably SunSoft.

SunSoft acquired the INTERACTIVE systems product that in 1990 was projected to be gaining market share as SCO was losing it. However, SCO still commanded a dominate market share overall of over 60 percent of the PC UNIX market. SunSoft has claimed that it is already the leader in the 32-bit UNIX operating system market in terms of units shipped. SCO will also face pressure from Microsoft's NT and from Novell, and from UNIX Systems Laboratory.

SCO followed Compaq in withdrawing from the ACE initiative. There are a considerable number of resellers and OEMs of PC UNIX who are watching SCO's strategy and could either jump ship or remain with SCO as it determines its new strategy.

SCO UNIX

Based on:	System V and XENIX
User Interface:	Open Desktop
Networking:	NFS, TCP/IP, UUCP, SCO XENIX-Net
Price:	Not available
Notes:	DOS file sharing, XENIX compatibility

3.4.7. The Wollongong Group

The Wollongong Group provides, on a contract basis, requirements analysis and development services for the design, integration, and implementation of complex network information systems. Wollongong sells a variant of UNIX known as EUNICE as well as integrated networking software. EUNICE is targeted mainly at DEC VMS users who want to utilize UNIX. Wollongong also sells to computer system OEMs.

3.4.8. UNIX Database Management Solutions

In addition to UNIX software vendors, database vendors are among the largest software companies in the UNIX market. A brief summary of the top four UNIX database vendors is provided below.

Oracle Corporation. With overall software revenues in excess of $1 billion and UNIX software revenues in excess of $250 million in 1990 and $680 million by 1992, Oracle is the largest software company selling its products into the UNIX market. Oracle Corp., based in Redwood Shores, California, offers a range of products including a relational database management system as well as a range of database and software engineering tools. Oracle supports a number of its software products on some 40 UNIX platforms and databases. UNIX is Oracle's fastest-growing market with growth estimated at 57 percent in 1992 with much of that growth coming from Europe. Oracle is expected to remain the largest software vendor in the UNIX market.

Oracle announced Oracle 7 for enterprise computing in the summer of 1992. Oracle is working with various UNIX platform vendors on its Parallel server technology and also brought its application software business into full swing in 1992. Its financial, government financial, human resources, and manufacturing applications have been gaining momentum and UNIX applications represented around 65 percent of Oracle's application revenues overall.

Informix Corporation. Informix, with 1992 revenues of $250 million has remained in the number two spot in the UNIX software market. Over 90 percent of the company's revenues come from its UNIX business operations. Informix revenues in 1992 grew 52 percent over 1991. Informix profited the most from Oracle's problems during 1990. The company reported UNIX revenue growth of 77 percent in 1990 over the previous year.

Informix sells a number of UNIX-related products including graphical spreadsheet software that runs with SCO's Open Desktop, Motif, and Open Look, and that supports interfaces that allow users to import data into the spreadsheet—known as Wingz—from an Informix backend database server.

INGRES Corporation. INGRES's 1992 UNIX revenues were just under $180 million. UNIX accounted for 60 percent of INGRES's business in 1992 and representing growth of over 50 percent over 1991. The company is regarded as being number four in the UNIX software market.

ASK Computer Systems of Mountain View, California, acquired INGRES Corporation during the latter half of 1990. The ASK merger may work to both companies' advantage. ASK was already using INGRES software in the development of its own future products.

During 1990, INGRES introduced INGRES Windows 4GL, which was designed for software developers or end users wanting to create a graphical user interface for their database application. Its latest database management software was upgraded to support multiple INGRES database backends and ensure update integrity.

Sybase, Inc. Sybase had 1992 revenues of just under $190 million, 80 percent of which were UNIX based. Sybase acquired Gain Technology, Inc. in 1992 in an effort to shore up its software development tools, an area Sybase is generally considered to lag its competition.

Sybase, based in Emeryville, California, was the first database platform designed on UNIX for distributed hardware environments supporting the client server model. Sybase was also the first relational database that was designed specifically for high-performance transaction processing applications. During 1990, Sybase acquired SQL Solutions of Burlington, Massachusetts, which specializes in providing professional services and tools for developing relational database management applications. It also introduced a family of products that integrates the IBM MVS mainframe into the expanded client server environment. In 1991, Sybase assimilated the SQL Solutions operation into its general business.

Sybase expanded its business over 80 percent to $103 million in 1990. Revenues in the early years were attributed mainly to the Sun and VAX VMS platforms. To foster their growth more recently and in the future, the company now supports the major UNIX platforms including Sun, HP, AT&T, and IBM's AIX and has also formed marketing agreements with Microsoft.

3.5. SOFTWARE TRENDS IN THE PC AND UNIX INDUSTRY

Putting UNIX and PC Software in Perspective

The major competitors for the desktop of the 1990's will include Windows, Macintosh, and UNIX. UNIX weaknesses, and why it is projected to be the runnerup by most analysts to the other operating systems, has to do with its cost, the applications, and cost of applications available on UNIX and the lack of maturity of the distribution channel for UNIX software compared to PC software. Most analysts estimate that UNIX will grow from less than 3 percent of PC operating systems sold to as high as 10 percent of units sold by 1994. The following appear to be inevitable truths of the desktop operating system market:

- The PC channel does not understand UNIX.
- DOS and Windows will not go away, and Windows/NT will be a market force.
- UNIX applications have to be significantly differentiated from PC software.
- Growth in UNIX software takes place only with the maturing of distribution.

Trends in UNIX Software

The software industry in general, and the UNIX software industry in particular, are undergoing significant change. Some of the key trends include the following:

- Operating system wars are causing platform vendors to try to accelerate ISV ports to their new platforms. Some serious porting fees have been negotiated, and some platform vendors have even acquired or taken equity positions in ISVs they consider strategic.
- With all the attention and technology investment going into Open Systems, the cost of porting to more than one platform has been reduced to the point where ISVs are almost always supporting more than one system platform.
- Original Equipment Manufacturers (OEMs) may buy hardware from other companies and offer it under their own name as if they actually manufactured it themselves. Traditionally hardware OEMs who added primarily hardware value-add to their products are increasingly moving to become the systems vendors of both hardware and software. Some system vendors are effectively un-

bundling their software products and spinning out business subsidiaries or whole new businesses to focus solely on software. All this creates tremendous competition between ISVs.

UNIX software has unique distribution problems. While it shares some of the characteristics of MS-DOS software in terms of lower cost compared to software used with mainframe or midrange systems, the channel of distribution for UNIX software is not even close to mature. PC software distribution is far more advanced in terms of the evolution of hardware independent distribution. The shrinkwrap nature of PC software by comparison to UNIX has also permitted an exceptional economy of scale that today is still largely the plan more than the reality. While MS-DOS application software is hardware vendor independent and can be distributed through independent distribution channels, it can only be operated on a single relatively fixed-size system and, therefore, will be more limited in the range of applications compared to what UNIX software can address.

UNIX software sales in 1990 were estimated to be approximately $3 billion worldwide. Tremendous growth has occurred in spite of the diversity of UNIX software products, the uniqueness of the marketplace, and the immature nature of software distribution.

While the distribution of UNIX software can and will be facilitated by addressing technical issues that make the UNIX system platform environment more uniform, UNIX software vendors today are creating new types of distribution channels and inventing new models of software distribution.

UNIX software as a category is unlike any other software category. It is unique for many reasons principal among these the fact that UNIX software can run on a very wide range of system platforms. UNIX software is rarely developed for a single vendor's architecture and operating system. UNIX software is frequently deployed in networks and over multiple network topologies. UNIX software is written to operate across these networks and to interoperate in peer-to-peer and/or client server relationships.

UNIX platform vendors can be divided into five major segments:

1. Low-cost UNIX PC operating system platforms for Intel and IBM clones

    Examples: SCO, ESIX, SunSoft/INTERACTIVE Systems

    Expectations: Low price, ease of use, available through all channels—distributors/value-added resellers; thousands of applications available.

Purchasing: By credit card or purchase order, evaluation and purchase in days to weeks.

Application Software Distribution: Retail, mail-order, distributors, VARs, and direct only to major accounts.

2. Workstation vendors with RISC supporting RISC and Intel-based platforms in uniprocessor and multiprocessor configurations
   Examples: Sun/SunSoft, DEC, HP-UX

   Expectations: Bundled with cost of workstations, available through multiple changes, VARs, and OEMs; thousands of applications but a few hundred leading packages. Software requires power of workstation.

   Purchasing: Corporate procurement in the main.

   Application Software Distribution: Software sold direct or through resellers who may also handle hardware.

3. Multiprocessor system vendors offering MP/MT UNIX
   Examples: Sun/SunSoft, HP, DEC, Sequent, Pyramid

   Expectations: Operating system normally costed above and beyond hardware. RDBMS software leads as software platform.

   Purchasing: Corporate procurement.

   Application Software Distribution: Sold direct. Resellers and OEMS to lesser extent.

4. Exclusively OEM suppliers
   Examples: USL, OSF

   Expectations: Will license for royalty to system vendor or software reseller.

   Purchasing: Licensing terms.

   Application Software Distribution: Not applicable.

So how do Desktop UNIX systems stack up overall? We explore several dimensions of the answer to this question in the following analysis.

In terms of *Intel architecture support*, SCO holds the largest installed base; Novell and SunSoft are both serious contenders for future PC UNIX market share.

In terms of *RISC support*, SunSoft is the clear winner with a commanding lead in RISC and SPARC architecture installations in particular. No SPARC clone has offered a significant challenge to Sun overall, but several SPARC vendors continue to prosper.

In terms of *applications availability*, the picture is less clear. SunSoft has a powerful set of leading edge PC ISV's committed to Solaris, but SCO has a huge number of microsystem ISV applications and resellers. It is too early to declare either company the winner and in fact they appear to be addressing very different markets; SCO—continuing its focus on the microprocessor server and to a lessor extent the ODT desktop and SunSoft focusing on the desktop with Sun Microsystems Computer Corporation focused on making Solaris a success on both the server and the desktop.

In terms of *standards compliance*, SunSoft and Univel are quite advanced. The difference is that SunSoft has the installed base to reference whereas Univel mostly has a good story.

3.5.1.   Different Channels for Different Types of Software

Even in the early stages of evolution, there appear to be unique channels of distribution evolving to fulfill the needs of different market segments.

1. High-volume, low-cost, horizontal software such as personal productivity software such as spreadsheet software or desktop publishing or even utilities such as calendar manager.
2. Low-volume, niche application market, horizontal software such as low cost CAD/CAM software or accounting software.
3. Low- to moderate-volume, high-cost horizontal software such as relational database management solutions (e.g., Oracle, Sybase).
4. Low-volume, moderate to high-priced vertical solution software targeting specific industries and line of business-oriented applications (e.g., legal software or banking software).
5. Low-volume, high-priced, often highly customized software such as MRP II or OLTP applications.

There are also very different characteristics in market segments made up in terms of type of buyers:

1. End users, whether individual or corporate buyers
2. Developers
3. System or network administrators

Each of these groups differs in terms of technical orientation, buying process, and so forth. Large software purchases will often involve all of these groups. The end user department in a corporation may drive the acquisition, but internal developers may have to evaluate and make recommendations about the tools surrounding the application. The system or network adminstrator will influence the selection of software especially when the hardware and operating system platform is already set.

3.5.2. Current Issues of UNIX Software Developers and Distributors

Software channels of distribution for UNIX are immature and still in a formative stage. This is in sharp contrast to the PC software market where channels of distribution are mature and relatively stable. Figure 3.4 shows the typical organization of software channels of distribution. SI stands for Systems Integrators.

There are many issues faced by developers and distributors of UNIX software. The different versions of UNIX and UNIX window systems often means that the multiplatform software vendor must have a rela-

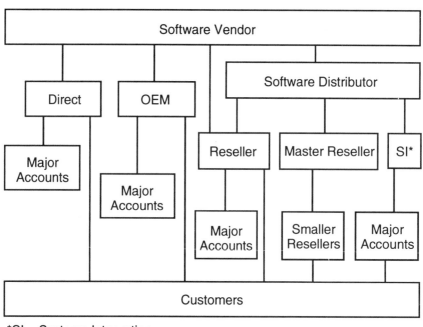

*SI = Systems Integration

Figure 3.4. UNIX software channels of distribution.

tively large number of stock-keeping units (SKUs). Whether distributed by the software vendor or through independent channels, multiple SKUs impact the cost of distribution and the profitability of the product.

Pricing strategies are a real issue since the software may be used on a single-user platform or multiuser platform having very similar price performance characteristics. The pricing issues are also complicated by a variety of licensing issues associated with development environments, run-time licenses, network licenses, and so forth.

Most software today is priced based on either the number of users active on the platform (in the case of multiuser or networked solutions) or based on the size or class of the system. Pricing strategies are normally implemented by creating multiple SKUs.

Like all software developers, UNIX software developers face the same problems of protecting their software in order to maximize revenues. UNIX software often uses license management mechanisms that they may have developed or may be supplied by either the system platform vendor, their distribution partner, or an independent software vendor. Networked UNIX workstations and multiuser systems offer an additional challenge for the software developer and add complexity to mass-market distribution.

Perhaps one of the greatest challenges lies in the rapid technological change in the computer industry itself. Product life cycles are decreasing dramatically and vendors are launching major new products and/or major new operating system releases once a year. This requires developers to work very closely with system platform vendors to stay current with what they are introducing and selling. It creates complex product management problems as well since changes in the underlying system software or platform often affect software product binaries and therefore the inventory and profitability of the software distribution channels.

The Linkage between UNIX Software, System Platforms Vendors, and System Platform Resellers. *Reseller News* conducted a survey in 1990 that showed the following:

- Close to 50 percent of resellers resold UNIX workstations.
- 50 percent sold multiuser applications.
- 70 percent sold to commercial users (e.g., small business or smaller departments of larger companies).
- 75 percent sold to companies with less than 100 employees.
- 22 percent sold to companies with between 100 and 1000 employees.
- Less than 3 percent sold to companies with over 1000 employees.

Resellers support activities (read value add) derived from installation, systems integration, training, modification of applications, and development of applications.

Recent research by Networked Publications has shown that resellers tend to get most of their inquiries and leads from software vendors and that many customers tend to make software decisions before they make platform purchasing decisions.

Network Publications in conjunction with Computer Intelligence and InfoCorp conducts and publishes annual surveys of UNIX ISV programs for system platform vendors, software vendors, and consortia. System platform vendors recognize that application solutions are what help sell their hardware. There is increasing competition between system vendors to offer effective ISV programs. Nearly all vendors' design programs are tiered to provide special support to the most important software partners.

Challenges Facing Buyers of UNIX Software. The buyers of UNIX software face numerous challenges in locating and procuring the right software products. While there are numerous software catalogs available, there continues to be a sense that there aren't enough applications—or as many as are available on MS-DOS, for example. We believe this has more to do with UNIX software distribution than with any shortage of applications per se.

UNIX International estimates there are over 18,000 UNIX applications running on UNIX System V release 4 (SVR4) based systems. Hundreds of hardware vendors maintain third-party catalogs of software applications. There are many vendor independent UNIX software catalogs including:

UniForum Product Directory

Ziff-Davis Computer Directory

ICP Directory

Large software vendors, most notably RDBMS vendors such as Oracle, Ingres, Informix, and Sybase, all have catalogs of third-party software as well.

So why do buyers still have problems locating the right software? They either don't know where to look for applications or they don't get exposure to applications until they have made a platform decision (e.g., opposite the way many companies actually buy). They don't see applications marketed by cohesive independent distribution mechanisms.

Some progress is being made by companies like UNIX Central, Qualix, and Highland Software. Each of these companies is trying to function as an independent distribution mechanism for UNIX software. UNIX Central is taking the printed catalog approach. Qualix and Highland Software, the CD-ROM approach.

Hardware vendors are also beginning to recognize the opportunity in distribution and setup subsidiaries to handle software direct marketing and distribution. SunExpress, a Sun subsidiary, was established for this reason. SunExpress carries not only Sun software but other third-party software as well. Vendors such as Digital and SGI have similar programs. The most traditional method at present that users locate software is through the ISV programs of the system vendors.

3.5.3.   ISV Program Evolution

Providing superior ISV support has become a fact of doing business for system vendors. Even companies like Apple, which hasn't put much effort into ISV programs in the past, have developed formal ISV programs. We predict that the next few years will see platform vendors reassess and continually improve their ISV support programs in order to strengthen their relationship and thereby leverage additional business through their ISVs.

But especially in the UNIX market, where Open Systems and interoperability are at the center of so much of the technology focus and innovation, the end user/customer is beginning to play an increasing role through the adoption of a standards-based, information-based information architecture. Figure 3.5 shows the typical hardware distribution channels.

These standards, together with the increasingly sophisticated application binary interfaces and application programming (source level) interfaces (called APIs), are making it possible for ISVs to support essentially one source code tree which, once compiled for a particular processor architecture, is binary compatible (in theory) for all platforms supporting the ABI. For other processor architectures, a recompilation is required to port the software to a platform with a different processor architecture but which otherwise supports the API standard.

Standards-Based Applications Required. Many customers are not particularly concerned with what the ISV has to do internally to get its software onto the platform it opts for. However, customers are increasingly looking for hardware independence, and if they decide to change hardware, they don't want their investment in software, data, and

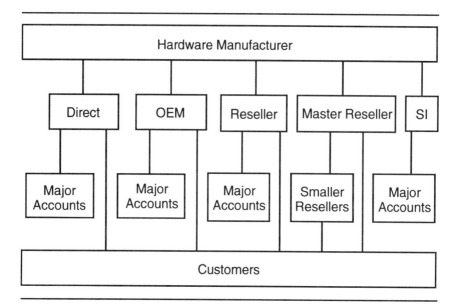

Figure 3.5. UNIX hardware channels of distribution.

training to become obsolete. They would also like to get their software as cheaply as possible. They would like cross-platform upgrades, for example. The less work it is for the ISV to port, the fewer the costs that have to be passed on to the customer.

The other end user consideration, which is especially true with large corporations or institutions, is that in addition to the software they buy, they still build software. Whether it's from scratch or it's tailoring a package or it's interfacing and integrating applications, many organizations have an "internal ISV." They resemble, in almost every respect with the possible exception of sales and marketing, the commercial ISV. They have to develop software, often for more than one platform, they have to quality assure it, and they have to install it and train users on it.

The ISV—System Platform Vendor Relationship. Most ISVs will never have enough money to create brand awareness via marketing communications and PR for their company. The expenses associated with developing a distribution channel that consists of some direct as well as indirect sales are neither trivial nor risk free. Increasingly, ISVs are interested in leveraging their platform vendor for joint development, marketing, and sales. In this context how the system vendor manages its relationship with the ISV can have a profound effect on the quality and effectiveness of the ISV-vendor relationship.

3.6.   USER DEMAND FOR UNIX SOFTWARE

Why are users using UNIX? Among the key reasons:

- Access to cheaper computer power, throughput, and multitasking
- UNIX fills a gap between low-end PCs and high-end systems; this gap is filled with networked workstations and servers.
- Many users have made heavy use of communications. The Internet has grown up largely with UNIX.
- UNIX is almost synonymous with Open Systems computing, and to most people represents the center of a rich layered standards-based system environment.

But perhaps the principal and sometimes overlooked reason people want UNIX is because of the applications, and the applications development environment. From its early history, innovative tools and applications have been available on UNIX.

Historically, Bell Labs and AT&T developed and adapted UNIX since it was a portable operating system and they could better control the evolution of their own internal solutions built on an operating system platform under their own control. Clearly, this was and is now well beyond the means of corporations. But try to imagine the costs of thousands of proprietary computers AT&T was acquiring. UNIX, originally developed in 1969 on the PDP-7, was ported to the PDP-11 and by the late 70s, the 32-bit VAX. UNIX, *the cult*, grew out of the research and educational institutions fueled largely by the aggressive actions of the Berkeley Software Distribution (BSD) version of UNIX funded by DARPA.

By the late 70s and the early 80s, UNIX variants were springing up everywhere. UNIX was proving to be a cheap way for companies to bring new system platforms to market. A large number of small computer companies jumped into the fray. In many cases, these systems were aimed at specific applications markets, and UNIX was essentially hidden to the user by design.

The fragmentation of UNIX bore little similarity to the emerging PC industry with its shrinkwrap MS-DOS software on the one hand, nor to the 32-bit systems market featuring numerous high-value business applications on the other. Many of these early UNIX system companies quickly became history. But it was far from over for UNIX. With the availability of commodity chips, the rise of RISC, and the meteoric rise of the workstation industry, new blood was pumped into the UNIX Industry.

Historical Summary of UNIX Applications

In 1986, the primary UNIX platforms were BSD on DEC VAX and Sun, AT&T's System V on various machines, ULTRIX on DEC VAX, XENIX on PCs and microprocessor based multiuser systems like Altos, and SunOS on Sun. The primary applications during this period included CAD/CAM, CASE, DBMS, communications, Email, and text/word processing. Around 85 percent of software sold with UNIX was sold with maintenance agreements, and more than half of the systems were networked, with communications software purchased from the system platform vendor.

By 1990, UNIX had established itself as one of the most important growth markets with over $15 billion in sales and growing at almost 25 percent per year. UNIX dominated the workstation marketplace and was rapidly becoming the norm in the midrange multiuser systems market. Many system OEMs were shifting toward becoming ISVs. Even UNIX systems vendors, recognizing the potential for software, started spinning out strategic business units and porting their software to multiple UNIX platforms. This was in part driven by a desire to establish their software as an industry standard much the way Sun did with its NFS software.

The 1990s will see growth in several segments of the UNIX market.

- Downsizing trends will fuel increased use of client server solutions. Mainframes will still play a role, albeit reduced, in managing the most complex update-intensive, transaction-processing environments. Many of the current mainframe applications that require read-only access to data, for example, and decision support, will rapidly migrate to database servers and high-performance clients for analytics.
- The midrange systems market will increase as the availability of vertical applications increases and far exceeds the quantity and quality of applications available on proprietary midrange systems such as the IBM AS/400, DEC VAX, and HP MPE-based platforms.
- The workstation market will continue to grow due to the superior price performance and integration offered by workstations.
- The low end of the UNIX market will rapidly increase based on the

availability of standards-based UNIX products designed for use with a wider range of PC platforms and the rapidly increasing power of PC processors, making them far more appropriate for supporting UNIX than PC platforms of the past.

In both the workstation and PC spaces, UNIX growth will go hand in hand with applications availability. UNIX applications will be differentiated from PC applications in several ways. They will be oriented toward the high-performance needs of knowledge workers. They will be based on open-application architectures, or "hubs," which allow for the integrated use of systems and applications development environments offered. All of this implies tremendous demands for software and a much more rapid pace of software innovation than in other parts of the computer market.

3.6.1. UNIX on Personal Computers

One of the most important and interesting developments in the UNIX industry is the growth of UNIX at the low end of the market. Due to the high number of unit shipments involved, this will be one of the most attractive markets for software vendors. There is currently a wide variation in the projections of industry analysts as to the growth of PC UNIX.

To be sure, Windows/DOS and the MAC will continue to represent major competition for UNIX. Cost, applications availability, and established distribution all seem to be working against UNIX. While no one is projecting the demise of dominant PC operating systems, even the most skeptical cannot argue with the attractiveness of UNIX in terms of comparative growth rates and the higher pricing and therefore higher margins than the commodity PC market products.

There are real opportunities for UNIX to complement the use of MACs and PCs in what is referred to as the "interoperability" applications. In such applications, work groups will be heterogeneous platforms with client-side software available on a variety of platforms and with a central back end on UNIX servers. In this model, ISVs will provide solutions that provide services to clients, making it possible to use existing equipment. Over the years, this creates the opportunity for UNIX-based hardware to compete more directly with traditional desktop platforms in replacement and upgrade situations.

While this prognosis is optimistic, the reality today is that PCs are cheap, and the PC channel still doesn't understand UNIX. UNIX applications growth is more complex, as will be discussed in the next section, due to the unique and less-developed nature of the channels of distribution for UNIX.

3.6.2. Summary of UNIX Software Distribution Trends

The UNIX market much more resembles the minicomputer market of the last decade than it does the PC market. Most vertical applications are sold through VARs or direct by ISVs. Most horizontal applications are OEMed and sold by system platform vendors or sold direct to major accounts and through indirect channels when possible.

With the rapid trend toward downsizing, with a free fall in prices for commodity hardware, and with the commercial market for UNIX based solutions projected by virtually every market analyst about to explode, the traditional model of distribution for UNIX software is no longer going to satisfy the requirements. The UNIX software market is going to look more and more like the PC market of the last decade.

With the above segmentations in mind, we now look at key trends in software distribution:

- Price trends:
  — System software represents 10 percent to 25 percent of platform initial value sold.
  — Key application software can represent anywhere from 50 percent to two or three times the platform initial value sold. For example a C++ software development environment costs roughly the same per user as users' base hardware does today.
  — UNIX customers require more support and they appear to be willing to pay for it.
- Competitive trends:
  — Software competition is stiff, especially for horizontal software. This is due to the large number of competitors (oversupply leads to rapid price/profitability erosion). As if the number of ISVs weren't high enough, many of the system platform vendors themselves are spinning off strategic business units and porting their software to other platforms. Examples include SunSoft porting to Intel and HP porting NewWave to Sun.
  — Pricing is quickly becoming a key differentiator, due more to the need to meet expectations of the PC market than anything else. There is a clear trend toward spreading the cost around using network licensing schemes, upgrades, support, and other techniques. Distribution is also becoming a competitive tactic, not

just in terms of shipping units sold, but also as advertising and for evaluation copies.

3.6.3.   Update on Emerging Technologies for UNIX ISVs

There is a variety of important new technologies that ISVs should plan to incorporate in their plans and products. This section gives a summary overview and provides references for further reading and research.

The technologies discussed here have tremendous potential to cut software development costs, increase the flexibility with which software can be licensed, and promise to radically alter the way software is advertised and distributed in the future.

* Object-oriented programming tools
* COSE API's and verification test suites
* CD-ROM
* Electronic bulletin board systems
* Network licensing

3.6.4.   Views of UNIX Distribution Channel Participants

The most successful UNIX ISVs have become so because they have created their own distribution channel. Oracle is the best example. Many ISVs have attempted to implement value-added reseller programs or to negotiate OEM agreements with large hardware manufacturers. But only about a third of the UNIX VARs will resell or package software products.

Software vendors recognize they cannot use the same distribution methods associated with successful MS-DOS packages. The PC software distributors are often targeting large, easily identifiable, business-oriented customers reachable through relatively low-cost marketing techniques. The fit of products like Lotus 1-2-3 to these channels relates to the characteristics of the spreadsheet and the target market of the channel.

For developers to be successful selling through distributors in the UNIX market in a similar way, they will have to develop their software and ensure that it is ABI compliant for example with UNIX System V Release 4. This ensures the widest possible market opportunity for example for SPARC-based systems, for the 88 open-based systems and the Intel iABI program participants.

Much of the software created for the UNIX market is not written for a broad market. Vertical industry applications and high-value software written for multiuser systems may be highly successful with sales of only a few thousand or even hundreds of units.

Scalability and heterogeneity, two of the widely recognized strengths of UNIX systems, can actually become obstacles for software developers who need to resolve the distribution question.

3.6.5. The Distributors' View of UNIX

Successful volume software distributors have become so because of the large market created by MS-DOS and the personal computer. Sales growth of PCs can be attributed to their relatively low cost and uniform characteristics of the market. Software distributors have been able to minimize the number of inventory items. If these PC software distributors were able to maintain the growth rate, and maintain profit margins, there wouldn't be much incentive to change. In reality, the PC software market has naturally migrated to a commodity market. Software distributors are loosing the battle to maintain profit margins. Most have attempted to offer value-added services, including marketing services, lead-referrals, systems integration support for their customers, support for the third-party software products they carry and so forth as a means of differentiating themselves other than in terms of price.

The traditional PC software distributor is coming under increased pressure from direct marketing, software catalogs offering very name-brand software very inexpensively on a mail order basis. Such inexpensive distribution also threatens retail operations selling PC software with the possible exception of computer superstores.

Many of the software distribution companies have been considering or are just now entering the UNIX systems marketplace even though UNIX is much smaller (in terms of unit volumes) and more complex (in terms of different versions of UNIX, GUIs, and APIs) than MS-DOS/Windows. But why? Software distributors find that UNIX systems have some of the best characteristics of the MS-DOS market.

There is minimal vendor control of the market. There is strong competition between hardware and software suppliers. Software products that can operate across platforms from different hardware suppliers create new opportunities. In addition, the average selling price of UNIX software is higher than on MS-DOS, and there is strong demand for value-added services both from the end users and from the software developers themselves.

UNIX is also poised for take-off in the Intel-based PC platform marketplace. SCO and INTERACTIVE Systems Corporation have been joined by a number of other suppliers who are targeting UNIX on high-end PCs. Most notably among these companies is SunSoft, a division of Sun Microsystems, which has announced its intention to market Solaris, an SVR4-based operating system.

3.6.6.   Hardware Suppliers' Views of UNIX Software Distribution

The days of the hardware supplier providing a single source for all hardware, software, and service are over. No single vendor can provide a single point of contact to meet all the needs of users today. Hardware suppliers understand that software sells hardware. They want to ensure that their systems are implemented in a way that allows the largest possible number of third-party applications software to run. This is one of the major reasons that hardware vendors are ensuring their systems comply with industry standards including application binary interface standards (ABIs).

System vendors are beginning to realize that just providing a compatible platform does not ensure that third-party applications will run on their systems, nor that there will be adequate distribution channels for these applications.

In general, hardware suppliers limit the extent to which their direct sales forces function as a distribution mechanism for third-party applications software. This is not only because it is difficult to properly train their sales force, but they also have to be careful not to play favorites with one software vendor in such a way that it negatively impacts other similar, competing software vendors on their platform.

Hardware system suppliers face a dilemma in the sense that they want to differentiate themselves in terms of the third-party software they have available on their platform but at the same time having to limit how far they can go in supporting the distribution of the third-party software. Hardware suppliers are desirous of seeing independent distribution channels arise for software that will provide the flow of applications to customers expanding the market as a whole.

Channels of UNIX Software Distribution. Software developers normally will want to use their own direct sales force to distribute products (as long as the cost of the sales force provides acceptable margins). There are several advantages to having a direct sales force for software. These include control over the sale, control over the salesperson, control over the sales process and quality of sales relationship and image, and most importantly, control over the customer (loyalty that translates into account control).

The cost of a direct sales force, however, is very high compared to the cost of indirect channels of distribution. Most large ISVs who can afford a direct sales organization, supplement it with indirect channels such as relationships with OEMs, VARs, or other ISVs.

The problem for the small software developer is that even though they would like to use indirect channels, demand for the product is small, and their name brand recognition is nonexistent. They are forced to either accept the cost of using direct distribution or give away a considerable percentage of their profitability to a distribution partner.

Mail order houses reach the end user through the use of catalogs. Most of the orders are placed over the telephone. Most mail-order houses have active outbound telemarketing sales activity as well. Many UNIX products are either too expensive or too complicated to sell through mail order catalogs.

UNIX Software Distributors, Resellers, and Catalog Companies. Table 3.2 is a partial list of distributors, resellers, and other companies. We've attempted to categorize each as follows. We have used best efforts to indicate the basic type of business model each company has as follows:

VAR	— reseller
MVAR	— master reseller
CAT	— catalog operation
PC	— established in PC software distribution
RCHN	— master reseller, retail operations
OS	— Operating system company that may OEM and/or distribute
UNIXD	— UNIX Distributor
ISV	— primarily ISV but may offer distribution and/ or OEM relationships

Final Notes on Software Distribution Strategy. As previously mentioned, a software developer should understand that distributors' and resellers' main role is to fulfill demand. They expect their developers to help create demand. The developer has to create an image for their company; they have to make customers aware of who they are. They have to

Table 3.2.   The largest UNIX software suppliers and form of distribution.

Access Graphics (MVAR)	McKenzie Brown Canada, Inc.
Advanced Data Products, Inc. (VAR)	Merisel Inc. (PC)
Andataco Inc. (VAR)	MicroAge Inc. (MVAR)
Analogous Solutions (VAR)	Novell (OS, MVAR)
Arrow Electronics (MVAR)	Nynex (MVAR)
Avnet Inc. (VAR)	Prior Data Systems (VAR)
CompuAdd Corporation (RCHN)	The Programmer's Shop (CAT, UNIXD)
ComputerLand (RCHN)	Qualix (UNIXD)
Corporate Software (PC)	Robec Distributors (UNIXD)
Dickens Data Systems (VAR)	Santa Cruz Operation (OS)
800 Software (PC)	Softmart, Inc. (PC)
ESIX Systems, Inc. (OS)	SunExpress (UNIXD, ISV)
Gates Distributing, Inc. (PC)	SunSoft (OS)
Highland Software (ISV, UNIXD)	Systrade AG (Switzerland)
Hunter Systems Software, Incorporated (ISV)	Tech Data Corporation (MVAR)
Ingram-Micro D (PC)	Unimac APS (Denmark)
INTERACTIVE Systems Corporation (OS)	Unipress Software (ISV)
ISE-Cegos (France)	Novell USG (OS)
J.B. Marketing (Canada)	Vitronix Corp. (ISV)
	Western Pacific Data Systems (VAR)

MVAR: Master Reseller   OS: ISV of UNIX OS
VAR: Reseller   ISV: Software Vender
RCHN: Retail Chain   UNIX D: Distributor of UNIX Software
PC: PC Softwre Dealer

create awareness and stimulate demand for their products. This should not be taken to mean that resellers don't ever create demand. Resellers can play a big part in creating demand through promotions. The real point is that resellers often rely on their suppliers for program development and they get involved as the program is rolled out.

Many resellers and distributors have very powerful telemarketing groups that can do an excellent job selling the product. Since distributors or resellers are basically in it to get orders, ask yourself, if a distributor or reseller has a choice between a product that people know about from a company people know about, are they more likely to have success than with a product nobody ever heard of from a company nobody ever heard of. The issue is not whether distributors or resellers create demand or not, because clearly they can, and many do. The real issue is that you can't abrogate marketing responsibility to these channels. You have to invest to make them successful.

For the same reasons you don't see retail companies providing in-depth sales support on the functionality of the software products they carry, you can't expect distributors and most resellers to proactively market your product. The role these companies perform is mainly to make it easy for customers to locate and buy your product. This is simple, yet we believe often misunderstood by developers.

So if distribution companies don't create awareness and demand, then how can the small software company? The answer is not simple and depends on the specifics of the product and the market. Advertising and promotion are the simple answers, but these marketing activities do not universally offer immediate or even attractive return on investment. These activities create leads for direct or indirect sales channels.

The best models of software distribution we have seen involve a special mix of marketing activities that support both direct and indirect sales. The formula is to use direct sales for major accounts and to leverage resellers everywhere else. If your product sales achieve sufficient volume, then you would use distribution for the most high-volume, low-cost products in your portfolio. Finally, to achieve the highest possible profitability, software companies should develop their own strategic marketing systems so they always know who their customers are. We will later build the case for investing in database marketing and database driven sales as the method for maximizing reach while retaining profits from the sales of product upgrades and sales of new products to existing customers. Your customer database, your house list, should represent your best database for surfacing leads for new business.

One interesting trend that has been observed in the PC market, is that companies who initially used distributors to fuel growth and market share have begun to evaluate creating their own subsidiaries to perform these functions in-house. The lesson here is that marketing and distribution are really business dynamics that need to be reassessed as a business grows. Each component within the overall marketing and sales process should be re-examined and optimized.

3.7.   UNIX COMPARED WITH MS-DOS AND OS/2

MS-DOS is the dominant PC operating system. MS-DOS licenses number in the millions, but each is a single user. While the number of UNIX licenses (of all UNIX systems) is far fewer, one must remember that many of these UNIX licenses are multiuser, meaning the UNIX system supports multiple users via terminals or workstations.

A large percentage of desktop computers today are 16-bit micropro-cessor-based. This includes Motorola 68000 and Intel 80286. These devices lack a flat address space, run graphics slowly, and have limited display capabilities. Similarly, the 16-bit Mac lacks memory management, has slow I/O, and can't support any large applications since it provides no direct memory access.

The PC industry set UNIX back 10 years. However, it looks like UNIX in the 1990s has turned the corner and is poised for creating another mass market. This will mean UNIX will be used for many applications, well beyond those it has historically been associated with, such as CAD/CAM and software development. New applications will include electronic mail, networking, end-user productivity tools, and all the general business applications like word processing, accounting, and the like.

The early 1990s will see tremendous action in the PC market as many new vendors increase their focus on UNIX. Commodore is just one example. It started shipping UNIX System V Release 4 in late 1989 and by 1990 had over a thousand SVR4 units in the field as well as an earlier release of SVR3.

PC-oriented UNIX products are becoming available through an increasing number of companies, including the ones mentioned below—to name only a few:

Novell (SVR4.2) UNIXWARE

SunSoft Solaris 2.x

SCO (SCO UNIX and SCO XENIX, Open Desktop, etc.)

SunSoft's INTERACTIVE Systems (Architect Applications Platform), UNIX System V/386 Operating Systems, UNIX OS/Multiuser)

Multiport (UNIX System V/AT, System V/386)

Everex (ESIX)

UHC (System V Release 4)

PC-based UNIX machines are increasing at almost 60 percent per year and represent a market with a base of around 1 million units in 1990. The reason for UNIX's growing popularity is largely its versatility in terms of providing single- and multiuser support, multitasking, and a rich set of networking and communications facilities. PC UNIX shipments have increased significantly as DOS applications compatibility has become possible.

OS/2 once seemed to be the heir apparent to MS-DOS, but to date, OS/2 lacks the momentum of MS-DOS/Windows. It is also receiving a serious challenge from UNIX. Many MS-DOS users find their PC solution to be too slow and/or limiting. MS-DOS users who want to upgrade to UNIX have at least three options:

1. Run UNIX on their PC hardware.
2. Upgrade from MS-DOS to DOS under UNIX on a UNIX system.
3. Go straight to UNIX on new hardware. UNIX on MS-DOS-based PCs.

PCs based on chips such as the 80386 32-bit processor are now powerful enough to be legitimate platforms on which to run UNIX. UNIX on DOS products allows the DOS user to use UNIX commands on an MS-DOS-based PC. MKS tool kit from Mortice Kern Systems of Waterloo, Ontario, is an example of this type of product.

MS-DOS to OS/2 or to UNIX? UNIX will compete with OS/2 in a bid for market share as users evaluate OS/2 versus UNIX. OS/2 offers several advantages over MS-DOS. For example, it eliminates the 640K-byte memory limitation, supports multitasking and multiprocessing, and provides an expanded API with dynamic linking and Presentation Manager for a window user interface. Both MS-DOS and OS/2 have incorporated many features of UNIX. For example, with the introduction of MS-DOS 2.0, Microsoft offered a hierarchical file system, input output redirection, pipes, and UNIX-like system call extensions.

It is important to note that OS/2 is not a simple product line. There are 16-bit versions, the Extended Edition, versions with and without Presentation Manager, and 32-bit versions. The number will only increase as Microsoft introduces Virtual OS/2 versions. Whether it is UNIX or OS/2, the move from MS-DOS will be traumatic for most users because it implies buying new hardware or significantly modifying existing hardware. UNIX is very different from MS-DOS and is not yet available through the traditional PC vendor channels of distribution.

How is UNIX different from MS-DOS and OS/2? MS-DOS has 50 to 60 commands and utilities. UNIX has over 200, although the user doesn't have to know all of them. UNIX also has a large number of subroutine libraries, utilities, and even language support built in. MS-DOS and OS/2 are single-user environments, while UNIX is multiuser.

Many basic commands of UNIX, MS-DOS, and OS/2 have similar counterparts, but UNIX commands give different results and have options for command line arguments that provide more power and versatility at the expense of added complexity. The UNIX command parser is also upper-case/lower-case sensitive.

Table 3.3 summarizes major differences between MS-DOS, OS/2, and UNIX. The number of UNIX applications is rapidly increasing. Since MS-DOS runs as a guest under many UNIX systems as an option, UNIX systems can potentially support a very large portion of the MS-DOS applications now in existence. The opposite is not true. Whereas MS-DOS is tightly controlled by Microsoft, variants of UNIX are readily available on all types of new technology.

Migration Issues. To ease the transition for MS-DOS users to UNIX, MS-DOS is often supported under UNIX. MS-DOS can be emulated in software, or PC-compatible boards can be plugged into UNIX systems as coprocessors. In either case, MS-DOS under UNIX is increasingly common as a bridging device for MS-DOS users and to help users preserve their software investments already made in MS-DOS.

DOS under UNIX is offered by several vendors: VP/ix from INTER-ACTIVE Systems and DOS Merge 386 from Microport, to name only two. Not all DOS software will run in DOS under UNIX environments, however. Limitations exist where the application software uses low-level PC hardware, is timing sensitive, or performs low-level access to the DOS file system. Performance can also be an issue where MS-DOS is emulated in software.

Hardware-based emulation is another matter altogether. PC compatible boards that plug into the backplane of UNIX systems tend to provide nearly flawless MS-DOS environments—as fast as real DOS. Some of the most popular MS-DOS software, like Word Perfect and Lotus One-Two-Three, are gradually becoming available on UNIX.

On MS-DOS and UNIX. There are different approaches to providing DOS under UNIX compatibility. Some UNIX environments support Windows. There are several companies offering UNIX under DOS. One of the major differences between DOS and UNIX lies in the tools that come with each operating system. DOS tools hide the fact that you are using DOS. They don't take advantage of the underlying operating system. UNIX development systems are much more standard than DOS development systems because there are so many more tools to choose from.

Table 3.3. Differences among the major personal computer operating systems.

OS	MS-DOS	Windows/NT	OS/2	UNIX's
GUI	Windows 3.x	Windows 3.x	Presentation Manager	X.11 Open Look Motif
Networking	NS/Networks NetWare	NetBUEI NetBIOS API MS-NET	Lan Manager NetWare	TCP/IP & OSI
Architectures	386/486 Only	386/486 MIPS R4000 DEC Alpha	386/486 Only	Many
Applications	25,000	N/A	1000	30,000 All Vendors
Multiuser	Not inherent	Not inherent	Not inherent	YES
Interoperability	Poor	N/A	Leading edge	Leading edge
Standards	De facto	POSIX (subset)	Limited	Many
Configuration	640K Memory 40Mb Disk	2-8 Mb Memory 60Mb Disk	2-4 Mb 30Mb Disk	4-16 Mb 80Mb Disk
System Security	None	Protected Mode	Protected Mode	User Password Group level Permissions
Strength	Large base of Applications	TBD	IBM Support	Portability Large base of Applications
Weakness	Memory Limited	Newness	Lack of Applications	Complexity (w/o GUI)

3.8. UNIX AND OS/2

IBM bundles OS/2 on its PC platforms. OS/2 unit shipments on PC's can be expected to be higher than unit shipments of UNIX on IBM's PCs. However, OS/2 will not ship on more powerful PCs and workstations and UNIX will gain greater share of high-end PCs and workstations. OS/2 as a LAN server does not utilize the full processing power of servers as well as UNIX. OS/2 is not expected to gain significant market share relative to MS-DOS and Windows or Windows/NT. IBM should realize that in this marketplace, Windows is dominant and most users and ISVs are not going to want to support Presentation Manager for OS/2. On the server side, while OS/2 has become a more solid product, interest in OS/2 seems limited to a small number of major companies which have made commitments to it. IBM has priced OS/2 very aggressively in order to try to capture market share from IBM.

OS/2—still Lagging in Terms of Innovation. IBM began shipping its 32-bit version of OS/2 2.0 in early 1992. OS/2 2.0 offers true multitasking and allows concurrent execution of multiple software programs. OS/2 does not utilize the X Window System. It uses the Workplace Shell, which is built around the concepts of object and uses drag and drop functionality.

OS/2 graphics comes from third-party video card and drivers. It does not address high-resolution 3D graphics or other acceleration features. OS/2 bundles 25 some odd utilities and can run up to 240 DOS applications provided enough disk space. Terminal emulation, 3270 and SNA host communication, and SAA protocols are supported. OS/2 2.0 also features a context sensitive help. Drivers for OS/2, performance monitoring tools, are provided by third parties.

OS/2 2.0 supports native OS/2 programs as well as DOS and Windows 3.0 applications. It supports application multitasking and concurrent execution of real and standard mode Windows applications. OS/2 represents advanced technology by comparison to Windows 3.1. Given its aggressive pricing by IBM, customers who are evaluating Intel-based platforms may choose OS/2 over Windows, especially if the customer is already an IBM-dominated account.

OS/2 runs only on Intel-based platforms and is only sold by IBM on Intel-based PCs. It is not ported to the RS/6000 or any other hardware platform. IBM plans to release OS/2 with a Mach-based microkernel that could support personality modes for OS/2, Windows, POSIX and others.

OS/2 has numerous strengths, but it lacks functionality to be used as a multiuser operating system except where the application or database provides the multiuser application services. IBM's innovation in the OS/2 Workplace Shell GUI is seen by most analysts as a risk. There is still no rush of ISVs to OS/2 which may ultimately doom it to success only in niche markets. OS/2 lacks full support of Windows (e.g., in enhanced mode) and the operating system is fairly complex to install and administer.

While IBM positions OS/2 as competitive to UNIX, OS/2's main competitor is going to be Microsoft. OS/2 lacks many features that UNIX has. We do not expect OS/2 to detract much from UNIX and would not be surprised to see OS/2 evolve to become much more compatible with UNIX over time.

Outside of IBM's Boca Raton, Florida facility, OS/2 is not widely considered to be a long-term strategic platform even within IBM. As IBM is giving OS/2 its full marketing attention, its customers are taking notice, and IBM believes it will be able to unseat Microsoft and position OS/2 as a replacement for Windows and be a formidable competitor for Windows/NT.

OS/2 now supports in excess of 1000 software applications after over two full years of IBM and Microsoft trying to get ISVs to support OS/2. IBM is confusing its own customers with so many conflicting messages about hardware and software strategies. Its focus on AIX and the RS/6000, its PS/2 product lines, its commitment to AS/400 and other mainframe operating systems, all in addition to OS/2 is a confusing set of messages. Now with IBM aligning its future development with Taligent and Apple, it is impossible for most customers to understand IBM's strategic direction and how to manage their migrations into the future. OS/2 is a product that is finally delivering on its promises even though it has limitations. If OS/2 is indeed strategic to IBM, perhaps it will port it to other platforms—including RISC and non-IBM or Intel architectures and license it more freely.

Many DOS ISVs were badly burned by Mircosoft's attempt to make OS/2 successful. Nevertheless, many of these ISVs are turning their attention to Windows and Windows/NT, and this is taking priority away from OS/2 ports. Many ISVs are still taking a wait and see attitude about OS/2. Converting 16-bit DOS applications to 32-bit OS/2 is not without effort. Apart from the technical development, porting, and support issues, ISVs have to perceive that they will benefit from marketing programs launched by the operating system vendors and hardware platform vendors and their distribution channels. IBM has to convince ISVs that they create demand pull for the ISVs solutions over all the other noise in the industry.

ISVs Will Ultimately Make or Break OS/2. ISVs drive the innovative solutions and get real work done for users. ISVs create tools so users and other ISVs can architect their applications solutions. The key to operating system success is getting ISVs to write to the APIs for the platform operating systems. There is a significant cost associated supporting multiple platforms. ISVs have to make critical decisions concerning where they port and develop their applications. A lot of the bad will that Microsoft is suffering at this time is due to the change of course that Microsoft made shifting their support from OS/2 to Windows during 1989 to 1990, this after a number of key ISVs had invested heavily in OS/2 development.

ISVs perceptions about the success of an operating system depend on many factors. If ISVs perceive that there is a stampede on in moving to a given platform then it further accelerates the pace of change. They rationalize they need to be there before their competition to maximize their market share.

3.9.   A COMPARISON OF SUNSOFT'S INTERACTIVE AND SCO'S OPEN DESKTOP

These two operating systems currently are nearly matched in terms of market share for PC UNIX. This section provides a high-level comparison of the two.

Company data. SCO has slightly higher market share, estimated at around 50 percent of the PC UNIX market. SCO has developed strong relationships with ISV who market SCO products first.

SunSoft's INTERACTIVE has closed the gap in terms of market share, estimated at around 45 percent of the market. INTERACTIVE has had a rich history of development of core UNIX technology and it has a very technically solid product.

Technology. SCO has less mature technology than SunSoft's INTERACTIVE business unit. INTERACTIVE has introduced new functionality earlier, for example support for X11.4 and has better overall system performance. INTERACTIVE's X11.4 performance is significantly faster.

INTERACTIVE's installation is reliable and it's 3.0 release is comparable to SCO. SCO installation and configuration could be more robust.

Compatibility. INTERACTIVE runs most XENIX, SCO UNIX and some ODT applications. SCO runs XENIX, SCO UNIX, and ODT applications.

Security. INTERACTIVE has C2 extension available. SCO has more advanced security features but they are nonstandard.

Technical Support. SCO's support is slightly better and may be used more frequently by some estimates. INTERACTIVE's support is used less frequently and there is also room for improvement.

Extras. INTERACTIVE 3.0 comes with Looking Glass and online annuals. SCO comes with a free version of the INGRES database and online manual pages.

3.10. COMPARISON MATRIX FOR UNIX SOLUTIONS

The features and attributes of alternative UNIX systems shown in Table 3.4 should be evaluated for each product that makes your shortlist. Not all of the features listed here will be of importance to your application. These are just suggestions to help in the formulation of your list of required and desirable features.

3.11. SUMMARY

Major computer systems vendors have historically positioned themselves to offer full solutions to customer needs. This was not only a ploy to lock the customer in but a necessity in providing integrated solutions where proprietary operating systems were concerned. In today's computing environments, however, it is nearly impossible for one vendor to supply everything, and this is causing a shift in the structure of the computer industry. Base computer hardware was originally a sufficient differentiator for system suppliers. Today, and increasingly in the future, software is providing the leverage and differentiation. Sharper divisions will occur in the supply side of the UNIX industry between the system vendors and the software vendors. Hardware suppliers will have to focus on the system hardware and software platform and less on the "solution," while the software vendors will focus increasingly on personal, work group, and vertical industry-oriented software solutions.

Just as there has been a trend toward the integration of computer systems through networking, the future will see this trend extended to information processing through the integration of application solutions. The environment in which these applications are developed will carry over into the environment in which they are deployed. The UNIX operating system is going to play a key role as the basic system software platform on which this environment will be based.

Table 3.4.   Features of alternative UNIX operating systems.

Feature	Function/Benefit/Why care
UNIX Name and Version	Compatibility with other systems and application software
Compatibility	With previous releases With other UNIX variants
Type of compatibility	Source Level (must recompile) Binary (no recompilation required)
Architectures Supported	
Types of Architectures 16, 32 or 64-bit	Intel, SPARC, Mips, etc. Access to large address space
Number of installed sites	Time-tested proven product in production environment
Interface Definition	Standards conformance
SVID Release 2 SVID Release 3 SVID Issue 2 Edition 3 POSIX Conformance FIPS Conformance (U.S. Government) X/Open (XPG3/XPG4) Branding ICCM Conformance CD-ROM ISO 9660 ANSI C Verification Tests e.g. SVVS	Compliance can be tested System V Verification Suite
Kernel Features	
VM Support Source code availability Loadable modules	For running large programs System Programming Ease of linkable software and low overhead
Dynamic linking/Shared libraries	Efficient use of system memory and other resources
Asynchronous I/O Multitasking and multiuser support Symmetrical multiprocessing support	For efficient database I/O Client Server Asymmetric versus symmetric

Continues

Table 3.4. *Continued*

Feature	Function/Benefit/Why care
Real time preemptive kernel support	Realtime
Shell Availability	For compatibility and customization
Bourne Shell	
Korn Shell	
C Shell	
Other Shells	
Streams Support	Software development and compatibility
Developer Considerations	
Languages Supported	Software development and availability of runtime licenses
C	
C++	Object-oriented programming
FORTRAN	
Pascal	
Assembly	
Cobol	
Lisp	
Prolog	
Basic	
Optimized compiler backends	
Optimized for multiprocessing	
Software engineering tools	
GUI tool kits	
Object oriented	
Device driver development tools	
Graphics APIs	
XGL	
PHIGS	
GKS	
PEX	
PEXLIB	
GL	
XLIB	

Continues

Table 3.4. *Continued*

Feature	Function/Benefit/Why care
DPS	
XIL	
Network file systems	Ability to access remote file systems
NFS	De facto UNIX and UNIX PC System
RFS	Compatibility with SVR3
Diskless client support	Lower cost per seat and ability to add clients without disruption
PC networking support	PC NFS
Networking and communications	Communications
DECNET	DEC connectivity
X.25	Wide area and international
SNA 3270	IBM connectivity
SNA RJE	IBM remote job entry
LU 6.2	IBM connectivity
PU2.1	IBM connectivity
Defense Data Network (DDN)	U.S. government DARPA protocol
Ethernet—TCP/IP	De facto standard UNIX networking
Sockets	
Streams	
TCP/IP Network Configuration Control	
Honey DanBer	Easy setup for TPC/IP Networking
NFS, RFS, Name services	
Other (OSI, GOSIP, X.400, X.500 etc.)	
DBMS Support	Database management
Informix	
Ingres	
Oracle	
Sybase	
Object-oriented database	
Window Systems	Ease of use and S/W development
X Windows	UNIX de facto standard
Open Look, Motif	Graphical user interfaces
Window tool kits	Window system independence
Postscript support	Efficient laser printer interface
Graphics libraries	Software development

Continues

Table 3.4. *Continued*

Feature	*Function/Benefit/Why care*
Object-oriented drag and drop	Ease of interface across system utilities and applications
MOOLIT tool kit	Development of Motif or Open Look GUI for reduced development time
Adobe type manager support	Support for font technology
UNIX Extensions	Compatibility
BSD 4.2	
XENIX	
NIS	
Multiprocessing	
Software Limitations	Built-in limitations you should know
Maximum number of files	
Maximum number of processes	
Maximum file system size	
Maximum number of local mounted file systems	
Minimum amount of disk required for single user	
Minimum and maximum number of users supported	
Hardware Limitations	Constrains use of software
Minimum and maximum memory configurations	
Minimum and maximum number of processors	
Processor architectures supported	
Processor upgrade path	
Emulation of MS-DOS, Windows, etc.	Reuse of PC software
DOS partitions	
DOS file transfer	
DOS as a task under UNIX	
DOS cross development environment	
Apple emulation	
Support for enhanced mode Windows	
System administration features	

Continues

Table 3.4. *Continued*

Feature	Function/Benefit/Why care
System installation scripts	Ease of installation Compatibility with other systems Uniform system administration
System and network management	SNMP
Network management tools	
High availability extensions Disk mirroring Dual porting Online backup Failover	
International language support features	
MNLS 3.2—8-bit support Code set and character processing Message handling XPG3 messages, commands, date, and time	
Utilities	
Multivolume backup	
System V utilities	Compatibility
Editors (vi, emacs)	Compatibility
System accounting	
Documentation	
Quality	
Online	Immediate, specific documentation on demand
Other features	
Real time	Data acquisition User controlled process scheduling
Security extensions	
B1, C2, etc.	U.S. government compliance
Kerberos Authentication	

Continues

Table 3.4.   *Continued*

Feature	Function/Benefit/Why care
DES and Login	
System level security	
Network level security	
Enterprise wide security	
Multimedia	
Video	
FAX	
Audio	
Computer conferencing and whiteboard	
Deskset utilities	
Cost of ownership	Assessment of full cost
Purchase price (initial)	Minimum to get started
Add-on costs	Add-on hardware and software
Software licenses	
Single user / desktop	
Multiuser / Server	
Runtime (e.g., compilers)	
Source code	
Maintenance	
Personal assistance	
Answerline	
Upgrades	
Upgrade options	
Bundled versus unbundled extensions	
Cost of media and documentation	

Significant opportunities on the supply side of the UNIX market will also be created for system integrators. These integrators will provide the expertise to bring together the right components from the systems and applications sides of the market. At the low end, value-added resellers (VAR) will help address niche applications or geographical markets. At the high end, major systems integrators like Arthur Anderson, Litton, and EDS will undertake large projects implementing state-of-the-art systems, such as factory information systems, automated branch exchange for banking, and so forth.

The supply side of the UNIX market will see a redefinition of the boundary of competitive interests. UNIX system vendors will have to work in partnership with the drivers of their systems businesses without competing with them and encroaching on their partners' value-added.

In a market where most products look alike, customers are hard-pressed to choose among them, and vendors are under even greater pressure to get customers to choose their products. As in other competitive industries, the fight for market share often boils down to the biased claims of marketing and sales forces, often under the guise of technical information.

On the one hand, some vendors will try to win customers by claiming that UNIX is portable and reliable. They will purport to conform to industry standards and make the sort of claims they think their customers want to hear. But on the supply side of the market, you don't want the next vendor to come along with a more modern system and steal your customers. UNIX suppliers must create some differentiation into their UNIX solutions as a "barrier to entry" to the competition. Vendors may call this "value-added." It can take the form of proprietary software packages, graphics packages, proprietary hardware, or user-friendly software that makes use of special keyboard layouts.

The enlightened UNIX suppliers see the pitfalls in their similar-but-separate ways and cooperate on standards. This is why standards conformance in the UNIX market is essential to its growth. As UNIX vendors integrate their own support for multiprocessing, networking, internationalization, graphics, database, and window systems, the UNIX kernel looks less and less familiar. You can end up with a nightmare that doesn't look like UNIX at all. When vendors upgrade to the next standard version of UNIX, they've got a long and tedious reintegration process to face. The same is true of the application software. Changes in UNIX often cause users to lose time getting their applications to run under the new versions.

Who is making money?

Prices are dropping on hardware and operating systems as more companies are getting into the UNIX business. There are now more spreadsheets, database managers, word processors, and other business applications available for UNIX than ever before. There is a notable increase in the interest of corporate buyers who are viewing this unfolding of the promise of UNIX. The above notwithstanding, UNIX alone does not ensure commercial success. The following is a quote from the December 6, 1990, *Wall Street Journal*:

Red Ink Flows Freely at Makers of UNIX Systems

UNIX, the increasingly popular computer operating system, has lured a number of big computer companies to stake their futures on its promise to become the lingua franca *of data processing . . . But consultants are starting to ask: If UNIX is so great, why are so many companies losing so much money on it? . . . Although times are tough all over in the computer industry, it wasn't supposed to turn out this way for the UNIX folks. They counted on phenomenal growth in the market for the industrywide standard operating system that can run on computers made by many different manufacturers. They weren't mistaken about UNIX's popularity: International Data Corp., a market researcher, estimates that growth of computers using UNIX will be 29 percent of the hardware sold in 1994, up from 10 percent in 1990.*

The problem is that computer companies have jumped into the market even faster than the UNIX pie has grown, intensifying competition.

Computers that run UNIX have rapidly become commodity items. Overlooking economic fundamentals isn't the only major miscalculation involving UNIX. The have-nots of the computer industry figured they could use UNIX to end the reign of the haves.

The problem is that the have-nots not only turned up the heat on such big competitors as IBM and Digital Equipment Corp., they turned up the heat on themselves. Young companies that have devoted themselves exclusively to UNIX, such as Sun Microsystems Inc., Sequent Computer Systems Inc., and Pyramid Technology have handled that just fine. But industry analysts suggest that many of these companies haven't gone far enough in cutting costs or in changing their marketing focus to make up for slim margins. Old-line companies trying to move their installed bases from proprietary systems to UNIX also will have problems because existing customers will insist that the manufacturers invest heavily to keep their non-UNIX lines up to snuff.

UNIX software market potential promises to reshape the market. The UNIX market is creating new opportunities in software, and it isn't only new software companies that are taking notice and positioning themselves to capitalize on this. Some examples include the following:

INTERACTIVE is now offering the popular DOS-based Norton Utilities package on its UNIX operating system technology, porting of which was done in conjunction with Peter Norton Computing and Segue Software.

Sun Microsystems, DEC, and HP have all announced and are aggressively porting and working on partnerships to make their unbundled software available on multiple UNIX platforms.

Sun licensed SunOS to INTERACTIVE Systems and numerous SPARC clone manufacturers, and based on its recent announcements of its SunSoft and Sun Technologies subsidiaries, it is planning to extend this practice to other products.

HP has been working with Unipress to port and make its NewWave windowing system available on multiple platforms.

The UNIX operating system is built into the fabric of many strategic industry alliances and into several product and technology plans. This commitment, and the growth experienced by many companies in the UNIX industry as a result, have caused software developers to identify the UNIX system marketplace of the 1990s as potentially the broadest and most lucrative ever to emerge.

Chapter 8 presents specific information on market research companies and on UNIX publications—in particular, the UniForum Product Directories publication. The latest data can be most easily obtained directly from the vendors, but this leaves to the buyer the task of comparing and critically analyzing the offering.

3.12. MANAGING CHANGE ON THE SUPPLY SIDE

Trends on the supply side are mirrored by trends on the demand side. Just as profits are shifting from hardware to software for traditional suppliers of computer systems, users are also paying more for software. We see several profound changes taking place on the supply side of the industry.

An article entitled "The Computerless Computer Company" in the *Harvard Business Review* set out the basic arguments that the computer business is moving to much more of a commodity status. It is clear nearly every traditional systems vendor is re-evaluating their approach to their business. The last few years have seen several companies break out divisions to focus on a given line of business. We believe that this represents a change in the way business is going to be done in the world of open systems, a change that could prove especially difficult for companies who are paying a premium for support and enjoying the relative simplicity of living in a proprietary world in which they basically do what their supplier tells them to do.

Competition in the computer industry has reached a critical point at the same time there has been an overall economic slowdown. This creates real pressures on cost and therefore the profitability model for the suppliers' line(s) of business. System vendors can no longer support the cost of sales they used to absorb even when selling relatively high-margin products.

Some of the major changes we see ahead are as follows:

A general recognition that hardware is nearly a commodity—therefore we predict continued industry consolidation for system vendors.

A general recognition that software is what is driving business. We predict traditional system vendors will have to break out their software development and marketing groups and design, market, sell, and support their software like any other software vendor. This means they will have to support multiple platforms. We predict related changes in the nature of the relationships between software and systems vendors. The emphasis will shift from a catalog of 5000 applications to a suite of complementary applications that are better integrated and supported as a whole than if they were obtained separately.

Within the UNIX market, we see tremendous potential for future embedded applications. The systems used in a legal office, or in a medical practice, or in vertical applications areas in a number of industries could care less what the operating system is. If the UNIX philosophy and model produces more robust applications, the fact it is UNIX won't matter. The fact it is standards-based, however, will matter a great deal as users become increasingly knowledgeable about total cost of ownership and the role standards play in preserving assets as well as managing change.

4

The Demand Side of the UNIX Market

This chapter provides a detailed overview of the demand side of the UNIX market. From this information managers will learn about the markets where UNIX had gained acceptance. Few people want to be the "guinea pig" in an experiment. Most managers and decision makers want to know where others have succeeded and have a better feel for where they are following suit, rather than being the trailblazers in terms of adopting new technology in general and UNIX in particular. While one might argue that the market data provided in this section is not really of interest to most managers, an understanding of where UNIX has been applied successfully has everything to do with predicting how it can be applied in the future.

There are distinct communities within the UNIX community. There are UNIX users who aren't even aware they are using UNIX, and there is a community of UNIX users. The first community—which may be the fastest-growing segment of UNIX users—might be referred to as application users. Application users may or may not even know that their application is being run on UNIX. Like the mainframe or minicomputer environment, there are technically knowledgeable people who set up and maintain the system. Examples can be found in retailers, in users of network services like AT&T Easy Link, banks, and a considerable array of additional applications. These users have an "applications' view" of the system. The underlying operating system is often completely hidden from the application user. This first group might as well be running VM, MVS, or VMS. It just so happens that the applications they need to run on UNIX and UNIX systems offer excellent price performance and lower total cost of ownership. This is the fastest-growing group of UNIX users. These users may not even know they are running on UNIX. For many, UNIX may be the invisible tool.

The second group of UNIX users is comprised of technically adept users such as software developers, engineers, analysts, and knowledge workers of other types. These users tend to have an appreciation for what an operating system is and does. At the center of this group is an almost cult-like group of professionals who have advanced technical knowledge usually involved with systems administration and utilities or programming. These UNIX-adept users are comprised of people who probably also use applications, but they are people who understand and use the operating system in some level of detail and depth. At one extreme in this group are the near-cultlike technological users who understand the inner workings of the UNIX operating system.

Both communities of UNIX users have come to take for granted file sharing, network printing, remote application execution, client server program support, and multiuser access. The X Window system has helped make graphical user interface another standard part of the environment. NFS has helped make workstation environments network integrated graphical applications environments.

4.1. OPEN SYSTEMS ARE BUILT, NOT BOUGHT

It is becoming abundantly clear as UNIX and Open Systems evolve, that it is really the role of the user base, not the vendors, to define and implement Open Systems, and it is the vendor's role to supply technologies and services that are needed to help these users achieve their goals. In this on the demand side of the market, we will explore how users are implementing Open Systems. We will examine the options and tradeoffs they are making. We will try to make sense out of the real role that standards play for the end users.

Just as the effects of standards and Open Systems are impacting the vendors on the supply side of the market, so to are these effects being felt by the end users. What is behind users' investments in UNIX-based small systems and their use in LANs? Why do more users claim they are implementing an Open Systems strategy than pursuing a UNIX-oriented Open Systems strategy? Why are communications, development environments, and database technologies (what some call middleware) becoming just as critical to information architecture as the operating system and hardware?

There are so many technologies involved, so many different choices, how are users coping with all of these components? What are the key tradeoffs that need to be made in moving to a new strategic information architecture? Will any one strategic framework evolve, supporting multiple platforms, offered by multiple vendors? What are the attitudes of users toward UNIX?

4.1.1.   Open Systems is Driving Demand for UNIX

While UNIX may not be the only factor driving demand for Open Systems, Open Systems is still one of the major driving factors for UNIX. When users feel they have a need to change, the majority of companies using computers in commercial applications are considering an Open Systems strategy. Most of the users making the decision to change are also considering UNIX as a strategic platform.

Traditionally, commercial users are concerned first with the availability of an application solution. If they believed that the application that best met their requirements was not available on UNIX, this would often drive the acquisition of a non-UNIX system. This is still the case to some extent today. But today, there is a marked increase in the end user's awareness of the importance of an overall architecture, that no system or application is an island.

Nonetheless, the application is perhaps the most critical factor driving the acquisition of UNIX-based systems. The success of UNIX is directly tied to the availability of a great variety of application software and a healthy software industry. The most relevant segmentation of UNIX-based systems requires looking at how people use UNIX systems. That means to look at applications.

4.1.2.   How Do Users Derive VALUE from Computing?

This is really the most fundamental question. Users benefit when computers enable the following:

- Achieve cost-effective computing
- Continuously assimilate improvements in technology smoothly
- Capture data, move it, and find it
- Share data
- Share system resources
- Improve the ability of applications to work together
- Avoid lock-in to any particular vendor or technology
- Ease the effort required to manage their environment

- Develop and deploy applications rapidly
- Use systems with ease

4.2. SEGMENTING THE DEMAND SIDE OF THE MARKET

The challenge is to find ways of segmenting the UNIX market to make it meaningful to management decision makers. The UNIX market can be segmented and sized in various ways, for example, geographically, by establishment size, by installed base, by industry, and by primary application areas. A variety of analyses will be provided in the subsections of this chapter.

Market segments and size estimates provided here are based on information made publicly available from market research companies as well as our own estimates. This information illustrates the magnitude and pervasiveness of UNIX and describes where it is and is not being used today.

Perspectives on the Demand Side of the UNIX Market

Since the market for systems based on the UNIX operating system is one of the fastest-growing segments of the computer industry, the factors that are responsible for driving these changes will first be discussed.

During the 1970s and early 1980s, no one organization or entity took responsibility for UNIX, although AT&T was its developer and held all rights to license, sell, or modify it. In the absence of firm standards, many vendors developed their own versions, which resulted in a situation where users had to choose from a proliferation of incompatible versions, releases, and types of UNIX.

The momentum behind the industry-wide adoption of UNIX as a universal operating system began in the engineering, scientific, and education communities, where workstations were fast becoming the primary hardware system. Independent software vendors rallied behind UNIX to develop engineering and scientific applications. From a user's point of view, having a large number of applications ported to a nonproprietary operating system reduces the problems encountered when integrating software across different operating systems. It also further reduces users' dependence on a specific vendor's hardware, making it possible to rapidly adopt the newest and best system products coming on the market.

Large corporations such as GM and Boeing began standardizing major aspects of their data processing operations on UNIX. The U.S. government and other governments throughout the world began specifying UNIX System V and other standards in their large distributed systems procurements.

Together, customers and vendors are driving an irreversible movement toward Open Systems. Users have recognized that UNIX can provide relative compatibility across multivendor hardware architectures, as well as effective single- and multiuser multiprogramming environments. For users who have major investments in proprietary systems, UNIX provides both distributed processing capabilities and a rich source of applications, most of which can coexist with the installed systems.

Customers are finding the promise of UNIX's flexibility appealing. It means they won't get locked into any one vendor long term that can simply charge what it wants for its hardware. Some have called this free market computing. Free market computing is a movement toward complete computer systems based on comprehensive standards. The standards define the technical characteristics of the software operating system and applications environments. This provides users with unparalleled flexibility and freedom of choice in selecting a hardware platform.

Keen interest in UNIX by users and suppliers worldwide underscores the tremendous importance of UNIX in mainstream commercial data processing. We are entering an era of open, vendor-neutral computing standards. Indeed, the position taken by OSF, and by IBM and DEC in particular, is evidence enough that UNIX has been accepted as a de facto standard in the industry. UNIX is and will continue to be a viable alternative to proprietary operating systems. Users can only benefit from the flexibility and freedom of choice that true openness implies.

For UNIX to realize its full potential, commercial market conditions must exist and help to create the opportunity for systems and applications suppliers to meet the needs of customers. Most standards are driven by votes, but UNIX is a standard that is being driven by customers who are voting with their wallets.

4.2.1.   Size and Shape of the UNIX Market

Consider the following statistics:

According to AT&T, in 1987, there were over 700,000 UNIX licenses worldwide. One estimate places the total number of UNIX licenses by the end of 1990 at over 2,000,000. This number grew to just under 4,000,000 by the end of 1991.

One market observer estimated that the number of UNIX-based systems increased over 70 percent in the last four years alone.

Based on a survey of the top five system suppliers, there are in excess of 15,000 applications provided by independent software vendors now supporting UNIX. This number is much larger if one considers that many UNIX systems feature MS-DOS compatibility, so many MS-DOS applications can run under UNIX but not vice versa.

The value of the UNIX market in 1987 ranged, according to various sources, from $9 to $13 billion in total value of hardware and software for UNIX systems vendors. By 1990, the UNIX market size ranged anywhere from $15 to $25 billion, depending on whose estimates you wanted to believe.

By IDC and Dataquest estimates, the UNIX marketplace will grow faster than any other segment—nearly 30 percent annually over the next several years. UNIX-based systems could account for as much as 35 percent of the overall commercial computer market by 1995. The commercial markets will be the last holdouts of the proprietary systems throughout the 1990s, but UNIX will continue to make significant inroads.

4.2.2. Installed Base of UNIX Systems

The UNIX-installed base is a market comprised of System V, XENIX, and BSD-based systems. Dataquest has estimated that AT&T leads with 40 to 50 percent of the installed base on System V, XENIX is second with approximately 30 percent, and BSD accounts for 15 to 18 percent. This leaves 3 to 5 percent of the market for the other variants, including AIX and Mach.

An estimated 200,000 AT class machines were running XENIX, not DOS, in 1987. This number was estimated to be around 350,000 by 1993. Sun has sold in excess of 500,000 workstations worldwide since it was founded in 1982. Sun is the UNIX market share leader in both units and revenues. SunOS is predominant in technical markets, but has been making strong gains in commercial markets in recent years. Sun is now selling well over 150,000 workstations a year.

Most XENIX systems were used for small business, multiuser environments. BSD was used predominantly in the technical workstation market and in multiuser environments to support technical and scientific applications in manufacturing, the telecommunications industry, and the government.

AT&T's System V is used in various areas, but tends to be concentrated in low-end to midrange business system environments. The specific UNIX operating systems in approximate order of usage as of early 1993 is shown below:

SunOS

UNIX System V releases 3

USL SVR4

SCO UNIX System V/386

INTERACTIVE

HP-UX

AIX

4.x BSD

ULTRIX

XENIX

Novell UnixWare (recently released)

SunSoft Solaris (recently released)

OSF/1

The relative ranking is subject to rapid change as some products have just been released. The above data is provided for illustrative purposes to give the reader a sense of the major versions of UNIX that are being used today.

4.3.   MARKET SEGMENTATION AND SIZING

Figure 4.1 shows the overall market estimates for computer systems revenues for multiuser and distributed UNIX systems, compared with the overall computer systems market.

An analysis of Figure 4.1 reveals the following: The 1990 UNIX market has been estimated at $13 billion, growing to as high as $35 to $40 billion by 1993 worldwide; this will account for almost 20 percent of the overall computer market. Compound annual growth is estimated at approximately 30 percent per annum.

The UNIX market can be segmented into four major classes of systems: UNIX PCs and workstations; small systems like those from Altos, which are typically small, commercial multiuser systems; medium-range systems; and large systems. By far, the UNIX PC and workstation market is the largest in terms of both revenue and shipments.

UNIX is not a unified market. The main areas of growth for UNIX have been in situations where a cost effective "hot box" was needed in an applications area.

Although it hasn't been proven through research, it is believed that UNIX growth is tied to the maturing population of individuals who have

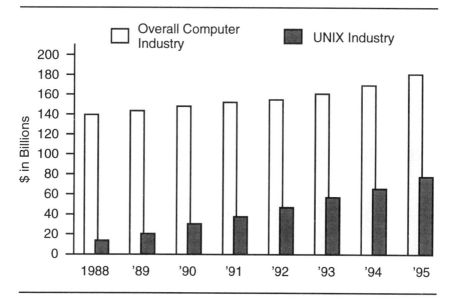

Figure 4.1. UNIX compared to overall computer industry. UNIX is predicted to continue to grow quickly and already accounts for nearly 30 percent of the entire computer industry revenues. Networked Publications estimates.

come out of universities and colleges around the country trained to some level of proficiency in UNIX. On average, the people who work with UNIX are younger and cost less than, say, the people who work in MIS today.

UNIX's growth can be directly attributed to the success of the Intel 386 chip and to RISC processor technology. It is an accident that UNIX fits with these processor architectures as well as it does, since neither of them existed when UNIX was first being developed.

The largest UNIX market segments are also oriented toward network computing. This includes workstations and servers as well as networked multiuser systems of all sizes and types that are used in large computer networks as well as remote offices, distribution centers, retail outlets, and bank branch locations.

As new applications that exploit the power and versatility of UNIX are introduced, one can expect significant future growth in UNIX personal workstations and servers where PCs and PC-LANs are prevalent today. Segmentation and sizing presented in the next sections are based on the above estimates.

4.3.1. Geographic Segmentation

The adoption of UNIX on a worldwide basis is very important because many large companies are facing increasing worldwide competition. These are also the companies that consume the most computer systems to support their business. The widespread use of UNIX internationally will also be important to software developers who want to reach the widest possible market.

The major geographical segments and the percentages of the overall UNIX market are shown in Figure 4.2.

UNIX is an increasingly international phenomenon. The Pacific basin and especially Europe are poised for major growth. The rest of this section briefly explores some of the specific market trends and characteristics of these major international markets.

USA—the Largest Market. The U.S. market for UNIX has been analyzed by most market research companies. For a summary of market research companies and the type of products they offer related to the UNIX market, consult Section 8.1.

For years, industry observers have talked about the coming of UNIX. For years, it didn't really come. Now, it finally seems to be taking off. Why? There are two major reasons. The first has to do with a trend in the computer market itself, which, while not directly related to UNIX, is occurring at the same time. This is the trend of distributed downsized and networked computing. The second reason has to do with the unification of numerous versions of UNIX into what promises to be two dominant code bases that have significantly similar technical characteristics.

What most of these studies point to is that UNIX is predicted to break out from its position of strength in technical markets and certain niches, notably microprocessor-based workstations and lower-end multiuser computer systems. This is evidenced by the fact that all significant computer systems vendors in the United States, including the largest established systems vendors, are entering the market. In order to really understand the trend toward UNIX systems, it is necessary to put it in the context of the computer industry overall.

Several industry analysts are predicting that networked computing will be the next major wave of growth in the computer market. The first wave was mainframes; the second wave, minicomputers; and the third wave, personal computers and personal workstations. This new fourth wave, they predict, will come about as computers are linked into networks and as users begin to think in terms of resources on the network instead of the resources of the system they are on.

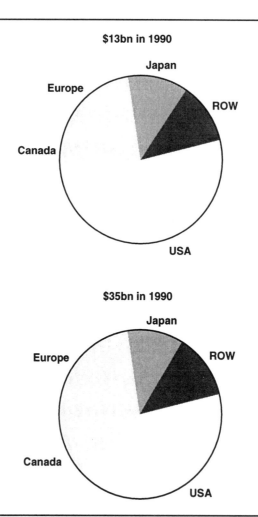

Figure 4.2.   UNIX overall segmentation by geography.

This trend implies a downsizing and a distribution of computing resources, away from mainframes and even centralized minicomputer approaches. These traditional architectures will give way to networks that have computing resources located on them where needed, disk storage where needed, and so forth. These devices will all be connected by high-performance networks. Such networked architectures are the subject of Chapter 5.

As a result of the trend toward networked computing, a general softness in the midrange minicomputer market is expected to occur in the 1990s. Companies will turn to networked computing as they realize the advantages and flexibility inherent in treating computer facilities as a coordinated whole and increasingly evaluate new systems in terms of their price/performance, connectivity capability, and the level of commitment of the systems supplier to industry standards. This is exactly where UNIX fits, and it is one of the primary reasons that even the established companies are putting an increased emphasis on UNIX.

Canada. In late 1988, the Canadian market research company DMR was commissioned by /usr/grp/cdn to conduct a survey of the UNIX market in Canada. The information in this section is drawn from DMR's report. A copy of an executive summary of this report can be obtained by contacting The DMR Group (see Section 7.1.3 for the address).

/usr/grp/cdn is an independent affiliate of the international UNIX group UniForum. It was founded in 1985, and its mission is to produce a UNIX produce catalog, issue bimonthly newsletters, and organize conferences and trade shows. It is sponsored by major systems vendors operating in Canada.

/usr/grp/cdn encouraged this project in order to learn more about the actual penetration of UNIX in Canada and how Canadian computer users looked at the benefits and risks of implementing UNIX. The Open Systems report, which was completed in late 1988, is over 500 pages long.

DMR found that the installed base of UNIX in Canada was probably smaller than others had estimated. However, it was growing at a fast pace. They found that among Canadian users, there was a widespread lack of knowledge about UNIX, but that a widespread interest in learning more about it existed at the same time. Of the companies surveyed by DMR, representing a sampling covering most major industries, just over 30 percent employed UNIX for general-purpose computing, while almost 80 percent used UNIX in their operation for some specific function or application.

DMR estimated that the UNIX market in Canada would grow from $140 million in 1988 to $560 million by 1992, representing a compound annual growth rate in excess of 40 percent. UNIX was estimated to account for 6 percent of all hardware revenues in 1988 (desktop, small system, midrange, and large), growing to 19 percent in 1992. The four most dominant UNIX applications were reported to be general data processing, office automation, scientific and technical and software development. These projections turned out to be conservative.

Europe—Rapidly Adopting Standards and UNIX. Almost all European system vendors are offering UNIX-based systems. The backers of X/Open represent a formidable group of major European suppliers, including ICL, Siemens, Nixdorf, Group Bull, Olivetti, Norsk, and GEC. Every vendor, with the possible exception of Norsk, has established a major line of UNIX products.

It is generally felt that standards efforts by major European (and American) system vendors, X/Open's efforts in particular, have served to promote more widespread use and interest in UNIX throughout Europe (including the United Kingdom).

The UNIX market in Europe in recent years has been growing faster than in the United States, although from a smaller base. Growth was estimated in excess of 170 percent in the last few years (according to *Electronics*, October 1987) and is estimated at around 60 to 80 percent in 1990, with percentage growth slowing as the size of the installed base grows larger.

One of the fastest-growth areas outside of workstations has been the small and medium-sized multiuser systems. These support 4 to 16 terminals. Commercial users in Europe are choosing UNIX as the strategic platform for their core businesses. The commercial UNIX market in Europe is expected to grow at over 35 percent annually. Germany represents the largest market, followed by France, the United Kingdom, and Italy. The EEC has now mandated the use of UNIX even for its mainframes.

Europeans tend to push harder for standards and tend to develop alliances and partnerships unmatched by U.S. firms. UNIX has been a vehicle, especially with pure European systems suppliers, for banding together and promoting a standard that until only recently was not a significant factor in their competition from large U.S. companies like IBM and DEC.

Spain and Germany are among the fastest growing European UNIX markets. Inflation has hit the hardware sales market but seems to have had much less of an impact on the UNIX market. Small-scale multiuser systems represented a major growth area in the United Kingdom.

1991 saw total UNIX systems revenue in Europe increase to $6.9 billion from $6.0 billion in 1990 according to IDC. IDC predicts 20 percent per annum growth between 1993 and 1995. Contrary to the UNIX-on-the-desktop skeptics, the fastest-growing sector will be the UNIX PC marketplace with compounded annual revenue growth estimated at 28 percent.

Japan. Japan is the second-largest UNIX market in the world. Localized versions of UNIX are required. Operating systems products, systems, or applications software must handle kanji and be prepared to follow the rapidly changing Japanese market including system platforms, new operating system releases, new and different competitors, and special product features that will be required.

In Japan, UNIX dominates the engineering workstation market, but has been slower on the uptake in business applications. At the low end of the systems market, Sony, Hitachi, Toshiba, and NEC have all entered the UNIX 32-bit multiuser systems market. There are more than 25 indigenous UNIX workstation and system suppliers in Japan. The big names in the Japanese UNIX market include: Nihon Sun, YHP, Sony NEWS, NEC, Omron, Fujitsu, Hitachi, Toshiba, and IBM.

UNIX has being actively promoted in Japan over the last decade. AT&T had operated a company called AT&T UNIX Pacific that delivered English-language versions of 386 System V and a Japanese application environment called JAE 2.0 for the 386.

The Japanese government, through MITI, backed a project started in 1985, called SIGMA, with over $120 million (25 billion yen). SIGMA, which stood for the Software Industrialized Generator Maintenance Aid project, was an attempt to create a standard platform for software developers. It was similar in concept to Europe's X/Open and claimed a membership in excess of 175 companies including users. SIGMA's strategic objective was to produce a large population of software developers. Increased software development was expected to come from a common development environment, standards for which were developed by SIGMA.

SIGMA OS Version 1 (VOR1) had been derived from AT&T's UNIX System V2.1 with support for streams, shared libraries, and Berkeley extensions. AT&T UNIX System V2.1 has been the commercial system of choice for UNIX systems in the Japanese market. NFS/RFS networking, database facilities, and X.11 windows were also to be included in the project. SIGMA was to also feature Japanese character set support, including phonetic Katakana and ideographic Kanji.

It was expected that SIGMA would target commercial software, such as retail or banking systems or other commercial niche markets where there was felt to be a lack of applications software on UNIX today. VOR1 was also targeted at applications such as process control, science and research, C, FORTRAN, and COBOL development environments, and it features software tools, editors, and debuggers.

SIGMA, as a company, tried without much commercial success to offer services in the areas of networking and database management consulting. In certain respects, SIGMA was trying to be like the X/Open consortium in that it designated standards. It was also developing a profile of standards-based implementations of features required for localization of software within the Japanese market.

SIGMA was expected to be more of a long-term research project within Japan. It was unlikely that it would ever receive much attention outside of Japan. Over the last few years, SIGMA has gone the way of other consortia that start off with a bang and die off slowly. SIGMA ran through 1990 and never quite achieved its goals for developing UNIX-based support tools as well as reusable code on a national basis. SIGMA did not succeed in its goal of disseminating on a major national basis a set of practical existing technology. Reportedly the project would be better characterized as having become somewhat academic and a failure in terms of gaining momentum and consensus behind its goals.

SIGMA was not the first UNIX based software project in Japan. In his book on Japan's Software Factories, Michael Cusumano describes numerous projects, a minority of which have actually involved UNIX. The SMEF (Software Maintenance Engineering Facility—1985–1989) was formed by leading Japanese firms to work on Interoperable Database Systems. This effort was eventually to be eclipsed by OSI.

Japan's IPA, or Information-technology Promotion Agency is over 30 years old and is managed by the Japanese Ministry of International Trade and Industry (MITI). The Joint Systems Development Corporation (JSD) was established in 1976. It consists of hundreds of companies including large Japanese banks. It was recently converted from a nonprofit organization to a corporation. JSD has become an aggregation of specialists in application and systems software development. JSD has several projects which involve UNIX. The SEG (Software Engineering Group) involves joint research targeted at solving software development issues including optimization of UNIX tools. FASET (Fast Approach to Software Environment Technology) develops software systems that will support all phases of software life cycle. SIRUS (Simple Input and Retrieval Information Utility System) was a project focused on standardization of office automation and document processing.

4.3.2.   Establishment Size and Usage

Because UNIX has been used on smaller multiuser and single-user systems, one might suspect that its penetration would be greatest in smaller companies. However, this is not to be the case. This distribution owes to the fact that the larger the establishment, the more likely that there will be some technical applications using workstations like Sun, HP/Apollo, or DEC running UNIX. These percentages indicate the number of companies that use UNIX in any function but do not imply that these companies use UNIX exclusively or even predominantly.

Table 4.1 shows that larger enterprises (e.g., Fortune 1000 companies) tend to buy the most systems. These same companies are most

Table 4.1. UNIX segmentation by establishment size. Historically, larger companies have made the strongest commitment to UNIX, but the numbers are changing.

Establishment Size Number of Employees	Percentage of Companies Using UNIX	
	1990	*1993*
>1000	75	85
500–999	30	45
100–499	19	50
25–99	8	45
1–25	5	8

Source: Networked Publications Estimates

likely to also have leading-edge users, especially in the area of technical computing. Servers and midrange multiuser systems supporting UNIX often offer very attractive price/performance. Larger companies interested in supporting many distributed locations or offices find this a compelling advantage.

UNIX-based systems have historically been sold through system vendors' direct distribution channels. The distribution of UNIX systems shown in Table 4.1 tends to show that UNIX is mainly being sold through direct distribution or, if indirectly, in close collaboration with systems suppliers. We believe the future trend will be more toward UNIX moving through a combination of direct and indirect distribution channels.

The smaller the company, the more important the availability of commercial software such as office automation, accounting, and the like. Name-brand PC software has only recently been making the move to UNIX. In the 1990s, as more applications become available, the demand for UNIX in small establishments will increase dramatically.

4.3.3. System Hardware Platforms

It is clear from the number of vendors of all classes of computer system platforms that the UNIX operating system is an ideal means of providing commonality over different machine architectures. An analysis of Table 4.2 indicates UNIX is offered on nearly half the computers sold today. Yet it only accounts for about 10 percent of those systems' revenues. UNIX is

Table 4.2.   UNIX and computer system architecture. UNIX supports more architectures than any other operating system.

	Number of Architectures	Offer UNIX
Large systems	25	30%
SUPERCOMPUTERS		
PARALLEL COMPUTERS		
MAINFRAMES		
Clustered Processing Systems	9	97%
MULTIPROCESSOR ARCHITECTURES		
LOOSELY COUPLED		
Mid-Range systems	35	97%
MINICOMPUTERS		
SUPERMINICOMPUTERS		
SERVERS		
Low-end systems	54	60%
MULTIUSER INTEL PCs		
SMALL RISC SYSTEMS		
Single-user systems		
WORKSTATIONS	26	100%
PERSONAL COMPUTERS	68	86%
LAPTOP COMPUTERS	15	10%
Embedded Systems		
INDUSTRIAL CONTROL DEVICES	100s	30%

gradually replacing the system revenues from proprietary product lines. UNIX is selling with most new hardware architectures. Not only is it inexpensive for the system vendors, but numerous applications become immediately available.

UNIX is rapidly becoming the de facto standard in technical computing and will be found on the smallest and the largest systems platforms launched into technical computing markets. Traditional mainframe environments supporting large corporate data processing functions will be slow to migrate over to UNIX as a replacement to, say, IBM MVS-based mainframes. This is not to say that there aren't UNIX-based systems that can be viewed as alternatives to mainframes. Sequent and Pyramid are examples of UNIX-based systems vendors that offer competitive mainframe-class products and are competing for niche applications. The UNIX mainframe market was on the order of $1.3 billion in 1989 world-wide and was growing at an estimated 30 percent CAGR.

The market for UNIX-based midrange systems and very high-end workstations with similar average selling prices in the $100,000 to $1 million range represented a $2.5 billion market in 1989. Midrange multiuser systems were growing at an estimated rate of 11 percent CAGR, while workstations were growing at 35 to 40 percent CAGR.

Workstation markets are dominated by UNIX-based operating systems. High-end PCs will also increasingly be offered with UNIX. UNIX inroads into PCs in general will be gated by ease of use and applications availability. The major players here are Sun, HP/Apollo, DEC, and IBM.

The UNIX PC market in 1990 is estimated at around $5 billion worldwide and growing at 45 percent CAGR. The UNIX market is focused mainly in workstations and midrange computers. While UNIX is the dominant operating system in supercomputers and also runs on mainframes, these are comparatively small markets for UNIX.

4.3.4.   Industry Segmentation

The purpose of this section is to explore which industries UNIX has most successfully penetrated in terms of general industry categories. Table 4.3 provides a breakdown. Figure 4.3 depicts that data presented in Table 4.3. It shows for future years a rough estimate of the market size and stage of evolution overall.

Reference points for Figure 4.3 and Table 4.3 are as follows: Dataquest has estimated that in 1991, business applications in commercial markets will account for over 55 percent of all UNIX revenues, while approximately 30 percent will be government purchases and only 8 percent schools or educational purchases.

InfoCorp has also identified commercial UNIX as one of the fastest-growth segments. It is projected to be as large as the technical segment by the middle of the 1990s. The commercial, engineering, and scientific market segments combined represented over 40 percent of the world-wide UNIX market in 1991. Much of this is reflected in the manufacturing industry. Government represented the second-largest segment in 1990, with over 18 percent of the overall market.

Public services and utilities accounted for over 9 percent of the market, with most business attributable to the telecommunications industry in particular. UNIX is perhaps most highly developed with the Regional Bell Operating Companies.

Small to medium business applications accounted for nearly 14 percent of the overall market. Mainstream corporate and business applica-

Table 4.3. Adoption of UNIX by industry segment. UNIX penetration by industry has been linked to application solution requirements.

INDUSTRY	1990	1993	APPLICATION
Manufacturing			
Process	Early	Advanced	Process control
Discrete	Growth	Growth	CAD/CAM
Aero/Auto	Advanced	Advanced	CAD/CAM
Government			
Military	Advanced	Advanced	Many areas
State/Local and Fed. Govt	Early	Advanced	D.P.
Public Services			
Utilities	Advanced	Advanced	CAD/CAM
Communications	Advanced	Mature	Telecomm.
Transportation	Advanced	Advanced	Mapping
Service Industry	Early	Growth	D.P.
Education			
Research	Advanced	Advanced	CASE and scientific
Academic	Early	Growth	Administration
Finance/Banking			
Financial Service	Mixed	Advanced	Many
Banking	Embryonic	Growth	D.P.
Insurance	Embryonic	Early	D.P.
Services Industry			
Transportation	Early	Growth	D.P.
Retail	Embryonic	Early	Point of sale
Wholesale	Embryonic	Early	Back-office
Health	Embryonic	Early	D.P.

tions accounted for nearly 12 percent of the market, with considerable penetration made in securities trading workstations and advanced applications areas with the finance and banking industries.

4.3.5. Application Solutions

This analysis, shown in Table 4.4, decomposes the UNIX market in terms of its adoption in generally recognized software application ar-

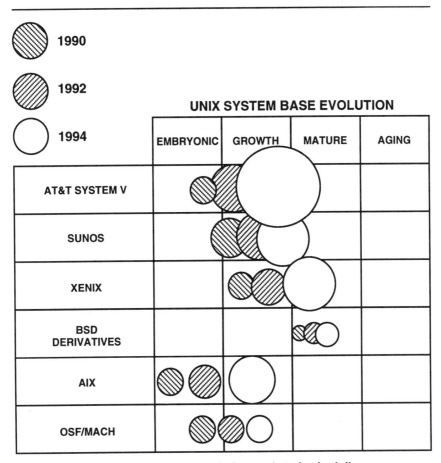

The size of bubble demonstrates relative market size in dollars.

Figure 4.3.   Adoption of UNIX in major industry segments. UNIX is poised for excellent growth in nearly every segment. Manufacturing may account for as much as a third of the total market by the mid-1990s.

eas. Figure 4.4 illustrates schematically the estimated size and relative stage of maturity of UNIX by major category of application.

The technical market is by far the most advanced and largest. CAD/CAM and scientific and engineering applications represented over 55 percent of the entire UNIX applications market in 1990. There is general agreement that significant growth will come from new commercial and general data processing applications areas in all industries.

Table 4.4.   Adoption of UNIX by application segment. Technical applications today are more advanced than commercial applications, although commercial applications are advancing rapidly.

APPLICATION	1990	1993
TECHNICAL		
Drafting Documentation	Advanced	Advanced
CAD/CAM/CAE	Advanced	Advanced
Software Engineering	Advanced	Advanced
Communications	Advanced	Advanced
Graphics	Advanced	Advanced
Earth Resoures	Advanced	Advanced
Technical Publishing	Advanced	Advanced
Real Time Data Acquis.	Early	Advanced
Medical Imaging	Early	Advanced
GENERAL OFFICE		
Accounting	Growth	Advanced
Office Automation	Growth	Advanced
Business Graphics	Advanced	Advanced
GENERAL COMMERCIAL		
Data Management	Early	Middle
Accounting	Early	Early
Office Automation	Early	Middle
Payroll/Personnel	Embryonic	Early
Sales/Distribution	Embryonic	Early
Decision Support	Embryonic	Middle
Manufacturing Planning	Embryonic	Early
Human Resources	Embryonic	Advanced

Among the oldest and most mature UNIX applications areas are telecommunications and teleprocessing. These will likely be among the most rapidly growing areas in data processing as enabling technologies in many other vertical applications. UNIX and its associated networking capabilities offer the advantages of power and versatility as applications move online. Applications in this area not only include telecommunications but utilities-oriented applications like geographic information systems as well.

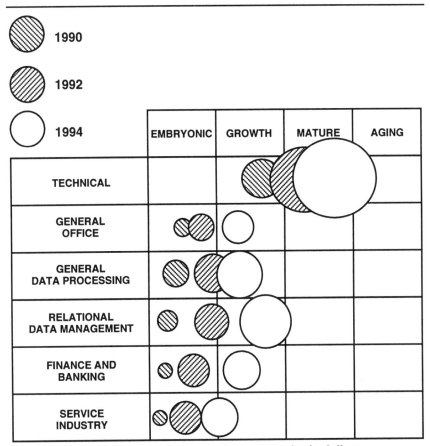

The size of bubble demonstrates relative market size in dollars.

Figure 4.4.   Adoption of UNIX in application segments. There is considerable growth in all segments. Commercial applications are now rapidly emerging.

Applications with longer life cycles will be slowest to move. For example, MRP II in manufacturing environments has a life cycle between 5 and 15 years. Even in these applications, however, it is expected that surrounding software, such as decision support and, in the case of MRP II, factory scheduling and work-in-progress tracking, will likely be migrated to UNIX. So even though those portions of the centralized database application may continue to be run on the traditional mainframe or minicomputer, other adjacent workgroup applications will likely be distributed. CIM accounted for under 9 percent of the UNIX applications solutions market in 1990.

Growth in UNIX hardware and growth in UNIX database software are not in lock step, but the two are certainly intertwined. Major trends in data management and applications development tools also carry the UNIX database market. The compound annual growth rate of database software on UNIX is as high as 80 to 90 percent.

4.3.6. UNIX in Technical Applications

What are technical market applications? Technical applications include engineering design and analysis computing, laboratory, and scientific computing, and industrial computing such as factory data collection and shop floor control. Technical computing spends the majority of its computer time supporting research and development or special types of operations, as opposed to the day-to-day commercial operations described in the next section.

UNIX is the de facto operating system for technical markets. Technical applications, in conjunction with distributed and high-performance computing, are rapidly being dominated by UNIX. Historically, several major trends have combined to drive the adoption of UNIX as the standard operating system for technical markets. These include the following:

Availability of high-performance CPUs and the fact that they can get to market fastest by running UNIX.

Advances in computer graphics.

Adoption of distributed computing environments, which achieve an optimal balance between interactivity and computation.

Standards (especially UNIX, NFS, and X Windows).

The use of C and the availability of C compilers with UNIX.

UNIX becoming the de facto standard operating system for workstations and workstations meeting the computation needs of technical users in a wide variety of application areas.

Historically, DEC made major inroads into the technical market with its PDP-11 and VAX systems. DEC has a large installed base in technical markets. PDP and VAX users run UNIX, especially BSD; ULTRIX, DEC's own version of UNIX; and VMS, the proprietary VAX operating system.

DEC's technical computing customers have traditionally favored departmental multiuser systems. DEC is facing competition from workstation and high-performance computing vendors as it tries to move its technical base forward. DEC's UNIX strategy and OEM arrangements with MIPS represent moves against the stiff competition it faces in technical markets from workstation vendors like Sun, Silicon Graphics, Inc., HP/Apollo, and so on. DEC must also defend itself from minisupercomputer vendors such as Convex, Alliant, and Sequent, which all support UNIX.

The major technical UNIX software by 1995 will include the following:

CAD/CAM/CAE

Scientific applications

CASE

Real-time applications

Graphics intensive applications (e.g., visualization, animation, GIS, etc.)

Industrial automation

4.3.7. UNIX in Commercial Applications

Defining "commercial" Commercial applications include word processing, email, accounting transaction processing, financial modeling, inventory, and so forth. All these applications are performed at the enterprise, divisional, departmental, or work group level and are used by managerial and production employees. Commercial sites spend most of their computer time using these types of applications to support their business functions.

According to the Hyannis, Massachusetts-based market research firm, the Standish Group, the market for OLTP on UNIX platforms will grow at 119 percent from $900 million in 1991 to $20.8 billion in 1995. Throughout UNIX history, detractors have always downplayed its potential impact in commercial markets. UNIX has achieved much of its current acceptance by chipping away at the market share of proprietary systems. A careful examination of the history, however, will reveal that where UNIX has made significant inroads into the commercial market, these inroads have had little to do with user demand for UNIX per se.

According to Bob Marsh, one of the founders of /usr/grp, much of the initial success of commercial UNIX-based systems, notably multiuser, microprocessor-based systems, was due to the efforts of hardware vendors that delivered integrated application solutions to users. Their users really didn't care about UNIX. Many of these commercial UNIX system

integrators or resellers were early licensees of AT&T, BSD, INTERAC-
TIVE Systems, or XENIX. They were attracted to UNIX because it was
cheap, readily available, and "no frills," creating an opportunity for
significant added value, and it had an excellent development environment offering portability and ease of integrating the latest disk and
other technologies. In fact, this group of commercial licensees was really the driving force behind the initial standards efforts in 1985 when
/usr/grp joined forces with IEEE to develop the ideal standard interface
specification that has become known as POSIX.

Driving forces

UNIX growth in commercial computing is coming from the adoption of
networked desktop computers as well as from low-end systems. In the
1980s, as PCs began to change the way computers were used on the
desktop, users demanded increased compute power, creating a need for
more powerful workstations.

Small business computing systems are sold primarily through Value-
Added Resellers (VARs). In the UNIX market, VARs will be key to
driving sales of UNIX-based systems into commercial markets. With
the introduction of more powerful multiuser microprocessors like Sun's
SPARC, Intel's 486, or Motorola's 68040, UNIX offers an ideal single
and multiuser operating system for small companies or work groups.
The multivendor characteristic of UNIX will continue to drive reseller
interest in it.

4.3.7.1. The Trend Toward Distributed and Work Group
Computing. The UNIX operating system is ideally suited for the time
sharing, multiuser, and networking required in distributed environments, which tie the mainframes and the PCs together. The top three
system's vendors selling UNIX in the commercial midrange market,
NCR, IBM, and AT&T, also have strong distribution and selling capability in major corporate environments.

An interesting development occurred in the last decade, as certain
systems vendors such as NCR first developed alternate sales and support channels for UNIX and then managed a transition to a mixture of
direct and indirect sales.

Finally, governments—the U.S. government in particular—are
striving for and increasingly insistent on compatibility among their systems for communications, applications, and development. At present,
approximately 70 percent of all government RFPs specify UNIX.

Strengths and weaknesses of UNIX in commercial markets. UNIX has both strengths and weaknesses in the commercial market. Its strengths include the following:

- Open and available on many hardware platforms
- Multiuser and multitasking (OS/2 is multitasking but not multi-user; PICK is multiuser but not multitasking)
- Optimized for applications development
- Strong in communications
- Thousands of tools and applications, including many leading commercial database products
- Portability of applications
- Relatively low cost

Its weaknesses include the following:

- Not yet fully optimized for large-scale centralized transaction processing—as a direct replacement to mainframes—for example, lacking in standardized system administration tools
- Lacking "big iron" applications (as a result of small business and VAR solution emphasis historically)
- Lacking an existing standard (multiple versions of the product still exist, which makes it less attractive to independent software vendors supporting MS/DOS or PC/DOS, although this is now changing)

All factors considered, the future of UNIX in the commercial market is virtually guaranteed. It is in the best position of any existing operating system to meet the needs of the commercial marketplace. Its success will have less to do with replacing the installed base of minicomputer systems than it will with capturing new applications that are designed to take advantage of UNIX and other new styles of networked computing.

UNIX will satisfy commercial application requirements in areas such as general data processing, financial analysis, compound commercial document management, office automation, numerically intensive business analysis such as statistical analysis, networking, and where high-resolution graphics are needed, such as facilities and space planning, and commercial art, and industrial design. One of the largest opportunities for UNIX in the mid-1990s will be in OnLine Transaction Processing (OLTP). While OLTP solutions today are mostly developed internally, standard applications will emerge in the 1990s and stimulate major growth in commercial applications areas such as accounting, human resource systems, manufacturing requirements planning, and other solutions oriented toward business operations. UNIX OLTP products will be integrated with executive information systems and decision support systems and will be increasingly used in "mission critical" business environments. Section 5.9 provides an overview of transaction processing with UNIX.

The major commercial UNIX software by 1996 will include the following:

Management and administration (e.g., including RDBMS)

Electronic publishing

General data processing

Business applications

Sales and marketing systems

Analysts have characterized 1991 and 1992 as transition years for commercial UNIX, with many vendor plans and promises but little in the way of real deliverables. 1993 to 1994 could be a turning point for the following reasons:

- There will be multiple alternatives for commercial-quality UNIX and well-configured symmetrical multiprocessing systems from multiple leading vendors.
- An acceleration in the trend toward client-server application architectures, along with the beginnings of significant shifts in dominance in commercial systems will occur as vendors with strong client-server offerings gain relative strength over those who do not have the technology or their market positioning to exploit the building wave of client-server computing.
- HP and IBM will retain strong commercial presence in managing the transition of their proprietary system business. IBM will incrementally increase its share, and HP will continue to migrate its base in the midrange commercial UNIX. We expect Digital Equipment to continue to struggle despite a new cycle of technology. NCR will remain a strong niche market player, and second tier vendors such as Sequent and Pyramid will lose share as the major players enter their market spaces with equivalent or better technology.

4.3.7.2. Commercial UNIX Market Growth. Overall, the rate of growth in the UNIX market (see Figure 4.5) has been impressive and

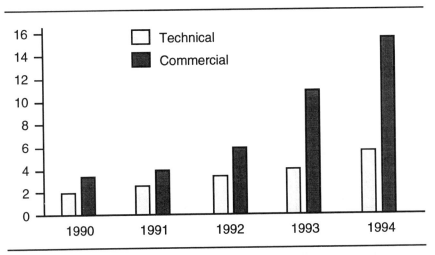

Figure 4.5.   Overall UNIX market size, $ billion/year. The UNIX market has been growing at an overall compound annual growth rate (CAGR) of 35–40%. In 1990, commercial utilization outstripped technical applications. Source: Composite InfoCorp and IDC estimates.

has been driven by more than just system performance. Studies such as the annual Cowen-Datamation survey and others have consistently shown that application portability and interoperability are major factors in users' purchase criteria, in many cases more important than performance. The increasing acceptance of UNIX for mainstream commercial as well as technical applications lends credence to the claims that today's Open Systems technology gives users the best of both, delivering both interoperability, and the assurance of leading-edge price/performance.

UNIX systems have not only become robust enough for production commercial applications, they have become the leading choice for major corporate rightsizing efforts. UNIX systems offer the best interoperability, development environment, and applications availability, combined with major advantages in price/performance. These improvements in the UNIX environment have manifested themselves in a steady increase in the adoption rate of UNIX systems in both commercial and technical environments.

Figure 4.6 shows how commercial applications are keeping pace with technical applications. Many analysts predict that by 1995, com-

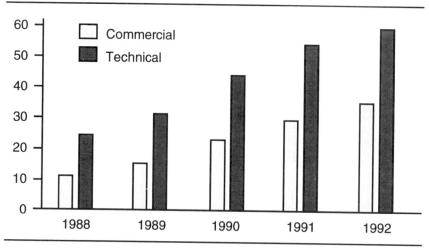

Figure 4.6. Percentage of new applications implemented in UNIX. The acceptance of UNIX can be seen by the increasing plans for UNIX as an implementation environment. Almost half of all applications planned will be implemented on UNIX systems. Source: InfoCorp/Gartner composite estimates.

mercial will overtake technical market percentage-wise (Figure 4.6) although not in absolute terms. Another bellwether indicator is the number of Fortune 500 sites with an installed UNIX system.

Shipments of midrange multiuser systems grew by approximately 45 percent to $3.5 billion in 1991. 1992 growth was running at an estimated 30 percent, with an estimated end-of-year probable market size of $4.6 billion. By this metric, Hewlett-Packard was estimated to be the leading dollar value vendor of the multiuser commercial UNIX world at the end of 1991, with an estimated 38 percent of revenue. With slightly less than two years of RS/6000 shipments, IBM has jumped from a negligible share to become a strong contender. Details of the midrange systems breakdown are shown below in Figure 4.8.

This analysis, the numbers for which are shown in Table 4.5, while certainly emphasizing HP's growth in commercial UNIX business (some of which is the result of converting its installed base of proprietary MPE systems) over the last three years, tends to seriously understate other vendors, and in particular Sun's potential strengths and the momentum it is building in emerging commercial applications. Sun strengths may unfold over the next few years as downsizing and the shift to client-server

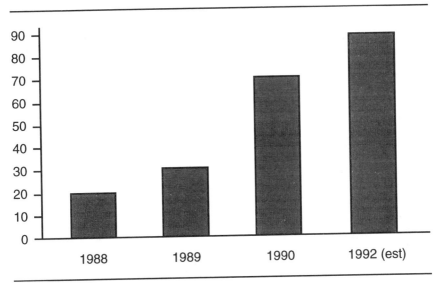

Figure 4.7.   Percentage of Fortune 500 sites with UNIX installed. By 1992, almost all Fortune 500 sites will have UNIX systems installed. Source: ComputerWorld 3/91 and analyst estimates.

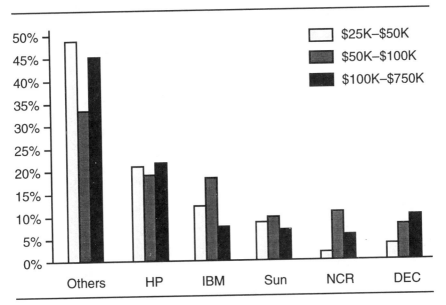

Figure 4.8.   Worldwide Initial Value, 1992 (all operating systems combined).

Table 4.5.   Supporting data—Worldwide Initial Value, 1992.

	$25K–$50K	$50K–$100K	$100K–$750K
Digital Equipment	4%	8%	10%
Hewlett-Packard	22%	19%	23%
IBM	13%	18%	8%
NCR	2%	11%	6%
Sun Microsystems	9%	10%	7%
Others	49%	34%	46%

Source: InfoCorp

applications allows Sun to convert its corporate strengths and focus as well as its large installed base and lead in client-server applications into major growth across a broad front of commercial applications.

4.3.7.3. The Trend Toward Client-Server Computing—Sun in Commercial. The past two years have established the reality of the trend toward application downsizing and client-server computing. Almost all research shows that the pace of implementation of client-server applications is increasing, and as both client and server technology and software continue to mature, increasingly complex and mission-critical applications are being re-engineered as client-server applications.

Early market share dominance in client-server computing is a good predictor of future strength as client-server applications become a mainstream technology, and the vendor with the largest base of users experienced in client-server computing will be well positioned to exploit the coming waves of growth in client-server computing. InfoCorp's numbers for server installations show Sun with a dominant lead over both HP and IBM, as shown below based largely on the success of the SPARCserver 600MP series which was initially introduced in 1991. Figure 4.9 shows an analysis of worldwide server shipments. The related numbers are provided in Table 4.6.

The evolution of Sun's position has to some extent mirrored the evolution of the UNIX market, with its initial strengths in technical markets, branching out into software development and commercial desktops, and its emerging focus on serious commercial midrange and departmental applications. This evolution would seem in lockstep with a developing market which has left Sun with a large installed base distributed across a wide spectrum of applications and companies—

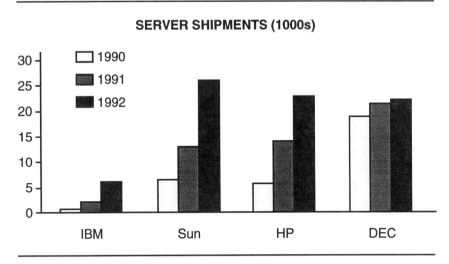

Figure 4.9.   Worldwide Server Unit Shipments (1000s). Source: InfoCorp and R.M. Fichera Assoc. estimates. Aggregate numbers derived from uniprocessor server shipments and SMP shipments.

during the critical growth years of the mid- and late 1980s in the UNIX market, many people who became acquainted with UNIX and UNIX networking did so on a Sun system.

Installed base—seeds for future expansion. Sun's legacy of a large installed base has translated into mind share within user organizations that leaves it well positioned to compete for commercial business with both current and planned products. Financially, Sun is in very sound shape. It is a profitable, growing company with a current run rate of approximately $4 billion, and over $1 billion in the bank. Sun is no

Table 4.6.   Supporting data—Worldwide Server Shipments.

	1990	*1991*	*1992*
Hewlett-Packard	6.1	14.5	23.1
Sun Microsystems	7.2	13.07	26.6
Digital	18.5	22.8	21.7
IBM	.9	3.7	7.1

longer an "emerging" company. It is a solid first-tier supplier, with one of the largest and most rapidly growing bases of any of its competitors. Sun, for example, is larger than the UNIX systems business of Digital and IBM combined, as of mid-1992. Sun's RISC architecture has been cited by InfoCorp as having the largest installed base of any desktop RISC system.

An additional strength that Sun carries forward is a proven track record as a low-cost manufacturer. In many consumer as well as technology segments, upward market penetration from a high-volume, low-cost product base gives a vendor major advantages over competitors who have been higher-cost suppliers—better channels, efficient internal operations, and lower manufacturing costs. Sun today is running at approximately $300,000 revenue per employee per year, 50 to 100 percent better than its competitors.

As Sun has expanded its systems' offerings upward from low-cost desktops, it has retained its cost-sensitive orientation and produced midrange offerings that are consistently lower in cost compared to many alternatives. As part of its coordinated client-server product line, Sun has also continued to enhance its low-end workstation products.

User demands continue to escalate. Research into midrange system user requirements reveal common trends among current and prospective midrange users:

- Demands for more processing power for midrange distributed applications
- Desire for flexibility in distributing computing resources
- Increasing budget pressures, with increased pressures on MIS to buy scalable upgradable solutions

User reaction to these pressures is clearly shown in recent surveys by InfoCorp which indicate a clear trend toward adoption of SMP technology as a base platform by a wide class of commercial user. Acceptance of Symmetrical Multiprocessor (SMP) architectures will accelerate over the next two years and expect that the majority of midrange systems will be SMP by 1995. InfoCorp research indicates that midrange user requirements include the following:

- Desire for incremental scalability
- Desire for cost-effective upgrade
- Desire for high-availability and "fail-soft" features for mission critical applications

Modern SMP systems are excellent matches to the requirements articulated by users, particularly those with OLTP requirements. Based on all available data, we strongly believe that multiprocessors will become the dominant architecture for OLTP over the next four to five years and that vendors without effective SMP solutions will be at a relative competitive disadvantage.

Our forecast for SMP adoption, shown with both aggressive and moderate SMP adoption assumptions, shows that by 1997 at least 60 percent of multiuser UNIX systems can be expected to be multiprocessor systems, a minimum CAGR of 17 percent (units).

This strong bias in favor of vendors with SMP offerings is one reason we believe that UNIX vendors are well positioned for sudden expansion of its commercial segment share in 1993–1995 as shown in Figure 4.10. Another critical element will be system granularity.

We believe that systems with 100–1200 TPC-A throughput will be the bulk of the midrange market in 1993–1995. The following chart shows the alternatives available to vendors in the 1993–1995 time frame for reasonable SMP system configurations. The shaded areas represent where we expect to see product configurations that answer the majority of market requirements.

System vendors will have many choices to implement these sys-

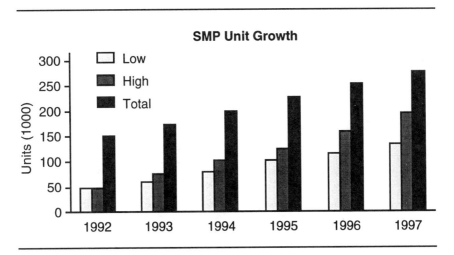

Figure 4.10.   Forecast unit growth for SMP systems (1000s). Source: R.M. Fichera Associates

tems, but vendors that can offer 50–100 TPC-A granularity in scalable SMP systems will have product offerings that will better match the requirements of midrange users for scalability and for multiple distributed processing nodes in 1993–1995 as shown in Table 4.7.

4.3.7.4. Multiprocessor Servers. Sun has quietly emerged in 1992 as the largest and fastest-growing vendor of SMP UNIX systems. Its multiprocessor SPARCserver 600 series, ranging up to the four processor SPARCserver 690, outstripped all competitors as of mid-1992, and by the end of 1992 appear to have an installed base close to the total of its next two competitors combined. In 1993 Sun introduced new servers featuring higher levels of multiprocessing.

InfoCorp's 1992 installed base estimates for UNIX SMP show Sun as a clear leader with their SPARCserver 630, 670, and 690 systems (see Figure 4.11). InfoCorp's estimates of year-end installed base do not highlight the explosive growth Sun is experiencing in SMP systems. Sun's 600 series has only been shipping in volume since the beginning of 1992, while their competition has been shipping, in some cases, since the early 1980s. Sun's mid-year run rate of 7,800 by June is running well ahead of estimates.

Detailed benchmark and configuration comparisons can be made to show almost anything—the fact remains that Sun is selling their SMP systems at a rate exceeding all of their competitors and building a large reservoir of users who will be candidates for upgrades and additional systems in the future. We also expect that when these users convert to Solaris 2.0, they will get a boost in performance from Solaris' efficient SMP support. Arguments that attempt to downplay

Table 4.7. TPC per processor.

TPC per Processor	Number of Processors				
	1	4	8	16	32
50	50	200	400	800	1600
75	75	300	600	1200	2400
100	100	400	800	1600	3200
150	150	600	1200	2400	4800
200	200	800	1600	3200	6400

Source: R.M. Fichera Associates

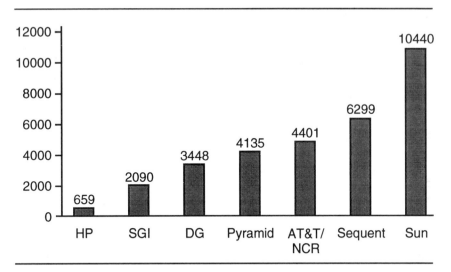

Figure 4.11.   1992 installed SMP UNIX systems. Source: InfoCorp

Sun's success on the basis that some large fraction of these systems are only acting as file servers are, we feel, exaggerated. Our surveys have uncovered enough users who are implementing commercial applications, many of them DBMS-based OLTP applications, to convince us that a large portion of Sun's 690 servers are being used in real commercial applications.

The recent announcement of the SPARCcenter 2000 and SPARCserver 1000 have filled in the previously missing link in Sun's product line—high-end expandable servers with performance that exceeds the SPARCserver 600 series. R.M. Fichera Associates expects that the SPARCcenter 2000 will deliver performance in the range of 1000–1500 TPC-A performance, depending on database software and OS tuning. We expect that the SPARCcenter 2000 performance will overlap anticipated offerings from HP, Digital, and IBM through 1993 and well into 1994, offering a platform for growth into large enterprise-critical, client-server, and OLTP applications with thousands of clients and high-transaction volumes while maintaining low per-user prices. In addition, the architecture of the SPARCcenter 2000 appears to be capable of supporting upgrades to future higher performance processors.

4.3.7.5. Commercial UNIX—Vendors Add the Missing Pieces.
UNIX has traditionally been regarded by commercial MIS developers as

cranky, buggy, unstable, and unsuited for serious enterprise computing. Until recently that perception has been more than a little true. Early UNIX has suffered from significant deficits, particularly in overall stability, file system robustness, security, and manageability. With the immense revenue potential of an emerging market at stake, vendors have been motivated to address these shortcomings. The past two years have seen major enhancements to the UNIX operating system environment to address the requirements of production commercial environments, including the following:

File system reliability and I/O performance. UNIX uses a hierarchical-linked block file system similar to many proprietary operating systems. Enhancements to the UNIX file system has raised its efficiency and robustness to the point where it is suitable for enterprise critical applications. UNIX file system performance has also improved. Many vendors have added memory-mapped I/O for direct transfer from the file system to user space. This is the same architecture used by many other proprietary commercial operating systems and delivers the same high throughput in commercial applications.

File system functionality. Modern UNIX file systems contain many advanced capabilities that are attractive to commercial users, including the ability to redefine file system partitions, add new devices while online, and have files and partitions span physical devices. These capabilities, usually referred to as "logical volume management," have been added to UNIX by many vendors. Modern UNIX systems now have all of the major features previously provided only by proprietary vendors. Another commonly added feature is disk mirroring, which allows users to maintain duplicate copies of data for backup and data availability. The inherently modular nature of UNIX makes it easy for third-party software component vendors to make new features available for special requirements.

Location independence for distributed file systems. Sun's Network File System (NFS) provides a de facto standard for network interoperability in a heterogeneous environment. NFS capabilities on clients and servers is a key facility for implementing today's distributed applications.

Backup. UNIX backup is now fast and robust. Almost every vendor has added online and network backup extensions such as Sun's Backup Copilot. Additional features such as hierarchical storage management are also available from multiple sources.

High availability. UNIX now has high-availability features ranging from disk mirroring and RAID disk arrays through automatic system fail over. The diversity of UNIX high-availability offerings allows users to select exactly the method that is appropriate for their particular application. This especially important to RDBMS and transaction processing environments.

Printer sharing. UNIX printer services are now on a par with those provided by proprietary environments. They provide support for multiple queues and devices, variable priorities, and better control and status monitoring.

Security. UNIX system vendors have invested large sums of money to bring it up to C1 or better security. Except for certain government bids, C1 level is adequate for commercial environments. Selected users will want some B level security features, such as access control lists. Products such as Sun's ARM and ASET allow administrators to create customized security environments that help protect their UNIX networks from security breaches.

Administration. Vendors have implemented interactive tools for online administration. The best of these also keep a history database to allow administrators to track revisions of the environment. UNIX system administration tools today are better and easier to use than proprietary administration utilities and more suited to administering distributed environments. With their convenient Mac-like windowed interfaces, they are easier to use than older character-based tools.

Shared libraries and run-time loadable modules. A common misconception about UNIX is that it lacks shared libraries and run-time loadable modules. Sun's UNIX operating system, for example, has had these features for several years.

Performance monitoring and tuning. UNIX vendors, particularly those selling multiprocessor systems, have added the advanced performance monitoring and tuning tools to allow production users to optimize their configurations for their particular applications.

Database and OLTP performance. Many UNIX systems offer a highly tuned environment to efficiently run major Relational Database Management Systems (RDBMS). Most RDBMS vendors now use UNIX for their development environment, ensuring efficient operation under UNIX. Several high-performance Transaction Processing (TP) monitors are available that enable high-transaction throughput and support for hundreds of users.

Most Open Systems vendors can now offer operating environments that are fully production ready for enterprise-oriented, even mission-critical, OLTP applications. Significantly, Sun, while not the absolute leader in all areas, has managed to remain at least in the middle of the pack in all significant areas.

Innovation is now occurring within a context of adherence to standards but still costs money. Sun has one of the largest, if not the largest, group of people working on UNIX than any other vendor. In addition to making its own investment in resources, Sun has also been a leader in allowing third parties to add additional value to its products.

4.3.7.6. The Commercial Multiuser Competitive Constellation.
Commercial Multiuser UNIX in 1993 and beyond will be dominated by a group of five vendors—IBM, HP, Sun, DEC, and NCR.

IBM. A previous review put IBM in the place of Hamlet, lamenting "to AS/400 or RS/6000, that is the question." Although IBM's recent announcements have clearly demonstrated that IBM intends to compete to the limits of its ability with its POWER RISC architecture, the fundamental internal schism still exists. The AS/400 Line of Business is still many times larger than the RISC Line Of Business, and we believe that IBM will still sell substantial quantities of AS/400 systems for at least the next three to five years. IBM field sales organizations are not about to pass up the revenues and margins associated with their flagship proprietary midrange system.

Internal issues aside, recent enhancements to the RS/6000 line, including the high-end Model 580 and 980, with 122 and 160 TPC-A, respectively, and CICS transaction processing software, firmly demonstrate IBM's commitment to commercial UNIX and its willingness to tolerate competition between the AS/400 and the RS/6000. On the deficit side are serious product shortcomings at least through the end of 1993 and the lack of an internal culture that is attuned to modern issues of downsizing, client-server computing, and networked UNIX application support.

IBM's major product deficit will be its lack of a multiprocessor system until at least 1994. The lack of multiprocessors leaves them with a serious gap in their product line. To compensate for this, IBM will be emphasizing various high-availability and clustered system offerings, driven with a combination of IBM and third-party software. We believe that clustered systems will only partially answer IBM's requirements for SMP systems for several reasons:

Clusters will be most effective in replacing large batch mainframes—Networked batch monitors have proven highly effective in batch throughput applications, and we expect them to prove effective in commercial environments for those limited number of users who are migrating batch environments to UNIX.

Cluster performance is not well understood for OLTP—For the more common paradigm of OLTP applications, clustered systems will have erratic performance. Limited user and vendor experience and lack of adequate simulation tools will make it difficult to predict and tune system performance in a loosely coupled clustered environment. When a clustered system is tuned for a particular application, it may not perform well if the application mix changes. For most users, SMP systems will remain a more attractive choice.

IBM's lack of an internal client-server "culture" has led them to create a large internal client-server group, with thousands of people and large resources. The formal charter of this group will be to integrate client-server applications for its customer base, with an informal charter to raise the level of client-server competency within IBM. Being IBM, they will probably flounder for a couple of years and still land some very large contracts within their large installed base. IBM will prosper, and due to its market coverage and huge installed base, they will certainly be one of the top three commercial multiuser UNIX vendors in the 1993 to 1995 time frame.

HP. HP is currently the leader in commercial multiuser UNIX, and we do not expect them to easily relinquish this title, even though the gap will narrow appreciably. HP is one of the few vendors in adequate financial shape. In the last two years HP has pulled out of a period of poor UNIX performance, particularly in workstations, and has turned successive quarters of good results, heavily driven by its very aggressive PA-RISC workstations and servers. HP is approximately $13 billion in revenues, with about 70 percent from computers and computer-related products. HP has moved from selling MPE first to selling UNIX first, and in the process has turned over much of its installed MPE base.

Unlike any of its competitors except IBM, HP has world-class inhouse expertise across a wide range of technologies—printers, storage technology, processor architecture and design, systems architecture, and semiconductor production. This advantage makes for an attractive marketing pitch, but in the real world has little impact since competitors can obtain parity output and storage technology from a number of OEM suppliers.

Like Sun, HP's major strategic challenge is to break into the "glass house"—major enterprise OLTP applications with $1 million+ systems that are controlled and purchased by the central IS groups in the world's largest corporations. HP's recently introduced Model 890 systems, with up to 575 TPC-A throughput offer the performance necessary for these applications. HP product technology is strong. Its major deficits are its large performance granularity and relatively high price for its SMP systems.

HP and Sun are in fact very similarly positioned relative to MIS applications. Both companies have exceptional hardware price/performance and commercial quality UNIX offerings. Both HP and Sun, in common with other aspiring vendors, must find the correct mix of software, service, and support to convince conservative IBM-oriented management to take the risk of a new vendor and new technology. Particularly noticeable is a lack of CICS, DB/2, or IMS compatibility tools.

Digital Equipment. In 1993–1994, Digital will be going through a period of major transition and is in the throes of both a major reorganization and a major product transition. Its major priority is to preserve and grow its installed VMS base. Although they will market an effective line of Alpha-based UNIX technology in 1993, we still see UNIX as a secondary focus for Digital. Despite a showing of support for UNIX, Digital's survival strategy is built around successfully migrating its installed VMS base to Open VMS on its new Alpha platforms.

NCR. NCR will establish itself as a solid niche player in commercial UNIX, coming off several years of relative success with their Tower series. Their Series 3000-based Intel SMP systems are solid performers with good price performance. We believe that they will still be a relatively narrow niche player, although their strengths in vertical markets and their integration expertise will give them a steady stream of large contracts in their market niche. NCR will be a solid contender for the number five slot in commercial UNIX.

4.3.7.7 *Significant UNIX Commercial Application Software.*
These are the most significant UNIX DBMS products:

Ingres	Ask Computer Systems Ingres Division
Oracle	Oracle

Progress	Progress Software
Empress	Empress Software
Sybase	Sybase
InterBase	Borland
Focus	Information Builders
Informix	Informix
Informix	Online
Informix	SE
Unify	Unify

These are the most significant 4GL products on UNIX:

Ally 4GL	Ally
JAM	JYACC, Inc.
Accell/SQL	Unify Corp
UNIFACE 4GL	Uniface
Magic	Magic Software Enterprises
SQR and APT	Sybase
SQL Forms	Oracle
SuperNOVA	Four Seasons Software

Transaction Processing solutions on UNIX:

Tuxedo/T	Ally
Encina	Transarc
Tuxedo/T	ITI
Topend	NCR

Object-Oriented Database Management software on UNIX:

Gemstone	Servio, Inc.
Objectivity/DB	Objectivity, Inc.
ObjectStore	Object Design, Inc.
ONTOS DB	ONTOS, Inc.
Versant ODBMS	Versant Object Technology Corp.
ITASCA	Itasca Systems, Inc.

Integrated UNIX Office Systems on UNIX:

Alis 2.x	Applix, Inc.
BBN/Slate	BBN Systems and Technologies
Rapport	Clarity Software
Goldmedal	Decathlon Data Systems
Teamware	Decathlon Data Systems
Cliq	Quadrtron
Uniplex II Plus	Uniplex Integration Systems, Inc.
WordPerfect	WordPerfect Corp.
Frame	Framemaker

4.3.7.8. Conclusions. The gap between the top three vendors will narrow considerably. HP's momentum will slow relative to IBM and Sun, and Sun's will accelerate as it begins to capture an increasing share of emerging commercial business. These are our summary forecasts:

- Sun will increase its share of the midrange commercial UNIX market substantially over the next three years. With the SPARCcenter 2000 to fill in the high-end gap in its product line and new management focus on service and support offerings, Sun can potentially equal HP in commercial market share by 1995. (Sun will remain a leader/center of innovation in basic UNIX technology.) An optimistic forecast, weighted by Sun's success in client-server computing, might even put Sun in first place.
- HP will still remain a strong contender and could hold on to its number one position, but its momentum will likely slow. HP's early dominance in multiuser commercial applications was to some extent due to its early focus and its conversion of its MPE base. Over the next few years HP will be facing focused and capable competition from both Sun and IBM, and its relative lead will erode.
- IBM will likely be number two or number three, although the first three positions will be extremely close. IBM's cluster computing initiative will not meet with widespread commercial success except as a replacement for batch mainframes or in accounts where IBM exerts significant account control. Its products will stay competitive as uniprocessors but will have continued weakness in high-end client server and OLTP applications until they begin shipping SMP systems in 1994, this despite IBM's investments into marketing CICS-compatible technology on AIX and the RS/6000.

- NCR and DEC will be fighting for fourth and fifth positions. NCR will close the gap slightly over the next year, but the momentum could shift to DEC by 1995–1996. Distribution between the low and high ends will vary between vendors, with IBM having the largest share of high-end UNIX business and Sun proportionately stronger at the low and midrange. (See Figure 4.12 and supporting data in Table 4.8.)

4.3.8.   Use of UNIX in Government

In terms of standards support SVR4.2 supports all the U.S. government and large corporation requirements including POSIX, FIPS, X/OPEN XPG, B1/B2 security, OSF AES, and IBCS (Intel Binary Compatibility Specification).

UNIX accounts for 18 to 25 percent of all federal, local, and state government computer system spending. In 1987, Digital Equipment Corp. protested the $4.5 billion U.S. Air Force computer acquisition

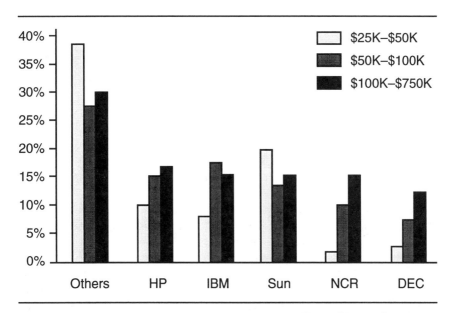

Figure 4.12.   Market Share Forecast, 1996, by Price Class—Support.
Source: InfoCorp forecast adjusted by R. M. Fichera Associates and Networked Publications

Table 4.8. Supporting data—Market Share Forecast, 1996, by Price Class.

	$25K–$50K	$50K–$100K	$100K–$750K
Digital Equipment	39%	28%	31%
Hewlett-Packard	14%	18%	17%
IBM	11%	18%	17%
NCR	3%	15%	16%
Sun Microsystems	21%	13%	16%
Others	7%	11%	14%

Source: RFMG

known as the AFCAC proposal. This called for the acquisition of 20,000 small, multiuser computer systems that conform to SVID. DEC challenged the government's right to specify SVID in procurements, but the GSA board of contracts ruled against the company, stating that the government could specify SVID because the RFP requirements do not restrict competition, that UNIX is not proprietary because it is supported by a number of vendors, that anyone could license it, and that it was equally available to all. The AFCAC RFP also specified that the selected operating system be able to migrate to conform with POSIX.

The NIST (National Institute for Standards and Technology), formerly the National Bureau of Standards, defines all of the functional areas that need to be addressed to promote applications portability. This profile is defined by the Federal Information Processing Standards group (FIPS) until it is available from POSIX.

UNIX is used in the government in the full spectrum of applications, including the most sophisticated such as those used by the intelligence community, NASA, and the IRS.

New Developments in Government Procurement. Over the last several years, there has been a constant stream of new developments in government procurement of information technology. The economy, changes in technology and government policies have all demanded improvements in the way the government acquires products and services.

The Corporate Information Management (CIM) program was instituted in the Department of Defense. CIM was unique in that it forces the support of top management by involving them in the process. It also had the effect of making MIS technology managers an integral part of the management team. The Office of Management and Budget put some teeth into this by stating that the CFO should have line responsibility for Information Resource Management (IRM) or alternatively be a "full participant" in Information Resource Management councils. This means the CFO must play a meaningful role related to financial systems.

CIM was not just a computer initiative. It was about organizational effectiveness. It analyzes business practices to determine what the organization was doing. It helps to establish organizational outcomes and to use information technology to leverage changes in accomplishing those outcomes.

CIM was intended to become way the DOD does strategic planning. It was a structured methodology tied to the planning, programming, and budgeting system. Over time it was expected to become the way budgets are justified. As a strategic planning process it was oriented around better business practices.

CIM considers information as a resource, as a corporate asset for the accomplishment of the mission. Information technology is viewed as a tool, a means to an end, and not an end in itself. CIM deals with the entire management process. Middle managers need to be involved, sold on the process, and turned into converts. If the justification process is tied to accomplishments of outcomes and outcomes are tied to dollars, you can justify things that usually get the short end of the stick in tough times.

It is clear that the federal government now recognizes that for agencies and departments that have largely technology-based missions such as the IRS and Social Security, there is a need for establish a Chief Information Officer (CIO) function. Such a role brings together business functions and operations in an information engineering scheme— relating business areas and business functions and the technology.

Executive Information Systems (EIS) brings together financial and other kinds of information used to make decisions. The CFO should play a lead role in EIS, bringing together financial data and performance and operational data to support the head of the agency.

Government Perspective on Open Systems. What the government would like from Open Systems is nothing short of complete interoperability. This means the flexibility to take any piece of hardware or any part of a network, substitute a new piece of equipment, hardware, network, or software, without adversely impacting the existing environment. It means that application software should be portable from one platform to another. It should be able to run from the desktop to the mini to the mainframe. The governments supports this idea of Open Systems because they spend enormous amounts of money converting applications from one box to another over the years.

This is not an easy thing to do because it's an immature process. It is evolving. It's a moving target. It's not just one standard, it's a plethora of standards that are all under the evolutionary process of being implemented. Procurement decisions have to recognize the nature of evolving processes. It's hard with a standards based procurement process to have to insist on full compliance and at the same time get the latest and greatest.

4.3.9.   UNIX in Education and Research

From the discussion of history, it is clear that the government's sponsorship of work at Berkeley promoted the adoption of UNIX within institutions also receiving government funding or wishing to take advantage of the technical benefits of UNIX. Briefly, these are the technical benefits of special appeal to the academic community:

*   It is a multiuser and multitasking operating system, as opposed to DOS and OS/2.
*   Programs and routines could be reused, making it easier to develop new programs by stringing operating system commands together with reusable programs and looping statements in shell scripts.
*   Programs can be easily interfaced to each other so the output of one program can be directed as the input to another. This permits preexisting code to be used to rapidly prototype or build new applications.
*   Availability of UNIX operating system source code has been a key factor in its gaining popularity within educational and research environments.

Source-level portability across a variety of multivendor architectures allows the use of a wide range of hardware where applications can be converted, often requiring only recompilation.

UNIX offered (and still does) a rich environment for the software developer, often providing access to the latest state-of-the-art tools (like the C language, for example).

4.4.   KEY UNIX INDUSTRY TRENDS

The five most significant trends in the overall UNIX market include the following:

1. Emergence of industry-wide standards, standards compliance, and Open Systems standards are perhaps inevitable in any product mov-

ing towards becoming a commodity. While it may at one time have seemed as if expensive computers would never become a commodity, UNIX is certainly moving them in that direction. Computing standards are not simple, however. Today's average computer user is only beginning to understand the importance standards will play.

2. **Strong movement toward distributed computing.** The 1970s saw the near-demise of the mainframe market. It would seem that history is repeating itself, only this time, it is the midrange computer market. Users want to make the next step from computing for personal productivity benefits to computing for work group productivity. To be effective in this respect, computers engage in cooperative processing.

3. **Increase in network distributed computing.** Users want to tie their computers together into networks. This trend is not restricted to any particular type of computers. The trend is toward using networked computers in truly cooperative fashion. Figure 4.13 illustrates the rapid growth projected in networked computing.

The vertical axis in Figure 4.13 represents the percent of the total computer market growth that is attributable to each of the types of computing, such as mainframes, minicomputers, and so forth.

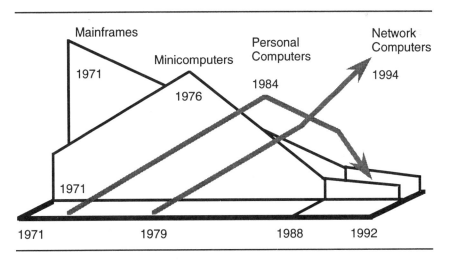

Figure 4.13.   Growth of UNIX in networked computing. Source: Sanford Bernstein.

4. Consolidation of UNIX variants toward a single standard. The score of UNIX variants and clones is very rapidly consolidating. It would appear that there will only be two UNIX systems in the 1990s. Both will be based on System V and extensions from the other dominant versions of UNIX: BSD and XENIX.
5. Commercial marketing muscle put behind UNIX. There is an enormous potential for UNIX in the commercial market where it has a relatively insignificant penetration today. As UNIX becomes easier to use, and as more commercial applications become available, it will gain rapid momentum as a departmental operating system of choice in most environments during the 1990s.

4.5. THE FUTURE OF THE UNIX INDUSTRY

The future of UNIX in the near term will only be limited by three major factors:

1. The emergence of world-class UNIX applications software, particularly in high-value commercial areas such as accounting and business operations solutions.
2. Federally mandated requirements that will have a stimulating effect in the commercial sector.
3. The strength of users' demand for multivendor solutions and the importance they will place on preserving their investments in software, training, and data over the long term.

Applications for UNIX will be found across a wide spectrum of applications and computing environments. PC users will adopt UNIX as ease of use is improved and as mainstream PC applications are ported to UNIX. Workstations will continue to be used, with distributed computing displacing timesharing in application areas that require the performance, graphics, and networking advantages available with UNIX products. Multiuser midrange and mainframe systems will increasingly be based on UNIX, taking advantage of networking and other technology. These systems will also offer significant price advantages over proprietary systems.

4.6. MANAGING CHANGE AS A USER ORGANIZATION

UNIX growth in commercial will depend on innovation that closes the functionality gap with proprietary systems. In particular, high-availability features must be incorporated in UNIX and UNIX applications to support more demanding mission-critical application requirements. Clustering and high-availability functionality are two of the emerging areas of differentiation for UNIX vendors. These are not, strictly speaking, server requirements, although considerable server functionality is involved to improve system resiliency, data integrity, support in fault isolation, and utilities that permit continuous systems operation. Fast recovery and failover schemes that can be customized to meet unique customer requirements are also being demanded in more sophisticated commercial applications areas.

UNIX server vendors, especially those involved with high-end servers are already using high availability as a strategic differentiator. Features such as disk mirroring, online backup, fast file system recovery are expected. More sophisticated functionality such as failover is being used as a differentiator today but will be expected as base functionality in the next few years.

4.6.1.   The Focus Is Shifting to New Structures and Needs

Companies are moving away from their traditional emphasis on rigid structures and centralized power to new organizations that are smaller, more flexible, and more responsive to change. Mass-production and mass-merchandising are yielding to the more modern concepts of modular design and customization, while at the same time businesses are learning to standardize the design and manufacture of products or services that are now built and distributed around the globe.

In periods of radical change, ways of doing things are reformulated, and new standards and new requirements begin to emerge. This creates new opportunities for those who understand the nature of change. An increase in emphasis on software design is going to occur in the 1990s. Powerful computers won't just be on desktops and in datacenters; they will be a nearly ubiquitous force, hidden in a great range of products and services. Software is what is going to make these computers do meaningful work. Designing software is still relatively difficult and time consuming. Faced with tremendous time-to-market pressures, the need to standardize the design of products made around the world, and the desire to modularize and customize these products, the industry will turn to off-the-shelf tools to help tap the power of computing. Innovation in software will be the hidden agent of change providing customers with the ability to harness powerful new technologies and new ways of working.

4.6.2.   Migrating to a Standards-Based Architecture

If Open Systems offer so many benefits, why is it that more companies aren't migrating to them? The answers range from simple lack of awareness and knowledge to the lack of a process whereby organizations can assess the merits of a standards-based architecture and then proceed to its definition and implementation.

There is a great deal of confusion in the marketplace regarding technology, standards, and management issues associated with Open Systems. Many information systems executives do not yet have the knowledge or expertise in their organizations to even evaluate the merits and disadvantages of Open Systems. To many, the task of moving to Open Systems may seem overwhelming. Users must determine whom to involve, how to get started, what areas make sense to look at, and how to fund what seems like such a massive change in technology.

In the X/Open Strategies for Open Systems program, a process is recommended where past investments in systems are protected, but new investments are examined for compliance with the desired future Open Systems-based information architecture rather than in perpetuating the past. It has organized an approach for organizations to define and implement an architecture based on standards and address some of the key migration and implementation issues.

The standards-based architecture is based on a number of elements that may not appear in traditional information systems technology plans. These include a new approach to architectural principles and the definition and modeling of an information technology infrastructure consisting of components that are common across the enterprise, based on industry standards, and are supported by products and technologies that adhere to those standards.

4.6.3.   The Emphasis Should Be on the Planning Process and Not the Plan

Inherent in a new approach to architecture will be a new culture and new vision. As such, organizational change is perhaps the greatest single challenge. A participatory process, involving both the information systems group and the end users, needs to be evolved starting with the joint development of this new vision.

End users must become stakeholders and share in the responsibilities for information systems as they become more dispersed throughout the organization. The goal is to achieve a real and positive change in the enterprise, not an interesting planning document.

The information architecture should tie business and technology policy together. This requires that a high degree of attention be paid to business practices and policy and how key business drivers are linked to key architectural models.

Another example of the importance of process can be found in the area of transition or migration plans. The focus should be on migration and not exclusively on the new target architecture. How to get from here to there is as important as defining the ultimate destination.

Finally, it is important to recognize that the only thing that is constant is change. An architecture should be designed for continuous change and iteration. Principles such as the adoption of standards will apply over longer planning horizons. This does not imply, however, that short-term results providing short-term benefits to the organization shouldn't be possible through short-term actions suggested by the planning process. The most critical linkage between the planning process and the construction of architecturally compliant systems and the acquisition of technology lies in the planning process driving the actual selection, sourcing, and delivery of systems, end users' tools, and facilities.

New Styles of Computing

Distributed computing technology has only recently come into vogue, and with so much discussion of distributed computing among vendors, the press, and analysts, numerous and often conflicting statements and definitions are creating confusion among users. The same applies to other new trends in computing such as windowing systems. Several of these trends, such as windowing and client-server computing, have "grown up" with UNIX and bear a special relationship to it, although they may also be supported in proprietary operating system environments. Their growth and popularity and that of UNIX are part and parcel, with cause and effect blurred. No book on the industry surrounding UNIX would be complete without a discussion of their relevance.

This chapter explores new styles of computing. With advances in technology that facilitate these new styles of computing, a new language for networked computing is fast developing. New concepts such as "networked computing in a heterogeneous environment" and "client-server computing" have sprung up. Windowing systems, tool kits, and "look and feel" are all relatively new concepts for software application architectures of the future. For example, Figure 5.1 illustrates how windows on the desktop computer display screen enable the user to access jobs running throughout the network. Here, the user can see and interact with different processes in each window. These processes may be run locally on his or her desktop computer as well as on other remote, even distant, nodes in the network.

According to most of the leading computer industry experts, distributed computing will be the next major stage in the evolution of the computer industry. Some industry researchers have projected that "client-server" computing will be a $50 billion total market in the mid-1990s.

The distinction between PCs and workstations is fading, and indeed many of the traditional terms and concepts used to describe computers, such as "batch processing," "timesharing," and "minicomputer" are no longer adequate in explaining this recent evolution in the industry. Many terms, such as "distributed processing," "requester server," "cooperative computing," and "client server" are now being widely used, although it is hard to find simple definitions for them. New terminology is being coined to describe these emerging concepts. We are experiencing a paradigm shift in computing, and this chapter is intended to help you cope by reviewing some of the basics.

In Figure 5.1, the user's desktop allows him or her to interface to any of the other computing facilities on the network. These facilities might include accessing printers, transferring files from other devices to the user's own system, and running terminal emulation software, which allows the window on the user's desktop to appear to the IBM mainframe like a 3270-type terminal, for example. These jobs could range from a simple transferring of files from the Apple/Mac to running simulation software on the Cray.

To achieve such access, each system needs to be networked. Figure 5.2 shows how devices are connected via a LAN (local area network). One of the nodes in the LAN shown below is a gateway that connects the LAN to a WAN (wide area network). This is one example of how networks may be combined into larger enterprise-wide network configurations.

The purpose of this section is to define and explain, through examples, what is meant by the "client-server" model of distributed network computing. We start by looking briefly at the history of styles of computing. We then give several examples of client-server configurations and applications. We summarize with a brief analysis of the benefits of the client-server model and why we expect it to emerge as one of the major new trends in modern computing. We conclude the chapter with a discussion of windowing systems, the X Window system in particular.

5.1. HISTORICAL PERSPECTIVE OF COMPUTING STYLES

Commercial computers of the 1950s and early 1960s processed jobs fed into the computer through punched cards or tape. This was called batch data processing. As databases were implemented on these systems, all

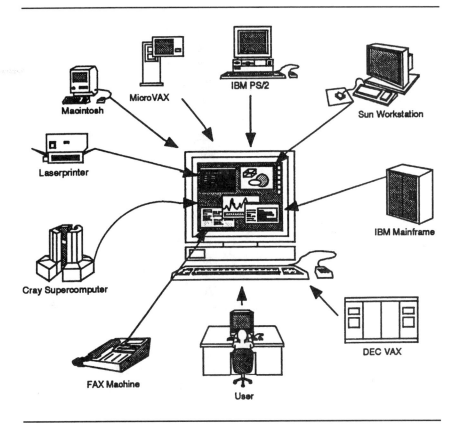

Figure 5.1. Heterogeneous networking. Window system environments take the place of multiple terminals and provide the user with an interface to applications running on their system or any other system in their network.

transactions against these databases were handled by mainframe computers, which performed centralized data processing functions. During the 1960s, IMS became IBM's premier database for transaction processing.

During the late 1960s, a new style of computing known as timesharing became more prevalent. Timesharing was typified by a standalone system with terminals attached to it. The terminals relied on the system for all processing and for interaction with any other devices. Timesharing gained popularity among programmers and computer users of both large mainframe computers and smaller minicomputers during the 1970s.

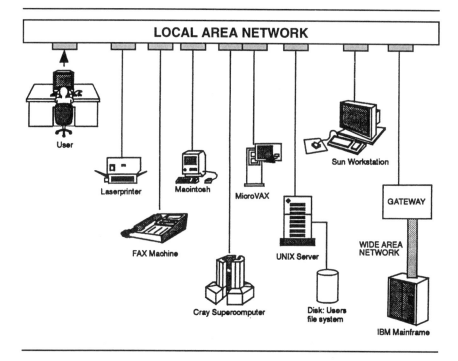

LOCAL AREA NETWORK

User

Laserprinter   Macintosh   MicroVAX   Sun Workstation

FAX Machine   UNIX Server   GATEWAY

WIDE AREA NETWORK

Cray Supercomputer   Disk: Users file system   IBM Mainframe

Figure 5.2.   The network is now the computer. A network provides connectivity and access to the resources in the network.

In the case of mainframe computers, the central processor was, by comparison to today's technology, low-performance (e.g., the IBM 360 processor). As more users were added to the system, it got bogged down handling terminal interactions. User complaints forced IBM to respond with a product known as CICS, which serves as a front-end communication service. This increased the number of users who could be added to the application's timesharing configuration.

As minicomputers came on the scene and increased in popularity, there was strong user demand to allow these computers to communicate and share data and peripheral resources. While magnetic tape or disks had served as the vehicle for exchanging data between systems, new interactive techniques had to be developed to allow users on one system to communicate interactively with another system. Terminal and communication emulation capabilities were developed.

In the early 1980s, the third wave occurred with the advent of personal computers and workstations. PCs provided a means of both dispersing and distributing processing. With advances in windowing, the processing required to support an applications user interface was handled by the desktop computer, while a minicomputer or mainframe computer was commonly used for number crunching, data management, resource sharing, and other functions that weren't practical on the desktop computer. It was not uncommon that the desktop computer ran one operating system (e.g., MS-DOS), while the "backoffice" computer ran a different operation system (e.g., MVS or VMS).

The 1990s will see a move toward networked computing and the growth of systems and applications that take advantage of the benefits networking offers in greater flexibility and adoption of computers and other network appliances in the workplace. As applications move from offline to online, and as the number of electronic office appliances like facsimile machines, copiers, and even telephone systems proliferate, there will be major advantages in integrating these systems.

Table 5.1 shows this evolution to the present.

The logical extension to this evolution is what some people are calling mobile computing. This simply means that the network technology will be very highly advanced and will free computers from the desktop the same way cellular phones freed the telephone.

Table 5.1.   Evolution of styles of computing. Software and hardware technology is progressing rapidly to distributed computing.

Year	Style	Software	Interfaces and Appliances
1960s	Batch	Centeralized	Cards/printouts
1970s	Timesharing	Dispersed	Dumb ASCII terminals
1980s	Networked	Dispersed processing	PC and workstations with bitmapped graphics and intelligent terminals
1990s	Networked computing	Distributed processing	Workstations and PCs Multi-media Hand-held devices
2000	Mobile computing	Distributed processing	Wireless networking Ultra miniaturization Personal devices (PDA's)

Multiprocessing, which employs multiple processors, has the advantage of providing smooth upgrade and increased performance to support timesharing and number-crunching programs. Where multiprocessors are used in networks, they can function as servers, but in and of themselves do not constitute a client-server architecture because they cannot be flexibly allocated physically around the network.

What is behind this new wave of network computing is pressure to put powerful compute capability close to the users. The extent to which this shift in information technology has been driven by technical progress—as opposed to user demand—could be debated, but there should be little doubt about the impressive growth in the workstation market, that users want more powerful desktop computers, and that power users are buying the most powerful workstations.

5.2. COMPARING PCS AND WORKSTATIONS

From an analysis of product introductions in recent years, it is clear from a technical standpoint that high-end PCs and low-end workstations are close in terms of price, performance, functionality, and suitability for various applications. But there are still significant differences.

PCs were designed to function primarily as standalone nodes capable of functioning without dependency on any other processor or server or network. On the other hand, workstations were designed to be used primarily as part of a network.

PCs tend to run operating systems that support one user (as opposed to several). Until OS/2, PC operating systems didn't support multitasking or the ability for the operating system to run several jobs simultaneously. Workstations commonly support windowing environments where each window is essentially running a different job in a multitasking environment. Workstations' networking capabilities support running multiple processes in a largely transparent fashion. These processes can be running locally and/or on remote processors in the network. This multitasking support requires more local processing power. Workstations have faster processors and support larger memories than PCs.

Apple Macintoshes, which are among the best PCs with respect to built-in networking, can share disk space, printers, and (with some effort) modems. Workstations can share disks, printers, modems, and most importantly, processors because of the functionality of the operating system.

Sun workstations, which have been among the best workstations with respect to price/performance and networking, run UNIX exclusively and support a rich topology (different ways of connecting them) in various configurations. Sun's success has helped accelerate the pace of change toward networked computing with UNIX.

The next section examines the new terminology of state-of-the-art computer developments, particularly the components in networked computing environments.

5.3.   NETWORKED COMPUTING

UNIX Networking

UNIX has a rich and at the same time not very well understood relationship with networking. It is rich in terms of the number of technologies and products as well as the integral role it plays in supporting high-performance distributed client-server computing. However, when it comes to products and integration of software and hardware in a heterogeneous environment, it can be confusing.

The world of UNIX networking is rapidly advancing to a world beyond the technology of computer communications. Electronic mail, list servers on the Internet, bulletin board systems, and a whole new information industry is evolving in terms of network-intrinsic applications. Networking is a critical technology in the integration of businesses. Examples such as electronic data interchange (EDI), remote teleconferencing, and other advanced applications are not only becoming feasible but also represent strategic competitive components in companies' information architecture strategies.

Nowhere is the influence of standards more advanced than in the general area of computer communications. Such standards are critical to the industry acceptance of new products and services. Networking is inherently a cooperative effort.

The most advanced form of computer hardware today is the workstation. Hardware is but one part of what makes up networked computing. Distributed network computing has four distinct components:

1. Network computing nodes
2. Cross-computer operating system support and services
3. The physical network connecting computing nodes and networking appliances
4. Distributed applications

5.3.1.   Network Computing Hardware

Network computing nodes, depending on how they are used, can support any combination of client and server processes. Client-server architecture will be explained in the next section in detail. Nodes do not have to be computers, although they must possess some computer technology to interface intelligently to the network. Hardware on the network can include input devices—for example, an automated teller machine and output devices such as a printer or laserwriter. One can expect to see an ever-widening array of network appliances.

5.3.2.   Cross-Computer Operating Systems

The UNIX operating system offers one of the best cross-computer operating systems for network computing. It maximizes flexibility in configuring different hardware in the distributed network and excels in permitting cross-vendor operating system compatibility. The initial objective of UNIX was to run the same operating system on different computers and enable data communications between them. Almost from the beginning, the architecture of UNIX was designed with networking in mind, and more than any other factor, its utility in network computing is responsible for the current migration to UNIX. Early on, UNIX utilities such as electronic mail and naming services exploited UNIX's interprocess communication and data-sharing capability.

PC LANs are used to connect personal computers into networks. Some of the more popular PC LAN technology is based on the notion of a network operating system, or NOS. NOSs such as Novell and Banyon for example are proprietary, although they may be ported to multiple equipment manufacturers' hardware. UNIX with networking extensions is a different Open Systems approach to solving the same problem. The same (or essentially the same) operating system running across multiple platforms represents a major step toward achieving compatibility and interoperability between the different resources in the network.

The NOS model used by Novell, the leader in the PC LAN market is shown in Figure 5.3. In the Novell network operating system, Figure 5.3 illustrates the interaction between an application running on a PC client and the PC operating system. When the application or user requests a particular file, the "interface shell" which resides on the PC intercepts the DOS commands from the user or application program. The shell determines whether the request is for a local file or a remote file on the Novell server. If the information is located on the local disk, the request is passed onto DOS and handled as a normal I/O operation. Otherwise, the request translator issues a read request to the file server that locates the file and transmits it to the reply translator which converts the information into a form that DOS can handle. DOS then provides the applica-

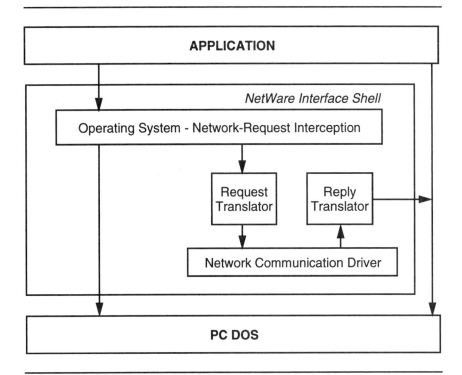

Figure 5.3. The Novell NOS model. The Novell model is mostly used for networking PCs. Network Interface Shell (Copyright 1986, Novell Inc., all rights reserved)

tion program with the data. Novell accomplishes file service and other functions using its own proprietary SPX/IPX protocol. In the last few years, Sun, Novell, and Netwise have jointly developed transport layer independent protocols so that the remote procedure calls used for writing client-server software on Sun and those for used by Novell applications both use a common transport independent interface. This has moved Novell and Sun closer to network protocol transparency.

Novell has progressed from offering a network operating system featuring printer and file services to LAN connectivity to mainframe computers via gateways. LAN connectivity to mainframes is not user friendly, and gateways require considerable knowledge about using the mainframe. The major emphasis has been on accessing mainframe applications and not on peer-to-peer communcations between microcomputer programs and the mainframe. Peer-to-peer communcations and user transparency still pose significant changes and represent the next stage of LAN technology evolution.

Novell's Open NetWare is a version of NetWare that is portable to many operating systems including VMS, OS/2, UNIX, and so forth. Portable NetWare lets the minicomputer or server running it act as a NetWare server. The implementation of portable netware is differentiated from "native NetWare" which is optimized for the Intel 80x88. Portable NetWare users are able to communicate with these Open NewWare servers both as terminals and as network workstations. As terminals they can run minicomputer and mainframe software. Otherwise, the services available to NetWare clients are broadly similar to those available from a native NetWare server. Unlike PCs with NetWare, UNIX usually has TCP/IP networking services built in.

5.3.3.   UNIX Network Hardware and Software

A UNIX network provides for high-speed intercomputer communications required to support requests for information and provide facilities for network processing carried over the network that are expected by UNIX users. UNIX Networking consists of both hardware and software components. In the UNIX markets, TCP/IP and Ethernet have historically been preferred communications network standards. As previously discussed this networking was one of Berkeley's major contributions to UNIX technology. UNIX networking was actually advancing in lock step with the ARPA network and later the NFSnet and Internet. Unlike Novell, UNIX networking was built with Wide Area remote communications in mind. Novell technology has historically been a protocol used to provide resource sharing for a small number of nodes in a local area network. This is not to say that Novell can't be used for enterprise-wide communications.

The most common communications medium used in UNIX environments to physically link systems into a LAN is Ethernet, invented by Xerox Corporation. Ethernet is a set of specifications that covers multiple physical media types. Media types include coaxial cables (thick net, thin net, or cheaper net), twisted pair, and fiber optic cabling. Twisted pair and fiber optic are now gaining the most in popularity.

The best way to think of the network itself is to think of it as comprising two major pieces: network hardware connections, which are the controllers, cabling connectors, and data conversion devices (also called internetworking devices), and network software interfaces, which consist of one or more of the following:

- High-level file transfer and file system services
- Translators
- Network interface drivers that talk to controllers

LANS and WANS. Networks can be categorized as either local area networks (LANs) or wide area networks (WANs). A local area network (LAN) handles high-speed data communications over a limited distance or area, typically throughout a building. Multiple local area networks can be tied together to form a campus-wide network to support communications between several buildings at a given site. The LAN itself is usually purchased and owned by the company that purchases the computers and network connection equipment.

A wide area network (WAN) may include a large number of different systems, which can be close to each other or separated by large distances. The transmission medium may be telephone lines, cable, or even satellites. WANs are typical in organizations that need to connect parts of their business in different locations. Usually, only large or specialized companies own their own wide area networks. Many WANs make use of telephone networks, which are owned and leased by the telephone companies. This technically facilitates systems being loosely coupled to a network through the use of modems.

Switching systems that allow remotely connected terminals access to various computers on a network, without being physically cabled to the system, provide great flexibility in permitting the user to log in to various systems without any reconfiguration. UNIX remote login provides this same function for networked machines.

The network software interfaces function as the support mechanism for network services. Network services include different types of utilities or applications that provide a service (literally) to users who are connected to the network. Such software can run on either clients or servers and usually has some component on each. The following are the most common network services associated with UNIX:

Network file services—server provides files that diskless, dataless, or even datafull clients require either to boot up or to execute. Email—mail servers enable users on a network to exchange messages with other users on any connected network.

Printer services—server handles printing of files for other systems on the network.

Communications services—server functions as a gateway, connecting one network to another.

Naming services—server looks up computer users' names; this is usually called the lookup service.

Distributed applications—software written both to operate and to take advantage of the networked computing environment.

5.3.4.   Internetworking Plans and Strategies

Just because there is some sort of cable connecting machines doesn't mean that workers at both ends are going to be about to work effectively in accessing and exchanging information.

What Is an Internetwork? There are at least three types of internetworks. The first type is local—for example, confined to a work group or floor of a building. The next is campus—the network that connects all the floors in a skyscraper or the network that connects different buildings in an office park. The next type of internetwork might be called metropolitan and so on. But these definitions are no longer clear or generally accepted. Network hierarchies like organization heirarchies are being flattened.

A small, homogeneous network is comparativly simple to design, install, and manage. But such networks are rare in all but very small organizations. The truth is that users who need to access resources across dissimilar networks, for example networks that combine PCs, Macs, and UNIX workstations and servers will find themselves blocked at numerous points. Users don't want to know how it all works, but as they gain experience they are going to demand ever-higher levels of support from their suppliers and from their systems and network administrative support groups (be they in MIS in a large company, or provided by outside service firms such as systems integration or Resellers).

In a special interoperability report, UnixWorld offered 10 suggestions or steps for users in search of interoperability. We have expanded on these steps. But before any of the steps below are taken, you have to get familiar with your information architecture.

Before a networking design can be undertaken, an organization's basic physical infrastructure should be mapped out. The organization should be functionally decomposed into logical groupings. A common set of services required should then be defined. Especially since certain options can cost a lot of money, it is important to define the business purposes and objectives for the systems and networks. Which users need access and to what should be determined. The bandwidth required should be estimated so the speed implications of the selected networking solution can meet the proper requirement. All of this should be contained in sections of your company's information architecture (see Chapter 7 for more details).

Step 1—Getting Wired. Desktop computers should be connected to a network (most probably in the form of a multiport transceiver using standard telephone wire or "cheaper net" if cost is a real issue. Local PCs, workstations should be able to share work group devices like servers, printers, fax modems, and so forth. The local networks might be hooked up to an enterprise network later on in a step known as internetworking—but the first objective should be to get co-located desktops onto a local area network.

The main consideration at this stage should be the ability of your existing or planned operating systems to support the network adapters for your desktop systems. With PCs you will have to add the network adapter. With workstations and servers, they should be integrated already.

Standardizing on network technology is smart. Otherwise you will have to consider internetwork hubs, bridges, or routers to mix different types of networks. If you have mixed media already, you might want to look at hubs such as those available from Cabletron or Synoptics. These hubs can link mixed topology and support Ethernet, fiber optics, and token ring all at single point.

Step 2—Getting Connected. Ensure your operating systems can communicate with each other and share data. In its simplest form this may mean ensuring that your operating systems support NFS so you can transparently share data files. There is usually some policy decision at this step since naming conventions and inherent differences between different operating systems may handle things differently or have inherent differences (like the number of characters that can be used for file names). There is at least one additional and very basic form of interoperability that should be addressed at this time. This is to be able to support the basic utilities of Telnet (e.g., basic UNIX networking technology) so that once you open a connection between two machines, users can perform remote login and other simple functions including terminal emulation. At this stage it should be possible to implement simple dial-back modems to allow people to connect with your system from remote sites. This can be great for people working from home or for people to tie into from their laptops or terminals when they are away from the office. You can also immediately begin to communicate in simple terms with your customers and suppliers through modems.

At an extreme, adapting a network operating system like Novell NetWare, or solutions from vendors like Banyon Vines or 3Comm might make sense. But this is probably the best path if you don't plan to ultimately expand the network to outside the work group.

Step 3—Getting Networks Interconnected. Networks grow to the point that they hit limitations in the number of nodes that can be connected. Breaking networks up into smaller subnets and then tying these subnets together through the use of internetworking devices like bridges, routers, and gateways is quite common. Most computer systems also support their own form of communications such as SNA, TCP/IP, IPX/SPX, and so on. These internetworking devices can be used to perform the conversions that allow different types of networks to communicate. In one strategy, you might have one physical local area network for your PCs running Novell and another physical network running TCP/IP for workstations and servers. These two networks could be bridged. In addition to protocol conversion, internetworking devices may offer other functionality for filtering and forwarding data. Such functions can be essential in large networks to reduce network traffic and also to add a level of network security. Some of these devices also support a wide range of telecommunications methods, so you can tie in dial-up lines, dedicated circuits such as T-1 and T-3 high-speed transmission lines as well as support X.25 "packet switching" for wide area network connectivity.

Step 4—Get a head start on managing things that are connected. This is the software side of step 3 and it breaks down into two parts. You need to use software in addition to these internetworking devices. Low-level software may already come with your operating system, but you have to investigate the compatibility issues and project your future connectivity requirements. The second part of the software you should evaluate is in the area of network management. By now, even if you are dealing with 20 machines, it probably makes sense to implement SNMP and start thinking of the network as a system that needs to have administrative tools. There are a number of different packages in this area. Software products may be available through the internetworking device supplier or the supplier of the transceivers in step 1. Synoptics, Cabletron, Sun Microsystems, HP, and many other vendors offer standards-based network management solutions that you should think seriously about at this step. Network management is fundamental to the diagnosis and maintenance of networks and will be the first step in managing distributed computing resources.

Step 5—Getting network-ready software and communicating with the outside world. You are now ready to give your users some networking software. Email is perhaps the next step to take. With most UNIX systems, there is basic email built into the operating system, so you might not have to spend anything to get started. Email has all the problems of compatibility one might expect of an electronic "tower of Babel." But there are different strategies for implementing email gateways to forward mail between different types of systems. It is also possible to link your network to outside service companies like Compuserve or MCI and even the Internet. In the case of networking with other UNIX systems, getting connected to the Internet through UUNET or one of the commercial internetwork exchange companies like PSI, ANS, Alternet, or some other service usually will require that you take additional security precautions building a "firewall" gateway through which you effectively control how your internal network can be accessed by others on the public data network.

Step 6—Getting applications to connect is a distributed network. Application interoperability is the next step. There are increasingly more sophisticated levels of applications interoperability. The most basic is having software applications that can transparently access files on remotely connected systems. This is usually not the sort of information you can read about at the store when you buy software. Whether you can use applications across different machines depends on what RPC (remote procedure calls) the programmers used when they first wrote the software. In connecting application front ends and back ends on different architectures, part of the solution may lie with the operating systems, but just as likely you will need some "middleware" either from your software vendor or a third-party software vendor they recommend. For example, Oracle has a suite of network connectivity products known as SQL*NET. These products have portions of software implemented on each system that want to communicate.

Another useful suggestion is to consider using the same application on multiple platforms across dissimilar networks. For example, FrameMaker has versions that run on most popular models of PCs, Macs, and UNIX workstations. FrameMaker files are designed to be accessible by a variety of clients.

Users often learn that application standardization is the only way to go. Even when the applications provide some file conversion facilities, it is often the case that these conversions invariably loses some of the richness of the native file format. Standards in this area, like CCITT's SGML (structured general markup language) and Adobe System's Carousel are slowly progressing.

Step 7—Gaining consistency in user interface. Virtually all desktop environments support graphical user interface technology. It should be an objective that users who know one platform's user interface can easily understand any other platform. This is usually very simple in purely text-based communications such as those discussed in step 2. But in getting PC desktops to take advantage of UNIX servers, it is going to be necessary to have X Windows supported by the window system on the desktop. There are a number of products that turn a Microsoft Windows window into an X server and therefore can run the graphical user interface of an application running on another machine including a UNIX server on the Windows desktop. But few corporations can do everything they need with software they buy off the shelf. This is also the stage for evaluating and selecting a graphical user interface builder which allows the same application to be run in a variety of target window system environments. A whole new set of "portable" interface builders is on the market. This step is where you should get X Windows applications and tools working.

With MAC, UNIX, and MS-DOS/Windows users all running X server software, the same applications can be supported on all desktops. While some of the uniqueness of each environment is lost with this approach, it can resolve the internetworking problems effectively creating an integrated logical network. The opportunity to run standardized applications, all supporting X, can be compelling.

Step 8—Special power tools and policies. This step involves getting deeper into the tools that allow application developers to write software that is portable by design across a wide range of systems. Cross-platform tools let programmers write applications with front ends (the part the users see) running on the desktop and back ends on servers or other systems. Today you find these types of tools available from Data Base Management software companies and in some cases from operating system developers (e.g., Sun's Tooltalk). This right set of tools depends on what you are trying to do. Often, in addition to acquiring tools and integrated development environments, programmers need to adopt new policies and procedures to ensure portability. Many companies have found it necessary for example to define a subset of ANSI standard C constructs that programmers are allowed to use.

Step 9—Distributed applications re-engineering. The tools in step 8 usually are a quick fix when it comes to getting software written for deployment across multiple systems. This next step really involves the adoption and management of programming practices as they relate to the use of standards-based API's (or application programming interfaces). The goal is to write to the API once and at most have to recompile code on different machines that support that API. Setting internal standards for using APIs and enforcing the practice in design reviews with programmers can improve programmer productivity since they are working on the application functionality and not the utilities below the application logic. Traditional programmers have evolved libraries they reuse in writing new applications. Often these libraries are not compliant with APIs.

Step 10—Getting people connected. Interoperability is not just about computers and technology. It is also about people. Networks should hide the complexity of what is happening from the user. Users should not have to understand all the intricacies of networking. But they will often require new skills and training as well as education concerning new policies and practices as they relate to open networking. Your smarter users, say engineers, should understand that even though they know how to do certain things, that they are not allowed to mess with production networks. Email users need to understand that there is such a thing as email etiquette, and that there are good and bad practices and fair-use rules on the Internet for example. Networking should not restrict people, it should have exactly the opposite effect. Whether its exploring the Internet or reading newsgroups on network services, users will find a rich set of resources opening up to them. They should be educated and not just expected to understand this potential.

Open network computing is the key to solving business problems and empowering people to work together better. Whether it is using email, teleconferencing, or simply sharing data files, networking is the way of the future. And don't forget that in terms of administration, "the network *is* the mainframe."

5.4. DISTRIBUTED COMPUTING: COOPERATIVE PROCESSING THROUGH CLIENT-SERVER

Distributed applications are architected to take full advantage of the processing capabilities throughout the network. Programs are split into client and server modules. The user interface runs on the desktop as a client process and accesses data and software services on the server(s) across the network. A client-server architecture is the result of combining these network computing components. Examples of current applications areas that exploit the client-server include CASE (Computer Aided Software Engineering), CAD/CAM (Computer Aided Design and Manufacturing), and relational data management.

5.4.1.   Servers

A server that supports client machines (client is defined in Section 5.4.2) with the same architecture as the server is called a homogeneous server. A heterogeneous server supports clients of the same and different architectures as the server.

The most common example is the file server. A file server is a computer that stores and archives files for various clients. When a client needs a file, it accesses its file server; but it must share that server with other clients. Examples of PC file servers are Novell, 3COM, Banyon, and Sun's PC NFS.

Technically, a workstation can be called a server in the sense that its computer serves multiple windows running on that computer. Each window is a client, and each window must contend with other windows on that machine for the shared resource; in this case, that resource is the machine's CPU, local disk store, and so on.

A compute server is a computer resource that various compute-intensive jobs run on. Each process is a client, and each contends with the other jobs for the CPU, memory, and disk of that compute server.

A database server is a computer that maintains a central copy of a data structure. Various clients can manipulate that data, but each client must access the data in a manner that is controlled by the server. Here, the data is the shared resource, and the clients all access that shared resource.

A PC LAN server is a server dedicated to supporting desktop computers in a local area network, while a site server is a computer that provides support to another server or client at the site or around a campus.

A communications server is a computer that provides support for communications functions—for example, providing a wide area network gateway between the local network and a remotely located computer or network.

One computer could be used for any or all of the above services. The point of distributed computing, however, is to spread the processing power around in the network and match the requirements of each service with the appropriate level of processing power, memory or disk capacity, and type of peripherals supported. This provides better overall resource utilization and more predictable performance.

5.4.2.   Clients

A client is a process typically running on a computer system or node on a network that handles the user interface and runs the application program. The client makes requests to servers in the network. Sun Microsystems defines three types of clients.

A diskless client is a computer that has no disk. It must be attached to a local area network. It uses the network as the means of communicating with one or more servers. A diskless client relies on a server to begin operation; it runs the UNIX kernel locally and can execute applications programs locally. It can support peripherals like a graphics display, input devices like a mouse or joystick, and even a printer or a plotter. Computations are done locally, consuming little or no server resources. The server is only used to access files and programs and to provide the client's virtual memory swap space.

A dataless client is like the diskless client, except that it has its own local disk, which is used to hold system software. This decreases the need for the kernel and programs running on the client to page over the network, which decreases both the load on the server and the network and allows more clients to be supported per server.

The datafull client has its own local disk and does not require a server either to start up or to execute on a continuing basis. A standalone system can function completely independently of a server and any other device on the network. By being attached to a network, the standalone system can gain access to services provided by servers on the network, such as electronic mail.

Terminals do not run an operating system. Thus, they are not clients. They may be connected directly to a computer or be connected to terminal concentrators, which in turn are connected to a network. Terminals are often connected to nodes (either hosts or clients) on the network but can access any other node in the network.

A terminal is a device that usually sends and receives character data. It does not run any programs and supports no peripherals. A terminal is completely dependent on a server for its operation.

A windowing terminal is a terminal that has enough local intelligence and processing power to run portions of a windowing system locally at the terminal. Unless these systems run downloaded software, they are not clients, strictly speaking.

5.4.3.   Distributed Applications

We have selected three different examples of applications that are architected to exploit the client-server model. These are CASE, CAD/CAM, and DBMS.

Computer-Aided Software Engineering (CASE). Advanced software engineering tools and utilities have been among the first applications to take advantage of client-server architecture. There are clear advantages in UNIX and its multitasking capability coupled with powerful workstation compute engines. This allows developers to handle concurrent activities such as documentation, source code update, online debugging, compilation, and execution with graphical windowing user interfaces. Client-server architecture not only allows the single developer to use network resources—for example, running long compiles on a server—but also is ideal for supporting teams of developers with servers that function as repositories for source, executable programs, documentation, and so forth.

Computer-Aided Design and Manufacturing. Another type of engineering activity that has moved rapidly and almost totally to client-server is CAD/CAM. In these applications, design and engineering are now implemented on workstation clients that support local processing and interactive graphics. The server provides resources for numerically intensive analysis and simulation as well as storage and archival of engineering data.

Data Management. A rapidly emerging application taking advantage of client-server is data management. In particular, Relational DBMS and Object-Oriented DBMS are implemented on a variety of client-server architectures. In these applications, the client handles the user interface (possibly the terminal management) and applications processing resulting in a query. This query or request is sent out over the network and is processed by a server. The server is running the database back end and will actually do reads and writes to the database. The server then sends replies to the client over the network, and the client continues to process, for example, postprocessing data from the database into presentation graphics. In a fully distributed database management architecture, there is a single logical view of the database, even though the actual physical data is stored in multiple locations throughout the network.

In client-server applications, the database manager, library services, and core application software run on the server while the client processes the client portion of the application logic and handles the user interface.

5.4.4.   Advantages of Client-Server Architecture

The client-server model offers several advantages over traditional methods of computing. Users can build up their networks gradually, adding and replacing nodes in the network to accommodate both additional applications and new users. Often, the alternative is to completely replace the existing computer and software investment. The client-server architecture permits a smooth incremental upgrade of computing resources throughout the network.

Since no vendor supplies the entire solution for most customers, the client-server model, together with de facto industry standards, permits the user to get out from under the "house arrest" of a single computer vendor whose proprietary products will not easily plug and play.

Users can localize special processing capability and resources where they are required in the network. For example, certain nodes in the network may require fault tolerance. An expensive supercomputer can be accessed and shared by several departments in a company instead of each department having its own system. The network architecture itself provides a level of high availability, so that even when certain nodes on the network go down, other nodes can continue processing.

Sophisticated graphical user interfaces especially suited to the work group are enabled by the combination of technologies made possible by client-server computing. Indeed, a new generation of software, called groupware is emerging, which exploits the ease with which data is accessible to users in a group without limitations. Examples can be found in electronic mail, calendar management software, teleconferencing, and a widening array of multimedia applications that combine data, voice, image, and fax.

5.4.5. Future Technology

Client-Server and Future Technology. The client-server computing model will become more pervasive with technological advancements. New technologies such as voice, image, CD-ROM (compact disk), and AI (artificial intelligence) will be linked to client-server architectures for two major reasons. First, the most advanced CASE developments will be exploiting client-server. It is clear that client-server will not only be a preferred development environment for such advancing technologies, but will also serve as an effective deployment platform. Second, users will want to adopt these new technologies but with minimal impact to their ongoing operations and systems. So adding clients and/or servers and extending existing facilities with networking will be a preferred approach to implementation.

Client-server in heterogeneous networks Figure 5.2 illustrated the layered communications software architecture supporting a heterogeneous Ethernet local area network consisting of workstations, PCs, and a UNIX server.

For software to be efficiently developed to take advantage of client-server, common application programming interfaces, or APIs, must exist across multiple vendors' platforms. This is an area currently receiving much attention. You can look for increased standardization of interfaces, which eventually will greatly increase the plug and play capability of software in client-server environments.

Flexibility is not being tied to a single protocol—for example, SNA, or a particular LAN technology available from only one vendor. Increasingly, future computing environments will be multivendor. This trend will be driven not only by advances in technology and price/performance but also by changes in the approach to sales and distribution of information technology. As standards emerge in virtually every area of technology, such as RISC, UNIX, and SQL, components in the client-server architecture will be able to be sourced from a variety of vendors. Value-added resellers, systems integrators, and large computer companies will all be competing with each other to bring the best components together to install networks and create solutions for their customers.

Significant technological advancements are expected in several areas, including network throughput, network management, and computer price/performance, to name only a few. These will help to further accelerate the trend toward client-server models of computing.

5.4.6.   Wrestling with Interoperability

A handful of small start-up companies have been wrestling with the interoperability issue of PC and Mac software emulation facing UNIX as it moves toward increased use as a desktop computing operating system platform. Several small companies are moving to supply products that allow current and future off-the-shelf, shrinkwrapped Windows or NT applications to run on UNIX.

SunSoft has acquired Praxsys Technologies Inc. of Norwood, Massachusetts. Bristol Technology of Ridgefield, Connecticut while it was readying a solution to the task of running Windows applications on UNIX. Echo Logic, a spin-off of Bell Labs Inc. and funded by AT&T Venture Partners has announced a pact with Apple Computer Inc. for its multipass binary compiler technology, FlashPort which permits existing shrinkwrapped Mac applications to run on Apple's anticipated PowerPC RISC UNIX boxes when they arrive. Quorum, of Menlo Park, California also offers software that allows Mac users to easily migrate to UNIX environments. Their software has actually turned out to be popular for software developers themselves to take advantage of the power of the UNIX software development environment for software which will be sold for use mostly on Mac platforms.

5.4.7.   Network Services and Value-Added Networks

In the 60s and 70s, only the government or the largest corporations had the resources to have a wide area communications network, normally connecting major data centers. Over the last decade, there has been an explosion of private and public network services. Some of these are described in this section.

The Electronic Frontier Foundation (EFF). The Electronic Frontier Foundation was founded to organize a new public interest advocacy organization to educate the public about the democratic potential of new computer and communications technologies and to work to develop and implement new public policies to maximize civil liberties and competitiveness in electronic social environments. The EFF's primary mission is to ensure new electronic highways emerging from the convergence of telephone, cable, broadcast, and other application technologies. The EFF is trying to ensure that the rules, regulations, and laws are being applied to emerging communications technologies.

The Commercial Internet Exchange Association (CIX) was formed in 1991 as a trade association open to all commercial Internet carriers. The primary goal of CIX is to provide connectivity among cooperative carriers with no restrictions on the type of traffic allowed.

At the end of 1992, CIX members consisted of BARRnet, CERFnet, EUNet, Performance Systems International (PSI), Unipalm Limited, UUNET Technologies, and US Sprint. Over 3000 commercial firms can be reached through CIX member services.

General Atomics, Performance Systems International, Inc., and UUNET Technologies, Inc. signed an agreement in 1992 to provide commercial internet exchange (CIX) facilities that will allow Alternet, CERFnet, and PSINet users to exchange Internet traffic directly, with no additional cost, regardless of which network the user gets service from. The three competing firms provide nearly all of the commercial TPC/IP-OSI internetworking services in the United States.

The Internet is a 20-year-old international network that links over 3 million users in 30 countries. The Internet is a vital part of another effort known called NREN.

NREN is intended to link research and educational institutions, government, and industry in every state. Agencies responsible for implementing NREN will work with state and local agencies, libraries, educational institutions, and organizations.

5.5.   NFS AND SUPPORT OF REMOTE FILE SYSTEMS

In the case of a network file server, the principal service provided by the server is file system access. In a traditional computer system, the file system is always integrated with the processing system, the way the record player was built into the hi-fi cabinet. You can now buy a different brand of record player (or CD, for that matter) and put it in another room if you want to. The desktop computer only needs enough local storage to meet the requirements of the application(s), and most data files and programs can be stored on one or more remote file servers in the network. Remember that file service is just one example of network services.

To encourage the development and propagation of network services to a wide range of machines, Sun Microsystems developed NFS, the Network File System, and placed the key building blocks and specification of the NFS protocols in the public domain. NFS provides remote file system access capability. File sharing between remote nodes on a network was made simple and transparent by NFS.

Because file sharing provides the most straightforward and tangible example of the benefits of distributed computing, NFS has become the best-known multivendor distributed service in the computer industry. Six years after its introduction, NFS is supported by hundreds of system and software vendors and is run on more than one million nodes and is an integral part of nearly every UNIX network and most TCP/IP networks. Remote machines' file systems are mounted locally and appear as if they were attached to the user's (client's) own system.

Under NFS, any node in a network can be either a client or a server. A node becomes a client or a server by simply issuing the appropriate system calls and/or commands. Adding a client node to the network is a simple operation. NFS provides a set of operations to allow servers to import or export file systems to the network and clients.

A client gains access to an exported file system when the file system is mounted, as if it were on a local disk. When a file system is mounted, NFS is given the location of the file system to be mounted on the network.

A networked file system can be built up from some combination of network (remote) and local file systems. A client can issue any ordinary UNIX I/O calls on any file in the file system. The physical location of the file in the network file system is transparent to the user. This is analogous to calling someone on the phone and being connected to your party without having to specify all the intermediate connections that need to be made. Virtually all UNIX applications, commands, and utilities can operate properly with network files.

Figure 5.4 shows the typical configuration of a network file server and summarizes the functions performed on the client versus the server in this context. One workstation and both of the PCs shown have a local disk. Three of the workstations shown are diskless. In the case of a device with local disk, the user might execute a command to start a program running. The program could be stored on the local disk; in this case, it is put into memory and executed. But let's say the user now needs to access a large data file to do analysis. Further, let's say the data file is too large to fit on the local disk. In this case, the data file could be stored on the file server. The application running on the desktop (client machine) requests the file server to provide access to the file physically stored on the file server.

In the case of the diskless workstations, they have no local storage at all, only local memory. In this case, the user requests that a program be run. The kernel running on the desktop has to request the program from the file server, load it into its memory, and then execute it. From

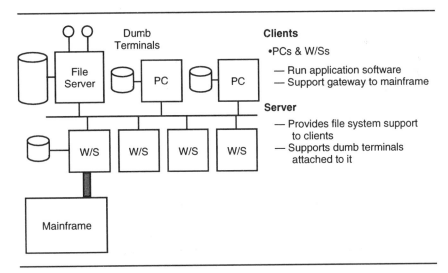

Figure 5.4.   File server configuration. The file server manages clients' file systems. Workstations (W/S) or personal computers can use shared file servers and be configured with minimum local disk required.

here, the example is the same as in the last paragraph with the desktop whose local storage could not accommodate the data file for analysis.

Figure 5.5 illustrates how the NFS remote file system actually works. The application on the local or client machine makes a system call into the file system layer. To process the call, the kernel does a lookup into the VFS/V-node layer to determine the location of necessary file system procedures.

Since the file is remote, the V-node pointer is set to identify the NFS file system. The kernel is directed to specific procedures within NFS that will process the request. The client NFS requests the server NFS to perform the requested function. The NFS daemon ("daemon" is a special name for a process running in the background) processes the request using the VFS/V-node interface to the appropriate file system.

The server in this example contains the appropriate file system in which the file exists. It could have just as easily been on another NFS file system on another node in the network, in which case the NFS file system would go out to the next host.

The virtual file system eventually determines whether this file can be accessed on any server whose file system is mounted. If the file can be accessed, the local virtual system accesses it locally and returns data to the NFS daemon, which in turn passes it to the RPC (Remote Procedure Call). The RPC provides a standard way for programs running on different operating systems to call each other, passing arguments and returning results. Programs that use RPC are shielded from the calling conventions of the different operating systems. The RPC on the client calls the RPC on the server just as it would in any local procedure. The RPC on the client translates the call into a standard format and sends it across the network to the appropriate server.

The RPC on the server then receives the remote call data, translates it into standard form, and then performs the necessary functions required in the server environment by invoking procedures on the server and passing them the appropriate parameters. For example, the file to be accessed might have special restricted access permission, in which case the password parameters are passed on. Results are returned by retracing the same steps in reverse order.

The XDR is a software layer that takes data input to it and converts it into a representation that can be passed between different machines. XDR shields programs from byte ordering, data structure packing, and other operations that vary from machine to machine and from operating system to operating system. Since the specifications of both the RPC and XDR are such fundamental techniques supporting interoperability, Sun

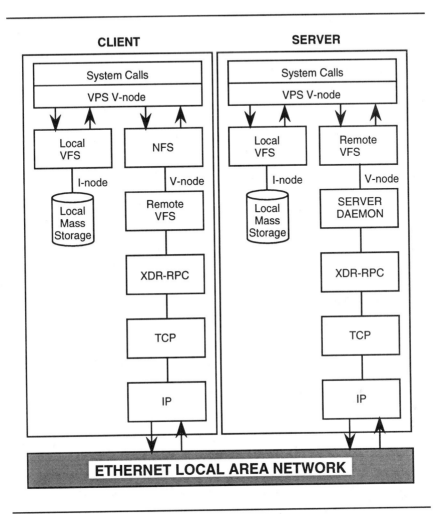

Figure 5.5.   NFS software architecture. NFS is the most widely used
technology for remote file sharing. The user or
application program can access files transparently from
any physical location on the network.

has placed them in the public domain. Today, there are nearly 300 system vendors who support Sun's NFS.

NFS does not totally emulate the UNIX file system, however, since
remote devices, such as tape drives, cannot be accessed by NFS. NFS

sacrificed support of remote special files, and a few other UNIX file system support details in order to have a stateless protocol, enabling simple, quick recovery from system crashes. (Devices are inherently statefull.) This allowed Sun to implement the most important file system operations with a higher level of performance and reliability than would have been possible with a complete statefull implementation. NFS is a good example of an ad hoc standard, given that it currently runs on so many different computer systems. The software architecture of a heterogeneous network is shown in Figure 5.6.

NFS and other PC LAN servers provide a method of file sharing and printer sharing. File sharing is passive in the sense that the client has to

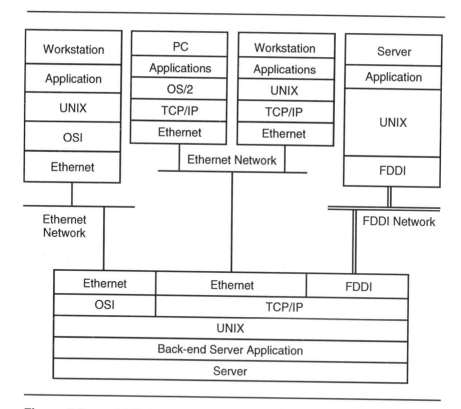

Figure 5.6. UNIX/Ethernet networking example. Ethernet and FDDI provide the physical interconnection. TCP/IP (and OSI) transport is the current standard for networked UNIX/ Ethernet configurations.

initiate active participation of the server. Typical file sharing implementations are not really examples of a distributed computing solution.

In a distributed computing environment, the network is hidden from the application. The system software is sophisticated enough to set up the environment required on a system in the network and then allow access to it dynamically. In most examples today, the user has to worry about setting the environment ahead of time.

Figure 5.6 illustrates how the UNIX operating system fits in the overall scheme of communications. UNIX is one layer in the communications support architecture. Ethernet is the physical layer, and TCP/IP is the transport layer that connects the networking subsystem to the UNIX operating system. Above the operating system is the application software.

TCP/IP Functions.

Telnet—a virtual terminal service

Rlogin—a UNIX dependent virtual terminal service

Tftp—trivial file transfer protocol

Ftp—file transfer protocol

SMTP—simple mail transfer protocol

Routed—a routing daemon (Ethernet to Ethernet)

Rcp—remote copy

Rsh—Remote shell (remote execution)

Differences between NFS and RFS. RFS is the remote file system provided by AT&T in System V versions of UNIX. RFS is intended to completely emulate the System V file system semantics over the network. NFS does not try to do this. This means that applications may work over RFS but not NFS (for example, if mandatory file locking is required). RFS allows the mounting and operating of devices such as a tape drive for example, over the network; NFS can't do this.

RFS uses a connection-based transport (like TCP), while NFS uses a connectionless transport (like UDP). There are situations where in a given network topology, RFS may have better performance than NFS using UDP. RFS and NFS also differ in the way they handle error recovery from severe failures. With hard NFS mounts, the NFS client can wait forever for the server to recover and never notice that the server was away (the server just appears to be very slow). RFS clients receive a signal when the server dies, so recovery is not transparent.

NFS is a heterogeneous protocol, available on UNIX and non-UNIX platforms. RFS is only available on UNIX systems. There may be cases where you want to use RFS and cases where you want to use NFS. UNIX allows support of multiple file systems concurrently.

5.6. EXAMPLES OF CLIENT-SERVER CONFIGURATIONS

This section provides some examples of client-server implementations and applications. Note that in each of the examples that follow, the computing resources are distributed to different nodes in the network.

5.6.1. Compute Servers

A compute server is a network resource that is potentially accessible to anyone on the network. The idea is quite simple. Users on personal computers and workstations may prepare input data and set up data files to transfer to the compute server. The user can then remotely log in to the compute server and start up an analysis job that takes this data and performs the compute-intensive work without placing any load on the user's personal machine resource.

In a compute server configuration as that shown in Figure 5.7, the user can open up a window to monitor the job running on the compute server. When the job is finished, data is transferred back to the user's system for postprocessing or graphical display of the results. Visualization workstations provide color 3-D simulations and usually need local disk to achieve the desired level of performance.

5.6.2. Database Servers

A database server is a slightly more complex type of configuration. In traditional database-oriented application software, the application program and the database management system are both executed on the same centralized machine. The traditional database application program consists of a user interface, a data manipulation or calculation section, and a section of code for database access.

A database server could support this same application, but more modern application programs are structured in a different way (see Figure 5.8). The application's user interface and perhaps some of its data manipulation and calculation portions would be run on a desktop machine or a terminal server node, while the database back end is executing on the database server. Several commercial database management products on the market support this type of execution. The

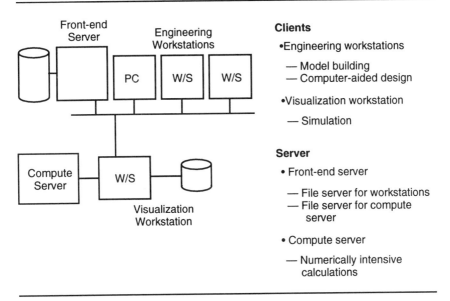

Figure 5.7.   Compute server configuration example. A compute server provides clients with numerically intensive calculation support. Workstations and PCs handle all the pre- and post- processing functions.

subdivision of computing offers numerous advantages and is being made possible because of the emergence of SQL (Structured Query Language), which is a comprehensive, English-like "language" that allows the user (application program) to perform complex searches and calculations on a database.

One of the technology leaders in this area is Sybase, founded in 1984. The company's objective was to address the shortcomings of existing relational data management systems for handling online applications. Sybase has optimized its product to run on networks of servers and workstations. Its client-server architecture splits the DBMS into a front end (called the DataToolset) and a back end (the DataServer). The DataServer handles data management functions for all users on the system. The DataToolset provides the user interface and a set of window-based tools for building and running applications. The front and back ends can run on the same or on two different machines. The Data-Server allows many applications running on many different machines to share a common database across the network. Sybase was one of the

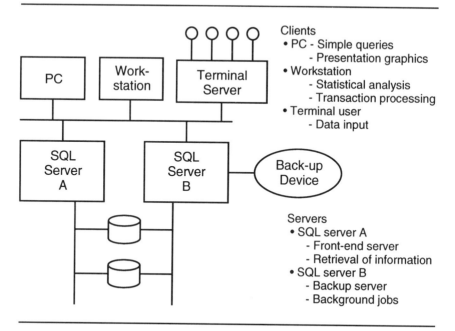

Figure 5.8. Database server configuration. The database server is the back-end database engine and repository for the physical database. Modern servers also provide a means of implementing all the business rules and access privileges.

first database vendors to implement a single-process back end, with extended SQL commands and the ability to store integrity rules and procedures in the data dictionary.

Sybase is essentially a "database operating system" that runs on top of, and largely independent of, the UNIX (or other) operating system. For performance, Sybase, like other DBMS systems, tends to use "raw I/O" instead of the UNIX file system.

Sybase has worked with Microsoft and Ashton-Tate to implement the Sybase DataServer for the PC world and the SQL Server running under OS/2. Sybase is building toward what it calls "presentation independence," which will allow Sybase applications to be adaptable to different user interfaces and windowing systems. This will offer the flexibility of distributing application front ends among PCs and workstations while running the SQL server on a Sun or DEC VAX server. Other vendors such as Oracle and ASK/INGRES have also enhanced their products with similar features.

5.6.3.   Image and Document Processing Networks

An image server is a relatively new concept. It is a server that incorporates an optical disk storage system capable of supporting many gigabytes or even terabytes of data storage. Multiple optical disks can be handled in a jukebox configuration, which, just as the name implies, features an arm that retrieves the proper platter and "plays" it. This is an example of what is called "near-line" storage (see Figure 5.9).

There are many working examples of image servers in workstation networks that support image processing applications. Sun Microsystems and other vendors offer products and reference accounts that implement image applications and data servers running UNIX.

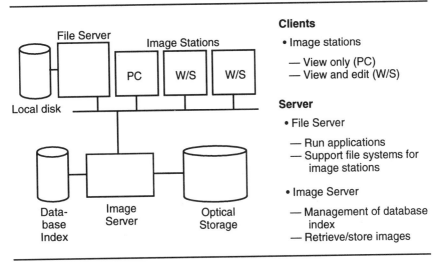

Figure 5.9.   Document image processing configuration. An imaging network server is a special case of a database server. In the image network, clients are used for scanning and editing online or as transaction front-end workstations, while the server provides the central index of files stored online or on near-line optical storage.

5.6.4. Team Software Engineering Environments

It is widely recognized that workstations are ideal platforms for computer software development. UNIX environments are also well suited to software development. The processing power of the workstation platform, its ability to handle multitasking, and the support of window systems combine to make the workstation the platform of choice in most technical software engineering environments today. Simultaneously, the programmer can be editing source in one window, compiling in another, and executing a symbolic debugging package in another. A symbolic debugger allows the programmer to step through the execution of a program, effectively tracing its execution in terms of the source code equivalent.

Not only does UNIX offer a very rich set of software engineering tools, but it has an advantage in being a common environment for software development and deployment. This is in contrast to PC development environments where code is developed, edited, and compiled on PCs but then must be executed and tested on the target environment. In Figure 5.10, the file server doubles as a compile server. It also houses the source code management system. (See also Section 2.5.3.)

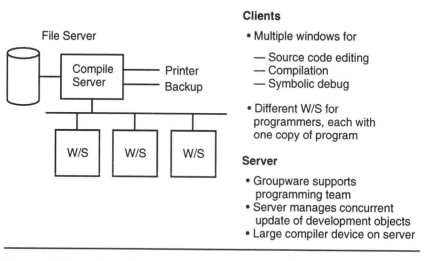

Clients

• Multiple windows for

   — Source code editing
   — Compilation
   — Symbolic debug

• Different W/S for programmers, each with one copy of program

Server

• Groupware supports programming team
• Server manages concurrent update of development objects
• Large compiler device on server

Figure 5.10. Compile server—work group parallel programming configuration. Programmers use the server as a file server, a database server, and a compute (for compilations) server.

A growing number of specialized development environments provide integrated sets of tools for all phases of the programming development cycle. They usually focus on a particular developer market such as ADA for the U.S. government, C and FORTRAN for scientific and engineering, or COBOL and data management-oriented, fourth-generation languages for commercial.

These environments are also rapidly moving from a focus on individual programmer productivity to groupware solutions that address the productivity of a team of programmers working together on complex software development projects.

5.7.   WINDOWING AND GRAPHICAL USER INTERFACES

UNIX makes the computer multitasking; windows make *you* multitasking. The entire computer industry has recognized the importance of standardized graphical user interfaces, and almost every system vendor now offers at least one windowing product. These products are all similar in basic concept to Apple's Macintosh user interface. Users who are familiar with any GUI interface can become productive almost immediately with any GUI interface. GUI interfaces can also be customized by users to look and act very similarly.

Consistent "look and feel" across all applications is an ultimate goal because it allows users to perform the same mouse/cursor movements and mouse clicks to achieve similar types of results on different platforms. The historical roots of graphical user interface or GUI go back to Xerox PARC in 1970s. Smalltalk and later Xerox Star were the first fairly complete implementations of all the concepts that one thinks of as GUI today.

The are five major GUIs in today's desktop market. The first commercial GUI to market was Apple Desktop Interface based on work at Xerox PARC. In the UNIX environment, there are two prominent GUIs, Sun Microsystem's Open Look, which is marketed by Sun and USL as part of SVR4, and Motif, which is marketed by OSF and distributed in versions from system suppliers or other OSF OEMs. Both of these GUIs have received support in the UNIX community and with ISVs. Neither is in a clear leadership position over the other.

The fourth GUI is IBM's presentation manager called the Workplace Shell—built around the product called Presentation Manager. The most popular interface is Microsoft Windows. Windowing systems are a still a battleground in the war to win market share in the desktop computing marketplace. Several forces in the market are lined up, and major battles will continue to ensue during the next few years as hardware vendors seek to influence the software industry and consumers seek to adopt particular user interface standards.

There are those who believe that the UNIX operating system will dominate the desktop market of the 1990s, much as MS-DOS governed the personal computer market in the last decade. But UNIX's progress has been slow because UNIX is widely regarded as having a particularly cryptic user interface. For UNIX to gain wide acceptance, it must be simplified or its complexity hidden behind a window system unless the user chooses to open a special window running a shell that accepts typed UNIX commands. Most UNIX suppliers have window systems featuring graphical user interfaces and mouse-based controls for UNIX, which make it much simpler for the novice.

Graphical user interfaces (see Figure 5.11) benefit users by reducing the training costs and the investment required to learn how a computer or particular application works. They free the user from having to remember locations of files and long, complicated commands, or sequences of commands.

For most users, UNIX command syntax is a maze of command strings with pipes and options that can make DOS look like plain English. UNIX GUIs provide an easier-to-use UNIX environment so users can navigate the system and understand what the computer is doing. There is considerable marketing hype about GUIs today, and this will

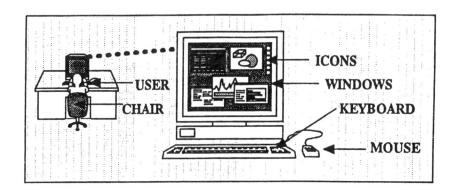

Figure 5.11. Graphical user interface. Today's computer users have the option to take advantage of powerful windowing tools and graphical user interfaces are much easier to use and cost effective.

continue for the next several years. Sales, not press releases, are the best measure of success for GUIs. Another measure is the number of applications that use the GUI.

Developing a GUI is no longer academic. But the changing nature of the technology and the confusion that exists are partly because UNIX has made GUI one of its more popular battlegrounds. This technology is only starting to stabilize and the terminology gel.

The graphical user interface (GUI) effectively frees the user from direct interaction with the operating system. Therefore, the exact type of OS under the GUI will become less important as long as it provides the functionality required by the user and operates in the overall distributed computing environment.

The mouse is a pointing device. It has one or more buttons that are pressed to make selections execute commands or control the movement of the cursor. Icons are symbolic images displayed on the screen that, when selected and opened, perform the same function as if the user had typed in a set of commands via the keyboard. The use of the mouse and of pull-down menus in a window system can greatly reduce (and in some cases eliminate altogether) the amount the user needs to type in order to interact with the computer.

Figure 5.12 illustrates the applications and windowing functions typically performed on the client and the server. There is potential for confusion here, especially where X Windows (see Section 5.8) is concerned. Clients are normally thought of as desktops and servers as back-end host computers. Yet in X Windows, the X "window server" is the software running on the workstation or PC client, while the X client is software running on the server. The X "window server" is software that manages the screen and interacts with the user. The window server passes on requests to processes (running inside windows) that it has opened for the user. These requests are then handled "somewhere else," transparently to the X window server. The user owns the window server, but applications must know how to speak to it.

The explanation of client-server is made more complex because the definitions differ depending on context. From a pure software context, the client and server are just processes running on a computer. Generally speaking, one can have multiple client or server processes running on either a front-end or the back-end machine. In most workstation and PC applications, both the window client processes *and* the window server processes run on the front end (client machine). It is up to the developer—or in some cases, the user—to decide which processes will run on which nodes in the network. For performance reasons, both processes are usually run on the same platform.

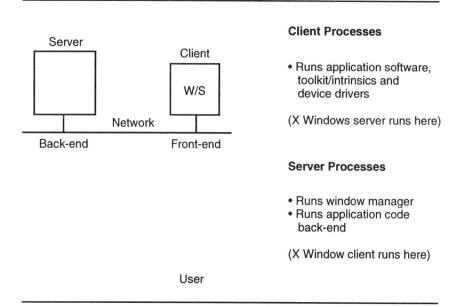

Figure 5.12.   Window systems and client-server. In the X Window system, the X server usually runs on the client, and the X client process runs on the server running the application.

With X Terminals, or, by extension, in network applications based on the X Window system, the front-end machine runs only the X Window server and the back end runs the application code and the X Window client. This is the timesharing model with windowing terminals. In this case, all the processing is going to be done by the back-end server system. The network in such cases can present a bottleneck, since the X protocol has to be transmitted over the network. Even a simple operation like resizing a window or figure can mean having to transmit a substantial amount of data from the X client to the X server over the network.

One of the real advantages of a window system that incorporates Adobe's Display PostScript is that the images on the front end can be manipulated with minimal data retransmission to the device over the network. In X Windows, different interactions at the front end (for example, rotating an image) require that the back end (X client) perform the manipulations and retransmit the entire image again to the client.

This is far less efficient than using the imaging model of Display PostScript or Sun's X.11/NeWS to perform these manipulations locally at the front end. (NeWS is essentially a PostScript emulator with input extensions.) While the efficiency of PostScript is important, its most fundamental benefit comes from the way it can handle high-level objects with variable resolution and from other technical advantages such as the ability to write extensions to the fixed PostScript command set. These are some of the details application programmers are most familiar with.

What is PostScript?

Adobe's trademarked PostScript language has become the de facto standard printer language. Every large system vendor has historically changed the language of its printers, but now, with the PostScript language gaining widespread acceptance, most vendors support PostScript or provide some emulation capability, and nearly all vendors support the use of printing devices that support PostScript. PostScript is device-independent, producing an identical or nearly identical image on any of the many printers from different vendors that provide PostScript an interpreter.

PostScript is a graphics language with extensions. It is like Pascal, Cobol, Ada, Lisp, or C, featuring variables, arithmetic commands, procedures, stack manipulation functions, and so forth. It looks like C.

PostScript is portable, extensible, and flexible, offering significant benefits over conventional printing. It handles characters, lines, shapes, and halftone images and can be used to generate complex images that can't be drawn on most printers. The basic advantage of PostScript lies in the fact that the language processor is built into the printer—so the most CPU-intensive work, especially mathematical operations, can be done at the peripheral offloading the host.

Procedures are written to eject a page, draw boxes and standard labels, and, once downloaded, can subsequently be passed only the parameters, cutting down on the amount of data needed to be sent to the printer. PostScript provides powerful graphics functions, including boundary clipping and pattern fill, and it supports multiple fonts in firmware—with more capable of being downloaded.

PostScript offers two advantages over Xlib: (1) it offers a richer set of graphics functions, and (2) it matches the graphics imaging model. Images are created by creating a layer of "ink" that may form characters, lines, shapes, halftone images, or other patterns. The ink is then pressed onto the page through an arbitrary set of "stencils," which can range in complexity from a border to a string of characters so that the raw image fills in the character outline. This capability makes it possible to easily create complex text and graphics images. Text can be drawn in black, shades of grey, as black or grey outlines, or filled with arbitrary patterns. PostScript allows fonts to be scaled and rotated arbitrarily.

One can expect to see PostScript client-side previewers and X window server extensions that support Display PostScript with client-side Display PostScript libraries.

Adobe's Transcript programs are a set of programs for UNIX that provide the capability to print UNIX files on PostScript printers. Plain ASCII files, plot files, and Tektronix 4014 graphics can be printed. In addition, certain UNIX utilities such as the text formatter TROFF can produce PostScript output. There are over 4000 applications today that "speak" PostScript, and over 55 output devices that have PostScript interpreters.

Windowing over Wires and Networks

Another consideration is the network itself. Some window systems support more limited connectivity options between the front-end and the back-end devices. Most UNIX desktops use TCP/IP and Ethernet. Some windows systems will run over the network configuration transparently. Some are even able to run over voice grade phone lines—for example, twisted pair at low baud rates. M.S. Windows can't do this.

Components of Graphical User Interfaces

The same layered systems approach used earlier in explaining the UNIX software environment is used in Figure 5.13. This shows the major components of the GUI with an overview of different vendors' products and how they fit. A high-level description of each of the major components is provided.

> *Style guide and look and feel.* This is a specification for how the GUI is implemented so that it is consistent on all systems and on all applications. It is a document, not a piece of software.
>
> *Toolkit and components.* These are software elements used by the window system to generate menus, scroll bars, and icons. They are like subroutines. They are also called "widgets" in the vernacular of X Windows. Application development tools are also becoming available. These tools help programmers and in some cases, end users design graphical user interfaces and then function as program generators outputting the software that uses the appropriate widgets

	APPLE	Windows/ NT	Presentation Manager	IBM	HP	DEC	SUN
STYLE GUIDE LOOK AND FEEL	Desktop Interface			Nextstep Motif Metaphor	NewWave	DEC-Windows Motif	OPEN LOOK
TOOLKIT COMPONENTS	Built In	Graphics Device Interface		Various	HP Widgets CXI	XUI	XVIEW
API LANGUAGE BINDING AND TOOLKIT	Built In	WIN16 WIN32S	Controlled by user interface	Xlib Nextstep	Xlib		Xlib NEWS
IMAGING MODEL	Quick Draw	GDI Output	Graphics API	X.11 Display Postscript	X.11 Display Postscript		X.11 and NEWS
OPERATING SYSTEM	MacOS	MS-DOS	OS/2	UNIX MS-DOS OS/2	UNIX		
CPU ARCHITECTURE	Motorola 680x0	Intel x86		Intel RT-RISC	Motorola H-P RISC Apollo RISC	VAX Mips	Motorola Intel 386 SPARC

Figure 5.13. Layers of windows systems. There are several choices for windowing systems. X.11 is playing a major role as the de facto and official standard on which other tools and environments are being based.

393

and conforms to the application programming interface, or API, for the window system.

APIs (Application Programming Interfaces). These are software development interfaces and corresponding tools and subroutine libraries for the application programmer. They make the job of writing and implementing a GUI easier than if the programmer had to start from scratch.

Imaging model. This defines how text fonts and graphical objects will be defined and displayed.

When you purchase a software application that uses windowing, it relies on the fact that the appropriate window environment exists to support it. But how do programmers actually create windowing applications?

Figure 5.14 shows the relationship between the tools used for applications development (namely, the tools for development of application programs within the graphics environment in which the application will execute). This environment will ultimately control the look and feel of the application.

Tools are usually intended for programmers already familiar with 4GLs, Cobol, FORTRAN, or other high-level languages. Widget editors provide WYSIWYG tools to accelerate the GUI design process as well as produce X-coded applications. They can create standard X widgets such as buttons, sliders, and scroll boxes to control applications.

Window management tools go beyond this to provide developers with a much more comprehensive set of tools, including icons and other pictures that represent important elements in the application, and utilities for making graphs and maps, as well as capabilities that allow visualization of changing data in real time.

Some tools work with multiple graphics environments. A good example can be found in IXI Ltd.'s (Cambridge, England) product called X.deskterm. Products of this nature have been referred to by some as GUI translators, since they can permit the same software to run compatibly with more than one window system such as Open Look, Motif, and Windows.

Windowing technology is going through rapid development at this time. There are numerous products being offered and, in some cases, multiple products by the same system platform vendor. Like UNIX, vendors will take the basic windowing system from a de facto standard, such as the X Windows system, and then implement their own extensions to it. X Windows and X-based windowing environments and tools

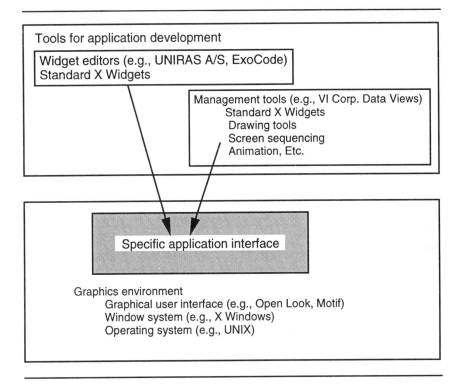

Figure 5.14.   Windowing and applications development environments.
Application interface gets its look and feel from the
graphics environment but its contents from the
application development tool.

are the way to go if you want to provide tools and applications that run on both MS-DOS and UNIX.

In the final analysis, (prior to COSE) we conclude that stressing standardization of a single GUI has been exaggerated. An end user of Motif would be no more dumbfounded by Open Look than a Lotus user would be by Excel. For the internal applications developer, tools such as X.deskterm will ease the migration of applications to X Windows and make it possible to exploit multiple window environments. The UNIX industry will agree on a single window environment, the COSE desktop. X Windows continues to be the UNIX windowing standard that is here to stay.

Window Wars—How Should You Compare Window Environments?

Here is what *ComputerWorld* found was important to users (in order of decreasing importance):

Compatibility

- Does it run the application(s)?
- Is it supported by a large number of ISVs?

Local area networking capabilities

- What are the performance implications
- What functionality is supported?

Ease of use

- How easy is it to customize
- How visually appealing is it?

Multitasking

- Does it support true multitasking—does the OS stay up when an application crashes?

Performance

Vendor service and support

Memory management

- How much memory and at what cost?

Documentation

- Is the documentation all online?

Ease of installation

Utilities

File management facilities

In a survey in 1992, users rated OpenLook over Motif, Windows, and OS/2. Market research point to Microsoft Windows the hands-down winner of market share on MS-DOS, with Motif and OpenLook tied for market share but Motif edging out OpenLook in terms of the perceived number of users—given the number of ISVs that support variants of Motif.

5.8.   X WINDOWS

While its not perfect, X is the best multivendor client-server environment available. X Windows was developed in 1984 at MIT with the goal of giving every student a windowing-capable workstation. It was clear that the campus environment would have hardware from many vendors, so X Windows was originally designed to be independent of both hardware and the network. The result was the specification of a hardware-independent protocol for sending graphics around the network. The development of this protocol eventually led to the development of the X Window system.

By 1988, MIT had formed the X Consortium to continue developing X Windows with leading workstation manufacturers, and soon thereafter the X Window system was adopted as an ANSI standard. As we have seen, X has its own special jargon. It is a distributed, network-transparent, device-independent, multitasking windowing and graphic system. It allows the display of multiple windows on a display screen. An application that uses X Windows can use as many windows as it likes subject to memory limitations.

When applications are written to the X programming interface, they can be viewed on any X Terminal or desktop computer that supports X Windows. X Windows does not specify or require a standard user interface or a so-called "look and feel." In turn, this allows users to choose whatever user interface they like.

Xlib is a library that provides programmers with graphical objects like lines, arcs, pixels, and so forth. X Intrinsics is a tool kit that uses these elements in defining graphical entities such as scroll bars, dialog boxes, or menus. The X Toolkit is a collection of different entities, also called "widgets," such as dialog boxes, scroll bars, menus, file system interface, and so forth.

Virtually every major computer hardware and software vendor in the UNIX industry has adopted the X window standard protocol. But several vendors have their own window tool kits, which are used by application software developers in building application software. Despite the availability of better graphics software, more elegant and efficient than X Windows, the fact is that X Windows is becoming the standard windowing protocol. Therefore, tool kits, such as Motif from OSF, DECwindows from DEC, and Open Look from Sun and AT&T,

will have to be compatible with the X Windows protocol. A large number of applications can be expected to support X Windows over the next few years. As the performance of X-based applications meets and exceeds the use of proprietary windowing technology, the pace at which software vendors adopt X Windows will increase.

The most important thing in ease of use isn't the specific windowing system you use—for example, Open Look versus Motif versus Presentation Manager graphical user interfaces. It is the *predictability* you get from dedicating computers to users. There have been and will continue to be religious wars around window systems in the UNIX industry. But almost everyone will concede that Windows from Microsoft is far and away the de facto standard for windowing systems given the volume it has achieved and the number of applications written to Windows. With Windows/NT, Microsoft has made Windows what it should have been to begin with. Windows can now support 32-bit applications. With one more major crank of the development cycle, Microsoft will have really narrowed the gap in terms of Windows functionality and ease of use compared to the Apple Macintosh. We believe that the entire industry will adopt the WIN32S API in the future. This will permit applications written for Windows or Windows/NT to easily run in UNIX environments.

Window managers

By itself, X Windows is not usable by an average end user and requires a layer of software called a window manager (also GUI) to provide the "look and feel" to the user. MOTIF and Open Look are the two common window managers used in X environments. These window managers are functionally comparable, but they are incompatible, and have different development tool kits. As we will describe later in this section, there are development tool kits which will support either window manager.

Developers are rapidly moving to the use of windowing systems in applications to provide software that has a rich, graphically oriented user interface incorporating state-of-the-art presentation technology. X is receiving the most widespread acceptance in the UNIX industry. X is also making inroads in the PC world with software that runs an X server in under Windows. This is an easy way to provide PC users with access to applications running on powerful UNIX servers on the network.

Users have different options available to them. They can put X Window applications on PCs. They can purchase X Terminals which are like special purpose stripped back workstations that run X Windows servers software. They alternatively purchase workstations. These options represent alternative strategies for distributing applications in a distributed client-server architecture. Figure 5.15 shows four typical configurations.

The first is the X Terminal model. In this model all application processing and application I/O is performed on the application server (which could be a workstation, a server, or almost any other kind of computer that supports multiusers and multitasking). Conceptually

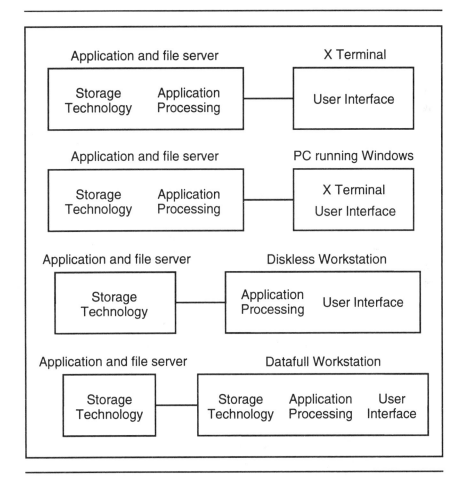

Figure 5.15.   Distributed processing options. There are several choices for configuring X Window-based applications in networks.

similar is emulating what the X Terminal is doing on a PC. The typical workstation processing model is also shown in which both the application processing and the X server run on the same device with other services, like file services provided by the server.

X Terminals take the X user interface and localize it in a terminal leaving the application on the server or desktop. Figure 5.15 shows various configurations for running X Windows and showing its flexibility to support X Terminals, allow PC users to run applications on any X client as well as the traditional model of the diskless and datafull workstation. There are several software packages for PCs and Windows which emulate the X Terminal server on the PC.

Several companies market X.11 server software, which allows PCs and Macintoshes to act as X.11 Terminals. Most products are priced between $300 and $500, but the software on a typical PC or Mac tends to have much lower performance than an X Terminal itself. Most run out of memory with only three windows displayed and are rather slow at graphics. Most only work with one or two of the many Ethernet cards available for PCs (Ungerman Bass, 3COM, etc.).

PC-based X.11 display software

PC and PS-2 X.11 software suppliers include Locus Computing's Xsight, Integrated Inference Machines' X.11/AT, Graphic Software Systems' PC-XView, and Visionware's XVision. Suppliers for the Mac include White Pine Software's eXodus and Apple's MacX.

X Terminals

X Terminals are generating lots of interest. But what exactly are they? Who makes them? What limitations do they have? How successful will they be? Where do they fit?

X Terminals are graphics terminals that bring a windowing graphical user interface to a centralized computing environment. They are terminals that run the X.11 display server. They look like a workstation (high-resolution bit map display, mouse, and cursor). The X.11 server is run typically on an embedded Motorola 68000 microprocessor. An X Terminal usually comes with one to two MB of RAM with expansion capability to up to eight MBs total. Some provide character emulation (e.g., VT100 or 3270) and most are compatible with TCP/IP and support both thick and thin wire Ethernet options. Some feature serial ports.

X Terminals do not run an OS. They are designed to run a single program. Since X.11 requires only a few megabytes of memory and a modest microprocessor to run, the price of the X Terminal tends to be lower than the price of workstations if looked at in isolation from the rest of the network cost of ownership.

What can they do, and what are their limitations?

X Terminals can display windows. They are usually connected to a host via Ethernet using terminal concentrators. The load they tend to place on the host is greater than that of a terminal, however. Each window on the X Terminal could have a complete process operating on the host. The X Terminal can end up looking to the host like a number of terminal sessions. The X Terminal offloads no processing from the host, so just like "dumb" terminals, X Terminals suffer from the same performance drawbacks associated with timesharing.

In low-duty working environments, with spare cycles on the host, X Terminals can represent a reasonably cost-effective way of adding a windowing desktop to an existing network. However, for only a few more dollars, it may be possible to get a workstation that does much more. X Terminals do not provide the same functionality as do PCs or workstations since they have no processing power. Nor do they improve the efficiency of the host—in fact, they may dramatically increase the host's workload. They don't work with traditional minicomputers as well as they do with state-of-the-art servers, which are tuned for Ethernet and multiuser performance.

They also tend to complicate system administration and are not as easy to set up and administer as terminals in this regard. X Terminals often have add-on features and embedded ROM that changes with releases of new software.

Evaluating X Terminals—what to look out for

Make sure the applications supports X.11 and can be demonstrated.

If you have a network in place, check for compatibility with existing wiring.

Check the X Terminal's memory expandability and cost options. ("Out-of-memory" errors can be highly frustrating to the users.)

Make sure the resolution of the display is sufficient for the software that is to be run.

Determine which options you may need and their total cost, for example, TCP/IP, 3270 emulation, VT100 emulation.

Check to see if the terminal will support connections for both RS232 and Ethernet RS232 for remote connection.

Ask to see the terminal running on a loaded system, preferably with the application you intend to buy.

Try to crash the terminal in the configuration you want to buy (with respect to the amount of memory) by opening several windows simultaneously.

Make sure the X terminal can be upgraded to a workstation in the future for a reasonable price! You'll be so close in cost you will want to know this option is open.

5.8.1.   X Windows for PCs

The PC X Server market grew by more than 200 percent during 1992, and rapid growth is expected to continue through 1993 and beyond. According to the X Business Group, PC X server software outnumbered X terminals for the first time in 1992. Out of 2 million X capable seats worldwide, 400,000 were comprised of X terminals, while over 450,000 were X-capable PCs.

The X Business Group projects the X server market will be $125 million by 1995 compared to the entire desktop connectivity market, which will be $862 million. The growth of Microsoft Windows, low-cost PCs, Macs, and workstations and the proliferation of notebook and laptop computers has fueled the need for remote modem connects to corporate networks. Many organizations have also been adding UNIX-based systems to the mix of installed host hardware, and interest in X Windows among corporate users has followed in most UNIX installations.

Most organizations want to upgrade their PCs and find ways to connect them to their host platforms. As end users want more access to the resources of corporate-wide networks, MIS managers want a greater degree of control than has traditionally been the case with PCs and PC Lans. X Windows is increasingly being viewed as an important part of achieving multiplatform integration and interoperability for distributed computing. X Windows is no panacea, but it does provide cost-effective, reliable, and upgradeable connectivity for all major host platforms including DOS, MS-Windows, Mac, UNIX, and VMS.

There are several providers of X software for DOS and Windows-based PCs, including the following:

AGE Logic, Inc.
9985 Pacific Heights Blvd.
San Diego, CA 92121

tel/fax (619) 455-8600 / (619) 597-6030
email address: sales@age.com

Hummingbird Communications Ltd.
2900 John Street, Unit 4
Markham, Ontario, Canada L3R 5G3
tel/fax (416) 470-1203 / (416) 470-1207

Network Computing Devices Inc.
350 North Bernardo Avenue
Mountain View, CA 94043
tel/fax (415) 694-0650 / (415) 961-7711

White Pine Software
40 Simon Street, Suite 201
Nashua, NH 03060-3043
(603) 886-9050

(The above is not a complete list of software suppliers with products in this area.)

5.8.2.   How Will X Windows and Associated Technology Change in the Future?

Interesting parallels can be drawn between X Windows and terminal emulation. Terminal emulation has historically been one of the major applications used on corporate PCs since users require some means of running legacy applications on host platforms. With the appropriate networking support, running X servers on PCs (desktop platforms in general) represent a natural evolution. As the use of X Windows increases, higher levels of integration with common desktop interfaces will evolve. Such integration will facilitate interoperability of desktop environments with remote applications and network services. Special network services extensions for email management, file conversion, and network connectivity even in the area of mobile connectivity can be expected.

5.8.3.   Microsoft Windows in UNIX Environments

By any objective analysis, the number of Microsoft Windows applications and users is huge in unit terms compared to UNIX Open Look and Motif combined. The market opportunity associated with running MS Windows applications in the UNIX, X Windows environment has not gone unnoticed. While major PC software vendors like Lotus and Word-perfect have moved their software to UNIX, many PC software companies—most notably Microsoft and Borland—have no plans to support UNIX or associated graphical user interfaces. Given the underpinnings DOS provides for the Windows API, wouldn't it be useful to be able to move Windows applications to a more robust operating system and in particular to UNIX?

It is far from simple to provide a Windows-compatible API for developers to simply recompile their applications and run on UNIX. Many features of Windows are not present in Motif—for example, such as Dynamic Data Exchange (DDE), Object linking and embedding (OLE), context-sensitive help, consistent printer support, and Dynamic Link libraries (DLL), as well as widgets that don't exist in the UNIX Motif tool kit. Many of the features of Microsoft Windows not found in X Windows, however, are found in the UNIX operating system environment, high-level window management software, or system software extensions. The problem for ISVs is that unless and until COSE unifies the APIs for graphical applications environments, ISVs have to support a number of different tools in UNIX, whereas they can use Microsoft's more integrated, albeit proprietary environment.

The above problems notwithstanding, there are vendors who have tackled this challenge. SunSoft's Wabi, Neuron Data's Open Interface, and Bristol Technology of Ridgefield, CT are among a growing list of vendors addressing this opportunity to varying extents.

5.8.4. UNIX Environments Will Offer Increased Compatibility for MS Windows Applications

The key to MS Windows compatibility lies in the support of a full set of APIs normally provided by the Microsoft Software Development Kit (MS SDK). All of the MS SDK functionality is translated into equivalent X Window and Motif function calls in the case of Wind/U from Bristol technology. This requires extensive mapping of low-level X Window events to equivalent Windows messages. Despite considerable development, the differences between Windows and Motif are great enough that some issues require manual modifications and corrections. Bugs in particular, which may never show up in MS Windows, don't port very well.

Converting from 16-bit Windows to 32-bit Windows presents many of the same difficulties for programmers as does converting Windows for use with a library such as Wind/U for UNIX.

Will Win32 Become a UNIX Standard? We believe the market pressures are quite significant for creating a de facto standard GUI API around Microsoft Windows. This would bring developers the promise of having a single API to write to in order to deliver applications to any Windows or Motif platform. Tools like Bristol Technologies Wind/U demonstrate the feasibility of cross-development at the API level between MS Windows and Motif. Other technology can be expected to handle MS Windows applications at the binary level using a Windows ABI emulation facility.

But the lesson is clear from COSE that vendors of Open Systems want technologies that are built on standards and open specifications. Will Microsoft eventually submit some of its technology for possible inclusion in X/Open? Not very likely. Microsoft indicated it would sue Sun over intellectual property rights should the company bring its WABI (Windows ABI) product to market.

It would appear that Microsoft sees itself as having market share that places it almost above industry standards. To date Microsoft has provided no overt support and has not become directly involved in any efforts to propagate Windows outside its own proprietary product set. It has indicated a willingness to license the technology but does not seem to feel any need to make it an industry standard any more than it already is as a proprietary technology.

5.9.   UNIX AND TRANSACTION PROCESSING (TP)

As UNIX moves into mainstream commercial applications, transaction processing will become a central issue for UNIX applications developers. By transaction processing we mean to imply all forms of transaction processing applications that include batch, online (OLTP), centralized, and distributed transaction processing. TP and OLTP are used interchangeably in this discussion.

Transaction processing has until recently been the exclusive domain of large mainframe-class computers. Over the last decade, however, there have been a number of research programs focused on the state of the art of transaction processing on UNIX. These have included the following:

The Argus (MIT) programming language

The Quicksilver project at the IBM Almaden Research Center

Research on persistent storage at the IBM Watson Research Laboratory (CPR on IBM RT/PC)

Carnegie Mellon's Camelot (distributed transaction processing for Mach and DARPA internet)

In the UNIX industry, several vendors who offer large-scale systems, such as Amdahl or Sequent, as well as midrange system vendors like AT&T and Unisys, have offered special extensions to their UNIX operating systems for support of transaction processing applications. These tools are being ported to more versions of UNIX, and independent software vendors have also identified the opportunity for integrating available software tools in creating new environments for transaction processing on UNIX.

Whether in a traditional centralized mainframe environment or in a UNIX environment, the notion of OLTP is the same; that is, multiple users share common, online access to databases concurrently. Often OLTP applications are mission-critical to the business. Special UNIX operating system and hardware features are often required to meet the requirements of such applications in terms of scalability, reliability, and security.

A transaction is simply a set of operations transforming a database from one consistent state into another. Transaction processing applications are often found in applications where batch-oriented, back-office functions have been brought online. Examples may be found in numerous areas such as banking, retail, and manufacturing. Everyday examples include airline reservation systems and credit card validation systems. Transactions have traditionally taken the form of terminal-based data entry. In traditional OLTP applications, the user gets limited control over the computer-based working environment. Often the user's only knowledge or view of the system is a so-called terminal view of the system.

OLTP applications handle a large number of users concurrently and try to provide consistent response times independent of the number of users on the system. The data processing environment of the transaction processing application must provide a high level of reliability and data integrity, so that partially completed transactions can be rolled back and restarted in the event of a system crash, for example. Traditional OLTP environments have provided not only this transaction management functionality but also terminal management, print spooling interfaces, recovery capability, and special command languages for designing user interfaces via alphanumeric screens (also known as maps).

The traditional OLTP environment is shown in Figure 5.16. In recent years, transactions have taken on a much wider range of user interfaces. Bar code readers and magnetic stripe readers have been replacing terminal interfaces. Wireless data entry devices have become commonplace, for example, in grocery store inventory applications. More intelligent "cash registers" and automatic teller machines are also commonplace. Not only has the user interface of transaction processing expanded, so too has the system's architecture.

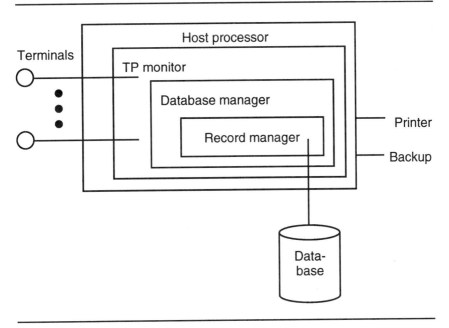

Figure 5.16.   Traditional centralized TP environment. TP monitors manage terminal I/O and database locking, queueing within the host environment.

Network computing has driven migration outward from centralized systems to numerous smaller networked processors. Front-end workstations with multitasking window systems and graphic displays are connected to back-end networks of processors handling file updates, backup, and other functions. Much of this innovation, and particularly the distributed networking involved, makes UNIX an ideal candidate for implementing such capabilities. This is especially so in a heterogeneous computer environment.

5.9.1.   Alternatives to Traditional OLTP

There are actually several alternatives now available to the traditional centralized OLTP applications architecture. Existing applications can be ported from their proprietary TP environment to UNIX.

UNIX can be used as the development environment, with applications then deployed on mainframe-class systems. Here the UNIX systems offer an excellent development environment over PCs and a much less costly and more productive development environment than the mainframe.

Another advantage of the UNIX development environment is that it can incorporate a full testing environment. Development and testing of new applications is possible on UNIX-based platforms, whereas it is not normally possible to TP test applications in a PC development environment except in very limited ways.

One can develop and deploy new applications faster on UNIX. Using newer tools like fourth-generation languages and relational database management, it may be possible to write applications faster than it is to port existing applications. It is often also the case that new applications will be better able to take advantage of state-of-the-art features than existing applications that are ported to UNIX.

Finally, one can use UNIX to implement distributed OLTP. Here a state-of-the-art front end for the application can be developed on UNIX, while the back end remains the same. An example might be a very large database existing on a mainframe. An interactive front end could be developed on UNIX that interfaces to the transaction processing back end.

A workstation-based application, for example, could process queries against the database while running 3270 terminal emulation, electronic mail, and numerous other applications or basic system functions. The single workstation in effect provides a means of integrating multiple related applications and a single user interface to multiple back-end processes.

It can be seen that UNIX offers many alternatives to traditional OLTP development and deployment environments. These traditional environments, however, are the product of decades of development and are in many cases very sophisticated. The UNIX systems environment may not provide all the same features or the same level of sophistication.

5.9.2.   Drawbacks to UNIX in OLTP Applications

There have been several historical drawbacks to the use of UNIX in TP applications. These limitations may be found in the following areas:

Scheduling. Traditional OLTP systems were designed to handle thousands of users who are timesharing off the same centralized system.

Thus, processing was not functionally distributed and complex algorithms had to be implemented to ensure that performance was tuned to online response. In UNIX, all users by default get the same priority.

File System Limitations. In UNIX, data files are stored as a sequence of bytes. Files are not usually preallocated; rather, they are stored in blocks that are not necessarily contiguous. A logical read frequently consists of two or more physical reads. The discontinuous nature of UNIX data storage can significantly affect seek delay in the I/O subsystem.

Security. In UNIX, a superuser can bypass all permissions and protection controls. Much more elaborate security is often found in traditional OLTP environments. There may also be numerous systems platform features required to satisfy high-availability requirements of the application as well. Such features may not be supported by different versions of UNIX. This points out the general problem that in the case of sophisticated OLTP applications, certain operating system features may be required that are not yet standardized in UNIX (e.g., real-time support).

5.9.3.   Growth and Acceptance Are Increasing

Despite these and other limitations, UNIX offers many attractive advantages for the OLTP application, and the necessary features required in OLTP applications are being provided by UNIX system suppliers, UNIX software suppliers, and independent software vendors.

The main drivers of UNIX transaction processing include the following:

1. For mission-critical applications—UNIX and standards will help preserve software investment (this is true even though TP-specific standards are only now emerging).
2. UNIX offers an excellent software development environment for OLTP applications development.
3. UNIX and UNIX-based relational database management solutions or other third-party software offer significantly better price per transaction than traditional proprietary systems—largely the advantage of RISC architecture.
4. UNIX is the platform on which technological advances occur first in a number of areas that are important to TP applications, such as relational DBMS, GUIs, RISC, and distributed application software architectures.

5. Some of the limitations of UNIX can be overcome with additional software that layers above the UNIX operating system itself or can be easily added to it.
6. Relational database management solutions are readily available on UNIX and help mask many of its deficiencies for OLTP.
7. With the TP application decomposed, independence is gained between the front-end and back-end processes. Clients request services in the same manner regardless of how a particular service is implemented. This modularity leaves clients unaffected by changes made to services.
8. By adding new services on network computing platforms, applications can introduce functionality in discrete parts without disturbing the functionality already in place.

The growth of UNIX is now causing users to look at integration issues on two levels: the applications portability level and the data integration level. UNIX-based TP achieves a higher level of machine independence and operating system independence. SQL has emerged as the tool for data integration, allowing applications access to databases that take care of the definition, storage, recovery, backup, security, and multiuser access required in TP applications. Relational database management systems are now the database technology of choice for most OLTP applications, and a number of excellent products are widely available to run with the most popular versions of UNIX.

Figure 5.17 illustrates how SQL is used in the TP application context. In a distributed (client-server) environment the client could communicate over either X.25 via a UNIX gateway to a UNIX local area network or through a channel attach to the mainframe environment using TCP/IP. Terminal emulation on the clients using 3270 is also common.

5.9.4.   Traditional UNIX and Transaction Processing (TP)

As previously described, traditional UNIX has a number of limitations when it comes to providing a comprehensive environment in support of TP applications. This section provides a more in-depth look at how UNIX solutions fulfill TP requirements in each of the following areas:

1. System platform requirements
2. Features of the TP environment
3. TP software migration
4. TP applications development

Centralized host environment

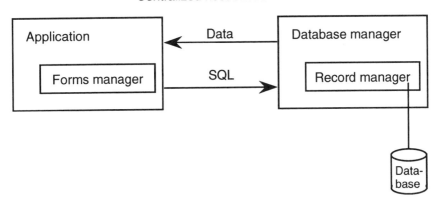

Distributed client-server environment

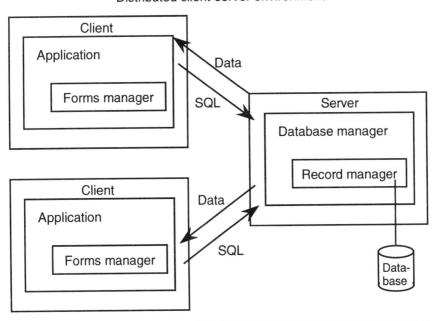

Figure 5.17.   Applications talk to DBMS through SQL. SQL is the means through which most applications will communicate with the database server. Many (clients)– to one (server) relationships are most commonly configured.

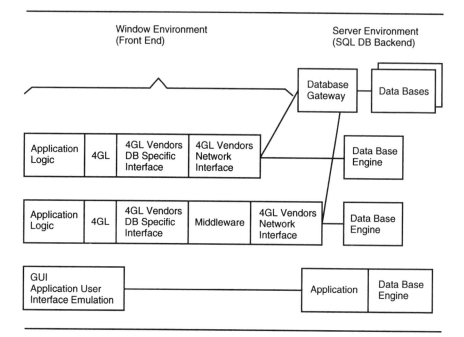

Figure 5.18. Data access for GUI-based applications. This illustration depicts alternative methods of providing an application with a graphical user interface access to an SQL server.

It should be noted that TP is used here to mean either batch or online transaction processing.

5.9.4.1. System platform requirements

Support for Large Databases. (Multigigabyte Databases). This requires support of virtual disks and logical volumes, both of which are supplied by many UNIX vendors today.

Mirrored Disks for High Availability. Mirrored disks provide for two or more copies of a file system on separate physical disks at all times. Each is an exact duplicate, so if one disk goes down or its I/O channel fails, the other disk(s) can be accessed and the data retrieved. Another option is to use RAMDISK. Many file systems have areas that are frequently accessed. RAMDISKS are virtual disks that reside in memory.

Large memory configurations. While demand-paged virtual memory provides a large address space for large applications, I/O performance can quickly become a bottleneck during paging. Large memory and RAMDISK help eliminate I/O channel and disk access times.

Copyback cache ... rather than write-through cache. In write-through cache, main memory is updated simultaneously with cache each time the CPU performs a write operation. In copyback cache, processors assume the notion of ownership of blocks of data, which translates to a more efficient processing algorithm consuming fewer system resources.

System Throughput. High-performance UNIX servers now provide more than just compute power. They are increasingly providing high performance (mainframe-class I/O subsystems) for balance, allowing the system to achieve exceptional transaction throughput as measured by TPS benchmarks and Specmark tests.

5.9.4.2. Features of a TP Environment

Scalability. The ability to gracefully expand the number of users, disks, and so on is provided by UNIX support of loosely coupled client-server-networked configurations and by multiprocessor technology that may offer smooth expansion of centralized functions. UNIX TP environments normally provide functionality above the level provided traditionally by UNIX for ease of administration as users are added or changed.

Online Availability. Dual ported disks, disk mirroring, and other system features may be required. These features are readily available on most UNIX server system platforms in some combination of software or hardware.

Recovery after failures occur should be automatic and involve low MTTR (mean time to recovery). Failover software may not be provided with UNIX. This functionality, which is used to bring a system back online following a system crash, is usually a combination of system administration procedures and additional software within the OLTP environment.

Time to Recovery. Fast recovery—without loss of data—is usually made possible by the TP environment in conjunction with the database manager. Predictable time for reconfiguration is the same.

Connectivity. The TP environment should provide strong communications links to corporate and end-user databases. Most of the networking support services are normally provided by UNIX and/or the system platform supplier.

The environment should support the ability to exploit PC- and workstation-based computing resources.

Integrity. Versions of data must remain consistent, and recovery must be as simple as possible, even in distributed applications environments.

Security. Security can be provided by a combination of UNIX functions, TP software functions, and RDBMS functions.

Performance. Performance is the result of the integration of components, including response times and throughput. UNIX I/O performance is often improved by the database vendors through the use of raw disk rather than the UNIX file system.

5.9.4.3. TP Software Migration. This section describes the process normally required for migrating or developing TP applications on UNIX. Looking at migrating applications first:

1. It helps to have well-documented applications to begin with. Problem areas include the following:
   Use of assembler language

   CICS internals use

   EBCDIC to ASCII conversion

   Language compatibility (COBOL adherence to ANSI 85 standard)
2. The UNIX operating system will normally be augmented with additional tools to address the following:
   TP monitor

   Database

   Manager/record manager

   4GL

   COBOL on UNIX

   COBOL compiler compatibility (ANSI 85)

   Record manager

   Relational Database supporting embedded SQL

   Other applications development and test tools
3. Migrating COBOL code, which involves: Defining tables in the new environment, for example:

File Control Table (FCT) (used for VSAM—IBM's virtual sequential access manager—file name equivalents and key paths)

Terminal Control Table

Program Control Table (relates transaction identifiers and key values to application programs)

Processing Program Table (used to identify programs under CICS)

Conversion of COBOL Copybooks

Compile and link COBOL code (may require precompilation —e.g., for CICS macros)

BMS source code (maps) conversions and linking to executables

Embedded SQL calls in COBOL

4. Record manager (e.g., VSAM) substitute. Most of the above should be provided by the OLTP development environment running on UNIX.

5.9.4.4. TP Applications Development. It may be possible to implement new TP applications faster than porting existing applications. This is because of the advancements in both database management and fourth-generation language technology. A wide variety of tools exist on UNIX today for this purpose.

5.9.5.   Commercial TP Software Solutions and UNIX

Today, many computer system vendors and ISVs have commercial UNIX-based TP products available. These vendors include, to name only a few:

Tolerant (Pathway)

AT&T (Tuxedo)

NCR (POS, TPSX)

Unisys (TP system)

Carnegie-Mellon (Mach/Camelot)

VISystems Inc. (VIS/TP)

Unicorn (UniKix)

Independence Technologies, Inc. (iTRAN)

Transarc (Encina)

Transvik, Inc. (OLTP for financial services companies)

UNIX database vendors (especially Oracle, Sybase, INGRES, and Informix)

AT&T's Tuxedo System/T is one of the best-known UNIX transaction managers. It is used in numerous production environments today and has been OEM'd to other system and software vendors. Unisys and NCR's TP solutions are derivatives of System/T technology. Vendors such as Independence Technologies, Inc. (ITI) recognizing the significant market potential for OLTP solutions, are implementing customer solutions with new TP environments based on the integration of existing components. System/T has been designed to work with several of the leading database management systems that run on UNIX, including Oracle, Sybase, and Informix.

Vendors like ITI, based in Fremont, California, provide services similar to those provided by the more sophisticated in-house MIS development groups in large corporations. ITI uses off-the-shelf components such an enhanced version of AT&T's Tuxedo System/T, Oracle's RDBMS product, and the Open Look GUI. Together with standards such as SNMP for overall system management, ITI integrates these components and provides the "glue" to tie them all together into a comprehensive TP environment.

Transarc, a company based in Pittsburgh, Pennsylvania, has been working with IBM, HP, Stratus, Sybase, Informix, and JYACC in developing and integrating a collection of components, including a distributed transaction service and a transactional RPC. Transarc's technology is not yet an end-user product. Transarc expects its technology to be easily ported across UNIX platforms as well as other proprietary platforms.

While much attention is being focused on TP monitors and OLTP environments on UNIX, other technologies may provide alternatives when traditional applications are to be re-architected or redeveloped. These alternatives include using 4GLs, tools provided by RDBMS vendors, and computer-assisted software development tools that support database migration and applications migration through reverse engineering. Reverse engineering tools can be used to assist in the migration of applications from proprietary environments to UNIX. A good example is Language Technologies, Inc. (LTI), which offers products that assist in converting COBOL source code to a higher level of abstraction so that it can be automatically restructured and converted back into COBOL or into another language, such as C. Similar tools are becoming available that allow database structures to be mapped from one system to another, easing at least part of the difficulty of migrating applications between databases. The availability of such tools is important to users making the move to relational database.

With the increased availability of such tools, developers will increasingly re-architect rather than just port most applications. There are many who believe that transaction monitors and database technology will converge as distributed OLTP becomes one of the major trends in data processing of the 1990s.

5.9.6.   The TP Environment on UNIX—A Conceptual Overview

Figure 5.19 provides a conceptual overview of the layered software environment that supports a distributed UNIX-based TP application. In addition to the operating system, the following subsystems are often required in TP applications.

Database Manager. The database provides the environment for the database processing required to process each transaction. The database server may also provide the functionality for backup security and transaction logging. To marry database requirements of transaction integrity to UNIX, database developers have evolved transaction logging techniques. These are used with standard UNIX file synchronization

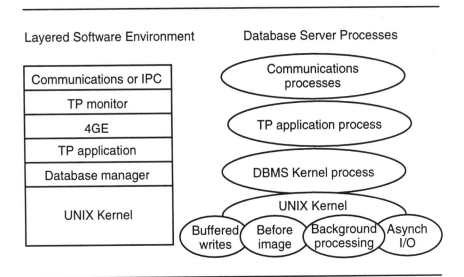

Figure 5.19.   Transaction processing environment on UNIX. This figure illustrates how TP processes map against the UNIX layered systems environment.

operations. Periodic file synchronizing flushes transactions to disk, allowing them to be logged as committed.

Application. The application provides the environment where the transaction is processed. It also submits SQL requests to the database server. The application is logically separate from the communications and database processes and can be physically separated as well. The trend here is to develop the applications in an object-oriented fashion. Vendors such as ITI provide the tools required to marry the object-oriented application world to the relational database management world.

4GE/4GL. Fourth-generation languages provided either by a database vendor or independently by another software vendor can greatly enhance the ease with which new applications can be developed. Examples include Informix-4GL from Informix, iSCREEN from ITI, FOCUS from Information Builders, Inc., Powerhouse from Cognos, and ALLY from Ally Software, Inc., to name only a few. The trend here is for vendors to provide tools which work in conjunction with windowing systems.

Transaction Monitor. The TM sits between the application program and the operating system. It frees the application from managing, scheduling, and prioritizing transaction processes, which can involve the support of a large number of access methods.

The use of a TM gives implementors a standardized component to work with in place of a proprietary TP solution. TMs have evolved to solve distributed computing problems not solved by the underlying operating system, DBMS, and network. In particular, they support multithreaded processes, message routing, queuing, and system management and recovery, as well as transaction abstraction (two-phase commit) in some cases. TM functions are starting to be found in both database and operating system products, and over time the need for TMs may diminish. The transaction monitor is the key element that interfaces the components of the distributed application solution.

Communications Support. For local area networking, Ethernet and TCP/IP are the standards. For wide area networking, X.25 is the standard. In addition vendors are providing application development tools that work in conjunction with the TM to ease application development. Network independent APIs allow a set of server applications to be developed that will support different network protocols without changing the application logic.

5.9.7.   Standards and OLTP

There is considerable work in progress regarding standards for transaction processing. The two bodies most actively involved include X/Open, ANSI, and OSI. The X/Open XTP committee in particular has issued a standard known as XA. XA is an API that defines the interface between the transaction monitor and the database. The database passes a transaction ID to the transaction monitor, for example, to start, open, and roll back transactions. This is equivalent to functionality provided by IBM's DB2 and CICS products.

The UNIX International and OSF vendor consortia can also be expected to put forth proposed standards in this area. AT&T is advancing System /T, which is XA-compliant and has been in production use especially by the Regional Bell operating companies for over seven years. OSF is working with Transarc for future products.

SQL is a standard across a wide number of vendors, providing a means of more readily mixing and matching server requestor database application designs between different vendor environments. But SQL is not a simple standard. For example, there is the base standard referred to as the ANSI SQL standard of 1986, a DB2 SQL standard, and a later, wider standard known as the ANSI SQL 2 standard. The DB2 standard has features not found in the ANSI standard and vice versa. For the time being, SQL architectures will be built around gateway technologies, although UNIX vendors are moving aggressively to establish a comprehensive interoperability standard based on distributed SQL standard formats and protocols.

This standards consortium, known as the SQL Access Group and comprising leading database vendors and leading UNIX system vendors, is working on the problem of lack of transparency associated with distributed databases.* Members hope to come up with a standard RPC

---

*Distributed database and distributed access are easy to confuse. Distributed access means that the database resides on one server. Applications executing on separate servers have access to the databases. Only one database is modified within a transaction. Distributed access is made possible by network transparency—that is, access to the data is transparent to the client applications running on the same network. Distributed database implies that databases reside on more than one server. Modifications of multiple databases happen within a single transaction. Access to multiple databases occurs within a single application. Distributed data is accomplished through database location transparency and the use of gateways, and it implies that the database management system supports two-phase commit.

that will eliminate the present need for the multiple layers of software required in supporting database gateways.

Most importantly, standardized benchmarking techniques for transaction processing are finally emerging. The traditional TP benchmarks are known as the TP1 and debit-credit benchmarks. The TP1 benchmark has been grossly abused; mostly because it has never been well defined. Each vendor has implemented its own approach to the benchmark, making it extremely difficult to compare benchmark results.

In August of 1988, 35 major computer companies and software vendors formed the Transaction Processing Council (TPC). This group has developed and trademarked a suite of new benchmarks, which are well-documented workloads intended to reflect different aspects of database and transaction processing applications. The extent to which a customer can achieve the results reported by a vendor is highly dependent on how closely the TPC benchmark approximates the customer's application.

In addition to the benchmark results, the vendor is required to file a full disclosure report of the implementation details. The TPC benchmarks represent a major improvement over past practices. They should not be used as a substitute, however, for specific customer application benchmarking when critical capacity planning and/or product evaluation decisions are being made.

The TPC-A benchmark formalizes and updates the debit-credit benchmark. It is a full-system benchmark that tests connectivity as well as throughput. The TPC-B benchmark formalizes and updates the TP1 benchmark. Other benchmarks are being developed, including the TPC-C for order entry and TPC-D for decision support.

5.9.8.   The Trend Toward Downsizing and Distributed Computing

Downsizing usually means implementing new applications on smaller system platforms, which are usually located within work groups or departments instead of a corporate data center. Downsizing cuts mainframe-related data processing costs, provides more local control over departmental applications, reduces communication costs, and can achieve a higher level of system availability even though a wide area network or central host is down. Closely coupled with the concept of downsizing is distributed computing.

Distributed computing, also referred to as cooperative processing and client-server computing, implies the functional decomposition of OLTP into a networked computing environment. This trend is being driven by the need for improved user interfaces incorporating graphics and imaging, access to desktop applications, local help, and other capabilities for local editing and validation.

As network computing drives migration outward from centralized systems to smaller networked processors, we will see increasing use of UNIX-based front-end workstations, with multiple windows and graphical displays connected to back-end networks of processors handling file update, backup, and administration. UNIX is an ideal operating system to use in such applications given its capability to help integrate heterogeneous system platforms.

Some OLTP applications have tended to be highly specialized, requiring different environments with conflicting constraints such as real-time response, reliability, security, and so forth. Typically, these distributed systems will continue to use existing (possibly technically obsolete) equipment because it supports some key application or solution component that cannot be easily moved to a newer UNIX-based platform. In such cases, facilities to test coexistence and interworking with existing systems will be important. This will demand an approach to designing TP solutions that will support gradual and continuous evolution instead of periodic total replacement. Some of the most complex business problems are being solved by new Open-Systems-based commercial processing environments based on the client-server architecture.

The client-server architecture offers the benefits of interoperability between different machines, increased data access, and expanded networking capabilities. Client-server architecture also allows systems to be scaled to meet performance requirements in small, incremental steps. Software components are modularized and distributed.

In a client-server model, extensive intelligent desktop processing power is used. The intelligent workstation front end not only provides the graphical user interface, it also offloads communications overhead from the back-end server processes. The client-server architecture is achieved through a layered systems environment, as shown in Figure 5.20. The database is a critical component in this environment.

Client-server databases support distributed access and distributed computing. For OLTP, distributed computing functions are key. Sybase and INGRES deliver this through stored procedure facilities that combine the desktop user interface with the server-based logic. As databases are integrated with TP monitors, such as Tuxedo, they will acquire enhanced configurability and interoperability.

In the case of terminals, point of sale, or other devices that would not be considered intelligent clients, front-end processors may be used as communications servers that process the transaction and return results to the transaction device.

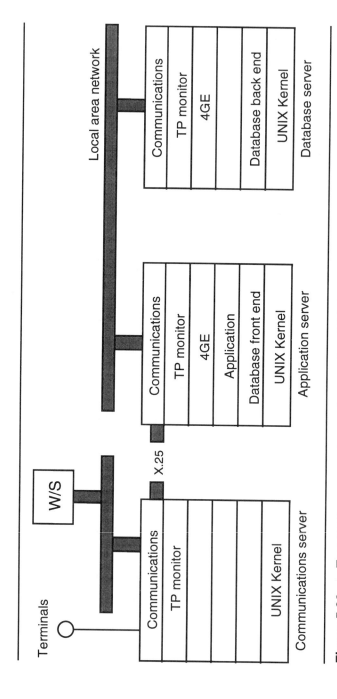

Figure 5.20. Transaction processing environment on UNIX. TP monitors are being used to integrate the distributed transaction processing environment.

The advantage of multiple application servers lies in the ability to scale processing resources in small incremental steps without adding large new back-end database servers.

Transaction monitors may be integrated with the communication server and the back-end servers so that transparent routing of requests can be efficiently handled. The front-end processors can be sized to support the appropriate number of client processors and handle the load associated with routing transactions to the most appropriate application server in the network.

The communication and application processes could both reside on an intelligent workstation front-end platform. Processes running on a multitasking workstation could include the user application (client side), a report writer, an application generator, a query tool, and electronic mail, as well as support for 3270 or some other terminal emulation.

5.9.9.   OLTP and Decision Support

Decision support can be viewed as one of a variety of database applications (viz., accounting, manufacturing, distribution, inventory management, point of sale, and customer service).

Decision support tools are used to help build, analyze, and extract data for the purpose of reaching decisions or confirming actions. Decision support systems are used for statistical analysis, executive information systems, and many other types of applications. Decision support tools may include report writers, end-user query facilities, or forms generator capabilities.

Whereas OLTP applications can be thought of as "update intensive," decision support applications are "read intensive." Most decision support applications today work with database extracts for performance and data integrity reasons. Extracts and replicated copies may not reflect the actual state of the database, which can create problems in trying to implement transactions against the replicated decision support database instead of the live or online database. With two-phase commit and replicated data, it will be possible for database update transactions to be queued. These technological advances, together with network computing configurations, will create an opportunity for a tighter integration of OLTP and decision support applications.

5.10.   GROUPWARE

Groupware is one of the great new buzzwords to originate in the last year. The easiest way to define groupware is to draw an analogy to today's typical PC software. Just as software for personal computers is intended to support an individual user, groupware is software to support people in work group environments. It represents a technology that is as much a way of working as it is just a piece of software. Groupware, like most new buzzwords and technologies, is heavy on potential benefits and light on concrete case studies of successful implementations and installations. An underlying theme in groupware is to make group work processes more efficient meaning making decisions faster, producing something faster, taking less time to respond to requests and so forth. Groupware is often closely tied to work flow and information flow processes. It might audit and document communications; it makes accountability more visible. Groupware software solutions are coming, some are here already. It's turning out that to really take full advantage of groupware, there usually has to be a major commitment to examine and change the associated business processes. For this reason, groupware software is often piloted and is staged into successively more complex areas as experience is gained.

Groupware's ability to increase work group productivity will become commonplace in networked environments. It will have its most dramatic benefit in terms of transforming the way work is actually accomplished in organizations.

5.10.1. What Comes First, Groupware or the Group of Workers?

Like the "chicken and egg" circular argument, groupware represents a subject of debate and there are different points of view about whether the technology can transform the workplace or the workplace has to transform to take full advantage of the technology. Technology inevitably changes the way people work, but the change is not necessarily what was expected. There can even be negative consequences. Consider electronic mail as a form of groupware. Before you had email, it was all on paper or voicemail. Now you put an email system in and you find yourself getting 10 times the amount of information you used to get. This is progress, right? Like technology-oriented organizational transformations in general, groupware will require active business process re-engineering and policy setting. The larger the work group, the more policy and process redefinition will be a requisite for success.

A calendar program that is groupware-ready will probably work for one individual on a standalone machine. Just installing the calendar manager on several machines on a network does not automatically mean that everyone is going to start using it as groupware, but people might use it as individual productivity tools at first and then migrate to the use of the same tool in a work group setting.

A lot of software already has all the characteristics of groupware. Database management, email, calendar tools, teleconferencing, authoring systems, software development frameworks are all good examples. Information sharing tools like Lotus Notes and scheduling tools from companies like Action Technologies are already here.

5.10.2.   The Link Between Groupware and Legacy Applications in Re-engineering

Workflow-oriented groupware will manage legacy applications and their data making it available to users by information sharing workflow as well as the traditional applications and query tools.

Workflow groupware will be concerned more with managing workflow than with changing or updating information at an atomic level. It will work like a database manager to a database of compound objects and is likely to play a role in downsizing by encapsulation legacy applications. It will help programmers to start off by using legacy applications as the functions or the logic under the groupware's control. Over time such embedded legacy applications will more gracefully replaced from the users' point of view.

5.10.3.   Groupware Makes the User a "Server"

Groupware is going to change the way users interact with computer applications by turning the user into a "server." Groupware will ask the user to do some work and take the results and transmit these results as appropriate to the next stage in the workflow process, that is, it will forward the work to the next user server down the line.

In summary, most groupware will come to market in the form of tools that interoperate with each other rather than integrated full-featured packages from a single vendor. Once the tools are good enough, the only thing that will hold an explosive growth in groupware will be the users' business understanding, the knowledge of workflow processes, or alternatively, the customer's consultant—who will have to be paid to learn about the customers' business and workflow. Chapter 7 is dedicated to discussing this same point except in overall terms of an information architecture. One of the most positive aspects of Open Systems will derive from users taking a hard look at their organizations, business structures, and decision-making work group processes as they rethink their company's enterprise and work group-level information architectures.

5.11.   LOOKING AHEAD

We believe that the industry is entering a new stage of development. Just as the 1970s saw the demise of the mainframe in many applications, the 1990s will see the demise of the midrange system (or at the very least a dramatic consolidation in the market). The trend toward work group computing and connecting work groups through networking will accelerate.

As users have experienced the benefits of applications offering advanced graphics user interfaces, they have begun to demand them. Windowing, while once unique to engineering design or business graphics software, is now a technology used in every type of application software you can think of.

It is easy to project into the future that computers will get faster and faster. What will this mean? It will mean that almost everything will become interactive. Computer user interfaces will become much more sophisticated, offering sound and video in addition to very high-resolution color and monochrome displays. Very fast networks will carry information around. The network itself will no longer look hierarchical. Accessing a system on the other side of the earth will look the same as accessing the system sitting in the next office. All interactive work will be done not only at the desktop computer but with a higher degree of mobility, just like car phones. Servers will manage the databases and support all of the services on the network.

Networking promises to be a critical technology for the future. The design of good system solutions in the future will call for open and extendable network architectures. Network standards are certain to change. It will be essential that as new technology is introduced, it doesn't break what is there already and it provides a smooth path to what is coming. Distributed computing technology is not static; it evolves over time. An important criterion of open, distributed, computing architecture is the ability to function within internationally recognized standards as they emerge without hampering the developers, the innovators, or the users.

As quoted in a June 1990 *UNIX Today* article,

> *Ritchie reminded the audience that Steve Jobs stood at the podium a few years back and announced that X was brain dead and would soon die. "He was half-right," Ritchie said. "Sometimes when you fill a vacuum, it still sucks."*

The area of windowing and graphics technology is quite complex, and its lack of standards is a serious issue facing developers. X Windows is far

from perfect, and there is considerable room for advancement and innovation. The real battleground in the future will be over applications. The
windowing system that offers the most applications will come out on top.
It is highly doubtful that there will be one windowing system any more
than there will be one version of UNIX. There will no doubt be room for
future innovation within a standards framework in the next few years.

The pace of market development and growth is subject to debate. If
you were to go back and look at what the pundits said about the PC
industry in the mid 1980s, you would see that it was estimated to grow
to a few billion dollars by the 1990s. By some recent estimates, the
figure has reached $25 billion already. This same explosive growth po-
tential in network computing is possible, and no one really knows for
sure what will happen.

5.12. MANAGING THE CHANGE TO DISTRIBUTED COMPUTING ENVIRONMENTS IN THE FUTURE

Architectural Evolution

Over time, application architectures have evolved allowing the gradual
separation of functions. Figure 5.21 depicts this evolution. The traditional software application results in a large monolithic executable.

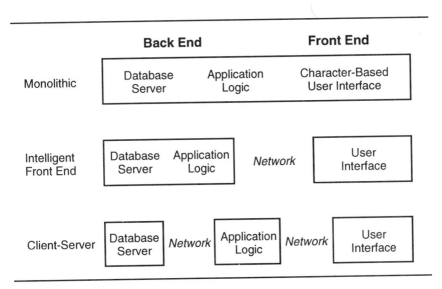

Figure 5.21. Evolution of application architecture.

There is no front end or back end per se. The database access, application logic, and user interface code are all contained in this single executable. As intelligent terminals and PCs were used in front-end processing, the functionality of the software evolved into the back end, handling database server and application logic and front ends, typically connected to terminal servers or PC LANs.

The evolution has taken an additional step with the separation of the application logic and database server on the back end. Modern relational database software allows the programmer to implement business rules in the database server. These rules ultimately determine who gains access to what data or who is allowed to update what data.

In the past, business rules and other logic had to be coded in the application logic. Removing this logic from the application not only leads to more efficient application software program development but also helps accomodate change. The programmer can make changes once to the back end to implement a new rule, for example, without having to change the application logic.

A slight variation of this model can be found when intelligent front ends are used in place of character-based terminals. PCs can be used for increasingly sophisticated purposes. They can support terminal emulation or can run an applications front end. In this environment some of the application logic might be implemented on both the front end and back end.

In the architecture labeled Client-Server, because the functional elements are separated, the user interface, application logic, and database portions of the application solution environment can each be distributed and run on the appropriate node in the network. For example, a typical setup would be to run the user interface and application logic portions on the client nodes and share a common database server back end between clients. The terminal used to be the sole method of interfacing to the user. PCs were then used to emulate terminals. Applications on PCs like spreadsheets could also manipulate the data—downloaded to the client, and it could then be uploaded when completed.

As PCs and windowing has evolved, PCs have become even more intelligent displays and were able to handle processing portions of the applications logic. This often necessitated rewriting the back end of the application however. Workstations are often preferred in applications that demand high-performance processing, high-resolution graphics, or integrated networking.

As CPUs on the client side grew faster, they have been able to support more of the application logic. Fast networks and powerful back-end servers are optimal for providing centralized database services.

Back Ends   **Front Ends**

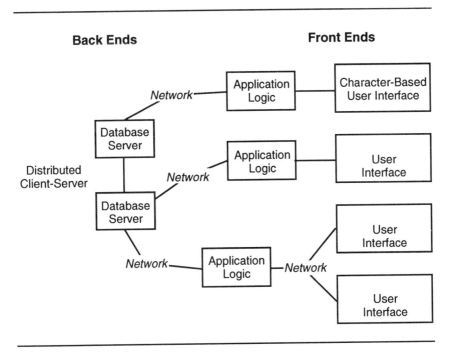

Figure 5.22.   Fully distributed application environment.

In a fully distributed architecture, a DBMS may reside on multiple systems. With a distributed architecture, applications can access databases as if they were a single database. The DBMS and network handle the details of locating, accessing, storing, and retrieving the appropriate data. The application does not have to concern itself with these factors.

A distributed information system is a collection of information service providers (servers) and information service users (clients) communicating over a high speed network as depicted in Figure 5.22.

Open Systems, Standards, and the UNIX Industry

The relationship between open standards and technology is changing, particularly in the way standards are developed and deployed today and in their impact on business. In addition to integrating mature standards, the industry seems to be heavily invested in nurturing and promoting new fledgling standards. It is hard to make sense out of what one hears and reads in the press.

Users and Standards—A Reality Check

An IDC survey in Europe a few years ago found that almost two-thirds of European corporate users have not decided to use X/Open's XPG3. Over three-fourths of them remain doubtful about POSIX standards and most have little or no interest in the OSF DCE, DME, and UNIX International's Atlas. More than half have no policy on specific UNIX versions, and more than three-quarters have not standardized on a choice of graphics user interface. Over a third of the users actually found standards an obstacle to the effectiveness of their UNIX systems. Can this be true? Is it possible that most of the "noise" about standards is just so much press?

By and large, open standards have proven beneficial to vendors and users since they foster the proliferation of high-volume applications. The supply side of the industry understands this is required to maintain dramatic market growth. However, standards represent a challenge for vendors. They must deliver the best-performing, best-integrated products that fully support standards. On the other hand, each generation of standards represents a baseline to build upon. The more stable standards are influencing the overall system design to the point the path to best performance is only achieved through a standard!

In the past, standards in the computer industry dealt mostly with technical issues. They were, and to some extent still are the concern of engineers and designers. But today, standards are becoming a business issue and the concern of the executive suite. In the past, participation in standards activities required little or no investment. Today the situation is quite different with significant resources required to participate in and comply with industry-wide alliances and standards.

Industry-wide cooperation and alliances are on the increase. In cases where standards do not exist but are needed, vendors and users try to find ways to work with each other through standards-making organizations.

As we will develop in this chapter, much of the standards work in the UNIX Industry has been carried out by supply-side vendors. However, the last few years have seen the emergence of numerous alliances of end-user groups.

1991 and 1992—The Years of the UNIX USER GROUP

The Petrotechnical Open Software Corporation (POSC), the User Alliance for Open Systems (formerly the Houston 30), and other formative bodies have declared themselves as alternatives to the vendor-dominated consortia. X/Open, the Corporation for Open Systems and UniForum would all seem to share the same generic concerns and would like to carry and represent these groups' concerns under the auspices of its own organization. While these user groups may have joined and send representatives to the established UNIX consortia, they still feel a need to press closer alliances within the user community.

Historically, UniForum provided the venue for such user groups interested in UNIX to come together. But over the last few years UniForum has apparently retrenched and become mainly focused around running its trade show. Its original charter and mission would seem to be outdated by industry developments. UniForum (formerly /usr/grp) started out as consortium of UNIX users who sought to influence AT&T's UNIX development and licensing policies. That was then and this is now. UNIX International is now a larger, mainly vendor-dominated group that seeks to influence USL.

With changes in its board of directors and its executive director, it is an open question whether UniForum will revitalize and provide leadership within the UNIX user community bringing diverse user groups such as POSC and the Houston 30 together in some fashion.

Open Systems and Standards

Open Systems represents a very significant change from the long standing legacy of proprietary hardware and software. This legacy is so strong that it represents a barrier to migration in many companies.

The User Alliance for Open System, a consortium of corporations, defines Open Systems standards as "those which allow unimpeded access to the information required to do one's job."

Standards encompass many different aspects of computer software; user interface, data access, communications, foreign language support, computer languages, development environments, and operating systems. What we call a standard and the character of the bodies bringing forth these standards have changed. In the past, standards were either official or government based. Today, there are also de facto and consortium-backed standards. Standards activities can be found at nearly every level of technology.

Relational databases, object-oriented programming and databases, and machine-independent operating systems are all driving the trend toward standardization. The migration of software standards is increasingly important in computer and software purchasing decisions.

Unfortunately, almost every hardware and software vendor uses the words open and standard to include their product or technology. It is not really possible to give a single succinct definition of what a standard really is. It is just as important to understand what a standard does and to understand what it is.

Standards are neither applications nor features of applications. They define the interface between different components or layers in a system environment. Standards are not themselves components or interfaces. They are specifications. Components, even ones that adhere to standards are proprietary unless they are in the public domain or are available to be freely licensed. NFS is one of the best examples of a UNIX industry standard. Sun was the trend setter with NFS. NFS was licensed to by Sun to anyone that wanted to acquire it. The specifications for NFS were placed in the public domain. Anybody could implement a version of NFS based on the public domain specifications. Hundreds of hardware and software companies incorporated it. It became a de facto industry standard. It was eventually recognized as a standard because its use was so prevalent. An open standard is one that is broadly available to anyone in the marketplace. It is not controlled by any one company.

Standards and Change

Open standards should enable change and diversity. If you think of a standard as a well-defined connection between two independent parts of a solution, the components on either side of the standard can change as long as they still meet the common standard defining the connection.

Standards represent a means through which new upgraded parts can be connected to other older parts in a "standard" fashion. The parts can evolve and change independently. The standard has the effect of isolating parts from each other and therefore isolating them from change.

Without standards, compatibility becomes a big issue as system environments become more complex and are built out of numerous parts. Standards are not a panacea. They come about slower and sometimes through somewhat questionable means. Standards committees are populated by people from companies who have very specific interests at stake. The politics of influence that occurs with certain types of industry standards can be disconcerting.

Standards also evolve and change. There are also many areas where standards do not exist. Fortunately, many companies pick their own standards, and in doing so, often decide to buy applications rather than build them internally. Standards have yet to evolve in the areas of application development environments and application software in general. Software technologies are especially complex. There is intense competition between competing technologies and the issue of standards is clouded by a host of arcane points of technology.

The Marketplace Ultimately Determines Standards— Because They Work

At the end of the day, the marketplace votes for standards with their wallets. Success is based on what works and what is popular. Marginal technology will be outpaced by more capable approaches. Future technologies that become standards are simply going to be those that get there first and work. The proof will be in a company that is successful in creating a market for their product. The existence of profitable, growing companies selling applications based on these technologies proves that the software platform can make it competitively.

One should be extremely wary of vendors or consortia that claim they have a standard when there is no evidence that their agreed-upon specification is commercially viable. Standards have been abused and history has shown that just because a group of vendors join together for joint press announcements and marketing activities for a new technology—and just because you hear about it a lot in the press—doesn't means that it's real.

There are many types of standards. Each standard is most easily understood as the definition of the interface between two layers. It defines the way these layers communicate and connect to each other. For example, the user interface connects the user and the application. The query language (SQL) connects the application to the database engine. SQL allows broader access to database information.

Data format standards are critical to promote data exchange between applications. File exchange is an example of this. For example, standard file form definitions allow files of one spreadsheet or desktop publishing package to be used with another.

Data format for graphical information, fax, sound, video, as well as data exchange in applications such as electronic data communications are very critical not only in preserving our assets in data but also in improving productivity through application interoperability. OS standards allow the same operating systems to run on multiple hardware platforms. The value of the hardware standards is to protect investments in the software and data. Networking standards allow physical communications between machines and between applications and between applications on different machines.

An open standard is one broadly available to anyone in the marketplace. MS-DOS is a de facto standard, but it is not an open standard. Open standards are not controlled by any one company. Their definition should be freely available and in the public domain, and the evolution of that definition should not be controlled for competitive purposes by either one company or any consortia of companies. The openness of the standard comes either from the agreement of a group of manufacturers and users (de jure) or from a company opening up a popular product (de facto). IEEE POSIX is a good example of the former, while UNIX, spun out by AT&T, is an example of the latter.

The relevance of standards for vendors and users are different. Standards like POSIX and SVID are more relevant to the system platform and operating system platform vendors than to users. Open standards do not carry a tax. That is, people can implement to the standard without paying a license fee. A measure of openness in this context has to do with the number of companies offering implementations of the standard for resale or licensing.

The opposite of standard systems are proprietary systems. Proprietary means under the control of one vendor, protected by the patent or copyright or creating some other barrier to competition, for example, in the way the standard is evolved.

An Introduction to UNIX and Related Standards

There are many examples of standards in everyday life. For example, there are emission standards for cars, power plants, and radiation (VDE, PTB, DHHS, and VCCI); there are safety standards (UL, CSA, TUV); and there are ergonomic standards (DIN and VDE). From an historical perspective, standards such as coins, interchangeable parts, railroads, and now computer systems have helped drive the globalization and widespread adoption of new technologies.

But why are standards in computing necessary? Hasn't survival of the fittest and the force of natural selection been working for years in the computer industry in the absence of standards? What is at stake in endorsing or not endorsing a standard? How is this different for vendors and users? What is important about standards to a company manager who is responsible for implementing UNIX? These and other questions are explored in this chapter.

Computing standards are intended to ensure that any device or software can communicate or interface with another device or software through conformance to an interface. The standard defines this interface—but doesn't specify exactly how the device or software itself is written.

Standards help system vendors avoid developments that rapidly become technologically obsolete. They are able to rely on standard-compliant products in place of internally developing their own products, thereby decreasing development costs. Standards enhance portability, but they do not guarantee it. For users, standards also provide a hedge against technological obsolescence. They offer the promise of greater flexibility, in particular, decreasing reliance on a single systems vendor's products. If there are going to be standards, who should be the keepers of the standards? Who will the movers and the shakers be that drive these standards? Whose interests are really at stake here?

Standards come into being because a consensus arises on the way to go about something. Vendors find that standards encourage banding together and agreeing to joint development. When customers want standards, vendors have to comply.

What Makes an Industry Standard Interface a Standard?

The growing popularity in the mid-1980s of UNIX—the first multivendor operating system used in microcomputers—opened the door to standard interfaces, as opposed to the proprietary single-vendor interfaces that prevailed before then. A standard interface is, by definition, the dominant interface implemented and actively used on products being shipped in volume. In the UNIX industry, a number of mechanisms push an interface along the path to dominance:

Early availability of the interface on products that ship in high volume

Endorsement by an industry consortium or a particular interface or product containing the interface

Broad licensing of an implementation of the interface

The adoption of the interface by official standards organizations such as IEEE POSIX, and federal purchasing requirements (FIPS)

Vendor/press announcements of commitment proclaiming specific support of the standard interface

Today's key driving standards include

IEEE/ANSI (keepers of the "official" U.S. standards)

NIST (influences government standards)

ISO (primarily European)

X/Open (originally European and government standards)

UNIX International (vendor consortia supporting UNIX System V release 4)

OSF (vendor consortia supporting OSF, Motif, and DCE)

Most of these are described in the following sections of this chapter.

Standards Groups Not Covered Here

The following addresses are provided for two major standards bodies that are not covered here: ISO and ANSI.

International Organization for Standards (ISO)
1, Rue de Varembe
Case postale 56
CH-1211 Geneve 20
Suisse

American National Standards Institute (ANSI)
1430 Broadway
New York, NY 10018

6.1. THE EVOLUTION OF UNIX AND RELATED STANDARDS

From history, we know that UNIX was developed and nurtured by Bell Labs. At the outset, a group of software developers created UNIX to meet their own needs and those of a small group at Bell Labs, where eventually it was widely used as it was at several universities. AT&T and DARPA, through the University of California at Berkeley, have continued to develop UNIX through many stages. As the interest in and use of UNIX spread, several companies began to adopt and "tweak" it for their own purposes. In many early commercial applications for UNIX, systems vendors were delivering a solution to their customers, and the fact that it was UNIX-based really made no difference so long as their product did what it was supposed to. A proliferation of UNIX variants and clones sprang up as a result.

A nonprofit organization called UniForum (formerly called /usr/group) was formed to share information on UNIX and to see to it that UNIX continued to advance. Within /usr/group, a core group formed bound by a common aim of formulating a standard definition of the UNIX interface. They were worried about the proliferation of variants hampering the goal of interoperability of applications on UNIX.

While AT&T actually owned UNIX, this group wanted to ensure that their voice would be heard concerning the direction of UNIX and the definition of UNIX standard interfaces. Several technical committees were formed to address technical aspects of UNIX implementation in an effort to continue to advance the state of the art—but to do so in a more orderly fashion.

AT&T continued to advance the UNIX standard in terms of System III. But as a profit-seeking systems vendor, it was under no obligation to implement the suggestions of /usr/group or anyone else. The /usr/group went to IEEE and submitted their UNIX specification, which led to the formation of POSIX, a special-interest group within IEEE.

While UNIX was being called a de facto standard, there were (and still are) a number of variants. How could UNIX be a standard when there were so many versions of it? The answer lies in part in the fact that what these variants had in common was their foundation on USL: UNIX system releases and interface definitions.

AT&T licensing practices, which have differed between releases, stipulate that a particular variant of UNIX is compliant with AT&T's System V Interface Definition if it is able to pass a compliance test called the SVVS (System V Verification Suite). This verification suite also differs between AT&T's releases. Before System V Release 2, any variant could be licensed without passing this conformance test. With Release 3, AT&T tightened its licensing requirements to include compliance testing. As AT&T released System V specifications, BSD UNIX was simultaneously being advanced at Berkeley.

While UNIX hadn't always stood as a standard, by 1985 it had grown in importance to the point that its standardization became critical to its growth potential. Bill Joy gave the keynote speech at UniForum in 1985, at which time he promoted the need to unify the different variants of UNIX and to reach a single standard. Sun Microsystems, Joy's employer, was actively involved with AT&T and Microsoft, seeking to accomplish this goal.

IEEE and X/Open, both nonprofit groups involved in establishing standards, evolved separately and have very different scopes. However, both are based primarily on UNIX System V Interface Definition (SVID). X/Open has published interface definitions that are more comprehensive, as they address the entire applications environment, while the IEEE via POSIX is more tightly focused on the UNIX system interface definition (the seven volumes of the XPG3).

UNIX must evolve, grow, adapt, and even specialize to compete in the world of proprietary operating systems. What effect will standards have on innovation? The answer is that the standards bodies are focusing on many new areas or extensions that need to be addressed to advance UNIX. These standards organizations are populated by both vendors and users. In addition to developing new capabilities in UNIX, they are trying to carefully control the impact such changes will have on the installed base.

Classifications of standards

De Facto Standards. These are standards arrived at due to volume and widespread market acceptance. Compliance with the standard is ensured through technology and source licensing and market pressures (often rising from customer demand). Examples are Sun's NFS, X Windows, MS-DOS, and UNIX SVID.

Official Standards. There are two types of official standards, country standards, and international standards. These are officially recognized national or international bodies that set standards in a number of different areas. These standards normally have a certification procedure and/ or a policing organization to monitor compliance. Official standards are consensus-driven. Examples include POSIX IEEE, ANSI, ISO, and Underwriters Laboratories.

Industry Standards. These are set by consortia typically comprised of industry groups and are enforced by technical source licensing and/or certification processes. Examples include X/Open, USL's SVID, and OSF. Industry standards are driven by consortia.

Government Standards (De Jure). These are official and set by the government as a prerequisite of doing business with federal agencies. Products bid to the government must meet these specified standards in order to be considered. The U.S. government often adopts other official standards such as MIL-STDS (military standards) and FIPS (federal information processing standards).

How Many "standards" Are There?

There are other standards organizations such as ISO, NIST (formerly NBS), IEEE, and X/Open. This presents a rather confusing picture to the typical computer user. With the exception of very large corporations, most of these standards groups aim to drive standards on the supply side of the UNIX market and are therefore primarily the concern of the systems vendors. In the future, however, the community of users will need to become more conversant with computing standards in order to benefit from them. Before we go on to discuss standards that are important to the UNIX user, we first want to describe the granddaddy: what Scott McNealy of Sun Microsystems termed in a 1988 *MicroTimes* article the "Coca-Cola Classic of UNIX"—AT&T System V.

UNIX System V—Coca Cola Classic of UNIX

First, don't confuse the standard and the product. USL offers a product called UNIX System V. Other system vendors can be System V-compliant without having to actually use USL's product at all. Rather, they have to comply with USL's licensing terms and conditions and comply with the System V Interface Definition.

Just what does the USL's System V Interface Definition consist of? The SVID version 3 (SVR3) is a published specification that includes the following:

Base system

Kernel extension

Base utilities extension

Advanced utilities extension

Administration systems extension

Software development extension

Terminal interface extension

Network extension

System V compatibility requires conformance to all base-level system calls and library routines, user commands and utilities, key System V features such as streams, the System V tty (teletype) driver, and other popular facilities and extensions such as shared memory, semaphores, messages, and named pipes.

In layman's terms, the SVID defines the syntax of UNIX commands and utilities as well as the software interfaces provided by the operating system.

System V Interface Definitions (SVID)

* Volume 1
    Base system
    Kernel extensions
* Volume 2
    Basic and advanced utilities
    Software development support
    System administration
    Terminal interface
* Volume 3
    Streams
    Networking
* SVID 1989 (current release for SVR4 also known as SVID 3)

The API is the Holy Grail of UNIX

In the early days, UNIX was usually distributed as source, and the user compiled and built the operating system and programs. Operating system source is still a UNIX tradition, although it is required in far fewer situations today with the advent of APIs and ABIs (application programming and application binary interfaces, respectively). Commercial software, on the other hand, is usually provided in binary form. Software supplied in binary form normally works only with one vendor/architecture. Software conforming to an ABI will run on any vendor that supports the ABI, which is usually architecture-dependent.

An API enables the ISV to leverage portable code and users to avoid vendor lock-in. POSIX, SVID, and X/Open are all converging attempts at defining APIs. While ABIs are difficult to implement, software written to APIs need only be recompiled to run on different architectures.

The ABI is a contract: the system vendor promises to run any software that conforms to the ABI, and the software developer promises to write applications that run on any ABI platform. The ABI is a document that comprehensively defines the binary system interface between applications and the operating system on which they run.

The definition and support of an ABI is the enabling technology for shrink-wrapped software. In an environment (industry) that is rapidly evolving with many competing vendors, it has become essential to provide ways for software to survive into the future. The ABI gives access to the ISV across a variety of hardware platforms and hardware vendors access to a diverse and growing software base.

The ABI specifies more than an operating system interface. It completely describes the run-time environment that the application can depend on, including which programs and libraries are guaranteed to be available. An ABI describes the following:

The standard distribution format

The installation and configuration procedures

The convention for file formats and organization

The calling conventions and libraries

6.2. IEEE AND POSIX

The IEEE (Institute of Electrical and Electronic Engineers) is well supported by vendors, users, and academic groups. IEEE has large peer review groups and standards require a 75 percent vote. Standards normally take three to five years to make it through IEEE, which means that by the time a standard is endorsed by the IEEE, it has been in use for several years—although there may be slightly different versions being used. Final IEEE standards become ANSI/ISO standards.

POSIX

POSIX stands for Portable Operating System Interface for Computing Environments. It is a programmatic-level interface standard for portable operating systems being created by a number of different committees organized through the aegis of the IEEE. POSIX was initiated by a technical committee of the /usr/group standards committee in 1981.

POSIX refers collectively to a number of standards specifications. At the time of writing, the only approved specification was POSIX 1003.1, which deals with the operating system's system call interface. POSIX 1003.1 was recently approved by IEEE as a full-use standard. It has also been made a requirement for U.S. government tenders. POSIX 1003.1 Draft 13 was adapted by IEEE in 1988. It has been adopted by the National Institute for Standards and Technology via the FIPS (Federal Information Processing Standard) or FIPS 151-1. POSIX has also been adopted by the American National Standards Institute (ANSI), and at the time of writing, its adoption is pending by the International Standards Organization (ISO).

The POSIX 1003.1 standard has received commitments from user groups, systems vendors, and major companies. POSIX 1003.1 was an attempt to skirt the issue of whose UNIX was really UNIX. A system that is POSIX 1003.1 compliant is not necessarily UNIX, but for a short term may satisfy major US Federal Government procurement specifications. Because POSIX does not specify what cannot exist on a system, most vendors become POSIX compliant by adding a set of POSIX compliant command interfaces to their systems.

Other POSIX groups are described below:

P1003.0 — POSIX working group: the overall working group chaired by the National Institute of Standards and Technology (NIST)

P1003.1 — Systems services interface: standardization of OS calls

P1003.2 — Shells and utilities

P1003.3 — Verification methods

P1003.4 — Real-time systems interfaces

P1003.5 — Ada language

P1003.6 — System security and system extensions

P1003.7 — System administration extensions

P1003.8 — Networking extensions

P1003.9 — FORTRAN

P1003.10 — Supercomputing

P1003.11 — Transaction processing

P1003.12 — Protocol independent interfaces

P1003.13 — Namespace/directory, services

P1003.14 — Real-time profile

P1003.16 — Multiprocessing

P1003.17 — Supercomputer profile

Critics argue that POSIX may have an advantage as a consensus standard, but that P1003.1 in particular is too skimpy and watered down. Indeed, proprietary operating systems can be POSIX-compliant. Consensus standards, by their very nature, take time to become entrenched because vendors who have different interests must reach agreement. It might take years before POSIX extensions like shells, tool specifications, and real-time extensions are defined. POSIX lacks many utilities and applications, such as system administration tools and certain interfaces. The standards bodies and the user community will no doubt argue whether these tools are important in maintaining applications across different vendors' machines. But so long as vendors have a vested interest in their own proprietary tools or extensions, this debate will continue, impeding progress in advancing the standard to cover new areas.

POSIX will be increasingly important to system programmers who have a desire to write their software to a specification that will be source code-compatible and run without modification on the widest possible range of hardware.

The POSIX standards definitions and other publications of interest can be obtained from the IEEE Computer Society for a nominal fee.

The major drawback of IEEE standards is their consensus strength. They cannot resolve major schisms in the industry. Examples of this are Ethernet versus Token Ring and Open Look versus Motif. In cases like these, the resolution has been to vote multiple standards or vote for a standards which is the union of the two.

IEEE
Computer Society
12662 Los Vacqueros Circle
Los Alamitos, CA 90720
Tel (800) 272-6657 outside California
(714) 821-8380

Other publications can be obtained through IEEE's main office at (202) 371-0101.

IEEE Standards Office
P.O. Box 1331
445 Hoes Lane
Piscataway, NJ 98855

6.3. X/OPEN

In 1984, several European computer vendors who had been competing with each other formed a nonprofit consortium called X/Open. Its goal was to identify an operating system architecture for which they could all develop or adopt compliant hardware systems in order to lower their development costs. X/Open originally started with a charter to bring a European voice into what was seen as U.S. dominated UNIX standards environment. X/Open has become much more international with participation from 11 U.S., 6 European and 4 Japanese industry participants.

Headquartered in Reading, England, X/Open was originally founded as a nonprofit corporation in November 1984 and became an international organization and a fully independent company as of September 1987. X/Open's mission is one of specification, verification, certification, and branding of open, interactive computer applications environments. Its strategy is to adopt existing industry standards, either de facto or established, as part of a cohesive common applications environment.

X/Open is very influential in Europe and has been growing in acceptance in the U.S. although it is not as well know in the U.S. X/Open now conforms to both ANSI and ISO standards and does not innovate individual standards. What is does define is a minimum packaging of standards, which enforces minimum functionality across vendor offerings. X/Open defines a Common Applications Environment (CAE) with conforms to ANSI and ISO, and is documented in the X/Open Portability Guide.

XPG 3—X/Open Portability Guide

The X/Open Portability Guide or XPG, is a set of Open Systems specifications that combine both formal standards and marketplace de facto standards. It is driven by a qualitative market requirements research study, called the X/Open Xtra Program, which is focused on portability and interoperability. Products displaying the X/Open XPG brand conform to the portability guide and provide increased investment confidence.

XPG3 is the current release and incorporates several key standards such as POSIX 1003.1 and the X Window system. The XPG3 verification suite contains a structured set of more than 5500 tests, that verify XPG3 system calls, libraries, C language, and ISAM functionality.

X/Open is now a joint undertaking of many of the world's largest computer suppliers. They include AT&T/NCR, DEC, HP, Unisys, Sun, Bull, Ericson, ICL, Olivetti, Nixdorf, Philips, Siemens, and (relatively recently) IBM. What makes X/Open unique is that it comprises many important users, not just vendors. In fact, vendors are now in the minority.

X/Open is not a standards-making body. X/Open adopts interfaces that are either internationally recognized and accepted or have been agreed to by other standards bodies such as IEEE or AFNOR.

X/Open specifies and promotes what it calls the CAE, or Common Applications Environment. CAE is an integrated environment that features a comprehensive applications environment interface defined now by the XPG3 specifications. The following areas are currently in the works to be standardized:

Base operating system—based on USL System V Interface Definition to be

POSIX-compliant with extensions

International support

User interface—X Windows tool kits and look and feel

Graphics guide

Source code transfer

Transaction processing

Commands and utilities

Security, DOD C2 guide

Networking—PC

Interconnect, transparent interface

Languages—ANSI C, FORTRAN 77, Cobol 85, ISO Pascal, GSA ADA

Data Management—ISAM, embedded SQL

X/Open has published interfaces for the System V operating system (POSIX P1003.1), ANSI C language specification, CISAM, Microfocus Cobol, ANSI X3, FORTRAN, Pascal, and SQL. X/Open has reportedly invested more than $40 million in executing its charter.

X/Open is actively involved in other standards organizations and in producing porting guides. The X/Open Portability Guide describes how to produce portable systems and software with respect to the X/Open effort. Most of the documents developed by X/Open are available through Prentice-Hall. X/Open has merged its software catalog with over a thousand applications from over a thousand vendors in the UniForum Products Directory.

Open Systems Business Specifications Under Development

In early 1992, the X/Open board agreed with a proposal that would restructure X/Open's User Council with a goal of producing a business specification for Open Systems. This moves X/Open's orientation toward that of becoming driven by end-user requirements. Such a business specification would be a nontechnical document that would sell the Open Systems philosophy to information technology users. It would be developed in parallel with X/Open's technical specifications for Open Systems that are sponsored by the supply side of the industry.

Such a business specification is intended to serve as a blueprint that organizations or departments could use to help understand and justify the business benefits of Open Systems and how companies can go about getting started with Open Systems. Over time it intended to provide a means of leveraging end-user needs and requirements in such a way that will help focus vendors to address unfulfilled promises associated with interoperability, application portability and standardization among other priorities.

No doubt X/Open would like to increase the profile of its User Council. X/Open has established a new chairman of the User Council. The User Council consists of a six-person executive committee and some 42 commercial and government organizations. We expect that this process will be in full swing by early 1993. Just as it is proving very difficult to get the supply-side consortiums together, it would be equally difficult for X/Open to formally integrate other UNIX end-user groups into its User Council and this is not expected to happen. We believe that X/Open's move to become more end-user oriented is very positive and encourage readers to contact X/Open to learn what is new and available through the programs of the User Council.

XPG4 Launched in Autumn 1992

XPG4 specifications where announced expanding the requirements necessary to receive branding. Substantial upgrading and conformation testing is required to have a product branded as XPG4 compliant. XPG4 specifications can be ordered from X/Open for $395.

> X/Open Company Limited
> Apex Plaza
> Forbury Road
> Reading
> Berks RG1 1AX
> England

> X/Open Company Ltd.
> 1010 El Camino Real
> Suite 380
> Menlo Park, CA 94025
> Tel (415) 323-7992
> Fax (415) 323-8204

or

> 3141 Fairview Park Drive
> Suite 670
> Falls Church, VA 22042-4501
> Fax (703) 876-0050

6.4. UI (UNIX INTERNATIONAL, INC.)

Largely in reaction to OSF, a group of 18 companies formed what was called the "Archer Group" on October 18, 1988. The name is said to be derived from the name of the conference room in which the initial meeting was held. These vendors announced their intention to introduce and support UNIX products based on AT&T System V Release 4. Their primary stated objective was to ensure the continued evolution and compatibility of UNIX systems to meet the needs of the current installed base.

On November 30, 1988, UNIX International, a group of major computer companies and software companies, was announced. The organization was established to guide the future development of AT&T's UNIX System V operating system. Each of UNIX International's members has a major UNIX product line. UNIX International's members include companies such as Amdahl, Arix, AT&T/NCR, Computer Consoles, Inc., Concurrent Computer Corporation, Control Data Corporation, Convergent, Data General, Fujitsu, Ltd, Gould, HCR, ICL, Intel, Informix, INTER-

ACTIVE Systems, Motorola, Microfocus, NEC, Oki Electric, Olivetti, Oracle, Prime Computer, Pyramid, SCO, Sun Microsystems, Texas Instruments, Tolerant Systems, Toshiba, Unisoft, and Unisys. At the time of writing, there are over 150 member companies.

One of the major goals of this consortium has been to reemphasize the major purpose of System V release 4.0, which is to provide a migration path for all the applications existing on Berkeley, XENIX and System V platforms. System V release 4 represented the culmination of two years of effort to unite these major variants of the UNIX system.

UNIX International will promote UNIX, in particular, for the development of end-user applications to independent application software vendors (the so-called ISVs), as well as guide and direct Novell and X/Open in technology, marketing, and licensing.

In early 1991, UNIX International started a special program for ISVs. By mid-1992, the ISV Product Catalog had over 5,500 entries which represents a subset of the 18,000 documented UNIX SVR4-compatible applications. The catalog has over 1,000 system software packages, over 2,250 horizontal applications, and over 2,250 vertical applications.

SVR4 is UNIX International's answer to protecting existing UNIX software investments while pursuing optimal price/performance in hardware. SVR4 has the distinct advantage of having a wealth of applications that ran on previous generations of System V, XENIX and BSD and their derivative systems. SVR4 is based on time-tested code that has run on a variety of hardware architectures and has had its bugs systematically eliminated. It comes with internal interfaces for the file system, virtual memory, network, scheduler, and device drivers. A new file system can be introduced without risk of being incompatible with future releases. SVR4 has all the basic networking functionality of BSD and SunOS, including sockets.

SVR4 combines all the major functions from BSD, System V.3, and SunOS:

BSD 4.2 and 4.3

64 open files per process

Name server

Net

Buffering

Security

Subnet support

System V.3 SVID compliance

Tty drivers

Utilities

Streams

SunOS

NFS

Diskless clients

Windowing

SVR4 is going to offer the promise, for the first time, of shrink-wrapped UNIX application software. It will offer generic ABIs for Intel, Motorola, SPARC, and other processors, and it will be available from a number of vendors, including both system vendors and independent software distributors. It will be compatible with 80 percent of the installed base of System V, BSD, XENIX, and SunOS systems. The AT&T graphical user interface (Open Look) will be a part of the basic system, as will TCP/IP networking support.

Finally, SVR4 is SVID-and POSIX 1003.1-compliant and ANSI "C" X3.159-1989-compatible. It is also XPG3-branded. SVR4 will always be a superset of existing standards, as it represents the introduction of new and evolving technology that may or may not have been fully addressed yet by slower-moving standards bodies. Waiting for the standard to develop before introducing new technology would effectively throttle the computing industry at large and discourage innovation.

Sheer volume sets de facto standards because software firms develop to the platform offering the widest availability and market potential. Technology distribution is often as important as the technology itself. Viable market solutions will provide solid technology and a large base for applications developers and vendors.

UNIX International's Roadmap which includes establishing standard systems management components would appear to be ahead of schedule. The Tivoli-based object framework level, compatible with OSF's DME effort, was agreed and the first reference applications, print management and network management were developed. Other applications in such areas as backup and restore, license management, journaling and more are close behind. In the area of transaction processing, considerable work remains to be done to make UNIX suitable for both online and batch processing. A stored requests facility along with the ability to share CICS transactions—participating in some of a mainframe applications' workload are under development.

UNIX Internationals roadmap shows a clear splitting into client and server components over the next few years, with SVR4.2 and follow-on products as the client and the merge of V4.ES (extended security) and MP (multiprocessing) in 1993 as the main server portion.

Development versions of UNIX System V Release 4 Enhanced Security/Multiprocessing (ES/MP) were released by USL in 1992. In ES/MP USL has a fully multithreaded kernel and can support up to 30 processors. Other enhancements include a compilation environment that allows users to build and install uniprocessor or multiprocessor versions of the system as well as system management commands for administering the multiprocessor features and the preliminary version of the application programming interfaces for multithreaded enhanced security features. General availability was planned for mid-1993. ICL, Fujitsu, NCR, Pyramid, and Sequent are some of the companies who were working with USL in the development of ES/MP.

The Atlas Distributed Computing Framework (DCF)

All of the major OSF members are ONC licensees and continue to support the ONC protocols, including RPC. OSF intends to provide a gateway as part of AFS, so AFS servers can support NFS clients. ONC and OSF DCE will support many of the same distributed services such as Kerberos, X.400, X.500, and NTP.

DCE remains unproven technology. It will be years before DCE is available for such platforms as DOS or mainframes. Most customers, including those of the major systems vendors such as IBM, DEC, and HP, will continue to use ONC/NFS.

Distributed object management will be the enabling technology for next-generation distributed computing. The Distributed Object Management Facility, or DOMF, defines an advanced method for using and sharing information on networked computers from different vendors. The DOMF specification currently supports both the Sun ONC and HP NCS network services.

UNIX International does not compete with any vendor. All specifications are freely available to developers. Software manufacturers desiring compatibility with Atlas may do so without charges or fees.

UNIX International, Inc.
Waterview Corporate Center
20 Waterview Blvd.
Parsippany, NJ 07054
Tel (800) 848-6495 or
(201) 263-8400
outside North America
Fax (201) 263-8401

or

UNIX System Laboratories
190 River Road
Summit, New Jersey 07901
Tel (908) 522-6000

6.5.   OSF (THE OPEN SOFTWARE FOUNDATION)

On May 17, 1988, seven leading computer companies announced the formation of the Open Software Foundation. The original group was called the Hamilton group, reportedly named after the building in which the first meeting was held—a DEC installation on Hamilton Street in Palo Alto, California.

OSF incorporated as a nonprofit research and development organization that would define specifications, develop an operating system, and promote an open and portable application environment. OSF develops versions of UNIX and UNIX-based software products that are licensed to computer vendors or software vendors. Initial funding for OSF came from its sponsors, including Apollo Computer, Groupe Bull, DEC, HP, IBM, Nixdorf, and Siemens. OSF members also include universities, software development firms, and other computer companies. OSF founders have devoted millions of dollars to the OSF. The founding members, who have put up the largest amounts of money, are in the best position to call the shots, especially the "big three": IBM, DEC, and HP. However, OSF claims that its own technical staff will make final decisions concerning all OSF developments.

OSF's stated goal is to provide a clear and easy migration path for application developers and users. The OSF system OSF/1, released in late 1990 to OEMs, includes features to support System V and BSD UNIX-based applications. OSF's stated goal is also to provide specifications and technology to the industry, not to a specific set of vendors. In practice, however, such technology is getting to the industry through a specific set of vendors. (This is no different for AT&T's USL and SVR4.)

OSF demands no commitment from its members for the marketing of products it develops. Following the initial release of OSF/1, it is no small effort for those system vendors in OSF to integrate it with their own products and bring the result to market along with requisite third-party application software. Several vendors may take years to do so.

The scope of OSF is not limited to "versions of UNIX." OSF is trying to provide its system vendors with a complete environment. OSF/Motif, for example, runs on both UNIX and non-UNIX-based systems. In fact, any system that supports X Windows will also support either Motif or USL's Open Look. The organization intends to develop and market software and license its products back to its member organizations.

OSF has an open process that actively involves membership participation and feedback. Vehicles such as special interest groups, focus groups, and member meetings, and documentation and project plan reviews by the membership have some influence on OSF's technical specification and direction processes. But OSF is not a consensus-based organization. OSF staff solicit and receive member input, then make relevant decisions independent of the membership. OSF delivers specifications as well as technology. The specifications are available regardless of licensing status.

OSF changed its original plans to use AIX's kernel and has now incorporated Mach 2.5's kernel and a parallelized file system. Much of OSF/1 comes from AIX from IBM. OSF/1 release 1.0 includes commands and libraries as well as some kernel technology from AIX v3.1. OSF has also included technology from several other vendors, which is being integrated for the first time. Each technology supplied to OSF is viewed on a case-by-case basis as new releases of OSF/1 are planned. TCP/IP support comes from Encore Computer. Security software comes from SecureWare.

OSF's use of the Mach kernel, and technologies from other vendors, makes OSF more of a developer than originally envisioned. It is not yet clear exactly when and how and on which platforms, HP, DEC, and even IBM will actually use OSF/1, although they have public commitment to it. The interested reader should contact these companies for specifics.

OSF and X/Open

OSF quit X/Open in late 1992. It cited as reasons the fact that it viewed X/Open as almost completely UNIX-centric. This irked X/Open which described itself as the last bastion of product independent specifications in the industry. According to its senior officials, X/Open is far more concerned with Open Systems than with UNIX. X/Open has said that it twice refused a proposal to standardize on the UNIX System V interface definition (SVID). When it was formed in 1984, it did take some parts of the SVID issue 2 for its system interface definition and added some of its own specifications such as internationalization. Further countering OSF's assertions, X/Open pointed to 28 specifications it had issued in 1991 of which 16 concerned interoperability, an area it claims to spend more than half its time and resources. OSF's new position would seem to contradict its position that OSF/2 will be XPG compliant. As OSF gave up its million-dollar seat on the X/Open board, it sought a slot on the ISV Council instead. X/Open turned OSF down since it isn't an independent software vendor.

OSF has scored a win in its Motif GUI. Ironically, Sun Microsystems, which had staunchly refused to support a Motif-based product, was the single largest platform on which Motif has been shipped. Sun believed Open Look to be superior technology and if customers wanted Motif, it was available from various third parties. There would also seem to be momentum building around DCE. But OSF/1 has not been the success that might have been expected when OSF first formed several years ago. Now part of COSE, even Sun has agreed to support Motif and DCE.

Open Software Foundation
11 Cambridge Center
Cambridge, MA 02142
Tel (617) 621-8700

6.6. ANALYSIS OF OSF AND UNIX INTERNATIONAL

OSF is both a marketing and an R&D organization. UNIX International (UI), on the other hand, is largely a technical marketing organization that seeks to influence AT&T's USL (UNIX Software Laboratory), which is responsible for UNIX software technical and business development. By early 1989, UNIX International was interfacing to AT&T's UNIX subsidiary, USL, which AT&T organized in early 1989. Following the acquisition of USL by Novell, UNIX International relationship to USL remains unchanged.

UI is open in its technology and product planning, with participation from its members and X/Open. OSF is open to participation in its technology procurement but prevents participation by its members in the specification and direction-setting process.

USL analyzes requirements and creates a development plan and schedule for new functionality to be incorporated into SVR4. OSF requests specifications and technology from the industry and then chooses implementations of technology. OSF is creating its own product.

UI is an industry organization that controls the specification and direction of UNIX System V. It is converging UNIX technologies into one enforceable standard. OSF is an ISV that is developing an alternative UNIX operating system that it will license in competition with UNIX System V.

UI was founded by and consists of major UNIX players. UI members have a vested interest in expanding the UNIX market. OSF was founded by and consists of the majority of proprietary system vendors. Some of OSF's members have a business interest in the continued success of their proprietary operating system products, and it will be interesting to see how they reconcile these interests with their commitments to UNIX and OSF.

OSF has a stated goal of distributing technology to its sponsors, who in turn seek to incorporate OSF products in their own commercial products. UNIX is only one of many components in the OSF software environment. OSF has a number of products and initiatives under way that are beyond the scope of this book.

UNIX International and now Novell's focus is on UNIX System V and the System V Interface Definition as the basis for Open Systems. The emphasis centers on transportability and interoperability across the platforms, with UNIX System V as the base operating system. Any software that adheres only to the interface definition of SVID should be source-compatible with future releases of Novell's UNIX or any other SVID-compliant UNIX implementation. AT&T had had a broader system environment for application portability known as AOE, or Application Operating Environment. Since the formation of UI, AT&T deferred to UI's support of the X/Open Portability Guide (XPG) and all but dropped AOE. System V is a released product as of this writing, and System V and its variants span a very wide installed base. Novell's SVR4 has as its foundation tested and proven technology. By comparison, OSF/1 is newly integrated and unproven although its components are drawn largely for existing proven technology.

Comparing Novell SVR4 and OSF OSF/1

- The two products, from OSF and Novell, are comparably priced. The system software is usually a small fraction of the total cost of the system ownership.
- Most commands and basic system calls will be the same—both are POSIX 1003.1-compliant. It is not clear whether Mach is POSIX 1003.1-compliant.
- Users will see differences in user interface and in certain utilities and some system administration utilities. Multiple windowing graphical user interfaces are expected to be supported on both operating system platforms.
- The number of applications on SVR4 is much larger than the number on OSF/1, since each OEM of OSF will drive the porting of

important software to its own variant based on OSF/1 and won't have the advantage of SVR4's binary compatibility.

- SVR4 and OSF will have different operating system kernel source code structures.

- OSF does not offer compatibility with SunOS which has the leading RISC/UNIX market share of over 66 percent in 1990. While OSF makes no claim about SunOS compatibility in OSF/1, the system does include an NFS-compatible file system as well as all BSD4.3 commands (with the exception of machine-specific ones).

- OSF has published an "Open Road" document that outlines the evolution of OSF technologies. One of the key requirements for OSF/1 release 2, according to OSF, is source and binary compatibility with previous releases. UI also updates its "roadmap" quarterly, and each successive release of SVR4 is supposed to have full source and binary compatibility.

There is little difference between the type of customers (system vendors) USL has and those OSF has. Both USL and OSF had made their technologies generally available. At the time of writing, Novell appears to have about a one-year lead over OSF in terms of vendors bringing product to market based on their new releases of SVR4 and OSF/1, respectively.

OSF and USL/UNIX International versions of UNIX did not differ significantly. For OSF to do otherwise would have created major problems migrating the XENIX, BSD, and System V installed base and applications software for vendors.

OSF has to remain committed to much of the System V Interface Definition through its promise to comply with X/Open's XPG3 and POSIX 1003.1. In fact, OSF users will have a built-in license to System V release 3, since AIX itself is based on this license.

OSF came up with a list of standards in what it called its "Level 0" specification. Its endorsement of X/Open's CAE was a critical item. It created a wider point of commonality among all key vendors from the point of view of the layered systems environment.

X/Open's XPG has yet to include other important areas of functionality for which there is no de facto standard. Areas such as graphical user interface, real time, transaction processing, and wide area networking still remain to be developed or agreed upon. X/Open is moving forward on most of these areas.

USL had shipped UNIX source tapes for SVR4. USL and its licensees were shipping operating systems based on AT&T's System V releases 3 and 4. AT&T and Sun developed SVR4, and it started shipping as planned by USL in 1989.

OSF/1 pricing is not based on total cost of a system. The pricing of both source and binary royalties is based on the cost of OSF/1 plus the prerequisite System V license. For systems priced under $280,000, OSF pricing is comparable to that of SVR4. For higher-end systems, the cost of SVR4 can be higher. These costs are carried by the system vendors. The final price of the system software is often bundled in the overall price of the system, especially in the case of high-end systems.

Some companies are betting on both racehorses, and there is nothing to prevent them from joining both groups. OSF and UNIX International are separate and competitive. Initially, they have had little or no bearing on each other. By virtue of each group's commitment to support standards such as POSIX 1003.1, users can only benefit from the competition. At a technical level, once all the marketing smoke clears, users should be the benefactors because applications portability and intervendor cooperation will drive the computer market further toward "openness" than ever before.

The Battleground Will Shift During the 1990s?

The schism between OSF and UI is no longer as wide as people might like you to believe. These organizations have publicly stated their intentions of working together on multiprocessing as well as other important emerging technology such as internationalization. Both groups support X/Open and its CAE (Common Application Environment) specification and COSE. They have also announced their intentions to collaborate on common verification technology aimed at ensuring compatibility. Most UNIX vendors support source-level standards, X/Open's Portability Guide, and IEEE POSIX.

One thing is certain. All companies bringing UNIX products to the market are going to have the effect of educating the market about UNIX. As is usually the case in competitive wars, users will benefit from the increased competition, but they will also be confused by conflicting marketing messages. For the novice, it will become more difficult to separate hype from reality.

As far as OSF and UI are concerned, there has been considerable speculation in the press that the two parties were negotiating with each other, trying to find common ground. Such speculation was put to rest when OSF and UI both issued formal statements that they could not reach agreement in 1992. OSF reportedly wanted AT&T to spin out the UNIX development group and merge it with OSF into a new corporation. It is suspected that AT&T's valuation at the time, of its organization and UNIX itself, was set at around $400 million. A mutually satisfactory business arrangement could not be put together.

How Does OSF/1 Stack Up Against SVR4 Technically?

A comparison of OSF/1 and SVR4 is shown in Table 6.1. The comparison, while highlighting technical differences between implementations, points out that much of the core technology is comparable. Assessing the impact on end users is more difficult, since it is not clear how system or software resellers will add value to address unique customer requirements. Other key points of comparison, such as how many vendors and system product lines will support each operating system, and the performance of each, are not possible to quantify.

Looking at file systems, one should bear in mind that most UNIX systems actually run multiple file systems, although this may be transparent to the end user. In addition to those mentioned in the table, support of PC File System(s) and High Sierra for use of CD-ROM-based file systems could be important for some users.

Networking Interfaces are particularly important to the UNIX community. Streams and TLI permit any networking functions to operate as transparent to the actual network transport layer. Sockets and BSD networking support is built on top of streams, which is an older although simpler method for implementing interprocess communications.

Graphical user interfaces will be supplied by both systems vendors and independent software companies. It should be expected that almost any window system or other tools for building window-based applications will be available on any platform that is shipping in volume.

Security extensions are normally provided by system vendors who sell in the government marketplace. The fact that security is supported by either OSF or SVR4 implementation is more relevant to system vendors in terms of saving costs of internal development.

Disk mirroring can be done in either hardware or software. Many vendors support disk mirroring today as an extension to their UNIX or system hardware offerings. Disk mirroring is one key part of addressing high-availability requirements—by writing multiple copies of data, it tries to ensure that that data can always be read, even in the event of a disk outage—a head crash.

Logical volume support means that files that are larger than a gigabyte, and that can't be broken down in size, can be supported. There aren't that many examples where this requirement is crucial in normal data processing.

Multiprocessing support is important if you have a multiprocessor system and if the software you are going to run—or how you intend to use the system—actually exploits multiprocessing. The test is found in assessing an application's throughput with one processor and then as-

Table 6.1. Features of OSF OSF/1 versus USL SVR4.

Feature	OSF	SVR4	IMPACT
File Systems Supported			
System V	y	y	Compatibility
BSD FFS	y	y	
NFS	y	y	
RFS	n	y	
RAMDISK	n	y	
customer defined	y	y	
Networking Interfaces			Network
			Transparency
Streams and TLI	y	y	Compatibility
Sockets and BSD networking	y	y	
OSI stack	not announced	announced	
Graphical User Interfaces			
X11R4	y	y	
OSF/Motif	y	y	
NEWS X11R4	n	y	
Open Look	n	y	
Security	B1	B2 announced	Gov't business
Disk Mirroring	available std.	announced	High availability
Logical Volume	available std.	announced	Huge Disk Files
Multiprocessing	User level threads	Full SMP	People with multiprocessors
	Full SMP announced	announced	
Applications Compatibility	Incomplete, ANDF under discussion	ABI's for Intel 80 × 86, i860, Motorola 68000, 88000, MIPS, SPARC, WE3200	

sessing its throughput with multiple processors. Is the application even close to "n" times faster when "n" processors are used?

On the issues of kernel-level multiprocessing, security, supported file systems, logical volumes, graphical user interfaces, and memory mapped files, OSF/1 and SVR4 have strong similarities. Unlike SVR4, OSF/1 provides no binary interface standard. Developers will have to support more ports than for SVR4-based computers with application programming interfaces, which, at a minimum, necessitate recompilation.

For obvious reasons, only a small number of applications currently claim to support OSF/1, in part because the motivation of software vendors is not driven by compatibility with OSF/1. Rather, they may want to run on computer hardware that may be running OSF/1. OSF and/or system vendors will have to work aggressively with software vendors to help them port. It is highly doubtful that OSF/1 will achieve any significant volume until the applications are there and working. Given the nature of OSF/1, and its support of System V and BSD interfaces and functions, porting shouldn't present a very serious technical challenge.

On the other hand, migration to SVR4 will be more like a migration than a port. The application binary interface supported by SVR4 will mean that applications, such as the majority of the SCO 386 Release 3.2 software, will run without modification on SVR4.

OSF/1 Commitment Builds Slowly

Major computer systems vendors like IBM, DEC, and HP are making public commitments to UNIX and pledging to support OSF/1 in addition to their proprietary operating systems. But few, so far, have provided timetables and details of how they will merge their current UNIX-based products with OSF/1. Many of these vendors today have SVID-based versions of UNIX (AIX, ULTRIX, and HP/UX, respectively). But when will they converge their current UNIX products with OSF's?

OSF/1 as a whole will initially represent new, untested technology, even though components of the system have been taken from existing products. The same can be said of system vendors who merge their existing UNIX variants with OSF/1. It normally takes about one year to make a port of a UNIX operating system; test it thoroughly to ensure high quality of software, documentation, and training; and ensure critical applications are compatible and run with acceptable performance.

As to which vendors will support OSF/1, DEC seems to have the furthest-along plans for providing their ULTRIX 5.0. IBM has stated it is planning to support OSF/1 on the current AIX family of systems, although it has not publicly set a timetable for doing so (at the time of writing). IBM has been very cagey about letting its OSF plans be known.

IBM has said only that it is planning to experiment with OSF/1 on the PS/2, the RS/6000, and its mainframes. For the time being, IBM plans to continue using its System V-based AIX on its own line of workstations, the RS/6000, and other platforms.

HP announced its intention to provide a port to one of its four workstation lines late in 1991. Other vendors are slower in moving to OSF/1 because it means letting go of their own versions of UNIX, unbundled software they have to port to OSF/1, and third-party applications software that may not be easily ported to OSF/1 for commercial as much as technical reasons.

Several of the OSF sponsors have stated that OSF technology is in their long-term direction. They have announced spot products will support OSF (e.g., DECstation 3100) or products that are not yet shipping in volume. Leading industry analysts agree that for OSF to be successful, the top vendors need to move quickly to support OSF/1 on their strategic platforms (vis., IBM RS/6000, DECstations and DECsystems, HP Precision-Architecture minicomputers, and Motorola workstations, for example). The major OSF sponsors face a tradeoff between short-term gains with their existing products and longer-term transitions to OSF. ISV's will not take OSF seriously unless they are convinced that these major vendors have clear transition strategies for their strategic (and high-volume) hardware platforms.

OSF/2 is supposed to be based on a microkernel implementation of Mach. Interface definition, object approach to server construction, performance, security and support for distributed systems all would seem to be problem areas that have to be resolved and could push the commercial availability of the new version out as far as 1995 or beyond before there is really useable code available beyond the normal cycle of early releases for product developers.

SVR4 picks up steam—moves towards commodity market. SVID was originally a single vendor's (AT&T's) specification. UNIX International and USL changed that. At UniForum in January 1991, SVR4 was everywhere, running on all kinds of platforms from PCs to RISC. USL and Intel had recently named INTERACTIVE Systems as "a principal publisher" of UNIX System V release 4 on Intel systems. INTERACTIVE said it would ship by mid-1991. Everex claimed it would be shipping even sooner. The price for a complete package from Everex—including the base OS, X Window (with Open Look), TCP/IP, and software development tools—would be "less than $1,000," according to their spokesman.

USL was planning for a number of new releases of SVR4 including SVR4ES, SVR4MP, and SVR4ES/MP. The ES version would offer extended security support for government and demanding commercial customers. The SMP version would provide fully symmetrical multiprocessing support. The ES/MP release is an integration of these other two releases. The migration plans for these releases are available in roadmap documents provided by USL and now Novell.

All of Novell's future releases are planned to be fully binary compatible with previous releases of UNIX. USL had been conducting tests to verify this claim. USL claimed that of testing done to date, 55 percent of the binary applications run "out of the box," and 25 percent will run but require care in using installation scripts. So, SVR4 is about 80 percent binary compatible. Of the remaining 20 percent, over half of these had incompatibilities due to bad programming, or intentional "use" of bug features.

As of the summer of 1991, the following vendors were offering SVR4-based or SVR4-compliant products: AT&T, ICL, ISC, MICROPORT, Novell, NCR, NEC, Pyramid, Sony, Sun Microsystems, and UHC. The rest of the members of the UNIX International consortium were well into the development and beta testing of new versions of their products based on SVR4.

Summary

UNIX International has one definition of Open Systems and OSF has another. The two groups have to accept what each other actually is. UNIX International, for example, has to accept that OSF is an industry-funded research and development organization. OSF does not want to be UNIX-centric like it perceives UNIX International. And yet, OSF saw UNIX International and USL's expansion with Tuxedo and Atlas as "restricting what users can implement." In the meantime OSF and USL negotiated over USL licensing OSF technology. This creates a rather confusing picture of just how UNIX International influences Novell.

OSF and Novell are, by nature, very different organizations. This makes talks between UNIX International and OSF even more difficult. Things seem to be evolving to the point in the industry where UNIX International is like the sheriff of the UNIX vendor community. X/Open is the vanguard of Open Systems, and OSF and Novell are software developers. OSF itself would like to move toward more self-sufficiency from a business point of view. OSF would like to derive maximum commercial benefits from its various technologies even though it is nonprofit. OSF would like to spread its contributed funding, currently on the order of $4.5 million per annum from each of its remaining six founder members, across a broader base of members as well.

Nonetheless, the two consortia are trying to find ways of working together. The main obstacle appears to be IBM and DEC issues. Apparently, HP and Siemens-Nixdorf are now convinced, via their respective partnerships with Sun and USL, of the potential for advancing the state-of-the-art in IT by working through competitive collaborations. To the extent IBM and DEC agree—as they have strong impact on OSF, then there will be more significant levels of cooperation.

It is now commonly understood that the only way to create a volume standard that has any chance of competing with Microsoft is to band together as UNIX moves more toward a mass UNIX desktop market. Microsoft and NT may provide the force required to make COSE happen.

6.7. STANDARDS AND LAYERED SYSTEM ARCHITECTURE

Figure 6.1 shows the relationship of major computing standards to the microview of the layered system architecture. Many of these standards have been previously discussed.

- Software library standards such as GKS, PHIGS, PHIGS+, and PEX exist especially for CAD/CAM and graphics programs to be more easily ported between different machines.
- Window system standards and server protocols such as X, PEX, IEX, VEX, and PostScript are used in the implementation of graphical user interface environments.
- File-based interchange standards such as CGM, IGES, PDES, TIFF, and so forth are used to promote CAD/CAM application data exchange.
- Networking standards such as Ethernet, FDDI, HPPI, NFS, and ISDN facilitate communications.
- Mass-storage interface standards such as SCSI and DSCSI as well as System Bus and Serial Bus standards allow a high degree of system component connectivity.

But today's standardization is not limited to system components. More recently, standards have come to a whole new and diverse set of activities.

- Standards in the areas of benchmarking, include SPEC, TPC, and NCGA's GPC for example. Application development environment bodies such as Object Management Group (OMG), the CAE Framework initiative (CFI), and ISO SC24WG1.

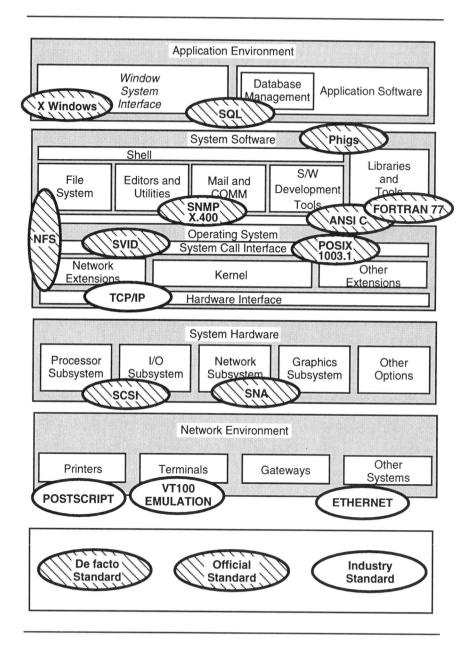

Figure 6.1.   Standards fit with layered system architecture. Standards usually apply to specific interfaces in the layered systems context. A group of standards taken together are called a profile.

Consortium-backed standards include X, PEX, IEX, CD-I, DVI, Motif, OpenLook, MIDI, SPEC, GPC, OSF/1, SVR4, Ethernet, and XPG. These categories are not always so clear cut. For example Ethernet can be categorized as both an official (IEEE 802) and consortium backed (i.e., Xerox, DEC, Intel). In fact, many of these processes overlap and the organizations must work with each other to leverage each other's efforts.

No vendor is immune to the accusation that they have added nonstandard functionality to UNIX in order to enhance their system's performance and functionality and/or provide differentiation. Common extensions can be found in areas such as multiprocessing, systems management, OLTP extensions, and data center—high-availability type extensions.

6.8.   SUMMARY OF STANDARDS AND STANDARDS-MAKING BODIES

Various standards bodies have been previously described, and others will be described later in this section. The summary in Table 6.2 is intended to help the reader understand the nature of different standards organizations in terms of their primary audience.

Below are addresses for standards organizations that are not provided elsewhere.

> 88Open
> 100 Homeland Court
> Suite 800
> San Jose, CA 95112
> (408) 436-6600

> MIT X Consortium
> Massachusetts Institute of Technology
> 545 Technology Square
> Cambridge, MA 02139
> (617) 253-0628

> Object Management Group
> Framingham Corporate Center
> 492 Old Connecticut Path
> Framingham, MA 01701
> (508) 820-4300

> SPARC International
> Suite 210
> Menlo Park, CA 94025
> (415) 321-8692

Table 6.2. Examples of types of standard by type of standards bodies.

Government Agencies	NIST (formerly NBS)
	DOD
Government Procurement or Legislative	CALS
	FIPS
Independent Bodies and Trade Associations	ISO (OSI standards)
	IEEE
	ANSI
	UniForum
	ACM
	X/Open
Vendor Consortia	UNIX International
	Open Software Foundation
	X Consortia
	SPARC International
Customer Consortia	GM MAP/BOEING TOPS
	POSC
	User Alliance for Open Systems

User Alliance for Open Systems
1750 Old Meadow Road
Suite 400
McLean, VA 22102
(703) 883-2817

6.9. PORTABILITY AND PORTING

This section examines issues associated with porting of software among UNIX systems, and between UNIX and other proprietary operating systems. It discusses the implications of portability in four subsections:

1. For porting the UNIX operating system itself
2. Application software between UNIX systems
3. From proprietary systems to UNIX
4. Operator (user) portability issues among UNIX systems

Source Code Portability. Source code portability implies that an environment can be transported from one computer to another without rewriting the source code program. It requires the use of compilers, which recompile the source code to operate on different architecture.

Binary Portability implies that the binary or executable image of the program can be transported and run without any recompilation or linking. It implies source file and object code compatibility. For binary compatibility to exist, computer system architectures have to use the same instruction set. Defining a binary standard means specifying a number of hardware-dependent characteristics. These include file data format, kernel entrance after a system call, media size and density, graphical and windowing interfaces, network interfaces, and the user process layout in memory.

Binary compatibility offers the ultimate level of portability for an operating environment. Some examples of binary compatibility can be found in various systems vendors' product lines, such as DEC's VMS-VAX line, Microsoft's MS-DOS, and Sun's SPARC.

For source code portability to exist, an application development and execution environment must provide the mechanisms that ensure compatibility. Obviously, the subject of portability is complex and extends well beyond the operating system or the language in which an application is programmed. Several standards groups and consortia of vendors, and an increasing number of users, are defining their own portability profile. Consider the NIST Applications Portability Profile shown in Table 6.3. It defines the standard for each functional element in the layered application architecture.

Standards constitute a strategy for achieving portability. Both the development and the execution environments should be based on standards. Standards are important in general software development, network management and communications, and for the integration of application software tools through the use of common underlying capabilities such as data management.

In the following sections, we will explore the issues of portability, at the operating system and applications levels and for the user.

6.9.1.   Operating System Portability

Why is OS portability important to system vendors? UNIX-based operating systems are available on more computer systems than any other OS. Technically, UNIX is programmed almost exclusively in the C language, while most other operating systems are programmed for efficiency in the assembly language of a target machine.

Systems vendors have a commercial incentive to license UNIX instead of developing yet another operating system. The major reasons

Table 6.3   Applications portability profile.

Function	Standard	Specification
Operating System	Extended POSIX	FIPS 151-1
		Shells and Tools
		(POSIX.2)*
		System Admin.
		(POSIX.7)
Database Management	SQL	FIPS 127
	IRDS	FIPS 156
Data Interchange		
Document Processing	ODA, ODIF	ISO/IS 8613
	SGML	FIPS 152
Engineering Data	IGES, PDES	NBSIR 88-3813
Graphics	CGM	FIPS 128
Network Services		
File Management	TFA	POSIX.8/4*
Data Communications	OSI	FIPS 146
		(GOSIP)
User Interface	X Window System	Version 11.3
Programming Services	C	X3.159
	FORTRAN	FIPS 069-1
	Cobol	FIPS 021-2
	Ada	FIPS 119
	Pascal	FIPS 109

*Not yet a full-use standard

for this are cost savings and the fact that supporting UNIX enables them to run the wide range of applications already ported to UNIX.

Why is OS portability important to users? Simply put, the standardized operating system greatly increases the potential for hassle-free porting of software between systems and enhances the use of systems in cooperative processing arrangements. It must be stressed, however, that UNIX (or any operating system) may facilitate or hinder portability. Portability is something that is to a large extent intrinsic to the software application itself. Software should be designed with portability in mind. UNIX itself was designed with portability in mind, from the very start. The UNIX operating system is much better designed for portability than much of the commercial software on the market today.

When the UNIX OS is licensed by Novell, for example, and system vendors port it to their hardware, they have to demonstrate conformance with specifications by successfully executing a set of verification tests known as SVVS. Similarly, standards groups usually define verification test suites to ensure conformance with the standards.

Most users and independent software vendors (with the exception of those intending to remarket a UNIX-based operating system) never have to worry about porting the UNIX operating system itself. They only have to understand which version of the OS has been implemented together with exceptions and/or extensions to defined standards that may affect application software.

6.9.2.   Porting Application

Since UNIX is available on many computer architectures and from different companies, many software developers choose UNIX. In contrast to many other operating systems, UNIX offers relative ease of porting software from one UNIX OS to another.

UNIX has a complete set of tools for software development and debugging. To the extent they're exploited, both the code and the software development environment used to build and manage the software development project can also be ported.

Porting C source code from one UNIX to another is usually a straightforward task. However, even C programs that are written for a specific machine architecture can present problems during porting, since the libraries they need or other elements in the layered systems software architecture may not be available or may be inconsistent across UNIX platforms.

Another factor that can limit a program's portability can be found where programs attempt to increase performance by packing bytes into words. This sort of operating won't affect porting between systems with the same system architecture, but may require recoding of the source program otherwise. Certain programming constructs that make assumptions about low-level byte alignment may be incompatible between CPUs, even from the same computer vendor. One example: DEC's hardware licensed from MIPS Computer versus the systems available from MIPS itself.

Good programming techniques to maximize portability of software require the isolation of machine-dependent sections of code so they can be easily identified and replaced. Such machine-dependent libraries can be written once and used for numerous application programs.

6.9.3.   Application Software Porting—Proprietary Operating Systems to UNIX

Truly portable software is extremely difficult to write. This is especially true when the application uses many system features or when performance has been optimized for the particular underlying platform architecture. It is common for "portable" code to include machine-dependent portions for each machine it has to be ported to.

There are several factors to consider when porting application software to UNIX from a proprietary operating system, or from one version of UNIX to another where the application is more complex or sophisticated:

Compiler compatibility

Cross-compiler availability

Multilanguage code support (e.g., C calling FORTRAN)

Software development tools

Shell programming

System library support

Determining compiler compatibility is relatively straightforward if the compiler exists, is standards-compliant, supports extensions, and has adequate performance. Cross-compilers are tools that produce software for multiple computer architectures. Moving from one architecture to the next only requires recompilation.

An application that contains modules written in several languages is not uncommon today. In such a case, the intermodule communication requirements may require that different languages interact—that is, they have the ability to call each other. Not all compilers support such a capability.

Software development tools include editors, source code control mechanisms, text preprocessors, and other utilities used by the programmers. Shell programming refers to the support of common shells or, in cases of moving from one UNIX system to another, porting shell scripts.

A system library used by an application program—for example, a math library—may not be available in both environments. Calls to UNIX software libraries should be examined for incompatibility between UNIX versions.

The architecture of an applications user interface (its use of a windowing system, graphics library, and user interface tool kit) can have a very significant impact on its portability. The fewer the changes in the user interface, the easier it will be for users to learn. To the extent the same architecture is used between applications, it is easier still for users to learn new applications. User interface is an area where standards are only now forming. It is a difficult area in which to achieve complete standardization given the radically different types of devices, particularly in the case of graphics displays.

6.9.4. Operator and User Portability

Operator portability refers to the user's ability to move from one application or system to another, given appropriate access, with little or no retraining. Achieving this goal requires a portable operating system environment. It also implies the availability of applications that have consistent user interfaces on a system and across different system environments. A consistent user interface is necessary, but not sufficient, to achieve operator portability.

To achieve the goal of user portability, the UNIX system environment must be consistent from one machine to another. Compatible UNIX shell and shell scripts can greatly assist in this regard. It is the responsibility of the user to customize the UNIX shell's start-up files to achieve this goal, especially where systems from multiple vendors will be used.

When it is decided to move users from a proprietary OS to UNIX, there are many new concepts and commands and utilities that must be learned. The transition can be eased by customizing the UNIX environment to emulate the original environment and thereby bridge users over to UNIX with minimal retraining. This includes the implementation of consistent system administrative practices, such as setting up directory organization, file naming conventions, and the like.

There are commercially available software packages that provide command language and editor emulation for proprietary systems under UNIX.

6.10. LIVING WITH MERGED KERNELS IN THE FUTURE

Mach, OSF/2, Chorus, Windows/NT are all examples of microkernel implementations which will support "multiple personalities." In recent years, many system vendors are moving to support merged kernels. In the past, people had their favorite variant of UNIX.

System V was generally considered to have better system administration than BSD. BSD provided user-friendly features like the C-shell and other commands. A particular variant of UNIX also used to be chosen for software portability. If we write software to the SVID interface definition and use good programming practices, the code will be fairly portable to SVID-compliant variants. Code written for one platform may use compiler features not available on another platform. The same is true for libraries. Device driver code is not usually portable between variants. Scripts may not be portable if they use commands not available on the target environment.

To solve this problem, vendors offer merged kernels. They support commands and features in multiple variants, but this can be done in different ways that may have drawbacks. There are (and will be many more) versions of merged kernels beyond UNIX variants. There are merged UNIX and Pick OS, VMS and UNIX, DOS and UNIX, and so forth. Windows/NT is to support 16-bit Windows APIs, 32-bit Windows APIs, OS/2, POSIX, and so forth.

There are two ways vendors implement merged environments. There are those that provide most of the UNIX standards as wholly separate and those that are primarily one system but have facilities to emulate the other variant(s). The first is sometimes called separate-but-equal, dual universe. The other is called separate universe.

In dual universe implementations, the system can be administered in either style. Some dual universe implementations require both systems be set up correctly, which can increase their administrative complexity greatly. You may have to be careful that if you use some system administration utilities, they will cause conflicts with the other universe.

Supporting a Standard Does Not Guarantee Compatibility

POSIX, ANSI, and SVID are all standard APIs that in a sense compete with each other. There are differences in these standards and in their libraries. OSF/1 is advertised as compliant with POSIX, XPG4, XTI, AT&T SVID Issue 2, 4.3BSD, and so forth. But resellers of OSF/1, for example, do not have to use the compilers and other tools that come from OSF.

XPG is a product-based standard from the European consortium. Standards that are product-based use a mixture of existing products as models for the standard rather than building a standard from existing standards and inventing new standards for everything else.

6.11. BENCHMARKS—A MEANS OF COMPARATIVE UNIX SYSTEM PERFORMANCE

Scottish author Andres Lang (*EDN*, November 1990) wrote, "Most micro-processor vendors use benchmarks as a drunken sailor uses lamp posts for support rather than illumination." Benjamin Disraeli, the British statesman, *almost* said, "There are three kinds of lies: lies, damned lies, and benchmarks."

Benchmarks don't have to be confusing and deceptive. Application software test suites that bear a resemblance to your software, consistently applied across a range of systems of similarly configured systems, can be helpful in selecting hardware.

Benchmarks are commonly used as a means to compare alternative systems. There are basically two types of benchmarks: marketing benchmarks and custom benchmarks. The later is normally ported to the target environment and run. The former are published by system vendors or other performance standards groups such as Aim Technology. Marketing benchmarks may or may not be reproducible and while interesting to see and compare are no longer used as the only comparative measure of performance. Not only are marketing benchmarks difficult to reproduce, but often their results do not serve as a basis for comparison with normal workloads.

Benchmarks are generally broken down into computational benchmarks (Whetstones, LINPACK, Khornerstones, SPECmarks), multiuser throughput benchmarks (SPEC SDM, AIM, Neal Nelson), and transaction benchmarks (TPC-A, TPC-B, TPC-C, RAMP-C). Benchmarks are a standard set of tasks used to compare system performance. Ideally they are reproducible and consist of server components including a set of tasks, a methodology for timing the tasks, and a standard format for comparing results.

Different benchmarks have applicability to different systems resources or features. For example, Dhrystones measure the arithmetic logic unit. Whetstones, LINPACK, and SPEC benchmarks measure the arithmetic logic unit, the floating point unit and the compiler efficiency. AIM measures all of these plus memory and disk I/O performance. A number of marketing benchmarks commonly used for UNIX systems follow:

6.11.1. AIM

The AIM suite of benchmarks are marketed by AIM Technology, Inc., located in Santa Clara, California. AIM uses a number of different benchmarks to measure and report the performance of computer systems. Among these is the AIM Suite III V3.0 benchmark for example which measures multitasking throughput. This benchmark is comprised of 31 different tests. Each test is a C program that performs different functions such as arithmetic calculations, system calls to exercise memory management, and disk I/O. A standard mix of these is used to derive the overall peak performance which is expressed in Aim's (a measure relative to the VAX 11/780—considered the standard system at 1 AIM), the AIM user load rating of the maximum user or task load where the system's performance becomes unacceptable, and the maximum throughput that the system attained in terms of jobs/minute. The curve of the system throughput versus the user load applied shows the capability of the system to sustain performance with increasing work load. AIM results are reported by AIM Technology in a four-page performance report.

6.11.2. Dhrystone

Originally it was created in 1984 in ADA as a synthetic mix of instructions modeled after a total of about 31 million instructions from real applications implemented in many languages. The Dhrystone is reported in MIPS (1757 Dhrystones = 1 MIP, based on DEC VAX 11/780). It was rewritten in C and posted in USENET, hence its popularity. The Dhrystone is a rather small piece of code and it fits into most small caches exaggerating their effectiveness. The Dhrystone is believed to qualify as a good indicator of efficiency in development work especially if done with C on UNIX. The Dhrystone is heavy on string handling and call/return functions. It does not emphasize I/O operations, floating point, or system calls.

6.11.3. Whetstone

The oldest CPU benchmark, originally published in 1976 in Algol and subsequently converted to FORTRAN, the Whetstone is a synthetic mix of elementary Whetstone instructions. Whetstone instructions are modeled using statistics from about 1000 scientific and engineering applications. Whetstone is another small benchmark and may be prone to particular treatment by optimizing compilers. It is very sensitive to transcendental and trigonometric functions and very dependent on fast or add-on math coprocessor(s). Versions of this benchmark are usually run in single and double precision. Whetstones are expressed in MIPS and for years were used as an indicator of systems performance. With changes in system design that made subroutine calls less of a bottleneck, and compilers that can now optimize the Whetstone benchmark, it has fallen out of favor.

6.11.4. LINPACK

The LINPACK benchmark was developed at Argonne National Laboratory and has become one of the most widely used applications benchmarks for scientific and engineering environments. This benchmark consists of the solving of a 100 x 100 system of linear equations. It has single and double precision versions in rolled and unrolled versions. The benchmark is particularly sensitive to floating point computation. Systems with hardware floating point capability look best. It is easily vectorizable and therefore very dependent on the run-time libraries. LINPACK does not fit in cache(s) and therefore qualifies as a good memory benchmark. LINPACK is commonly used as the basis for MFLOPS (millions of floating point operations per second) ratings. LINPACK is a better predictor of performance of matrix structured algorithms rather than complete applications. LINPACK can be thought of as more of a practical limit rather than as an actual application performance predictor. LINPACK results tend to correlate reasonably well with real-world scientific performance.

6.11.5. MUSBUS

This test was designed at the Monash University in Australia. This benchmark involves a multiuser simulation. The workload is constituted by 11 UNIX commands and 5 programs. This benchmark is complete in that it tests CPU speed, C compiler efficiency and UNIX quality, file system performances and multiuser capabilities, disk throughput and memory management implementation.

6.11.6. TPC

Some interesting UNIX systems-based database performance testing suites have been developed over the last few years cooperatively by vendors and users. TPC stands for the Transaction Processing Council (TPC). TPC-A focuses mainly on transaction processing while TBC-B focuses on update intensive database services. The TPC-A is oriented toward real-time online terminal sessions, significant disk input and output, and moderate systems and application execution time and transaction integrity. TPC-B concentrates on the database server and on activities on that server. It involves only significant disk input and output, moderate systems and application time, and transaction integrity. TPC-C, the newest and most advanced TPC benchmark, simulates an online transaction processing environment that is based on a multiuser order entry application. The inventory is distributed across 10 warehouses, each of which has 10 districts. Each district has 3000 customers. The TPC requires vendors to report both TPC results in terms of transactions per second and information on the five-year total cost of hardware and software. From this a cost-per-transactions is calculated.

Competition in the UNIX systems market is so fierce that companies will do almost anything to improve their benchmark numbers in the price/performance stakes. Once they have gotten all the performance they think they can, they will look for ways to improve their price competitiveness. For its TPC-A and TPC-B benchmark tests for the RS/6000, IBM used Applied Digital Data Systems Inc. terminals and Digichannel terminal concentrators since they were cheaper than their own. This sort of data is all public and contained in the TPC submissions vendors must make to the TPPC. The Transaction Processing Council can be reached in San Jose, California at (408) 295-8894.

6.11.7. SPECmarks

SPEC is a nonprofit organization of over 21 manufacturing companies. Members have cooperated to develop standard benchmarks to measure system's compute and memory performance. The benchmarks are intended to measure acknowledged real-world applications rather than isolated components or traditional units of measure like MIPS or MFLOPS. SPEC first released the SPEC 1.0 in 1989.

SPEC benchmarks are developed by the System Performance Evaluation Cooperative, a nonprofit organization formed to develop benchmarks that measure system performance. The SPEC Release 1.0 measures compute performance and consists of a benchmark suite of tests with the GNU C compiler, Espressor, Spice 2g6, Doduc, NASA Ames Kernel, LISP Interpreter, Eqntott, Matrix3000, Fpppp, and Tomcatv. Three reporting formats are provided, the SPECmark—the geometric mean of the 10 SPEC ratios because is gives all the programs equal importance the SPECint, the geometric mean of the integer benchmarks, and SPECfp, the geometric mean of the floating point benchmarks. Individual benchmarks are in the public domain and generally available applications. SPEC ratings should be obtained from SPEC. SPECmarks are commonly presented now in place of MIPS or MFLOPS as a more legitimate measure of performance. SPEC publishes a newsletter and benchmark results for a number of different hardware configurations.

SPEC Newsletter is published quarterly. It costs $450 for 4 issues and one copy of the benchmark tape or $150 for 4 issues without the tape. For more information call (415) 792-3334 or contact the Systems Performance Evaluation Cooperative.

SPEC c/o Waterside Associates
Systems Performance Evaluation Cooperative
39510 Paseo Padre Parkway
Suite 350
Fremont, California 94538

Standard Performance Evaluation Corporation
Fairfax, VA
(703) 698-9600.

6.11.8. MIPS

Millions of instructions per second is the rate at which the central processing unit performs instructions of all types. This is a general measurement (not a benchmark test) with little actual consistency from one vendor to another. A MIP is based on performance relative to a VAX, and VAX is a CISC machine. RISC machines do not implement 80 percent of the CISC architecture instructions. Is this really a fair measure standard?

There are many other benchmarks such as CONFIG, UTAH, TOOLS, BYTE, SAXER, TEST C, DODUC, and BSD. The ultimate purchasing decisions should be based on testing a group of final-cut candidates in real-world environments. Published benchmarks may represent "snapshot" indicators of relative performance, but they are rarely an accurate representation of real-world applications.

We believe a new trend will develop over the next decade where the emphasis will shift from highest performance to highest level of proven functional integration. This reflects the fact that functionality, and in particular the ability of software to interoperate with other software running on a system or within a network, will be valued quite highly.

6.11.9. Neal Nelson Benchmarks

Neal Nelson benchmarks are multiuser benchmarks designed to emulate commercial environment. It measures time to complete scripts for variable numbers of users. It contains some questionable benchmarks, for example, using AWK to measure floating point. Neal Nelson is loosing popularity to AIM and SPEC. A major problem with the Neal Nelson benchmark is that it uses the AWK UNIX utility which is particularly inefficient compared to optimized C for floating point operations.

6.12.   HOW WILL OBJECT ORIENTATION FACILITATE OPEN SYSTEMS?

Object-Oriented technology—fact or fiction?

The proponents of object-oriented technology contend that once it is established, it will obsolete 90 percent of today's software engineering technology. James Martin has made a major investment in Versant Object Technology Corporation. Sun's Bill Joy has started a new company inside Sun called the Sun Aspen Small Works which is reportedly developing system software and application products that will reach the market in three to five years. Object World 1992 featured Microsoft, Borland International Inc., SunSoft Inc., Taligent, and NeXT Inc.

"Can the horse evolve into an automobile?"

Steve Jobs, in rhetorical response to a Microsoft
presentation on its object management strategy

What is Object-Oriented Technology?

Object orientation allows the building of software out of components instead of creating software monoliths that are difficult to modify and extend. This modularity changes the business dynamics for suppliers of these components. Application vendors are getting involved in setting standards, for example, in electronic mail, taking over some of the territory currently held by the operating system vendor. Cross-OS portability will become more and more common in software.

But interoperability has a flip side—interdependence. Foundation classes, those that provide basic objects, will likely take on some of the role the operating system plays currently as the defining platform. You can develop foundation classes without owning the operating system, but it's clear that every OS vendor will want to be in this game. Higher-level classes, such as database and communications classes to say nothing of application frameworks, will be designed to work across foundation classes (and operating systems).

Object orientation means that it will be easier to mix software from various sources. It is unlikely that a single vendor will dominate the market in the way Microsoft does in the PC market today. There will be market leaders, but the computer business will become more and more integrated into the business world. Everyone will buy and use computers, more and more firms will sell software as an adjunct to or vehicle for whatever product or service they sell. Value-add in computers is software, value-add in software will be applications, and application-specific market knowledge will drive differentiation in high-value applications.

Object orientation promises a technology that will help customers to acquire and assemble solutions from a fragmented supplier community. It is potentially the ideal technology to facilitate Open Systems. In the interim, any company that can prove its ability to assemble and customize available components—for example, perform systems integration, will have an opportunity to exploit the current market conditions.

CASE Interoperability Alliance

The charter of this alliance is to establish a common set of messages for communication between software development tools for the purposes of better integration. Frame, Interleaf, Cadre, IDE, Centerline, Visix, Softool, SunPro, SunSoft, and Digital Tools were among the vendors participating.

CASE interoperability is beneficial to ISVs to achieve a common messaging specification. It will allow end users and developers to take advantage of plug and play levels of integration. Software development requires the use of multiple combinations of tools. These tools exist in the marketplace today, but most of them do not communicate with each other. The process of getting information from one tool to the next during the software development process requires a fair amount of effort with data often having to be entered. With competing vendors, it is difficult to achieve coordination between them. What is required is a set of common messages that each class of tool can use when fitting into a software development environment.

SunSoft's Tooltalk and HP/Softbench are prominent capabilities in this area. Tooltalk uses object-based messaging, enabling developers to begin creating these next-generation integrated applications.

Even SGI, Sun's arch-enemy in the workstation market endorsed Tooltalk and planned to ship it on its Iris workstations. Sun lined up ISVs including Frame, Interleaf, Applix, Island Graphics, Visix, Softool, TeamOne, Procase, Digital Tools, CaseWare, and Silvaco. These vendors have formed the Case Interoperability Alliance for defining common messaging mechanisms between applications and publishing their formats in the "Case Interoperability Series." Other alliances have also formed in areas such as EDA, desktop publishing, and productivity tools.

Object-oriented technology

Object management is one of the most futuristic developments within the computer industry. Object management is a technology that requires collaboration and unified approaches be adopted between competitors for it to fulfill its promise. The Object Management Group (OMG) is chartered with producing a standard specification and supporting commercially available technology with object technology. These standards will mean faster development of exciting new applications for workstation and servers, such as shared whiteboards, compound documents, and integrated multimedia applications.

In early 1992, SunSoft and HP jointly proposed the "Distributed Object Management Facility" (DOMF) to the OMG in response to their request for technology entitled "Object Request Broker." NCR and Object Design also submitted a proposal and have since supported the SunSoft/HP proposal.

Sun Labs, the research arm of Sun Microsystems is working on a future object-oriented technology code named Spring. Spring is a collection of core object technology projects which Sun hopes will help catalyze the evolution of operating system and software development environments. Some of the work is already being incorporated in Sun and HP's joint development with the Object Management Group.

Object-oriented technology is the next software development paradigm. HP discovered the penalty to be paid for moving into a major new technology area too early with its object-oriented NewWave environment. It had to delay its introduction of a UNIX version of its technology until sufficient buy-in and momentum could be achieved. The Object Management Group and Sun also became partners with HP in the effort. Sun also agreed to incorporate significant new functionality in the UNIX version. One of the key enhancements will involve support for distributed objects, something that is not in the Windows PC version of the NewWave environment.

HP signed an agreement with Science Applications International Corp. to convert, distribute, and support the Motif-based Visual User Environment on the Sun SPARCstation. HP says the environment will support Open Look as well as Motif applications and traditional UNIX applications without modification. Sun machines were the first non-HP platforms on which the environment has been ported and made available. It is one of the components of the NewWave Computing strategy. HP also offers its OpenView network management server software, SoftBench software engineering integration framework and TaskBroker network optimiser on Sun machines.

6.13. NETWORKING STANDARDS—NFS AND DCE

Network interfaces have proliferated and span UNIX versions. Networking standards are extremely important for users. Communication interfaces are typically the most difficult part of a distributed application to debug and the one that users are the least willing to change. For this reason, communications tend to be quite persistent and stay around for a long time after the original environment for which they were defined has disappeared.

Some of the key UNIX networking standards are NFS, RFS, Ethernet, TCP/IP, Token Ring, Sockets, and Streams. This section mainly describes NFS and DCE. NFS is also described Chapter 5. See the glossary for definitions of these other terms.

6.13.1. RFS

RFS stands for the Remote File System. It was AT&T's original answer to NFS. It corrects certain shortcomings of NFS that are described in Chapter 5. RFS is used at comparatively few sites and is most popular with AT&T UNIX users and Regional Bell Operating Companies.

6.13.2. Sockets and Streams

Sockets and streams are two UNIX APIs for interprocess communication. Sockets defines a simple point-to-point connection. Streams is a more complex and flexible interface first introduced in UNIX System V3.2. Streams is most popular at SVR4 sites. Users who depend on streams tend to have applications that are dependent on it. Sockets versus streams takes on an almost religious significance (like window systems) with some programmers and users.

6.13.3. Ethernet and Token Ring

ANSI made both of these approaches standards despite the fact that they have overlapping functionality and represent disjoint protocols. There are numerous technical differences between the two in terms of architecture, response characteristics and the way they degrade under heavy load. Ethernet is the de facto standard for multivendor Open Systems interconnection. Token Ring is generally a PC and IBM environment.

6.13.4. NFS and DCE

At the present time, NFS is the de facto standard for distributed file systems and UNIX networking is the de facto standard for "remote" computing. A new consortia-backed standard known as DCE is receiving considerable attention these days as a possible successor to NFS.

The Open Software Foundation has developed the DCE specification for supporting applications interoperability and cooperative processing in distributed computing environments. The idea of computers sharing and cooperating is referred to as distributed computing. This idea is not new; the computer industry has been advancing this idea for some time.

With all the press on DCE it is actually difficult to find a simple explanation of what it really is. Indeed, an entire book has been recently published entitled, *Getting to know DCE*. DCE from OSF consists of a set of services, a distributed file system, and a global directory service. The core services it provides include remote procedure call, threads support, and directory and security services. What services are provided to customers depends on specifics of OSF's DCE OEMs or other companies whose products are compliant with OSF DCE specifications. Most vendors who are planning to offer DCE are licensing source code from OSF for redistribution on their proprietary architectures.

DCE was first announced by OSF in the second half of 1990. In early September of 1991, the first specification of DCE was released. OSF shipped DCE development kits to its OEMs in 1992. DCE expects to release a new version of the DCE specification in 1993 and it will be 1993 to 1995 before applications that support DCE begin to appear in any volume.

DEC faces significant challenges before it will find widespread acceptance and use. In planning its fit in a long-term architecture, it's important to understand what it can and can't do. DCE is a suite of services for a well-defined set of programming problems.

DCE will support only distributed applications, particularly those being developed for large multivendor environments. DCE services are for new DCE-compatible applications. DCE may make the most sense when functionality beyond NFS is needed and when applications are intended to run on 10 or more computers of different kinds (assuming DCE is available on these different types of systems) and that it is available for reasonable cost compared with alternate products (e.g. ONCT).

DCE does not single-handedly deliver application interoperability. It will not in and of itself make current applications interoperable. Applications will have to be developed to use DCE services. "Well-behaved" applications that adhere to the DCE specification should be able to be recompiled on different platforms that support DCE.

DCE does not provide network management capabilities. These are part of another OSF specification called DME, distributed management environment. DME lags behind DCE in terms of both standard specification definition and development.

As stated earlier, the idea of distributed computing isn't new. Sun

Microsystems' network file system was working on an estimated 4 million computers in 1992. DCE services will have to offer some level of compatibility with the current NFS de facto standard. In many ways, OSF's DCE is following Sun's strategy of making DCE not just for UNIX users but also for use on proprietary platforms.

OSF will license DCE technology to its OEMs, it is not in the business of selling to users. It will try to spread the acceptance and use of its specification into the software industry. DCE-compliant implementations will be sold by system and system software vendors. DCE will cost hundreds of dollars per PC or workstation and perhaps thousands of dollars for servers or other high-end systems.

DCE is an interesting example of a good story that makes the news and occupies a very prominent position in futures statements of major vendors. However, to date, only a few vendors have actually released products based on DCE such as Gradient Technology and Transarc. OSF's claim that the industry has committed to DCE is backed by its claim that 113 vendors have licensed it. Vendors like IBM and DEC do not actually have to license DCE in order to be compatible with the specification.

History would seem to indicate that not everyone who licenses technology actually brings it to market. History also shows that vendors have to position and manage existing products with new technologies like DCE. Transitioning their software partners and their customers from their existing architectures to a new architecture like DCE tends to take many years.

DCE and Middleware

Middleware is a relatively new buzzword that is used to describe a class of software that runs above the operating system and below the application. The simplicity of the concept obscures a complicated set of technical and commercial issues.

UNIX International has created a framework for distributed applications called Atlas. UNIX International has positioned Atlas as accepting DCE as one way of providing distributed computing services. NFS is another alternative within the Atlas framework. Compatibility issues between DEC and Atlas services still have to be worked out.

Putting DCE in Perspective

Within the UNIX community, application interoperability was initially accomplished through streams and sockets. Programmers had to write to this level of interface. Sun introduced NFS which eventually became the de facto standard for networking file services. It included the RPC or remote procedure call interface. The original RPC mechanism initially relied on BSD sockets for the transport layer. Sun, Netwise, and Novell then collaborated on the development of a transport independent RPC mechanism which could use streams or Novell SPX. Thus applications could be developed once and be used in environments supporting different transport layers.

Not only was the RPC mechanism used by programmers for network-intrinsic applications but it was also used in implementing UNIX utilties. DCE has some technical advantages when compared to NFS, namely it supports a cache file system, logging, and asynchronous RPC. Similar functionality is being added by SunSoft to NFS, which makes either the NFS RPC mechanism and the DCE mechanisms technically indistinguishable.

Just as the programming interface moved from sockets to RPCs, most of the state-of-the-art development in application interoperability now involves objects. The Common Request Broker Architecture is what most developers are really working on. RPCs are what people use today but within a few years will be largely passé. Its short technological life cycle together with its relatively high price as an add-on product creates some doubt as to DCE's long-term viability. DCE is intended to help with application interoperability in heterogeneous environments. It is not clear how fast DCE-based products will actually be supported. Finally, it is not clear whether DCE will become available and viable for the PC space.

TCP/IP Cooperative Challenges OSF's DCE

Growing out of Sun's NFS Connectathon compatibility testing, the ONC/NFS Development Cooperative formed in 1991 by software vendors who develop applications based around the public domain NFS specification and de facto industry standard. Sun's annual Connectathon has now become an annual trade show known as the Connectathon Interoperability show held annually in San Jose, California.

DCE is based on the old Apollo remote procedure call (RPC) technology which is incompatible with the NFS RPC. ONC/NFS environments dominate the industry today while DCE is a new amalgamation of some new and some old technologies. OSF created a storm of controversy in the industry when it originally ignored Sun's submission to its request for distributed computing technology leading many to question its motives. Using the NFS RPC mechanisms, a broad coalition of software vendors are creating applications allowing UNIX, MS-DOS, VAX/ VMS, OS/2, Windows, Macintosh, and even IBM mainframe users to share resources and create a distributed computing environment. Applications will include electronic mail systems, system backup software, database services, printer services, and other applications that will run across different hardware platforms using the de facto TCP/IP networking standard and other network transport protocols enabled by the transport independent RPC mechanisms developed by Sun, Novell, and Netwise. The Transport-Independent Remote Procedure Call interface, TI-RPC, combined with source code technology from Netwise, is part of the ONC RPC Application Toolkit announced by Sun in 1992. The platform enables software applications to run unmodified across a range of operating systems, hardware platforms and networks such as TCP/IP, OSI and Netware's IPX/SPX. Novell, Borland, Lotus, and AST Research have endorsed the approach.

The cooperative is building on a standard rather than attempting to build another one. These are applications being built entirely on public domain software.

The Cooperative is not a standards-making body, nor a formal entity. They have no logo, no standing committees, no formal corporate entity. Sun has no direct involvement in this group of software companies. The five founding companies include TGV Inc., Interlink Computer Sciences Inc., InterCon Systems Corp., FTP Software Inc., and Beame and Whiteside Software.

A reference port of each application will be developed and published along with protocol specifications and an application programming interface for developers. The members of the cooperative will then incorporate the base technology into their products which will be targeted at UNIX, PC, and Mac users.

USL and DCE

USL was still looking to formulate an agreement with OSF for DCE on SVR4 when a small Massachusetts company called Gradient announced such a capability. One of the problems that occurred between OSF and USL in coming to terms on an agreement for DCE was the fact the OSF had apparently never considered the need for a master distributor agreement with USL.

While USL seemed to be interested in offering a productized version of DCE it may all be for naught. For all the marketing hype behind DCE, users may find the bill for DCE interoperability excessive by comparison to ONC/NFS.

6.14. OTHER OPEN SYSTEMS AND STANDARD GROUPS AND CONSORTIA

Corporation for Open Systems (COS). The Corporation for Open Systems is an industry group funded by parties interested in participating in Open Systems Interconnect. OSI is being developed by ISO/IEC JTC 1 and virtually every standards organization is participating in the effort. The orginal purpose of COS was to rally support for the standard by promoting the use of OSI standards. COS then moved into the certification and conformance testing arena.

SPARC International. SPARC International, apparently taking a leaf out of 88open's book is creating a class of shrinkwrapped software that will run on SPARC machines regardless of architectural distinctions. The effort will propagate the newly cast SCD 2.0 as the specification software houses and end users write to. Documentation, tools, and white papers have been packaged onto a CD-ROM called the Developer's Tool-Chest. Software written to ToolChest will be able to bypass costly compliance testing on all the various SPARC boxes. None of the software created under ToolChest can be optimized for any particular SPARC configuration without forfeiting compliance. Compliant software will be branded.

UNIX Business Association of Japan. The UNIX Business Association was formed in Toyko, initially consisting of over 73 companies, mainly small to medium-sized software houses involved in application development. The group also includes UNIX International and hardware vendors such as Sun, HP, and Omron Corp. The organizers of this group came out of the research arm of the Personal Computer Software Association. The main function of this group is to serve as a forum for exchange of information, for the promotion of Open System applications developed by members, joint marketing, training of UNIX staff, lobbying the Japanese government, and market surveys.

6.15. MANAGING CHANGE THROUGH STANDARDS

It may be easier to write software with portability in mind than to re-architect sophisticated systems that already exist. This is perhaps the main reason that many experts in the UNIX industry believe that we will see, and indeed are already seeing, new applications written to standards with both the development environment and the deployment environment in mind. Standardizing the UNIX environment in the development environment translates to benefits as the application is moved into production and makes business sense. UNIX and standards normally associated with UNIX are important not only to the developers but also, ultimately, to the user community.

To the novice, standards seem like a sort of holy scripture, but to the true professional in computer science, they are more of a reflection of an agreed-upon interface and specification by the parties involved. Standards are snapshots in time. They are usually living documents.

Standards that are not established by formal bodies such as IEEE or ISO are valid only to the extent of their acceptance in the open market. In other words, de facto standards are usually reflected by the volume of real buyers in the market putting money down on what they believe in.

Open Applications Lag a Decade Behind Open Systems

The definition of standard software components lags as much as a decade behind the definition of standards in hardware and lower-level system platform standards. Standards in the area of graphical user interface are still quite immature, for example.

Like other standards, the goal of software standards are to increase vendor independence on any single vendor, increase the portability of software and solution components between environments supported by different vendors, increase interoperability allowing applications to share data and communicate with each other.

Just as memory, disks, and other hardware components have plug and play compatibility with hardware systems, plug and play software standards also implies greater interchangeability of parts. Software is much more difficult and does not lend itself as readily as hardware. This is due not only to the technological complexity of software but also to the considerably more diverse nature of the supply side of the software industry. The best examples of software standards are found in the areas of operating systems and networking software.

How Standards Will Change

The purpose of interface standards is to protect the rest of the system from a change in one of the functional layers of the system. Evolution occurs and occurs differently at each layer. Independent evolution of these components would be impossible without standards.

Much of the in-house developed applications software that is in use today is not based on any standards. Such software is therefore highly susceptible to any change in underlying platforms such as database, networking, operating systems, and even hardware.

The challenge in managing change lies in understanding how to apply the relevant standards, how to assess how well the standards are defined and developing an understanding of how the standards will evolve.

The most significant change in standards will represent a shift toward increased relevance to end users. We believe there will be a gradual shift in industry standards intended to increase their relevance for the end-user community. Many of the standards today tend to focus on the way suppliers of systems or software implement their products. Of course, this has an impact on the end-users community, but the shift we envision is different.

Companies do not want computing, like health care costs, to become a large component of their expense base. And yet, information technology and its integration within the enterprise and providing external reach for interenterprise are bound to increase the costs associated with computers, applications make/buy, systems and network administration, and reskilling and training the people who work with computers, be they managers, knowledge workers, end users, or programmers.

Companies will have to develop information architectures to manage all this change. These information architectures will have to incorporate standards prominently. Large investments will be made as much on the predictable direction technology is going as on what it can do at the moment of purchase. But the standards are themselves changing. Which standards should customers watch and how will it help them manage change?

X/Open's branding represents the Open Systems' version of the seal of approval of Underwriters Laboratories (UL). When X/Open launched XPG3, it was 18 months before tested and compliant systems were available. X/Open branded solutions were registered for both proprietary systems and UNIX. X/Open has devised a process which illustrates the evolutionary nature through which they will manage change in terms of the introduction of new components in XPG4 which remain compliant with XPG3. For XPG4 products to be branded, they must pass the VSX4 test suite comprised of over 7500 conformance tests. The XPG profiles provide the vital link between standards and the practical procurement of Open Systems technology. The fact that X/Open and XPG3/XPG4 are independent of any particular technology or single vendor is very important in achieving Open Systems.

ISO—Watch This Spot

European-originated standards like OSI have not achieved projections. But the ISO, which is not exclusively European, should not be underestimated. Europe represents a significant market opportunity. ISO standards represent a key linchpin in unifying and building this common market. ISO quality standards, and particularly quality standards in information technology we believe will be led by the Europeans.

When Is a Standard Relevant? (Look at Volume and Practical Relevance)

With so much complexity and news in the press about standards, and with new technologies and products invariably being introduced as "the new standard for . . . ." users have to make determinations about the relevance of standards.

Scott McNeally said, "Standards without volume are meaningless." But volume (read installed base) versus volume that is projected has to do with pain versus gain. For example, OSI is still not taking off—in volume terms, that doesn't make it meaningless, but it surely implies that there is more pain than gain in the migration to OSI.

We believe that de jure and de facto standards which evolve will have the most practicality to users. Examples include the success of ANSI C and FIPS specifications in government procurements—especially in the area of security for de jure standards (orange book) and SPX/IPX, SNA, TCP/IP, ONC/NFS as examples of de facto networking standards. Users have to migrate from where they are today to where they want to be. Whole new "standards" that don't plug and play with what is accepted as standard practice may be doomed to failure despite the marketing prowess of the suppliers pushing the standard.

POSIX has now reached the status of the 10 commandments—but it is almost meaningless with OpenVMS, MPE-IX, and POSIX supported by IBM and Microsoft. POSIX has a long way to go before it can deliver on its promise of applications portability.

Standards and vendor value add their relevance to customers' environments. Figure 6.2 depicts the layering of standards that would seem to be emerging from the end user's perspective. At the base of the standards profile are a group of base standards including those shown. Above this base, there are a set of de facto standards that are supported because they are so prevalent. On top of these are the proprietary standards representing vendor value add.

The past few years has seen some significant changes in the world of Open Systems standards.

- Standards are only now being recognized as product attributes. They are gradually becoming a factor in the procurement of products and

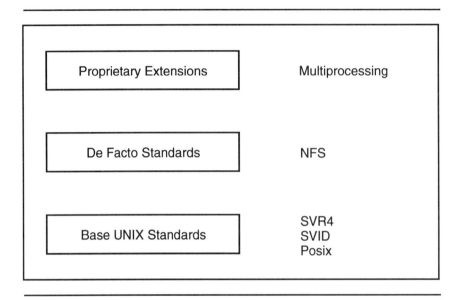

Figure 6.2.   Simple applications portability profile.

services and this in the case of commercial companies. Users see the benefits in using standards.

- Standards are getting away from being technical issues and are finally becoming part of the business discussion. Companies faced with complex migrations from their existing information systems are making the move because of their confidence in the power of standards. If they didn't believe in the power of standards, they wouldn't be changing in the first place.
- End users are finally getting active in terms of participating in the standards process. They are finally taking an active role that is projected to match that of the supply side of the industry. End user organizations want to be informed and want to take a more active role in driving standards. The most intense interests are coming from industries where standards are an important factor in driving change and market acceptance. Industries such as telecommunications, aerospace, manufacturing, petroleum, and of course government are all extremely proactive in standards.
- The idea of "self-certification" is going out. There is more push for formal verification. Some groups that set standards are also looking at verification and compliance testing as a new revenue source. For the supply side of the industry, certification can be very costly.

GOSIP certification testing for one configuration can cost $250,000—and for small companies and ISV, some certification testing is already creating barriers to entry.
- Standards in IT are gaining greater acceptance. This is particularly true in Europe with the demands of EC92.
- Finally, the level of confusion is growing about standards. With so much noise in the system, many users are looking for anything that is simple and easy to get their arms around. As standards become a business issue and are elevated to a higher plain of discussion, this trend toward viewing standards somewhat simplistically can be counterproductive.

The world of computer standards is clouded and confused even for the experts. There are 10,000 ISO standards, and some 4,000 of them in the area of information technology. There is very little integration between standards—making them all the more complex.

Standards are now coming ahead of innovation. Usually standards lag behind technology, but now a new model seems to be developing where standards are developed even before there are reference implementations. With standards agreed, vendors see it as "safe" to invest in implementations.

How to Manage Changing Standards

Users are demanding product implementations, but in standards committees, the emphasis is on interface specifications—not product implementations. If you have a product, and it becomes a standard, it creates disadvantages for other possible vendors of competing products based on that standard.

Users See Standards Are Moving too Slowly

Users see standards as giving them multivendor compatibility. Are products only available from a single vendor risky? Unfortunately, if you look at the press, the front page of the industry trade magazines is full of coverage about standards. It is clear that within the computer industry, the losers are people who didn't see change coming and get control. The winners are companies who set the standards—usually the de facto standards—anticipated change and were there with the implementation ahead of the market.

If you only read the press, you get a warped view of just who the agents of change really are. The press covers OSF and DCE, Microsoft and NT, Intel and Pentium . . . all examples of monopolistic strategies. Each of these companies is focused on particular implementations of standards. Those who adhere to the standard are also forced to OEM these companies products. True standards like X windows, UNIX SVR4, networking specifications like FDDI are all taking back seat in the press.

These traditional standards simply aren't as exciting. With the commercialization of standards, a company's marketing rhetoric seems to be all that some companies need to hear

Users are revolting. Large companies buy 10 of anything and things just don't work together. Many companies expect standards to solve this problem and are moving into the standards process and becoming agents of change. Standards need to be viewed as base building blocks on which solutions can be layered. In the future, companies will increasingly use standards and compliance as a filter to determine how to shortlist prospective suppliers. Attention to standards is most notable in companies that are moving toward an enterprisewide information architecture.

Standards represent different things to different people. There is not unanimity on an overall architecture for standards. There is disagreement between organizations and individual rationales and goals for participation in the standards process. There is a great deal of confusion about standards only exacerbated by the use of standards as a marketing tool. This is often reflected in the popular press making it all the more difficult for IT users to get a handle on things.

There is no unified body of knowledge and indeed no formal program for users and IT professionals to stay on top of what is happening in the world of IT standards. Only the larger or highly specialized companies who can afford it actually participate in the standards process. As previously described, this is especially true of users who concentrate in a given industry and find that the benefits of cooperation outweigh the potential conflicts. In some industries and specific applications areas, IT is used to build barriers to entry. Where such a strategy exists, it is often impossible for companies to disclose their strategies.

For the IT user community in general, standards currently play an important role, but the depth of understanding of standards and the process of standardization is low. This drives many companies to simply seek out what appears to be a "standard" because they read enough about something in the popular press or they want to believe their vendor's sales and marketing rhetoric.

It is easy to be suckered into believing what companies say, to placing trust in some new industry direction through a sort of IT "herding instinct," and to simply make a decision that something is a standard and will be a standard for their company without any real depth of understanding. Users can hardly be faulted for this since the world of standards is so complex, clouded, and confused.

So how can you manage change through standards? First you have to make an investment in understanding them. If you have read this chapter you have hopefully begun to demystify this complex area. Here are a few suggestions of practical steps you can take from here.

1. Do a little research on new books and literature in this area. Many people understand the general confusion that is out there and see it as a business opportunity. We expect to not only see new books in this area but information coming out of conferences and user groups that is being developed by the MIS community itself.

    In particular, look to some of the user groups within the standards organizations and see what they may have. X/Open, ANSI, UniForum, IEEE, ISO, CCITT can be approached by users. You can request overview information as well as information on specific technical working committees.

    Other standards bodies include the following:

    ECMA—European Computer Manufacturers Association

    CEN and CENELEC—European telecommunications bodies

    AFNOR—Association Francaise de Normilisation

    JISC—The Japanese Industrial Standards Committee

    BSI—The British Standards Institute

2. Beware of monopolistic standards. Here is how you can tell a monopolistic standard when you see it:

    The standards is really an implementation and that implementation is controlled by one vendor or consortium. If there aren't multiple implementations available from different companies, then somebody has a monopoly on the implementation. Usually, there is a lockin or some hidden cost in these situations.

    If there isn't a clear interface specification that is freely available, you should wonder just how "standard" something that has undocumented specifications can be.

    If there is a significant upfront licensing cost for suppliers who want to support the standard, then you have to evaluate just how open the standards process really is. The profit motivation behind the standard might be a hint of a monopoly.

A standard without multiple reference implementations is a sure sign of a monopoly. "Multiple" should not mean one or two but many reference implementations.

Beware of standards that emerge from predominantly vendor sponsored and controlled consortia. These standards can come close to violating the spirit of antitrust regulations. When a group of vendors decides to collectively endorse the implementation of a product—you are in oligopoly territory—monopoly with a slightly different spin. A test is to examine how the consortia is funded, how much users have a say in the process and whether the standards process is in fact being leveraged for a hidden profit, for control, or for disguised competitive reasons.

3. Don't believe everything you read in the popular press. There are ample examples of IT standards, especially those that are built around vendor dominated consortia, which come out with a bang— and go out with a whimper. Take a little time to study failed attempts at standards like ACE. It's amazing how short the memory can be. Remember that companies are now using standards more than ever as a marketing tool. If they can capitalize on the confusion and encourage an "IT lemming effect" then they will usually get some unknowing companies to walk right off the end of the cliff. Just because you read alot about an industry standard for example doesn't mean it is real.

4. A technology that appears to be multivendor, that is available on a number of platforms, does not necessarily make it open or standard.

Open Systems and Information Architectures in Transition

Information Is the Competitive Battleground of the Future. Whether the existing information is broken, or it just can't deliver what the organization needs, or it falls short of meeting user expectations, every organization sees the issues from a slightly different angle.

Existing information systems have normally been built an application at a time, writing usually within the context of a division or self-contained unit within the company. There has been no real reason to consider the unifying architecture overall, other than perhaps in the area of communications. It is ironic that we call our business systems "management information systems," when they are most likely supporting very basic operational needs like accounting or order processing and are more a source of frustration to management, failing to support their needs.

7.1. BARRIERS TO CHANGE

Existing systems can be roadblocks to change. It's not just the existing information systems alone that creates barriers to change. The organization can be locked into predetermined structures and procedures related to the existing generation of information systems that make change difficult. For example, departmental systems that may have proliferated without much centralized control, may be highly entrenched. Change in information systems must often be accompanied by change in organization.

The role existing systems play in decision making and careful analysis of how systems support information distribution is critical to understand where bottlenecks exist or may arise in the future. The building blocks of corporate strategy are not products and markets but business practices. Success depends on transforming key processes into strategic capabilities that provide superior value to the customer. The central focus on an information strategy should be to support the business strategy. Computer decisions should relate back to the central problems the business faces. Providing the information needed to implement the business strategy is the fundamental reason for information systems.

7.2.   A SURVIVAL GUIDE FOR "NEW AGE" MIS

Planning, designing, and implementing information systems is an exercise in decision making at many levels within an organization. Decisions are made to include or exclude certain options, and different decisions determine certain ways of solving a particular problem. It only makes sense that the process through which information systems are evaluated and purchased be treated as a series of decision points, each of which contributes to the success of a given project.

Those involved in the decision process include upper-level general and IS management as well as IS staff with responsibility for specific functions such as system design and development and operations. Upper-level management needs to make business decisions and provide guidelines for the organization including both the end-user organization and the IS department. Information systems design staff lay out the system in a general sense. With the help of the development staff, the layout often includes selecting hardware and software to be used in the project. System designers actually build the system. Installation and maintenance staff are then responsible for getting the systems implemented. This usually includes the training of end users and defining the ongoing maintenance of the system. Different levels of the organization therefore have different types of concerns.

Business requirements should always drive computing decisions. Upper-level management should state its goals and needs in noncomputing terms. It should clearly state in business terms why it wants to do it and what bottom-line return it expects from any new IS project. General management should make clear, in business terms, how it sees IS as helping to meet its business goals. For example, the focus may be on "faster access to information," "ability to better integrate and analyze disparate pieces of information," or "better communications between remote offices." General management should commit to a maximum cost figure for each project and provide a target date by which the project should be implemented. Such cost and target date objectives should include both IS and non-IS aspects, computing resources and personnel resources, from development and through to production and ongoing maintenance.

Obviously there are limits to what an information system will do relative to what is expected bottom-line by general management. General management goals may or may not be achievable based on the estimates of the IS department or whatever group may take responsibility for the design and implementation of a new system. Such estimates come later in the process and are constrained by the general limits set by general management. IS projects without these kinds of business-oriented goals objectives and limits often fail for lack of support as real costs go beyond general management's ability or willingness to meet those costs.

As computing becomes more integrated with the business, more groups get involved with computing. The decision as to who will build and support a particular piece of the information system, a question that in the past usually had a single clear answer, "MIS," is now more complicated. Most organizations realize that groups outside MIS must now perform functions once thought to be the exclusive domain of MIS. With increasing ease of use and ease of system administration, end users can perform IS tasks with considerable competence. With network management and remote system administration, it is also possible for MIS to continue to support such distributed systems. An excellent example is found in the area of file services where, in most organizations, pockets of end users turned to local area networking to obtain services and applications that central computing facilities were unable or unwilling to provide for whatever reasons. Today, end users' organizations may actually have more experience in dealing with aspects of a LAN-based work group solution than does the central IS staff.

Stratification of Decision Points

Below we summarize one possible method for stratifying decision points. In this example, five groups are identified, and then key questions are developed within each area.

Upper-level general management
— What are the business requirements?
— What are the key benefits expected?
— What are the budgetary constraints?

— What are the personnel constraints?

Upper-level general and IS management

— Who are the users and how will they benefit?
— Who should undertake the development?
— Who will own the maintenance?
— How will the project be funded?
— How will the quality of the project be monitored and measured?

System design and development and upper-level IS management

— What are the projected requirements for capacity, performance and so on?
— What level of security and management are required?
— What are the project's estimated component costs and benefits?
— How much should be spent on the project?
— What are the requirements for disaster recovery?

System design and development

— What are the applications platform requirements?
— Will current hardware or applications be involved?
— What alternatives exist (applications make versus buy)?
— What alternatives exist (current systems versus newer technology)?
— What are the detailed functional requirements for services (e.g., database, file services, and so on)?

System design, development, and operations management

— How will files and data be structured?
— How will data and processing be distributed?
— What are the operational considerations, for example, backup?
— Who will install and maintain the system/network?
— What training is required?

Today's task of deciding who will design and implement systems is much different from the traditional decision process in organizations that have IS organizations. Concerns such as technical knowledge, fiscal responsibility, ownership, and trust are involved. The more mission-critical the project—such as supporting primary data entry and data processing—the more likely it will heavily involve a central IS organization. Other applications (e.g., providing access to secondary or downloaded data) will make it more likely the local IS staff or end-user organization will be in design and implementation.

Is Your Technology in Control or Are You?

Too often the business strategy is lost among relatively unimportant but numerous and complex issues of technology. Without an Information Architecture, the absence of strategy it's easy for companies to bounce back and forth with technological issues, not business strategy and process taking center stage.

What impact should technological change have on your information strategy? Some experts suggest it should have no impact. Technology provides a set of alternatives through which the information strategy is implemented. Technology direction is often designed to solve the problems of MIS itself, not the problems within the organization as a whole.

Is Your Vendor in Control or Are You?

Companies with proprietary environments are more likely to make decisions guided by their vendors. At an extreme this is like abdicating responsibility to the vendor. I once had a conversation with a senior MIS executive who told me: "If I use your systems and it fails, I will get fired. If I use IBM and I fail, my management will understand that the job couldn't be done." Companies realize they don't want to be at the mercy of their vendor. They also realize they have a continuous problem analyzing their systems and the vendors' offerings. Many mainframe customers turn to research companies like the Gartner group to help them stay on top of the vendors' strategies and changes that could impact their systems. In UNIX and Open Systems, companies will need to rely on numerous sources of information to stay current. System vendors, VARS, software suppliers, integraters, consultants, and so forth will all be important sources of information.

No organization is exempt from change. Companies are looking for ways to gain more control over their business operations. By organizing independent business functions, different forms of control can be exerted. These business units can receive more investments and be permitted to grow at their natural pace, or they can be spun off during times of corporate consolidation. Independent, strategic business units are becoming the norm.

This change is especially evident in larger organizations. The change is driven by a need to improve time to market. Companies need to be able to react quickly to market changes and opportunities. The complexity of a large organization's decision-making process within the corporate structure is perhaps one of the more detrimental consequences of large or poorly structured corporations.

Decisions are made through layers of management. Top-down decision making works best when things change slowly. Like turning around a large boat, it takes time for decisions made at the top to work their way to the bottom of the organization. Hard information about business transactions and financial performance take a long time to generate and compile. The upper levels of management of most corporations do not know what is happening until weeks or months after the fact. This time lag makes it difficult to react to fast-changing events.

Basic Business-Related Questions

1. What are your longer-term business objectives?
    The answers to this question and the way the organization will measure its achievement of these objectives are fundamental to the IS strategy.
2. What are the priority areas for strategic planning?
    You just can't do everything at once. You have to solve the problems by breaking them down into manageable projects. Your organization can only accommodate so much change. You have to demonstrate results. You have to gain management agreement about where you place your resources.
3. What are the needs of the organization for information?
    The point of this question is to ask how better information handling can improve business process and the decision-making processes.
4. How much change can your organization assimilate?
    This question should be asked at two levels. The first concerns how quickly the new systems can be implemented. This might depend on the user organization's ability to assimilate the change. The second issue concerns the ability of the organization to react to the changes made possible by information systems.

Computers can outstrip an organization's ability to deal with change. For example, in manufacturing, resource planning may be run weekly generating work orders for the factory. It could be run daily or even hourly, but this wouldn't make sense. It would be like giving someone directions to do something and just as they get started telling them to do something else. The real benefits of change come from making changes that combine new information processing with new business processing. This type of comprehensive change may require a dramatic shift in the way information management decisions are made.

Companies try to close the gap and improve response times by flattening the organization—eliminating layers of management. This pushes decision making down. This sort of organization transition is not well supported by traditional monolithic centralized mainframe-oriented data processing. A networked, distributive data processing architecture that puts power where the decisions are made represents a fundamental change in companies that are mainframe based.

Downsizing describes the process of restructuring a corporation to meet its competitive challenges. Like the organizational restructuring of an organization, the restructuring of data processing resources is becoming a competitive issue. Downsizing means moving an organization away from a dependency on centralized corporate mainframe for transaction processing. As the pace of change increases, the layers of management and business processes have to change to meet the needs of the business. Layers of management usually have to be eliminated and a move to a more decentralized information systems model is required. But there are serious risks in making these types of changes without a clear strategy and plan.

7.3.   THE "DOMINO EFFECT" IN DOWNSIZING

What happens when an application is taken off a mainframe? The business unit that was using the mainframe may no longer be billable by MIS for the time, facilities, cost of personnel, and so forth associated with their mainframe use. But someone still has to pay for the mainframe. Those who remain on the mainframe may experience an inflation in their data processing costs. The internal politics of making a change can easily spark interdivisional discord. In many companies, divisions planning to make such a move keep it quiet until it is a fait accompli. Other divisions can be blindsided by unplanned increases in the cost of data processing as the base of billable applications in the data center shrinks. The domino effect occurs as divisional executives who are using the mainframe start wondering what will happen if they are the last out the door. Smart executives would just as soon be first out the door. Any corporation that discourages profit centers from reducing their controllable costs dooms the entire organization.

As organizations try to adjust to the increasing pace of change, they frequently discover that the existing generation of systems act as a roadblock to that change. Information systems can lock an organization into predetermined structures and procedures that can handicap the organization and limit its ability to respond to competitive threats or meet market opportunities. This can be especially true in organizations that try to delegate control to strategic business units, improve quality and productivity by giving people more decision-making responsibility. Existing systems can be bottlenecks in developing and deploying applications and distributing information that these people require to make decisions. Independent business units are the norm in corporations today. Even divisions in large corporations are expected to act like independent business units. Corporations realize that the traditional large company structures simply can't respond to the pace of change in the market. By flattening the organization, the goal is to shorten the amount of time required for decision making. Just as the organizational hierarchy of the corporation is flattened, so is the hierarchy of information systems. Networking is making this feasible. In the future, the network will become the mainframe—the enterprise computing resource.

Downsizing means moving mission-critical applications off the centralized mainframe and distributing them throughout the company. Many companies saw the PC as a possible answer. PCs have proliferated tremendously, but the focus has been on the wrong type of software if the goal was to achieve the goal of effective distributed computing. The real problem here is software.

The proliferation of PCs and computer systems in general has aggravated the problems of information flow within large corporations. Distributed computer power in the form of PCs, workstations, and minicomputers provide computer power, but if the data in them is disconnected from the flow of information through the company, they can actually exacerbate the problems. Increased compute power, availability of applications, sophisticated networking technology do not necessarily translate to "better" information for the organization.

PCs give individuals tools for personal productivity: word processing, spreadsheets, database tools, and so forth. These systems store information in their own individual system. They replace typewriters, calculators, file cabinets—not mainframes. They are great for creating reports and doing analysis, but they are rarely tied into data processing based on information flow from business activity.

The real value of documents and analysis depends on its information content. Personal workstations can create nice looking reports quickly but rarely have been integrated with systems which control the main flow of information and real work in the business.

Personal workstations need an adequate flow of information in order to increase the information content of documents or analysis performed on them. Activity-based information like sales orders or shipment data usually comes out of the information system as data processing reports. It is not unusual for this data to be re-entered manually from computer printouts.

Just connecting PCs in a network doesn't solve the problem either. The applications available on PCs can make the data look prettier and the reports more graphical, but this isn't real value add. Using a PC to emulate the host application software user interface might create a much easier-to-use interface for the user, but it suffers because nothing is really changing in the rigid centralized data processing environment. The need is to connect the document-processing capabilities of the personal workstation together with the transaction-processing capabilities of transaction-specific information systems.

Minicomputers in the 70s and 80s provided a much less expensive alternative to transaction processing, especially in terms of system and software initial costs and maintenance costs. There quickly developed a wealth of transaction-processing software. This software was no more flexible than traditional mainframe software, and because these minicomputers were usually implemented as standalone systems, an information fragmentation problem was created. Applications didn't share data, nor was the data on the system well maintained or managed especially by comparison to the mainframe environment. Connectivity has traditionally been an add-on to minicomputers rather than something built in. Applications interoperability across the communications interfaces were restricted to file transfer and terminal emulation.

In companies with mainframe computers, minicomputers were purchased because they provided access and control of information. This same sort of functionality was only available on mainframes at much higher cost. The mainframe transaction processing applications environment was also more restricted in the kind of access and control of information it offered the users. The use of minicomputers resulted in a number of separate flows of vital information all disconnected from one another. When these decentralized systems were used for transaction processing or consolidation of information from transaction processing, the information managed, like the data on PCs, became disconnected from the rest of the organization and the flow of other business information. These minicomputer systems often became islands of information and were trapped within certain levels of the organization.

The greater the number of systems in a corporation, the higher the potential for database proliferation and fragmentation. Redundant databases proliferates incorrect information. People in different parts of the organization don't communicate changes, so databases get out of synchronization.

7.4. TRANSITIONING FROM MAINFRAMES TO UNIX

The transition of mainframes to Open Systems is a hot topic of industry conversation. But what is really going on? Is there evidence that companies are actually unplugging mainframes and moving to UNIX-based systems? While there are a number of well-publicized examples who have made this switch, it would seem that there is much more going on here.

The reduction in mainframes is due to many factors. Companies are consolidating their data center operations. Companies are downsizing and moving applications off their mainframes to other proprietary computer architectures such as the AS/400s, DEC VAX/VMS, as well as other UNIX-based alternatives. UNIX suppliers such as Pyramid Technology Corp. and Sequent Computer Systems have had some success among large IBM users, but there is little evidence of a string of migrations following these wins. Mainframe suppliers other than IBM, such as Unisys, ICL, and others would seem to be more vulnerable than IBM in terms of its mainframe business downsizing to UNIX and Open Systems.

While statistics might suggest that it will be years before UNIX-based systems displace mainframes in running mission-critical applications in large corporations where IBM mainframes have previously been used, this does not mean that most corporations are not interested in UNIX. UNIX is especially interesting for new and distributed applications. Many companies seem to be planning to maintain certain of their core business systems on mainframes but surround these mainframes with "report server" architectures. Data entry, decision support, and other applications will be migrated off the mainframe. Such a surround strategy will facilitate the eventual replacement of the mainframe.

7.5.   THE CHANGING ROLE OF MIS

The traditional role of MIS must evolve as a company moves to an Open Systems strategy.

- More attention to the competitive market
- Plan to reduce support and maintenance through the use of standard operating systems and use of common tools and utilities (languages, database system, etc.)
- More outsourcing of applications
- More decentralization
- New skills development and acquisition
- More systems integration
- More emphasis on network management
- Use of standards to ease integration burdens
- Shrinking in size

- Smaller project teams
- Less dependency on outside suppliers

Resistance to change

- Financial
- Short-term costs will be higher; long-term costs may also be higher. The difference depends on whether the information systems improve the bottom-line of the business.

As Richard Foster writes:

"The major cultural difficulty in managing through technological discontinuities is making skill transitions. What any company amounts to, no matter how large its asset base, is the skill of its people. If that skill base is rendered useless, if other skills turn out to be more relevant, then management faces a very difficult problem because it takes so long to fix. You can't just change people's skills overnight . . . Anticipation is the key. A company has to start early. The less time it has, the more money it will have to spend to accomplish the transition."

Especially in applications re-engineering or downsizing programs, companies should expect some problems with both MIS personnel and with users.

7.6.   HOW DOES THE IS ORGANIZATION MANAGE THE CHANGE TO NEW MODELS OF INFORMATION SYSTEMS?

As Information technology evolves toward client-server, Open Systems, distributed computing, what are the implications of managing the change?

Budgets will reflect major shifts in hardware, software, and services.

Budget allocation and charge-back policy will shift toward decentralization. New expense alignments and tradeoffs will have to be made.

Business re-engineering will cause significant restructuring of the business policies and practices. Business modeling will become critically important to executive decision making. The work process will become highly integrated with systems delivery.

Architecture will require detailed internal and external plans that map out transitions and migrations with contingencies.

The organization and its users skills will have to be carefully factored into the introduction of new technologies. Outsourcing may be required. Application acquisition "make buy" decisions will shift to buy whenever possible.

New staff will be required with new responsibilities as decentralization occurs, and users become more literate and understanding.

Vendors will become strategic partners, a perspective of the strategy and ability/commitment of vendors to deliver against their promises will be a critical factor in qualification and acquisition.

How do you determine vendor neutrality? One way is through frameworks of standards that link the applications development to the applications deployment.

Information systems frameworks are evolutionary processes that start with today's products, processes, and standards, and evolve them overtime by the transition to and addition of new products, processes, and standards.

7.7.   THE IMPACT OF OPEN SYSTEMS ON INFORMATION ARCHITECTURE

One of the most frustrating things to many senior executives is the ongoing uncomfortable feeling that the money they're pouring into computers isn't being well spent and that somehow there should be "a better way." Interestingly, they're right on both counts. Yes, large amounts of money are being wasted. Yes, there is a better way.

A recent global study showed that "75 percent of all systems development undertaken was never completed or, if completed, not used." This pervasive problem with developing and installing new computer-based systems is one of management's most common complaints when discussing their companies' computer-related expenses.

Remarkably, this problem is nothing new. It's been with us almost since the very beginning of the use of computers in general business activities in the early 1960s, almost 30 years ago. In the following we provide answers to the two obvious questions: "Why is this the case?" and "What can be done about it?"

Fundamentally, the "Why" has, as described below, two answers: poor planning and closed systems. Many firms have good plans and already recognize the value of Open Systems. Those that do should find the following useful as a sanity check and (hopefully) as a modest addition to what they already know about these important topics. Those other firms that suspect they could be doing better, should find the following useful as a test of their suspicions and as a guide to improvement.

7.7.1. Regarding Poor Planning

From virtually the very beginning of the use of modern electronic digital computers, people have all too frequently avoided even the most basic forms of good planning. If ever there was a tool where the old saying "Measure twice and cut once" applied, the computer is it. The absolute essential element of good computer planning is a realistic Information Architecture. In essence, this is a fairly simple concept—basically a clear and concise statement of a company's information delivery mechanism as it is desired to be, starting with the computer and telecommunications network up through the data delivery facility, then through the "applications," and ultimately to the information user.

The reason for having an Information Architecture is equally simple since an Information Architecture provides—as nothing else does as well—an unambiguous framework (somewhat analogous to the architectural plans for an office building) to insure that the goals of a company's Information Systems (IS) function are in agreement with those of the company as a whole.

Can anyone really imagine building a building without a set of plans? Well, that is almost exactly what many people do when it comes to building an information system! Information Architectures have three levels of ever-increasing detail. Typically, they start at the top by defining the 5 to 10 most important business processes (and their related information) that must be performed to manage the business. Often, this also includes a description of how information will be delivered (for example, "online via a workstation").

Whereas the top level is very nontechnical, the next level begins to define the supporting databases stating in a general way what, where, and how data will be stored, how it will be accessed, and the level and manner of integration. This level focuses on the more technical aspects of "applications" and the data delivery facility.

In most companies, this last level involving systems, is the only one ever addressed and, even then, only in the vaguest of terms—such as "We're an IBM shop" or "We use DEC/VAX's" or something similar.

A vendor's product line does not (except by a considerable stretch of the imagination) equal an Information Architecture. The key omissions are openness (discussed later) and connectivity—a scrupulously precise definition of how the entire complex of computers, local area networks, workstations, PCs, EDI connections, and so forth are going to take in data, store it, and spew it back out when needed.

If well thought out, this three-level structure can have some powerful virtues:

- Flexibility to respond quickly to business changes, thereby enabling a company to outmaneuver its competition
- Internal cohesiveness to cover all of a company, encompassing the totality of the company's information-providing activities
- Longevity—the ability to serve a company well beyond the year 2000

The opposite of the above virtues (rigidity, fragmentation, and a short life span) are the much too common negative consequences of not having an Information Architecture. These consequences continue to impact many businesses in spite of the fact that the development of an Information Architecture is not all that difficult.

Who is involved? Typically, the more senior members of a company's Information Systems organization along with the company's Executive Committee/Senior Management Committee/whatever it calls itself.

How is one prepared? First, the overall business goals of the company are defined. Then, the major items of information needed to achieve those goals are identified (along with their related core business processes, data sources, and interrelationships). Finally, the three architectural levels mentioned earlier are developed with explicit clarity.

An overarching concern in the whole process is very often that of the "buy-in" by top management that is required to make an Information Architecture "real." If such "buy-in" is not obtained (and retained), the whole thing becomes just another "exercise."

Information Architectures should not be developed by "outsiders" (i.e., consultants). Outsiders can help facilitate the process, but we are aware of no success story referring to an outsider-developed Information Architecture. The importance of internal "buy-in" is just too great.

How long does it take? In most companies, the development of an Information Architecture takes from three to six months—with a large part of that time devoted to factfinding and, later, consensus building. The task involves senior personnel and, often, major financial decisions. These can sometimes include the "un-buying" of expensive computer hardware and software identified as not a part of (or, in conflict with) the newly specified Architecture.

When (with respect to budget timing) should it be developed? An Information Architecture is a long-term decision. Once made, it transcends budgets cycles. However, it should (must?) have related to it a long-range Information Systems Plan (ISP) that serves as the tangible vehicle for insuring the implementation of the Architecture. That is, a detailed, explicit, tactical plan—all elements of which are consistent with the directions and goals identified in the Information Architecture.

How are strategies, budgets, plans, architectures, and so forth related? Strategies and architectures articulate long-range concepts, goals, and objectives. They specify the context within which are developed the more mundane management tools such as annual budgets and tactical plans.

7.7.2.   A Second Wave Of Chaos

While many Corporate Information Systems organizations continue to focus on their highly centralized mainframes, personal computers have snuck in and achieved a very high level of penetration in their user community. As this has progressed, the problems of apples versus oranges have gotten worse, not better. "Users" are now doing their own thing, creating their own information. Even more recently, these PCs have begun to be replaced by far more powerful workstations—thus introducing a second wave of chaos.

There is no question that this second wave of chaos has the potential to be much worse than the first if it is allowed to progress without the structuring benefits of an Information Architecture including an intense focus on the following:

- Integration (of data)
- Openness (of structure) allowing everyone easy, quick, and reliable access (within the constraints of good security control)

A recent study by an IS consulting firm can serve as a useful example. For Company X, a multibillion-dollar Silicon Valley electronic equipment manufacturer, the consultants were asked to assist in the selection of an entirely new and comprehensive "Order Fulfillment" system. The field had been narrowed to two major contenders, one clearly consistent with the company's then recently defined Information Architecture and the other being functionally slightly superior but having a nonconforming database that would have made integration of data difficult (at best).

Working closely with a user and internal IS team, the consultants constructed a small set of "critical success factor" selection criteria, traveled to several vendor and company sites throughout the United States—

and ultimately concluded that there was virtually no really persuasive difference between the two contenders except for the one point regarding conformance with the company's Information Architecture.

In a memorable meeting at the company's corporate headquarters, the user+IS+consultant team presented its recommendation to "go" with the architecturally consistent contender, although slightly functionally inferior. The team made its presentation three times in one day to ever-increasing levels of management. By end-of-day, top management accepted the team's findings, and the winner and loser were informed by phone.

In the two years since that meeting took place, the company has continued to hold to its now accepted architecture. Multiple subsequent decisions have been made—but these have all been made within the context of the architecture—which now is no longer thought of as easily subject to exception. After over a decade of frustrating system integration problems, Company X's systems are finally beginning to come together and our latest (October 1991) word from them is that they view that memorable meeting as a major (and positive) turning point in their company's Information Systems saga.

While a well-thought-out Information Architecture is the essential cornerstone for a good computer plan, it isn't sufficient by itself. There must be a real plan that the users buy in to, that is both (1) an excellent fit with the business needs of the company, and (2) technically viable.

Many companies have learned the lesson of "good fit with business needs" but still, as a consequence of the momentum of tradition, follow a technical plan that implies an underlying computer framework that is closed. Such closed frameworks are a tie to the past, a tie that greatly complicates integration, that stifles flexibility, that prevents a company from benefiting from the recent 100x increase in desktop computer power and the concurrent 100x increase in ease of connectivity.

As the pace of business increases, the most successful companies of the 1990s will be those that harness the practical power of the computer to support corporate GROWTH WITH FLEXIBILITY. They will do this not through "closed systems" but, rather, through the pathway afforded by Open Systems as made real by the power of modern workstations and the integrating power of modern (relational) database management systems.

7.7.3.   The Move from Closed to Open Systems

The early computers conformed to few, if any, standards. If you bought product X from company Y, there were many cases where product X+1 was incompatible, where programs that you laboriously developed for "X" had to be almost completely rewritten to run on its new/larger/more powerful brother "X+1." Rather quickly, the major computer companies started producing families of products. This simplified things if you wanted to use exclusively "Family X" from company Y. However, if you wanted to use a hierarchy of computers and have them all interconnect and have them all use the same set of programs in hopefully the same way, you had—until very recently—no hope.

In the early 1980s a few companies (most notably, Sun Microsystems) began to see a market for computers that could really be called interchangeable. Almost at the same time, the various international standards organizations started developing practical standards to make this happen. The merged consequence of these two concurrent streams is "Open Systems."

In an ideal implementation of Open Systems, components plug in and play with each other like the components of modern stereo systems. This allows the mixing and matching of these components in creative ways, leveraging individual component strengths (from possibly multiple vendors) to achieve an optimum result.

A key feature of the Open System concept is vendor independence— a feature that could not have been achieved without the now broad-based support for standards in the computing and telecommunications industries. Open systems allow far more cost-effective use of computer power and offer a true sea change in flexibility. Whereas in a Closed System environment, a complex and expensive assemblage of interfaces and gateways were needed to connect one such system to another, in an Open Systems environment, a better level of connectivity is achieved far more simply and at much lower cost.

Open Systems are the essential ingredient for what is quickly becoming the preferred computing model for the 1990s. This "model" is called "client-server computing" and refers to an environment wherein a company's systems are run on a network of microcomputers and workstations instead of mainframes. The network is composed of "clients" such as PCs and workstations (along with printers, modems, and so forth) that are all linked to "server" devices (often other microcomputers) that store and manipulate data.

The key feature of client-server computing is that both data and processing are distributed to the desktop, allowing a company to bring data out of the back room (usually on a mainframe) and put it, along with a tremendous amount of computing power, at the disposal of its employees.

This move of data and computer power from the mainframe/backroom to the desktop is paralleled by a progression from using computers for Operational purposes to one of using computers for Strategic purposes. Although still relatively rare, Strategic Information Systems (SISs) and Systems for Competitive Advantage (SCAs) are no longer just academic dreams—and it is the enabling combination of Open Systems operating within the context of client-server computing that is making them real.

There have been many failed attempts at Strategic Systems—often as a consequence of poor tools plus the pressure to give "first attention" to the Operational systems and work on the "strategic stuff" only when time allowed (which was rare if ever). However, now in the early years of the 1990s we are beginning to see a few successes. These are, most often, systems that have evolved, slowing taking shape on the desk of a CEO or CFO through personal tinkering on their part and, generally, out of a long-brewing sense of frustration—suspecting that it could be done but not being able to get anyone to do it.

7.7.4. The Swiss Cheese Pyramid

The Swiss Cheese Pyramid depicted in Figure 7.1 emphasizes what has for so many years been "The Problem." Fundamentally, most of today's information systems are full of holes: confused assemblages of interfaces, systems that can't talk to each other, hardware that is inadequate for timely, online delivery of decision-focused information. Complicating all this is the gap between the data resident in tactical information systems and the strategic information systems that need that data.

Today, with client-server Open Systems + the power of modern workstations + the power of modern (relational) database management systems + more than a bit of constructive premeditation (i.e., careful advance planning), the benefits of Strategic Information Systems and Systems for Strategic Advantage can be obtained at relatively low risk. The data gap between tactical information systems and strategic information systems can finally be closed. The tools exist; we have but to use them . . .

The key to a successful client-server environment is the integration of the resources on the network. Rather than just an assemblage of connected workstations, the systems on the network should be linked so seamlessly that the network itself becomes the computer. This allows employees in a company to do the following:

- Communicate and share information resources in a highly fluid manner, no matter where they reside in an organization

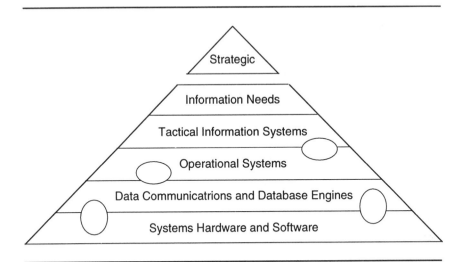

Figure 7.1.   The "Swiss Cheese Pyramid."

- Leverage the processing power, applications, information, and other network resources without having to know where they are or how to access them

The following are some of the more specific benefits of client-server computing:

Lower costs. One company, a $100+ million electronics manufacturer now performs all of its information systems using a microcomputer network with a systems budget of less than .5 percent of gross revenues—compared to the industry average of 1.7 percent.

Use of information as a "strategic tool." The easier access to information and the decreased time required to develop specially tailored analytical reports gives action value to information in contrast to the often only historic interest of mainframe data.

Faster development and implementation. A prominent West Coast publisher replaced essentially all of its systems with new ones better tailored to current market conditions in less than half the time that had been estimated using traditional methods.

Easier adaptation to changing needs and market conditions. The distributed design of client-server computing enables these systems to accommodate workload increases without major computer changes. One firm grew by a factor of four in gross revenues in three years while concurrently making only modest computer hardware upgrades (and virtually no software upgrades) to its client-server based systems.

KEEP IN MIND IN ALL OF THE ABOVE, THE ESSENTIAL IN-GREDIENT IS A VENDOR-INDEPENDENT ASSEMBLAGE OF COMPUTER PRODUCTS THAT INTERCONNECT WITH EASE—I.E., AN "OPEN SYSTEM."

Another recent IS consulting study can serve as a useful example. Company Z is in the business of facilitating the electronic transfer of information, providing services such as electronic mail, conferencing, bulletin boards, text search and retrieval, and access to information in databases. The nationwide customers of this service both put information into the system and access data put in by other customers. These services are now provided by a central mainframe accessed via dial-up telephone lines. Though acceptable when first installed several years ago, as the number of customers grew and the business evolved, two major shortcomings emerged.

1. Each time information is added or updated, assistance from the client's information services (IS) personnel is required.
2. Customers, becoming more accustomed to the speed and ease of use of applications running on their PCs and other dedicated worksta-tions, are asking for similar features on our client's system.

The consultants were asked to suggest a replacement for the current system and, in response, proposed a solution based on an Open System architecture using products conforming to widely accepted standards. The new system is now under construction.

It will be a distributed network of client and server systems con-nected via a high-speed wide-area network. The required functionality will be provided using a small number of commercially available pro-grams, tied together by a small program, which also controls data flow and access within the network. The following are among the benefits of the proposed system:

A wide range of workstations and LANs are supported. PC-compatible computers, Macintoshes, and UNIX-based workstations, as well as many kinds of LANs, can be connected into the network and used to provide or access information.

Services can be provided from any platform located on the network. Information can be stored on any of the platforms connected into the network. To a future information user, it will be unimportant that one file is on a UNIX workstation while another is on a PC.

Easier to use. A much improved user interface (called a Graphical User Interface or GUI) will make it much easier to both access information and to make information available on the network.

Higher-speed network. The use of a wide-area network utilizing high-speed lines will significantly improve response time.

Limited need for customized programming. Use of commercially available programs will significantly reduce the need for customized programming.

7.8.   HOW TO MAKE IT HAPPEN

The daunting task facing many firms is the replacement of their aging, fragmented, accumulated-over-time, no-longer-effective set of computer-based information systems now held together by too-numerous human beings used as the connecting "glue."

Reflecting on the preceding pages, many of these firms will choose to accomplish this task via an Open Systems approach—an approach that, heretofore, would have been both expensive and a very considerable developmental challenge. Now, as described below, the concepts of Information Architecture and the technological tools of Open Systems provide a means that is both financially within reason and of relatively low technical risk.

The first step in this replacement process is the selection of exactly what to replace. If this is a company's first excursion into Open Systems, it is wise to move forward carefully. Start with something relatively small such as offloading from the mainframe a data entry and editing system or a decision support system or perhaps a highly user-interactive mathematical or statistical analysis system. Given success on one or two of these, then move forward to something bigger, such as the reconstruction of a system based on an antiquated database management system.

Not too surprisingly, the fundamentals of the following process are no different than those encountered in "standard" Information Systems projects. The key Critical Success Factor is collaboration—both among a company's many different business functions and between a company and its suppliers of Information Technology.

It is important to stress the point of collaboration with "the suppliers." Open Systems, by their very nature, involve more than one vendor—and often many. A good, collaborative working relationship between the company and all of its vendors (of mainframes, workstations, servers, networking components, relational database management packages, developmental "tools," application software packages, and so forth) can be uncommonly helpful. Vendors are most often the best source of detailed technical advice when things "don't seem to be quite working as expected." Further, they can provide information on their future plans so that their client firms can comment on them, plan for them, and so on.

Within the context of a collaborative environment, there remain all the typical nontechnical project-impacting factors: company politics, traditional management practices (i.e., the factor of management inertia), multiple geographically dispersed sites, and so forth. Complicating these is the impact of the use of a new technology (i.e., the factor of technical inertia). Given highly visible, widely communicated, ongoing commitment from senior management and a well-managed development process, these negative factors can be effectively ameliorated.

And . . . the ultimate value of the project—much improved core competencies and competitiveness through the use of Information Technology that is finally truly synchronized with the company's business needs—makes the project worth the time and effort. At the outset of any project of such importance, there are some "trouble causers" that need to be watched out for:

- Fence sitting and excessive analysis through unclear delegation of responsibilities
- Avoidance of "people" issues such as (1) poor human communications, and (2) the natural fear of something new

plus all the other common project problems that are best addressed "up front":

- Winging it (i.e., poor planning)
- Gross cost underestimating
- Overfocusing on technology, forgetting the original problem that was to be solved

With these trouble causers and up-front problems satisfactorily addressed, most Information Technology projects have an excellent chance of success—if a carefully premeditated, logical process is followed, one that is communicated and well understood by all of the participants. There are many examples of such processes. The common threads found in the better ones include (1) an intense focus on carefully defined business requirements, (2) an explicit means for ongoing human communication, (3) a formal structure for migration planning, and (4) a careful integration of project management and developmental method.

There is an old aphorism along the lines of "well started, half-finished." This is particularly true in the case of Information Technology projects and even more so in the case of Information Technology projects that use new concepts such as Information Architecture and new tools such as Open Systems.

Given a collaborative environment, senior management commitment, avoidance of inertia (and similar) factors, trouble causers, up-front problems, and the like plus the use of good human communications, a consistent focus on the people issues, and an effective developmental process—the project at hand will be truly well started.

7.9.   THE NATURE OF CHANGE

Any shift from the status quo represents a change. People, organizations, industries, societies constantly experience change and find themselves adjusting to it. Managing change involves both dealing with whatever is causing change as well as with the consequences and implications of change, short term and long term.

Change may be caused by industry consolidation, your computer system vendor gets acquired or a new software application becomes available that you think can help your business. Your company reorganizes, or a new computer system is needed to replace an old system that no longer meets your business needs. Maybe you get a new job as a UNIX system administrator.

The implications of such changes, finding a new supplier and migrating your existing users to new applications, setting new objectives for your business, educating users on the new computer applications you've installed, forming new relationships in your new position, all have the potential to turn out positive or negative experiences for all involved.

Change can be costly and involve many types of risks, personal, professional, economic and so forth. Change may be self-initiated or it may be initiated by others or events outside your control. Change may have effects on individuals, on work groups, on an organization and even large constituencies.

Work environments are increasingly impacted by change for a number of reasons. There are more problems, issues, tasks, and people. In business environments, there are increasingly complex interdependencies between people and groups of people both inside and outside the enterprise. There is often a lack of resources, time and people to get the job done. Market conditions and business climate can combine to make things very unpredictable. It is no wonder that many people find it difficult to deal with change and even resist it.

Organizations that work to maximize the positive impacts of change and minimize the negative, tend to develop more formalized approaches to proactively managing change. Most often, various types of programs are used to facilitate change such as communications programs, training, and reward systems. These are used to facilitate and ensure that successful change initiatives occur.

The impact of change should be the realization of new opportunities. A company's ability to meet the challenges associated with change represents its most strategic competitive advantage. Change in Information Technology is driven by a wide range of factors such as the following:

- Government regulations
- Incorporation of new technology or processes
- Merger or acquisition or business changes
- Competition
- Incorporating new processes in a business
- Cost containment or downsizing of an organization

While software and hardware are the most obvious components that are required in Information Technology change initiatives, people are perhaps the most important component required to successfully integrate Information Technology into the business environment. A variety of people issues are involved in dealing with Information Technology change. New management techniques and even organizational structure may need to evolve. Installing a new network might require hiring a new network administrator.

Responsibilities may shift especially from a centralized to a distributed system. Data ownership and system administration are good examples. Authority and control may be redefined. Security issues may increase with the introduction of new networking services. Communication patterns may change. Electronic mail often radically impacts the frequency and types of communications.

7.10.   CHANGE MANAGEMENT AND OPEN SYSTEMS

Open Systems provides a unique set of opportunities as we have described. It also presents a unique set of risks and dangers. Open Systems itself represents a fundamental change in thinking. People will resist what they don't understand. In today's aggressive business environment, people will resist change until the pain of the status quo is greater than the cost of the transition to a new status.

Unless and until a process exists for consciously surfacing certain information in order to generate the appropriate level of pain associated with the status quo, the critical mass to support major forms of change will not be realized. Pain drives change—at both personal and organization levels. In a business, the loss of market share to a competitor is painful. Job security may be threatened. Pain may result from the inability to reconcile information or reports for different sources.

Pain also occurs when you are missing an opportunity. Timeliness of implementing changes may be a factor in gaining competitive edge or taking advantage of a business opportunity through immediate action. The opportunity cost of missing an anticipated opportunity—capturing customers today because in the future you will be able to offer them some new products or services.

Much of the marketing and competitive positioning by computer systems companies, software vendors, and even systems integrators tends to create a confusing picture as to what motivates people to change. Customers are interested in the benefits offered by technology. They want to be able to relate these benefits to the pain they are experiencing. Sales of high-value computer systems and applications always involve consultative selling. Sellers often must help their customers to understand their problems and formulate their requirements for change. These requirements then become the basis for new procurements of products and services to support the customers' change initiatives.

One of the impacts of Open Systems involves changes in the nature of the supplier-customer relationships. Presales support is now far more involved due to the complexity of the users' environment. Postsales support involves working issues associated with products and interactions between products. Customers find finger pointing most frustrating and they tend to look to platform vendors to support them when they have problems integrating solutions.

When is it time to change and why? What is creating the pressure and pain to change?

- Importance of information capture and distribution
- Expansion of scope of IT across the enterprise
- Expansion of scope of IT between enterprises
- IT as the basis of strategic competitive advantage
- Cut down time frames of business processes
- Increase productivity and production

When will the pain be great enough to necessitate action?

- When restructuring occurs (major reorganization, acquisition, merger, etc.)
- Business regulation
- Redeployment of assets
- Downsizing and redeployments or layoffs
- Lost opportunity cost

What are the strategic alternatives?

- Do nothing
- Incremental change—incremental refinements
- Radical change
- Strategic change

What is your company's current business position?

- What are your business drivers?
- How does the operating model tie with Information Systems?
- Where are your company's business information centers and what are the key information entities?

The turning point:

- When will you freeze further investment in nonstrategic architectures (legacy environment)?
- When will you limit investments in applications that don't conform to the strategic information architecture?
- How will the information architecture support key business information centers?
- How is the strategic architecture communicated throughout the organization?
- What individuals have the mandate to change?

What is the opportunity?

- Internal computing to support internal business processes?
- External computing (e.g., EDI) to support external business operations?
- How can you use IT for competitive advantage?
- How can new IT strategies support current or develop new centers of competence?

- How does the IT strategy link to and support key elements of the business strategy?
- How can you give power to the people?

7.11.   STRATEGIES FOR FACILITATING CHANGE IN INFORMATION TECHNOLOGY

When most people think of change in computer systems or applications, they first think of the technicians or experts who are responsible for implementing the new systems or applications. In most companies, the MIS group has had the responsibility of planning and managing changes in the companies' information systems.

However, as computers have become more pervasive in the workplace, especially with the increase in the use of PCs and workstations, a shift in emphasis is taking place. This shift is most evident in companies that have established CIOs, or Chief Information Officers. The CIO and "enlightened" MIS technicians now understand that the most important role they play is making their users productive and happy. They don't just develop and manage systems, they include the users in the definition of the system, carefully plan, and implement the migration of users to the new system. In short, they see their roles as more than integrating hardware and software, they see their roles as integrating people and technology. The overall goal is to optimize the relationships not just between people and technology but also between people through the proper application of technology.

Managing change can be thought of in terms of managing risks. By analyzing failure factors, strategies can be evolved. Failure factors might include the following:

- Wasted resources
- People feeling their job security is threatened
- Loss of confidence in management and confusion about management's commitment to change
- Organizational resistance to change
- Lack of skills required to make the change

Attention to the assessment of failure factors is key to ensuring successful implementation.

Special attention needs to be paid to those people most disrupted and affected by change initiatives. In a traditional MIS environment planning to adopt Open Systems, MIS itself may require such attention.

Strong and visible management commitment is essential. Senior management must play an active role in sponsoring and championing change. Management must transfer a sense of ownership down to lower levels of management in order to foster a climate for organizational teamwork.

Management strategy must take into account that resistance to change is natural. Especially in dealing with technicians, the paradox of change is that while careful implementation planning is required, there must also be tolerance for some ambiguity in accepting the process of change. Strategy for managing change should incorporate ongoing analysis and development of tools for people involved in making change or who will be affected by change.

7.12. SITUATION ANALYSIS

Are the objectives of the change initiative clearly stated? Is there an assessment of the problems associated with implementation? What are the impacts of change, both positive and negative? Are the roles and responsibilities clear in terms of who is making the decision to change, that is, who is championing the change initiative? Who has the responsibility to implement the change? Who is impacted by the change? What groups, which individuals?

How does the change impact existing responsibilities, behavior, and organizational structures? Will business policies or practices change along with information systems? Where and how will change control be applied?

Implementation Plans

Have implementation plans been drafted with sufficient time for review by those involved and those impacted? Has organization change been factored into the implementation plan? Has a specific strategy for communicating the planning process been developed to maximize organizational awareness and to promote teamwork?

Have the skills of your organization been assessed? What is the level of confidence in different parts of the organization concerning the feasibility of making the change? What system of communication will be used to keep the user base informed of the intention to change and the progress being made? What reward system will be used to ensure that change actually occurs?

7.13. MANAGING ORGANIZATIONAL TRANSITIONS

While executives are usually knowledgeable about the basic mechanics of change, they usually do not understand why people resist change. Within the context of information systems, resistance to change often starts because of a failure to bring existing activities to a satisfactory closure or ending. For example, most companies have significant applications backlogs. Leaving the unfinished business associated with this backlog open will create such frustration and resistance to change. This can doom change efforts to failure. It is crucial for executives to include transition planning in preparing for changes that lie ahead.

A change is characterized by a stop and a start. Transition is the human component of change. William Bridges has described a model of transition management involving three phases of transition:

1. The ending phase
   — Letting go of the old
   — Dealing with uncomfortable feelings (fear, despair, etc.)
   — Coping with a sense of loss (loss of turf, attachments, competence or control)
2. The neutral zone
   — Experiencing "no-man's-land" (caught between the old and new)
   — Disorientation and a sense of confusion about direction
   — Handling a sense of things falling apart (loss of a familiar process or system)
   — Trusting that incubation and reorientation can lead to creativity
3. New beginnings
   — Developing new competencies
   — Getting used to new procedures
   — Establishing new relationships
   — Building new plans
   — Setting new priorities
   — Finding new purposes

Managing change in the organization means finding ways of dealing with each of these phases.

7.13.1. The Ending

Some companies have gained closure in very aggressive ways. One of the largest and most progressive Wall Street Financial companies sold its MIS group to a major systems integrator and then planned to hire them back to manage the outsourcing of their data center as well as to deal with unfinished and critical backlog and maintenance issues associated with the extensive mainframe information systems. This may be an extreme example, but it sent a pretty clear message to the remaining employees concerning the end game for the current system.

Whether the MIS staff or the end-user community, there are bound to be negative feelings associated with making transitions. Management should accept these feelings and appreciate that they are natural and are not directed at individuals so much as to the situation. It is important that people know their objections can be worked through if they are recognized and regarded as important.

It is important to immediately make clear who will have to let go of what so that people's fear of loss is based in reality. If the sense of loss is turf, negotiate interest-based, not position-based territory to reallocate. If loss of meaning and value, restore meaning by assuring individual(s) of worth. If loss of future, establish career and life planning. If loss of competence, offer training and development in new competence. If loss of control, involve individual in creating future.

7.13.2. Neutral Zone

Be prepared to communicate regarding what lies ahead and eliminate confusion. Understand that productivity and effectiveness can break down this phase, but open discussion can speed up the process of reorientation.

An open process architecture that examines major business processes rather than looking at local solutions can enforce a higher degree of process discipline maintaining standardization across the business environments. Shift the thinking to "the business problems." Use this incubation period to re-examine popular assumptions and entertain unconventional ideas.

7.13.3. New Beginnings

This is the time to articulate the vision of the new reality, the big picture that will serve as a foundation upon which the future will be based. This is where the Information Architecture fits in. It should be a clear plan that will produce visible results. Spell out the following in the plan: how the future will work and logical reasons for the changes; what the future will feel like; and how everyone will fit into it. Create new channels of communication.

7.14. INTEGRATING ADVANCES IN TECHNOLOGY WITH RAPID ORGANIZATIONAL CHANGE

People in companies all around the world are doing exactly the same thing, which is everybody is going through a lot of change. Everybody is trying to figure out how to manage change. In the face of this change, CIOs and IT directors and MIS managers have to decide what to do to help their companies prosper over the next 10 years.

If you think of the 80s as focused on capital and financial engineering, the 90s may turn out to have a special focus on time—where is time in your business process, and why is it there and what are you going to go do about it? Time is competitive advantage, flexibility, cost, quality, and customer satisfaction. Time is the enemy, and the most successful companies have really strived to get time out of their business process. What we're seeing take place now on a worldwide basis is more and more firms understanding that if they're going to survive, if they're going to compete effectively in the 90s, they too have to worry about time and treat time as the enemy and figure out a way to get time out of there.

To get time out takes change: changes in the way people think, in the people you have, in your organization structure, in your business processes, and in your business systems. And as soon as you think you've got your systems right, people are going to walk in the door and tell you now they really understand what they were trying to do, and the design they'd given you two years before to implement is totally wrong, and they now need some other way. That is going to be life in the 90s, as we figure out how to go and make this all happen.

But change is a very complex thing. It has become a vortex in which you really have so many forces going on that you really have a constant state of disequilibrium. You have a goal, and the goal can be straightforward—how to get time out of my business process. Then you can decide how to address it—do you address it through the organization, do you address it through the process design? And you get the cycle of time and process re-engineering and organizational design working. But literally every one of those steps involves people and systems. People interact with the systems/the systems interact with the people. So if you think you have a simple, one-step process here to go make this happen, you're wrong. This is something that is going to be interdisciplinary and run across the whole company. It begins to affect the fundamental values of the company, how you operate, where you're going, and what you plan to do with the business over time as you move forward.

Information systems are strategic. Everybody understands that now. CIOs are increasingly key players in the business. People understand that your information systems are the cutting edge. It has been said that all commerce is now effectively electronic in the global world. The way we run our business in commerce is electronic. The physical movement of goods and services is becoming secondary to the movement of the electronic information and exchanges that take the order, manage the order, and confirm delivery.

Has MIS Become Outdated?

Information technology, as it is called in Europe (information services in the U.S.), is now recognized as a much bigger challenge. It's really good to feel wanted and to get attention by being MIS. Unfortunately, however, MIS soon discovers that meeting new expectations is very hard. The classic dilemma for any MIS director or IT manager is if your people are very responsive and really step up to the business partners and say, "Yeah, we're there with you all the time," you run the risk of getting fired because you don't deliver on those promises. And if you say on the other hand, "Don't promise anything more than I can deliver," you find out that you're fired for being unresponsive. So how we manage expectations can be a very difficult challenge that will ultimately drive success or failure for the organization.

Application lives are always getting shorter. Today they are much shorter than just a few years ago. In technical applications, rapid application life cycles have been the norm for some time—an average life cycle for CAD/CAM software for example may be 3 to 5 years maximum. But in commercial applications, an average application life for manufacturing requirements planning for example might be 10 to 15 years.

But how long are the business processes that these applications support going to survive? The challenge is always to keep growing. There's a whole new set of challenges coming our way that we haven't even begun to focus on. Just as we think it's going to be safe, that the change is complete, we will find a whole new set of things to do.

7.15.   A COUNTERCULTURE OF SHRINKWRAP APPLICATION SOLUTIONS IS COMING

It is important to recognize that there is another whole counterculture out there that is focused around shrinkwrapped applications and databases, claiming that these are really going to solve the problems. MIS may see these today as toy applications. MIS exists to provide competitive advantage to business and has traditionally been focused on something very different from shrinkwrapped applications. There is a a growing counterculture in computing that believes shrinkwrapped is all you need. But there is no way core, mission-critical business problems are all going to be solved by shrinkwrapped applications—at least not in all but the most trivial businesses. MIS will use them, see them as necessary tools—but MIS does not believe that shrinkwrap applications represent the essence of competitive advantage.

We believe companies will increasingly be faced by the challenges of very rapid change in business practice. Business will probably have to change every one of their business practices every three to five years. The exact time frame is largely dependent on the nature of the change factors such as growth in the business and in the nature of change in the industry. But it puts real demand on the people in the IT organization because they will have to respond and they have to learn to change very quickly in response to what the company, its business partners, and its customers are asking for and demanding as time goes forward.

Most companies have a checkered "systems history." A review of how their legacy systems came into being would probably reveal a general lack of overall planning. The result, a semifunctional hodgepodge of components. Many pieces of the system that are in operation have probably been there for some time. The design specification for these systems when they were bought may not have much relationship to the current situation. In point of fact, we believe most companies have ended up running their companies using minicomputers and mainframes without any overall information architecture at all. MIS maintains control of the operational—mission-critical systems. Individual groups and departments make decisions to procure other systems. Many system projects may never have been fully implemented. Business practices changed in the process. Projects probably took longer and cost more than was originally thought.

Most companies expect a lot from their vendors, but the vendors probably weren't able to deliver completely. Let's try to be realistic. You cannot expect to completely replace your information systems every few years. You might like to have a whole new generation of software, all GUI-based, all client-server, all fully interactive, all fully distributed— and deployed in operations throughout the company.

One of the measures that we use to manage the company is total cycle time. This concept is a very Japanese-style concept. It's vendor days lead times through day sales outstanding. It's the total amount of time that a company has to commit capital in order to service a customer order. So it starts when the company first places an order for parts, and it ends when the customer pays.

Reducing total cycle time drives everything good about a business:

it improves quality, lowers cost, improves asset efficiency. There's nothing wrong with reducing total cycle time. To give you one measure—reducing total cycle time in this way can give you the ability to put millions in incremental cash onto your balance sheet.

To do this might mean changing almost every aspect of your business process. You might have to change the way you do the following:

- Take orders
- Fill orders
- Bill orders
- Forecast
- Run the factories
- Distribute

You do have to figure out how to run your company, how to solve business problems.

7.16.   KEYS TO SUCCESS

There are four keys to success in making this happen:

1. One global network infrastructure and network management framework
2. Delegation and establishment of self-sufficient work groups
3. Scalability
4. Distributive computing

These are things you must do in an Open Systems client-server environment using products from multiple vendors at the same time. These are the most important issues that you have to face if you decide you need to go forward and build your information systems to respond to the need to drive business process and business change.

7.17.   TYPES OF DATA

Operational data is data from production processes, databases, and data created by applications. Informational data is the data used by knowledge workers and management for tracking, reporting, analysis, and forecasting as part of decision making in the business process. Informational data is operational data that is summarized, combined, abstracted, and enriched by adding some value to it. The operational and informational data required to support business processes may differ considerably between different areas and management levels within areas.

With advances in computer systems and applications and decrease in cost, almost all data is now online, meaning there is some level of interactive access. In high-volume transaction environments, such as order processing, users (e.g., telesales people) need quick access to the order information on a real-time basis. The person placing the order may be on the phone waiting for confirmation. These people have a requirement to access and update data.

Forecasts based on the sales data collected over the last six months is an example of informational data. This type of data does not update the operational data, read-only access to information is required. The operational data in the last 24 hours might not even be required.

In order to ensure high-performance throughput, information processing strategies are often employed to dedicate one or more systems to transaction processing. Queries, like those supported for forecasting, do not have to be run on the same systems supporting the transaction processing environment and they also don't have to be run on the same database as is being accessed in real-time by those doing transaction processing. Network computing permits a high level of flexibility in distributing processing to accomplish this strategy. Rarely is this accomplished in a purely automated fashion.

Operationally oriented decisions need to be made, for example, when and how to replicate operational data for decision support applications. Such decisions often must consider issues such as data security, data integrity, and data distribution.

7.18. NETWORK INFRASTRUCTURE

Most modern corporations will have thousands of computers. One global network will eventually connect most of these computers. There will be computers from many different vendors used for different purposes. You will no doubt be using a mixture of machines. Heterogeneous environment will be the norm even if there is one dominant architecture. This network is not a LAN, it is more like a data center. This is an area where you will need more tools to improve the management capability. For every 100 or so desktops, you are going to need a system administrator. This ratio should be constantly improved through the use of tools.

The mainframe and minicomputers become simply a network resource. The mainframe now appears to people as an application, and literally sitting at their workstation they don't even know unless you're reasonably sophisticated that it's a mainframe-based application. It just looks like any other application running on your workstation. This network is the plumbing for electronic mail that runs on this net and will carry information which is the lifeblood of the company. You can't run a modern company without email messages.

The traditional use of the corporate network has been to fill the reservoir—and you view the network as a river feeding into the reservoir—taking information from out in the nether parts of the company and putting it together into the central reservoir. I think that the essence of how you do quick management through rapid organization, integrate technological change, bring about re-engineering is to change the direction of the river and you have the river flow from the reservoir out to the places that need it. So you really view it as instead of the network flowing in, the network is flowing out. And this is a real mindset change. Once you understand that that's the way it should go, there's no question that you need a single network. It is very much a philosophical issue which I've discussed with a number of CIOs. You really have to believe that the network feeds the rest of the organization; it doesn't draw information from them. That's a fundamental psychological change that I think you have to go through to survive in the 1990s.

7.18.1. Delegation and Decentralization

The second point is delegation and establishment of self-sufficient work groups. MIS has to be structured with a balance of resources within corporate support and within other divisions, departments, or other groups of people who run on the network backbone. You can't possibly support all the different kinds and paces of change in the organization. So what we want to do is find a way to drive the change down. You have to delegate responsibility and give the capability to the line for their information systems. It's easy to give responsibility—it's very difficult to give responsibility and capability, particularly if everyone comes back to a mainframe.

One problem that you might find is that no matter how you try to push projects down, they come back around to your mainframe solutions. You really have to try to change that and push things out. I think there are three factors that are important to make that happen:

1. Self-integrating environment
2. Small manageable projects
3. People skills

7.18.2.   Self-integrating Environment

You need your systems to be self-integrating. Systems should be as small and as module as possible and depend upon the standards-based features of UNIX and networking products to put them all together. Between a Windows environment, an X-Windows environment, a network file system, the network, the operating system—you can glue these pieces in the complete solution but use the system to integrate them. So write your systems so they're self-integrating by design.

Small Manageable Projects.   Your projects should be small enough to be almost self-managing. Your projects should be managed by a steering committee (half users, half developers). Management should not intervene except when things seem to be going off-course. Program process should be documented in emails that reach management for review. A rule of thumb for a small project might be 10 people for a year at around a million dollars at the outside.

  You should try to manage these small projects locally with the business through these committees with a clear focus on business practice change. MIS organizations have too much in life to do than to go and drive a change that doesn't support a change in business practice—it isn't worth it, the user isn't going to be committed, the risk of failure is very high, and you're not going to be doing a lot for your business in the end.

People Skills.   Your people have to change, too. They need new skills and new training. The best way in the world to train people is at the time and place of need. The training should occur there. Look at your information systems as a delivery mechanism for training. People can train themselves as they need it, particularly when they have relatively lower-skilled, high-turnover occupations like customer support reps. So this is a key issue, but if you can run your company and your MIS organization around self-integrating systems, self-managed projects, and self-educating users, you've got a huge step forward on giving value to your business and surviving in your job as you go through the decade.

7.18.3.   Scalability

The third point is scalability. Scalability is the ability to move functionality around the network backbone—from the desktop to server easily—because they run the same binary image. What this means is you can have the flexibility to put the right amount of computer capability where you need it. If you only have to have one design center, you can use a small server; if you have a big country, you use a big server. It's very easy. If instead you have to have a PC design center, a mini design center, and a mainframe design center. You also have to have all the interoperability between them. How much can you save by eliminating the need to have all sorts of "middleware"?

You get resource flexibility, being able to move functionality over time between the desktop and the server so that you can bring up an application as usage grows on it; you can move it out to the desktop and try to keep a flat load on your network. And then something that's very, very important is it's very easy in a scalable environment to do front-end and back-end applications. Now front-end and back-end applications make up 90 percent of what I do, at least in my organization. They probably make up at least that of what you do. And it's just so much easier when you're able to move information and processing back and forth between the environments as opposed to having different development environments. Just try to do a debug where you've got everything sitting on one machine—and do a debug when you've got two different computers talking across two different network protocols of different development environments. You can save a factor of 10.

7.18.4. Distributive Computing

The fourth one is distributive computing. Separate out tiers of computing functionality. Separate the presentation layer from the application layer. Separate the application layer from the data layer. In this way, you have flexibility in separating database-intensive functions from other processing. The database processing can be optimized to provide database services to clients throughout the backbone optimally. Hardware and software are basically cheaper than people, so you look for ways to manage coordination by eliminating the need.

You can achieve enormous simplicity by having the ability to run most applications on dedicated servers so that there's accountability—the application team owns that server and can run that way. So design, build, and operate your systems as modules. Modularity is important.

7.19. LESSONS

Lesson #1. Coordination is complexity. If there's one big hidden cost in MIS today, it's coordination. We still have a spaghetti bowl set of systems and applications. Coordination is the biggest single cost, hidden or explicit, that you have in your company.

Lesson #2. Robustness over efficiency. Robustness means it still works well if the assumptions are wrong. Assume the assumptions are wrong—build for the worst case. It doesn't cost that much money when you've got cheaper hardware and more powerful machines.

Lesson #3. Duplicate data consistently rather than share it. Data sharing is very complicated. It takes a lot of coordination. This is expensive and very difficult to do. It's much easier to build multiple databases and then worry about keeping those databases in sync than it is to try to share data. It doesn't work to share data compared to building copies of data and building around those copies.

Lesson #4. You can never have too much modularity. Don't let anybody ever tell you any different. Force the design to be modular. People tell you it's going to be harder to build. It may be, but the gains downstream are just massive in development, testing, and reusability. Build the systems that are immune to organizational change. Don't let organizations focus on databases or data. Get them to focus on functionality, on what they need, and move the pieces around to give them what they need.

Lesson #5. Minimize training requirements. If you're going to change, you can't have a system that takes six to nine months for people to learn how to use. So you'd better go and build GUIs, and you'd better go and build the ability to train at the time and place of need.

Lesson #6. Use client-sever as a strategy to manage network computing. This one may surprise you. This is a message that everyone needs to come to understand because it allows you to change the way you relate to your business partners, to change, to everything that's going on in your organization. Client-server lets you change the way you manage computing, and the changes are all for the better.

As a global company with rapid change we must do all of our education, communication, training as a first resort on the workstation, and do it at a time and place of need. This is a big challenge. This suddenly gets much more into the human resources world, the education world, the training world. And then right around the corner is multimedia, whatever you want to call it—human metaphor, person-to-person communication—but the ability to have instant one-to-one videoconferences on the workstations. They want video email, audio email, to be able to record a video message and then mail it off to somebody as opposed to sending them text. This technology is not that far off; it's all running in the labs of a number of vendors. This represents a whole new set of challenges for MIS directors. Just as you think it's safe, there is going to be a whole new set of challenges to go worry about, and two to three years from now, conferences are going to be focused on computer-based education again. It's not going to be separate. It's going to be an integral part of the system. And the same will be true about communication.

1. You have to drive out time to make your business successful.
2. You have to drive out complexity to make your system survivable.
3. You have to go to client-server, Open Systems computing as a key step.

7.20. IMPORTANCE OF THE APPLICATIONS DEVELOPMENT ENVIRONMENT

Most (60 to 70 percent) of mainframe software, software on large minicomputers, and software applications that involve transaction processing are not "off the shelf." This software is largely custom applications and will likely never come in shrinkwrap format. Much of this type of software has been developed internally by large corporations up to the 1980s. During the late 70s and 80s, high-value software in core applications like Financials and MRP II became available on minicomputers. Minicomputers helped create a whole new software market opportunity. Hundreds of companies and thousands of products became available. Many companies who acquired these applications solutions realized that they still had to tailor them to meet specific requirements of their business process. A classic example can be found in the area of sales order processing. Few companies approach this process the same way and most companies have to develop or highly customize software for their own purposes.

Maintenance and customization costs of such software is where the real expense comes in. A tremendous amount of money and time is consumed trying to deal with the applications backlog that is often associated with these high-value applications whether built or bought. The software developers themselves are also lagging in meeting the demands of their customers. This situation has created an opportunity for application development tools that are often sold as add-ons to high-value software. These tools range from report writers to forms packages to administrative utilities.

The need for more and better applications development technologies is driven by the fact that the demand for applications outstrips the industries' ability to generate them. This situation is not likely to change.

Enter Applications Re-engineering

When a company decides to make a change in a major application, the process of change can be quite complex and risky. Such a decision for major change comes from a recognition of the limitations of the base technology employed by the application. That base technology often has to do with the database platform and the development tools. Companies decide to recreate the appropriate parts of their existing system and add enhancements not possible with the existing systems by exploiting new technologies. In many cases, these new technologies didn't exist when their original applications were created. New applications may be built with fourth-generation languages, utilize a modern relational database, support distributed networking, imaging, and other technologies.

Evolution in Development Tools

The driving forces in the development of new tools for applications software development are increased productivity to 1) reduce application development complexity and time, 2) minimize the knowledge required to develop and use software, so that ideally even the end user could write simple application on the one hand and the user will find the application easy to use without requiring lots of training, and 3) to increase the supportability of software, thereby decreasing maintenance related expenses.

Getting time out of the development cycle is only partly a matter of running development tools on fast workstations. If not more significant are the issues associated with design, development, and test. Case tools, high-level languages, and automated testbed software as well as bug tracking software all address this issue.

Reducing the knowledge required to develop applications is supported not only through tools but development frameworks that help encourage the creation and reuse of software components. "Ease of use" is the phrase often used when describing the characteristic of applications that are built with modern, consistent graphical user interfaces. Such applications are almost self-documenting. Knowing how to operate one application module helps you understand how to use another one that is based on the same user interface.

Keeping applications running in a changing environment is a challenge. It drains resources to keep up with enhancements and maintenance away from new applications developments. Application maintenance over time is one of the most important characteristics development tools can help address. Ease of changing applications, managing the process of change, and the ability to easily propagate changes into the production environment are critical features to examine when evaluating application development tools.

Building vendor-independent applications requires an application development environment that is open in multiple dimensions. An open-application development that produces portable applications is one of the key steps in the transition to Open Systems. The key question is: What application environment can a large enterprise adopt to produce portable code?

There is considerable complexity to this issue, much of it deriving from its multiple dimensional nature. First one must consider the range of applications for which the development environment will be applied. Technical applications tend to have more limited scope by comparison to commercial applications. Database management plays an important role in commercial applications both in terms of providing a suite of applications access to a common database, as well as lessening the dependence of the applications on a proprietary database that runs on one or a limited number of platforms. The next dimension involves the extent to which the application development environment permits the developer to freely integrate other tools and methodologies.

The term ICASE refers to an integrated computer-aided software engineering environment. ICASE solutions usually work within a particular CASE methodology and there is a high level of integration between individual tools. The suite of tools that make up the application development environment use a fully integrated repository, a common user interface and themselves developed with a common toolset. ICASE tools are proprietary and usually available from a single vendor.

The alternative approaches to ICASE for application development environments include the following:

- Use of a specific case tool
- Mix and match of best of breed tools
- Repository based mix and match of tools
- Repository based best of breed mix and match of tools

Open Systems-oriented application development tools are immature by comparison to single-vendor proprietary environments such as IBM's AD/Cycle or DEC's Cohesion. These environments may represent a practical short-term approach for some users, but the drawbacks over the long term are significant if the object is to develop portable software.

Since most large corporations are multivendor in nature, they will need to adopt interim strategies recognizing the limitations. By careful analysis and attention to evolving standards, they will leave themselves a mechanism to incorporate new technology regardless of its source.

Such interim strategies may involve the use of tools and platform software like 4GLs and relational and object-oriented database which are hardware vendor independent. Application development environments should be evaluated against the following standards:

- ANSI COBOL, C, FORTRAN
- ANSI SQL
- XPG
- POSIX

Such tools should be able to run on a variety of hardware platforms and on a variety of operating system platforms.

Application developers should make sure that run-time services are supplied to support a ported application on the same variety of operating systems and hardware platforms and that appropriate licensing permits cross-vendor application porting. Several important Open Systems standards related to application development are only now receiving attention. In particular these include standards for repository and OLTP. Open Systems standards for case tools and repositories are evolving. An example can be found in the Atherton software backplane.

7.21.   MIGRATION TO DISTRIBUTED APPLICATIONS

Everyone is looking for a single infrastructure supporting any to any connectivity, transparently integrating users and applications and supporting application interoperability. Client-server is not necessarily a cost-saving tactic. In fact, it may require more powerful desktop systems and the use of servers surrounding traditional systems. In client-server architecture, data distribution is the key issue.

The ultimate justification of rightsizing is its use as a catalyst for changing the information architecture to reflect new functional requirements of doing business. In the case of downsizing mainframes, it forces the disassembly of often monolithic solutions and the redesign of several, more complete applications.

The fundamental challenge of client-server architecture lies in the "middleware" that will be the applications to the hardware and operating system platforms. The problem is that for most customers, such an architecture normally falls short of supporting the migration and evolution of legacy systems.

The author believes that UNIX and "middleware" open-network computing standards emerging from the UNIX industry will gradually become the dominant trend in commercial computing by the end of the century.

MS-DOS is technically impoverished, MS-Windows does not provide an Open System alternative. OS/2 is good technology, but has its limitations. Windows/NT is still vaporware and the Macintosh is still viewed as a niche system.

7.22.   INFORMATION STRATEGY DEVELOPMENT FRAMEWORK

Suggestions:

- Separate planning and operations.
- Planning should focus on integrated architectural framework.
- Prototypes and pilots should be invested in.
- Operations should focus on service delivery.
- Information Architecture should be developed and evolved.
- Strategy process should be decoupled from investment decision process.

Investments:

- Application introduction and ramp up (user training)
- Application software environment (development)
- Application software environment (deployment)
- Data model, data management, and data distribution
- Systems platforms and administration
- Communications utilities and administration
- Network and communications infrastructure

Applications:

- Personal productivity applications and tools
  — Word processing
  — Spreadsheets
  — Personal database

- — Personal information systems
- — Calendar tools
- — Voice mail
- Work group applications (examples)
  - — Email
  - — Lotus Notes
  - — Calendar tools
- Transaction processing applications
  - — Mission critical
  - — Operational support systems
  - — Decision support frameworks
  - — Report servers
  - — Executive Information Systems (EIS)
- Workflow analysis (examples)
  - — FileNet
  - — Plexus ImageFlow
  - — Xerox XDOM
  - — JTS OpenImage
  - — Action Technologies Workflow

Applications Environment Attributes:

- Data access
- Distributed access
- Reuse / reapplication
- Reduction in numbers
- Common administrative frameworks
- Open APIs

Information Centers:

- Production
- Planning
- Sales
- Product distribution
- Financial controls
- Facilities
- Regulation
- Market intelligence
- Geographic
- Employee
- Information servers database

Levels of Information Center Management and Access:

- Enterprise
- Divisional
- Work group
- Individual

Business Process Automation Elements:

- Authentication
- Approval
- Software distribution
- Backup and archival, and restore functions
- Audit trails, disaster recovery

7.23.   OUTLINE OF AN INFORMATION ARCHITECTURE EXECUTIVE SUMMARY

1. Executive overview
   - Overview of study team (whose recommendation this architecture represents)
   - Scope and implications
   - Process through which architecture has/will evolve
   - Goals of architecture
   - Information System Architecture
   - Vision statements
   - Road map—overview of future
2. What is an Architecture?
   - Business processes and drivers
   - System re-engineering guidelines
   - Style guides for creation of new business processes
   - Development system framework
   - Process for determining customer needs for information services
   - Recommendations for technologies
3. Business model
   - Business process evaluation process
   - Business drivers
     —Market competition
     —Global enterprise
   - Implication of business drivers
     —Lower prices and margins
     —Multilanguages

        —Distribution related issues
        —EDI and Information Technology services for suppliers and
        customers
- Process definition
  - —Major business processes
  - —Supplementary processes
  - —Applications requirements
- User community involvement
  - —Roles and relationship
  - —Cross-communications
  - —Joint analysis objectives
  - —Business analysis (User)
  - —Systems recommendations (Systems)
  - —Process Analysis (User)
  - —Systems Analysis (Systems)
  - —Process Design (User)
  - —Systems Design (Systems)
  - —Implementation
- Business process optimization
- Analysis and documentation methods

4. System model
   - Information system solutions for business problems
   - Business drivers and system implications
     - —Market share
     - —Reduction of operational overhead
     - —Global enterprise
     - —W/W EIS/DSS and system support through time zones
   - Development approach
     - —Global and centralized development
     - —Localized development
     - —New technologies
   - Key elements of architecture
     - —Transaction systems
     - —Reporting tools
     - —Data repositories/registries
     - —Information flow
     - —Supplier linkages
     - —Distribution channel linkages
     - —Point of sale information
     - —Service data
   - Application families
     - —Applications area

—Primary business functions
—Business process satisfied
—System characteristics
—Key features
—Integrated system map
—Major system recommendations

5. Vision
    • System and technology implications on business drivers
    • Globalization
    • Data exchange
    • Customer interface
    • Use of portable computing
    • Technology frameworks
        —Key elements—application life cycle
        —Internal systems
        —Systems for external use

6. Transition road map
    • Application migration
        —Application family
        —Business functions impacted
        —Application/method
        —Long-term recommended application
    • Application migration considerations
        —Development considerations
        —Priorities
        —Make vs. buy
        —Migration checklist
        —Transition dependencies and timing
        —External dependencies
        —Ghantt charts

7. Conclusion
    • Architecture highlights
        —System model
        —System requirements
        —Technology vision
        —Transition road map for future environment
    • Key issues
        —Resource allocation
    • Key concerns
    • Next steps planned

Appendices as appropriate

What IS NOT Included in the Architecture

- Detailed project plans
- Cost estimates
- Resource requirements
- Functional specifications
- Start/end dates

These items should be determined by project teams as requirements and investigated and understood. The architecture facilitates the efforts of many diverse and dispersed groups in the creation of a new systems environment.

7.24. INFORMATION ARCHITECTURE

7.24.1. Objectives, Strategies, and Policies

1. Architecture Objectives
    1.1 Development environment in place by . . . (date)
    1.2 Production environment in place by . . . (date)
    1.3 New Architectural principles agreed upon
        —Data access
        —Information centers
        —Repository and data dictionary
        —Desktop integration, client interface environment
        —Systems infrastructure
        —Network infrastructure
    1.4 Future developments and plan for conformance to new architecture
    1.5 Freezing and downsizing of legacy systems and applications
2. Objectives for data access (examples)
    2.1 Production decision support in place by . . . (date)
    2.2 Reference data uniquely identified in terms of owner, location, etc.
    2.3 New policies and procedures in place for data
    2.4 Data extraction, propagation, collection and maintenance controls and procedures in place to ensure data integrity and reliability.
3. Objectives for data capture
    3.1 Access by Legacy Systems to reference data
    3.2 Integration of third-party software not compliant with architecture
    3.3 Make vs. buy for new applications and plans for integration

    3.4 Consistent design templates for new software
       —modular
       —shareable
       —reusable
       —message-based

4. Objectives for repository
    4.1 All data defined uniquely and consistently with repository data dictionary.
    4.2 Rules of data and system ownership and custodianship established and agreed.
    4.3 Reference data specifications, data capture-to-access extraction specifications, desktop integration authorization profiles and user preferences stored in and accessible from the repository.
    4.4 Case tools and methods with repository metadata.

5. Objectives for desktop integration
    5.1 All "new architecture" applications appear on the desktop with consistent, intuitive, and easy to use graphical interface.
    5.2 Access to enterprisewide data and services on the network is managed transparently by client-end service modules that present external resources and services as natural extensions of the desktop.

6. Objectives for systems infrastructure
    6.1 Bandwidth
    6.2 Throughput
    6.3 Reliability

7. Objectives for systems development and maintenance
    7.1 New systems are built from modular, shareable, reusable, message-based software modules.
    7.2 CASE tools and procedures integrated into systems development and maintenance processes.

8. Objectives for interoperability between new and legacy (old) architectures
    8.1 Applications can access data from relational databases.
    8.2 New architecture GUI front ends and custom-built applications access and update reference data in both data capture and data access modes.

9. Objectives for commercial package integration
    9.1 Purchased application software packages compliant with the new architecture can be integrated directly into the environment via industry-standard linkages (SQL).
    9.2 Purchased applications that are not compliant with the new

architecture can be integrated into the environment via data warehouse and repository.
10. Objectives to migration of existing legacy applications and systems
    10.1 All data and applications can migrate to new environment based on technical needs, business needs, and so on.

7.24.2. Supporting Policies, Strategies, and Standards

1. Graphical User Interface standards for Applications Development
    1.1 Develop and promulgate GUI standards
2. Interim Architecture policy implementation, extensions
    2.1 Develop and make accessible "approved standards and tools" list.
    2.2 Create and implement approval process for new and substantially modified information systems.
    2.3 Data ownership policy
    Define management responsibilities for data and system ownership.
    2.4 Develop process for amending Architecture
    —Data dictionary
    —Platforms and locations
    2.5 Use software engineering to create modular, platform-independent, network-tied systems composed of standard components shareable and reusable.
    2.6 Evaluate new information systems proposals against architecture.
    2.7 Manage information as shareable corporate resource organized for transaction processing and decision support at minimum cost.
    2.8 Reduce reliance on mainframe processing power.
3. Communications, education, and marketing strategy
    3.1 Spread awareness.
    3.2 Seek inputs.
    3.3 Gain agreement on basic architecture directions.
    3.4 Identify key constituencies and internal partners.
    3.5 Identify key external partners.
    3.6 Establish user notification methods encompassing
    —Business practice changes
    —Organizational changes
    —Responsibility changes
    —Information resources project status

  —Technology evaluation
4. Staffing and training strategy
 4.1 Hire new staff as required.
 4.2 Develop and implement training plans for key groups and individuals.
  —Developer and programmers
  —Analysts
  —Departmental end users
  —Senior management
5. User support strategy
 5.1 Ensure users of information systems, resources, and services in new environment are supported.
  —Central consulting services
  —Departmental experts
  —Other resources
 5.2 Establish central point of contact for user initial inquiries.
 5.3 Determine user expectations for new services.
6. Operations and maintenance strategy
 6.1 Implement production service model for client-server systems operating in new environment.
  —Availability
  —Security
  —Reliability
  —Backup
7. Interoperability strategy
 7.1 Allow applications to read and write RDBMS data directly.
 7.2 Network-based applications and support services.
 7.3 Access services through open, client-server, technology-based connections.
8. Vendor and external partner liaison strategy
 8.1 Coordinate vendor development directions with company directions.
 8.2 Perform architecture conformance review for vendor products in use or under consideration.
 8.3 Coordinate site-license and purchase agreements.
 8.4 "Accredit" consultants to work within the architecture, listing and providing references for those who are qualified to work on new architecture projects.
 8.5 Negotiate relationships and engagements with external consultants as necessary.
 8.6 Maintain communications with other institutions and companies pursuing similar architectural initiatives.

9. Migration strategy
   9.1 Source or build tools and capabilities for migrating existing applications incrementally to new environment.
   9.2 Develop processes, procedures, plans, and teams to support the migration of current operational systems into the new environment.

7.24.3. Phase Strategy / Milestones

1. Establish information resources organization structure for new architecture.
   1.1 Determine roles and responsibilities.
      —Application development
      —Application support
      —Architecture
      —Geography managers
      —Strategic planning
      —Project management structures
      —Project leaders
   1.2 Establish bug reporting and escalation mechanism.
   1.3 Establish service request and feedback mechanism.
2. Establish user-client group for major business processes.
   2.1 Determine user-client goals.
   2.2 Determine user-client metrics and methodologies for successful solutions.
3. Establish priorities.
   3.1 Establish program prioritization process.
   3.2 Establish funding utilization mechanism.
   3.3 Determine how projects will be assigned.
4. Architecture review process for all major projects.
   4.1 Design reviews encompassing all phases.
      —Proposal
      —Detailed functional review
      —Detailed system design
      —Pilot / prototype
      —Establish roll-out criteria
      —Determination of implementation and transition impacts
   4.2 Establish formal signoff process involving:
      —Project leaders
      —Functional managers
      —End-user management
5. Establish baselines for project plans.

5.1 Requirements definitions
5.2 Requirements specifications
5.3 Design issues
5.4 Implementation plans
5.5 Well-defined goals and measurements/evaluation criteria

7.25. MANAGING ORGANIZATION CHANGES AND INFORMATION TECHNOLOGY

Consider the following:

- Legacy applications are taking 50 percent and often greater percent of development staff time. Application backlog and maintenance for legacy applications is a huge problem.
- Re-engineering is being pushed by top management, but in many companies the end-user organizations have not bought into the change process and don't feel an equal partnership with the MIS organization.
- There is a lot of planning going on related to internetworking. MIS-IBM'rs are having problems understanding how they control things if the answer isn't SNA.
- CIOs have a flat or smaller budget each year to experiment with. CIOs fear for their jobs especially in the glass house environments.
- Companies are having to be downsized or are remaining flat. In many cases, there is no business plan that documents the basic business strategy making the MIS of designing and planning information architectectures that much more difficult.

The challenge for MIS in the 90s is to become the catalyst for achieving strategic business objectives. Businesses must change to survive. The rate of change is increasing. To be competitive, businesses must reduce the time and cost it takes to deliver their products. The same is true for MIS.

MIS must create effective information systems to support the business demands for information services. It must find ways to reduce the cost of delivering these services AND deliver the services quickly. Maximizing the value of existing information systems investments in equipment, software and people is desired but may not always be possible.

Too often, monolithic proprietary computer systems have been unable to meet these needs and the challenges of change. It is often necessary to initiate a comprehensive set of programs to migrate from an existing computing environment to a new distributed architecture.

The challenge in business computing in the 90s will be to encompass a number of architectures and system technologies from the last 20 years. Isolated systems at a department level or a personal system level need to be tied together before organizations can work together and share data.

The architectural problems arise when large monolithic applications on large centralized computer systems hold the data which is needed to make business decisions. Users often find it difficult or impossible to get the data they need. Even if they can find the data, it is hard to distribute and share this information with other users.

Some of the major shifts that have occurred include the following:

- Single-source to multiple-source hardware architecture
- Multisource operating systems
- Proprietary de facto networking standards to open de facto—IBM, SNA, and NetWare to TCP/IP and UnixWare
- From single-vendor application software to multivendor environments
- Competition among a few to open competition
- Shift from competition between architectures, e.g., Intel vs. SPARC to competition within architectures, e.g., Intel vs. AMD

Issues Faced by CIO

CIOs are faced with a number of issues as they move into the implementation of new distributed environments.

CIOs must first deal with the embedded base of business critical applications. The transition away from these legacy applications in mainframe environments can actually cost more over the short term in terms of mainframe costs. For example, the applications that move off the mainframe cut the number of mainframe customers who share the expense of the mainframe. With the shift toward distributed applications, more complexity in system and network administration is encountered. The tools for applications development and testing of GUI-based, network intrinsic applications are immature, and care must be taken in tool selection.

CIO organizations quickly realize that there is no one solution. Cross-product and vendor interconnectivity requirements demand greater awareness of and adherence to standards. Access to the technical roadmaps for implementation of product implementations become very important for long-term planning.

Roles and responsibilities have to been redefined. There should be no confusion about what end-user groups versus MIS is responsible for. Responsibility extends beyond programming or applications engineering to applications and systems support. Capital allocation priorities have to be rethought. Hardware ownership can be confusing. Who buys the development machines and who buys the production machines? Development has to buy new machines to write applications—they cannot borrow time on a centralized mainframe as is often the model in centralized mainframe environments.

The following summarize key success factors in managing migrations:

Successful migrations are staffed fully, even overstaffed.

Successful migrations have champions.

Successful migrations enjoy broad-based support at many levels in all organizations involved.

Successful migrations are designed to accommodate change.

Migration Strategies

Migrations from current systems to new systems are carried out for various reasons. This section summarizes some of the alternative strategic reasons for change.

Decreasing Costs

- Provide the same level of services for less cost.
- Improve level of services at same cost.
- Provide significantly greater services at more cost.
- Provide new analysis applications, e.g., exploit new visualization technologies.

Strategic Migrations

- Legacy systems have a number of inherent barriers inhibiting incremental improvements. Rigid data structures need to become more flexible.
- Legacy tools require IS staff intervention—greater flexibility is required to empower work groups to build their own applications within the guidelines of a company's information architecture.
- Legacy systems are not suited for ad hoc query—new query server or report server architectures are required to support management decision making.

Strategic Applications

- Driven by business needs, not by control or migration of computing costs and applications.
- Address time-sensitive customer service needs.
- Batch processing too slow.
- Existing systems overloaded—costly to upgrade.
- Information access limited and inflexible.
- Need for real-time queries.

Making Operating System Transitions

One of the ongoing challenges will be to keep pace with technological advancement. While it potentially introduces significant dislocation, operating system transitions are a fact of life in information systems environments. Whether it is a transition to a new release of the same operating system or the migration to a whole new operating system, a number of lessons can be learned and techniques applied to managing change in information architectures.

First, there should be a formal migration planning process. A strategy needs to be laid out. First identifying work groups that share servers and applications. Outline the software and the types of systems users are using. Take the opportunity to rethink the network and network management strategies.

Determine what applications need to be upgraded and when these upgrades will be ready. Consider the use of tools that may be available to help in scanning existing applications or help in applications re-engineering. If you expect to continue to run applications in a compatibility mode, e.g., VAX VMS code on Alpha or SunView applications on Solaris, then explore special related issues related to performance implications.

Stage in a new release by starting with a diskfull workstation and build out from there. Become familiar with new methods of system administration in a simple environment first.

Use this staging system for developing new scripts as required to support your operations. Start the migration within a single group and resolve all of their problems before moving onto the next group. Involve your system administration in your group's migration.

System administrators should investigate tools that can help make the migration proceed smoothly. Consider the impact on the user community. Make sure users understand how the new operating system is being staged in and make them aware of new facilities that may be available to them.

Getting Connected

Something interesting about UNIX, especially now that it is receiving considerably more commercial interest than in the past, is the wealth and intensity of information available about it. With so many sources of information, a resources roadmap can help you find the information you need.

This chapter summarizes various resources that are available to anyone who is interested in learning more. There is such a large number of information sources, particularly concerning local trade associations or reference books, that it is clearly beyond the scope of this document to describe all of them. The approach taken here is to give pointers to some of the most reputable and comprehensive resources available. By understanding these information resources, and by following the leads or pointers provided, you stand to profit in any number of ways. For example, you might be able to find a particular software application solution you need, or you might learn enough about a particular trade show to avoid going or sending someone whose time and energy might be totally wasted. You will better understand where to get readily available journals, books, or periodicals that will keep you up to date on the latest market or product announcements. Whether for you or for someone else in your organization, the following sections summarize several important resources that will improve your productivity in getting better connected to the UNIX world.

While system suppliers will continue to be important sources of information, you will find that there are many other places to look.

Historically, mainframe users have relied very heavily on their system suppliers for information and products, while PC users have tended to go to their local computer retail outlet or use mail-order catalogs to get what they need. The UNIX market is becoming more commercially oriented and is rapidly moving in the direction of the commodity mass market of personal computing.

8.1. UNIX MARKET RESEARCH AND CONSULTING SERVICES

Several market research companies provide products and services with special focus on the UNIX market. Most provide a subscription service that entitles subscribers to periodic reports as well as limited access to market research analysts. Many also issue newsletters and regular updates on selected subjects. Most market research companies offer custom consulting services to meet very specialized needs.

The output of most market research companies is oriented toward either the user community or toward the vendor community. While the primary customer base of many market research companies is the hardware or software vendors, there is a clear trend toward repackaging information for users who prefer to rapidly survey a field of interest to find out which players or products are worthy of closer examination. Be forewarned, however, that most of these services are expensive and could prove of limited value if not carefully evaluated. It is not unreasonable to ask for some references and some samples of previous reports or newsletters to gauge the caliber of the product before you purchase a subscription service.

The companies presented in alphabetical order in the next section offer products or services that may be worth further investigation. Many of them put on conferences or special seminars that can be very interesting to attend. It is a good idea to get on their mailing lists and let them know your specific areas of interest. A limited number of free passes to these conferences may be included when you buy one of their subscription services. It is best to contact these companies directly to learn current details concerning their products, services, and pricing.

8.1.1. Datapro Research Group

600 Delran Parkway
P.O. Box 7001
Delran, NJ 08075
(609) 764-0100 or 1-800-328-2776
Fax (609) 764-8953

In April 1989, Datapro began to offer a new service on UNIX systems and software. This new service provides detailed product descriptions and expert analysis of market trends. Datapro's *UNIX and Systems Software* reports were continually issued as the marketplace changes and new products were introduced. A monthly newsletter called *UniStrategy* was also included that provided timely articles written by Datapro's UNIX editors. This resource cost approximately $500 a year. Datapro's service contained some of the same information contained in other less costly sources such as UniForum Product Directory. However, Datapro publishes very comprehensive and specific product summaries and analysis.

Datapro has revamped its service and raised its prices slightly. The new *UNIX Systems and Software* service consists of starter volumes and monthly issues bringing you the latest in UNIX systems and software technology. The monthly issues provide in-depth reviews, management-oriented reports on standards and strategies, detailed product profiles, overviews of technology areas and profiles of value-added resellers and computers running under UNIX. The UNIX reports in the United States now list for $840 annually or $1,502 for a two-year subscription. Datapro offers just under 40 similarly priced components of its services. These services cover all sorts of different areas including, Communications, Software, Office Technologies, Work Group Computing, Computer Systems, Managing Information technology.

We recommend this service but caution that it is not always up to date. This is more a reflection of the breakneck pace of change in the industry than problems with the inherent quality of Datapro's reports—particularly in UNIX. For example, there was mention of the ACE consortium that was totally out of date in an evaluation copy I went through recently. Notwithstanding issues of currency, Datapro may represent excellent value for the money depending on your needs.

Datapro may loan you binders to evaluate. This might prove a useful way to best determine what value they offer.

8.1.2.   Dataquest

1290 Ridder Park Dr.
San Jose, CA 95131
Tel (408) 971-9000
Fax (408) 971-9003

Dataquest is one of the more established market research companies and one often cited in the press. They provide overall forecasts and analyze trends in a large number of markets. They have been analyzing UNIX for over four years now. Dataquest can provide market share estimates that can tell you who the major vendors are in a particular segment. They also estimate and predict market size in terms of revenue and unit shipments.

Dataquest subscriptions provide reports and updates, limited access to market analysts, and relevant portions of their database, which can be used to make different cuts on the data than those normally published. An annual subscription fee to one of Dataquest's services will run around $15,000.

Like most major market research firms, Dataquest provides services that are mainly targeted at larger systems vendors and larger software companies.

8.1.3.   The DMR Group

43 Front St.
East Toronto, Ontario
Canada M5A 1N1
Tel (416) 363-8661

or

50 Fremont Street
Suite 1410
San Francisco, CA 94105
Tel (415) 597-4400
Fax (415) 597-4411

DMR is Canada's largest market research consulting firm. In 1989, they completed a large multiclient survey on UNIX in Canada. They commenced a similar study in the U.S. marketplace during the summer of 1989, which has now been completed. While the final reports from these studies will only be available to sponsors, the DMR Group does publish executive summaries for release to the public.

DMR's extensive survey of Canadian vendors and users was aimed to determine the size of the UNIX market and the characteristics of the companies and applications where UNIX is, and will be, used in Canada. The slant of their current study, while similar to the one done in Canada, covers not only UNIX but also Open Systems. It promises to be an interesting primary research project that will help document uses and users' requirements for Open Systems.

8.1.4.   INTECO Corp.

102 Halls Road
P.O. Box 1054
Old Lyme, CT 06371
Tel (203) 434-1644

INTECO normally specializes in providing continuous subscription services covering computer systems and value-added resellers. In 1988, it completed a survey focusing on users of smaller UNIX-based systems, both in the United States and in Europe, analyzing how the users plan to expand the use of their systems. INTECO usually markets this service to systems vendors and larger corporations.

8.1.5.   International Data Corporation (IDC)

5 Speen Street
Framingham, MA 01701
Tel (508) 872-8200

IDC is one of the larger market research companies offering continual information services in a number of areas, including UNIX. It publishes what it calls "data books" as well as special reports, and its subscription services also include limited inquiry services. An annual subscription service costs around $15,000. Individual reports can usually be acquired independently.

IDC has several databases. They do surveys and publish the findings in reports. Their system census is probably one of the most authoritative in the industry. IDC has a UNIX service that focuses on the supply-side analysis of the UNIX market.

8.1.6.   InfoCorp

2880 Lakeside Drive
Suite 300
Santa Clara, CA 95056
Tel (408) 980-4300

or

289 Great Road
Suite 307
Acton, MA 01720
Tel (508) 635-9950

InfoCorp is one of the more established market research companies.
They are a spin-off of people from Dataquest, and historically they have
focused on low-end systems, personal computer markets, and distribution channel analysis for these products.

InfoCorp specializes in tracking system and product vendors. Various services, such as their software service and their midrange computer systems services, provide information on UNIX as part of the
overall market analysis. InfoCorp also offers a specific UNIX service
that focuses on operating systems, standards, and related applications
software. InfoCorp has a unique integrated database model on which
they develop overall market estimates on the performance of specific
make and model numbers of competitive systems or products in the
market. Their subscription services run upwards of $12,000 per year.

8.1.7.   Novon

Research Group
3360 Dwight Way
Berkeley, CA 94704-2523
Tel (415) 548-7800
Fax (415) 540-6150

Novon maintains a database of users and vendors and periodically
conducts in-depth surveys. Novon's subscription service includes copies
of quarterly reports, limited access to analysts, and database access.
Novon makes its database available either in hard copy or in magnetic
form. The subscription fee ranges from $16,000 and up per year.

8.1.8.   Patricia Seybold's Office Computing Group

148 State St.
Suite 612
Boston, MA 02109
Tel (617) 742-5200
Fax (617) 742-1028

This firm publishes different newsletters that cover the UNIX marketplace. The most notable is *UNIX in the Office*, a monthly research report featuring an analysis of major new product announcements or other subjects of interest. The firm also provides consulting services to vendors or users to assist them in strategic planning.

8.1.9.   The Yankee Group

200 Portland St.
Boston, MA 02114
Tel (617) 367-1000

The Yankee Group offers UNIX-related reports as part of its subscription service. Two reports have been published since 1987 specifically dealing with UNIX: *UNIX 1987: A Promise Kept* and *UNIX in Manufacturing*. The latter examines the role of the UNIX operating system in current and future technologies. Yankee subscription services start at around $17,000 per year and include limited access to analysts, reports, and newsletters.

8.1.10.   Albert Consulting Group

P.O. Box 2085
Saratoga, California 95070
Tel (408) 464-0600

This group performs specific studies rather than publishing general reports. Vendors of UNIX workstations use their services in planning strategic directions, while end users and software developers often seek their help in making purchase decisions. The firm also trains salespeople and distributors of UNIX-based products. The Albert Consulting Group expertise is centered on CAD/CAM/CAE and on advanced topics such as concurrent engineering.

8.1.11.   Esther Dyson Newsletter

EDventure Holding Inc.
375 Park Avenue
New York, NY 10152
Tel (212) 758-3434

Esther Dyson is a well-known speaker and writer in the computer industry. She publishes a newsletter called *Release 1.0* on a monthly basis. It covers PCs, software, CASE, groupware, text management, connectivity, artificial intelligence, intellectual property law. A companion publication, *Rel-EAST*, covers emerging technology markets in Central Europe and the Soviet units. Subscriptions are $495 per year, $575 overseas.

8.1.12. Open Systems Advisors, Inc.

268 Newbury St.
Boston, Mass. 02116
Tel (617) 859-0859
Fax (617) 859-0853

Nina Lytton, who previously worked at the Yankee Group, started the Open Systems Advisors, which offers a monthly newsletter for supply siders and end users alike who are interested in tracking trends in Open Systems. Nina is also very involved in the trade show industry and provides consulting services to trade show companies. She has contributed to the success of Interop and has also worked with UniForum. She has helped to design and coordinate Executive and MIS sessions for these and other conferences.

8.1.13. Networked Publications

16680 Shannon Road, Cabana Suite
Los Gatos, CA 95032
Tel/Fax (408) 356-4059

Networked Publications is a new Silicon Valley start-up company owned and operated by Ed Dunphy. Networked Publications specializes in research and writing about Open Systems software. The company markets its publications through established market research companies. The company makes its reports available in print, through an online information service as well as on CD-ROM media. Networked Publications consists of a large "loosely coupled" network of individuals who regularly research and contribute toward the company's Information-Ware products. Contact Networked Publications if you are interested in its products and services for ISVs, for MIS management and application software developers, and for Open Systems consultants. If you interested in learning more about Network Publications products and services, or if you are a writer who would like to participate in the company's different ventures, contact Ed Dunphy at Networked Publications.

8.2.   PROFESSIONAL SOCIETIES AND CONSORTIA

This section describes various professional societies and consortia that may be important in terms of the role they play in UNIX and Open Systems.

8.2.1.   UniForum

UniForum is best known today as one of the most popular and largest trade shows featuring UNIX solutions. But it actually started out a user consortia.

UniForum and /usr/group are trademarks of UniForum. It was founded in 1980 and published the first independent catalog of UNIX product and services in 1981. Today, it offers several services of interest to the UNIX community, including biweekly newsletters, technology guides, an annual products directory, and various other materials and services. Membership costs $100 per year, which includes a copy of the directory.

One of the largest, if not the largest, UNIX-oriented user group also called UniForum (formerly known as /usr/grp) has about 7000 current members. The slash("/") is a designation for a directory in UNIX, and the name is a pun on the UNIX hierarchical file system. UniForum is a vendor-independent, nonprofit trade association dedicated to the promotion of UNIX products.

In addition to UniForum, with members drawn from all over the world, there are national, regional, and local user groups that share a common interest with the mother group.

For more information see also under section 8.3.1 or contact Uni-Forum.

UniForum
2901 Tasman Drive
Suite 201
Santa Clara, CA 95054
Tel (408) 986-8840
Fax (408) 986-1645

8.2.2.   88open

The 88open Consortium was founded in April 1988 to assist companies working with the 88000 RISC microprocessor. Its mission is to help these companies—hardware vendors, software suppliers, end users, or others—achieve success in their businesses through cooperative activities. Founded in 1988, 88open represented a new way of doing business in the

Open Systems industry. Much of its work has been to develop Open Systems standards that allow greater sharing of products and opportunities among the community while reducing the costs of doing business for all. As a result, 88open has created one of the first shrinkwrapped software environments for UNIX in the market.

88open has published *Sourcebook*, a guide to binary-compatible hardware systems for six manufacturers. Each certified system in the *Sourcebook* has been tested to meet the consortia's standards for portability. 88open has over 55 members.

88open
100 Homeland Court
Suite 800
San Jose, CA 95112
Tel (408) 436-6600

8.2.3. MIT X Consortium

Founded in 1988, the MIT X Consortium sets interface standards for its members and the entire industry for the X Window System which is the base technology in UNIX graphical user interface environments. Examples of these standards are the X protocol, the X lib software library, and the X Toolkit Intrinsics. The X Consortium is administered by employees of the Massachusetts Institute of Technology where the X Window System was developed. It is financially self-supporting through membership fees and membership is open to any operating corporation willing to execute a participation agreement with MIT. There are over 90 members, mostly large computer systems or software companies.

MIT X Consortium
Massachusetts Institute of Technology
545 Technology Square
Cambridge, MA 02139
Tel (617) 253-0628

8.2.4. Object Management Group (OMG)

The OMG is an international organization that promotes the development of software based on object-oriented technology (not strictly UNIX). Working with its members, standards organizations, and related industry groups, OMB develops specifications for object-oriented technology for heterogeneous applications environments. OMG was founded in 1989 and currently has over 100 companies as members.

Headquartered in Framingham, Massachusetts, with marketing operations in Boulder, Colorado, the OMG is an international organization of systems vendors, software developers, and users founded to promote the theory and practice of object management technology for object-oriented applications based on industry guidelines. The adoption of the OMG framework will make it possible to develop a heterogeneous applications environment across all major hardware and operating systems.

OMG Marketing Group
3823 Birchwood Drive
Boulder, CO 80304
Tel/Fax (303) 444-8129/(303) 444-8172

OMG Headquarters
492 Old Connecticut Path
Framingham, MA 01701
Tel/Fax (508) 820-4300/(508) 820-4303

8.2.5.   SPARC International

SPARC International is an independent association of corporations and institutions interested in promoting RISC microprocessor design developed in the mid-1980s by Sun Microsystems. It is like 88open in a way, except the emphasis is on SPARC. There are over 150 organizations in SPARC International, many ISVs as well as hardware manufacturers. Member services include administrative support and development of standards (especially SPARC Compliance Definition or SCD), technology, and marketing programs. SPARC International also develops tools to assist in the conformance testing of hardware and software.

SPARC International—Focusing on SPARC ABI. The SPARC architecture represents the third largest installed base of systems behind Intel-based computers and Apple Macintosh in terms of units. SPARC systems currently represent approximately 60 percent of all UNIX shipments.

As availability of applications is a strong factor in end-user platform preference, and as there is a growing requirement among users for applications that are compatible across multiple SPARC-based architectures, SPARC International has established a program and process through which programs can be branded and such that binary compatibility can be warranted between applications and SPARC-compliant hardware.

For ISVs, SPARCware decreases the costs of software quality assurance and support. SPARCware compliance is achieved by porting a set of binary interface specifications for SVR4-based systems called the SPARC Compliance Definition 2 (SCD 2). Created by SPARC International members, SCD 2 contains the application-visible interfaces common among platform providers and optional interfaces that may be supplied by only some vendors. SCD 2 documents the interfaces available in commercial operating systems running on SPARC-based platforms. By porting to a common set of binary interfaces rather than an operating system, ISVs are guaranteed a stable set of interface specifications.

Compliance to SCD 2 is facilitated by SPARC International's System Compliance Test (SCT). The SPARC Application Verifier (SAV) is another tool ISVs use during the development and testing of software.

Application software vendors can obtain the SPARCware brand if the ISV develops or ports the software application using SAV to isolate and correct compliance issues. SAV can be self-tested on any conforming system at any site chosen by the ISV. Having completed the conformance test, the ISV submits the conformance test reports to SPARC International for verification. SPARC International validates the application and sends the ISV a trademark license for the SPARCware brand.

We believe X/Open will adopt a similar process to that developed by SPARC International for compliance testing and verification.

SPARC International
535 Middlefield Road
Suite 210
Menlo Park, CA 94025
Tel (415) 321-8692

8.2.6. User Alliance for Open Systems

Previously known as the "Houston 30," the User Alliance for Open Systems is a group of large corporations concerned with end-user issues and Open Systems technology. Officially formed in late 1990, the alliance is part of a larger group called the Corporation for Open Systems International (COS). The primary objective of the User Alliance is to development a process to influence Open Systems information technology. The Alliance does not officially endorse or support any specific technology or operating system. It has published a guide called *Overcoming Barriers to Open Systems Information Technology* which identifies nine of the most common barriers to Open Systems and recommendations on how to over-come these barriers. The Alliances' parent group, COS was founded 1986 and has over 50 members.

User Alliance for Open Systems
1750 Old Meadow Road
Suite 400
McLean, VA 22102
Tel (703) 883-2817

8.2.7.   IMA—The Interactive Multimedia Association

The Interactive Multimedia Association is an international trade asso-ciation with more than 240 corporate members representing the full scope of the multimedia industry, including applications developers, hardware and software suppliers, system integrators, publishers, dis-tributors, educators, and users.

The problem, according to IMA, is that each system or software vendor develops its own specific multimedia systems based on different services, data, and file formats. A multimedia application or title was capable of being played back only on that system for which it was designed.

In the interest of driving interoperability, the IMA publishes Re-quests for Technology, or RFTs, to define a robust set of requirements that will establish a strong foundation on which application developers can create applications that perform with predictable and consistent results across a wide variety of platforms and networked environments.

International Multimedia Association
3 Church Circle, Suite 800
Annapolis, MD 21401-1933
Tel/Fax (410) 626-1933/(410) 263-0590

8.3.   TRADE SHOW EXHIBITIONS AND TRADE ASSOCIATIONS

Tradeshows offer the opportunity for tens of thousands of people to get acquainted with the state of the art in UNIX systems, peripherals, soft-ware, and services such as consulting and training. There are more news and more product announcements and more changes in direction evident at each new show. In the future, trade shows will showcase different applications because UNIX will be taken for granted. In the long run, vendors with standardized UNIX will not be very exciting.

There are several relevant computer conferences, exhibitions, and trade shows. Many if not all of these will be attended by UNIX system suppliers. For the user interested in finding application solutions, there are several industry-oriented trade shows and exhibitions, such as:

SIGGRAPH (ACM)—computer graphics
NCGA—computer graphics and CAD/CAM
Autofact—manufacturing
SME—manufacturing
Electronic imaging—image processing
AEC—architecture, engineering, and construction

There are also several general-purpose computer exhibitions and conferences, including:

NCC—National Computer Conference
COMDEX
SICOB—France
Hanover Fair—Germany

Trade shows that specialize in technology include:

Xhibition for X Windows
Interop for networking

Trade shows that specialize in UNIX include:

UniForum
UNIX EXPO

8.3.1. UniForum

UniForum is tailored more for UNIX literates such as programmers, system administrators, and so forth. There are usually some sessions dedicated to the manager and the novice, but this show tends to draw a more technical audience. It focuses more on UNIX itself and systems technology and less on application solutions. It is similar to ACM's SIGGRAPH as opposed to UNIX EXPO, which is more like NCGA. The Xhibition usually addresses a wider group.

The annual UniForum conference is sponsored by UniForum. It is dedicated to the promotion of products and services based on UNIX. UNIX systems and software vendors are represented on a worldwide basis. Workshops and tutorials can be very valuable and of practical use to attendees, although they are generally aimed at the more technical users.

Conference registration forms and announcements can be obtained by contacting UniForum. The conference usually costs a few hundred dollars, the tutorials about the same unless you're a member. The vendor exhibits and tutorials held concurrently with the conference can be excellent sources of information and can provide a forum for attendees to exchange information.

UniForum is a nonprofit, vendor-independent trade association dedicated to promoting environments running UNIX and later Open Systems. Specifically, UniForum is concerned with promoting the establishment of vendor-independent standards related to UNIX. UniForum's primary function evolved over time to become one of the major forums for the users, developers, and vendors to exchange information about UNIX and the software and applications it supports. UniForum is today the world's largest UNIX user organization.

UniForum was founded in 1980, continuing the work of an association then known as /usr/group. It published its first catalog in 1981. It is perhaps best known for its annual trade show. Over 32,000 people attended last year's show in San Francisco.

UniForum is a trade association and as such provides services to its membership including publications such as *UniForum Monthly*, *UniNews*, and the *UNIX Products Directory*.

UNIX Products Directory

This directory is published annually just before the UniForum trade show held in January. Vendors who have been in a prior directory are contacted mid-year to update their product information for the next edition. Approximately 10,000 *UNIX Products Directories* are printed annually.

To order copies of the *UNIX Products Directory* or to join UniForum, you must complete a membership application. These are located in the back of the *UNIX Products Directory* or can be obtained from UniForum.

The *UNIX Product Directory* features the following:

* 7,689 vendors, including 428 worldwide
* 3,460 vertical and horizontal software packages

- 2,097 system software, application development tools and commu- nications products
- 800 hardware peripherals from modems to printers
- 329 books, magazines, newsletters, catalogs, and directories
- 311 consultants
- 154 training vendors

UniForum members enjoy the news value and product information found in its publications and events it sponsors, most notably the an- nual UniForum conference and exhibition, the world's largest exposi- tion of UNIX and Open Systems products and services with more than 300 vendors exhibiting at the 1992 show.

UniForum has approximately 9000 members worldwide. Its mem- bership is growing at approximately 20 percent per year. UniForum operates out of its headquarters office in Santa Clara, California. See Contacts. Its channels are essentially its membership and its affiliate groups which are listed in the *UniForum Products Directory*.

Dedicated to UNIX and Open Systems, it focuses on communica- tions about products, including hardware, software, and services. UniForum itself consists of corporate sponsors, and affiliate organiza- tions. The *UNIX Products Directory* program itself has no tiered struc- ture. It costs $100 for general membership to UniForum. The *UniForum Products Directory* is provided free to general members of UniForum; affiliate members pay a discounted price. Associate mem- berships cost $50 and give discounts on UniForum publications. Corpo- rate memberships cost $2,500 and are geared mainly toward UniForum exhibitors.

Vendor's editorial listings in the *UNIX Products Directory* are free for the first listing of any product in any category. Subsequent listings in other product categories cost $200 per listing. The only restriction is that the product or service listed must be UNIX-specific. Published material is based on information received in standardized product en- try forms. All vendors listed must verify the accuracy of their product listings in order to be retained in the directory from issue to issue. Products that are not updated are dropped from subsequent editions.

UniForum does have a Technical Director who can help answer ISVs' or members' questions. UniForum does not actively get involved in conversion or implementation of third-party software.

For information on advertising or future editions, or to be added to the vendor mailing list, contact the UniForum office at (800) 255-5620 or (408) 986-8840. UniForum sells its mailing list of around 14,000 total names of which over 7,000 are members and another 7,000 are people interested in remaining on UniForum's mailing list. Members can obtain this list for $300; non-members pay $500.

UniForum
2901 Tasman Dr., #201
Santa Clara, CA 95054
Tel (800) 255-5620 or (408) 986-8840
Fax (408) 986-1645

UniForum (Trade Show Management)
2400 East Devon Avenue
Suite 205
Des Plaines, IL 60018
Tel (800) 323-5155
(312) 323-1349 in Illinois and Canada
Fax (312) 299-1349

8.3.2.   UNIX EXPO

UNIX EXPO is one of the best shows for the layman as well as the novice in UNIX. It is held every autumn in New York City and consists of a three-day conference and exhibition. Tutorials and computer labs are run by AT&T. This is strictly a commercial show. The emphasis is on how UNIX is used in real-world applications.

National Expositions Co., Inc.
49 West 38th Street
Suite 12A
New York, NY 10018
Tel (212) 391-9111

8.3.3.   Xhibition

The Xhibition conference and exhibition, usually held in San Jose, California, proves that the X11 protocols and the X Window System from the Massachusetts Institute of Technology are making great strides year to year. Xhibition is a small but growing product exhibit floor and technical conference. X11 is a fast-emerging common denominator in UNIX, if not the entire computer industry. Everything short of an IBM MVS mainframe, from UNIX workstations and X Terminals to Apple Macintosh and IBM personal computers, is demonstrated rigged up as X servers (the workstation component, in X lingo), while the client is the host that runs the application. (see 8.3.6. for phone number)

8.3.4.   Vendor User Groups

Most major computer vendors have user groups that hold annual meetings. In many cases, these groups are run autonomously by a user group board of directors and independently of the vendor. It is usually possible to attend these meetings whether or not you are a user. This can be an excellent way to learn rapidly from the experiences of other users.

8.3.5.   Local User Groups

UniForum publishes contacts for local user groups all over the world in the *UNIX Products Directory*.

8.3.6.   Summary of Industry Trade Shows and Exhibits

Case World (508) 470-3880	Programmers
COMDEX (617) 449-6600	PC users
Computer Graphics Show (301) 587-4545	Graphics, CAD/CAM/CAE
Database World (508) 470-3880	MIS, programmers
DBEXPO (415) 941-8440	MIS, programmers
Downsizing Expo (508) 470-3880	MIS
Executive UniForum Symposium (617) 742-5200	CIOs, MIS
Federal Computer Conference (800) 343-6944	MIS, programmers
Interop (415) 941-3399 x900	Network professionals
LAN Expo* (617) 449-6600	Networking professionals
NetWORLD Expo (415) 780-3708	Novell NetWare/UnixWare
Object Solutions* (508) 649-9731	Programmers
Open Systems Europe* (508) 879-6700	MIS, programmers
PC Expo (800) 829-3976	PC users
SCO Forum (800) 553-9939	SCO users
Seybold Pub. Conf. & Expo (213) 457-5850	MIS, desktop publishers
Siggraph (312) 644-6610	Graphics, imaging
Software World (508) 470-3880	Programmers

Sun Open Systems Expo (800) 289-3976	Sun, SPARC clone users
UniForum (800) 323-5155	UNIX users, MIS, programmers
UNIX EXPO (508) 879-6700	UNIX users, MIS, programmers
Usenix (714) 588-8649	Programmers
Windows OS/2 (510) 601-5000	Programmers
Xhibition (617) 621-0060	Users, programmers
XWorld (212) 274-0640	Users, programmers

8.3.7. UNIX Reseller Trade Show and Exhibition

UNIX Reseller is sponsored by Computer Reseller News and VARBUSINESS. It is the largest all-reseller UNIX show in the industry. Almost 80 percent of UNIX suppliers rely on UNIX resellers to provide products and services to customers who use UNIX. UNIX Reseller is a conference designed to give resellers all the business and technical information they need about UNIX products and UNIX reseller programs. It is one of the premier forums for manufacturers to meet with resellers. The Educational Foundation for Resellers of Open Systems (EFROS), which sponsors this conference, also provides practical education and training. It has built up an independent and objective professional network for resellers of Open Systems. EFROS can be reached at (800) 766-3976.

> Educational Foundation for Resellers of Open Systems
> 500 College Road East
> Princeton, NJ 08540

8.4. SOURCES OF UNIX APPLICATION SOFTWARE

Historically, computer systems vendors have published third-party software catalogs that provide descriptions of the software that is available for use with their systems. This is still one of the best and fastest ways to learn where to find application software.

Because software porting from one version of UNIX to another can be relatively straightforward, there is a large list of software promoted by AT&T that runs with System V and can usually be made available for use on any System V-compliant operating system. Caution should be exercised in determining specific details concerning compatibility on a case-by-case basis. With UNIX, one need not feel limited to the software available in the vendor's third-party catalogs. There may be other software that can be easily modified and supported that can be ported from another vendor's catalog.

There is also a huge amount of public domain software running on UNIX, mainly coming through universities or user groups. These are the best sources of application software for UNIX:

- Your system suppliers and their third-party software
- UniForum *UNIX Product Directory* (see Section 8.5)
- Database or other software vendor's applications catalogs
- Datapro (see Section 8.1)
- Archives for free source code on The Internet (see Section 8.9.3)
- *UNIX International Product Catalog* (see also UNIX International Section 6.4)
- *The UNIX System V Release 4 Product Catalog* from USL lists some 5,000 applications

8.5. BOOKS, DOCUMENTATION, AND REPORTS

If you have looked, you have probably noticed that there are relatively few readily available books on UNIX in your local retail computer store, especially by comparison to, say, MS-DOS or OS/2 or the Apple Macintosh. The reason for this is that UNIX is commonly used with high-end personal computers and workstations, as well as with multiuser computer systems. It is typically used for business or commercial purposes as opposed to personal use, although this is rapidly changing.

Most UNIX books are reference manuals. They can provide a good basis for learning UNIX from a hands-on point of view. Books on UNIX that are commonly available tend to have a technical user orientation that tries to improve on information or documentation available from AT&T or other UNIX system vendors. Such books go beyond a description of the syntax of UNIX commands and try to tell the reader more about how and when UNIX commands should be used or how they actually work.

In addition to UNIX reference manuals, there are numerous specialty books dealing with topics such as programming techniques, writing shells, and system administration, which appeal to a very specific audience.

AT&T, John Wiley & Sons, and Prentice Hall are excellent sources for System V manuals. Microsoft, Inc. sells XENIX manuals.

Through your local UNIX user group or professional society, you can usually learn about the latest books and documentation coming on the market. There are book critics who regularly review UNIX-related books, and their reviews are often published in journals and periodicals. To find the best general sources of UNIX documentation, we suggest you consult your system vendor for available documentation or write to publishing houses that specialize in computer science texts:

Prentice-Hall (Englewood Cliffs, NJ)

QED Publishing Group (Wellesley, MA)

John Wiley & Sons (New York, NY)

Computer Literacy Bookshops (Sunnyvale, CA, (408) 730-9955)

Computer Systems Resources, Inc. (Atlanta, GA, (800) 323-8649)

The following books are recommended for specific areas of interest:

Beginner/Introductory UNIX Books

UNIX for People (Birns)

The UNIX Environment (Walker, UK)

Exploring the UNIX System (McGilton and Morgan)

The UNIX System (Kaare)

The UNIX System (Bourne)

UNIX for the Superuser (Foxley)

UNIX, the Book (Banahan and Rutter, UK)

UNIX System Administration (Fiedler and Hunter)

Shells

UNIX C Shell Desk Reference (Arick)

UNIX C Shell Field Guide (Anderson and Anderson)

UNIX Shell Programming (Kochan and Wood)

The Korn Shell Command and Programming Language (Bolsky and Korn)

The UNIX Shell Programming Language (Manis and Meyer)

UNIX Hacking

The C Programming Language (Kernigan and Ritchie)

UNIX Programming Environment (Kernigan and Pike)

Advanced UNIX Programming (Kochan and Wood)

Advanced UNIX—A Programmer's Guide (Prata)

UUCP/USENET/Communications

THE TCP/IP Companion (Arick)

USENIX Association (Berkeley, CA, (415) 528-8649)

Managing UUCP and USENET (O'Reilly & Associates, Inc.)

UNIX Communications (The Waite Group)

Using UUCP and USENET (Nutshell)

InterNetworking with TCP/IP (Comer)

Miscellaneous

UNIX Papers (The Waite Group)

Tricks of the UNIX Masters (Sage)

UNIX System Security (Wood and Kochan)

UNIX in a Nutshell, A Desktop Quick Reference for BSD or SYS-TEM V (O'Reilly & Associates, Inc.)

Improving the Security of Your UNIX System (Curry, SRI)

Publishers

USL. USL has established a publishing arm called UNIX Press. Chartered to provide authoritative and comprehensive System V literature, UNIX Press has compiled a complete line of audience specific guides and reference manuals.

UNIX Press has chosen to co-logo their catalog with Prentice Hall. The catalog can be obtained by contacting Prentice Hall, Box 11073, Des Moines, IA 50381-1073. Fax requests can be made to (201) 592-2247.

Reports and Newsletters

In addition to the special reports offered by market research firms, consortia, and user groups and alliances, there are a few companies who specialize in providing information specifically on business issues related to the UNIX and Open Systems Industry.

Networked Publications
16680 Shannon Road, Cabana Suite
Los Gatos, California 95032
Tel/Fax (408) 356-4059

Networked Publications publishes titles such as:

UNIX Vendors ISV Programs Report

Direct Marketing and Inside Sales For UNIX ISVs and Resellers

Matrix News. *Matrix News* is a monthly newsletter about cross-network issues. Networks frequently mentioned include USENET, UUCP, FidoNet, BITNET, the Internet and conferencing systems such as the WELL, and CompuServe. *Matrix News* is not about any single one of them. It is about the Matrix, which encompasses all computer networks worldwide that exchange electronic mail.

Online subscriptions are available in postscript or ASCII format. Special rates are available for students.

Matrix News
Matrix Information and Directory Services, Inc.
1106 Clayton Lane
Suite 500W
Austin, TX 78723
Tel (512) 451-7602/Fax (512) 450-1436
Email address: mids@tic.com

8.6.   JOURNALS AND PERIODICALS

These resources can be extremely valuable in keeping up with the latest developments in the market. Most are readily available in retail computer stores.

BYTE (McGraw-Hill Publication)

CommUNIXations (UniForum)

COMPUTERWORLD (CW Publishing/INC.)

CSN (Computer Systems News)

UNIX REVIEW (Miller Freeman Publications Co.)

UNIX Today! (A CMP Publication)

UNIXWORLD (A Tech Valley Publication)

COMPUTER Currents (IDG Communications Publications)

Micro Times, BAM Publications

Sys Admin—Sys Admin is a new journal for UNIX system administrators. It is published by R&D Publications, Inc. Inquiries concerning subscriptions should be directed to *Sys Admin*, 1601 W. 23rd St., Suite 200, Lawrence, KS 66046-2743, (913) 841-1631.

There are also several vendor-specific publications that can be useful, such as:

Sun Observer

SunWorld

DEC Professional

Digital News

8.7.   TRAINING AND EDUCATION

There is a growing number of sources for UNIX training as UNIX gains greater commercial popularity.

Some of the best:

Universities	Nearly all support some training in UNIX as part of their Computer Science curricula
Vendors	System suppliers offer customer education courses. Many offer them at their training centers or on-site. Ask your vendor or prospective vendor what types of education seminars and "course ware" they offer.
Self-training	There are several companies that offer computer assisted instruction. A good starting point to locate products can be found in the UniForum *UNIX Products Directory.*
Training	In recognition of the growing interest in UNIX, a number of companies now specialize in training services for UNIX. See the UniForum *UNIX Products Directory.*

There are small companies that offer quite interesting training products. One in the Bay Area is .sh consulting. .sh offers a series of 20 one-day seminars that can be taken independently or in combination with other seminars according to your training needs. A set of 15 seminar notebooks with examples has been developed. These course notes have been developed over the last 10 years. Course fees are $200 per course, per person based on pre-enrollment.

.sh consulting
3355 Brookdale Drive
Santa Clara, CA 95051
(408) 241-8319

8.8. GETTING EXPERT ASSISTANCE

Consultants for Users

There are times when companies need to find outside consultants to do things that they either don't know how to do or don't want to do internally. The good news is that the burgeoning UNIX market has created a cottage industry of consultants. UNIX system and software vendors usually have consulting groups that can be contracted to do special work.

The *UNIX Products Directory* provides a new listing each year of organizations that offer expert assistance. The broad range of available assistance, from students to needy programming wizards, from independent companies to system vendors, means that you should be able to shop around to find the type of help best suited to your needs.

SSC (Specialized Systems Consultants, Inc.). SSC was established in 1968 and has specialized in the UNIX operating system since 1980. SSC publishes pocket size *C and UNIX Command Summaries* and tutorials. The command summaries summarize user commands and command options. The C Library Reference includes the library functions and system calls organized by function area. Other books published include the *Korn Shell References, VI Reference, VI Tutorial, Emacs Reference, C++ Reference, C Library Reference for UNIX System V Release 4, ANSI C, RS-232 Card, System 5 (Bourne) Shell Tutorial,* and the *MS-DOS 5.0 Command Summary.*

SSC
P.O. Box 55549
Seattle, Washington 98155
Tel (206) 527-3385
Fax (206) 527-2806

8.9. SUBSCRIBING TO NETWORK SERVICES

Bulletin board systems such as UUNET and CompuServe provide information services over public networks such as USENET, the Internet, and AlterNet, a new commercial alternative to the government-funded Internet.

8.9.1. USENET

USENET is an informal network of UNIX sites which was first created at Duke University in 1979. Originally it was a way for members of the

USENIX association to read and post news to each other. A revised USENET program was developed at Berkeley in 1982. Today USENET reaches tens of thousands of users around the world.

How To Get on USENET and the USENIX Association. To get on USENET, you first need to find a nearby site that already has USENET that is willing to be your "feed." Ask your system vendor for possibilities, or find someone through a local UNIX user group. You should be prepared to pay the telephone bill for communicating with your feed via dial-up modems. Once you have a reliable physical connection, you need to be sure UUCP is there and working. UUCP is supplied with most popular UNIX systems.

With UUCP and a physical connection in place, you now have to get the latest USENET sources from your feed site. These programs are in the public domain and should be obtainable free of charge. Next, read the accompanying instructions and follow them through implementation. You will then be "plugged in."

The USENIX Association is a professional and technical association of individuals and institutions concerned with breeding innovation in the UNIX tradition. Membership information may be obtained by contacting the association at P.O. Box 2299, Berkeley, CA 94710.

UUNET and UUCP-Net. UUNET is a system that simply transports mail and news as a major node in a worldwide communications network. UUCP-Net is supported by commercial enterprises, educational institutions, and other individuals who are willing to dedicate resources to perpetuating the network. To provide access for users not already associated with one of the established nodes (since finding a feed site is not always possible), the USENIX Users Group created a dedicated node, named UUNET, to which anyone can subscribe. Now, the UUNET node has become a commercial service (known as the UUNET Communications Services) and offers access to the USENET news distribution. It also offers email forwarding to thousands of other nodes and several networks, including the Internet. USENIX started a commercial communication service in 1987. UUNET recently began offering a 900 number for anonymous UUCP access to its source archives. UUNET also provides subscription to AlterNet.

USENIX provides a mail gateway and UNIX archives that can be accessed by subscribers. UUCP-Net is available to anyone on a fee-paying basis. Contact the USENIX association (Berkeley, California) for the latest description of UUNET services and rates: (415) 528-8649 or (703) 876-5050.

UUNET Communication Services
3110 Fairview Park Dr.
Suite 570
Falls Church, VA 22042
(703) 876-5050

Public-Access UNIX Networks. There is a growing number of public-access UNIX systems that provide login service to all comers. Unlike UUNET, where information is downloaded to your computer, these systems let you log in and gain access to USENET and other services through their systems. Consult UniForum or USENIX for a complete listing to find the right location, type of system, and fee structure to meet your needs.

An Information Explosion in NETNEWS. In the last few years, the volume of data transmitted electronically has surpassed, for the first time, the amount of voice traffic over communications networks. Evidence of this data explosion can be found in the Internet itself, where there is a reported 25 megabytes a day of information posted to NetNews.

NetNews is an alternative to large email interest lists. There are well over a thousand newsgroups active and readable once you get on the Internet. News provides several advantages over email lists. With news, all messages about the same field are grouped together, and all news is separated from your email. While the details of specific mail readers may differ, nearly all of them allow easy elimination of news that is not of interest to you. Newsgroups are much less expensive in terms of network bandwidth and system administration.

There are several popular newsreaders; some are: rn, newstool, and gnuemacs/gnus. Your system administrator should be able to get these up and running on your system. Numerous newsgroups are usually available. They provide all sorts of information ranging from special interests like ham radios or fishing to technical papers. It is not unusual to have access to hundreds of different newsgroups. A new set of hypermedia-like tools are likely to emerge to help users cope with locating the right information becoming available over the network.

8.9.2.   Email and Conferencing Services

UUNET is not the only provider of electronic mail and computer conferencing. Several companies offer both computer mailboxes and various conferences. MCI Mail and Compuserve are well known providers of mailbox type services. These are national organizations you can find through the yellow pages.

Portal Communications (Cupertino, CA) is an example of a smaller private mailbox service company. For five years Portal has operated a for-profit store and forward service that competes with UUNET. Other groups are starting to provide services like UUNET and Portal. The Well is a popular conference and mailbox system based in Sausalito CA. BIX is a conferencing and mailbox service run by BYTE magazine in Peterborough NH.

8.9.3.   The Internet

The Internet has evolved from its root in the government and research community and into the mainstream of networked computing. It is a conglomeration of over 5000 networks in 33 countries around the world. Gigabytes of information can be accessed through the Internet and it continues to grow as more organization subscribe.

The term "internet" means something specific in the networking community. "The Internet" is not an individual network, nor is it an individual organization or even a network. It is a collective term for the many backbone, regional and site data networks.

Organizations join the Internet because it is convenient and because it is less expensive than establishing their own wide-area networks. The value of a network is in how it connects people. The Internet defines a common ground for internetworking communities and establishes a community of people who want to connect.

The applications, services, archives, and other sources of information easily fill up an entire book and there are a few of them you can obtain. ARPANET was one of the driving influences of the Internet. The Internet is a network designed originally to accommodate the needs for serious data communications within the government and government research groups. It was the mechanism that could share huge amounts of data and connect thousands of scientists.

Over the years, the Internet became so large it was beyond any single institution's capability to register users, etc. At this point Network Operation Centers or NOCs were established (like regional telephone companies) to administer the Internet in different geographic territories.

The Internet for many people, particularly programmers means "info-booty" according to John Quarterman, an expert on the Internet and internetworking in general. There is shareware, freeware, source code, documents, graphics, and datasets all available via file transfer downloads and from email servers. Sites like UUNET and The World each have several gigabytes' worth of publicly available archives. There is so much information on the Internet—so many archives that a group at McGill University in Canada put together the Internet Archive Server Listing. The "archie group" at McGill manages *archie*, a central database of information about Internet-accessible archive sites, plus server programs that provide access by *telnet*, anonymous file transfer protocol (FTP), email and the Prospero distributed computer system.

The Internet users today mostly include programmers, and the information that is available is mainly of a technical nature. The Internet is not that difficult to use, and kindergarten through twelfth-grade groups have sprung up within the Internet and the Free Educational Mail network of more than 150 bulletin board systems. Schools are connecting to the Internet in order to get into the ICS, an educational-oriented network conferencing group organized at the University of Michigan. It can be reached at the address ics@um.cc.umich.edu. Over 10,000 students from nearly 400 schools have been using ICS players.

8.9.4. Commercial Internet Exchange

The Internet was once restricted to research, education, and government agency activity. The Internet had a fair use policy that basically said for-profit usage was forbidden. As Public Data Internets offer commercial unrestricted connectivity, their users are bound by these limits for traffic only within and among the appropriate portions of the Internet. No commercial traffic like advertisements (junk email) are allowed for example on the NSFnet backbone used to connect NSF researchers. The Commercial Internet Exchange established by the PDIs enables PDIs to exchange traffic without sending it over the NSFnet. Hundreds of companies are turning commercial PDIs like Advanced Network and Services (Elmsford, NY), Performance Systems International (Reston VA) and UUNET Communications Services (Falls Church, VA) to be part of the Internet.

8.9.5. Making the WAN Connection Through the Commercial Internet

In the past, to connect to the Internet you had to locate the administrator for the regional network and work on getting a connection. Some people still do this, but there are a growing number of businesses who offer this type of service, which can greatly simplify the process for individuals or companies getting connected to the Internet.

Wherever you are, the location of your nearest network point-of-presence is important in choosing which commercial Internet provider to use. Before you go out and buy a modem, make sure your prospective commercial Internet provider doesn't provide one for you as part of their service. Its also a good idea to ask them to recommend the best equipment (modems, bridges, routers, etc.) to use for connections at your site.

While the cost of the modem, monthly fees, and usage fees add up, the benefit of using a commercial Internet provider is that they provide professional management for your wide-area network. They monitor your network connection(s) and make sure it's up. Most providers check the connections and don't wait until you call with a problem.

8.9.6. Commercial Internet Providers

Alternet, UUNET Technologies Inc.
3110 Fairview Park Dr., Ste. 570
Falls Church, VA 22042
(800) 488-6383, (703) 204-8000
Email address: alternet-info@uunet.uu.net

Cerfnet, General Atomics
P.O. Box 85608
San Diego, CA 92186-9784
(800) 876-2373
Email address: help@cerf.net

Colorado Supernet Inc. (Colorado residents only)
Colorado School of Mines
Computing Center
1500 Illinois
Golden, CO 80401
(303) 273-3214

PSInet, Performance Systems International Inc.
11800 Sunrise Valley Dr., Ste. 1100
Reston, VA 22091
(703) 620-6651
Email address: info@psi.com

Pipex Ltd.
216 The Science Park
Cambridge CB4 4WA, England

+44-2-23-424616 or +44-2-23-426868
Email address: pipex@unipalm.co.uk

(The above is not a complete list of suppliers.)

8.10.   CAREERS IN THE UNIX INDUSTRY

There are numerous career opportunities and career progression possibilities for people within the UNIX industry. Programmers have progressive ladders of positions, from junior to senior program, to project leader, to manager or director. Program managers, who need to really understand customer needs and determine how to deliver a solution will always be in demand. The ability of these people to break down complex projects into tasks can play a crucial role in the management of change. There are usually opportunities for people to move between the end-user community and the vendor community while staying within the same industry or area of specialization.

When looking for a job, networking is important both figuratively and literally. UNIX networks and bulletin board services have become common devices for advertising and finding programmers for example. Career centers have sprung up in most larger companies and these can be a good place to investigate job opportunities as well as more traditional methods such as universities or other institutions or trade shows. High tech career fairs are organized where you can meet with numerous prospective employers.

There are also more aggressive and creative techniques you can use to find a job in the UNIX Industry. You could take out an ad in one of the many magazines or trade publications. You could look into the ISV or VAR catalogs of the major vendors to find companies you might never otherwise have ever heard of.

There is strong demand for all sorts of people in a variety of areas. There are recruiters who specialize in UNIX, but with all the above suggestions, if you have the time, you might be surprised how much you can do on your own.

The following are hot areas of interest in technical and commercial skills now and for the foreseeable future:

Technical orientation

*   Programmers
    —C and C++
    —Relational and Object-Oriented Database
    —Programming in multiple window environments

- Network and system administration
- Network and systems integration

Business orientation

- Program management, project management
- Technical product marketing
- Business and process re-enginneering

Bibliography

Apgood, R., "A UNIX Primer, A Guide for New Users," *Sun Observer*, February 1989.

AT&T, *System V Interface Definition, AT&T*, AT&T Customer Information Center, Indianapolis, IN, 1985.

Bourne, S., *The UNIX System*, Addison-Wesley, Reading, MA, 1983.

Cargill, Carl F., *Information Technology Standardization, Theory, Process and Organizations*, Digital Press, 1989.

Christian, K., *UNIX Command Reference Guide*, John Wiley & Sons, New York, 1988.

Curry, D. A., *Improving the Security of Your UNIX System*, final report, ITSTD-721-FR-90-21, SRI International, Menlo Park, CA, April 1990.

Fiedler, D., and Hunter, B. H., *UNIX System Administration*, Hayden Book Company, Hasbrouck Heights, NJ, 1986.

Groff, J. R., and Weinberg, P. N., *Understanding UNIX: A Conceptual Guide*, 2d edition, Que Corporation, Indianapolis, 1983.

Jespersen, H., "Scaling the MIS Heights," *UNIX Review*, September 1987.

Kochan, Stephen G., and Wood, Patrick H., consulting editors, *UNIX Networking*, Hayden Book Company, Hasbrouck Heights, NJ, 1990.

Lee, E., "Window of Opportunity," *UNIX Review*, Vol. 6, No. 6.

Libes, D., and Ressler, S., *Life With UNIX, A Guide For Everyone*, Prentice Hall, Englewood Cliffs, NJ, 1989.

Lynch, Daniel C., and Rose, Marshall T., *Internet System Handbook*, Addison-Wesley, Reading, MA, 1993.

Nichols, E. A., Bailin, S. C., and Nichols, J. C., *UNIX Survival Guide*, Holt, Rinehart and Winston, New York, 1987.

Marshall, Kirk, McKusick, "A Berkeley Odyssey, Ten Years of BSD History," *UNIX Review*, January 1985.

Mohr, A., "The Genesis Story," *UNIX Review*, January 1985.

O'Dell, M., "Putting Unix in Perspective," *UNIX Review*, December 1986.

OPEN SYSTEMS: The UNIX in Canada Study Report, /usr/group/cdn, Ontario, Canada, 1989.

Porting Reference Guide for Sun Workstations, Sun Microsystems, Inc., Mountain View, CA, November 1988.

POSIX Explored, UniForum, Santa Clara, CA, 1987.

Realini, C., "UNIX in the Business Market," *UNIX Review*, November 1986.

Ritchie, D. M., "The Evolution of the Unix Time-sharing System. Language Design and Programming Methodology," Lecture Notes in *Computer Science 79*, Springer-Verlag, New York, 1980.

Schnatmeier, V., "A Banner Year for UNIX," *Unix World*, January 1988.

Schulman, M., *Open Systems: Facts and Fallacies*, Soloman Bros. Inc., NY, 1988.

"Shipments of UNIX Systems," *Electronic News*, January 19, 1987.

Stahlman, M., *Bernstein Research Notes*, Sanford Bernstein & Co., Inc., NY, June 29, 1988.

Strong, B., and Hosler, J., *The UNIX for Beginners Book: A Step-by-Step Introduction*, John Wiley & Sons, New York, 1987.

SUNOS Technical Overview, Sun Microsystems, Inc., Mountain View, CA, 1988.

"UNIX: Japan Jumps into the US Computer Marketplace," *Electronic Business*, March 1987.

UNIX: Products Directory, /usr/group, Santa Clara, CA, 1989.

UNIX Systems & Software, Datapro, Delran, NJ, 1989, 1990.

Waite, M., Martin, D., and Prata, S., *UNIX PrimerPlus*, Howard W. Sams & Co., Inc., Indianapolis, IN, 1983.

Wood, P. H., and Kochan, S. G., *UNIX System Security*, Hayden Book Company, Hasbrouck Heights, NJ, 1985.

X/OPEN, *X/OPEN Portability Guide*, Prentice Hall, Englewood Cliffs, NJ, 1989.

Young, J., and Manuel, T., "UNIX Looking Better," *Electronics*, October 15, 1987.

Glossary

Those of us whose work demands a knowledge of computer technology are constantly encountering new concepts and buzzwords. Over time, certain words tend to have "overloaded" meaning and can mean different things depending on the context in which they are used. This section will be useful to consult to clarify the author's definition of key acronyms, buzzwords, and concepts.

ABI (Application Binary Interface)

A specification that defines how executable UNIX programs are stored so that they can run on specific hardware architectures by relinking instead of recompiling. AT&T and Sun Microsystems have defined these interfaces for System V. The benefit for users and independent software vendors is that the software can be written once to the ABI instead of to each unique hardware architecture. This allows software written to the ABI to be run as interchangeably as the software that runs on personal computers today.

Access Control

A "trusted" process that limits access to the resources and objects of a computer system in accordance with a security model. The process can be implemented by reference to a stored table that lists the access rights to subjects of objects, for example, users to records.

ACM

SIGGRAPH (Association for Computing Machinery, Special Interest Group in Computer Graphics) SIGGRAPH sponsors a trade show and exhibition each summer covering the latest advances in computer graphics.

Ada

High-level computer language used by the U.S. government.

AIX (Advanced Interactive Executive)

A UNIX variant based on AT&T System V release 2 with Berkeley extensions. Originally developed by INTERACTIVE Systems under contract to IBM for the IBM RT/PC, AIX was initially selected by OSF as the basis for its future UNIX product.

ANSI (American National Standards Institute)

An organization sponsored by the Business Equipment Manufacturers Association (BEMA) for the purpose of establishing voluntary industry standards.

API (Application Programming Interface)

A high-level interface specification and programming language interface between the application program and the operating system. The interface allows the programmer to write once for the API instead of implementing numerous interfaces to different underlying operating system calling conventions. An application that adheres to the API need only be recompiled to run on any other operating system that supports the same API.

Application Environment Specification

This specification addresses the portability of applications at the source code level. It includes the application interfaces, operating system, and system extensions. These are consistent with POSIX, NIST, and X/OPEN's XPG.

Architecture

The underlying design of a computer that defines data storing methods, operations, and compatibility with other systems and software. Refers to specific components of a computer system and the way they interact with each other. Often, this refers to the type of CPU chip that is used as the basis of a computer system.

Batch System

An operating system function that schedules one job at a time through the computer's processing subsystem.

Booting

Powering up a computer system, testing to determine which devices are attached, bringing the operating system kernel into memory, running it.

BSD

(Berkeley Standard Distribution) A derivative of the UNIX system developed at the University of California at Berkeley.

Bug

A fault or mistake in the design or implementation of hardware or software that causes incorrect results or prevents successful processing.

Bus

A cable or circuit used to transfer electrical signals among connected devices.

C

A high-level computer language developed by Bell Laboratories, normally included as part of UNIX. C is a machine-independent language. It was originally developed by Dennis Ritchie at AT&T Bell Laboratories. When UNIX was rewritten in C, it became easily transportable to other computer systems. Today, C is a widely used language.

CALS

A Department of Defense standard for electronic exchange of data for computer-aided logistics systems.

CDE - Pg. 94

CD-ROM (Compact Disk—Read Only Memory)

An inexpensive and hardy medium for distribution of programs and data.

CGM (Common Graphics Metafile)

A standard for computer graphics data exchange.

Client (dataless)

Sun's definition from NFS is a node in a network that has its own disk and runs its own operating system but relies on other network server(s) for booting, its file systems, and other services.

Client (diskless)

Sun's definition is a node in a network that has no disk and relies on a networked server for file storage, booting, and other services.

COBOL

A high-level programming language used primarily in business applications.

Command

A directive to a computer program. Commands may be typed at a keyboard or invoked by choosing an option from a menu.

Command Interpreter

A program that reads lines typed at a keyboard and interprets them as requests to execute other programs. The shell is the UNIX command interpreter.

Compiler

A program that converts high-level source language input into a form that can be processed by the system.

COS (Corporation for Open Systems)

COSE   pg. 94, 90

CPU

Central Processing Unit. The hardware in a computer that executes machine instructions.

Daemon

A server process that handles system-wide functions and runs "invisibly" in the background. Daemons are initiated during system boot and activated automatically or periodically to perform some particular task. They provide resources to the host machine and/or network.

DARPA (Department of Defense Advanced Research Projects Agency)

Coordinates and funds research projects related to defense systems.

De facto

Refers to standards that are widely used even though they may not be sanctioned by any official standards bodies. According to actual practice. Protocols and architectures, such as Sun's NFS and IBM's SNA, are called de facto standards because they are so widely used.

Distributed Computing

The dispersion of discrete computing functions, such as processing, storage, and network management, among the various computers on a network, as determined by their specialized capabilities or availability. The goal of distributed computing is to place computing at the convenience of the user, with applications distributed optimally throughout the network. In this way, users can take advantage of resources on their network including applications, system, and service choices all without having to know the exact location where such services or data reside.

Driver

A program or portion of a program that controls the transfer of data from an input/output device.

Electronic Data Interchange (EDI)

EDI is a standard format for the exchange of business documents such as purchase orders and electronic fund transfer between businesses. The EDI process may consist of taking mainframe extracted data and moving it to the UNIX environment where it gets converted into standard EDI format.

Email (electronic mail)

A set of programs used to transmit information electronically within a network or to other remote networks.

Emulator

Hardware or software features that allow a computer, terminal, or other device to mimic another system. UNIX emulators make it look like you are running UNIX when it is not really there. Such implementations usually have performance or functionality shortcomings.

Ethernet

A commonly used local area network technology developed by Xerox Corporation.

Extensible

Software that readily permits features to be modified or added.

File system

An arrangement of directories of files on mass storage device(s).

Filter

A UNIX utility that reads data, operates on it in some way, and writes it out again.

FIPS (Federal Information Processing Standards)

Directives that specify requirements to be used in U.S. government computer-related purchases. FIPS are developed by NIST. The government has developed a test suite based on a subset of the AT&T SVVS to test conformance to FIPS.

Fork

A UNIX system call for copying the entire address space and context of a process to create two identical processes, the parent (original process), and the child (new process).

FORTRAN

A high-level programming language used mainly in scientific and technical computing applications.

Gateway

A node in a network that enables networks using different protocols to communicate with each other. Gateway refers to the logical interconnection of otherwise incompatible networks that perform protocol conversion via hardware and/or software, allowing messages to be routed between networks.

GOSIP
U.S. government communications standard.

grep
A UNIX utility that searches through text files for a user-specified string of characters.

Groupware
A new term used to describe a type of software solution that supports cooperative work group processing. Examples include calendar programs and teleconferencing systems.

GUI (Graphical User Interface)
Users typically select services using a mouse to point and click on selected icons which then invokes the appropriate commands.

Hacker
Someone who spends large amounts of time with computers; a workaholic programmer. "Hacker" is usually a term of endearment in the technical community, but it can connote an undisciplined or eccentric programmer to the MIS world.

Hard Mount
Default NFS mounts are hard mounts where the client tries to mount the directory even if the server does not respond. Any file systems that are read-write should be hard-mounted. See also Soft Mount.

Hardware-Independent
Software that is portable across a wide variety of computer hardware.

Heterogeneous Server
A server that can have clients of another architecture attached to it as well as clients of its own architecture.

Hierarchical File System
A method for storing groups of files on a disk (or other mass storage) system in a tree structure; for example, a "parent" can have many "children," but each "child" can have but one "parent."

High Availability

Usually, an architecture consisting of both hardware and software features that is intended to keep a system operating with very high reliability. The ultimate example is a fault-tolerant system virtually guaranteed never to go down.

Homogeneous Server

A server that has clients only of its own architecture.

Host

A computer system. Often, a larger system such as a mainframe computer in the network.

IEEE (Institute of Electrical and Electronic Engineers)

IGES (Intermediate Graphics Exchange Specification)

A NIST standard for expressing geometric data for interchange between CAD/CAM software.

Integration, Horizontal

One of the two essential elements of a truly Open System, a capability that provides the ability to integrate applications and data and interfaces across many different vendors' systems.

Integration, Vertical

One of the two essential elements of a truly Open System, a capability that provides portability and integration of applications from PCs and workstations all the way up through servers and into mainframes.

(The) Internet

A worldwide area network using internet protocol (IP), originally sponsored by DARPA (Defense Advanced Research Projects Agency).

Internet Address

The address of a system on a network.

Interoperability

Also called interworking; implies that computer systems and/or software between different vendors will work together in some complementary fashion.

Interprocess Communication

A mechanism that allows one process to communicate with another.

IRDS (Integrated Repository Definition Standard)

ISO (International Standards Organization)

International Standards Organization is a standards body based in Geneva Switzerland which is composed of a number of national standards bodies. ISO is one of the most authoritative producers of international standards including the OSI reference model.

Kernel

The master program set for the UNIX operating system that manages all the physical devices of the system, including the file system, memory, disks, tapes, printers, and communications. The kernel supports such functions as task synchronization, scheduling, memory allocation, and communications with other systems.

LAN (Local Area Network)

A group of nearby computer systems (nodes) tied together by a high-speed network.

Libraries

A collection of programs and packages that are made available for common use within some environment; individual items need not be related. A typical library might contact compilers, utility programs, packages for mathematical operations, and so on.

Mac

Nickname for the Apple Macintosh.

Mainframe

A large computer used for corporate data processing. Examples are an IBM 3090 and "IBM Plug Compatibles."

Minicomputer

A midrange computer system in the class of DEC VAX, Prime 50 Series, or Data General computer systems.

Minisupercomputer

A class of "sub-supercomputers." Examples are Convex and Alliant.

Mips

A computer systems vendor acquired by SGI. Mips is the maker of the R2000, R3000, and R4000 RISC processors.

MIPS

Millions of instructions per second. A general measurement—not a benchmark number that has little consistency from one vendor to another.

MIS (Management Information System)

A central group of specialists whose function is to support a corporate data processing center.

Modem

An electronic device connected to a computer system that enables communication between systems over telephone lines.

Motif

A graphical user interface from OSF based on the X-windows technology.

MS-DOS (Microsoft Disk Operating System)

The dominant operating system on IBM PCs and compatibles. An operating system developed by Microsoft for computers using Intel 16 and 32-bit family of microprocessors. It provides a set of software services for programs running in a single-user environment and a simple command line interpreter as its user interface. A major facility is a set of services for managing files and I/O devices.

Multimedia

Mixed data representations—voice, video, fax, data, and so on.

Multiprocessor

A computer whose processing subsystem consists of multiple identical processing elements.

Multitasking

Functionality in an operating system that allows users to run several tasks or programs at once that may access and change the same data simultaneously. A multitasking operating system assigns priorities to the processes competing for control of the CPU. The operating system processes have the highest priority. The longer any process waits for the CPU, the higher its priority becomes, until the operating system finally allocates memory and handles the swapping of the process.

Multi-threading (MT)

A form of code that uses more than one process or processor, possibly of different types, and that may on occasion have more than one processor or processors active at the same time.

Multiuser

Functionality in an operating system that allows multiple users to run several tasks simultaneously, providing independent access to the same files or data, to print documents or run programs at the same time on the system.

NBS (National Bureau of Standards (now known as NIST))

Name of NIST until 1988.

Networking

The interconnection of two or more computers.

NFS (Network File System)

A software system supporting access to files stored on one networked device by any other networked device. Developed by Sun Microsystems, NFS is now a UNIX industry standard.

NIST (National Institute for Standards and Technology)

Formerly called the National Bureau of Standards (NBS), the NIST is a U.S. government standards body that approves computer and networking specifications as standards. Vendors who want to sell products to the government must build their products in compliance with such standards. The FIPS standards were created and are managed by NIST.

Open Architecture

A seamless integration of client applications and information resources residing on distributed, heterogeneous hardware systems.

Open Software Foundation (OSF)

A vendor consortium formed in 1988 to develop an open computing operating system environment in reaction to AT&T's exclusive UNIX System V Release 4 development alliance with Sun.

Open System

A form of system (be it based on hardware chip, operating system, database, or user interface) that enables the consumer to reduce his/her dependence on single-source suppliers.

Open Systems

Computing devices that are relatively inexpensive, versatile, and compatible because of their reliance on industry-standard technologies and their conformance with industry-accepted specifications. Communications and computing capabilities that conform to standards and permit software portability and transparent networking.

Operating System

The basic software that runs the inner workings of a computer; the intermediary between the application software and the computer.

Optical Disk

Compact mass-storage device that will hold vast quantities of data.

Orthogonality

The property of independence among different functions, such that new functions can be substituted with little or no impact on other functions.

OSI (Organization for International Standards)

Originally, a European consortium defining standards for networking. Defines standard formats for messages sent across system boundaries.

PHIGS

(Programmer's Hierarchical Interactive Graphics System) A software interface standard including data structures for high-level 3-D applications.

Pipe

The ability provided by UNIX to allow two or more commands to be connected so that the output of one command becomes the input to the next command.

Portability

Used to describe software that can be easily moved from one computer system environment to another. "Easily" implies that minimal to no modification is required.

POSIX

A set of standards developed by IEEE specifying components of a portable operating system. POSIX is vendor-independent, and its goal is to allow the development of portable application software across different vendors' hardware.

PostScript

A text and graphics language created by Adobe Systems to drive laser printers and used in some display interfaces.

Protocol

A set of formal rules specifying how hardware and software on a network should interact in transmitting and receiving information.

RDBMS (Relational Database Management System)

A system that manages a database relationally as opposed to hierarchically. "Relationally" means that data can be accessed via a choice of routes instead of the rigid, top-down-only route of hierarchically organized data.

RISC (Reduced Instruction Set Computer)

A microprocessor architecture that optimizes speed and power by simplifying the computer's internal communications; has gained acceptance as an alternative to the complex instruction set computers (CISC) widely used today.

Scalability

Used in a hardware context to mean the ability to smoothly upgrade or downgrade system capabilities such as processing speed. Also used in describing how the basic system architecture design—for example, RISC—can be implemented in various manufacturing technologies such as CMOS, ECL, GaAS (Gallium Arsenide), and so on. Used in a software context to mean that the operating system or software can be used with a wide range of computers, for example, from PC to workstation to minicomputer to mainframe to supercomputer.

RPC (Remote Procedure Call facility)

This facility is a library of procedures providing a mechanism for a client process to execute a procedure or server process.

SCCS

Source Code Control System

SCSI

Small Computer Systems Interface

Semaphore

In AT&T System V, semaphores provide system-wide process state data. Like messages and shared memory, these are useful for communicating and synchronizing multiple processes.

Server

A computer in a networked system with a specific role to play providing other systems referred to as clients with services over a network. The server manages and coordinates the sharing of resources.

Service

A daemon through which processes access servers.

shell

A command interpreter in UNIX.

Shell script

A file consisting of commands and special constructs for shells.

Sockets

An interprocess communications channel. Once sockets are connected, processes can read and write for communications (presuming TCP, UDP are different).

Soft Mount

An NFS concept where the client does not retry the mount operation if the server does not respond to its first request. Directories that are read-only, such as the MAN pages, are usually soft-mounted.

SPARC

Scalable Processor RISC Architecture

SQL (Structured Query Language)

An ANSI standard language for accessing and implementing relational databases.

Standards

Products or procedures that have become the most common, or most frequently used, within the industry. Standards are not specific to one company though they may be owned and licensed from one source.

Standards, De facto

Standards that are licensable (such as standards that may be owned by a particular vendor but where that vendor has gone to the open market and freely licensed that standard, such as UNIX from AT&T and the Sun Microsystems SPARC architecture).

Standards, De jure

Standards set by bodies that are independent from manufacturers. Such bodies include IEEE (with its POSIX standard) and ISO (International Standards Organization with its OSI [Open Systems Interconnect standard]).

Standards, Multivendor De facto

"Standards" based on product alliances such as the OSF and the UNIX International versions of UNIX wherein a variety of different vendors have gotten together and agreed to package a common product in a way that it is supported on a wide variety of vendors' platforms.

Standards, Single Vendor De facto

"Standards" such as IBM's MVS operating system and NetWare from Novell wherein there is a single supplier of the product, but it is available on a variety of different vendors' platforms.

Streams

An implementation of interprocess communication first introduced in UNIX System V release 3. Provides a flexible mechanism for two or more processes to communicate with each other. A general facility and a set of tools for the development of UNIX system communication services. Supports the implementation of services ranging from the complete networking protocol suites, such as OSI or TCP/IP, to individual device drivers.

Supercomputer

A term generally referring to a very high-performance computer such as a Cray or other "number-crunching" computer system.

Superminicomputer

A computer in a higher-performance class than the minicomputer but less powerful than the so-called minisupercomputer or mainframe.

Superuser

A user with special privileges granted by the operating system that allow him or her to perform special system administration functions and have unlimited access to all parts of the system.

SVID (System V Interface Definition)

AT&T's documented specification for System V compatibility originally released in 1985. A vendor must implement to this specification in order to claim its product is System V compliant. The specification ensures a high degree of portability of software to any other SVID-conformant system. Applications written to the SVID can be executed with minimal or no modifications on any system that conforms to the SVID following recompilation of the software.

SVVS (System V Verification Suite)

A collection of tests that demonstrate compliance with SVID. SVVS was announced by AT&T in 1985. It is updated with each new release of System V.

TCP/IP

(Transport Control Protocol/Internet Protocol) DOD's ARPA network protocol implementation for layers 3 and 4 of the OSI model developed in 1982. Consists of a suite of byte stream protocols that ensure that data packets are delivered to their destinations in the sequence in which they were initially transmitted. TCP/IP is the most prevalent protocol for Ethernet.

Text Editor

A program used to enter and revise text and data.

Timesharing System

A computer system with dumb terminals attached to its serial ports. The terminals rely on the system for all processing and storage functions. Timesharing implies that a system is used simultaneously by several users.

UDP

(User Datagram Protocol) Uses connectionless datagram sockets. Also a network transport.

Unbundled Software

Software supplied independently of the operating system and usually at additional expense.

UNIX

A computer operating system rapidly gaining worldwide acceptance as a standard for both technical and commercial markets.

UNIX International

UNIX International, Inc. is an independent industry association formed by computer and software companies to guide future development of the UNIX System V operating system. The association will support products based on UNIX System V.

User Interface

The means by which a user communicates with a computer program.

USL (UNIX Software Laboratories)

A subsidiary unit originally set up by AT&T separately from the Computer Systems business unit. UI is responsible for the development, marketing, and licensing of UNIX system V software. USL works with UNIX International on product definition, licensing policies, and product release schedules. USL was acquired by Novell.

Utility Program

A specialized group of instructions that are used to perform frequently required operations such as system administration tasks, report generation, and so forth.

UUCP (UNIX to UNIX Copy Program)

A collection of programs used to copy files and execute commands remotely over telephone lines or networks.

Virtual Memory

A memory management technique used for programs that require more memory space than can be allotted to them. The operating system moves only those pages of the program needed at a given time into memory, while unneeded pages remain in mass storage.

Virus (computer virus)

A program that infects compilers and adds a particular program to others being compiled, thereby propagating itself.

WAN (Wide Area Network)

A network that extends beyond an area served by the dedicated communications lines of a LAN. Typically employs telephone lines for communications over long distances.

Windowing

Subdividing a computer display screen into multiple, overlapping, independent regions.

Word Processing

A computer-based system for preparing, editing, storing, and printing text.

Workstation

A high-speed desktop computer with a powerful multitasking operating system, a high-resolution graphics display, integrated networking functions, and connectivity to different computers.

Worm (computer worm)

A program that infects other programs by modifying them to include a copy of itself.

XDR (External Data Representation)

A standardized specification for portable data transmission. Takes the form of a library of routines.

X/Open

An international organization established to increase the number of applications that conform to X/Open's standards (XPG).

X/open's portability guide

X Terminal

A terminal with built-in local memory and processors that solely supports the X Window system and network communications. Generally employs ROM-based TCP/IP software using a built-in Ethernet card or a direct serial connection.

X Window System

A windowing technology developed and licensed by the X Consortium at the Massachusetts Institute of Technology. It provides a portable windowing environment for use on a variety of hardware platforms.

X.11

An industry standard for workstation window software from the MIT consortium of vendors, supported by many hardware and software vendors.

YP

The Sun Microsystems Yellow Pages network service, now called NIS+, which accesses read-only databases for administration of network-wide data.

Index